MINUTES

OF THE

Eighth Biennial Convention

OF

The United Lutheran Church in America

Philadelphia, Pennsylvania
October 12-19, 1932

THE UNITED LUTHERAN PUBLICATION HOUSE
PHILADELPHIA, PA.

THE UNITED LUTHERAN CHURCH IN AMERICA

CALENDAR, 1932-1934

OFFICERS

President—Rev. F. H. Knubel, D.D., LL.D., S.T.D.
39 East 35th Street, New York City.

Secretary—Rev. W. H. Greever, D.D., LL.D.
39 East 35th Street, New York City.

Treasurer—Mr. E. Clarence Miller, LL.D.,
1508 Walnut Street, Philadelphia, Pa.

EXECUTIVE BOARD

Term Expires 1936

Rev. E. B. Burgess, D.D., LL.D., 73 Haldane Street, Crafton Br., Pittsburgh, Pa.
Rev. E. P. Pfatteicher, D.D., LL.D., 1228 Spruce Street, Philadelphia, Pa.
Rev. A. Steimle, D.D., 174 West 93rd Street, New York City.
Hon. Wm. E. Hirt, Erie, Pa.
Robbin B. Wolf, Esq., 711 Plaza Building, Pittsburgh, Pa.
Hon. John L. Zimmerman, LL.D., Springfield, Ohio.

Term Expires 1934

Rev. Marion Justus Kline, D.D., 1407 Twelfth Avenue, Altoona, Pa.
Rev. Jacob L. Morgan, D.D., 612 S. Main Street, Salisbury, N. C.
Rev. Rees Edgar Tulloss, Ph.D., D.D., 1817 Woodedge Rd., Springfield, O.
Mr. John Greiner, Jr., 1317 Myrtle Street, Scranton, Pa.
B. B. Miller, Esq., Salisbury, N. C.
Mr. Wm. H. Stackel, 68 Crosman Terrace, Rochester, N. Y.

Members Ex-Officio

Rev. F. H. Knubel, President.
Rev. W. H. Greever, Secretary.
Mr. E. Clarence Miller, Treasurer.

Place of next Convention—Savannah, Georgia

Minutes of the Eighth Biennial Convention of The United Lutheran Church In America

THE SERVICE—INTRODUCTORY

CHURCH OF THE HOLY COMMUNION
Philadelphia, Pennsylvania.
Wednesday, October 12, 1932, 7.30 P. M.

Preparatory to the Opening of the Eighth Biennial Convention of The United Lutheran Church in America, delegates from the Constituent Synods, a large number of visitors and many members of the churches of the Convention City assembled to participate in The Service, at the Church of the Holy Communion, Philadelphia, Pa., on Wednesday evening, October 12, 1932, at seven-thirty o'clock. The Secretary conducted The Service, including the Order for Public Confession and the Administration of the Sacrament, and the Reverends J. L. Morgan, President of the Synod of North Carolina; M. R. Hamsher, President of the Synod of West Pennsylvania; H. H. Bagger, President of the Pittsburgh Synod, and J. Reble, President of the Synod of Canada, assisted in the Administration of the Sacrament of the Altar.

The text of the Sermon, which was preached by the President, was "Thou openest Thine hand and satisfiest the desire of every living thing": the theme, "God's Open Hand."

FIRST SESSION

BENJAMIN FRANKLIN HOTEL.
Philadelphia, Pennsylvania.
Thursday, October 13, 1932, 8.45 A. M.

Matins were conducted by the Rev. C. J. Shealy.

The President called the Convention to order, and, after the use of the Order for the Opening of Synods, declared the Eighth Biennial Convention of The United Lutheran Church in America open for business.

By general consent the report of the completed roll of delegates was deferred.

The roll, as finally established, follows:

5

ROLL OF DELEGATES BY SYNODS

1. Ministerium of Pennsylvania

Organized August 15, 1748

Clerical

Rev. Ernst P. Pfatteicher, Ph.D., D.D., LL.D.
Rev. Charles M. Jacobs, D.D., LL.D., L.H.D.
Rev. Henry Offermann, D.D.
Rev. A. Charles R. Keiter
Rev. John H. Waidelich, D.D.
Rev. Franklin T. Esterly, D.D.
Rev. William L. Stough, D.D.
Rev. George A. Kercher
Rev. Gomer C. Rees, D.D.
Rev. Arthur S. Deibert, S.T.M.
Rev. Aden B. MacIntosh, D.D.
Rev. Corson C. Snyder, S.T.M.
Rev William H. Kline
Rev. Paul C. Weber
Rev. Conrad Wilker, D.D.
Rev. Ernst F. Bachman, D.D.
Rev. George Gebert, D.D.
Rev. J. Henry Harms, D.D.
Rev. L. Domer Ulrich, D.D.
Rev. John C. Mattes, D.D.
Rev. Charles C. Snyder
Rev. Otto Kleine, D.D.
Rev. G. Harold Kinard, D.D.
Rev. James F. Lambert, D.D.
Rev. David F. Longacre, S.T.M.
Rev. Joseph H. Orr
Rev. Allen L. Benner, D.D.
Rev. Gustavus H. Bechtold
Rev. Henry K. Lantz
Rev. Nathan B. Yerger
Rev. Clarence M. Snyder
Rev. Wayne Z. Artz
Rev. Jeremiah J. Schindel, D.D.
Rev. Elmer L. Leisey
Rev. Jacob H. Sandt
Rev. George S. Kressley, Litt.D.
Rev. Emil E. Fischer, D.D.
Rev. Raymond A. Kline
Rev. William C. Schaeffer, Jr., D.D.
Rev. John C. Fisher, D.D.
Rev. Ira F. Frankenfield

Lay

Hon. Claude T. Reno
E. Clarence Miller, LL.D.
Mr. Peter P. Hagan
Ralph H. Schatz, Esq.
Mr. Oscar C. Schmidt
Mr. Henry F. Heuer
Mr. William H. Hager
Mr. H. Torrey Walker
Grant Hultberg, D.C.L.
Mr. Daniel F. Yost
Mr. Allen R. Shimer
Chester H. Rhodes, Esq.
Mr. William M. Mearig
Mr. Mathias L. March
Mr. John Greiner, Jr.
Mr. August Baur
Mr. H. C. Miles
Mr. William P. M. Braun
Mr. J. H. Wisler
Mr. A. R. Maberry
Mr. Peter Trumbauer
Mr. George W. Haag
Paul H. Price, Esq.
Mr. John Burkhardt
Mr. J. Milton Deck
Mr. Louis Welker
Mr. Joseph T. Evans
Mr. L. H. Gehr
Mr. T. C. Zerbe
Mr. Robert D. Raeder
Mr. Charles G. Albrecht
Mr. R. K. Martin
Mr. John H. Morgan
Mr. Herman Kersteen
Mr. D. M. Reitz
Mr. Harry Hodges
Mr. George Purper
Mr. Albert Broadmeyer
Mr. Otto W. Osterlund
Mr. Carl J. Sandhoff
James F. Henninger, Esq.

2. United Synod of New York

October 23, 1786

Clerical	Lay
Rev. Samuel Trexler, D.D.	Mr. Fred H. Wefer
Rev. Paul Andrew Kirsch	Mr. Jacob Wagner
Rev. Frederick Noeldeke	Mr. Joseph M. Lotsch
Rev. George L. Kieffer, D.D., Litt.D.	Mr. Raymond B. Fenner
Rev. Fred H. Bosch, D.D.	Mr.' Val C. Dorner
Rev. Theodore O. Posselt, D.D.	Mr. P. C. Lehman
Rev. Carl H. Hirzel	Mr. Frederick Henrich
Rev. Herman Brezing, D.D.	Mr. Arthur W. Kimman
Rev. Henry C. Freimuth	Heiby W. Ungerer, Esq.
Rev. Albert Heyd	Mr. Henry Beisler
Rev. Ellis B. Burgess, D.D., LL.D.	Ellwood M. Rabenold, Esq.
Rev. Herbert A. Bosch	Mr. Henry Walter
Rev. J. George F. Blaesi, D.D.	Mr. William H. Stackel
Rev. Carl E. Poensgen	Mr. Edgar Krauch
Rev John H. Dudde	Mr. Martin Wulff
Rev. Ernst H. von Hahmann,	Mr. Martin C. Schwaner
Ph.D., D.D.	Mr. William Eck
Rev. Robert E. Schlotter	Mr. Michael Frisch
Rev. Hugo L. Dressler	Mr. John Frederick Kahl
Rev. Herman Brueckner, D.Th.	Mr. George Hagemeyer
Rev. Franklin F. Fry, D.D.	Mr. J. F. Nubel
Rev. William F. Sunday, Ph.D.	Mr. Henry Streibert
Rev. F. H. Knubel, D.D., LL.D.,	Mr. James Gear *a*
S.T.D.	Mr. Philip Machemer
Rev. Siegmund G. R. von Bosse	Mr. John Stavnitzky
Rev. Howard R. Gold, D.D.	Mr. Charles Abb
Rev. Austin H. Roeder	Mr. Henry Durk
Rev. Andrew L. Dillenbeck, D.D.	Mr. Fred W. Rettenmeyer
Rev. Augustus Steimle, D.D.	Mr. W. W. Weller
Rev Arthur S. Hardy, D.D.	Mr. William Richters
Rev. F. R. Knubel	Mr. E. B. Fernschild
Rev. Dorr E. Fritts	Mr. W. D. Bruns
Rev. Chalmers E. Frontz, D.D.	Mr. Ernest Doscher *a*
Rev. Charles W. Leitzell, D.D.	Mr. Otto R. Brandenberger
Rev. Frederick C. Ellermann	Mr. Adolph Nutzhorn
Rev. Charles D. Trexler, D.D.	Mr. Harry M. Greenwald
Rev. Fridolin E. Oberlander, D.D.	Mr. Henry G. Pfeil
Rev. Paul E. Scherer, D.D.	Mr. Elmer Shinemann
Rev. William G. Boomhower, D.D.	Mr. S. F. Telleen
Rev. H. T. Weiskotten, Ph.D.	Mr. Paul G. Wehle
Rev. A. H. Holthusen, D.D.	
Rev. W. Frank Hersh	

* Date of organization of the Ministerium of New York and Adjacent States and Countries, which on June 5, 1929, merged with the Evangelical Lutheran Synod of New York (organized 1830, see Minutes U. L. C. A. 1926, p. 8) and the Evangelical Lutheran Synod of New York and New England (organized in 1902), to form The United Lutheran Synod of New York.

3. United Synod of North Carolina

May 2, 1803

Clerical	Lay
Rev. J. L. Morgan, D.D.	Mr. Charles S. Heilig
Rev. E. H. Kohn, D.D., Ph.D.	Mr. W. P. Hooker
Rev. M. L. Stirewalt, D.D.	Mr. E. W. Wagoner
Rev. S. W. Hahn	W. L. Kibler, M.D.
Rev. P. E. Monroe, D.D.	Prof. M. S. Beam
Rev. E. C. Cooper, Ph.D.	Mr. J. W. H. Futchs
Rev. J. C. Dietz	Mr. J. L. Fisher
Rev. H. B. Schaeffer, D.D.	Prof. K. B. Patterson
Rev. V. C. Ridenhour	Mr. H. E. Isenhour

* Date of organization of the Evangelical Lutheran Synod and Ministerium of North Carolina, which on March 2, 1921, with the Evangelical Lutheran Tennessee Synod (organized July 17, 1820) merged into the United Evangelical Lutheran Synod of North Carolina under an amended charter of the former of the two synods which merged.

4. Maryland Synod

Organized October 11, 1820

Clerical	Lay
Rev. J. Edward Harms, D.D.	L. Russell Alden, Esq.
Rev. William A. Wade, D.D.	Mr. F. W. Kakel
Rev. Ralph C. Robinson	George S. Yost, Esq.
Rev. Oscar F. Blackwelder, D.D.	Mr. M. P. Moller, Sr.
Rev. Robert D. Clare, D.D.	Mr. Virgil W. Doub
Rev. A. T. Sutcliffe	Mr. Thomas P. Hickman
Rev. J. W. Ott, D.D.	Edwin W. Herrmann, Esq.
Rev. John B. Rupley	Mr. Ira N. Hoover
Rev. M. L. Enders, D.D.	Mr. H. T. Wentz
Rev. Henry Manken, Jr.	Harry T. Domer, Litt.D.

5. Synod of South Carolina

Organized January 14, 1824

Clerical	Lay
Rev. C. A. Freed, D.D.	James C. Kinard, LL.D.
Rev. P. D. Brown, D.D.	Mr. R. C. Counts
Rev. C. J. Shealy, D.D.	Mr. W. Frank Hipp
Rev. Geo. J. Gongaware, D.D.	Mr. W. A. Rast
Rev. C. B. Foelsch, Ph.D.	Mr. E. H. Schirmer
Rev. Thos. F. Suber	E. L. Horger, M.D.

6. Synod of West Pennsylvania
Organized September 5, 1825

Clerical	Lay
Rev. M. R. Hamsher	Mr. Geo. P. Black
Rev. H. H. Beidleman, D.D.	Mr. J. E. Reisner
Rev. R. W. Lind	George E. Neff, Esq.
Rev. Earl S. Rudisill, Ph.D.	George E. Holtzapple, M.D.
Rev. W. R. Sammel	Mr. Wm. H. Menges
Rev. Mervin E. Smith	Mr. Alvin R. Nissly
Rev. D. S. Kammerer	Mr. C. C. Culp
Rev. S. L. Hench	Mr. Arthur E. Rice
Rev. J. H. Hege	Hon. Franklin Menges

7. Synod of Virginia
*August 10, 1829

Clerical	Lay
Rev. J. J. Scherer, Jr., D.D.	Mr. R. E. Mapes
Rev. R. Homer Anderson	Mr. L. C. Hassinger
Rev. L. A. Thomas, D.D.	W. T. Stauffer, Esq.
Rev. J. L. Sieber, D.D.	Mr. C. V. Henkel
Rev. A. M. Huffman	Prof. H. C. Ahalt
Rev. C. J. Smith, D.D., LL.D.	Mr. H. L. Snyder
Rev. A. W. Ballentine	Hon. J. L. Almond, Jr.
Rev. M. J. Klutz	Mr. C. M. Speese

* Date of organization of the Evangelical Lutheran Synod and Ministerium of Virginia, which, on March 17, 1922, with the Evangelical Lutheran Synod and Ministerium of Southwestern Virginia (composed of the former Evangelical Lutheran Synod and Ministerium of Southwestern Virginia, organized September 20, 1842, and the Evangelical Lutheran Holston Synod, organized September 29, 1860), merged into the Lutheran Synod of Virginia.

8. Synod of Ohio
*November 7, 1836

Clerical	Lay
Rev. Joseph Sittler, D.D.	Hon. John L. Zimmermann, LL.D
Rev. H. C. Getter	Mr. Francis Seiberling, M.C.
Rev. A. H. Smith, D.D.	Edw. Rinderknecht, Esq.
Rev. E. E. Flack, Th.D.	Mr. Earle C. Greiner
Rev. A. E. Bell, D.D.	Mr. J. W. Kahler
Rev. W. M. Hackenberg, D.D.	Mr. S. G. McCord
Rev. H. S. Garnes, D.D.	Mr. D. L. Keyser
Rev. R. E. Tulloss, Ph.D., D.D., LL.D.	W. F. Emery, M.D.
Rev. Arthur J. Hall	Mr. J. K. Linsenmayer
Rev. S. A. Metzger	Mr. C. E. Lindquist a
Rev. D. B. Young, D.D.	Mr. F. W. Mehl
Rev. W. J. Kratz, D.D.	Mr. M. E. Riggle
Rev. C. L. Warstler	Mr. W. F. Dill a
Rev. Franklin C. Fry	Mr. W. W. Pagan
Rev. D. M. Funk	Mr. R. A. Prentiss
Rev. C. C. Wessel	Mr. W. J. Rummel
Rev. R. A. Harshman	Mr. Wm. J. Fisher
Rev. M. I. Powell	Mr. Dennis Hiner
Rev. G. W. Miley	Mr. C. E. Koon
Rev. Paul R. Clouser	Mr. Walter Otte

* Date of organization of East Ohio Synod which, on November 3, 1920, with the Synod of Miami (organized October 16, 1844), Wittenberg Synod (organized June 8, 1847) and the District Synod of Ohio (organized August 26, 1857) merged into the Synod of Ohio of The United Lutheran Church.

9. East Pennsylvania Synod
Organized May 2, 1842

Clerical	*Lay*
Rev. W. C. Ney, D.D.	Mr. E. G. Hoover
Rev. George A. Greiss, D.D.	William H. Emhardt, Esq.
Rev. C. G. Leatherman, D.D.	Mr. Harold U. Landis
Rev. John F. Knittle, Ph.D.	Mr. O. R. Frankenfield
Rev. E. A. Chamberlin	Mr. E. S. Gerberick
Rev. E. H. Delk, D.D.	Prof. R. D. Owen, Ph.D.
Rev. E. M. Grove	Mr. John G. Kurzenknabe
Rev. L. C. Manges, D.D.	Mr. A. H. Durboraw
Rev. G. Z. Stup	Mr. J. W. Lauer
Rev. C. L. Mogel	Mr. J. A. Fisher
Rev. R. R. Gresh	Mr. H. A. Fritsch
Rev. H. S. Dollman	Mr. Frank T. Harpel
Rev. J. E. Rudisill	D. P. Deatrick, DD.S.
Rev. S. W. Herman, D.D.	Mr. B. B. Slifer

10. Alleghany Synod
Organized September 9, 1842

Clerical	*Lay*
Rev. H. C. Michael, D.D.	Mr. James E. Gable
Rev. E. L. Pee	Mr. Frank Howard
Rev. George O. Ritter	Mr. Joseph Biddle
Rev. C. H. Stong	Mr. Samuel Z. Miller
Rev. George W. Nicely, D.D.	Mr. Martin L. Wenrich
Rev. C. P. Bastian	Mr. C. H. Fetterolf
Rev. H. L. Saul	Mr. J. Ralph Detwiler

11. Pittsburgh Synod
Organized January 15, 1845

Clerical	*Lay*
Rev. Henry H. Bagger	Mr. Albert W. Smith
Rev. Frank W. Ash	Mr. R. H. McGraw
Rev. Ludwig Beisecker	Mr. W. M. Smith
Rev. Chas. E. Read	Mr. Jesse Martsolf
Rev. Chas. O. Frank	Mr. W. J. Shaughnessy
Rev. E. Clyde Xander, D.D.	Mr. N. H. Slonaker
Rev. G. E. Swoyer	Mr. J. Buortmes
Rev. J. R. Nicholas	J. W. King, Esq.
Rev. J. F. Flegler	C. Edward Miller, D.D.S.
Rev. E. F. Krauss, D.D.	Prof. O. F. H. Bert
Rev. J. C. Klingensmith	Prof. Roy H. Johnson
Rev. Geo. J. Baisler	Mr. J. E. Wulfetange
Rev. G. W. Englar, D.D.	Mr. Michael Alexi
Rev. Frank C. Snyder	Mr. W. B. Ferguson
Rev. J. L. Fischer	Mr. Scott S. Laughlin
Rev. Chas. W. Barnett	Mr. J. I. Nicodemus
Rev. P. H. R. Mullen, D.D.	Mr. H. S. Miller
Rev. C. A. Dennig	J. Warren Hunter, Esq.
Rev. A. M. Stump	Mr. W. P. Houser
Rev. David E. Maxwell	Mr. John E. Van Dyke
Rev. Henry F. Obenauf	Mr. Harry W. V. Johnson
Rev. A. W. Stremel	Mr. Frank H. Thurm

12. Indiana Synod
October 28, 1848

Clerical	Lay
Rev. Ira R. Ladd, D.D.	Mr. Charles H. Dahlinger
Rev. J. Earl Spaid	Mr. Stanley M. Burger
Rev. J. S. Albert	Mr. Bruce D. Maxwell
Rev. F. A. Dressel, D.D.	Mr. Edward H. Hasemeier
Rev. Allen K. Trout	Mr. Geo. A. Fisher

* Date of organization of the Olive Branch Synod which, on June 24, 1920, with portions of the Chicago Synod (organized 1896), united to form the Indiana Synod of The United Lutheran Church in America.

13. Illinois Synod
September 8, 1851

Clerical	Lay
Rev. W. Carl Satre	Mr. J. F. Hardel
Rev. Edwin J. Johnson	Mr. A. M. Johnson
Rev. H. Allen Leader, D.D.	Mr. S. G. Broeker
Rev. Jacob Diehl, D.D., LL.D.	Mr. Louis Riechmann
Rev. William J. Boatman	Mr. C. J. Driever
Rev. Fred J. Lottich	Mr. Paulus List
Rev. Roy G. Catlin, D.D.	Mr. Frederick Sachse
Rev. George P. Lottich, D.D.	Mr. Alfred Arnesen
Rev. C. E. Paulus, D.D.	Mr. C. W. Breitwieser
Rev. Edwin Moll	Mr. Monroe Ash
Rev. M. E. Boulton	Mr. John J. Low

* Date of organization of the Northern Illinois Synod which on June 10, 1920, with the Southern Illinois (organized 1856), the Central Illinois (organized 1862), and portions of the Chicago (organized 1896) Synods, formed the Illinois Synod of The United Lutheran Church in America.

14. Texas Synod
Organized November 10, 1851

Clerical	Lay
Rev. J. C. A. Pfenninger	Mr. O. C. Dittmer
Rev. Paul Bechter	Mr. P. L. Wahlberg

15. Susquehanna Synod
February 21, 1855

Clerical	Lay
Rev. W. M. Rearick, D.D.	Mr. J. Edward Harman
Rev. J. G. C. Knipple	Mr. R. L. Schroyer
Rev. F. P. Manhart, D.D., LL.D.	Prof. Frank P. Boyer
Rev. C. E. Arnold	Mr. M. L. Yarrison
Rev. O. E. Sunday	Prof. George E. Fisher, Sc.D.
Rev. M. F. Good, D.D.	Mr. I. A. Shaffer, Jr.
Rev. G. Morris Smith, D.D.	George B. Reimensnyder, Esq.
Rev. R. G. Bannen, D.D.	Hon. Charles Steele

* Date of organization of the Synod of Central Pennsylvania which, on September 5, 1923, with the Susquehanna Synod (organized November 5, 1867) merged under the name of the Susquehanna Synod of Central Pennsylvania of the Evangelical Lutheran Church. The newly organized synod held its first session May 22, 1924. The name was changed April 11, 1932, to The Susquehanna Synod of The United Lutheran Church in America.

17. Synod of Iowa
Organized July 25, 1855

Clerical	Lay
Rev. John W. Mangum	Mr. William Karow

16. Mississippi Synod
Organized September 3, 1855

Clerical	Lay
Rev. J. O. Simon, D.D.	Mr. J. L. Berger
Rev. M. A. Getzendaner	Mr. A. G. Heitman
Rev. F. J. Weertz	Mr. Frank Heidt

18. Michigan Synod
*October 27, 1855

Clerical	Lay
Rev. A. H. Keck, D.D.	Mr. H. J. Herbst
Rev. F. H. Bloch	Mr. Swan Nelson
Rev. G. C. Goering	Mr. P. C. Kantz
Rev. W. E. Watts	Mr. William Diedrich
Rev. W. C. Zimmann	Mr. J. P. Lantz
Rev. L. S. Keyser, D.D.	Mr. J. A. Lechler

* Date of organization of the Northern Indiana Synod which on June 10, 1920, with portions of the Chicago Synod (organized 1896), formed the Michigan Synod of The United Lutheran Church in America.

19. Georgia-Alabama Synod
Organized July 20, 1860

Clerical	Lay
Rev. W. A. Reiser	Mr. Wm. B. Clarke
Rev. H. J. Black, D.D.	Mr. A. H. Reu

20. Synod of Canada
*July 21, 1861

Clerical	Lay
Rev. J. Reble	Mr. A. W. Sandrock a
Rev. H. R. Mosig	Mr. Wm. E. Kraft
Rev. O. Stockmann	Mr. Gordon Hollinger
Rev. C. S. Roberts	Mr. F. C. Kalbfleisch
Rev. E. F. Sterz	Mr. J. H. Ziegler
Rev. C. Zarnke	Mr. D. Weppler

* Date of organization of the Evangelical Lutheran Synod of Canada with which, on June 12, 1925, the Synod of Central Canada (organized November 11, 1908) united.

21. Synod of Kansas
Organized November 5, 1868

Clerical	Lay
Rev. G. K. Mykland	Mr. L. T. Bang a
Rev. G. C. Schaub, Ph.D.	Mr. L. M. Rauch
Rev. E. Victor Roland	Mr. A. V. Lindell a
Rev. J. W. Peterson	Mr. R. E. Hangen

22. Synod of Nebraska

Organized September 1, 1871

Clerical	*Lay*
Rev. Fred C. Wiegman	Mr. Madious G. Leamer
Rev. G. N. Mendenhall, Ph.D.	Mr. Gus Prestegaard *a*
Rev. C. B. Harman, D.D.	Mr. J. Fred Smith
Rev. W. T. Kahse, D.D.	Mr. Marius Christensen
Rev. W. C. Heidenreich	Mr. J. Alfred Johnson

23. Wartburg Synod

Organized 1875

Clerical	*Lay*
Rev. W. F. Buch	Mr. George Musch
Rev. H. R. Pontow	Mr. Christ Hummel
Rev. Christian F. L. Pieper	Mr. E. W. Wischmeier *a*
Rev. C. W. Knudten, D.D.	Mr. Jacob Schafer
Rev. R. R. Belter	Mr. George Heitmann *a*

24. German Synod of Nebraska

Organized July 24, 1890

Clerical	*Lay*
Rev. F. C. Schuldt	Mr. William Prante
Rev. Otto W. Heick, Ph.D.	Mr. Hugo Polenske *a*
Rev. Martin Schroeder	Mr. Bernh. Havekost
Rev. E. V. Nussbaum	Mr. Henry Monke
Rev. M. Koolen, D.D.	Mr. Peter Clausen
Rev. O. Klatt *a*	Mr. J. F. Iburg
Rev. Paul Waldschmidt	Mr. Fritz Reuter *a*
Rev. J. Kupfer	Mr. Freud Wendte *a*

25. Synod of California

Organized April 2, 1891

Clerical	*Lay*
Rev. Earnest A. Trabert	Clarence B. Runkle, Esq.
Rev. Mark O. Heller	Mr. J. A. Sende
Rev. Louis S. Axe	Mr. R. M. Kuner
Rev. D. Edward Wright	Mr. Raymond Tambert

26. Rocky Mountain Synod

Organized May 6, 1891

Clerical	*Lay*
Rev. E. W. Harner, D.D.	Mr. E. H. Rights
Rev. Walter A. Voss	Mr. A. E. Johnson

27. Synod of the Northwest
Organized September 22, 1891

Clerical	Lay
Rev. Paul H. Roth, D.D.	Mr. J. K. Jensen
Rev. W. P. Gerberding	Mr. J. W. Jouno *a*
Rev. R. H. Gerberding, D.D.	Mr. Carl Gottschaik
Rev. A. A. Hahn	Mr. George Hemsing
Rev. A. A. Zinck, D.D.	Mr. LeRoy W. Fieting
Rev. P. W. Roth, D.D.	Mr. E. C. Bayerlein *a*
Rev. J. H. Dressler, D.D.	Mr. C. E. Anderson
Rev. Paul R. Siebert, D.D.	Mr. H. S. Brooks

28. Manitoba Synod
Organized July 16, 1897

Clerical	Lay
Rev. Thos. Hartig	

29. Pacific Synod
Organized September 26, 1901

Clerical	Lay
Rev. Daniel D. Kistler	Mr. Edgar D. Blood
Rev. Andrew Engeset	Mr. C. B. Taw
Rev. J. C. Kunzmann, D.D.	Mr. Jens Adolphsen

30. Nova Scotia Synod
Organized July 10, 1903

Clerical	Lay
Rev. L. F. Hartzell	Mr. Earle Morash

31. Synod of West Virginia
Organized April 17, 1912

Clerical	Lay
Rev. C. A. Portz	Mr. C. A. Pilson
Rev. A. B. Leamer, D.D.	Mr. B. F. Becker

32. Slovak Lutheran "Zion" Synod
Organized June 10, 1919

Clerical	Lay
Rev. Gustav J. Chernansky	Mr. Martin Zlejsi
Rev. Joseph Kavalek	Mr. Andrew Cerniansky

33. Synod of Florida
Organized September 24, 1928

Clerical	Lay
Rev. Theodore K. Finck	Mr. Carl M. Brubaker

(Associate Bodies)
The Evangelical Lutheran Church in the Andhra Country, India

Rev. Frederick L. Coleman   Rev. G. A. Rupley

Japan Mission and Church
Rev. L. S. G. Miller, D.D.

a. Absent.

On motion the reports as printed in the Bulletin were received.

On motion the order of business was adopted as follows:

PROGRAM OF THE CONVENTION

All meetings will be held in the convention hall at the hotel. The churches for the evening services are indicated in this program.

The offerings at all evening services will be applied to the deficit in the treasury of the Board of Foreign Missions.

WEDNESDAY, OCTOBER 12—Night, 7.30 o'clock.
At the Church of the Holy Communion, Chestnut Street, between Twenty-first and Twenty-second Streets.
The Service. President's Sermon. Sacrament of the Altar.

THURSDAY, OCTOBER 13—Morning, 8.45 to 12 o'clock.
1. Devotions. (Matins will be used. The Committee on Devotions will appoint those who are to conduct all devotions.)
2. Formal opening of the Convention.
3. Organization of the Convention — Roll. Receipt of reports as printed in the Bulletin. Order of Business. Appointment of special committees. General rules of procedure.
4. Approval of minutes of last convention.
5. Action on item 5 of the Executive Board's report entitled, "Duties of the Secretary."
6. Reports of the President and the Secretary.
7. Election of the President and of the Secretary.
8. Treasurer's Report, with audit.
9. Election of the Treasurer.
10. Executive Board.
    Actions at this and succeeding sessions to be taken on the following items from their report. Any delegate may call up for consideration or question other items, not included in the following. These are given in the order in which they are found in the report. Board of American Missions and the Year 1938. Establishment of a Bureau of Architecture. Proposed merger of Inner Mission Board, etc. Transfer of Immigrant Mission Work. Training of Pastors and Teachers. Co-operation with Suomi Synod. The Preparation of a Catechism. Budget. Synod's Relation to the Assignment of Apportionment. World Conference on Faith and Order. Place of next convention.

THURSDAY, OCTOBER 13—Afternoon, 2 to 5 o'clock.
1. Devotions.
2. Continuation of action on the Executive Board's report.
3. Committee on Plan of Apportionment.

THURSDAY, OCTOBER 13—Evening.
Banquet arranged by the Laymen's Movement.

FRIDAY, OCTOBER 14—Morning, 8.45 to 12 o'clock.
(Before the opening of the morning session the chairmen of synodical delegations must secure ballots in the voting room for those elections which are to be held this day at noon: Each chairman will distribute the ballots to his delegation.)
1. Devotions.
2. Minutes.
3. Reports of Nominating Committees as to members of the Executive Board, of the Commission of Adjudication, of the Church Paper Committee, and of the Executive Committee of the Laymen's Movement.
4. Commission of Adjudication.
5. Laymen's Movement.
6. Church Papers' Committee.
7. Board of Education.
8. Unfinished Business.
(Immediately after the close of the session the election will be held for membership on the Executive Board, the Commission of Adjudication, the Church Papers' Committee, and the Executive Committee of the Laymen's Movement. Each delegate must deposit his own ballots. Polls close at two o'clock.)

FRIDAY, OCTOBER 14—Afternoon, 2 to 5 o'clock.
1. Devotions.
2. Representatives and General Resolutions. (As arranged by the Committee of Reference and Counsel for this place and for stated places on following days.)
3. Committee on Army and Navy Work. Address by Major John Hall, Lutheran Chaplain.
4. Parish and Church School Board.
5. Board of Publication.
6. Board of Ministerial Pensions and Relief.

FRIDAY, OCTOBER 14—Night, 8 o'clock.
Service at Zion-St. Michael's Church, Franklin Street between Race and Vine Streets.

Address in recognition of the Washington Bicentennial—The Hon. Claude T. Reno.

Address in recognition of the Gustavus Adolphus Tricentennial—The Rev. Dr. G. A. Brandelle.

SATURDAY, OCTOBER 15—Morning, 8.45 to 12 o'clock.
> (Before the opening of the morning session the chairmen of delegations must secure ballots for today's elections.)
> 1. Devotions.
> 2. Minutes.
> 3. Report of Nominating Committee for today's elections.
> 4. Report of tellers upon Friday's elections.
> 5. Inner Mission Board.
> 6. National Lutheran Home for the Aged.
> 7. Board of Deaconess Work.
> 8. Commission on Investments.
> 9. Unfinished Business.
> (Immediately after adjournment the election will be held for membership on all boards and elective committees not included in the Friday election. Polls will close at 1.30 o'clock.)

SATURDAY, OCTOBER 15—Afternoon, 1.30 o'clock.
> Excursion and Patriotic Service. By automobile to Valley Forge, and thence to Trappe, where service will be held. Return by way of Mt. Airy.

SUNDAY, OCTOBER 16.
> The Philadelphia Committee has arranged and will announce the preachers at all church services, both morning and evening.
> In the afternoon at 2.30 o'clock.
>> City Convention Hall, 34th and Spruce Streets. A choral vesper service with foreign missionaries in evidence and an address on the world-wide mission of the Church by the Rev. Dr. R. E. Tulloss.

MONDAY, OCTOBER 17—Morning, 8.45 to 12 o'clock.
> 1. Devotions.
> 2. Minutes.
> 3. Report of tellers upon Saturday's elections.
> 4. Board of Foreign Missions.
> 5. Unfinished Business.

MONDAY, OCTOBER 17—Afternoon, 2 to 5 o'clock.
> 1. Devotions.
> 2. Representatives and General Resolutions.

3. Board of American Missions.
4. Committee on Evangelism.
5. Necrologist's Obituary Record.
6. Unfinished Business.

MONDAY, OCTOBER 17—Night, 8 o'clock.
St. Matthew's Church, Broad and Mt. Vernon Streets. Memorial
Service.
Tribute to the Rev. Dr. M. G. G. Scherer by the Rev. Dr. A. G. Voigt.
Tribute to the Rev. Dr. H. E. Jacobs by the Rev. Dr. N. R. Melhorn.

TUESDAY, OCTOBER 18—Morning, 8.45 to 12 o'clock.
1. Devotions.
2. Minutes.
3. Committee on Lutheran Brotherhood.
Hearing of the representative of the Brotherhood.
4. Committee on Women's Work.
Hearing of the representative of the Women's Missionary Society.
5. Committee on Associations of Young People.
Hearing of the representative of the Luther League of America.
6. Committee on Memorials from Constituent Synods.
7. Unfinished Business.

TUESDAY, OCTOBER 18—Afternoon, 2 to 5 o'clock.
1. Devotions.
2. Representatives and General Resolutions.
3. Committee on Moral and Social Welfare.
4. Commission on Lutheran Church Unity.
5. Commissioners to the National Lutheran Council.
6. Executive Committee of the Lutheran World Convention.
7. Committee on Women as Congregational Representatives.
8. Unfinished Business.

WEDNESDAY, OCTOBER 19—Morning, 8.45 to 12 o'clock, and afternoon 2 to 5 o'clock.
(Portions of the program for this day may be advanced to Tuesday
night, if the convention decides to hold a session that night.)
1. Devotions.
2. Minutes.
3. Committee on the Office of the Ministry.
4. Committee on Common Service Book.
5. Committee on Church Music.
6. Committee on Church Architecture.

7. Committee on Statistics and Church Year Book, including reports of the Statistical Secretary and of the Editor of the Year Book.
8. Committee on German Interests.
9. Committee on Publicity.
10. Committee on President's Report.
11. Representative to the American Bible Society.
12. Committee on Conference with Y. M. C. A.
13. Committee on Church and State.
14. Committee on Transportation.
15. Archivist.
16. Committee on Place of Next Convention.
17. Committee on Leave of Absence.
18. Lutheran Historical Society.
19. Lutheran Church Book and Literature Society.
20. Unfinished Business.
21. Printing of Minutes.
22. Final Minutes.
23. Formal close of the Convention.

There being no objection, the President ruled that Special Committees stand as appointed, without reading them.

SPECIAL COMMITTEES

COMMITTEE OF REFERENCE AND COUNSEL

This committee is appointed to consider all general resolutions before they are submitted to the Convention; to arrange with the President for the hearing of representatives sent to the Convention; generally to assist the president in the daily program.

Rev. Herman Brezing, D.D.
Rev. Henry Offermann, D.D.
Rev. P. E. Monroe, D.D.
Rev. P. D. Brown, D.D.
Rev. A. E. Bell, D.D.
Rev. George W. Nicely, D.D.
Rev. E. F. Krauss, D.D.
Rev. George P. Lottich, D.D.
Rev. F. P. Manhart, D.D., LL.D.
Rev. H. J. Black, D.D.
Rev. Mark O. Heller

Mr. L. Russell Alden
Mr. J. E. Reisner
W. T. Stauffer, Esq.
Mr. E. G. Hoover
Mr. Charles H. Dahlinger
Mr. P. L. Wahlberg
Mr. J. L. Berger

COMMITTEE ON PRESIDENT'S REPORT

Rev. William G. Boomhower, D.D.
Rev. Charles W. Leitzell, D.D.
Rev. Robert D. Clare, D.D.
Rev. L. A. Thomas, D.D.
Rev. E. H. Delk, D.D.

Mr. Daniel F. Yost
George S. Yost, Esq.
Mr. George E. Holtzapple
Mr. A. H. Durboraw
Prof. George E. Fisher, Sc.D.

Rev. H. L. Saul
Rev. J. Earl Spaid
Rev. Edwin Moll
Rev. R. G. Bannen
Rev. F. J. Weertz

Mr. J. A. Sende
Mr. E. H. Rights
Prof. M. S. Beam
Mr. M. P. Moller, Sr.

COMMITTEE ON LEAVE OF ABSENCE

Rev. Emil E. Fischer, D.D.
Rev. G. N. Mendenhall, Ph.D.
Rev. John H. Dudde
Rev. J. L. Fischer
Rev. Allen K. Trout
Rev. W. C. Zimmann
Rev. J. W. Peterson
Rev. C. W. Knudten, D.D.
Rev. Martin Schroeder

Mr. Charles G. Albrecht
Mr. E. H. Schirmer
Mr. J. F. Hardel
Mr. William Diedrich
Mr. C. A. Pilson
Mr. Martin Zlejzi
Mr. H. A. Fritsch
Mr. James E. Gable

COMMITTEE ON MEMORIALS FROM CONSTITUENT SYNODS

Rev. George A. Greiss, D.D.
Rev. Aden B. MacIntosh, D.D.
Rev. Augustus Steimle, D.D.
Rev. J. C. Dietz
Rev. C. B. Foelsch, Ph.D.
Rev. Earl S. Rudisill, Ph.D.
Rev. E. E. Flack, Th.D.
Rev. G. W. Englar, D.D.
Rev. Paul Bechter
Rev. F. H. Bloch
Rev. C. S. Roberts

Mr. William M. Mearig
Mr. William Eck
Mr. R. E. Mapes
Mr. J. K. Linsenmayer
Wm. H. Emhardt, Esq.
Prof. Frank P. Boyer
Mr. Wm. E. Kraft
Mr. George Musch
Clarence B. Runkle, Esq.

COMMITTEE TO NOMINATE EXECUTIVE COMMITTEE OF LAYMEN'S MOVEMENT

Rev. J. L. Sieber, D.D.
Rev. M. L. Enders, D.D.
Rev. G. E. Swoyer

James F. Henninger, Esq.
Mr. William Richters
Hon. Franklin Menges
Mr. C. E. Koon

COMMITTEE TO NOMINATE MEMBERS OF EXECUTIVE BOARD, COMMISSION OF ADJUDICATION, AND CHURCH PAPER COMMITTEE

Rev. William A. Wade, D.D.
Rev. S. G. R. von Bosse
Rev. Franklin C. Fry
Rev. E. Clyde Xander, D.D.
Rev. C. E. Paulus, D.D.
Rev. C. Zarnke
Rev. E. W. Harner, D.D.
Rev. L. F. Hartzell
Rev. A. B. Leamer, D.D.

E. L. Horger, M.D.
Mr. L. C. Hassinger
Mr. Joseph Biddle
Mr. R. E. Hangen
Mr. William Prante
Mr. Frederick Henrich
Edw. Rinderknecht, Esq.
Mr. J. E. Wulfetange
Mr. Carl Gottschalk

COMMITTEE TO NOMINATE MEMBERS OF ALL OTHER BOARDS

Rev. A. A. Zinck, D.D.
Rev. Otto Kleine, D.D.
Rev. Mervin E. Smith

Mr. J. L. Fisher
Mr. Stanley M. Burger
Mr. J. P. Lantz

Rev. S. W. Herman, D.D.
Rev. G. Morris Smith, D.D.
Rev. M. A. Getzendaner
Rev. H. R. Pontow
Rev. Louis S. Axe
Rev. Gustav J. Chernansky

Mr. Wm. B. Clarke
Mr. Madious G. Leamer
Mr. Jens Adolphson
Mr. Carl M. Brubaker
Mr. J. Milton Deck
Mr. Paulus List

COMMITTEE ON DEVOTIONAL SERVICES

Rev. George J. Gongaware, D.D.
Rev. Gomer C. Rees, D.D.
Rev. E. Victor Roland
Rev. Fred C. Wiegman
Rev. M. Koolen
Rev. Walter A. Voss
Rev. Paul H. Roth, D.D .
Rev. Andrew Engeset
Rev. Arthur S. Hardy, D.D.

Mr. Henry Streibert
Mr. E. W. Wagoner
Mr. Samuel Z. Miller
C. Edward Miller, D.D.S.
Mr. Edgar D. Blood
Mr. Earle Morash

COMMITTEE OF TELLERS No. 1

To conduct the election of the president and of the secretary, and also the Friday elections.

Mr. Henry F. Heuer
Mr. Heiby W. Ungerer
Mr. Thomas P. Hickman
Mr. C. C. Culp
Mr. D. L. Keyser
Mr. Frank Howard

Mr. George A. Fisher
Mr. O. C. Dittmer
Mr. William Karow
Mr. H. J. Herbst
Mr. Gordon Hollinger

COMMITTEE OF TELLERS No. 2

To conduct the election of the treasurer and also the Saturday elections.

Mr. C. J. Driever
Mr. H. Torrey Walker
Mr. W. A. Rast
Mr. B. B. Slifer
J. W. King, Esq.
Mr. Alfred Arnesen

Mr. R. L. Schroyer
Mr. A. G. Heitman
Mr. A. H. Reu
Mr. L. M. Rauch
Mr. J. F. Iburg

The following rules of procedure were adopted:

(1) That any delegate may, from the floor, move a resolution which fits perfectly to any report coming before the Convention, but that resolutions of a general character must be handed to the Committee of Reference and Counsel, with whom the mover may confer;

(2) That in discussion the time of speakers be limited to five minutes; and

(3) That the privilege of the floor be granted to members of the Executive Board, to all members of the Commission of Adjudication and to officers of other boards when their reports are before the Convention.

The President ruled that the Acting Secretary of the Church would be the Secretary of this Convention.

By common consent it was decided that reports shall not be adopted as a whole, action being taken only upon resolutions and recommendations.

A printed copy of the Minutes of the Milwaukee Convention, certified by M. G. G. Scherer as Secretary, and F. H. Knubel as President, under seal, was submitted and approved. The President thereupon declared it to be the official protocol of the proceedings of the Seventh Biennial Convention of The United Lutheran Church in America.

The Rev. C. P. Swank, Chairman of the Philadelphia Committee on Arrangements for the Convention, introduced Mayor J. Hampton Moore, who welcomed the Convention to the City of Philadelphia.

Response to the Mayor's welcome was made by President James C. Kinard, of Newberry College.

The Rev. C. P. Swank introduced the Rev. W. O. Fegley, pastor of Augustus Lutheran Church, Trappe, Pa., who presented President Knubel with a block and gavel made from one of the floor beams of Augustus Lutheran Church and inscribed with the motto of Henry Melchior Muhlenberg: "Ecclesia Plantanda." President Knubel responded to the presentation, and on behalf of the United Lutheran Church, thanked Dr. Fegley.

The item of the Executive Board's report concerning the Duties of the Secretary (I, 5) was presented, and on motion adopted. (See p. 40.)

The President presented his report, which was referred to the Committee on President's Report. (For action on this report see p. 449.)

REPORT OF THE PRESIDENT

At the close of the seventh biennium of the United Lutheran Church in America it becomes the president's duty for the seventh time humbly and prayerfully to perform the duty required in the By-Laws, that he "summarize the general conditions in the Church." It is to be regretted that the picture cannot be a rosy one, although one outstanding item of beautiful promise will be portrayed. We may also remember for our encouragement that even amid worst conditions God always has in the Church, as in Elijah's day, His thousands who have not bowed the knee to Baal.

It is commonly stated that a period of depression like the present one in the world's life is beneficial to the Church, and that a spiritual awakening is inevitable. Evidences, however, seem not procurable. An effort was made to gather testimony as to increasing Church attendances and greater desire for the Sacrament. The reports were, as at other periods, contradictory, and few seem to be greatly distressed or elated. The circulation of our Church papers has always been a disgrace and grows worse, but again nobody is distressed about it. Our benevolent gifts always were meager and have fallen lamentably, but once more only some officials seem to be distressed. Not just the facts, but especially the lack of emotion over the facts leads one to ask where the spiritual improvement in these times of depression is to be found. The truth is that no condition, prosperous or depressed, in the world's life is of itself favorable to the Church. The world is always in essence the same, and is not "a changing world." It is always what Paul called it, "this present evil world," and it is never helpful to religion, to the Church. A prime responsibility of the Church is to maintain her independence of the world, drawing her life from divine sources. The sad picture of present conditions now to be portrayed is just this, that the Church has not maintained her independence of the world, but has been a mimic of the world.

The United Lutheran Church in America was born amid the frenzy of Armistice Day in 1918. Since then the world has lived constantly in some form of feverish excitement. It has never become normal, and no man on earth could be altogether quiet. If the first page of the newspaper cannot thrill us with something startling the day seems out of order. Staggering news today must be overwhelmed by some colossal undertaking tomorrow. Everything must be exciting, must be big, and must produce quick results. And all of the excitement has centered around two old principles of "this present evil world," the bigness of material things and the bigness of man. Material things—bigger things to see, to hear, and to add up in figures, instead of bigger things to think and to believe in, like God. The bigness of man—Let the wonder of human life freely express itself, without any restraint, in youth and through all the years; give to big political leaders free rein, and give to big financial leaders unlimited salaries and bonuses; man is great, not God. A change has come in the last few years, but only a change to another form of excitement. The world has not sobered in the least, for its frenzy is now revealed in dazed bewilderment. Riches have flown and financiers have been found as fools, but for the depression men continue to cry that big plans be made, with quick results. Every radical proposition finds a quick following, and the imitators of a Mussolini are in every land. The bigness of material things and the bigness of man continue to control, even in the depression. Has the world thought of God? It is more than a century since such a flood of atheism as is seen today has swept all nations.

In all of this the Church has mimicked the world—in excitement, in huge undertakings for quick advance, in calls for great leaders, and above all in neglect of God. It began just after the war with the ambitious Interchurch World Movement. Even when that crashed, inflated projects continued steadily, as our memories may easily recall. The watchword has been that we must do big things, with the worldly emphasis on "we" and on "big." With all our Lutheran conservatism, even in our Church congregations and synods and institutions and boards have been led into exaggerated and impossible plans. As now the depression has come, we like the world are found in excited bewilderment. Above all the Church also seems to lack today awestruck consciousness of the greatness of God. Were that consciousness common among us, we would not be facing the atheism in the world with so much of religious ignorance among the members of the Church. Did we possess that consciousness, we would know that lack-luster periods like that of the judges in Israel's history, when God was their King, may be more lustrous than times such as when Israel did big things under her great leaders, her great kings. Then furthermore wonder would again possess us that God can use blundering men at all for His purposes. Sober steadiness and stillness would possess us, while we listen for His word. No doubt we in our busy ways have been interfering with His ceaseless activity. We have mimicked the world.

This forgetfulness and hindering of God is only a part of the picture of present conditions. To one who aims to understand the prevailing mood of the world today it seems unavoidable to believe that men generally desire above everything else to get out of present conditions and back to hilarious prosperity, no matter how. They are impatient over any other proposition. There is no satisfaction for them in a patient study of their own guilt for conditions, nor in the idea that fundamental changes in their attitudes are necessary—in their attitude toward wealth and economy, for instance. They are not deeply conscious that they were individually responsible for the sufferings of multitudes today. They are not seeking forgiveness, are not repentant. Without consciousness of God, they are unconscious of sin. They are only and thoughtlessly in a hurry to be through with the present time.

In this also it is sad to believe that the Church mimics the world. Let our hearts bear witness that we too are chiefly and impatiently "rearin' to go" again, without being ready to go. We have simply held in abeyance for a moment any old ambitions, extravagances, and big wilful plans of ours. We are not using this opportunity to restudy them deeply as to their Christian wisdom. We have not sought forgiveness because of our participation in the world's guilt, because of our forgetfulness of God. Is it not true that there is too little of sincere repentance in the Church today? We are not ashamed of our sins in the immediate past.

An excited forgetfulness of God and an impatient unwillingness to repent. What else? Our third look at the world of the last decade or two compels us to recognize its lovelessness. War hate, that tiger in the breasts of men, has brought forth its long-lived brood. Peace treaties, League of Nations, pacts and disarmament conferences have not subdued it. Hate and jealousy and fear still rage. Race prejudice is perhaps as strong as ever. Nationalism assumes evil aspects. Years of prosperity also favored selfish, loveless instincts, and in depression each man seeks to protect just himself and his own. Even the widespread giving during prosperity was clearly not born of pure love.

Has the Church been a mimic in this also? It would be a sufficient answer to remind ourselves of the Church's near surrender of human love in war-time, and (for those who know conditions in many lands) the Church's apparent advocacy of a false nationalism today. We may confine our test of her love, however, to her gifts. Christian love and its gifts are in essence something far beyond any mere thoughts of human welfare, of pity, yes even of stewardship and tithing. It is a love of all men, unloveable as they are, purely because constrained by the love of Christ; in self-surrender, self-effacement, and self-sacrifice it gladly gives its all. In the matter of giving, the Church must continue to note Christ's words to the rich young ruler, "If thou wilt be perfect, go and sell that thou hast, and give to the poor, and thou shalt have treasure in heaven: and come and follow Me." Have the Church's gifts, in prosperity or depression, been like that? Is her love today like that?

One naturally feels disheartenment over the above description of the Church as a mere echo or parrot to the world. What then is that outstand-ing item of beautiful promise in her present condition to which reference was made at the beginning? It is the fact that there is among us evident dis-satisfaction with our condition, voiced from various sources, and variously depicting our faults. It is all concentrated in the repeated calls for EVANGELISM. Protestantism throughout the world is discarding the empty message of modernism, has grown weary of the over-emphasis on social Christianity, and is heeding the call for a return to Reformation prin-ciples. At the meeting this summer of the International Missionary Council in Herrnhut chief attention was drawn to the great results which follow a more earnest evangelistic endeavor, and special note was made of that which our own people have not grasped, the caste movement towards Christianity in our own Telugu field in India. The meeting declared that the center of missionary work, demanding chief emphasis, "is to proclaim in word and life God's revelation and redemption in Jesus Christ. Apart from this there is no Christian mission. We desire to call the Churches and missions to a more earnest evangelistic endeavor. Our aim is the personal conversion of men." During the last biennium that call for a determined evangelism has grown ever more emphatic within the U. L. C. A. Ministers and lay-men have individually written and spoken to the president concerning it. Many of our synods have discussed it and some have memorials of that character before this convention. Several communities have undertaken noteworthy efforts. The editors of our Church papers have spoken repeatedly and emphatically.

This manifestation is a cheering one for two pertinent reasons. First of all, evangelism is the prime necessity of the Christian heart, for that heart must find others to win to the same faith. It represents the fundamental attitude of the Church towards the world, and is the one means whereby the Church maintains her necessary independence of the world. She can never be a mimic of the world, while she knows that the world needs evangelism, that the world is wrong and must be converted. She becomes the world's echo only when she ceases to preach salvation to the world.

We are cheered by these evidences, in the second place, because evangelism will necessarily and effectively purge the Church of that forgetfulness of God, that unrepentant spirit, that lovelessness which she has been absorbing from the world. Evangelism believes that God has acted in Christ to save men, and that only God could do it; that this simple but marvelous statement is true, "Look unto me, and be ye saved all the ends of the earth;" that true preaching is first of all the proclamation, the heralding of a divinely accomplished and revealed salvation. Evangelism must have primarily a changeless consciousness of and faith in a wonderful God. Further, evangelism insists that repentance is necessary from all men; that an unrepentant Church cannot impress the world with this need; that the true preacher is, therefore, not only a herald, but also a witness of his own repented sin and its forgiveness. Then also evangelism, the effort to win all men, can thrive only if there be in the Church a Christ-born love for them; if the preachers become, not only heralds and witnesses, but ardent pleaders with men. We seem to have lost in the Church's sermons such pleading as led Paul to cry repeatedly in love, "I beseech you, we beseech you, as though God did beseech you by us." Only love can speak in that fashion.

Remembering the three evils in which the Church has copied the world it is significant that Paul admonishes Timothy to the effect that our message is complete if it arise "out of a pure heart, and a good conscience, and faith unfeigned." Manifestly evangelism is a sure corrective of the three evils.

Since then this manifestation among us, this call for evangelism, is clearly the work of God among us, is His gracious effort to preserve us as a Church, it behooves us to note the inevitable paths along which we must follow His guidance. We must recognize our definite responsibilities in the conduct of our work with Him. These obligations of ours occupy the remainder of this report. Details of evangelistic operation cannot be included, but the practical principles of such operation must be designated. At least four of them are almost self-evident. We shall be sinning grievously in the face of Christ's evident care for us if we do not permit them to control us completely.

1. Evangelism is the constant task of the Church. Its spirit, as we have seen, maintains the Church from contamination by the spirit of the world. Evangelistic spurts, special efforts, cannot content us. Russia's seven-year plans and even Kagawa's wonderful five-year plans in Japan cannot be models for us. It is no doubt good to recognize the value of Lent as a peculiarly favorable season, but even Lent can do us harm if it suppress the

idea of evangelism for other periods of the year. The unevangelized everywhere are always a multitude, and the Christian life of the faithful will
fall to a low ebb if at any period the surge of loving desire for the unevangelized does not possess them.

2. Evangelism is the primary task of the Church. She has two other
great tasks, education of men and mercy to men, which are ordinarily equal
to the evangelistic task. They are, however, secondary in the sense that the
Church can operate in them only as she suffuses them with the blood of
evangelism, only as she aims by them also to win men ever more fully to her
Lord. The Church has more than concern and pity for the ignorant and
the distressed. She has love for them. This fact she has tried to prove to
men, though none too well. Yet she knows that mere education and mere
prosperity are all too readily curses to a man. Without the love of God in
his heart he does not know how to use them. Evangelism is the all-con-
trolling task of the Church.*

3. It is evident that just two centers of operation must receive chief
emphasis from the Church, in view of her evangelistic responsibility.

a. The congregations. These are always the primary bodies in the Church,
for they alone reach the individual members. Only as they are strong is
the Church strong. All other forms of organization in the Church are
absolutely secondary in importances. All agencies, institutions, officials,
etc., of the Church find their true place only as they can realize themselves
to be definitely and entirely serving the interests of the congregations. The
congregations are therefore primary for the evangelistic task we are considering. Their educational and merciful work must be manifest, but their
members are whole Christians and their congregational life is safe from the
world only as under a true pastor's leadership they are missionary-minded.
It may be worth a congregation's while to ask if any converted sinners are
kneeling at its altar along with the people who were always respectable.
Are the homes of its people shining Christian lights in their immediate
vicinity? Are the pastor and people watchfully ready to establish branch
preaching places and Sunday schools at nearby locations? It is evident that
the true security of each congregation in these times demands that it test
itself as to its evangelistic fervor. When doing so, it should ask if it is
saving its own immediate life by an interest as broad as its Master's. Does
it care for the neighbor Christ gave it at the other end of the United States
and Canada, and on the other side of the globe? This leads us to recognize
the second center of the Church's chief emphasis, namely,

b. The apportionment decided by the congregations themselves through
the conventions of The United Lutheran Church in America. This must
manifestly receive such pronounced emphasis as one of only two chief
centers, because over two-thirds of the total is devoted to purely evangelistic

---

* If any reader of this report doubts the president's intense concern for the Church's
educational and merciful tasks, he is asked to examine previous biennial reports.

endeavor—the amounts assigned to the Boards of Foreign and American Missions.

Let the Church exalt these two centers, and she will be answering aright Christ's urgent call in these times to the Church. She will no longer mimic the world.

4. The Constituent Synods are provided with an order of importance for the outstanding elements of their work.

a. The care of the congregations. Our Church leaves this tremendous and primary responsibility almost entirely to the synods. They should read again the deliverance of the Church in this respect found on page 87 of the minutes of the 1920 convention. They are responsible to guide into a fully rounded Christian life in the congregations, with the emphasis on evangelism, but with full attention to educational and merciful development. The synods are thus also the primary agencies for the promotion of the general benevolent gifts of the congregations.

b. Next in importance is the synod's cooperation with the Board of American Missions in the missionary development on the synod's own territory.

c. Third come the special educational and merciful responsibilities of the synod.

This report is brought to a close with a realization that the Church may decide to commit it and its suggestions to the Committee on Evangelism. That committee has always had a weighty responsibility. We cannot, however, as a Church, wash our own hands of the matter merely by such a decision. If the Church has erred by her imitation of the world and if our Lord is mercifully calling us to better ways through voices which have cried out from our own constituency, let us earnestly pray that our Church everywhere will repent and ask, "Lord, what wilt Thou have me to do."

The work of the president during the biennium was carried on as usual, and generally in cooperation with the other officers and with the entire Executive Board of the Church. Immediately after the last convention all special responsibilities from that convention were carried out, including the appointment of commissions and committees. In spite of difficulties involved, the new requirement that a man may not be a member of more than two committees was observed. The authorized Committee on Apportionment was not named until after the minutes were printed, and is therefore given here as a matter of record: Rev. E. B. Burgess, Mr. Arthur P. Black, Rev. Herbert A. Bosch, Mr. Robert F. Bowe, Mr. J. Milton Deck, Rev. C. B. Foelsch, Rev. Robert H. Ischinger, Mr. J. K. Jensen, Rev. Paul H. Krauss, Mr. E. Clarence Miller, Hon. Charles Steele.

A few elections in 1930 required that the individuals concerned, because of our constitution's requirements, withdraw from certain agencies. Thus Rev. J. L. Morgan chose to remain as a member of the Executive Board and resigned from the Board of Foreign Missions. Rev. P. D. Brown remained as a member of the Inner Mission Board and of the Parish and Church School Board, resigning from the Committee on Church Papers.

Resignations were as follows: Rev. Paul Krauss from the Committee on Apportionment. Rev. G. Albert Getty from the Common Service Book Committee. Rev. C. M. Jacobs from the Commission to the National Lutheran Council. Mr. J. Horace Frank from the Committee on Church Architecture. Death created the following vacancies: Mr. Albert F. Schenck on the Committee on Church Architecture. Rev. M. G. G. Scherer on the Commission to the National Lutheran Council and on the Commission to the World Conference on Faith and Order. Rev. H. E. Jacobs on the Common Service Book Committee. Appointments were made as follows: Rev. Carl R. Simon on the Common Service Book Committee. Rev. E. A. Fritsch on the Committee on German Interests. Rev. C. E. Krumbholz on the Commission to the National Lutheran Council, of which Rev. P. W. Koller was named as convener. Other vacancies were not filled, generally because they occurred near the end of the biennium.

Rev. H. J. Pflum and Rev. R. H. Gerberding were appointed as representatives to meetings of the Augustana Synod, Rev. W. P. Christy and the president himself to meetings of the Suomi Synod, Rev. H. H. Bagger to the American Federation of Lutheran Brotherhoods, and Rev. V. J. Hanninen to represent the Canadian Finnish Conference at the meeting of the Suomi Synod.

Certain special activities of the president are noted. An extended trip to the territory of our far western synods. Radio broadcasting arrangements with the National Broadcasting Company. Assumption of the tasks of the Secretary of the Church, during the illness of our much loved Dr. Scherer, until the appointment of an Acting Secretary just before his death.

The report of the Acting Secretary was then presented, and the memorials from Constituent Synods were referred to the Committee on Memorials from Constituent Synods.

REPORT OF THE ACTING SECRETARY

(For action on memorials see pp. 447, 449.)

On May 19, 1932, the Acting Secretary was informed by the Secretary of the Susquehanna Synod of Central Pennsylvania that the name of this Synod had been changed by a decree of the Court of Northumberland County, Penna., April 11, 1932, from the "Susquehanna Synod of Central Pennsylvania of the Evangelical Lutheran Church" to "The Susquehanna Synod of The United Lutheran Church in America." The new name of this synod is recorded in our roll of Constituent Synods.

Memorials from Constituent Synods have been received as follows: one from the Florida Synod endorsing the invitation of the Georgia Synod to hold the 1934 Convention in Savannah, Ga.; one from the Illinois Synod concerning a concerted program of evangelism; one from the Maryland Synod concerning principles of budgeting; two from the Nebraska Synod, one concerning a monthly periodical and one concerning the aim, function and budget of the Board of Education; two from the New York Synod, one concerning a national radio broadcast and one concerning our relation to the Federal Council of Churches; one from the Pacific Synod concerning an annuity for the Rev. J. C. Kunzmann; three from the Ministerium of Pennsylvania, one concerning our relation with the Federal Council of Churches, one expressing a welcome to the Philadelphia Convention, and one concerning a phonographic record of the ideal rendition of the music of The Service; one from the Pittsburgh Synod concerning army chaplains; one from the Virginia Synod concerning a Rural Life Sunday; and one from the West Virginia Synod, and one from the East Pennsylvania Synod concerning the holding of the next convention of the Church three years hence instead of two years hence.

ABDEL ROSS WENTZ.

The Convention proceeded to the election of a President, under the direction of Committee of Tellers No. 1.

Treasurer E. Clarence Miller presented his report.

REPORT OF THE TREASURER OF THE UNITED LUTHERAN CHURCH IN AMERICA

RECEIPTS FROM SYNODS
For the Year Ended June 30, 1931

	Apportionment	Specials
Ministerium of Pennsylvania	$256,105.06	$72,285.04
United Synod of New York	150,900.00	84,198.15
United Synod of North Carolina	25,915.13	6,995.26
Maryland Synod	96,747.12	18,570.60
Synod of South Carolina	25,206.43	4,806.10
Synod of West Pennsylvania	97,303.00	26,838.59
Synod of Virginia	16,713.83	9,056.18
Ohio Synod	119,000.00	41,605.53
East Pennsylvania Synod	101,763.00	35,924.00
Alleghany Synod	58,412.00	18,650.00
Pittsburgh Synod	135,029.69	32,596.52
Indiana Synod	22,583.38	5,735.30
Illinois Synod	61,000.00	20,435.20
Texas Synod	3,196.73	1,396.80
Susquehanna Synod of Central Pennsylvania	65,065.95	12,938.10
Mississippi Synod	415.47	104.77
Synod of Iowa	7,900.00	2,642.52
Michigan Synod	20,325.06	5,749.32
Georgia-Alabama Synod	6,179.67	3,606.24
Synod of Canada	6,505.17	5,522.23

Synod of Kansas	11,000.00	3,453.49
Synod of Nebraska	21,629.31	5,762.77
Wartburg Synod	5,200.00	1,888.77
German Synod of Nebraska	2,600.00	934.20
Synod of California	7,869.40	2,527.97
Rocky Mountain Synod	3,507.35	2,514.90
Synod of the Northwest	39,298.30	12,872.64
Manitoba Synod	1,550.00	670.87
Pacific Synod	4,000.00	2,489.16
Nova Scotia Synod	1,722.99	1,306.10
Synod of West Virginia	5,500.00	4,343.13
Slovak Lutheran "Zion" Synod	500.00	405.00
Synod of Florida	2,182.65	312.38
	$1,382,826.69	$449,137.83

CASH ACCOUNT
For the Year Ended June 30, 1931

RECEIPTS

	General Fund	Apportionment	Specials*	Trust Funds
Synods		$1,382,826.69	$449,137.83	
Women's Missionary Society			320,746.45	
General Donations		510.00	1,953.76	
Income from Trust Accounts			1,746.62	
United Lutheran Publication House	$25,000.00			
Bank Interest	1,886.48			
Income from Investments..				$2,364.74
Transfers from Apportionment Fund to General Fund	58,512.00	58,512.00		
	$85,398.48	$1,324,824.69	$773,584.66	$2,364.74

DISBURSEMENTS

Apportionment disbursed to Boards		$1,318,038.00	$757,652.48	
Unapportioned Benevolence and special apportionment items		3,450.00	15,932.18	
Salary of President	$7,500.00			
Salary of Secretary	6,000.00			
Salaries of Clerks	3,975.00			
Salary of Statistical and Year Book Secretary	800.00			
Traveling Expenses: President	432.38			
Secretary	11.70			
Expenses: Treasurer	205.30			

Board Members	1,265.19	....	....	....
Statistical and Year Book Secretary	204.09	....	....	....
General Expenses	372.93	....	....	....
Postage and Telegrams	159.93	....	....	....
Printing and Stationery......	100.89	....	....	....
Auditing	450.00	....	....	....
Milwaukee Convention Expenses	24,714.66	....	....	....
Convention Expenses, Bulletin and Minutes	5,000.46	....	....	....
Convention Expenses, Publicity	2,462.97	....	....	....
Luther League	7,000.00	....	....	....
Federal Council of Churches	3,000.00	....	....	....
Committees:				
Apportionment	172.60	....	....	....
Adjudication	156.51	....	....	....
Congress International Education	70.00	....	....	....
Church Architecture	245.67	....	....	....
Church Music	106.20	....	....	....
Church Papers	58.35	....	....	....
Common Service Book....	33.90	....	....	....
On Boards	7.24	....	....	....
Evangelism	230.03	....	....	....
German Interests	265.02	....	....	....
International Justice and Good Will	5.00	....	....	....
Investments	476.38	....	....	....
Lutheran Church Unity..	8.51	....	....	....
Lutheran World Convention	1,702.84	....	....	....
Necrology	297.00	....	....	....
Publicity	513.37	....	....	....
Special Delegate to Augusta Synod	5.00	....	....	....
Theological Problems	109.52	....	....	....
Theological Education ..	67.77	....	....	....
Transportation	14.82	....	....	....
Lutheran Women's Work	54.70	....	....	....
World Conference on Faith and Order............	250.00	....	....	....
Transferred to the Treasurer of the Lutheran Church House.				
For reduction on principal of mortgage	25,000.00	....	....	....
For Rent	2,878.50	....	....	....
For Telephone	143.78	....	....	....
Income paid under Trust Funds:				
To Boards, etc.	....	....	....	1,746.62

To Emma M. Schmauck 240.00

$96,528.21 $1,321,488.00 $773,584.66 $1,986.62

RECEIPTS FROM SYNODS
For the Year Ended June 30, 1932

	Apportionment	Specials
Ministerium of Pennsylvania	$222,206.47	$29,360.46
United Synod of New York	117,400.00	20,435.63
United Synod of North Carolina	23,502.13	2,467.74
Maryland Synod	86,794.97	12,227.97
Synod of South Carolina	14,275.00	2,036.15
Synod of West Pennsylvania	87,770.00	14,862.02
Synod of Virginia	15,658.24	4,718.34
Synod of Ohio	95,000.00	15,432.33
East Pennsylvania Synod	87,784.00	20,692.00
Alleghany Synod	46,471.00	7,946.63
Pittsburgh Synod	108,029.64	16,009.22
Indiana Synod	22,779.22	2,913.31
Illinois Synod	54,500.00	7,298.52
Texas Synod	1,974.13	2,796.93
Susquehanna Synod of Central Pennsylvania	51,332.71	2,941.38
Mississippi Synod	428.80	65.44
Synod of Iowa	9,450.00	696.35
Michigan Synod	19,182.20	2,053.93
Georgia-Alabama Synod	5,724.41	955.77
Synod of Canada	5,514.54	2,812.49
Synod of Kansas	10,701.15	1,174.70
Synod of Nebraska	18,733.78	1,836.12
Wartburg Synod	5,000.00	1,051.22
German Synod of Nebraska	1,700.00	118.50
Synod of California	6,512.51	1,204.06
Rocky Mountain Synod	2,968.53	488.96
Synod of the Northwest	33,447.58	6,471.47
Manitoba Synod	1,050.00	329.48
Pacific Synod	3,600.00	425.80
Nova Scotia Synod	1,987.39	191.52
Synod of West Virginia	3,700.00	2,066.80
Slovak Lutheran "Zion" Synod	....	683.00
Synod of Florida	1,813.77	100.79

$1,166,992.17 $184,865.03

CASH ACCOUNT
For the Year Ended June 30, 1932
RECEIPTS

	General Fund	Apportionment	Specials	Trust Funds
Synods	....	$1,166,992.17	$184,865.03	....
Women's Missionary Society	....	....	310,997.14	....
General Donations	....	180.00	3,305.42	....

Income from Trust Accounts			2,094.15	
United Lutheran Publication House	$25,000.00	10,000.00		
Bank Interest	543.62			
Income from Investments				$2,032.28
Transfers from Apportionment Fund to General Fund	50,032.00	—50,032.00		
Refunds on Insurance	11.23			
	$75,586.85	$1,127,140.17	$501,261.74	$2,032.28

DISBURSEMENTS

Apportionment disbursed to Boards		$1,127,018.00	$486,344.25	
Unapportioned Benevolence and Special Apportionment Items		2,950.00	14,917.49	
Salary of President	$7,500.00			
Salary of Secretary	6,000.00			
Salaries of Clerks	4,125.00			
Salary of Statistical and Year Book Secretary	800.00			
Traveling Expenses:				
President	74.49			
Secretary	3.10			
Expenses:				
Treasurer	1,038.30			
Board Members	794.20			
Statistical and Year Book Secretary	555.30			
General Expenses	266.08			
Publicity Expense	72.53			
Postage and Telegrams	165.79			
Printing and Stationery	197.73			
Auditing	296.25			
Lutheran World Convention	1,702.84			
Luther League	8,000.00			
Federal Council of Churches	3,000.00			
Committee and Delegates Expenses:				
Apportionment	6.74			
Church Architecture	901.48			
Common Service Book	472.97			
German Interests	209.60			
International Justice and Good Will	22.60			
Investments	230.03			
Transportation	13.77			
Necrology	17.60			
World Conference on Faith and Order	250.00			

Theological Education	11.00	....	....	....
Office of Ministry	225.66	....	....	....
Committee of Six	94.10	....	....	....
Miscellaneous Committee and Delegates Expenses	795.10	....	....	....
Transferred to the Treasurer of the Lutheran Church House:				
For reduction on principal of mortgage	25,000.00	....	....	....
For Rent	2,477.08	....	....	....
For Telephone	143.08	....	....	....
Income Paid under Trust Funds:				
To Boards, etc.	....	....	....	2,094.15
To Emma M. Schmauck ..	....	....	....	240.00

	$65,462.42	$1,129,968.00	$501,261.74	$2,334.15

SUMMARY OF CASH BALANCES AT JUNE 30, 1932

Balance, Apportionment Fund	$3,940.34
Balance, General Fund	8,886.40
Balance, Trust Funds	2,843.96
	$15,670.70

In hands of Treasurer..	$15,170.70
In hands of Secretary...	500.00
	$15,670.70

RECAPITULATION OF APPORTIONMENT RECEIPTS

For the Years ended July 31, 1919 to 1924, inclusive;
the Eleven Months ended June 30, 1925, and the
Years Ended June 30, 1926 to 1932, inclusive.

1919	$223,687*
1920	877,995
1921	1,014,567
1922	1,026,672
1923	1,074,187
1924	1,167,115
1925	1,104,403**
1926	1,258,381
1927	1,270,977
1928	1,408,113
1929	1,371,611
1930	1,422,919
1931	1,382,826
1932	1,166,992

* Partial year.
**Eleven months.

TRUST INVESTMENTS AT JUNE 30. 1932

EMMA K. SOTTER TRUST

Income for Home Missions and Church Extension:
    $3,000 Altoona and Logan Valley 1st Mtg. 4½s, 1933.
    500 U. S. Fourth Liberty Loan, 4¼s.
    3,000 Appalachian Electric Power 1st & Ref. 5s, 1956.
    3,000 Georgia Power Co. 1st & Ref. 5s, 1967.

M. S. HOTTENSTEIN TRUST

Income as determined by The United Lutheran Church in America:
    $1000 Hotel Chelsea 1st 6s, 1945

W. P. HUFFMAN TRUST

Income one-third each to: Lutheran Orphans' Home at Salem, Va.
    Home Missions.
    Foreign Missions.
    $2,500 Mortgage, 5407 Vine Street, Philadelphia, Pa.
    Guaranteed; 5½%.
    3,000 Georgia Power 1st & Ref. 5s, 1967.
    2,000 American Gas & Electric 5s, 2028.

C. PFLAUM, JR., TRUST

Income for Mission Purposes:
    $5,000 Times Square, 46th St. Building 1st 6s, 1953

REV. R. A. HAFER, TRUST

Income: Three-fifths to Missions.
    Two-fifths to Education and Ministerial Pensions.
    40 shares Northern Pacific Railroad Company
    10 shares Public Service Corp. of N. J. 7% pfd.
        Respectfully submitted,
        E. CLARENCE MILLER, *Treasurer*.

Philadelphia, Pa., July 23, 1932.

We have audited the accounts of the Treasurer of The United Lutheran Church in America for the Biennium beginning July 1, 1930, and ending June 30, 1932, and we hereby certify that in our opinion the foregoing statements of:

Receipts from Synods, for the years ending June 30, 1931, and June 30, 1932.

Cash Accounts, for the years ending June 30, 1931, and June 30, 1932.

Summary of Cash Balances at June 30, 1932.

Recapitulation of Apportionment Receipts for the years ending July 31, 1919 to 1924, inclusive; the eleven months ending June 30, 1925, and the years ending June 30, 1926 to June 30, 1932, inclusive, and

Trust Investments at June 30, 1932

are in accordance with the books of account, and are true and correct.

        TAIT, WALKER & BAKER,
        Accountants and Auditors.

It was moved and carried that the report of the auditors be accepted.

Committee of Tellers No. 1 reported that the Rev. F. H. Knubel had received 414 votes for President out of a total of 459 votes cast. The Secretary declared that Dr. Knubel, having received more than a three-fourths majority of the votes cast on the first ballot, was elected President of The United Lutheran Church in America.

The convention proceeded to the election of a Treasurer, under the direction of Committee of Tellers No. 2.

The Convention proceeded to the election of a Treasurer, under Committee of Tellers No. 1.

It was moved and carried that one ballot for Secretary be taken at this time and that if the first ballot should not result in an election further ballots for Secretary be postponed until tomorrow.

The Secretary presented the report of the Executive Board.

REPORT OF THE EXECUTIVE BOARD
I. CONCERNING THE EXECUTIVE BOARD
1. Members:

Ex-Officio: Rev. F. H. Knubel, Rev. M. G. G. Scherer, Mr. E. Clarence Miller.

Term Expires 1934: Rev. Marion Justus Kline, Rev. Jacob L. Morgan, Rev. Rees Edgar Tulloss, Mr. John Greiner, Jr., B. B. Miller, Esq., Mr. Wm. H. Stackel.

Term Expires 1932: Rev. A. Charles R. Keiter, Rev. Charles D. Trexler, Rev. Abdel Ross Wentz, Hon. Wm. E. Hirt, Hon. John F. Kramer, George E. Neff, Esq.

2. Committees of the Executive Board:

At the beginning of the biennium the following committees were appointed by the President:

Committee on Constituent Synods
Rev. A. Charles R. Keiter   Rev. Charles D. Trexler
Rev. J. L. Morgan

Committee on Boards and Committees
Rev. Abdel Ross Wentz   Rev. M. G. G. Scherer
Rev. Marion Justus Kline   Rev. Rees Edgar Tulloss
Mr. Wm. H. Stackel

Finance Committee
Mr. E. Clarence Miller   Mr. John Greiner, Jr.
George E. Neff, Esq.

Legal Committee

Hon. John F. Kramer   Hon. Wm. E. Hirt

B. B. Miller, Esq.

3. Death of the Secretary:

The Board has the sad duty of reporting the death of its Secretary, who was also the Secretary of the Church. The Reverend M. G. G. Scherer, D.D., passed into life eternal on March 9, 1932. The Board at its meeting on April 14, 1932, adopted the following memorial minute:

Minute on the Death of Dr. M. G. G. Scherer

Since the last meeting of the Board our hearts have been saddened by the departure of our beloved Secretary, the Reverend M. G. G. Scherer, D.D., who passed into life eternal on March 9, 1932. By his going away the Executive Board has lost a most valuable and efficient Secretary and The United Lutheran Church in America one of her noblest and most dependable leaders and counselors.

Dr. Scherer was born in Catawba County, N. C., on March 16, 1861. He was the son of the Rev. Simeon and Sarah Scherer and the grandson of the Rev. Jacob Scherer. The Scherer family played an important part in the work and history of the Lutheran Church in the South almost from its very beginning, as well as in some of the states farther west. Dr. M. G. G. Scherer himself was practically all his life a member of one or another of the Southern Synods, and gave unsparingly of both time and labor to help build up the Church of the Reformation in those Synods. However, when the time came for the organization of The United Lutheran Church in America, without losing aught of the love which he had for his Church in the southland, he became profoundly interested in the larger undertaking and threw his full strength into that movement.

Dr. Scherer was educated at Franklin Academy in Rowan County near Salisbury, N. C., and at Roanoke College in Virginia. He took his theological training in the Southern Seminary which was then located at Salem, Va. He served quite acceptably as pastor of churches in Virginia, Georgia, West Virginia, Pennsylvania, North Carolina and South Carolina. He was at one time Secretary of the North Carolina Synod, was President of North Carolina College, and was later called to become Professor in the Lutheran Theological Southern Seminary. For two terms he served as President of the South Carolina Synod. He was for a number of years Secretary of the United Synod of the Evangelical Lutheran Church in the South, and later on he was President of that body, which office he held at the time of the merging of the Synods into The United Lutheran Church in America. He was a member of the Ways and Means Committee for the Merger and helped to draw up the Constitution and map out a program for the organization.

When The United Lutheran Church in America was organized he was elected as Secretary of that body, which office he continued to hold and magnify, to the gratification of the whole Church, until the time of his death. As Secretary, Dr. Scherer not only kept accurate records for the Church and for her Executive Board, but he moreover helped to lay out programs and shape policies which gave direction to the life and mission of the newly formed United Lutheran Church. His discerning intellect and sound judgment helped to define the proper relationships which this new body should endeavor to maintain towards that of other Lutheran bodies in this country, which will have great weight in maintaining sympathetic understanding among one another.

Nor does his influence stop here, but it reaches even beyond the pale of the Lutheran Church out into other communions. This was evidenced in the part which he took, as a delegate, in the Universal Conference on Life and Work in Stockholm in 1925, and especially so in the World Conference on Faith and Order in Lausanne in 1927 where, by his clear and scholarly presentation of the Scriptural and historic Lutheran position concerning the ministry and kindred subjects, he won for the Lutheran Church fresh ecumenical recognition and prestige.

Dr. Scherer rendered valuable service also on a number of important boards and committees of the Church, among which we make mention of the following: namely, Board of Trustees of Mont Amoena Female Seminary, Board of Trustees of Newberry College, Board of Trustees of the Lutheran Theological Southern Seminary, Common Service Book Committee, Board of Managers of American Bible Society, Board of Trustees of American Tract Society, Member of the Statistical and Church Year Book Committee, Board of Managers of the Lutheran World Almanac, and Member of the Continuation Committee of the World Conference on Faith and Order.

He was not a voluminous writer, but he was painstaking and forceful in what he wrote. He was co-author of the Key Books of "Our Church," a contributor to the symposium in the book entitled "What is Lutheranism," author of "Christian Liberty and Church Unity," and editor of the now seven volumes of the Minutes of the Conventions of The United Lutheran Church in America. His sermons and addresses, many of which he wrote out in full, are also of high order and merit a place in permanent book form.

But Dr. Scherer was more than a writer or great Secretary and wise counselor, he was a great man. In fact he was great in his official capacities, because he was, first of all, great in himself. He was a man of great faith, and on this sure foundation he developed a scholarly mind with strong convictions which gloriously withstood the storms of the times through which he was called to pass. But withal he was forbearing, kind-hearted and sympathetic. He was cultured and pure-minded, a man of winning personality. And he enjoyed, as he deserved to, the confidence and esteem of all whose privilege it was to have known him and fellowshipped with him.

And now let us who remain give humble and unfeigned thanks to Almighty God for his gracious favors brought to us through the life and labors of this great man and, being inspired by his example, endeavor to consecrate anew ourselves to the cause of Christ which he loved so well.

4. Election of Acting Secretary:

The Executive Board elected the Rev. Abdel Ross Wentz as Acting Secretary until the next convention of the Church.

5. Duties of the Secretary: (For action on this item see p. 22.)

The Board considered the redistribution of work among the officers of the Church and recommends concerning the office of secretary in addition to the duties required of the secretary by the Constitution of the Church:

(1) That his office be located in the Church House.
(2) That he be in charge of the statistical work of the Church.
(3) That he be editor of the Year Book.
(4) That he be in charge of the publicity work of the Church.
(5) That he be in charge of transportation activities of the Church.
(6) That he be in charge of the operations of the Lutheran Church House.
(7) That he be subject to delegation by the President to attend meetings of boards or committees, and meetings of synods where official representation is desirable.

The Board further recommends that the President and Secretary, as arranged between them, read all minutes of meetings of boards and synods; represent the Church where desirable in important public gatherings, and give consideration to projects and undertakings which will promote the internal welfare of the Church.

6. Nominations to Fill Vacancies:

To fill vacancies occurring at this convention, the Board places the following in nomination: Rev. Ellis B. Burgess, Rev. E. P. Pfatteicher, Rev. A. Steimle, Hon. Wm. E. Hirt, Robbin B. Wolf, Esq., Hon. John L. Zimmerman.

II. MATTERS REFERRED

1. Minutes; Approval, Printing and Distribution: . (Minutes U. L. C. A. 1930, p. 602)

The Executive Board approved the Minutes for the last two sessions of the Milwaukee Convention at its meeting held January 8, 1931, and ordered that 4,200 copies of the Minutes of the Seventh Biennial Convention be printed and distributed. This work was done by our Publication House. The Minutes were mailed, according to a list prepared by the Secretary, early in January, 1930.

2. Financial Missionary Objective of the Luther League: (Minutes U. L. C. A. 1930, pp. 328, 334)

(a) **Annual Appropriation for the Biennium:** On recommendation of the Finance Committee the appropriation to the Luther League was fixed at $8,000 per year for the biennium.

(b) **Financial Missionary Objective:** The Luther League decided to assume the main building of the seminary in Japan, an item of $15,000, as its missionary objective during the biennium and asked the approval of the Executive Board. This approval was granted.

3. The Board of American Missions and the Special Year 1938: (Minutes U. L. C. A. 1930, pp. 264, 302)(For action on this item see p. 84.)

The Board of American Missions applied for permission to use the year 1938, the twentieth anniversary of The United Lutheran Church in America, as a time to conduct a campaign on behalf of Church Extension funds. We recommend that the year 1938 be reserved for the Board of American Missions to conduct a campaign for Church Extension funds, but that the final decision as to the advisability of a campaign be deferred.

4. Establishment of a Bureau of Architecture: (Minutes U. L. C. A. 1930, pp. 450, 451) (For action on this item see p. 84.)

The Board recommends that no Bureau of Architecture be established, but that a more liberal allowance be made for office and secretarial expense for the Committee on Church Architecture.

5. A Conference and Manual on Publicity: (Minutes U. L. C. A. 1930, pp. 208, 209)

A resolution of the Milwaukee Convention referred to the Finance Committee of the Executive Board a request that The United Lutheran Church in America include in its budget for publicity an amount not exceeding $3,000 to finance a "conference on church publicity" and the publication of a "Publicity Manual" for pastors. The Finance Committee recommended an appropriation of $2,000 for these purposes. The Executive Board voted that in view of present financial conditions it finds itself unable to act favorably on this recommendation.

6. Proposed Merger of Inner Mission Board, the Board of Deaconess Work, the Committee on Evangelism and the Committee on Moral and Social Welfare: (Minutes U. L. C. A. 1930, p. 339) (For action on this item see p. 84.)

The action of the Executive Board was as follows:

In the light of all the facts in the case we conclude that there is a distinct sphere and separate function for each of these four agencies in the life of the Church if they are properly administered and related. We therefore recommend

(a) That no action be taken looking toward a merger of these agencies, and

(b) That the President of the Church be instructed to attend meetings of each of these agencies in order to urge upon them a higher degree ol efficiency in their work and a more thorough correlation with one another.

7. Transfer of Immigrant Mission Work: (Minutes U. L. C. A. 1930, pp. 264, 302)

A recommendation of the Board of American Missions that the Immigrant Mission Work be transferred from the jurisdiction of the Inner Mission Board to the Board of American Missions was referred to the Executive Board. A conference was held with representatives of the Inner Mission Board and representatives of the Board of American Missions and it was felt that there are no compelling reasons at this time for changing the present method of administering the Immigrant Mission Work.

8. The Exchange of Students and Professors with European Universities: (Minutes U. L. C. A. 1930, pp. 147, 408)

The Executive Board considered the proposal, expressed its approval of the general idea and referred it for consideration to our theological seminaries, the conference of our theological professors and the Board of Education.

9. Training of Ministers and Teachers: (Minutes U. L. C. A. 1930, pp. 580, 581)

The Executive Board appointed a Committee of Six to initiate plans to present to a joint conference of the three agencies designated, namely, the Executive Board, the Board of Education, and the Synodical Presidents. The joint conference was appointed for October 11, 1932, and the action of the Executive Board as a result of the joint conference is submitted in a supplemental report of the Executive Board. (See Supplemental Report "A" of the Executive Board, pp. 61-72.)

10. Commission on Investments: (Minutes U. L. C. A. 1930, pp. 335, 336, 415)

The Board elected five men to the Commission on Investments and approved the Rules and Regulations of the Commission. See Report of Commission on Investments, p. 219.

In the course of the organization of the Commission on Investments the President of the Church was requested by the Executive Board to provide a ruling upon the relationship of Recommendation 7 to Recommendation 5, page 337 of the Minutes of the Milwaukee Convention (1930) for the benefit of the Commission and the Board. The ruling follows:

A careful examination of the report and especially the recommendations of the Commission on Method of Investing Endowment Funds reveals that in Recommendation 5 we have a *general* statement concerning "a plan" and in Recommendation 7 a *specific* provision which must be included in "such plan." The importance to the general plan of this specific item becomes manifest when one recognizes that Recommendation 6 is so worded as to be exactly parallel with Recommendation 7. Recommendation 6 is another *specific* provision which must be included in "such plan." In other words, the requirement for the merging of all funds (Recommendation 7) is of equal importance with the requirement that all funds shall be committed for safekeeping with banks and/or trust companies (Recommendation 6). The relationship of Recommendation 7 to Recommendation 5 is therefore the specification of something vitally essential to the general plan, without which the general plan cannot be devised.

This view is upheld by a realization of the fact that the debate at the Milwaukee Convention was focalized upon the provision in Recommendation 7. It is upheld also by the Commission's own emphasis in its report that "best results" would be achieved by the merging of all funds, and by the Commission's elaboration of six reasons in favor of this merging.

On the other hand and although the Commission is not fulfilling its instructions unless it plans now and definitely for a merger of funds, nevertheless its responsibility under Recommendation 5 will not have been fulfilled unless it also plans to bring under its supervision "all" funds even before they are ready for merging. The words "as soon as practicable" manifestly refer to the words immediately following, "to perfect and put into operation a plan" and not to the more remote words, "bringing under its supervision, etc." This view is upheld by the original purposes in mind when the idea of a commission was proposed and by the frequent repetition in the report of the phrase "all funds." It is upheld also by the statements in the Commission's introductory item 8 of its report. Any arrangement in the plan concerning funds not immediately to be merged must however be definitely regarded as temporary in its character and as merely preparatory to the inclusion of such funds also in the merged fund. To complete this ruling the introductory item 8, previously mentioned, must be given weight. It is clear from that item that the preparatory "supervision" of unmerged funds involves "the working out of all details with each endowed agency or with its duly authorized committee in order that due attention may be given to special situations." In other words the "supervision" becomes in reality an advisory or a consultative supervision.

11. Co-operation with Suomi Synod: (Minutes U. L. C. A. 1930, pp. **414, 415)** (For action on this item see p. 85.)

The Milwaukee Convention adopted certain agreements concerning Finnish work in Canada and relations with the Suomi Synod. The Suomi Synod proposed amendments to these agreements. A conference was held December 3, 1931, among representatives of the Suomi Synod, our Executive Board, our Board of American Missions and our Commission on Lutheran Church Unity. This conference adopted resolutions as follows:

(1) That the United Lutheran Finnish congregations in Canada be guaranteed the right to use the Finnish language as long as it is necessary in the conduct of their work in accordance with the Washington Declaration.

(2) That the United Lutheran Finnish congregations of Canada be free to use Suomi Synod publications in their congregational work, and in the education of ministers make use of the Theological Seminary of the Suomi Synod, in which the establishment of a Professorship by The United Lutheran Church in America for the Canadian Finns would be very desirable.

(3) That the United Lutheran Finnish congregations of Canada be united with the United Lutheran Church Synods on the territory in which they may be located and that arrangement be made for biennial meetings of all Finnish pastors in Canada.

(4) That the Executive Board of The United Lutheran Church in America, through the proper synodical authorities, arrange for visitors from the Finnish Lutheran Churches in Canada to the Suomi Synod meetings and festivals, these men to be chosen by the Finnish Lutheran pastors in Canada.

(5) That when the Canadian Finnish work has developed sufficiently in the estimation of the Mission Boards of The United Lutheran Church in America, the United Lutheran Finnish congregations in Canada be supported in their petitions to organize a Finnish Lutheran Synod in Canada.

(6) Recommended that the Suomi Synod be requested to appoint a commission to meet with the Commission on Lutheran Church Unity of the United Lutheran Church for the purpose of studying and cultivating the relationship between the Suomi Synod and The United Lutheran Church in America.

The Executive Board approved this action of the conference of December 3, 1931.

12. Uniform Report Blank for Delegation Chairmen: (Minutes U. L. C. A., p. 601)

In compliance with the instruction of the Milwaukee Convention the Executive Board prepared and placed in the hands of delegation Chairmen a uniform report blank to be used in making reports to the Committee on Leave of Absence.

III. SYNODS
A. In General
1. Apportionment to Synods, 1932 and 1933:

The budget of $2,400,000 adopted at Milwaukee for the years 1932 and 1933 was apportioned among the Constituent Synods as follows:

Apportionment for 1932

	Communing Membership	Apportion-ment
Ministerium of Pennsylvania	140,873	$507,028
United Synod of New York	95,196	342,628
United Synod of North Carolina	18,887	67,978
Synod of Maryland	30,983	111,514
Synod of South Carolina	13,222	47,589
Synod of West Pennsylvania	33,905	122,031
Synod of Virginia	12,203	43,920
Synod of Ohio	48,304	173,855
East Pennsylvania Synod	33,984	122,315
Alleghany Synod	20,563	73,986
Pittsburgh Synod	51,740	186,222
Indiana Synod	8,660	31,169
Illinois Synod	25,959	93,432
Texas Synod	2,882	10,373
Susquehanna Synod	25,662	92,363
Mississippi Synod	313	1,127

Synod of Iowa	6,248	22,488
Michigan Synod	9,755	35,110
Synod of Georgia-Alabama	2,721	9,794
Synod of Canada	12,015	43,245
Synod of Kansas	5,023	18,089
Synod of Nebraska	9,068	32,638
Wartburg Synod	5,835	21,002
German Nebraska Synod	6,352	22,869
Synod of California	4,254	15,311
Rocky Mountain Synod	1,725	6,209
Synod of the Northwest	22,464	80,852
Manitoba Synod	5,310	19,112
Pacific Synod	2,107	7,584
Nova Scotia Synod	1,628	5,860
Synod of West Virginia	3,129	11,262
Slovak "Zion" Synod	4,849	17,453
Florida Synod	999	3,596
Total	666,818	$2,400,000

Apportionment for 1933

	Communing Membership	Apportion- ment
Ministerium of Pennsylvania	140,996	$503,684
United Synod of New York	95,435	340,925
United Synod of North Carolina	18,931	67,628
Synod of Maryland	31,373	112,075
Synod of South Carolina	13,424	47,955
Synod of West Pennsylvania	33,977	121,377
Synod of Virginia	12,532	44,769
Synod of Ohio	48,322	172,622
East Pennsylvania Synod	34,072	121,716
Alleghany Synod	19,984	71,390
Pittsburgh Synod	51,740	184,832
Indiana Synod	8,401	30,011
Illinois Synod	26,531	94,777
Texas Synod	2,757	9,850
Susquehanna Synod	25,539	91,234
Mississippi Synod	325	1,161
Synod of Iowa	6,922	24,728
Michigan Synod	9,661	34,512
Synod of Georgia-Alabama	2,985	10,663
Synod of Canada	13,493	48,201
Synod of Kansas	4,974	17,769
Synod of Nebraska	9,959	35,577
Wartburg Synod	5,859	20,930
German Nebraska Synod	6,014	21,484
Synod of California	3,949	14,107
Rocky Mountain Synod	1,737	6,205
Synod of the Northwest	24,149	86,268
Manitoba Synod	5,461	19,508
Pacific Synod	1,865	6,662
Nova Scotia Synod	1,767	6,312

Synod of West Virginia...	3,190	11,396
Slovak "Zion" Synod	4,584	16,375
Florida Synod	923	3,297
Total	671,831	$2,400,000

See also VI, 4, of this Report, p. 53.

2.   Amendment to Model Constitution for Constituent Synods:

The Board amended the Model Constitution for Constituent Synods, Article IX, Section 1, Paragraph 2, by adding "and such other ordained Lutheran ministers engaged in extra parochial work of the Church, as have been elected to membership by the synod upon recommendation by the Examining Committee."

3.   The Preparation of a Catechism: (For action on this item see p. 85.)

The Board received from within one of the synods the suggestion that the Church prepare a catechism for the assistance of our pastors in their catechetical work. The Board recommends :

(a) That this Convention authorize the appointment of a special committee of three pastors and three professors of religious education or of practical theology to report to the Executive Board concerning the advisability and a plan for the preparation of such a manual.

(b) That, if the report of this special committee is favorable and approved by the Executive Board, the actual preparation shall proceed in accordance with the plan proposed by the special committee.

4.   Mode of Procedure in Merging Congregations:

In response to several requests for information as to the proper mode of procedure in the merging of congregations, the Board, through its Committee on Constituent Synods, accepted the following and refers it as a desirable method to the Constituent Synods and through them to congregations.

Order of Procedure for Congregations Seeking to Merge

Congregational mergers are generally of two distinct types, viz. (a) congregations belonging to the same synod which have determined to merge and (b) congregations belonging to different synods which have determined to merge.

(1) In either case if two congregations have reached the state at which they seriously consider a merger each of them should appoint a committee to represent it in negotiations and preparation for the merger.

(2) If these committees represent congregations of the same synod they should consult with the synodical president who will act in an advisory capacity throughout the proceedings. If the congregations they represent belong to different synods they should notify their respective synodical presidents who should act in a similar advisory capacity. For the best interests of all concerned no merger should be attempted without proper notification of and consultation with the officers of the synod or synods affected.

(3) The two merger committees should meet and organize into joint committee.

(4) The joint committee shall take into consideration all matters necessary for a successful merger. This consideration should not fail to include

the disposition of the properties of the merging congregations, the reallocation of such portion or portions of a parish to which either congregation may belong which portions may not be party to the merger, the future of such pastor or pastors as may be connected with the merging congregations, —and the name and place of worship for the new congregation. If the way seems clear they should prepare a constitution for the merged congregation based upon the model constitution for congregations prepared by the United Lutheran Church. They should also prepare a plan of merger outlining in detail the manner in which and the date on which the merger is to become effective.

(5) This constitution and plan of merger should be submitted to each of the congregations for approval. We are of the opinion that a two-thirds majority should be required to constitute such an approval.

(6) When the congregations have both approved of the proposed constitution and merger plan they should be called together in joint meeting as provided by the plan, for the purpose of giving effect to the merger and organizing the new congregation.

(7) The joint committee should arrange for someone to call the meeting to order and state its object. This might be the chairman or secretary of the joint committee, or an officer of synod or conference called upon for the purpose.

(8) The meeting should then elect a temporary chairman and a secretary.

(9) The joint committee should then submit to the meeting a report setting forth the approval by the constituent congregations of the merger plan and constitution and presenting the proposed constitution for formal adoption.

(10) The constitution having been adopted, the next step would be the election of officers for the congregation according to the provisions of the constitution. (The person chosen by the newly elected church officers to be their presiding officer should serve in a similar capacity for the congregation until a pastor has been called and has entered upon his work.)

(11) It will be advisable and probably necessary for the joint committee to have competent legal counsel in addition to the president of synod to meet with it and advise it, especially with regard to all matters of property and other matters requiring legal advice.

5.   An Official Interpretation of the Constitution:

(For action on this item see p. 85.)

The Executive Board requested the President of the Church to present to the Church a ruling as to the meaning of Article V, Section 1, of the Constitution, and to indicate the method of applying the interpretation in detail.

The following official interpretation is given to the Church:

"A 'pastoral charge' means primarily an organized group of Christians who are regularly ministered to with the Means of Grace by a regularly authorized minister as a pastor. What is commonly called a 'vacant congregation' belongs under this classification, because presumably it desires such ministration and its condition is merely temporary. A group of Christians customarily ministered to by more than one pastor is nevertheless only one pastoral charge. In the Constitution of The United Lutheran Church in America the term is furthermore manifestly intended to designate a group of congregations ministered to by one pastor as being only one 'pastoral charge.' Non-synodical congregations are naturally not to be included at all when synods decide upon the number of delegates to which they are entitled."

It is also recommended that the Convention instruct the Secretary of the Church to correspond with the officials of all synods for the purpose of a true adjustment in the number of delegates from all synods.

B. In Particular

Survey of Canadian Synods:

On invitation of two of the constituent synods, namely, the Manitoba Synod and the Synod of Canada, and at the suggestion of two of the boards of the Church, namely, the Board of Education and the Board of American Missions, the Executive Board authorized, the officers of the Church to appoint a commission to survey the work of our Church in Canada. The officers appointed the Revs. E. B. Burgess, Gould Wickey and E. A. Tappert. The report of the Commission, together with its recommendations, is submitted in a Supplemental Report of the Executive Board. (See Supplemental Report "B" of the Executive Board, pp. 72-84.)

IV. BOARDS AND COMMITTEES

A. In General

1. **Proposed Merger of Four Agencies:** See II, 6, of this Report, p. 41.

2. **Twenty-fifth Anniversary of Laymen's Movement:**

The Executive Board granted a request from the Board of American Missions, the Board of Foreign Missions, and the Laymen's Movement for Stewardship, for permission to designate a day in November, 1931, to commemorate the twenty-fifth anniversary of the Laymen's Missionary Movement.

B. In Particular

1. **Board of Foreign Missions:**

(a) **Undesignated Income from Trust Funds:** The Executive Board assigned all undesignated income from trust funds during the fiscal years of the past biennium to the Board of Foreign Missions to be applied against the indebtedness of that Board.

(b) **Offerings at Convention Services:** The Executive Board assigned all offerings at services during the Philadelphia Convention to the Board of Foreign Missions to be applied against the indebtedness of that Board.

(c) **Vacancies Filled:** Upon nomination of the Board of Foreign Missions the Rev. L. C. Manges was elected by the Executive Board to succeed the Rev. J. E. Byers, deceased, term expiring 1934; the Rev. P. E. Monroe to succeed the Rev. J. L. Morgan, resigned, term expiring 1936; Mr. Frank Howard to succeed the Rev. G. Albert Getty, resigned, term expiring 1936; and Mr. M. P. Moller, Jr., to succeed Mr. A. Y. Leech, resigned, term expiring 1934.

2. Board of American Missions:

Vacancy Filled: Upon nomination of the Board of American Missions Mr. Horace W. Bikle was elected by the Executive Board to succeed Mr. C. Lehmann, resigned, term expiring 1932.

3. Immigrants Mission Board:

Vacancies Filled: Upon nomination of the Immigrants Mission Board the Rev. F. O. Evers was elected by the Executive Board to succeed the Rev. S. N. Carpenter, resigned, term expiring 1932; the Rev. J. M. Francis to succeed the Rev. G. H. Rhodes, resigned, term expiring 1932; and Mr. H. F. Heuer to succeed Mr. Frank L. Fox, resigned, term expiring 1932.

4. Board of Education:

Vacancy Filled: Upon nomination of the Board of Education the Rev. C. H. Stein was elected by the Executive Board to succeed the Rev. Charles S. Bowers, resigned, term expiring 1932.

5. Inner Mission Board:

Vacancy Filled: Upon nomination of the Inner Mission Board the Rev. Rufus E. Kern was elected by the Executive Board to succeed the Rev. Joseph S. Schantz, deceased, term expiring 1934.

6. Board of Publication:

Vacancies Filled: Upon nomination of the Board of Publication Judge Claude T. Reno was elected by the Executive Board to succeed Mr. John M. Snyder, resigned, term expiring 1932, and Mr. W. G. Semisch to succeed Dr. Croll Keller, deceased, term expiring 1934.

7. Parish and Church School Board:

(a) **Leadership Training School Corporation:** The Milwaukee Convention approved the action of the Parish and Church School Board in forming this Corporation but recommended that the Parish and Church School Board consider the advisability of amending its Charter, if necessary, and of taking over the work of the Leadership Training School Corporation ana its assets and dissolving the latter corporation and that the Parish and Church School Board report its action to the Executive Board. For the information of the Church we report that the Parish and Church School Board finally decided not to dissolve the Leadership Training School Corporation and take over its assets.

(b) **Comprehensive Plan of Parish Education:** (For action on this item see p. 86.)

(For action on this item see p. 86.)

As instructed by the Milwaukee Convention (Minutes, 1930, p. 589) the Parish and Church School Board has been gathering information and preparing to formulate a comprehensive plan of parish education. The work of the Board was so readjusted as to enable the secretarial staff to devote all of their time to this undertaking. After much preliminary labor, nearly a whole year has been spent directly on the project. The work has been prosecuted on such an extensive and intensive scale that it has been physically impossible to conclude it within the time limit evidently intended by the Milwaukee resolutions.

A preliminary report of work done was submitted to the Executive Board on July 7, 1932. From this report and from a subsequent conference (October 5, 1932) between the Chairman of the Executive Board's Committee on Boards and Committees and the secretarial staff of the Parish and Church School Board, it appears that the Parish and Church School Board has laid very thorough-going preparations to carry out the instructions of the Milwaukee Convention, that information has been gathered with painstaking care and from the widest possible sources, that the work of analysis is about completed and comprises many volumes of classified data and many bulky packages of exhibits, and that several parts of the survey are yet to be completed, such as the preparation of summaries, the drawing of conclusions, and the statement of principles on which to base a comprehensive plan of parish education. Not until these preliminary and preparatory studies have been completed can the actual formulation of a plan begin.

The Executive Board took action (1) approving the method of procedure employed by the Parish and Church School Board in carrying out the instructions of the Milwaukee Convention, and commending that Board for the thoroughness with which it has prosecuted this work; (2) approving the work thus far accomplished on the comprehensive plan of parish education and instructing the Parish and Church School Board to carry the work to completion; and (3) commending the Board of Education and other agencies of the Church for their co-operation in this work.

The Executive Board recommends that the instructions of the Milwaukee Convention, both to the Parish and Church School Board and to the Board of Education, be continued, and that the time for the completion of the work by both Boards be extended as long as may be necessary.

8.   Board of Deaconess Work:

Vacancy Filled: Upon nomination of the Board of Deaconess Work the Rev. J. J. Schindel was elected by the Executive Board to succeed the Rev. C. T. Benze, resigned, term expiring 1936.

9.   Committee on Church Papers:

Vacancies Filled: Upon nomination of the Committee on Church Papers, the Rev. C. E. Gardner was elected by the Executive Board to succeeed the Rev. J. A. Leas, resigned, term expiring 1934; the Rev. W. H. Greever to succeed the Rev. P. D. Brown, resigned, term expiring 1934; and the Rev. A. J. Holl to succeed the Rev. John C. Horine, resigned, term expiring 1936.

C. Standing Committees, Commissions, etc.

1. Statistical and Church Year Book Committee:

Statistical Secretary: The Rev. George Linn Kieffer was elected Statistical Secretary for the biennium at a salary of $800 per annum.

2. Committee on German Interests:

(a) **A General German Conference:** On request of this Committee the Executive Board authorized the holding of a General German Conference during the fall of 1931.

(b) **Special Appeal for Martin Luther and Saskatoon Seminaries:** On petition of this Committee the Executive Board authorized a special offering in our German congregations on Whitsunday, 1931, for the benefit of Martin Luther and Saskatoon Seminaries.

3. Commission on Theological Education:

The Commission was dissolved and its secretary informed the secretary of the Church under date of January 15, 1931, that the papers of the Commission have been placed with the Archivist of the Church.

V. INSTITUTIONS

Privilege of Deferring Education Campaigns:

On October 8, 1931, the Executive Board took the following action:

Whereas, The year 1931 has been set aside by action of The United Lutheran Church in America for emphasis upon the needs of our educational institutions and for campaigns on their behalf; and

Whereas, We are passing through a period of economic distress of unprecedented severity, which is creating serious problems for many persons among our constituency, and it would seem impractical to undertake procedures looking toward the gathering of large sums through campaigns for special purposes,

Be It Resolved, That in cases where it is desired, we grant institutions and synods contemplating such campaigns the privilege of deferring the opening of these campaigns until such time as general conditions may show improvement, perhaps even as late as the year 1935.

Be It Resolved, That in cases where such postponement may create a serious or dangerous financial situation for an institution which has been depending upon the results of the expected campaign, it is suggested that such institutions and their supporting synods confer as to means by which the minimum current needs of the institutions may be met during the period of postponement of campaigns.

VI. FINANCE

1. At the meeting of the Board on October 8, 1931, the financial situation of the Church as affected by the financial depression was discussed at great length, and the officers of the Board were instructed to draft the sentiment of the Board on this subject. Following is the statement issued by the officers:

(1) The present conditions if spiritually considered and taken to heart may provide richer blessings for us than did all the seeming prosperity of

recent years. Self-sufficiency and dependence upon material wealth does not become those whose God is the Rock of their strength. This is a time for faith.

(2) Christians may be saved from worry and fear, not by optimistic worldly prophecies, but by listening to Him Who wishes to calm the storm in their own souls before He quiets the disturbance in the world without.

(3) In private and family and congregational prayer special petitions for the needy, for the Church, for the nations, and for their leaders are eminently fitting.

(4) Every congregation has before it the practical duty to promote a painstaking, personal, and continued effort on behalf of the unemployed and their homes within the parish.

(5) At this season of the Every Member Canvass there are actually multitudes of members who have reason for a thankful increase in their contribution to the Church and its causes. Let the pledges made bear the aroma of grateful sacrifice more than in any previous year.

(6) All of our Synods, Boards, Institutions, etc., should examine their obligations and expenditures in detail, with a view to ascertaining whether a definite and wise reduction is possible.

(7) The Finance Committee of the Executive Board is instructed to follow this course with its own funds, and to report to the next meeting.

All of the above is commended to the Church for calm decision, as our sacred obligation in a much disturbed period.

2. Auditors Appointed:

The firm of Tait, Walker & Baker, Muhlenberg Building, Philadelphia, Pa., was appointed as the auditors during the biennium.

3. Budget: (For action on this item see p. 86.)

With reference to the budget the Executive Board makes the following recommendations:

(a) That, as to the distribution of the budget among the agencies of the Church, no change in the present percentages be made for the biennium 1934-35, except as provided in (b).

(b) That for the biennium 1934-35 the percentage of the National Lutheran Home for the Aged be reduced from .60 per cent to .45 per cent, that the percentage for Tabitha Home be reduced from .40 per cent to .30 per cent, that the percentage of the Lowman Home be reduced from .09 per cent to .06 per cent. This recommendation is made with the expectation that the continued process of reduction will, after three more bienniums, entirely eliminate these charitable institutions from the budget of the Church and leave them to the budgets of their supporting synods.

(c) That the saving of .28 per cent effected by the reduction of the percentages of the three charitable institutions named above, be divided as follows: .15 per cent to the Parish and Church School Board making the total for that Board 1.10 per cent; and .13 per cent to the Inner Mission Board making the total for that Board 1.70 per cent.

(d) That the Church fix the budget for 1934-35 at $2,000,000 annually.

(e) That the Church rescind the action taken at the Milwaukee Convention, October 8, 1930, fixing the budget for 1933 at $2,400,000, and fix the budget for 1933 at $2,000,000.

(f) [Inserted by the Convention, see p. 86.]

On the basis of these recommendations the budget for 1933, approved by the Executive Board and recommended to the Convention is as follows:

	Amount	Percentage
Board of Foreign Missions	$600,000	30.00
Board of American Missions	760,000	38.00
Board of Education	180,000	9.00
Parish and Church School Board	19,000	.95
Inner Mission Board	31,400	1.57
Board of Minis. Pensions & Relief	235,000	11.75
Board of Deaconess Work	40,000	2.00
National Home for the Aged	12,000	.60
Tabitha Home	8,000	.40
Lowman Home	1,800	.09
National Lutheran Council	23,000	1.15
American Bible Society	5,000	.25
United Lutheran Church Treasury	84,800	4.24
	$2,000,000	100.00

and the budget for the years 1934 and 1935, approved by the Executive Board and recommended to the Convention is as follows:

	Amount	Percentage
Board of Foreign Missions	$600,000	30.00
Board of American Missions	760,000	38.00
Board of Education	180,000	9.00
Parish and Church School Board	22,000	1.10
Inner Mission Board	34,000	1.70
Board of Minis. Pensions & Relief	235,000	11.75
Board of Deaconess Work	40,000	2.00
National Home for the Aged	9,000	.45
Tabitha Home	6,000	.30
Lowman Home	1,200	.06
National Lutheran Council	23,000	1.15
American Bible Society	5,000	.25
United Lutheran Church Treasury	84,800	4.24
	$2,000,000	100.00

4. Apportionment to Synods: See III, A, 1, of this Report, p. 46.

On the basis of the budget recommended in 2 above the apportionment to the synods for 1933 is as follows:

	Apportionment
Ministerium of Pennsylvania	$419,735
United Synod of New York	284,105
United Synod of North Carolina	56,356
Synod of Maryland	93,395
Synod of South Carolina	39,962
Synod of West Pennsylvania	101,147
Synod of Virginia	37,307
Synod of Ohio	143,851

Synod of East Pennsylvania	101,430
Alleghany Synod	59,492
Pittsburgh Synod	154,026
Indiana Synod	25,009
Illinois Synod	78,981
Texas Synod	8,208
Susquehanna Synod	76,028
Mississippi Synod	968
Iowa Synod	20,606
Michigan Synod	28,760
Synod of Georgia-Alabama	8,886
Synod of Canada	40,168
Synod of Kansas	14,808
Synod of Nebraska	29,647
Wartburg Synod	17,442
German Nebraska Synod	17,906
California Synod	11,756
Rocky Mountain Synod	5,171
Synod of the Northwest	71,890
Manitoba Synod	16,257
Pacific Synod	5,552
Nova Scotia Synod	5,260
Synod of West Virginia	9,496
Slovak "Zion" Synod	13,647
Florida Synod	2,748

$2,000,000

5. Synods' Relation to the Assignment of Apportionments:

The attention of the Executive Board was called to the action of a number of the synods in revising and reducing the amount of the apportionment assigned them by the Convention of The United Lutheran Church in America. The Executive Board calls the attention of the synods to the fact that such action is in plain violation of the obligations which the synods assume when they become members of The United Lutheran Church in America. (Constitution of the U. L. C. A., Article VI, Section 5, and Article VIII, Section 8.)

6. Salaries of Officers of the Church:

In view of the request on the part of the officers that a revision of salaries be made, and taking into account that these salaries were not increased during the years of prosperity, we recommend the following action to go into effect October 1, 1932: That the salary of the Secretary be made $4,800 with an allowance of $900 for house rent, and that the salary of the President be made $6,000 with an allowance of $1,000 for house rent.

7. Income from Undesignated Trust Funds: See IV, B, 1, (a) of this Report, p. 48.

VII.   LUTHERAN CHURCH HOUSE
Report of Treasurer F. H. Knubel
CASH ACCOUNT
For the Year Ended June 30, 1931

RECEIPTS

	For Maintenance	For Towels Telephone Telegraph etc.	Miscellaneous	Total
Board of American Missions......	$2,300.00	$191.92	....	$2,491.92
Board of Inner Missions..............	775.75	41.63	....	817.38
National Lutheran Council	3,168.00	361.98	....	3,529.98
New York Synod	1,425.00	309.61	....	1,734.61
Executive Board U. L. C. A......	2,878.50	185.37	....	3,063.87
All Others	673.72	187.77	$4.35	865.84
For Mortgage Payment	....	....	25,000.00	25,000.00
Total Receipts	$11,220.97	$1,278.28	$25,004.35	$37,503.60

DISBURSEMENTS

Salaries and Wages	$3,488.50
Telephone	1,066.02
Interest	1,902.78
New York Steam	1,511.12
House Painting	1,056.86
Plumbing and Heating Repairs............	579.20
Electricity, Gas, Oil, etc.............	722.61
Insurance	103.33
Services	683.51
Telegraph	200.92
Supplies and Expense	681.00
Reduction of Mortgage	25,000.00
	$36,995.85
Installation of New York Steam............	1,100.00
Installation of Equipment	512.00
Total Disbursements	$38,607.85

CASH SUMMARY
July 1, 1930 to June 30, 1931

Balance, July 1, 1930...................	$3,148.46
Receipts	37,503.60
	$40,652.06
Disbursements	38,607.85
Balance in Banks, June 30, 1931............	2,044.21
Petty Cash	10.00
Total Cash, June 30, 1931.........	$2,054.21

CASH RECEIPTS
July 1, 1931, to June 30, 1932

	For Main-tenance	For Towels Telephone Telegraph etc.	Mis-cella-neous	Total
Board of American Missions	$2,142.00	$125.23	....	$2,267.23
Board of Inner Missions	907.03	108.33	....	1,015.36
National Lutheran Council	3,831.30	288.09	....	4,119.39
New York Synod	1,226.36	183.10	....	1,409.46
Executive Board United Lutheran Church	2,477.08	143.08	....	2,620.16
Lutheran World Convention	1,599.96	74.07	....	1,674.03
All Others	58.32	550.65	$20.72	629.69
Total Receipts	$12,242.05	$1,472.55	$20.72	$13,735.32

CASH DISBURSEMENTS
July 1, 1931, to June 30, 1932

Salaries and Wages	$3,644.80
Telephone	1,012.25
Interest	625.00
New York Steam	1,006.94
House Painting	428.00
Plumbing, Repairs, etc.	191.56
Gas and Electricity	588.27
Insurance	572.50
Elevator Maintenance	157.85
Telegrams	248.84
House Supplies	304.03
Services	570.35
Miscellaneous	247.66
Total Disbursements	$9,598.05

CASH SUMMARY
July 1, 1931, to June 30, 1932

Balance, July 1, 1931	$2,044.21
Receipts	13,735.32
	$15,779.53
Disbursements	9,598.05
Balance in Banks, June 30, 1932	6,181.48
Petty Cash	10.00
Total Cash, June 30, 1932	$6,191.48

F. H. KNUBEL, *Treasurer.*

Philadelphia, Pa., August 3, 1932.

We have audited the accounts of the Lutheran Church House for the biennium beginning July 1, 1930, and ending June 30, 1932, and hereby certify that the statements of Cash Receipts and Disbursements for the two (2) years under audit, as submitted by the Treasurer, are in our opinion, true and correct.

TAIT, WALKER & BAKER,
Accountants and Auditors.

VIII. NATIONAL LUTHERAN COUNCIL

The Executive Board on April 9, 1931, approved an appeal of the National Lutheran Council to our Church for Seventy Thousand Dollars ($70,000.00) for European relief. Included in this amount was an item of Fifteen Thousand Dollars ($15,000.00) for the operating expenses of the activities of the Lutheran World Convention in this country. A special report of our Commissioners to the National Lutheran Council will be received by this Convention of the Church. (See p. 420.)

IX. LUTHERAN WORLD CONVENTION

As the special committee of The United Lutheran Church in America for the Lutheran World Convention, the Executive Board reports that an item of Fifteen Thousand Dollars ($15,000.00) for the operating expenses of the activities of the Lutheran World Convention was included in the appeal of the National Lutheran Council authorized by the Executive Board on April 9, 1931. A special report of the Executive Committee of the Lutheran World Convention will be received by this Convention of the Church. (See p. 296.)

X. FEDERAL COUNCIL OF CHURCHES OF CHRIST IN AMERICA

Visitors were appointed to each of the annual meetings of the Executive Committee of the Federal Council of Churches that were held during the biennium: the Rev. A. R. Wentz to the meeting in December, 1930, and the Revs. E. P. Pfatteicher and J. J. Schindel to the meeting in December, 1931.

Dr. Wentz reported, April 9, 1931, as follows:

The Annual Meeting of the Executive Committee of the Federal Council of the Churches of Christ in America was held in Washington, D. C., December 2 and 3, 1930. The sessions were arranged in connection with the first North American Home Missions Congress. The undersigned was the only visitor from the United Lutheran Church.

Those who have attended these meetings repeatedly record their impression that this gathering of the Executive Committee was characterized by unusual interest in the spiritual state of the churches today. Certainly a genuine spiritual tone was sounded by Bishop McDowell in welcoming the members of the Committee and proposing a key-note for the meeting. It emerged again and again in the discussion of practical plans. It received special emphasis in the report of the Commission on Evangelism. It was emphasized, not once but often, that the leaders of the Church must become more genuinely Christian or the Church will fail to meet the present-day situation.

Most of the time of the meeting was consumed on the highly useful but secondary interests, such as race relations, world peace, and social service. In addition to the usual list, there were several special items this year, such as unemployment, war guilt, conscientious objectors, prohibition. It was interesting to note that the Commission on Evangelism inveighed against some of the theological positions that are characteristic of modern liberalism.

Two items in the transactions of the Committee will be of special interest to this Board. One is the retirement of Dr. Charles S. Macfarland, the Senior General Secretary, after nearly twenty years of service. The choice of his successor will be awaited with great interest. The other is the report of the Committee on Function and Structure, under the chairmanship of Dr. George W. Richards, which calls for a systematic series of conferences between that Committee and representative groups in all the cooperating denominations during the next two years for the purpose of studying ways and means by which the Federal Council can be of the largest service to the churches. The Federal Council has been criticized in recent studies and surveys, and an attitude of expectancy is abroad concerning the future turn of affairs. There are those who feel that the Federal Council should prepare to abandon its role as an agency for cooperation among the churches and should undertake to secure corporate union among those who will unite. This sentiment does not dominate the Executive Committee, but the report of the Committee on Function and Structure, which is to be presented at the next Quadrennial Meeting in Indianapolis, in December, 1932, will doubtless be scanned with great interest by members of The United Lutheran Church in America.

Drs. Pfatteicher and Schindel reported, January 14, 1932, that at the meeting of the Executive Committee of the Federal Council in Philadelphia, December 2-4, 1931, there was much earnest discussion on three points particularly:

1. Are any modifications of the structural organization of the Federal Council desirable? It was suggested

(a) That the Administrative Committee be composed exclusively of members directly named by the denominations.

(b) That the organization of the Council be simplified by combining the Executive and Administrative Committees into a single body meeting bi-monthly, and having the Council as a whole meet biennially, instead of quadrennially.

2. What Principles and Procedures should govern the Federal Council in its relation to the denominations in issuing pronouncements, studies and educational materials?

3. Can the programs of denominational agencies be coordinated in such a way as to make a united impact upon the community? Would representation of state councils of churches upon the governing bodies of the Federal Council help to accomplish this or other important ends?

The discussion on these points was particularly forceful in suggesting that the Administrative Committee be elected directly by the denominations—as over against the five-fold classification of today and that it be made up of men who can give their time and thought to the task rather than men whose names mean something. There was criticism of the publication of pronouncements which proceed from commissions as the voice of the Federal Council itself.

XI. WORLD CONFERENCE ON FAITH AND ORDER

Report of Commissioners: (For action on this item see p. 86.)

No meeting of this Commission has been held during the biennium, but the members have received regularly the reports of the Continuation Committee of the Conference and have been in correspondence with one another.

The Continuation Committee has held several important meetings and at High Leigh, England, in August, 1931, initiated certain changes in the organization of the work. These arrangements have constituted an Executive Committee composed chiefly of the officers of the Continuation Committee, the treasurer and the secretaries. Hitherto the members of the Continuation Committee residing in America have served as a sort of Executive Committee and have been also the Business Committee. The American Group continues to function, however, and will now establish its own Executive Committee and also a permanent Finance Committee. The new organization seems to look toward a more energetic effort for means of support of the World Conference from the European and other sections as well as from America.

At the meeting in High Leigh, it was also decided that another World Conference be held in August, 1937, at Lausanne, to carry further the work accomplished by the first. It was provisionally decided that the general subject of the Conference of 1937 shall be The Church in the Purpose of God. It is believed that the movement towards the unity of the Church can best be furthered at this time by promoting study of the question what, in the intention of God, the Church should be and do. The suggested list of subheadings is as follows:

(1) The Church and the Word
(2) The Church and the World
(3) The Meaning of Grace:
    (a) Grace and the Church
    (b) Grace and the Ministry
    (c) Grace and the Sacraments
(4) The Church's fellowship in life and worship:
    (a) The life of the Church as expressed in the Holy Communion
    (b) The Communion of Saints
    (c) The Church and the Churches: including such questions as those affecting Intercommunion, Federation, etc.

This list is however regarded as subject to free modification in the light of suggestions which may be received either from the Churches or from national or confessional groups of those interested in the movement.

A formal request has been received that The United Lutheran Church in America appoint not more than six representatives to this second World Conference.

Another communication asks that The United Lutheran Church in America repeat for 1932 its contribution of $250, which is the amount appropriated the last few years.

Among the plans for the conference in 1937, some attention has been given by the Continuation Committee to the membership. It has been proposed that this large committee itself (far over one hundred individuals) be seated as members of the conference, and a request has also come that fifty places be reserved for a representative Youth Group. The latest action of the Continuation Committee in response to these suggestions was "that a certain number of places be reserved for representatives to be appointed by the Churches, and that a certain number of places be otherwise filled in order to make the Conference as representative as possible." The natural question is, "representative" of what? We believe that the Continuation Committee should come to a definite decision as to whether or not this Conference is to be a Conference of the Churches. We cannot believe that individuals, with no actual constituency behind them and representing therefore only their own views or the views of groups, should have even a voice in a Conference of responsible representatives of Churches. We believe that any hope of true accomplishment by this Conference is futile unless it truly represents the Churches.

As Commissioners we recommend.

1. That the Executive Board appropriate $250 as a contribution for 1932, and that the next convention of the Church authorize the Executive Board to make later appropriations as seems wise and possible.
2. That the coming convention of the Church authorize the Executive Board, in its discretion, to name representatives (not more than six) to the proposed World Conference in 1937 and also an equal number of alternates.
3. That these representatives and alternates together constitute the Church's Commission on the World Conference on Faith and Order.
4. That The United Lutheran Church in America record its conviction that the next Conference should be composed as completely as possible of representatives officially appointed by the Churches.

The Executive Board adopted this report and its recommendations, and therefore recommends to the Church:

1. That the Church authorize the Executive Board to make appropriations to the World Conference on Faith and Order as seems wise and possible.
2. That the Church authorize the Executive Board, in its discretion, to name representatives (not more than six) to the proposed World Conference in 1937 and also an equal number of alternates.
3. That these representatives and alternates together constitute the Church's Commission on the World Conference on Faith and Order.
4. That The United Lutheran Church in America record its conviction that the next Conference should be composed as completely as possible of representatives officially appointed by the Churches.

XII. PLACE OF NEXT CONVENTION
(For action on this item see p. 86.)

The Executive Board recommends to this Convention that a special committee be appointed, consisting of the Chairmen of the several synodical delegations, to which shall be referred all invitations for the next convention of the United Lutheran Church, this committee to report before a vote is taken.

F. H. KNUBEL, *President,*
E. CLARENCE MILLER, *Treasurer,*
ABDEL ROSS WENTZ, *Acting Secretary.*

SUPPLEMENTAL REPORTS OF EXECUTIVE BOARD

A. THE CHURCH'S ARRANGEMENTS FOR THE TRAINING OF MINISTERS AND TEACHERS

(For action on this item see pp. 175, 452.)

Introduction

(1)   There is a widespread conviction within the Church that the existing arrangements for the training of her ministers and teachers are inadequate to her best interests.   That there is a desire for improvement is evidenced by the Church's actions upon the reports of the Commission on Theological Education at the Richmond, Erie and Milwaukee conventions.

(2)   While theological education, under our present church policy, is carried on primarily by the constituent synods and while in the last analysis they are responsible for supporting our theological seminaries and making them efficient agencies of the Church, nevertheless since

a.   ordination by one synod is recognized by all the other synods,

b.   the efficiency of the preachers and teachers in one part of the Church affects the efficiency of the Church as a whole, and

c.   the Church can best suggest and secure that cooperation of synods, or that coordination of synodical efforts necessary to strengthen our institutions for theological education and thereby produce a more efficient ministry,

there are certain aspects of the training of our ministers and teachers that must necessarily engage the attention of the Church as a whole and call forth its judgment.

(3)   Some aspects of theological education that must necessarily engage the attention of the general body at the present time are

a.   The objective of theological education.

b.   The status of the seminaries.

c.   The efficiency of each seminary as an educational institution.

d.   The establishing of new institutions.

I. The Objective of Theological Education

(4)   The primary objective of theological education is to prepare men to serve the Church in the ministry of the Gospel and in other fields of activity to which the Church may call them. (See Richmond Minutes, p. 525.)

(5)   For the achievement of this objective, the first requisite is a living faith in Jesus Christ and an eager desire to share that faith with others. This is especially true in Lutheran theological education, because the material principle of the Reformation, concerning faith, is central to and controls our entire conception of revealed truth and must therefore control the education of the Church's pastors. Our Seminaries must seek to broaden and develop the faith of their students, both by the quality and nature of their instruction and also by the pronounced religious life of the seminary community. Professor and students will not be satisfied with a purely scientific treatment of

the content of theological instruction, but will realize that the knowledge thus imparted is fruitless for a true ministry of the Gospel unless it is put at the service of a living faith.

(6)   The successful minister must also have knowledge. He must know the Bible, the central document of our religion, its interpretation and the application of its truth. He must know the origin, historic development and missionary expansion of the Christian movement as well as the content of Christian teaching. He must know his own Church, her history, confessions, life, work and outlook. He should be acquainted with religion in its Christian and non-Christian phases, and with such aspects of non-Christian thought as he may be likely to meet in his ministry. He must know man, his nature, needs, and possibilities and "the creative relations of the Christian religion to individuals and the entire social process." This, also, must be a concern of theological education.

(7)   Our theological schools must be mindful to prepare graduates for their actual tasks. They are to be preachers of the Gospel, shepherds of souls, teachers of Christianity, trainers of the laity in works of serving love, congregational directors, community servants, and loyal upholders of the Church. These facts also must be considered in deciding what the technical content of theological education is to be.

(8)   The Constitution of the Church refers to the training of teachers as well as ministers. It is evident therefore that the purpose of theological education must include more than the preparation of pastors for congregations. Provision must be made for the preparation of theological scholars, missionaries, editors, authors, administrators, experts in the field of Christian education, specialists in the field of Inner Missions, layworkers, etc.

II.   The Present Status of the Seminaries

(9)   Your committee does not believe that the Milwaukee Convention intended that a technical survey be made of the seminaries. We do believe, however, that sufficient data should be presented that the Church may have a fairly definite understanding of the "arrangements for the training of ministers and teachers," and that on the basis of this data, together with other considerations, definite recommendations may be presented.

1. *Number*

(10)   The number of seminaries in the United Lutheran Church in America is 13. This is one seminary for every 80,752 members (13 years and over. This basis is used so that we may have more adequate comparison with other denominations) and 253 ministers.

(11)   In contrast, it is interesting to note the following facts :

Name of Church Group	No. of Sems.	Ch. members 13 yrs. & over	No. of Min.	One Seminary for Members	Ministers
Lutheran					
American Lutheran....	2	344,057	1,554	172,029	777
Augustana	1	239,845	825	239,845	825

Norwegian	1	332,259	1,304	332,259	1,304
Missouri	2	762,207	3,361	381,104	1,680

Presbyterian

Presbyterian U. S. A.	11	2,009,875	9,767	182,716	888
United	1	171,571	920	171,571	920
Presbyterian U.S.Sou.	4	451,043	2,409	112,761	602

Reformed

Reformed in America	2	153,739	842	76,869	421
Reformed in U. S	3	361,286	1,323	120,429	441

Methodist

Episcopal, North	8	4,080,777	18,040	501,097	2,255
M. E. South	2	2,487,694	8,001	1,243,847	4,000

Baptist

Northern	9	1,289,966	8,786	163,329	976
Southern	3	3,524,378	22,907	1,174,793	7,636
Protestant Episcopal	13	1,859,086	5,926	143,006	456
Roman Catholic	98	17,095,904	27,065	174,448	276

2. *Location*

(12)   The seminaries are located at:

New York—

   90 miles from Philadelphia
   542 miles from Waterloo
   912 miles from Chicago

Philadelphia—

   90 miles from New York
   117 miles from Gettysburg
   147 miles from Selinsgrove
   348 miles from Pittsburgh
   570 miles from Springfield
   617 miles from Columbia
   832 miles from Chicago

Gettysburg—

   117 miles from Philadelphia
   80 miles from Selinsgrove
   207 miles from New York
   80 miles from Washington

Selinsgrove—

   80 miles from Gettysburg
   147 miles from Philadelphia
   385 miles from Waterloo

Columbia—

   617 miles from Philadelphia
   476 miles from Washington

Springfield—
     298 miles from Chicago
     570 miles from Philadelphia
Chicago—
     298 miles from Springfield
     420 miles from Minneapolis
     450 miles from Waterloo
     468 miles from Pittsburgh
     520 miles from Omaha
     574 miles from Fremont
     575 miles from Lincoln
    1334 miles from Saskatoon
Minneapolis—
     381 miles from Omaha
     436 miles from Lincoln
    1818 miles from Seattle
     900 miles from Saskatoon
Fremont—
     37 miles from Omaha
     50 miles from Lincoln
Lincoln—
     55 miles from Omaha
Seattle—
     957 miles from San Francisco
    1818 miles from Minneapolis
Saskatoon—
     900 miles from Minneapolis
    1281 miles from Omaha
Waterloo—
     385 miles from Selinsgrove
     450 miles from Chicago
     542 miles from New York

3. *Supporting Constituency and Synods*
    (13) The supporting constituencies and synods of the various seminaries
are as follows:

Seminary	Supporting Synods	Confirmed Membership
Hartwick	New York	155,563
Gettysburg	West Penna., East Penna., Maryland, *Alleghany, Susquehanna, W. Va.*	212,470
Southern	Virginia, N. Car., S. Car., Georgia-Alabama, Florida, Miss.	72,465
Hamma	Ohio, Indiana, *Michigan, W. Va.*	88,918
Susquehanna	Susquehanna and *Alleghany*	70,139
Philadelphia	Min. of Pa., *New York*	354,335

Chicago ....Illinois, *Michigan,* Wartburg.............................. 67,860
Western ....Nebraska, Rocky Mt., Kansas, Iowa and
       California (?) 40,525
Waterloo ....Canada and Nova Scotia (?)............................ 21,057
Pacific ....Pacific 3,294
Martin Luther ......German-Nebraska and Texas (?)...................... 14,774
Saskatoon ....Manitoba 7,697
Northwestern ....Northwest 31,292

(14) The italicized synods support more than one seminary. The synods with question marks after them do not regularly contribute to the institutions designated, so far as we could ascertain. The Pittsburgh Synod has representation on the Boards of the Philadelphia, Gettysburg and Susquehanna Seminaries.

(15) Gettysburg receives support from six synods, but has drawn students from ten different synods during the past six years. Hamma receives support from four synods, but drew students from fourteen synods during the past six years. Susquehanna drew from seven synods. Philadelphia drew from seventeen synods. Chicago drew from twelve synods. Western drew from six synods. Martin Luther drew from five synods. Northwestern drew from seven synods.

(16) The overlapping of synods and the competition among the seminaries is revealed by

 a. The geography of the synods. (See synodical boundaries.)

 b. The divided support of the synods. (See above facts.)

 c. The synodical source of the seminary graduates. An extensive study on this point is most revealing.

 d. Some seminaries draw students past other seminaries. A few seminaries are able to do this because of their superior faculties and equipment.

4. *The Financial Status*

(17) Although figures could not be obtained on the exact financial status of each institution on account of organic relationship with colleges, yet the following figures are sufficient for some basis of comparison.

Name of Seminary	Value of Property	Funds	Total Assets	Indebtedness
Hartwick	41,000	42,579	83,579	2,116
Gettysburg	400,000	686,707	1,086,707	3,439
Southern	171,500	106,050	277,550	800
Hamma	*107,480	272,414	*379,894	
Susquehanna...............	Assets not separated from the college			
Philadelphia	1,170,000	635,000	1,805,000	129,000
Chicago	464,340	452,916	917,256	97,500

---

* Values of land and library are not included since they are not separated from the college assets.

Western	26,000	39,659	65,659	10,000
Waterloo	Assets not separated from the college			
Pacific	77,500	80,000	157,500	
Martin Luther	42,100	3,000	45,100	
Saskatoon	71,800	5,584	77,384	22,457
Northwestern	62,600	194,675	257,275	

(18)   The year 1931-32 should not be considered typical, but nine out of ten seminaries reporting on current funds showed deficits amounting to $49,330, and ranging from $80 to $16,733.

(19)   For three of the above seminaries, the funded indebtedness amounts to more than 10 per cent of the total assets.

5. Professors, Students and Costs per Student

(20)   It is desirable to know the number of full-time professors and the number of regular students registered at the Seminaries. This enables us to ascertain the number of students per professor. In this connection, it is informing to note the expenses for the past year incurred at the seminaries and the consequent costs per resident student. These facts are shown in the following table:

Name of Seminary	Profs. Full-Time	Students Resident	Students per Professor	Expenses	Expenses per Student
Hartwick	4	16	4	$11,140	$696
Gettysburg	6	79	13	47,188	597
Southern	4	31	8	15,702	507
Hamma	6	30	5	29,039	968
Susquehanna	3	9	3	Not separated from college	
Philadelphia	8	109	14	71,689	658
Chicago	6	37	6	37,494	1,013
Western	3	19	6	11,827	622
Waterloo	3	11	4	Not separated from college	
Pacific	3	10	3	26,251	2,625
Martin Luther	2	12	6	13,174	1,098
Saskatoon	2	14	7	Not separated from college	
Northwestern	5	19	4	23,076	1,215

(21)   It will be noted that the number of full-time professors ranges from 2 to 8; that the number of students ranges from 9 to 109; that the number of students per professor ranges from 3 to 14; and that the cost per student ranges from $507 to $2,625. The average cost per student is $706.

(22)   The following figures regarding the similar facts at certain other Lutheran seminaries are interesting:

Name of Seminary	Full-Time Professors	Number of Students	Students per Professor	Cost per Student
St. Louis (Mo. Synod)	14	531	38	237
Luther (Norwegian)	8	162	20	330
Dubuque	5	59	10	592

6. *The Curricula*

(23) The Commission on Theological Education in its report to the Richmond Convention showed a rather extensive study of the problems connected with the curriculum. Your committee did not think that it should go into this problem in detail at this time. However, what study has been made of the curricula at our seminaries shows that considerable improvement has taken place in the past six years. More courses are being given; formerly neglected fields are being recognized, and students are given more opportunity to study a more varied program.

(24) The catalogs do not give sufficient information to obtain adequate descriptions of the courses. Titles of courses do not always give a clear indication of content.

7. *The Library*

(25) The Library is one of the most important parts of any educational institution. Most of our seminaries do not have adequate library facilities for effective instruction. Moreover, changes in the methods of instruction at some of our seminaries would utilize more largely the library facilities that are available at present and would cultivate in the students stronger habits of library reading and research.

(26) The libraries at our seminaries have the following number of volumes according to the latest reports:

Hartwick	7,000
Gettysburg	43,500
Southern	8,000
Hamma—included in institutional library—total	50,000
Susquehanna—included in institutional library—total	9,537
Philadelphia	37,000
Chicago	20,000
Waterloo—included in institutional library—total	4,000
Pacific	3,000
Martin Luther	3,000
Saskatoon	3,000
Northwestern	4,000
Western	5,000

(27) As a matter of informaton, we submit the number of volumes in the libraries of the following seminaries:

St. Louis (Missouri)	22,400
Dubuque (Am. Luth. Ch.)	14,000
Luther (Norwegian)	35,000

The Presbyterian U. S. A. Seminary libraries range from 5,000 to 133,000, with an average of 40,636.

(28) The committee has allowed the above facts describing the status of the seminaries to speak for themselves. These facts seem to indicate that theological education in the United Lutheran Church might be carried on

far more effectively, economically, and the interests of the Church served more adequately, if the amount of money, energy, and man power were employed in the maintenance and operation of fewer institutions. A reduction in the number of institutions would appear to be a truly worthwhile undertaking.

(29)   The committee made no attempt to study the charters and constitutions of the several seminaries. This was done to some extent by the commission reporting at the Richmond Convention. Some desirable changes have taken place since that time. Any future study of these documents will be dependent upon the action of the Church to this report.

(30)   Likewise, as already intimated, we did not think it within our province at this time to suggest how curricula "may be improved, enlarged and standardized in conformity with the ideals and cultus of the whole Church." This task is properly dependent upon the action on this report.

III. Probable Efficiency of Our Theological Seminaries

(31)   As a basis for determining the efficiency of our theological seminaries, we submit the following suggestions of minimum requirements for a first-class theological seminary in the United Lutheran Church in America. The submission of these quantitative standards is not to be interpreted as implying that final judgment of any one seminary or of all seminaries can be made on the bases of these standards alone.

1. *Curriculum*

(32)   The following fields of study should be recognized:

a. The Bible, including the English Bible, Old Testament (Introduction, Theology, History, Exegesis of selected books), New Testament (Introduction, Theology, Life of Christ, History of Apostolic Age, Exegesis of selected books), Hebrew, New Testament Greek, and History of Biblical Times.

b. The History of the Christian Church, including General Church History, the Origins of Protestantism, American Church History, History of Christian Doctrine, Studies of special Periods and Movements, Studies in the History of special Aspects or Activities of the Church.

c. The Interpretation of Christianity, including Dogmatics, Creeds and Confessions of the Church, Symbolics, Apologetics, Ethics, together with auxiliary studies such as Psychology of Religion, Comparative Religions, and Philosophy of Religion.

d. The Work of the Ministry, including Pastoral Theology (homiletics, worship, evangelism, cure of souls, congregational administration and community service), Christian Education (the theory and practice of Christian Education, history of Christian Education, Curricula of Christian Education, Catechization), and Missions (Home Missions, History and Theory of Inner Missions, History of Foreign Missions, Survey of the Mission Fields, and Religions of the Mission Fields), and Church Polity and Government.

(33)   It is understood that

a. Each student would do work in every field. While there will be opportunities for election of courses, special concentration in any one field should take place only in a graduate school or department.

b.   There will be a proper balance of subjects within fields and between fields.

2.   *The Faculty*

(34)   A curriculum, as outlined above, would require a faculty of from five to seven full-time professors.   This number may vary slightly, dependent upon the number of part-time instructors and lecturers.

(35)   However, the size of the faculty is not wholly dependent upon the curriculum.   In the interests of economy, there should be not more than one professor for every ten students.

(36)   While the qualifications of a theological professor may not seem to enter into this general problem, nevertheless, there are three requisites of which the Church and the seminaries must be mindful always:

a.   He shall be a man whose faith and piety are so outstanding and whose love for men is so sincere as to command the respect, the affection, and emulation of those who are his students.

b.   He should have had some years of special study and training in the field in which he is to teach.

c.   He should ordinarily have had experience in the practical work of the ministry.

3.   *The Library*

(37)   A library, adequate for effective instruction in the fields of study set forth above, should number at least 25,000 usable volumes, not including pamphlets and reports, properly housed, accessible, indexed, and should be in charge of a capable librarian.

4.   *The Endowment*

(38)   An endowment sufficient to carry out the program of theological education heretofore suggested, should amount to $750,000, allowing actual moneys received from supporting synods to be counted towards this amount on the basis that the synodical grant represents 5 per cent of a capital investment.

The annual income should approximate $40,000.

5.   *The Church Constituency*

(39)   To supply a student body and adequately support a standard seminary, the confirmed membership (or members 13 years and over) of supporting synods should number 200,000.   This figure will vary dependent upon different densities of Lutheran population and also Lutheran wealth.

6.   *The School Year*

(40)   It is desirable that theological schools adopt a standard educational year of thirty-six weeks.   Under such an arrangement the year would be divided into semesters or quarters, and a term would be conducted in the summer.   It would also be desirable to provide courses which would include field work for students in certain semesters or quarters.

(41)   After a study of our present seminaries with reference to these proposed standards, we find:

   a.   That no one seminary meets them absolutely in all respects.

   b.   That a few of our seminaries approach these standards closely.

   c.   That in the case of a number of our seminaries substantial advances must be made before they can be regarded as approximating these standards.

IV.   A New Institution

(42)   There is a general conviction "that no synod or group of synods should hereafter organize or locate a theological seminary without first securing the consent of the United Lutheran Church."

(43)   However, the needs of the Church for future professors of theology, editors, authors, and spiritual leaders demand specialized training in theological scholarship and in the various branches of church work.   To meet this demand the Church must soon make more adequate arrangements to provide such instruction.

(44)   The establishment of a post-graduate seminary to which graduates of all our seminaries might go would seem to meet in the best manner this situation.   We are not certain, however, whether the Church is ready or able at this time to take this step.   It can, however, ask some of its existing or proposed institutions to undertake certain phases of graduate instruction, in addition to the regular seminary courses.

V.   Considerations for the Realignment of Seminaries

(45)   The most feasible plan for effective, economic and adequate operation of our seminaries for the best interests of both the synods and the whole Church appears to be a merging of existing institutions.   Of course any plan of such character must bear in mind, besides any standards which may be set up, the following considerations:

1.   Proximity to other seminaries.
2.   Overlapping territory and unnecessary competition.
3.   Inadequate facilities.
4.   Ability to meet possible standards.
5.   Educational possibilities.
6.   Lutheran possibilities.
7.   Missionary possibilities.
8.   Linking of different ecclesiastical tendencies.
9.   Cultural background.
10.   Geographical area.
11.   Economies of mergers (favorable disposition of properties).
12.   Advantages of various locations from the standpoint of
     a.   Laboratory facilities, as found in the churches and social centers.
     b.   Cultural facilities, as found in universities and libraries.
13.   The advisability or inadvisability of operating a seminary in the same town or on the same campus as the Church college.

VI. Recommendations

(For action on these recommendations see pp. 175, 452.)

In view of the foregoing findings and for the best interests of The United Lutheran Church in America in the exercise of the power of advice and counsel which belongs to the United Lutheran Church in accordance with the decision of the Commission of Adjudication (Second Supplementary Report, Milwaukee Convention, Minutes pp. 409-412), we express it as our judgment and do hereby advise:

I. *As to the Number and Location of Seminaries, with Supporting Synods*

1. That Southern Seminary be continued, developed, and supported by the following synods:

Virginia, North Carolina, South Carolina, Georgia-Alabama, Florida, Mississippi.

2. That Hartwick, Gettysburg, Susquehanna and Philadelphia seminaries be merged, and be supported by the following synods:

Ministerium of Pennsylvania, United New York, East Pennsylvania, Slovak-Zion, West Pennsylvania, Susquehanna, Alleghany, Pittsburgh, Maryland and West Virginia.

3. That Hamma and Chicago seminaries be merged, and be supported by the following synods:

Ohio, Indiana, Michigan, Illinois, Wartburg.

4. That Western, Martin Luther and Northwestern seminaries be merged, and be supported by the following synods:

Northwest, Nebraska, German-Nebraska, Rocky Mountain, Kansas, Texas, and Iowa.

5. That a seminary on the Pacific Coast be supported by the Pacific and California Synods.

6. That, at least until the future of the Pacific Seminary has been determined, the Board of Education be asked to pay for the transportation of students for the ministry from the Pacific Synod to the proposed Western Seminary.

7. That recommendations regarding Waterloo and Saskatoon Seminaries be held in abeyance awaiting the report of the commission surveying the work of the Church in Canada.

II. *As to Specific Responsibilities*

8. That the Church ask the proposed seminaries to undertake the following specific responsibilities:

a. The proposed Eastern Seminary—A special department for the training of teachers, scholars, editors, foreign missionaries, etc.

b. The proposed Central Seminary—A special department for the training of layworkers and workers in the field of inner missions.

c. The proposed Western Seminary—The training of men to serve in churches requiring the use of other languages than English, and also the development of special training in the problems of the rural parish.

III. *As to a New Institution*

9. That the Church ask the Commission of Adjudication to inform and instruct it as to its constitutional right to establish and organize a post-graduate seminary, or a post-graduate department in connection with some one seminary, to be maintained and controlled by the whole Church.

IV. *As to the Effecting Agency*

10. That the Church request the Board of Education to approach the constituent synods and the theological seminaries with reference to the adoption of measures for effecting the program indicated in the above recommendations.

These recommendations were adopted by the Executive Board in conference with the Board of Education and the Presidents of the Constituent Synods, and are herewith presented to the Convention for the action of the Church.

> F. H. Knubel, *President,*
> E. Clarence Miller, *Treasurer,*
> Abdel Ross Wentz, *Acting Secretary.*

B. SURVEY OF CANADIAN SYNODS

(For action on this item see p. 294.)

Under date of August 11, 1932, the following petition of the Manitoba Synod was submitted to President F. H. Knubel of The United Lutheran Church in America:

"The Manitoba Synod is convinced that the time has arrived where it should invoke the assistance of the Executive Board of The United Lutheran Church in America, through petitioning the said Executive Board to appoint a commission, whose duty it would be to thoroughly inquire into the operations of the Manitoba Synod, its missionary endeavor and opportunities, its college and seminary, and such other operations of Synod as the said Commission might deem advisable, in order to point out the weaknesses of the work, and to give advice to the Manitoba Synod as well as to the Executive Board of The United Lutheran Church in America and to the United Lutheran Church in Convention, how the weaknesses can be best overcome and the promising work can be prosecuted more effectively and vigorously in the future."

At the meeting of the Evangelical Lutheran Synod of Canada (See Minutes of 1932, p. 19), the following recommendation of its president was adopted:

"That a committee of five, three pastors and two laymen, be appointed to study very thoroughly the history and present state of the Lutheran Church in Canada, to examine especially its immediate needs, to aim at a closer co-operation of the synods in Canada, and to invite to conferences representatives of the other synods in Canada of The United Lutheran Church in America."

This special committee of the Synod of Canada later invited the Commission to include Ontario and Quebec in the scope of its survey.

Favorable action having been taken by the Executive Board, July 7, 1932, the Board of Education, June 29, 1932, and the Board of American Missions, July 21, 1932, the undersigned were appointed to serve as a Commission on Canadian Survey and report to the Executive Board in advance of the Convention of the United Lutheran Church.

The Commission was keenly aware of the uniqueness of its position, serving as the agent of the United Lutheran Church on the sovereign territory of Constituent Synods and endeavored to discharge its duties in full harmony with our established church polity. It is a pleasure to report the fine courtesy extended in every part of the field under survey. In view of the limited time only one month could be spent in the visitation; but during that time contacts were made with all sections of the Church from Montreal to Edmonton. At each point where a number of pastors and laymen could assemble, the vital problems of the Canadian field were freely discussed. Constructive counsel was offered by the Commission on the preparation of the budgets of educational institutions and synods, the enrollment of non-synodical congregations, the use of the standard Parochial Blank, the unwise granting of supplementary pensions through a synodical budget, the place of national groups in synodical life and the adequate recognition of the spirit of young Canada in the literature of the Church. The employment of a chartered accountant for the annual audit of the accounts of all institutions and synods was recommended. All educational institutions of the Lutheran Church in Canada, regardless of synodical affiliations, were visited, and everywhere information was cheerfully given.

The investigations of the Commission centered about the problems of administration, home missions and education, and its report is formulated accordingly.

I. Administration

1. *The Synod of Canada.* In 1857 the Pittsburgh Synod became deeply interested in the German immigrants locating in Ontario, and began to organize them into home mission parishes. The Canada Conference of this Synod functioned from February 2, 1859, to July 22, 1861, when "The Evangelical Lutheran Synod of Canada" was formed. In 1901 the English congregations withdrew to become affiliated with the Synod of New York and New England; but in 1909 formed the Synod of Central Canada, which in turn federated with the Synod of Canada in 1925. At the time of merger the Synod of Central Canada enrolled seventeen pastors, seventeen congregations and 3,300 baptized members; the Canada Synod fifty pastors, seventy-five congregations and 22,488 baptized members. The territory of the Synod includes the provinces of Ontario and Quebec. The following table indicates its growth during the last decade.

Table of Progress
Synod of Canada
1922-1932.

Year	Pastors	Congregations	Souls	Property Value	Mission Appropriation
*1922	57	91	25,068	$1,183,800	$7,250.00
*1923	61	92	25,726	1,231,080	7,295.00
*1924	67	92	25,788	1,258,355	7,776.00
*1925	69	85	25,788	1,258,355	7,176.00
1926	68	92	26,360	1,355,430	7,547.00
1927	69	92	25,454	1,269,950	8,519.00
1928	67	90	25,339	1,303,879	9,259.00
1929	75	87	25,210	1,373,130	10,842.00
1930	72	87	26,001	1,432,955	11,954.00
1931	80	87	26,857	1,459,235	13,647.00
1932	85	96	28,041	1,491,884	12,936.00

* Combined statistics of Synod of Canada and Synod of Central Canada before 1925.

2. *The Synod of Nova Scotia.* The pioneer Germans of Nova Scotia settled in Halifax in 1750; of these a group of 1,453 settled in Lunenberg and vicinity in 1753. The successors of the Lunenberg pioneers form the synod of the present day. They have clung to the faith of their fathers, even when they found it necessary to surrender their language. From October 17, 1876, to July 9, 1903, they formed a Conference of the Pittsburgh Synod and then began to function as a separate synod. Because of the limitation of their field to three counties of the province, and also because of the declining population, it has been difficult to add much to the number or strength of the parishes. An opportunity to expand has come recently in new German immigration to New Brunswick, where the city of St. Johns should be investigated as a center of possible home mission operations.

Table of Progress
Synod of Nova Scotia.
1922-1932.

Year	Pastors	Congregations	Souls	Property Value	H. M. Appropriation
1922	7	29	5,052	$216,925	$1,300.00
1923	7	30	5,187	216,925	1,300.00
1924	7	30	5,105	222,050	1,800.00
1925	8	31	5,807	224,425	1,600.00
1926	8	31	5,946	227,875	1,300.00
1927	8	31	6,060	221,025	1,033.00
1928	8	31	6,012	220,725	900.00
1929	8	31	5,778	223,225	1,080.00
1930	8	31	5,351	229,474	950.00
1931	8	31	5,419	232,100	950.00
1932	8	31	5,498	239,800	950.00

3. *The Synod of Manitoba.* The life story of this missionary body, which covers the provinces of Manitoba, Saskatchewan, British Columbia

and Alberta, is confined within the limits of recent years. In 1888 the pastor of Trinity Church, Winnipeg, was alone in the field, excepting his Lutheran neighbors from Iceland. For the first eight years all missionaries of the German Home Mission Board of the General Council were connected with the Synod of Canada. The great distance between the natural Lutheran centers of eastern and western Canada led the Synod of Canada to encourage its fine frontier missionaries to organize the "Evangelical Lutheran Synod of Manitoba and other Provinces" in 1897. From 1900 to 1914 there was a great influx of settlers, and a corresponding increase in the strength of the synod. Other organized synods entered the field during this period, answering the calls which the older synod found it impossible to answer because of the lack of both men and money. During the period of the World War, 1914-1918, serious setbacks were suffered; but, with the organization of the United Lutheran Church, a better day dawned and the synod is now making the rapid advance indicated in the following table.

Table of Progress
Synod of Manitoba.
1922-1932.

Year	Pastors	Congregations	Souls	Property Value	*Mission Appropriation
1922	34	59	10,007	$251,532	....
1923	33	58	10,168	263,835	$14,969.00
1924	32	59	10,049	264,055	15,878.00
1925	39	68	10,517	277,125	15,345.00
1926	38	59	10,453	315,700	15,465.00
1927	42	75	11,164	327,050	18,860.00
1928	37	74	11,123	326,050	18,760.00
1929	44	84	11,967	334,080	18,407.00
1930	46	90	12,860	330,259	20,258.00
1931	47	103	13,471	341,078	23,715.00
1932	52	127	14,979	355,000	23,392.00

* Including salaries, interest grants and traveling expenses.

4. *Other Synods of the United Lutheran Church in Canada.* The following synods are also represented in the Canadian mission field:

   1. Pacific Synod—Prince Rupert, English.
      "   "   Vancouver, English.
      "   "   Vancouver, Finnish.
   2. Northwest—Winnipeg, English.
   3. Michigan—Windsor, English.
   4. Pittsburgh—Windsor, Siebenburger.

The reasons that led to this crossing of the international boundary will gradually disappear in time.

5. *Benevolence Policy of the United Lutheran Church.* In its contacts with representatives of the independent nationalist groups of the Canadian field, the Commission learned to its deep regret that the policies of the

Church in regard to apportionments had been seriously misrepresented. To clarify the situation, the following brief statement is offered for the consideration of the Church.

(1) It is the duty of every Christian to obey the Saviour's command and assist in the task of preaching the gospel to every creature.

(2) The United Lutheran Church in America possesses power to lay apportionments upon its Constituent Synods, but no power to collect them beyond the voluntary giving of her people.

(3) These apportionments are not regarded as a tax but as a guide to Christian giving; and no effort can be made to collect any deficits after the close of each fiscal year.

6. *The Future Church of Canada.* No question discussed by the pastors at the several conferences aroused deeper interest than the possibility of organizing a United Lutheran Church in Canada on the same broad lines as the United Lutheran Church in America, embracing the congregations of every synod now in the field. Young Canada was especially concerned. Difficulties in the way were clearly seen and understood; but the formation of such an all-inclusive body, holding pulpit and altar fellowship with all parent bodies in the United States, is a goal toward which every Canadian Lutheran may well strive.

For the present, the organization of all the United Lutheran Church congregations of Canada into one body, under the valuable Dominion charter of "The Evangelical Lutheran Synod of Canada" should be given careful study. It might furnish the basis on which to build greater things in the future. In the formation of such a general body, each group of Provinces or Nationals so desiring could be given a conference organization, charged with most of the duties usually pertaining to a synod, and hold an annual meeting every spring, while the general body, composed of delegates elected by the several conferences, could hold its meetings biennially, alternating with those of The United Lutheran Church in America. Delegates to The United Lutheran Church in America would be elected by the general body from nominees of the conference. The solution of this problem will not be found in a diplomatic quieting of the conflicting demands of the moment, but in a statesmanlike laying of broad and firm foundations on which the future Church of Canada may rise in strength and beauty.

II. Home Missions

The motivating spirit for the survey of the Canadian field came from the hearts of our devoted missionaries. In this spirit all Canada is beginning to share. Much as has been done, much more could have been accomplished had the Church been fully awake to her opportunities.

1. *The Land Factor.* The total land area of the eleven provinces of Canada is 3,510,008 square miles, of which 560,000 is considered suitable for agricultural or pastoral purposes, but only 115,770 improved. In addition,

82,260 square miles of timber land when cleared would be suited to agriculture. These figures indicate the possibilities of a virile population, that grew from 8,788,483 to 10,376,786 in the last census decade, a gain of 18 per cent. During the same period the growth in the number of Lutheran adherents was 37 per cent.

2. *The Immigration Factor.* Immigration from Lutheran lands set in at an early date in eastern Canada, the Germans having established themselves in Nova Scotia in 1750 and in Ontario in 1784. The larger German immigration did not begin, however, until after the year 1848. Germans from Ontario began to settle in Manitoba about the year 1872. With the exception of the Icelanders, who founded the "First Lutheran Church" of Winnipeg in 1876, they were the pioneers. Several Norwegian and Swedish settlements were also made at an early date in Saskatchewan and Alberta. The German immigration, which has provided our most fertile field, is of comparatively recent origin.

Table of National Origins
Census of 1921.

Province	German	Scandinavian	Finnish	Hungarian
Alberta	35,333	44,545	2,926	1,043
British Columbia	7,273	18,402	3,112	343
Manitoba	19,444	26,698	506	8,946
New Brunswick	1,698	2,142	35	6
Newfoundland	....	....	....	....
N. W. Territories	12	34	....	....
Nova Scotia	27,046	1,333	45	180
Ontario	130,545	12,716	12,835	1,737
Prince Edward Island	260	33	1	....
Quebec	4,668	2,219	76	89
Saskatchewan	68,202	58,382	1,937	828
Yukon	155	2,531	21	7
Total	294,636	166,757	21,494	13,179

It was the original intention of the Commission to report the figures for national origins from the census of 1931, showing such important facts as the growth of the Finnish population of Ontario and the development of British Columbia as a mission field; but these later census figures will not be released for publication for several months. Valuable data has been secured, however, for the guidance of the Board of American Missions.

3. *The Home Mission Factor.* Under the census regulations of the Dominion Government a return is made of the religious preferences of the entire population. In 1931, a return of 394,047 Lutherans was made as over against 287,496 in 1921. Many of these professed Lutherans have not yet been found by the missionaries; but it must not be forgotten that there are many "leaners" among them, who mean little to the Church. A study of the following table will be helpful.

Lutherans in Canada
1921-1931.

Provinces	Year	Census Adherents	Missouri Synod	U. L. C.	Other Synods
Alberta	1921	60,573	6,528	2,376	8,857
	1931	82,409	8,676	5,107	9,210
British Columbia	1921	17,659	412	197	805
	1931	36,627	2,338	366	1,157
Manitoba	1921	39,472	1,586	4,069	8,331
	1931	46,879	1,846	4,399	11,202
New Brunswick	1921	378	....	....	....
	1931	967	....	....	203
Newfoundland	1921	12	....	....	....
	1931	....	....	....	....
N. W. Territories	1921	11	....	....	....
	1931	64	....	....	....
Nova Scotia	1921	8,077	....	5,187	....
	1931	7,944	....	5,498	....
Ontario	1921	66,863	12,584	23,286	2,635
	1931	96,957	13,605	27,804	3,317
Prince Edward Island	1921	....	....	....	....
	1931	76	....	....	....
Quebec	1921	2,209	209	114	139
	1931	8,254	277	401	354
Saskatchewan	1921	91,988	8,041	3,745	20,440
	1931	113,631	12,535	4,180	25,545
Yukon	1921	254	....	....	....
	1931	239	....	....	....
Not Located	1921	....	....	....	....
	1931	....	....	1,714	....
Total	1921	287,496	29,360	38,974	41,207
	1931	394,047	39,277	49,469	50,988

Up to the present time the efforts of the Manitoba Synod have been confined chiefly to the churching of the large German-speaking immigration from Volhynia, Russia, Austria, Bessarabia, Transylvania and Bukowina; but the pastors are fully aware that many others are looking to them for spiritual care, and their home mission program is being readjusted accordingly. First of all, they would like to establish an English Lutheran Church in each of the centers of population; and, in harmony with this desire, the

Commission has made a survey of the Lutheran constituency of the twelve leading cities of the Dominion, and placed the same in the hands of the Board of American Missions. Among the Finns work is being done in Alberta, British Columbia, Saskatchewan, Manitoba, Quebec and Ontario. Thousands of Finns have located in Ontario during the last ten years; and new missions should be opened at Sudbury, Port Arthur and Timmins, as soon as possible. A valuable survey of the Finnish field has been made by Pastor Saarinen. Among the Letts and Esthonians, as well as the many scattered Scandinavians, our missionaries have found it possible to render a helpful ministry in connection with their regular parish work. Some of these missionaries are accomplished linguists; and one young man has recently entered Saskatoon Seminary, who will be able to preach in eight languages. Another open door before the Manitoba Synod is found among the Ukranian, former adherents of the Russian Orthodox Church, to whom the Lutheran Church is said to have the best approach. Within three years it is planned to send at least two Russian-speaking missionaries into this inviting field. In the prosecution of all this work, it has been found advantageous to make use of the system of traveling missionaries who make regular reports direct to the proper officials of the Board. It has also been found economical and practical to direct the incoming immigrants from their port of entry to definite locations in which the Church has already been established; and for that reason the Commission is of opinion that the Inner Mission work at Montreal, as well as the colonization work at Winnipeg and Edmonton, should not be abandoned. When the tide of immigration returns it should find the Church in a position to lend a helping and directing hand. It is the possession of these vantage points, the elimination of all unnecessary offices, and the education of young Canadians fortified for the field, that has enabled the United Lutheran Church to gather greater returns with a less expenditure of money than any other Lutheran group at work in Canada. The development within the last two years has been especially gratifying, during which the Synod of Canada added nine and the Synod of Manitoba thirty-seven new congregations to their parish rolls. The educational factor in missions will be considered in the next general division of the report.

III. Christian Higher Education

1. *The Educational Policy of Canada.* Education is under the control of the various provinces, each Legislature having authority within its own province. In each province there is a complete system of public and high schools, and also one or more universities, agricultural and technical schools, aided by the Government with grants. In connection with some of the universities, in addition to the courses in arts and sciences, there are faculties of medicine, law and dentistry.

In the sphere of higher education, the standards are determined by the one provincial university. The degree granting power resides in each of the provincial universities, generally speaking. Consequently, recognized degrees for work done in private and church colleges are granted by the university with which the college is affiliated.

An affiliated college is one which is so related to its central colllege or to the university as a whole that it has equal rights to conduct Pass Courses and Honor Courses as the university itself. Both together grant degrees, change the courses, set examinations and examine answer papers in common. The growth and life of the affiliated colleges, conducted by various denominations, is of interest to the central authorities. Affiliated colleges have representatives on the Senate and on all the vital committees of their universities.

2. *The Status of Lutheran Educational Institutions.* Visits were made to the Lutheran colleges and seminaries, established in seven centers. The United Lutheran Church has institutions in two centers, the Icelandic Synod in one, the American Lutheran Church in one, the Norwegian Lutheran Church in two, and the Missouri Synod in one. At each center, without exception, the most cordial conferences were held. There seemed to be an earnest eagerness to discuss educational problems.

The educational policy and program of any Lutheran group in Canada should take into consideration, not only the educational policy of Canada, but also the status of the educational institutions of other Lutheran groups, unless questionable and unnecessary, not to say un-Christian, competition be developed. Accordingly, as a matter of information, we submit some data regarding all the Lutheran educational institutions in Canada.

Name and Synodical Relation	Founded	Location	Value of Funds and Property	Faculty	Students	Disbursements
Canada Seminary	1911	Waterloo		S 3	11	
Waterloo College	1924	Ontario	$170,000	C 12	76	$31,697
U. L. C. A.						
Lutheran College (A)....	1913			A 2	16	
and Seminary	1919	Saskatoon	77,384	S 2	14	16,622
U. L. C. A.		Sask.				
Lutheran College (A)....	1911	Camrose	49,000	4	81	*
N. L. C.		Alb.				
Jon Bjarnason	1913	Winnipeg	76,000	3	87	8,426
Academy I. S.		Man.				
Luther College		Regina	140,000	10	123	*
(A and JC) A. L. C.......	1913	Sask.				
Outlook College		Outlook				
(A and JC) N. L. C.......	1916	Sask.	75,000	4	36	*

Concordia College (A and JC) M. S.	1921	Edmonton Alb.	200,000	5	42	*

Code: A—Academy
     C—College
     S—Seminary
     JC—Junior College

U. L. C. A.—United Lutheran Church in America.
I. S.—Icelandic Synod.
N. L. C.—Norwegian Lutheran Church.
A. L. C.—American Lutheran Church.
M. S.—Missouri Synod.

* The latest figures were not available.

All these institutions, with the exception of Waterloo College, do high school work. Waterloo College is the only four-year college, and has attained the highly desirable position of being able to offer honor courses, in affiliation with the University of Western Ontario at London, Ontario. Concordia College offers three years of college work but is not in affiliation with any university. Outlook College and Luther College at Regina have two years of college work and are affiliated with the University of Saskatchewan. There are two seminaries and both of them belong to synods of the United Lutheran Church. All other Lutheran groups train their ministers in the United States. Waterloo Seminary grants the degree of Bachelor of Divinity through the University of Western Ontario. The Saskatoon Seminary has its faculty recorded in the bulletin of the University of Saskatchewan and is given some recognition.

The distance between the cities in which these institutions are located, and also some cities in the United States is interesting information. From Edmonton to Camrose it is 55 miles, to Saskatoon 351 miles. Fram Saskatoon to Outlook it is 66 miles, to Regina 142, Winnipeg 470, Seattle 1,200, Chicago 1,334. From Winnipeg to Regina it is 356 miles, to Chicago 860 miles, Waterloo 1,200 miles. From Waterloo to Chicago it is 450 miles, to New York 542, to Saskatoon 1,670.

3. *Some Problems of Our Educational Institutions.* Although formal suggestions for greater economies and more effective programs have been given to the administrators, yet it is desirable to present a general picture of the problems of our institutions.

Jon Bjarnason Academy. While this institution belongs to the Icelandic Synod, yet it has been aided by our Board of Education for several years. This year $1,200 is allotted. Without such aid this academy would have had to close, is the measured judgment of those interested in its continuance.

This year they have their largest attendance of about ninety. About 30 per cent are Lutherans. A very large percentage of the students pass the provincial examinations, which is an evidence of the type of work done. It is supported only by voluntary offerings.

Saskatoon College (Academy) and Seminary. The buildings are located beyond the present limits of the city's water and sewer accommodations. The grounds and buildings are kept in good condition, commensurate with financial ability.

The academy offers Grade 12 (first year college) this year, because of the need of four students. The seminary did not offer any instruction in the English language during the past year. The curriculum and staff are wholly inadequate for proper bi-lingual instruction.

The Manitoba Synod, with 7,697 confirmed members, through its budget and special offerings, supported the institution to the extent of $1,801 during the past year. The Board of American Missions will give $3,450 during this year for the salaries of two theological professors. The Board of Education gives $7,000 annually. The indebtedness, including mortgages, bonds, taxes, unpaid salaries and local business accounts, is $24,724.44, or about 32 per cent of the total assets.

The president should be able to develop the interest of the churches and make proper contacts with both educational and civic circles. The seminary needs a professor who will give his whole time to instruction, through the medium of English language in Bible and Practical Theology. These and other needs necessitate a larger income. The academy should not attempt a larger educational program, and the Board of Directors should consider the advisability and feasibility of allowing the academy students to take all subjects, except Bible, at the local collegiate (high school).

Waterloo College and Seminary. Decided improvements were found in the appearance of grounds and buildings, a more definite educational program in the college, a better trained college faculty, and the scholastic background of the theological students.

The tutorial or high school has been discontinued. The college gives honor courses. The college enrollment is seventy-three, with 60 per cent of the classes having five and less students.

The Canada Synod, with 21,057 confirmed members, contributed through the budget and special offerings, in 1931-32, a total of $20,097. The Board of Education gave $5,000. The present indebtedness is $26,006 or 15 per cent of the total assets.

The present income is not quite enough to balance the budget. Without increasing materially the expenses, the college could serve one hundred more students, whose fees would more than balance the budget, but the constituency does not seem able at present to furnish more students. The program of the college cannot be enlarged without endangering the financial status of the institution.

4. *The Educational Policy of the United Lutheran Church in Canada.* The data and findings on administration and home missions show that the foundations for a great Lutheran Church in Canada are being laid. This must include an educational policy. There is enough truth in the declaration, "No Church is greater than its schools," to compel us to avoid the mistakes of the Lutheran Church in its early history in the United States. The church schools prepare the local leaders who direct the development of their Church. The Lutheran Church in Canada must educate its youth primarily for the sake of an intelligent and loyal church membership. But

no educational program dare be of such type that it becomes a financial burden to the Church and thereby prohibits the desirable expansion of the Church and the necessary attention to other phases of the Church's life.

Recommendations

(For action on these recommendations see p. 294)

1. That the Synod of Canada be encouraged to continue the consideration of its plan of reorganization, and form contacts with the Synod of Manitoba and the Synod of Nova Scotia, with a view to considering the possibility of uniting all under its Dominion charter of 1885; and that if such united body in time should be formed, it be given the place of the Synod of Canada on the roll of Constituent Synods of The United Lutheran Church in America.

2. That The United Lutheran Church in America will give its approval, if and when desired, to the organization of an independent United Lutheran Church in Canada, embracing all Lutheran congregations in the Dominion, provided no relationship be established with any other general body of Lutherans that is not established with The United Lutheran Church in America.

3. That the statement of benevolence policy, given in the body of this report and conveyed by the Commission to the Lutherans in Canada, be approved; and that the Executive Board be requested to consider the publication of a concise pamphlet, containing the administrative, linguistic and benevolence policies of the Church, for the assistance of Nationalistic Synods which may seek our fellowship.

4. That the Board of American Missions be requested to consider the practical use of summer canvassing by theological students, in the large cities of Ontario, as a means of assisting our mission congregations in the direction of self-support.

5. That the attention of the entire Church be called to the large increase in the number of Lutheran adherents in Canada during the last decade, and also to the eagerness of the new immigrants to be organized into congregations.

6. That the Board of Education be requested to confer with the Board of American Missions with a view to the gradual assumption of an undivided support of the seminary at Saskatoon.

7. That in view of the suggested reorganization of the Church in Canada and the advisability of training men from the field, on the field, for the field, the seminaries at Saskatoon and Waterloo be continued.

8. That the pastors of the drought-stricken sections of Western Canada be commended for their devotion to their people during the period of privation and want, and that the deeply appreciated relief work of the Church be continued through the coming winter.

Commissioners {
Ellis B. Burgess,
Ernst A. Tappert,
Gould Wickey.

These recommendations were adopted by the Executive Board and are herewith presented to the Convention for the action of the Church.

F. H. KNUBEL, *President,*
E. CLARENCE MILLER, *Treasurer,*
ABDEL ROSS WENTZ, *Acting Secretary.*

The item concerning the Board of American Missions and the Special Year 1938 (II, 3) was by vote postponed to the next convention of the Church.

The item concerning the Establishment of a Bureau of Architecture (II, 4) was adopted.

Action on the report of the Executive Board was suspended to hear the report of Committee of Tellers No. 2. The Committee reported that Dr. E. Clarence Miller had received 433 votes out of a total of 450 votes cast. The President declared Dr. Miller elected Treasurer.

Consideration of the Executive Board's report was resumed.

The item concerning the Proposed Merger of the Inner Mission Board, the Board of Deaconess Work, the Committee on Evangelism and the Committee on Moral and Social Welfare (II, 6) was on motion resubmitted to the Executive Board with the request that they take the necessary steps to correlate the work of the two committees and the two boards involved in this item.

At twelve o'clock the Convention adjourned with prayer by the Rev. C. J. Shealy.

SECOND SESSION

BENJAMIN FRANKLIN HOTEL.
Philadelphia, Pennsylvania.
Thursday, October 13, 1932, 2.00 P. M.

Devotions were conducted by the Rev. G. W. Englar, and the President called the Convention to order.

The President announced that the Rev. Ralph H. Long, Executive Director of the National Lutheran Council, was present, and with the general consent of the Convention, would be heard at this time. Dr. Long spoke to the Convention on the work of the National Lutheran Council. The President responded.

Committee of Tellers No. 1 reported that there was no election in the balloting for Secretary. The President announced that in accordance with the Convention's action this morning, the next ballot for Secretary would be taken tomorrow at this time. The Rev. A. R. Wentz, Secretary of the Convention, spoke to the Convention and insisted that the delegates refrain from voting for him as Secretary of the Church.

Consideration of the Executive Board's report was resumed.

The item concerning the Training of Ministers and Teachers (II, 9), as set forth in the Supplemental Report of the Executive Board, Item A, was then presented to the Convention, and on motion the consideration of this item was postponed for at least twenty-four hours. The President appointed Friday afternoon, four o'clock, as the time for the consideration of this item as a special order of business.

The item concerning Co-operation with the Suomi Synod (II,11) was taken up for consideration. It was voted to rescind the action of the Milwaukee Convention adopting certain agreements relating to Finnish work in Canada (Minutes 1930, pp. 414, 415). The new set of agreements approved by the Executive Board and presented to this Convention was adopted as a substitute for the agreements originally adopted by the Milwaukee Convention.

The item concerning the preparation of a Catechism (III, A, 3) was taken under consideration. On motion the recommendations were amended to read:

"(a) That this Convention authorize the Parish and Church School Board to report to the Executive Board concerning the advisability and a plan for the preparation of such a manual.
"(b) That if the report of the Parish and Church School Board is favorable and approved by the Executive Board, the actual preparation shall proceed in accordance with the plan proposed by the Parish and Church School Board."

On motion paragraph "(b)" was stricken from the item. It was moved to adopt paragraph "(a)". On motion it was decided to refer this entire matter to the Parish and Church School Board for report back to this body.

The item concerning an Official Interpretation of the Constitution (III, A, 5) was received as information. The recommendation "that the Convention instruct the Secretary of the Church to correspond with the officials of all synods for the purpose of a true adjustment in the number of delegates from all synods" was adopted.

The item concerning the Parish and Church School Board's Comprehensive Plan of Parish Education (IV, B, 7 (b)) was considered and the recommendation was adopted.

The Convention took up the consideration of the item concerning the Budget (VI, 3).

Recommendations (a), (b), (c) and (d) were adopted.

Recommendation (e) was taken under consideration. On motion it was decided to rescind the action of the Milwaukee Convention fixing the budget for 1933 at $2,400,000. The recommendation of the Executive Board to the Milwaukee Convention fixing the budget for 1933 at $2,400,000 was amended by substituting $2,000,000 for $2,400,000. The amended recommendation was adopted, thus fixing the budget for 1933 at $2,000,000.

On motion of the Rev. G. Morris Smith, paragraph (f) was inserted as follows:

"That the budget of $2,000,000 be accepted not as a retreat but as an advance to be actually secured by synods and conferences and congregations stimulated by the delegates here assembled."

The recommendations 1 to 4, concerning the World Conference on Faith and Order (XI) were adopted.

The recommendation of the Executive Board concerning the appointment of a special committee to report on invitations for the next convention of the United Lutheran Church (XII) was adopted. The President appointed as convener of this Committee the President of the United Synod of New York.

Postponing the item of the Executive Board's report concerning the Survey of Canadian Synods (III, B and Supplemental Report "B" of the Executive Board), the Convention proceeded to the report of the Committee on Plan of Apportionment.

The report of the Committee on Plan of Apportionment was presented by the Rev. E. B. Burgess, Chairman of the Committee.

REPORT OF COMMITTEE ON PLAN OF APPORTIONMENT

(For action on the recommendations in this report see p. 167.)

At the seventh biennial convention of The United Lutheran Church in America, October 7-14, 1930, memorials from certain constituent synods were referred to a special committee, consisting of Rev. Ellis B. Burgess,

Rev. C. B. Foelsch, Rev. Robert H. Ischinger, Rev. Herbert A. Bosch, Arthur P. Black, Robert F. Bowe, J. Milton Deck, J. K. Jensen, E. Clarence Miller, and Hon. Charles Steele.

The referred memorials are:

1. *Memorial of the Texas Synod.* See U. L. C. Minutes, 1930, page 142.
"To the convention of the United Lutheran Church in America concerning the distribution of the apportionment obligation to the constituent synods.

"We believe that the apportionment method, by which The United Lutheran Church now for several years has endeavored to raise the funds needed for its benevolent operations, has demonstrated the wisdom of such a method sufficiently to warrant its retention by the Church. We, furthermore, believe that the failure to raise a sufficient amount to satisfy the annual budget is due to a wrong principle of distribution.

"The Word of God (I Cor. 16:2) requires that the collection for benevolent purposes be made through free will offerings from every Christian in the measure with which God has prospered him. This biblical principle, we believe, has not been adhered to in the distribution of the apportionments to the several synods affiliated with The United Lutheran Church, but, contrariwise, without regard for the peculiar ability of the individual synod, each synod has been assigned the same per communing member, though it is evident that there is a marked difference in ability of each synod, as is evidenced by the value of congregational property described in the annual statistical reports of congregations and synods. The question before us then, brethren, is how we may measure the relative ability of the synods. This, it seems to us, could be accomplished on the basis of property valuation as shown in the last reports, less the indebtedness of each synod. Allowance should also be made in some equitable manner for the support which the individual synod must give to its charitable and educational institutions.

"We believe that by such a method the weaker synods and congregations who are much behind in meeting this obligation, would rather be encouraged when the amount is within their reach, while congregations and synods who have heretofore raised the full amount, would, according to Christian principle, not slacken their endeavor in this exercise of their Christian privilege and duty."

2. *Memorial of the United Lutheran Synod of New York.* Minutes U. L. C. 1930, page 140.
"That we memorialize The United Uutheran Church in America to use voluntary pledges, secured in advance from the constituent synods, as the basis for its annual budget."

3. *Memorial of the Ministerium of Pennsylvania.* Minutes, U. L. C., 1930, page 143.
"That the Ministerium of Pennsylvania memorialize the United Lutheran Church to adopt the two-fold basis of laying apportionment, namely, communing members and current expenses."

4. *Resolution of the Ministerium of Pennsylvania.* Minutes, U. L. C., 1930. page 144.
"Be it further resolved, That all of the constituent synods shall accept this principle, and shall meet their obligation to pay in full the annual budget for benevolence, it being understood that, in fixing the basis of synodical apportionment for the budget of benevolence, due consideration be given to the financial ability of the smaller synods of the United Lutheran Church."

The Committee on Plan of Apportionment met in Philadelphia, June 10, 1931, gave consideration to the principles of Christian giving involved in the several memorials, made a survey of apportionment methods now in use in eight of the leading Protestant bodies in the United States, and submits the following statement of its findings.

(1) The development of Christian stewardship and beneficence is a process of years, to which every agency of the Church should be made to render increasing service. No achievements of today can be regarded as other than the ground work on which the greater achievements of tomorrow will be built. The evangelical ideals of Christian giving are so lofty in principle that no basis of apportionment, expressed in terms of the business world, will long satisfy the mind of the Church. Dissatisfaction with present methods, found in Christian hearts, may be properly interpreted as the inner strivings of the Church toward her ideal.

(2) The memorial of the United Lutheran Synod of New York presents an ideal of Christian beneficence, for which every constituent synod of the United Lutheran Church might well strive. The proposition to make use of it in the distribution of apportionments to the synods, however, raises so many questions of practical administration, especially in dealing with the less developed synods, that the committee is not prepared to recommend it.

(3) The resolution of the Ministerium of Pennsylvania, asking that each synod of the United Lutheran Church accept full responsibility for the payment of 100 per cent of its apportionment would be neither just nor effective unless all synods were prepared to give it 100 per cent endorsement.

(4) The memorial of the Texas Synod, asking that consideration be given the weaker synods in the distribution of apportionments, contains an element of fairness which the older and more firmly established synods should recognize. The solution proposed in the memorial is not so convincing. Those church bodies now using net valuation of church property as one of their basis of apportionment, have found it such a variable factor as to be untrustworthy.

(5) The memorial of the Ministerium of Pennsylvania, requesting the United Lutheran Church to adopt the two-fold basis of laying apportionments, namely, communing members and current expenses, raises a specific question that was debated at length in the conventions of the Church before the present basis was adopted. It also raises the general question of the relative merits of narrower and broader basis of apportionment, the answer to which the committee attempted to find in the survey already cited. With a single exception, the returns from this survey indicated a general preference for the broader basis.

    a. The Presbyterian Church in the United States (Southern). A three-fold basis is used: membership, 50 per cent; gifts to budget purposes, 25 per cent; ministerial support, 25 per cent.

    b. The Presbyterian Church in the United States of America (North). A three-fold basis is used: per capita giving to all purposes, or the resource factor; per capita giving to Board quotas, or the willingness factor; and size of congregation, or the responsibility factor.

    c. The United Presbyterian Church. A dual basis, communing members, and "having regard as far as knowledge could reach to the financial ability of the constituency," is in use. This body lays special stress upon tithing.

    d. The Reformed Church in the United States. A five-fold basis is in use: membership, 30 per cent; congregational expenses over a three-year period, 30 per cent; benevolent contributions over a three-year period, 30 per cent; property above indebtedness, 10 per cent; moral ability, used only as an "adjuster."

e. The United Brethren in Christ. First, a four-fold basis was used: church membership; past giving to benevolences; pastors' salaries; net value of church property. To these bases it was found desirable to add two others: the development of church membership; and difference in the income of the people.

f. The Northern Baptist Church. At first the allotments were made on the basis of past giving; now a four-fold basis is being studied: membership; value of the church property over mortgage; contributions to local expenses; and contributions to local missionary and institutional work.

g. The Christian Church. A three-fold basis is used: membership, one-third; previous giving, one-third; local current expenses, one-third. Four general free-will offerings annually supplement the budget, chiefly for their educational value.

h. The Congregational Church. Apportionments are distributed by states; and, since the state organizations are autonomous, "there is considerable variety of practice in arriving at apportionment figures in the local church." This tendency is to the adoption of the voluntary principle.

(6) The Committee is of the opinion that a broader basis of reckoning in the distribution of the apportionment among the synods would be fairer to all sections of the United Lutheran Church, and submits the following plan:

1. The apportionment shall be distributed among the synods: 75 per cent on the basis of communing members, and 25 per cent on the basis of allocation.

2. The percentage basis of allocation at each convention shall be prepared by a Board of Allocation, appointed by the President of the United Lutheran Church, consisting of the chairmen of the several synodical delegations represented in the convention.

3. The treasurer of the United Lutheran Church at each convention shall furnish the chairman of the Board of Allocation the following data: first, the total sum to be laid upon the synods by allocation; second, the total sum of apportionment paid by each synod during the last four fiscal years; and third, the percentage of the entire apportionment receipts of the last four fiscal years paid by each synod.

4. This table of percentages, expressed to five decimal points, furnished by the treasurer, shall be the basis of deliberations for the Board of Allocation at each convention; and no changes shall be made therein except by a two-thirds vote of all members of the Board.

5. Should major changes occur *ad interim*, such as merger or division of synods, the percentages of such synods shall be calculated on the basis of the congregational records.

6. When this table of percentages has been reported to and adopted by the convention, it shall be the lawful basis on which the treasurer of the United Lutheran Church shall distribute 25 per cent of the apportionment to the synods for the ensuing biennium. The remaining 75 per cent shall be distributed on the basis of communing members.

ELLIS B. BURGESS,	C. B. FOELSCH,
E. CLARENCE MILLER,	ARTHUR P. BLACK,
CHARLES STEELE,	ROBERT F. BOWE,
J. MILTON DECK,	HERBERT A. BOSCH,
R. H. ISCHINGER,	J. K. JENSEN.

At five o'clock the Convention adjourned with prayer by the Rev. G. W. Englar.

Thursday Evening

On Thursday evening, October 13, in the Crystal Ballroom of the Benjamin Franklin Hotel, Philadelphia, Pa., a banquet for men was sponsored jointly by the Laymen's Movement for Stewardship and the Lutheran Social Union of Philadelphia. Five hundred and forty-one men were in attendance.

The Invocation was pronounced by the Rev. E. P. Pfatteicher. Dr. E. Clarence Miller was the Toastmaster. Mr. Francis C. Leupold, President of the Lutheran Social Union, presented the greetings of that organization. President F. H. Knubel presented the greetings of The United Lutheran Church in America, calling attention to the "Silver Anniversary" of the Laymen's Movement. The Rev. N. R. Melhorn was in charge of the group singing. The special music for the occasion was furnished by the Melody Ensemble of Philadelphia.

The address of the evening was delivered by the Hon. Ellwood M. Rabenold, of New York City, on "Individual and Social Responsibility." Mr. J. L. Clark, President of the Laymen's Movement for Stewardship, spoke on "Our Twenty-fifth Anniversary."

THIRD SESSION

BENJAMIN FRANKLIN HOTEL.
Philadelphia, Pennsylvania.
Friday, October 14, 1932, 8.45 A. M.

Matins were conducted by the Rev. A. B. MacIntosh.

The Convention was called to order by the President.

The Minutes of the First and Second Sessions were read by the Secretary and declared approved.

Because of slight typographical errors on the ballots distributed, it was on motion decided to postpone today's elections until Saturday, and to postpone Saturday's elections until Monday.

The report of the Commission of Adjudication was presented by the Rev. E. B. Burgess, a member of the Commission.

REPORT OF THE COMMISSION OF ADJUDICATION

(For action on these proposed amendments see p. 193.)

The Commission of Adjudication organized, for the biennium just closing, in Milwaukee, on October 11, 1930, and elected the following officers:

President—Rev. A. G. Voigt, D.D., LL.D.
Vice-President—Rev. Luther Kuhlman, D.D.
Secretary—Rev. H. C. Roehner, D.D.
Clerk—Hon. E. K. Strong.

It is a pleasing fact, indicative of the harmony that prevails in the United Lutheran Church, that no disputed questions of doctrine or practice came before the Commission for consideration during the biennium. It was therefore unnecessary to have any meeting until immediately before this Convention on October 12, 1932. The only business was of a somewhat formal character.

In consideration of the fact that questions are sometimes submitted to the Commission for adjudication by a convention of the United Lutheran Church, and also of the further fact that it is often highly desirable that a possible appeal from the decision of the Commission should be determined at the same convention, it has appeared to the Commission that the by-laws requiring ten days' notice in writing of an intention to appeal would invalidate the right to appeal. There are also other possible cases in which this form of notice, causing long delays, would not be equitable. Therefore, a committee was appointed by the Commission to recommend a suitable modification of the pertinent By-Laws. On the basis of the report of this committee, the Commission resolved to recommend to the United Lutheran Church the following amendments of the By-Laws: Strike out Section V, Division C, Items 11 and 12, and insert the following:

"Item 11. In all cases of appeal from any decision of the Commission of Adjudication rendered within the interim between Conventions of The United Lutheran Church in America, Notice of Intention to Appeal shall be given in writing to the President of the Commission at least ten days prior to the first day of the Convention following: Provided, however, that when decisions have been rendered at any convention, or within thirty days prior thereto, appeal may be made during the convention upon consent obtained by a two-thirds' vote of the delegates present. The convention shall thereupon fix a time when the appeal shall be made a special order of the convention.

"Item 12. An appeal from any decision of the Commission of Adjudication can be made only at the Convention of the United Lutheran Church at which such decision has been reported, and can be entertained only when Item 11 above has been fully complied with and the appeal shall have been submitted in writing by five delegates to said convention. After the submission and argument of the appeal it shall not be voted upon until the succeeding day, unless by reason of limited time, the Convention, by two-thirds' vote, shall decide to adjudicate the appeal on the same day. To sustain the appeal and reverse the decision from which the appeal is made, a two-thirds' vote of the members present and voting shall be necessary. In the discussion of any such appeal, the Commission of Adjudication shall be fully heard through any of its members whom it may designate, whether they be or be not delegates to the Convention."

A. G. VOIGT, President.

E. B. BURGESS, Secretary pro tem.

The President called the attention of the Convention to the fact that this constitutes due notice of proposed amendments to the By-Laws of the Church, to be voted on at the first session to-morrow.

The report of the Laymen's Movement for Stewardship was presented by Mr. A. P. Black, Executive Secretary of the Laymen's Movement.

REPORT OF LUTHERAN LAYMEN'S MOVEMENT FOR STEWARDSHIP

(For action on the recommendations in this report see p. 97.)

The year 1932 marks the twenty-fifth anniversary of our Lutheran Laymen's Movement for Stewardship, a volunteer organization of business and professional men, whose one purpose is to promote the benevolent program of our great Church as a whole.

A 100 PER CENT PROGRAM AND A BALANCED BUDGET

We rejoice in the fact we are privileged to report that in spite of the worst financial depression in the memory of our generation our Laymen's Movement has been able to function 100 per cent during this biennium—and with a balanced budget. This double blessing has been made possible by (a) drastic reductions in our overhead expense, (b) the loyal financial and moral support of our membership, (c) the wholehearted cooperation of local Brotherhoods, synodical officials, board secretaries, THE LUTHERAN, college and seminary officials, and pastors and lay workers generally throughout our Church, and (d) placing the major emphasis in all our work on the educational and spiritual. To all those who have contributed so effectively toward the working out of our program we want to say with sincerest appreciation and gratitude, "Thank you, and God bless you."

EVERY MEMBER VISITATION

Each year of this biennium has marked a distinct step forward and upward in the development of our Every Member Visitation program.

Our chief means of determining the progress made by the Every Member Visitation are (a) the number of orders for our promotional literature received during succeeding campaigns, and (b) verbal and written communications from pastors and lay workers. In last fall's campaign there were

2,567 pastors in our United Lutheran Church in America, each of whom was actually in charge of one or more congregations. Of this number 1,821, that is *seven out of every ten,* ordered our literature. This marks an increase over any preceding year of more than 100 pastors who made the Every Member Visitation for the first time, so far as our records show. The significant fact about the increase in the number of orders is that it represented a *general increase throughout our Church,* rather than spotty increases here and there.

To illustrate: actual increases were registered in twenty-one synods. In five synods the number of orders equalled the previous high record. In only six of the smaller synods was there a slight falling off in the number of orders.

The most gratifying increases were from our largest two synods—the Ministerium of Pennsylvania and the United Synod of New York.

Literature Well Received

During last fall's campaign we issued (a) 575,000 copies of a new Stewardship pledge card, printed in two colors, (b) 540,000 copies of a folder on "Worship and Regular Church Attendance," (c) 465,000 copies of a folder emphasizing the first fundamental principle of Christian Stewardship—"Divine Ownership," and (d) 415,000 copies of a new Annual Church Booklet, presenting a general survey of the work of our Church, copy for which was supplied by eleven secretaries. All told, approximately 2,000,000 copies of these four pieces of literature were distributed, (1,995,000 to be exact), all upon request, and *without cost to the congregations,* following our annual letter, accompanied by samples of literature and a postal card order blank, which went to all pastors the first week in September.

The total cost to the Laymen's Movement of last fall's Every Member Visitation exceeded $6,000. This represented an increase of more than $500 over the cost of the 1931 campaign.

Financial Losses More Than Offset

The gains resulting from our two Every Member Visitation campaigns this biennium have been educational and spiritual, if not financial. This fact has been reflected clearly in our correspondence. The following excerpts from a letter from one of the leading pastors in the middle west will serve as a typical illustration:

"Our Every Member Visitation last fall was the best ever—not from the standpoint of raising the budget (we didn't, by a considerable margin), but from the standpoint of the spirit of the Visitation, and the resultant general attitude on the part of visitors and those visited. Some of the visitors were pessimistic before they started out. When they came back they were optimistic, because they found that the people in general were ready to receive them, and ready to respond to their requests. Some few people were obliged to reduce their pledges. *Many increased pledges.* The remainder pledged as before. Everybody was seen and given a chance to pledge. Their manner of response was a heartening experience for the visitors. The visitors were given a good dose of the efficacy of prayer in advance, with some straight-from-the-shoulder experiences, and they were sold on the idea that the Lord was with them. When they came back to report they were all so enthused that it was really a wonderful experience. *We got an expression of loyalty from our people which said louder than words just how they felt about the whole matter."*

The experience of this pastor was matched by the experience of hundreds of pastors, and there is no scriptural reason why it could not be matched by practically every pastor. It will be when our pastors and church council-men generally become thoroughly awake to the facts that (a) the funda-mental principles underlying the Every Member Visitation belong to our Church as a whole; (b) the duty of enunciating those principles belongs to our Church as a whole; (c) the responsibility for keeping the machinery going to fulfill that duty is the responsibility of our Church as a whole; and (d) our Church as a whole is dependent upon its more than 3,800 *individual congregations.* **(See Recommendations 1 and 2.)**

STUDENT AID

During the first year of this biennium eighteen (18) students who had received aid from our Laymen's Movement were graduated from our seminaries into our United Lutheran Church in America ministry. This year there were seventeen (17). Of the 1931 group all but two are giving full-time service to our Church, at home or abroad. One of the two is doing post-graduate work in Yale University, and one has not been placed. Of the 1932 group, ten of the seventeen had been placed when this report was filed (the last week in June), one notified us he would do post-graduate work in the University of Chicago, and three had calls pending. All told the number of men graduated into the ministry, who received aid from our Laymen's Movement, totals 124, as shown from the following official tabulation:

In 1926	6
In 1927	16
In 1928	22
In 1929	28
In 1930	17
In 1931	18
In 1932	17
Total	124

The number of different students aided by our Laymen's Movement, for the whole or a part of their college and seminary course, totals 261.

Our Student Aid budget from the beginning, by years, has been as follows:

1923-4	$3,665
1924-5	5,350
1925-6	16,150
1926-7	23,795

1927-8	....	26,790
1928-9	....	27,275
1929-30	....	20,362
1930-31	....	15,675
1931-32	....	12,800
Total	....	$151,862

Our Student Aid budget for 1932-3 will be slightly more or less than $10,000, distributed among fifty or more students. The largest number of students carried on our rolls in any one year was 145 in 1928-9.

We are sometimes asked how many of our beneficiaries receive synodical aid also. Of the sixty-nine on our rolls the past year, twenty-four received synodical aid and forty-five did not. In other words, slightly more than one-third received synodical aid. The average for the decade 1922-1932 is slightly less than one-third. **(See Recommendation 3.)**

CHRISTIAN STEWARDSHIP BEING EMPHASIZED

This biennium has marked a distinct advance along stewardship lines throughout our Church. *More Conferences* than in any preceding biennium have given the principles of Christian Stewardship a prominent place in their programs. It has been my privilege to work in several where the entire program has been devoted to papers and discussions of those principles. *Synodical bulletins* from the majority of our synods come to my desk regularly. With hardly an exception they carry vital stewardship messages in every issue. *A growing number of the younger pastors* have written our office for stewardship information, and it has been our pleasure to loan books to some of them from our library. THE LUTHERAN printed a series of ten articles on "The Deeper Meanings of Stewardship," in the fall of 1931, and is printing a similar series this fall. *The Women's Missionary Society* had "Our Stewardship" for its leading editorial in the January, 1932, issue of its official magazine, LUTHERAN WOMAN'S WORK, and emphasized the stewardship of talents, time, and possessions, in its January, February, and March issues. Its local congregational missionary societies throughout our Church are making a special study of stewardship along with their study of missions. It is with the profoundest kind of joy we note the effective work being done in this vital field by the Women's Missionary Society through its branch societies. It is just possible our women may yet prove to be the deciding factor in making our United Lutheran Church in America more stewardship-conscious and more missionary-minded. Five years ago very few of our synods had a synodical stewardship secretary. *In this year 1932 practically every synod* either has a regularly elected or appointed synodical stewardship secretary, or committee, or both. Our next step is to have a stewardship secretary or director in every congregation. Congregations here and there already have taken this step. *Speed the day when every congregation will have the vision to make Christian Stewardship the basis of its permanent program."* **(See Recommendations 4 and 6.)**

VISITS TO SEMINARIES

One of the most fascinating and, we believe, most profitable adventures made annually by our Laymen's Movement is the visit to our seminaries by one of its official representatives. It was my high privilege to visit nine of our twelve seminaries last March and April, and have an hour with the seminarians to present and discuss the theme *"Suggestions to Seminarians About to Enter the Gospel Ministry."* Copy of skeleton outline of the presentation was left with each seminarian for reference purposes. In every instance there was the most cordial response and sympathetic reaction on the part of both seminarians and members of the faculty, and an invitation to return next year was extended. Several of our seminaries are experimenting with a course on "Church Administration," with encouraging results. Our prayer is that every seminary will give such a program a permanent place in its curriculum. It is not fair either to our Church or our seminarians to graduate them into the ministry without a working knowledge of administrative problems every minister faces from the day he assumes charge of a pastorate. **(See Recommendation 5.)**

RECOMMENDATIONS

1. That the annual simultaneous Every Member Visitation be re-endorsed, and every organization in individual congregations be urged to cooperate actively with the pastor and council (1) in the preparatory educational and spiritual campaign, (2) in making the actual visitation, and (3) in a systematic follow-up.

2. That congregations not using the budget, the duplex envelope, the pledge card, and the quarterly statement, be urged to use them, and congregations already using them be urged to make more effective use of each.

3. That the Student Aid program of the Laymen's Movement, as being worked out in cooperation with the president of our Church and the presidents of synods, be approved.

4. That the growing emphasis being placed on Christian Stewardship by our various Church agencies be given unqualified approval, and that continued cooperation be urged, to the end that our great Church may speedily become more stewardship-conscious and more missionary-minded.

5. That those seminaries not already experimenting with a course on "Church Administration" be urged to consider the advisability of giving such a course a permanent place in their regular curriculum.

6. [Inserted by the Convention see p. 97.]

Respectfully submitted,

J. L. CLARK, *President,*
ARTHUR P. BLACK, *Secretary.*

Recommendations 1, 2, 3, 4, and 5 were adopted.

On motion a sixth recommendation was added as follows:

"That the Church recommend to the congregations that there be a stewardship secretary or director in every congregation."

An invitation to all laymen to become members of this organization was extended by Mr. W. H. Hager.

It was moved and carried that the Convention express to the Laymen's Movement its appreciation for their work.

The report of the Committee on Church Papers was presented by the Rev. H. Offermann, Chairman of the Committee.

REPORT OF THE COMMITTEE ON CHURCH PAPERS

(For action on the recommendations in this report see p. 98.)

In the interests of economy your committee has held but two meetings during the biennium, one on May 15, 1931, and the other on June 28, 1932. The organization of the committee remained the same as in the preceding biennium with Dr. Offerman as chairman and Dr. Pfatteicher as secretary, the officers of the committee and Dr. Aberly constituting the Executive Committee.

Both regular meetings of the committee were largely spent upon problems of editorial policy frankly discussed by the editors with the committee, upon the unfinished item of personnel, and upon the problems of circulation and advertising with the business manager of the publication house.

In re editorial policy, the committee commended Drs. Melhorn and Tappert for vision and definiteness of purpose. The editors referred to difficulties which they encounter in seeking to cover the whole field adequately and promptly, in getting brief, snappy and popular presentations on the part of specialists in their respective fields, on their inability to get sufficient contributions from the really good writers we have without some guarantee that they will be printed in full, and of the diametrically opposite views of what a church paper ought to be expressed by letter writers. **(See Recommendation 1.)**

The item of personnel involves the desirability of adding an assistant editor to the staff of THE LUTHERAN from among the ranks of our younger men who have specialized in publicity and newspaper work. It was felt by your committee that in view of the report of the business manager of the publication house concerning the circulation of THE LUTHERAN, and the necessity of even now subsidizing it in part, and also in view of the splendid and intelligent editorial assistance rendered Dr. Melhorn by Miss Harriet Horn, who has a wide knowledge of both the Church and its paper, that this item be tabled for the present. **(See Recommendations 2 and 3.)**

In re problems of circulation and advertising, your committee commends the grasp of these items by Dr. Hultberg, who was present in person at both meetings and graciously and readily answered every question put to him. Reference was made to the splendid cooperation of our pastors throughout the Church in connection with the celebration of the Centennial of our Church papers in 1931. One of the two peaks reached by the circulation department was achieved last year—1918, 41,000—1931, 39,000. **(See Recommendations 4-6.)**

Your committee has faced necessary withdrawals from its membership by nominating to the Executive Board the names of Dr. C. E. Gardner in place of Dr. Leas, Dr. Greever for Dr. Brown, and Dr. Holl for Dr. John C. Horine.

Your committee has nominated the Rev. M. R. Hamsher and the Rev. E. P. Pfatteicher for re-election, and Mr. Henry Streibert to take the place of Mr. I. Searles Runyon, whose term expires and who is ineligible for re-election.

The recommendations of your committee are as follows:

1. That we endorse the recommendation of the editor of *The Lutheran* that he experiment upon a department of religious world news and a department of Lutheran world news; [Withdrawn.]

2. That we table for the time being further thought concerning the election of an assistant editor for *The Lutheran;* [Withdrawn.]

3. That we recommend the re-election of the Rev. Dr. Nathan R. Melhorn as Editor of *The Lutheran*, and the Rev. Dr. C. R. Tappert as Editor of *Lutherischer Herold.*

4. That for the present we discontinue the publication of *The Daily Lutheran,* heretofore issued as a convention news sheet; [Withdrawn.]

5. That we impress upon our pastors and congregations the necessity of conserving the circulation gains of 1931, and urge the designation of a society or person in each congregation to act as an active agent for our Church papers;

6. That we express our sincere gratitude to the Publication Board and to its business manager for making possible the continuance of our Church papers in times such as these.

7. [Inserted by the Convention see p. 99.]

Respectfully submitted,
For the Committee,
H. Offermann, *Chairman,*
E. P. Pfatteicher, *Secretary.*

There being no objection, recommendations 1 and 2 were withdrawn.

Recommendation 3 was adopted and the President declared the Rev. N. R. Melhorn elected Editor of *The Lutheran,* and the Rev. C. R. Tappert elected Editor of the *Lutherischer Herold.*

Recommendation 4 was withdrawn.

Recommendations 5 and 6 were adopted.

It was moved and carried to adopt the following as an additional recommendation in the report of the Committee on Church Papers:

"7. That, in order to conserve and increase the circulation gains and in order to co-operate more fully with the Church at large in the program of Christian stewardship, the editors and business managers of our official church papers refuse all advertising which shall appeal to the money-making desires of church organizations."

The report of the Board of Education was presented by the Rev. H. R. Gold, President of the Board.

REPORT OF THE BOARD OF EDUCATION

(For action on the recommendations in this report see p. 167.)

A BOARD OF SERVICE

"The object of this Board shall be to promote the general educational interests of the Church, to conserve the religious life of the students in the educational institutions of the Church, in State Universities, and in other schools; to stimulate the supply of candidates for the ministry; to administer the work of ministerial education for co-operating synods, and to render financial aid to educational institutions."—Constitution of the Board of Education, Article II.

It is quite evident that the Board of Education, as conceived and chartered, is a board of service. This idea the Board attempts to carry out in directing the activities of the secretarial staff. Four secretaries are employed: Mary E. Markley, Litt. D., the Reverend C. P. Harry, D.D., Mildred E. Winston, A.M., and the Reverend Gould Wickey, Ph.D., D.D., A major portion of the time of Miss Markley, Miss Winston and Mr. Harry is devoted to student work, while the remaining portion is given to promotional and research activities. Miss Markley counsels with our college officials, especially in administering the office of dean of women and in securing capable women teachers. Mr. Wickey, the executive secretary, devotes about one-half of his time to visiting and serving the colleges, seminaries and student centers, one-quarter to promotion and research, and one-quarter to administrative matters. In fulfilling their responsibilities, during the biennium, these secretaries have made 475 visits to 242 different institutions in twenty-six states of the United States and three provinces of Canada, travelling about 150,000 miles; have delivered 1,118 addresses and talks, reaching about 80,000 individuals, at educational institutions, conferences, synods, missionary conventions, Sunday Schools, Luther Leagues, and church services; and have written more than fifty articles and pamphlets, and edited regularly two news bulletins. The real contribution to the lives of individuals as well as to the educational centers cannot be estimated in quantitative terms.

But the Board of Education carries out the idea of service not only in the distribution of the time and activities of the secretaries, but also in the distribution of its income. During the biennium, the Board disbursed $246,950, of which $221,426, or 93.72 per cent, was for grants and service to colleges, seminaries, and student centers. Only 6.28 per cent was consumed in administrative expenses.

Conscious of the serious responsibility it carries, in endeavoring to leaven higher education with the spirit of Christ, the Board presents its eighth biennial report, describing the nature of its work and submitting a record of its stewardship.

I. BEACONS AND BUILDERS—OUR INSTITUTIONS

As beacons lighten the darkness of the land and sea, so the church college and seminary have functioned in areas of educational darkness. While this was quite evident in the eighteenth and the first part of the nineteenth centuries, it is still equally true in the field of Christian higher education. They hold aloft the light of the Son of God to direct men in the pathway of righteousness and Christian culture. But our colleges and seminaries are more than beacons; they are builders. They build personalities which resist all efforts to break down the fundamental principles of social living and endeavor to construct a more definitely Christian civilization.

These institutions belong to the Church; in their progress the Church is interested, and in their adequate maintenance and greater development the Church must be ever alert.

1. The Service of the Board

Grants and Visits

The Board endeavors to distribute in a most equitable manner grants to the colleges and seminaries. Since 1920 these grants have varied from $53,000 to $74,000. They are dependent upon the amount received from the Church. During the biennium the institutions received in direct grants $129,908, an average of $64,954 per year.

In accordance with the recommendations of the survey, which were adopted by the Church in 1928 with regard to the use of grants made by the Board, notices were sent to the colleges informing them "That the Department of Bible and Religious Education is to be aided first by said grant, and that then consideration be given to the promotion of the religious activities on the campus, provided such limitation of use of grant does not affect the standing of the institution with the accrediting agency."

It should be kept in mind that through the service of the secretaries the Board may be of more assistance to an institution than the grant itself. A visit of the executive secretary includes all or most of the following items: an address before the student body, private conferences with students, extended conferences with the president and members of the faculty, round table discussion with the faculty, and visits to classes. The type of advice sought by the institutions and given by the secretary covers general administrative problems, curriculum changes, teaching staff, student welfare, advertising and publications, and relations to the alumni and church constituencies. For example, the secretary showed one of the presidents that a certain office could be dispensed with and the duties thereof assigned to three other members of the administrative staff. By following this advice, the institution saved $3,000. In another institution the secretary counselled with the president in effecting a decrease in the budget for the ensuing year of more than $12,000.

Notwithstanding the increased recognition, even from a monetary point of view, of the value of secretarial visits, the Board is quite anxious that a large percentage of its income be distributed to the institutions. Accordingly, at its meeting in June, 1932, the following resolution was passed:

"That, in view of the vital importance of our educational institutions in the life of the Church, and in view of what we believe is the attitude of the Church at large, this Board endeavor to allocate not less than 60 per cent of its income to the support of our colleges and seminaries."

However, it must not be thought that the interest of the Church in Christian higher education is measured by what the Board of Education can contribute to the colleges and seminaries. Reports from synodical treasurers reveal that the synods of the United Lutheran Church gave, during 1931, $267,837. This sum added to what the Board gave, amounts to $332,791, distributed to thirteen seminaries and fourteen colleges.

While this sum appears large, yet it is hardly a third of what our Church should have given, when compared with the manner in which other Churches, including other Lutheran groups, support their higher educational institutions. We hope the day is not far distant when the Church will see fit to allot to the Board of Education a larger share of the apportionment. Let it not be said of our Church that when her colleges and seminaries grow stronger she withdraws her support from them. We dare not "penalize success."

Educational News Bulletin

During the past year the Board published, in mimeographed form, an Educational News Bulletin to fulfill the following purposes:

    a—To keep the colleges and seminaries informed of what the others are doing.
    b—To present summaries of educational projects being carried on by both Lutheran and non-Lutheran institutions.
    c—To give ideas for more effective and efficient administrative policies.
    d—To bring the Board and the institutions into closer co-operative relationship.

While the Bulletin was started as a venture, its status is now assured by the enthusiastic reception given it by the administrators. Some look upon it as a monthly visit by the secretary.

The value was of such degree that the National Lutheran Educational Conference asked the executive secretary of this Board, who is the secretary of the Conference, to prepare a Bulletin which will function in a similar manner for the colleges and seminaries holding membership in the Conference.

This Bulletin is mailed to the administrative officers of all colleges and seminaries, to pastors working with students, to synodical presidents, to the members of the Executive Board and the Board of Education, and to selected individuals both within and without the Lutheran Church.

Visits to Seminaries by Specialists

One of the ways in which an institution may be assisted is by extended visits from specialists. Such visits have the value not only of informing the faculty and students of that institution in those particular fields, but also of giving them a larger view of religious and theological problems in other sections of the Church. This whole plan was presented through correspondence and in person to various officials and professors of our seminaries. They believed the idea a good one and suggested that the operation of such a plan be initiated and supervised by the Board of Education. In accordance with this expressed wish, the Board at its meeting in June, 1932, passed a resolution favoring the general plan and appropriating a sum not to exceed $500 to cover the traveling expenses of the specialists.

Following Up the Values of the Survey

In our report of 1930 there were noted items of very definite progress which were effected to some degree through the Survey of Higher Education. In this report (see IV, Search and Research, sec. 2), there is recorded what has been accomplished in developing the religious life of the students at our colleges. It is now six years since the survey was started, and three years since it was published. It is possible to state some concrete values which have come to both the institutions and the Church.

To the institutions:

1. The confidence of assured knowledge. Many presidents knew of necessary changes, but the survey emphasized and supported the presidents in their appeals to their Boards and constituencies.

2. Numerous suggestions for economies, more effective organization, and constructive improvements.

3. Increased favor in the eyes of the standardizing and accrediting agencies. These bodies respect such surveys and look with favor upon the efforts being made to fulfill the recommendations thereof.

To the Church:

1. The Church and its Board of Education have a means of knowing the nature and quality of the service rendered by any one institution.

2. The Church knows in what direction efforts should be expended for the development of the whole educational program.

3. The Church, through the Board of Education, is offered opportunities to get into closer and more constructive touch with the institutions.

The existence of the survey does not mean that the institutions need no longer be concerned with a study of what they are doing. In fact, there must be a constant self-survey by each institution, if continued progress is to be effected.

Survey of Our Institutions in Canada

The Board endeavors to keep itself and the Church informed on educational situations and tendencies. It was with this in mind that the Survey of Higher Education was undertaken six years ago. It now appears desirable that a survey be made of the educational situation and possibilities in Canada, as concerns the United Lutheran Church in particular and the Lutheran Church in general. Accordingly, the Board authorized its executive secretary to carry out a resolution to this effect. Since the educational situation is tied up with the missionary situation, the Board of Education intends to co-operate with the Board of American Missions who favor a survey from their point of view.

A Duty to Seminary Graduates

The Board of Education is responsible for the recruiting program of the Church. We have reason to believe that the large number of young men in our seminaries today is partly the result of the recruiting efforts of the Board during the past years. This very condition makes us feel responsible also to some degree for the seminary graduates securing some field of service in the Church. We learned that on October 1, 1931, eight members of the graduating classes of 1931 were not placed, and on May 1, 1932, about half of the seniors of 1932 were placed. Because of the prospects of young men not being called to pastorates, and because many of the seniors were willing to serve the Church at a minimum salary, communications were addressed to the presidents of synods inquiring concerning prospective mission fields which might be developed and established churches which might be willing to take a seminary graduate for a so-called "clinical year."

In this effort to be of assistance to the graduates of our seminaries, many appreciative letters were received from seminary and synodical officials. It is highly improper for a Church to stimulate an interest in Christian Life Service and then have no positions available when the young people have completed their period of preparation. The Board is willing to act as a co-ordinating agency between such trained persons and synods and local parishes.

2. Matters Referred

The Training of Men for Bi-Lingual Ministry

At the 1930 Convention the United Lutheran Church adopted a policy for the training of men in a bi-lingual ministry. This policy places upon the Board of Education the responsibility of arranging for the adequate and effective training of students preparing for bi-lingual ministry. To supply the Church with pastors who can minister in more than one language has always been a problem with the Lutheran Church in America. This problem arises because of the principle of the Reformation that the Church must preach the gospel in the language of the people. Today the problem concerns more than the training of men to serve German-English parishes. We have congregations which must be served in other languages. Accordingly the Board, at its June, 1931, meeting, adopted the following resolutions:

"That the Board of Education stand ready to provide the salary (not to exceed $2500) of a professor, at one of our seminaries, properly equipped to assist in the training of men for the Slovak and Hungarian ministry.

"That the seminary, at which such training is given, shall be selected by the Board of Education in consultation with the Linguistic Department of the Board of American Missions."

Conditions during the biennium were such that it did not appear necessary to put the above resolution into effect. So far as German-English work is concerned, the Martin Luther, Saskatoon and Waterloo Seminaries appear to be able to supply pastors for such a bi-lingual ministry.

Closing of Kropp-Breklum Seminaries

In accordance with the action of the Church in 1930, authorizing the Board "to take the necessary steps leading to the friendly dissolution of our relationship with Kropp-Breklum," the Board continued its grant of $6,000 during the year 1930-31, and contributed $1500 during 1931-32. This latter sum was given to assist in closing their books without indebtedness. On July 1, 1931, the institutions were officially closed.

These institutions have sent to America some very valuable men who are now pastors and teachers prominent in the affairs of the United Lutheran Church. Others are serving diligently and sacrificially in little-known fields. For all, the Church thanks the Kropp-Breklum institutions. The closing of these institutions will no doubt bring a feeling of regret to the many friends in this country, but it must not be interpreted as failure. To have served a purpose in God's plan, is the highest type of success.

Case of Professor Boettcher

At the 1930 Convention the Church asked this Board, in connection with the Board of Ministerial Pensions and Relief, to consider the case of Christian Boettcher, for twenty-three years a professor of Kropp Seminary. Investigation disclosed that he had not been on the Kropp faculty for a number of years, but through sickness and general conditions in Germany was reduced to penury in his old age. It was believed that this was a case for the Board of Ministerial Pensions and Relief, if the United Lutheran Church had any connection with it at all. Our Board supported the petition of the Committee on German Interests to the Board of Ministerial Pensions and Relief for a grant or pension in favor of Professor Boettcher.

Extension of Christian Education Year

Because of the continued economic uncertainty, the campaigns planned for 1930 and 1931, as presented in our report to the 1930 Convention, had to be indefinitely postponed. The Executive Board became aware of the situation in which the colleges and seminaries found themselves, and graciously resolved at its meeting in October, 1931:

1. That, in cases where it is desired, we grant institutions and synods contemplating such campaigns the privilege of deferring the opening of these campaigns until such time as general conditions may show improvement, perhaps even as late as the year 1935.
2. That in cases where such postponement may create a serious or dangerous financial situation for an institution which has been depending upon the results of the expected campaign, it is suggested that such institutions and their supporting synods confer as to means by which the minimum current needs of the institution may be met during the period of postponement of campaigns.

This action is greatly appreciated by the institutions. They hope for the hasty approach of the time when the people may be able to assist them in their period of dire need. The Board of Education stands ready to assist any college or seminary in the promotion of a campaign.

The Exchange of Theological Students and Professors

The problem of exchange of theological students and professors with Germany, as submitted by the Executive Board of the Church to the Board of Education, has been given careful consideration. We believe that some sort of an exchange of professors would be desirable, and that the Board of Education might be the co-ordinating agency, but it is not possible to effect any plan at this time on account of the financial conditions.

3. SIGNIFICANT EVENTS AND FACTS

The by-laws of the United Lutheran Church require that the educational institutions shall report to the Church through the Board of Education. All the colleges and seminaries have reported on forms supplied by the office of the Board and otherwise. These reports have been analyzed and summarized in the following form, for the sake of economy of space and for a more effective presentation of the outstanding items.

Centennial Celebrations

Southern Seminary—On November 25, 1930, the one hundredth anniversary of the founding of the Theological Seminary by the South Carolina Synod was celebrated. The commemorative address was delivered by the Rev. J. L. Morgan, D.D., president of the North Carolina Synod; the historical sketch by Dean A. G. Voigt, D.D., LL.D., and an address on "The Philosophy of Faith" by the Rev. M. G. G. Scherer, D.D., secretary of the United Lutheran Church in America. The Board was officially represented by Miss Markley.

Gettysburg College—On May 26-30, 1932, Gettysburg College celebrated its one hundredth anniversary by presenting one of the outstanding educational programs in the history of the Lutheran Church in America. More than 2,500 people were registered, and the attendance at all meetings and events was far beyond expectations. There were symposia for doctors, clergymen, lawyers, scientists and industrialists, and educators. It is estimated that the average attendance at these meetings was more than 500. One of the unique events of the celebration was an Alumni Walk Around, during which, from various prominent buildings on the campus, speakers presented the following subjects: "Gettysburg in the Field of Science;" "Gettysburg in the Field of Christian Service;" "Gettysburg in the Field of the Humanities;" and "Gettysburg in Prospect."

Some of the prominent speakers were: Dr. L. F. Barker, Johns Hopkins University; Dr. Joseph Fort Newton, Philadelphia; Dean L. A. Weigle, Yale University; Dr. Frank P. Graves, Albany; Dr. C. S. Northup, Cornell University; Dr. W. J. Cooper, Washington, D. C.; Dr. L. P. Eisenhart, Princeton University; President James R. Angel, Yale University; President F. H. Knubel, New York City; Dr. John H. Finley, New York City.

"A History of Gettysburg College," written by Prof. S. G. Hefelbower, Ph.D., former president of Gettysburg College and now professor of philosophy, Carthage College; and a volume containing biographical data of graduates and former students, prepared by Registrar Stoever and Alumni Secretary Beachem, appeared in connection with the celebration.

The President of our Board was the official representative, and was honored with the degree of Doctor of Divinity. The executive secretary represented the Council of Church Boards of Education, and spoke in the Alumni Walk Around on "Gettysburg in the Field of Christian Service."

Conference on Curriculum

On December 20, 1930, at the invitation of the Board, twenty-two representatives of the colleges and seminaries assembled in Washington to discuss problems of Curriculum Correlation between Colleges and Seminaries, with special reference to courses in Bible, Religious Education, Christian Ethics, Church History and Apologetics, as they affect students for the ministry. Some of the subjects discussed were: "The knowledge of the Bible possessed by the average high school graduate;" "The sufficiency of Bible courses for entrance into seminaries;" "Where should courses in religious education be taken?" and "The study of ethics and apologetics."

The Conference unanimously adopted the following findings:

1. That the average high school graduate has very meagre knowledge of the Bible.

2. That the first course in Bible in our colleges should be a survey course.

3. That mere courses in the Bible are not necessarily sufficient for entrance into the seminary. The theological student needs:
    a. An intelligent interest in the Bible.
    b. An attitude of mind which secures a larger conception of God, man and life.
    c. The inner voice of holy scripture.

4. That colleges must not attempt to be miniature seminaries, and seminaries must not expect the colleges to do what they themselves (the seminaries) should do.

5. That students in college, intending to enter a seminary, should take the fundamental cultural courses.

6. That the Board of Education be requested to appoint a committee
    a. To investigate the present purpose and content of college and seminary courses in English Bible, Apologetics, Ethics, Church History, and Religious Education.
    b. To ascertain the possible contributions of General Education Courses, and of Psychology to Seminary Work in Religious Education.
    c. To define or redefine the specific purposes of each—college and seminary courses—growing out of a definite understanding of the existing situation.

In harmony with the above action of the Conference, the Board authorized its committee on institutions to proceed with a study of the problem of Curriculum Correlation. Considerable progress has already been made in the gathering and analysis of data. When all the evidence has been properly analyzed and the results studied, concrete suggestions will be given to the colleges and seminaries for the improvement and better correlation of the courses concerned.

Charter and Constitutions

Hartwick College was granted a permanent charter February 19, 1931, by the Regents of the University of the State of New York.

Newberry College completely revised its constitution and by-laws, incorporating the best principles of modern academic organization and procedures.

Hartwick Seminary is reported to have changed its constitution "for the best interests of all concerned." The Board of Trustees is enlarged from twelve to twenty-five, of whom a majority must be from the United Lutheran Synod of New York, while the remainder may be selected from the Lutheran Church at large.

Accreditation and Approval

Susquehanna, Lenoir Rhyne and *Newberry* were received into the Association of American Colleges. While this is not an accrediting organization, admission of a college is to a large degree dependent upon the scholastic work done.

Susquehanna and *Wagner* were accredited by the Association of Colleges and Secondary Schools of the Middle Atlantic States and Maryland.

Newberry was given a four-year "non-member" status in the Association of Southern Colleges.

Marion Junior had its Teacher Training Department accredited by the Virginia State Department of Education.

Martin Luther Seminary and *Newberry College* were placed on the approved list of institutions by the Department of Labor. This list indicates the institutions to which individuals from foreign countries will be allowed to come for educational purposes.

Church Affiliation of the Students in our Colleges

Reports from the colleges regarding the religious affiliation of the students is most informing and interesting. The data reveal that there are thirty-one different denominations represented. The Churches with the highest percentages are as follows:

Church	*Number*	*Per Cent*
Lutheran	2095	45.52
Methodist	692	15.03
Presbyterian	446	9.69
Baptist	294	6.38
Catholic	217	4.71
Reformed	207	4.49
Episcopalian	147	3.19
Christian-Congregational	131	2.84
No Affiliation	102	2.21

What significance have these figures? It would appear that the Lutheran College is a community servant. This is in harmony with the facts found at all colleges, namely, that a majority of the students come from within a radius of seventy-five miles. If our colleges are to serve the Church to the greatest degree, then they should be located where the Lutheran Church is most populous. If, on the other hand, a church college has primarily a missionary function, then it should be located in areas of unchurched population. If the purpose of a church college is only cultural, then it is a question whether the Church should attempt to compete with the state.

Encouraging Authorship

Are Lutheran faculties productive? The following constitutes an excellent answer for a period of less than a year.

"The Church Charismata and Ministry"—
  Professor John O. Evjen, Ph.D., Th.D., Carthage College.

"The History of Gettysburg College"—
  Professor S. G. Hefelbower, Ph.D., D.D., LL.D., Carthage College.

"A Botanical Survey of Hancock County, Illinois"—
    Professor Alice L. Kibbe, Ph.D., Carthage College.

"An Outline of Persian History based on the Cuneiform Inscription—
    (Revised Edition) Professor William Ahl, Ph.D., Susquehanna University.

"The Lutheran Church in American History"—
    (Revised Edition) Professor A. R. Wentz, Ph.D., D.D., Gettysburg Seminary.

"The Taproot of Religion and Its Fruitage"—
"An Introduction to Philosophy"—(an authorized translation of Jerusalem's revised and enlarged tenth edition)—
    Professor C. F. Sanders, D.D., Gettysburg College.

"Guide for the Study of Human History"—(a Freshman History Syllabus)
"The Struggle for the Control of the Mediterranean Sea Prior to 1848"—
    Professor J. E. Swain, Ph.D., Muhlenberg College.

"Dictionary of American Biography," article on Benjamin Harrison—
    Professor A. T. Volwiler, Ph.D., Wittenberg College.

Development of Curricula

Education deals with life. Life can never be static; it is always dynamic. The curricula of our institutions cannot remain the same from generation to generation. It is to be expected that during certain periods these curricula will be studied and constructively revised. Such a period was the past biennium. Significant changes have been made or authorized in the curricula of *Gettysburg College, Muhlenberg College, Roanoke College, Susquehanna University, Wittenberg College,* and *Philadelphia Seminary.* Other colleges and seminaries are studying their curricula with a view to changing them in harmony with the best principles of curriculum building.

Enrollments

For the year 1930-31 the total percentage increase in attendance at our thirteen senior colleges exceeded that of the whole country which was 3½ per cent. However, for the year 1931-32, the total enrollment at these colleges was less than that of the previous year, even though nine colleges reported increases. The total enrollment for 1929-30 in all departments and special schools of these colleges was 10,781, while for 1931-32 it was 9,508, making a net decrease in total registration of 11.6 per cent. However, it should be noted that the registration in the college departments alone reveals an increase of 2.6 per cent. This indicates that it is in the special schools where our colleges are having a decreased registration.

In regard to the seminaries, the total enrollment two years ago was 544. The figures given in the recent reports show a total registration of 581. This is an increase of 6.8 per cent.

Financial Campaigns

While the past two years were not conducive to financial campaigns, nevertheless a few of our institutions felt it necessary to go ahead with their plans.

The Midland College-Western Seminary-Martin Luther Seminary Campaign was set for $400,000, and they received in pledges $175,000 or more than 43 per cent.

The Thiel College Campaign goal was for $750,000, and they received more than $180,000 in pledges, or more than 24 per cent of the goal.

Gettysburg Seminary started a campaign for $100,000, to be used for a new chapel and depository of art and library treasures. About $25,000 in cash and pledges have been received. It is proposed to continue this work until sufficient funds for the chapel have been provided.

Dedications

Muhlenberg College dedicated at the 1931 commencement, the Egner-Hartzell Memorial Chapel, one of the most beautiful and impressive college chapels in America. This magnificent structure, erected at a cost of about $300,000, was made possible by the will of Mrs. Annie Egner Hartzell. The windows, organ, altar, stalls, and pews are gifts of individuals, groups, and classes.

Carthage College formally opened a new field house costing about $100,000.

Gifts and Legacies

Carthage College: Notice of a bequest of $15,000 from the estate of David A. Kistler.

Hartwick College: Bequest of $5,000, and a third interest in estate of Mrs. Addie B. Stilson, who had previously given the college a $10,000 annuity bond.

Gettysburg College: From the Carnegie Foundation, $10,000 for purchase of books for library.

Roanoke College: From the Carnegie Foundation, $8,000 for purchase of books for library.

Wagner College: Bequests of $10,000 from five sources. From the Carnegie Foundation, a grant for purchase of books for library.

Marion Junior College: A large part of the library of Dr. F. D. N. Painter.

Martin Luther Seminary: Three hundred and eighty acres of mineral and oil land in southeastern Oklahoma, and first mortgages on Los Angeles real estate.

Southern Seminary: Bequest of $10,000 from Mrs. M. M. Kinard.

Philadelphia Seminary: A gift of $27,644 from the estate of Amelia A. McCreary.

College and Seminary Leagues of Women

The women of our Church are playing an increasing part in the maintenance and development of our colleges and seminaries.

Gettysburg College has had a Women's League and local leagues in various urban centers for many years. These leagues were responsible for the erection of the Weidensall Y. M. C. A. building.

Muhlenberg College has for years had a strong support in the Women's Auxiliary. Its most recent gift is the splendid organ in the Egner-Hartzell Memorial Chapel.

Thiel College reports the recent formation of a Women's League with strong general and local officers and membership.

Martin Luther Seminary has a guild two years old with an enrollment of more than 600. It has for its object the upkeep of the interior of the seminary buildings and the promotion of Christian fellowship between the congregations and the seminary.

Alumni Funds

Carthage College, Susquehanna University and *Philadelphia Seminary* have recently formed Alumni or Living Endowment Funds, which will assist them in meeting current expenses and in establishing scholarships. In 1926, Harvard University formed a Harvard Fund, and recently reported that it has received nearly one million dollars from twelve thousand men.

Serving the Communities

Colleges and seminaries cannot exist within closed walls, serving the students alone. They have a responsibility for the Christian culture of their communities. Adult education, a new name for extension work, is awakening institutions to a sense of their duty to local communities. While our colleges are not in a position to stress this work, since it requires additional instructors, nevertheless no small amount of activity in this direction is found at *Hartwick* with 223 enrolled in eleven classes at seven centers; *Midland* with 82 enrolled in five classes at four centers; *Muhlenberg* with 683 enrolled in four centers; *Susquehanna* with 144 enrolled in fifteen courses at four centers; and *Wittenberg* with 825 enrolled in thirty-eight classes, not counting several non-credit groups. *Gettysburg Seminary* serves the community through an annual leadership training school conducted under the auspices of the Adams County Council of Religious Education and held in the Administration Building.

Changes in Presidents

Wagner College: President C. F. Dapp. Ph.D., D.D., resigned, effective October 1, 1930. The Rev. Herman Brezing, D.D., of Niagara Falls, N. Y., was called as president, took charge July 1, 1931, and was inaugurated

November 17, 1931. This was the first time a president of Wagner College was inaugurated.

Martin Luther Seminary: President J. Huebner died, and Professor O. W. Heick, Ph.D., was elected acting president.

Waterloo College and Seminary: The Rev. F. B. Clausen, D.D., Brooklyn, N. Y., became president January 1, 1931.

Pacific Seminary: President J. C. Kunzman, D.D., resigned as president, and the Rev. M. J. Bieber, D.D., was elected acting dean, beginning June 1, 1932.

Saskatoon Seminary: President H. W. Harms gave up the active duties of president in order to solicit funds in the East. His work was carried on by members of the faculty, and President Thomas Hartig, of the Manitoba Synod, conducted the official correspondence for the institution.

Changes in Seminary Faculties

Chicago Seminary: Professor E. S. Klotsche, Ph.D., D.D., formerly professor of Exegetical Theology at Western Seminary, was elected professor of Practical Theology.

Gettysburg Seminary: The Rev. John E. Sanderson was elected assistant librarian.

Hamma Divinity School: Professor Leander S. Keyser, D.D., retired after serving for twenty years as professor of Systematic Theology. The Rev. T. A. Kantonen, Ph.D., of Maynard, Massachusetts, was elected as his successor. Professor B. H. Pershing, Ph.D., was elected professor of Church History.

Pacific Seminary: Dean P. W. H. Frederick, D. D., resigned, and the Rev. H. W. Monesmith, A.M., was elected as his successor. The Rev. C. A. Miller, A.M., B.D., was elected professor of Religious Education   The Rev. K. K. Olafson, A.M., president of the Icelandic Synod, taught on a part-time basis.

Philadelphia Seminary: Two new professors were installed: The Rev. O. F. Nolde, Ph.D., as professor of Christian Education; and the Rev. Russell D. Snyder, A.M., as professor of Ancient Church History.

Waterloo Seminary: Professor George Sandrock, D.D., was installed as professor of Old Testament.

Western Seminary: Professor Holmes Dysinger, D.D., LL.D., resigned as Dean, and the Rev. J. J. Raun, Ph.D., was elected as his successor. Professor E. S. Klotsche, Ph.D., D.D., resigned, and Professor P. W. H. Frederick. D.D., was elected professor of Exegetical Theology.

Interesting Items

Hartwick College: The first commencement was held on June 13, 1932, with sixty-seven graduates.

Newberry College: Reorganization of the Music Department and the organization of a Department of Business Administration. Enlargement of the Department of Education in order to meet new requirements for the certification of teachers. The adoption by the Board of Trustees of a definite program of expansion over a period of years.

Wittenberg College: A plan of affiliation with the Dayton Art Institute, under the terms of which the educational facilities of both institutions jointly are made available for students who desire to combine training in art with academic or professional pursuits, has been effected. Another plan was approved by which the college and the city hospital will co-operate in establishing a standard school for nursing. The degree of Bachelor of Science in Nursing will be granted to persons who will combine three years' work at the city hospital with two years of resident study at Wittenberg.

Philadelphia Seminary: An interesting experiment in catechetical instruction is being conducted by the Department of Christian Education in the graduate school. Three distinctive features have characterized the experiment: First, the course for catechumens is based upon a psychological analysis of Christian experience. Basic to Christian experience is the Father-Child relationship as it is realized through Jesus Christ. Out of this relationship grows a prayer life or fellowship. Then there develops an increasingly intelligent faith and a desire to express that faith. Mere verbal expression of faith is inadequate. It is necessary to have standards for guides. When one recognizes his inability to meet these standards he becomes conscious of an infringement upon his initial relationship with God. He needs to be assured of God's forgiveness and love in his faith generally, and in the provision of particular opportunities in the Church. The five parts of the catechism in a somewhat different order than usual are used for the development of these elements of Christian experience. The second phase of the experiment is the provision of twenty-five study sheets or contracts bound in booklet form as guides for the catechumen's home work. The third phase is a series of lesson plans for the pastor.

Southern Seminary: Special courses were introduced in Public Speaking and Church music. A study of the courses taken by the students indicates that the majority prefer the curriculum that requires the study of Greek and Hebrew. Only 28 per cent chose the English Course.

Saskatoon Seminary: Students in the theological and high school departments are giving religious instruction in the Institution of the Deaf and the Mute, and are said to be teaching with great success.

4. A Section of Numbers

Two years ago the Board reported detailed statistical information from the colleges and seminaries. At that time the institutions did not keep their records according to the plan suggested by the statistical blank, and consequently there was an incompleteness in many items. This year reports in this regard are greatly improved.

The Church should know that the blanks for the colleges were prepared in harmony with forms proposed by the National Committee on Standard Reports. It is now possible to compare the situation existing at our colleges with that of other church schools.

It should be noted that in most cases the figures representing the financial status are for the year ending 1930-31, since most of the institutions do not end their fiscal year until July or August. Consequently the present status of some may be quite different from that given in the tables. The figures regarding the students and faculties are for the year 1931-32.

Complete figures could not be given on Susquehanna Seminary, Hamma Divinity School, and Western Seminary, because of organic relation to their respective colleges.

The figures for Marion College, although a Junior College, are included in the tables with the other colleges, in the interest of economy of space.

Although totals are not given in connection with the tables, attention is called to the following figures which are relatively correct and exhibit, especially in the grand total, an interesting picture of our thirteen seminaries and fourteen colleges.

	13 Seminaries	14 Colleges	Grand Total
Value of all Property	$2,634,320	$11,927,134	$14,561,454
Funds			
Permanent Endowment	2,305,650	6,957,546	9,263,196
Other Fund Assets	212,934	1,291,788	1,504,722
Total Fund Assets	2,518,584	8,249,334	10,767,918
Value of All Assets	5,152,904	20,176,468	25,329,372
Total Indebtedness	265,312	2,748,898	3,014,210
Current Funds			
Income	262,378	1,998,909	2,261,287
Expenses	311,708	2,053,350	2,365,058
Deficits	49,330	54,441	103,771
Total Volumes in Library	133,500	284,020	417,520
Total Faculties	81	401	482
Total Student Enrollment	581	9,628	10,209
Total Alumni	5,271	16,058	21,329

STATISTICAL TABLES—I. THEOLOGICAL SEMINARIES

THE PROPERTY

Index No.	Institution	Location	Founded	President or Dean	Campus Acres	Campus Value	Bldgs No.	Bldgs Value	Value of Real Property	Library Vol.	Library Val.	Furn. & Fix.	Val. of Equip.	Total Value of Property
1	Hartwick Theo. Seminary	Brooklyn, N.Y.	1797	Rev. S. M. Paulson, D.D.	40				$41000					$41000
2	Luth. Theo. Seminary	Gettysburg, Pa.	1826	Rev. J. Aberly, D.D.	6	$40000	9	$300000	340000	7000	$50000	$10000	$60000	400000
3	Luth. Theo. Southern Sem.	Columbia, S.C.	1830	Rev. A. G. Voigt, D.D., LL.D.		20000	5	140000	160000	8000	9000	2500	11500 Col.	171500
4	Hamma Divinity School	Springfield, Ohio	1845	Rev. R. E. Tulloss, Ph.D., D.D., LL.D.			3		95438 (See Wittenberg)				12042	107480
5	Susquehanna	Selinsgrove, Pa.	1858	Rev. G. M. Smith, D.D.	10			See Susquehanna University						
6	Lutheran Theo. Seminary	Philadelphia, Pa.	1864	Rev. C. M. Jacobs, D.D., L.H.D., LL.D.	15	350000	15	745300	1095000	37000	50000	25000	75000	1170000
7	Chicago Theo. Seminary	Maywood, Ill.	1891	Rev. L. F. Gruber, D.D., LL.D.	5	200000	11	218250	418250	20000	20000	19860	39860	*464340
8	Western Theo. Seminary	Fremont, Nebr.	1893	Rev. H. F. Martin, Ph.D., D.D.			5	23000	23000	5000	3000		3000	26000
9	Luth. Sem. of Canada	Waterloo, Ont., Canada	1911	Rev. F. B. Clausen, D.D.	14			See Waterloo College						
10	Pacific Theo. Seminary	Seattle, Wash.	1911	Rev. M. J. Bieber, D.D., Acting		65000	5	10000	75000	3000	2000	500	2500	77500
11	Martin Luther Seminary	Lincoln, Nebr.	1913	Rev. O. W. Heick, Ph.D., Acting		15000	2	25000	40000	3000	2000	100	2100	42100
12	Lutheran Seminary	Saskatoon, Sask., Can.	1921	Rev. H. W. Harms.	16	5500	7	57400	62900	3000	4350	4550	8900	71800
13	Northwtn. Luth. Theo. Sem.	Minneapolis, Minn.	1921	Rev. J. Stump, D.D., LL.D., L.H.D.			1	53000	53000	4000	6000	3600	9600	62600

NOTE: Cents are omitted.
Valuable totals are given on previous page.
Blanks indicate no report or nothing to report.
*Included is $6,230 of miscellaneous property not otherwise noted.

THE FUNDS: PERMANENT

Index No.	Productive Restricted	Productive Unrestricted	Unproductive Annuities	Unproductive Other	Scholarships	Total End'mt	Other Assets Interest Bearing	Other Assets Non-Int. Bearing	Total Funds	Grand Total Assets Property and Funds	Additions to Capital 1930–31	Additions to Capital 1931–32	Total Indebtedness
1						$42579			$42579	$83579			$2116
2	$38265	$520613	$34000		$68829	661707	$7000	$18000	686707	1086707	$26820	$13194	3439
3	64000		7600			71600	6700	27750	106050	277550	4750		800
4	45000	168414	54000		5000	272414			272414	379894			
5	See Susquehanna University												
6	50000	585000			37050	635000			635000	1805000	30000	5200	129000
7	1400	263166	152700		6000	452916			432916	911256			97500
8		32259				39659			39659	65659			10000
9	See Waterloo College												
10		18000	12000			30000		50000	80000	157500			
11	3000					3000			3000	45100	50		
12			2000	$100		2100	1440	2044	5584	77384		911	22457
13	2500	91975	200			94675		100000	194675	257275			

I. THEOLOGICAL SEMINARIES—Continued

THE FUNDS: CURRENT INCOME / CURRENT EXPENDITURES

Index No.	Endowment	Tuition	Fees	Dormitory Rentals	Total from Students	Synods	U.L.C.A.	Special Gifts	Miscellaneous	Total Annual Income	Administration	Instruction	Books Equipment	Operating	Maintenance	Dormitory Maintenance & Operation	Interest	Miscellaneous	Total Expenditure	Surplus or Deficit
1	$32210				$1829	$7177	$2416	$2534		$11140	$2387	$10540		$1068	$1147				$11140	
2	2319		$775	$1829	775	1971		966		8447	623	19111	$686	4385	1866	$2368	$470	$90	47188 d	$3438
3	13768		190	990	1180	11293		123	$1134	27498									15702 d	7255
4	See Susquehanna University.																		29039 d	1540
5	27754		2500		2250	18000	2305	260	6442	54956	7000	33000	5479	22910	3312		*11905	3300	71689 d	16733
6	23069					5452	1979	450	1541	32817	29596	7538		2518	523		600	1187	46000 d	13183
7	1716		320		320	2265		4244		6280	586		62						11827 d	5547
8	See Waterloo College.																			
9																				
10	1800	$590			590	900	2500	15999	3574	24773	7104	7029	100	1263	1735	5551	2135	6885	26251 d	1478
11	150					6446	2687	3250	281	13404	1513	4125	30	1935	3418			50	13174 s	230
12						1411		3578	1546	16542		6041	92	3139	232			6809	16662 d	80
13	5283	216			216	17132	9791	229	127	22771		19290			600			47	23076 d	305

* Includes $6,398 interest on annuity bonds.

THE FACULTY

Index No.	Number	No Degree	A.B.	A.M.	B.D.	S.T.M.	Doctor
1	6			1			3
2	6			2			4
3	4			4			
4	7			2			5
5	6		1	2		3	3
6	16	1	1	3	1		10
7	7						3
8	8			4			2
9	5	1	1		1		
10	6		1	3	1		1
11	6			2			2
12	3	3					
13	6		1		1	1	

THE STUDENTS

Index No.	Under-Graduate 1st Year	2nd Year	3rd Year	Special	Total	Graduate In Residence	In Correspondence	Total	Total Enrolled	College Graduates 1st Year	2nd Year	3rd Year	Special	Grad. in Residence	Grad. in Corresp.	Total Col. Grad.	Non-Lutheran	Alumni	May Women be Admitted?
1	5	4	3	4	16	3		3	19	5	4	1	1	3		14	6	305	Yes
2	21	30	20	8	79	13		13	92	21	30	20		13		84	8	1488	Yes
3	13	10	8		31				31	13	10	8				31		357	Yes
4	13	16	7	4	30	4		4	34	13	6	7	2	3		32	1	645	Yes
5		1	1	8	9	12		12	21		1	2	2	9		14	4	255	Yes
6	35	37	29	2	109	82		82	191	35	37	29	1	82		185	5	1400	No
7	13	11	11	2	37	8	41	49	86	13	11	11	3	8	41	85	3	400	No
8	7	5	5	3	19		2	2	21	7	5	5	2			19		206	No
9	3	3	2	9	11				11									59	Yes
10	3	1	4	1	10				10		6	2	1			5	4	19	
11	2	6	6	2	12				12			3	2					31	No
12	3	6	4		14				14									17	No
13	5		6		19	20		20	39					18		34		89	No

STATISTICAL TABLES—II. COLLEGES

The Plant and The Equipment

Index No.	Institution	Founded	Location	President	Type	Accredited by	Campus Acres	Campus Value	Buildings No.	Buildings Value	Value of Real Property	Library Vol.	Library Val.	Lab. Equip. and Mus.	Fur. and Fix.	Other Equip.	Value of Equipment	Total Value of Property
1	Gettysburg	1832	Gettysburg, Pa.	Rev. H. W. A. Hanson, D.D., LL.D.	M	1,2,3,4	42	125000	13	1050576	1175576	40000	100000	43987	70069		214056	1389632
2	Wittenberg	1845	Springfield, O.	Rev. R. E. Tulloss, Ph.D., D.D., LL.D.	M	1,2,3,4	54	332855	15	1571193	1904048	50315	46960	22391	252370	16590	299330	*2427306
3	Roanoke	1853	Salem, Va.	Rev. C. J. Smith, D.D., LL.D.	C	5	20	60113	10	459974	520087	18000	83325	12000	14921		137226	657313
4	Newberry	1856	Newberry, S.C.	J. C. Kinard, LL.D.	C		43	50000	10	295500	345500	20000	20000	12000	47000		79000	**509050
5	Susquehanna	1858	Selinsgrove, Pa.	Rev. G. M. Smith, D.D.	M	2,3,4	62	135515	18	497887	633402	9537	22000		100243		122243	755645
6	Muhlenberg	1867	Allentown, Pa.	Rev. J. A. W. Haas, D.D., LL.D.	M	1,2,3,4	75	566854	10	1560749	2127603	51000	51000	20999	52980	17855	142836	2270439
7	Carthage	1870	Carthage, Ill.	Rev. J. Diehl, D.D., LL.D.	C	2,3,4	38	23854	8	366030	389884	20494	21516	19761	47029		88306	478190
8	Thiel	1870	Greenville, Pa.	Rev. E. C. Xander, D.D.	C	2,4	35	35000	8	353000	388000	15000	15000	15000	44000		74000	462000
9	Wagner	1885	Staten Is., N.Y.	Rev. H. Brezing, D.D.	M		52	364000	11	710840	1074840	12000	11029		38558		49587	1124427
10	Midland	1887	Fremont, Nebr.	Rev. H. F. Martin, Ph.D., D.D.	C	2,3,4	36		5		335541	18000					26579	362120
11	Lenoir Rhyne	1891	Hickory, N.C.	Rev. H. B. Schaeffer, D.D.	C	2,3	36	90000	6	450000	540000	12000		12800	60000		72800	612800
12	Waterloo	1911	Waterloo, Ont. Can.	Rev. F. B. Clausen, D.D.	C	3	30	5000	8	80000	130000	4000	3000	2000	5000		10000	140000
13	Hartwick	1928	Oneonta, N.Y.	Rev. C. W. Leitzell, D.D.	C	4	97	40000	4	415000	455000	6674	13000	65000	35000		113000	568000
14	Marion Junior	1873	Marion, Va.	Rev. E. H. Copenhaver, D.D.	W	6	5	25000	5	125000	150000	7000	5000	1000	14212		20212	170212

The Funds—Permanent, Other Assets, Additions to Capital, and Indebtedness

Index No.	Restricted (Productive)	Unrestricted (Productive)	Annuities (Unproductive)	Other (Unproductive)	Total Funds	Scholarships	Loan Funds	Notes, Pledges, Etc. Interest Bearing	Notes, Pledges, Etc. Non-Int. Bearing	Total Other Assets	Total Funds and Other Assets	Total Value of Assets	Additions to Capital 1930–31	Additions to Capital 1931–32	Indebtedness Bldgs. and Grounds	Indebtedness Current Accumulated	Indebtedness Total
1	$53945	$746739	$43500		$844184		$10000			$10000	$854184	$2243816	$447169	$5169	$614000		$614000
2	192105	1356906	303272		1852284		63390	$22558	$86076	172024	2024308	4451614	20124		79300	$38356	117656
3		645513	3000		648513		7870		21222	29092	677605	1334918	35000	25000	119000	20000	139000
4		212000		$20000	232000			332528		332528	564528	1073578			72850		72850
5		368780	38600		407380	$1686			3973	5659	413039	1168684	2330		615000	26648	641648
6					891632						891632	3162071			143179	11118	154297
7	233997	616967	24400		875364		1000	713		1713	877077	1355267	3225		55000	170000	225000
8	166000		5000		171000			5000	100000	105000	276000	738000			308314	51387	359701
9	375182			326	375508				19795	19795	395303	1519730			72000	29827	101827
10	114931				152931		1338			1338	154269	516389	1850				
11	32500				381750				168000	168000	549750	1162550	5000		160000		160000
12			1750		30000						30000	170000			20000	6000	26000
13	30000			30000	95000	400	440000			440400	535400	1103400	10000	15000	65000	27000	92000
14	95000							1815	4424	6239	6239	176451			29000	15919	44919

Note:—Cents are omitted.
Totals are given at beginning of this section.
Blanks indicate no report or nothing to report.
*Included is $223,928 of dwellings and farm land not otherwise noted.
**Included is $84,550 for property and equipment at Summerland College, not otherwise noted.
†This deficit was wiped out by an accumulated surplus of $27,796.

Code:—M—Men; W—Women; C—Co-educational.
1. Association of American Universities.
2. The Regional Accrediting Association.
3. The State University.
4. The Regents (New York).
5. Four year "non-member" status in Southern Association of Colleges.
6. Virginia State Board of Education.

STATISTICAL TABLES—II. COLLEGES—Continued

THE CURRENT FUNDS—INCOME

Index No.	Educational and General — Students: Tuition	Less Remissions	Fees	Endowment	Gifts and Grants: Synodical	U.L.C.A.	Others	Other Sources	Total	Auxiliary Activities and Enterprises: Dormitories	Residences	Other	Total	Non-Educational Purposes: Annuities	Other	Total	Total Annual Income
1	$161315	$549	$13600	$31937	$21333	$1200	$3923	$11343	$211426	$10503			$10503	$1825	$9437	$11262	$233191
2	286463	47982	61526	108663		1167	21227	13710	433380	19819	$5884		25703				469083
3	41345		2185	37196		3417	745	1980	119080	2293		$2576	4869		305	305	123948
4	18400		7794	7028	1645	5400	1060	72	42992	4283		696	4979				48876
5	94817		14414	22280	7200	2900	3352	35658	142759	11245		59474	70719				213478
6	117813		8115	55338	18000	1200	279	2482	239854								239854
7	44482	5520	4206	23868	3150		1000	600	72941			3020	3020				75961
8	63000			9000	16000	2500	600		92100								92100
9	20619		3067	27102	24850	2500	3624		81762	8370		27002	19401			780	101943
10	55718		4635	5377	10189	9896	418	4158	90381				35372				127915
11	48000			16000	3000	3200			70200	900			68000			2162	138200
12	3754		300	869	19787	4583			29293								30193
13	46955			4265	22500	900	540							750	250	1000	78266
14	5044	500	937			708	258		6447	3036		17017	20053				26501

EXPENDITURES

Index No.	Educational and General: General Admin.	Instru. and Research	Library	Operation Maintenance	Total	Auxiliary Enterprises: Dormitories	Other	Total	Non-Educational Expenses: Annuities	Interest	Scholarship Student Aid	Other	Total	Total Expenditures	Surplus or Deficit
1	$61503	$129516	$2637	$30680	$224336	$21428	$2800	$24228	$2740		$15815		$18555	$242891	D $9700
2	37527	263178	11364	111675	423744		1854	1854	13810	15344	2389		31543	479514	D 10431
3	21382	64382	1845	6584	94193		5681	5681	180	7118	10527		17825	113873	S 10075
4	2999	29700	424	11656	41780		41886	41886		1715			1715	52175	D 3899
5	22413	103707	2186	25280	153586		8518	8518		7148	1700		8848	204320	D 9158
6	15658	120219	2400	59998	198275					33301			33301	240094	D 240
7	19358	51242	1185	8477	80263		20000	20000		6816			6816	87079	D 11118
8	16000	54000		20000	90000		13760	13760		10000		$5000	15000	125000	D 32900
9	35191	43446		18280	96917	1553	20390	21943						110677	D 8734
10	17031	64508	2436	14590	98565					5870		3873	9743	130251	S 2336
11	12500	4900	4700		66200		64000	64000					4000	134200	D 4000
12	26699			1408	28107					3090	500		3590	31697	S 1504
13	21479	43366	2296	8625	75766		1563							75766	S 2500
14	4630	8857		2298	15785	5148		6711		2316	1000		3316	25813	S 688

STATISTICAL TABLES—II. COLLEGES—Continued

THE FACULTY / THE STUDENTS — College of Liberal Arts

Index No.	Faculty M	Faculty W	Faculty T	Lutheran M	Lutheran W	Lutheran T	No. Degree	A. B. only	A. M. only	Doctor	Fresh. M	Fresh. W	Fresh. T	Soph. M	Soph. W	Soph. T	Jun. M	Jun. W	Jun. T	Sen. M	Sen. W	Sen. T	Spec. M	Spec. W	Spec. T	Grad. M	Grad. W	Grad. T
1	45		45	32		32		5	17	19	202		202	157		157	96	7	103	110	8	118	7		7			5
2	54	23	77	39	9	48	3	14	23	43	151	75	226	107	42	149	78	55	133	98	62	160	25	103	128	3	2	
3	21		21	11		11		4	12	5	121	42	163	76	15	91	48	1	49	26	1	27	5		5			
4	13	6	19	10	4	14		11	6	2	74	37	111	54	35	89	41	54	95	31	32	63	5	9	14			
5	28	10	38	19	7	26		14	15	9	49	31	80	42	28	70	42	31	73	45	33	78	3	3	6			
6	32		32	22		22		6	13	13	187		187	114		114	83		83	68		68						
7	20	8	28	15	5	20	1	10	13	4	45	37	82	47	28	75	33	9	42	38	16	54	10	5	15			
8	17	6	23	10	2	12	1	6	11	5	71	38	109	28	18	46	34	23	57	35	20	55	6	5	11			
9	10		10	7		7			4	4	44		44	26		26	11		11	22		22						
10	24	10	34	16	4	20	3	18	9	6	64	73	137	31	35	66	26	21	47	28	9	37	12	15	27	1	1	2
11	16	6	22	13	4	17	2	6	8		52	39	91	25	40	65	22	36	58	28	39	67	11	29	40			
12	9	3	12	8	4	12	4	3	5		8	8	16	9	2	11	9	3	12	11	3	14	6	2	8			
13	17	10	27	9	3	12				10	49	35	84	29	33	62	41	38	79	36	31	67		30	30			
14	2	11	13	2	5	7	2	3	6			36	36		34													

THE STUDENTS — Continued

Index No.	Total M	Total W	Total T	Luth. M	Luth. W	Luth. T	Acad. M	Acad. W	Acad. T	Spec. Schools M	Spec. Schools W	Spec. Schools T	Summer M	Summer W	Summer T	Ext. M	Ext. W	Ext. T	Grand Total M	Grand Total W	Grand Total T	Graduates	Ex-Students	Total
1	572	15	587				100		100				99	12	111				671	27	698	3359	2289	5648
2	462	339	801	218	135	353				28	65	93	198	342	540	273	437	710	868	1023	1891	3153	2978	6131
3	276	59	335	41	5	46							90	96	186				366	155	521	1521	4382	5903
4	205	167	372			187	152	56	208	19	55	74	33	210	243	63	81	144	238	377	615	1330	1500	2830
5	181	126	307	73	64	137							158	94	252	213	519	732	386	344	730	1348	1002	2350
6	452		452	228	228	228						78	260	203	463					1347	1347	2000		2500
7	173	95	268	85	56	141				6	72	78	7	23	30	2	4	6	177	120	297	1006	500	6406
8	174	104	278	71	44	115	25	25						58	104				299	282	581	922	5400	4922
9	103		103	53		53													138		138	275	4000	
10	161	153	314	62	108	148				167	296	463	80	270	350	30	106	136	323	630	953	522		
11	138	183	321			170									465			344			1130	500		
12	39	17	56	27	5	32	10	8	18							22	211	233	49	25	74			
13	161	139	300	26	29	55					16	16							183	350	533	74	49	
14		100	100		50	50		9	9											120	120	73		

II. FOLLOWING OUR STUDENTS

"The object of this Board shall be . . . to conserve the religious life of the students in the educational institutions of the Church, in the State Universities, and in other schools."

The *Student Division* carries on its work of conserving the religious life of the students of the Church in the institutions of the Church, in tax-supported institutions of higher learning, in privately endowed colleges and universities, in professional and technical colleges and schools.

The extent of the work of this division can be partially determined by the fact that from 1919 to July, 1932, the student secretaries visited 416 different institutions—Lutheran and non-Lutheran—in thirty-four different states and four provinces of Canada. Many of these institutions have been visited only once; in some cases contact has been kept through correspondence with students, faculty, or pastor. The most strategic student centers, so far as possible, are visited once a year by one of the secretaries. By correspondence and by publications of the Board, the secretaries are in touch with students, faculty, or pastors at many centers which have never been visited.

1. Visits of Secretaries

Visits to Lutheran Colleges and Seminaries

All of the colleges and seminaries of the United Lutheran Church and six secondary schools connected with it were visited by one or more of the secretaries. By special invitations, secretaries visited twenty-one different academic institutions of other Lutheran bodies. A secretary visiting a United Lutheran campus interviews the administrative officers and those members of the faculty who are especially concerned with the religious life and activities of students. Upon invitation, a secretary visits classes in Religious Education, Bible, or in other fields in which a general class discussion may be carried on. Meetings of organized groups like Y. W. and Y. M. C. A., Student Volunteers, Lutheran Student Association, are attended. Interviews with students individually and in groups become a major opportunity for Christian guidance. Through the pastors of the local churches attended by students, the secretary will get into touch with Sunday school classes, Luther Leagues, and Missionary Societies. In the theological seminaries, the secretary explains in detail the work of the Board, especially as it relates to the responsibility a future pastor faces with boys and girls preparing for or attending college. A secretary may be invited to speak at Convocation, in Chapel, or before other academic, church or civic groups.

Lutheran Institutions Visited

United Lutheran: *Colleges*: Carthage, Gettysburg, Hartwick. Lenoir Rhyne, Marion, Midland, Muhlenberg, Newberry, Roanoke, Susquehanna. Thiel, Wagner, Waterloo, Wittenberg. *Seminaries*: Gettysburg, Chicago,

Hamma, Hartwick, Martin Luther, Mt. Airy, Northwestern, Pacific, Saskatoon, Southern, Susquehanna, Waterloo, Western. *Secondary Schools*: Gettysburg, Hartwick, Collegiate, Lankenau, Konnarock, Saskatoon.

Other Lutheran Colleges and Seminaries: Augsburg Seminary, Augustana (Rock Island), Bethany, Capital, Concordia, Dana College and Seminary, Gustavus Adolphus, Luther Seminary, Phalen Seminary, Suomi College and Seminary, Jon Bjarneson Academy.

Other Lutheran Institutions: *Motherhouses*: Baltimore, Mary J. Drexel, Immanuel, Milwaukee. *Bible Schools*: Chicago and Minneapolis. *Hospitals*: Lutheran (New York), Norwegian (Brooklyn), Lutheran (Moline), Immanuel (Omaha), Milwaukee, Robinwood (Toledo).

Visits to Other Institutions

In places where a pastor is working with students, he sets up a visit by a secretary. Opportunity is given, if the visit occurs over a week-end, to speak to the congregation on the work of the Board and of its own privileges and opportunities, to the Sunday school, and to the Luther League or Student Association. Sometimes a secretary meets with Church Council, congregational committee on student work, or missionary societies. Interviews with individual Lutheran students and faculty are held, at least one group meeting of students, and a conference with student officers or cabinet is arranged. Through the pastor an invitation from the college administration to speak in convocation or chapel is sometimes received and accepted. The president, and especially the deans, of an institution are visited, as are faculty members who are directly in contact with the religious courses or activities of students. Secretaries of the Y. M. or Y. W. C. A. offer co-operation in meeting students, and secretaries occasionally speak at their group meetings. Where pastors of other churches are working with students, calls are made in order to understand better the part the Lutheran Church has in the whole program of Christian activities of students. In places where there is no student pastor or Lutheran congregation, the visit by a secretary is arranged for in advance by a student, a Y. M. or Y. W. secretary, or an interested dean. In other cases the secretary must arrange after arrival for the best possible contacts and future follow-up of work. Visits to a campus vary in length from one to four or five days.

An outstanding need of our students is to learn how to sustain and develop their Christian lives. The training in the parish fails to teach many of our young men and women techniques of prayer, Bible study, personal spiritual hygiene, and ways in which to express Christian love effectively in service. Secretary Harry has developed a number of *Talks on Techniques,* some of which he has given most successfully to groups of students in various types of colleges and universities. These talks include among others the following topics: How to receive God's guidance; How to develop and maintain an interesting and satisfying devotional life; How to use the Bible; Personal evangelism; Meeting intellectual difficulties. Students have shown marked interest and have expressed much appreciation of this type of service rendered during the visit of the secretary.

Institutions Visited

New York: *Metropolitan*—New York University, Columbia, Long Island; Municipal Teachers Colleges, Jamaica and Maxwell; Colleges: Adelphi, Barnard, Brooklyn, Hunter, Pratt, Teachers; Professional Schools: Union Theological Seminary and Biblical Seminary, and fifteen others; Hospitals, seven. *State*—Albany State Teachers College, Oneonta Normal School, Elmira, Emma Willard, Russel Sage, Sarah Lawrence, Vassar.

New Jersey: New Jersey College for Women, Montclair and Trenton Normal Schools, Rider.

New England: Harvard, Massachusetts Institute of Technology, Radcliffe, Simmons, Wellesley, Leland Powers, Sargent, Hospitals, two. Yale, Hartford Foundation, Mt. Holyoke, Smith.

Pennsylvania: University, Temple, Woman's Medical, Lehigh, Osteopathy, Bucknell, Penn State; State Teachers Colleges: Bloomsburg, California, Kutztown, Indiana, Lock Haven, Mansfield, Millersville, Shippensburg, Slippery Rock, Stroudsburg, West Chester; Colleges: Albright, Allegheny, Bryn Mawr, Carnegie, Cedar Crest, Elizabethtown, Grove City, Lebanon Valley, Moravian, Penn Hall, Pennsylvania College for Women, Swarthmore, Ursinus, Wilson; Hospitals, five.

California: California at Los Angeles, Southern California.

Delaware: University.

Georgia: Institute of Technology.

Illinois: University, Chicago, Northwestern, Millikin, National Kindergarten, State Teachers College, Macomb.

Indiana: University, Purdue, State Teachers College, Muncie.

Iowa: University, Iowa State, Iowa State Teachers College, Drake.

Kansas: University, Kansas State, Emporia, State Teachers College, Emporia.

Maryland and *District of Columbia*: University, Goucher, Hopkins, George Washington, Maryland College, Towson Normal, National Colored, Lucy Webb Hayes.

Michigan: University, Michigan State, State Teachers College, Kalamazoo; State Teachers College, Ypsilanti; Battle Creek, Kalamazoo, Detroit Hospital, Battle Creek Hospital.

Minnesota: University, Hamline, Macalester.

Nebraska: University, State Teachers College, Wayne.

North Carolina: University, Duke, State, N. C. College for Women, Boone S. T. C., Bennett, Catawba.

North Dakota: University, North Dakota Agriculture.

New Mexico: University.

Ohio: University, Ohio State, Miami, Toledo, Western Reserve, Case, S. T. C., Bowling Green; S. T. C., Kent; Muskingum, Oberlin, Kindergarten Training, Schauffler, Western, Wooster.

Oregon: University, State, S. T. C., Monmouth.

South Carolina: University, Clemson, Winthrop.

Virginia: Polytechnic, S. T. C., Harrisonburg; S. T. C., Radford; Staunton Military, Presbyterian, Richmond School Social Science.

Washington: University, Reed.

Wisconsin: University, S. T. C., LaCrosse; S. T. C., Oshkosh; Lawrence, Ripon.

Canada: University of Saskatchewan.

Work With Students in New York City

This biennium marks the termination of pioneer work among students in New York. Since 1919, under the direction of the Board of Education, various churches, in addition to the secretaries and fellows of the Board, have done much to promote Church interest among our students. During the past year the various interested agencies have become centralized, and the activities as a whole have received the Church and the campus recognition which finishes the foundation upon which more intensive work can be built. The largest academic center in America, with over 2,000 Lutheran students representing over fifty institutions, needs and is prepared for a full-time student pastor. The unusually large number of graduate, professional, and foreign students in New York makes for most important contacts.

In June, 1931, the Board of Education directed Miss Winston to give the greater part of her time during the academic year to New York City. This arrangement was made because of the inability to have a full-time student pastor, and because the time and money expended in the past did not warrant bringing in a new student fellow for one year. The objectives of the work for the year were: To maintain a personal relationship with students and faculties in Greater New York; to become more closely associated with local and national leaders in student religious activities; to co-operate with other agencies of the United Lutheran Church in the territory of the United Lutheran Synod of New York; to enlist the interest of other Lutheran bodies in students; to promote interest in the appointment of a full-time student pastor and the facilities necessary for his work. The progress towards each objective has been decidely encouraging.

Close co-operation has been given to the *Church of the Advent* in its work with Columbia University, (400 Lutheran students), and to *Holy Trinity* in its work with New York University, (700 Lutheran students). *Advent* has continued most generous in service to students. Pastor Steimle and Sister Pearle have enlisted a number of students in the work of the Luther League and the Sunday school; the leading parts in the pageant given annually for the Inner Mission Society were taken by twenty-five Columbia students. An increasing number of students attend the morning service; some have become guest members, an average of fifty attend the Sunday Twilight Hour Service. Effective work with student nurses have been carried on by Sister Pearle, especially in the larger nurses training centers.

Holy Trinity Church, Dr. Paul E. Scherer, pastor, is successfully establishing work in New York University. The well-attended monthly Sunday evening forums have resolved themselves into intimate discussions of personal religious development. Dr. Scherer is making many personal contacts with students, and has directed students who are residents in New York to churches in the community in which they live. At New York University a Lutheran is to be invited to become a member of the Board of Directors of the Religious Associations.

There are campus organizations at Columbia, New York University, and Hunter. Every school in which contacts have been made is a member of the Metropolitan Association, sponsored by the students themselves. The Metropolitan Association has had three meetings during the year. One meeting was in the form of a Conference, at which fifteen institutions were represented. Miss Winston has maintained a close relationship with these organizations, especially at New York University and at Columbia University, where Doctors Steimle, Markley, Harry and Werner were the guest speakers at week-day Columbia chapel services. President F. H. Knubel preached one Sunday at St. Paul's Chapel. The recognition by Dean Hawkes and Chaplain Knox of the work done on the campus is noteworthy.

Other Lutheran Bodies, such as Norwegian and Augustana Churches, National Lutheran Council, and the Lutheran World Convention, are manifesting increasing interest. This is largely in connection with the promotion of contacts among *Foreign Students.* Constant touch is kept with the American Scandinavian Foundation, Institute of International Education, Friendly Relations Committee, Foreign Students Christian Associations, Foreign Student Department of Y. W. C. A., Foreign Student Committee of the Foreign Missions Council, and International House.

Visits to Teachers Colleges and Normal Schools
There is no way that the Church can exert a greater direct spiritual influence upon the life of the nation than through its contact with the teacher-training institutions. The relationship of the pastor in the college town to the students affects their attitude toward social, personal, and academic problems. With the proper appreciation and experience of religious values,

the well-trained young teacher will be a positive Christian influence in the community through the classroom, and will be able and willing to render to the Church the same quality of service that she gives to the public school system.

The secretaries, since 1919, have visited sixty-five teacher training institutions in twenty-two different states and Canada. Of these thirty-one schools in fifteen states have been visited or revisited during the past biennium. In view of the strength of the United Lutheran Church in Pennsylvania, the following facts are of interest: The total enrollment in the thirteen teachers colleges is 9,551 students. Of this number 1,153 are Lutheran. (This does not include the municipal institutions in Pittsburgh and Philadelphia for which figures are not available.) In the towns in which three of these institutions are located—California, Edinboro and Mansfield—there are no Lutheran churches. In Slippery Rock a mission has been started. In West Chester the 200 Lutheran students have a strong campus organization, and during the past year have established an individual affiliated membership in the local congregation, and have representatives upon the Church Council. This congregation is a small mission under the supervision of the East Pennsylvania Synod.

In addition to the students from the regular teachers colleges, last year, 25 per cent of the graduates of the recognized colleges in Pennsylvania went into the teaching profession.

In New York State there are two State Teachers Colleges, Albany and Buffalo, and nine State Normal Schools. The number of Lutheran students is small, with the exception of the State Teachers College at Albany. In addition to these there are large municipal institutions, Jamaica and Maxwell, from which it is impossible to get the number of Lutheran students. However, on each one of the campuses there is a small number of Lutheran students with whom pastors and secretaries are in touch.

2. Lutheran Students: Numbers and Distribution

During the past three years the Council of Church Boards of Education has been making some careful studies of the church affiliations of students. The first study was published by Mr. Raymond H. Leach, the university secretary of the Council, in the October, 1931 issue of *Christian Education*. It covered facts concerning the enrollments of 1929-30 at ninety-eight different institutions.

A. Publicly Controlled Colleges and Universities in forty-eight states. Of the total number of students 253,811 enrolled in these institutions, eighty-seven per cent expressed a church preference. In the New England and Middle Atlantic institutions the percentage of preference was ninety-five; in the Rocky Mountain and Pacific institutions the percentage of preference was seventy-six. According to this survey the large church student groups rank as follows: (for convenience round numbers only are given): Methodist, 57,900; Presbyterian, 34,500; Baptist, 27,400; Congregational, 22,900; Roman Catholic, 20,600; Protestant Episcopal, 15,800; Lutheran, 11,600; Hebrew, 9,400.

The Lutheran students, according to this survey, are distributed as follows: In the publicly controlled colleges and universities of

New England and North Atlantic States	1,030
Southern States	1,283
North Central States	7,996
Rocky Mountain and Pacific States	1,336
Total	11,645

The figure in the first section is obviously most inadequate, and a study of the institutions omitted in the survey explains the reason. The publicly-supported institutions in New York State do not have to take or report church preferences; therefore, the College of the City of New York and Hunter College are not included. It is true, moreover, that in these states publicly controlled institutions are neither so large nor so numerous as those in the Middle West, for example.

B. Teachers Colleges and Normal Schools. Mr. Leach has also made a study of the church relations in this important group of institutions. (This study has not yet been printed but has been made available to all Church Boards.) Tabulations from this survey are surprisingly full of interest. Lutheran students in Teachers Colleges and Normal Schools in:

*Pennsylvania in 13 institutions			1,153	
Minnesota " 5 "			1,122	
Wisconsin " 9 "			1,254	
North Dakota " 5 "			1,458	
32				4,987
Ohio " 2 "			167	
Illinois " 6 "			183	
Michigan " 4 "			543	
12				893
Iowa " 1 "			271	
Nebraska " 3 "			130	
Kansas " 3 "			109	
S. Dakota " 4 "			244	
Montana " 2 "			108	
Washington " 2 "			115	
California " 5 "			126	
32				1,996

In fifty-six institutions in the other states, 667 Lutheran students were reported, making a total of 8,543 Lutherans in 132 different institutions.

(*We have added figures in this office for a few institutions from which Mr. Leach was able to get no response.)

C. Liberal Arts Colleges (enrolling fewer than 650 students). In January, 1932, issue of *Christian Education,* Mr. Archie Palmer, associate secretary of the Association of American Colleges, published the results of a study of church students at ninety-five small colleges in thirty-two states, of which eighty-four are church affiliated and eleven are independent. The sum total of student enrollment was 34,472. The percentage of church preferences expressed was 94.3; in Rocky Mountain and Pacific the percentage was 89.1; in New England and Middle Atlantic, 96.1. In this group studied five were Lutheran colleges. Eliminating those and the twenty-five small sectional colleges reporting no Lutherans, 1,085 Lutheran students were reported in sixty-five Liberal Arts Colleges.

The sum total of these three surveys brings the number of students reported as Lutherans up to 21,273.

D. To the figures of these *Three Surveys* of the Council of Church Boards of Education can be added the figures of Lutheran students in the great metropolitan areas where our Board has been working over a period of years. These figures are *not* duplications as they cover institutions not included in the three surveys mentioned above—independent universities, church affiliated universities, professional schools.

Boston ....Metropolitan Area...................................		300
New York .... "	....	2,000
Philadelphia .... "	....	1,100
Baltimore and Washington .... "	....	400
Pittsburgh .... "	....	400
Chicago .... "	....	500
Total		4,700

The grand total of 26,000 Lutheran students is a conservative estimate as there are many institutions not included in any of the three surveys or in metropolitan areas.

United Lutheran Students. It is difficult to get exact figures. Even our own colleges and junior colleges in reporting 2,095 Lutheran students do not indicate that they are all of the United Lutheran Church. The official religious census of any educational institution outside of the Lutheran Church naturally makes no distinction between students of various Lutheran bodies. Our own pastors working with students find it not easy to make this distinction. About half of the total, or 13,000, are probably United Lutheran students.

3. Pastors Who Work With Students

It has been a principle of the work of the Board among students that the local congregation is primarily responsible for the Christian welfare of Lutheran students (as of all Lutherans) in the college community where the congregation is located.   The pastors of 166 such congregations are rendering service to students of the Lutheran Church in non-Lutheran universities, colleges, or professional schools.   To these pastors the Board gives guidance and assistance through regular publications, and through study books and folders especially for students.   By visits and correspondence, the secretaries of the Board offer such assistance as is sought and needed.   To thirty-nine such congregations where the financial situation is such that work with students cannot be carried on without some assistance, the Board makes annual grants.   But by far the greater number of congregations and pastors work with students as one of the privileges in the upbuilding of the Kingdom.

LIST OF PASTORS WHO WORK WITH STUDENTS:

California Synod:

E. A. Trabert	Berkeley, Calif.	University of California
J. E. Hoick	Los Angeles	Univ. of Southern California
A. J. Soldan	Los Angeles	Univ. of California at L. A.
Wm. H. Derr	Pasadena	California Inst. of Technology
W. E. Crouser	San Jose	State Teachers College

Georgia-Alabama Synod:

J. L. Yost	Atlanta, Ga.	All Schools in Atlanta
L. B. Hamm	Macon	Mercer University

Illinois Synod:

Dwight P. Bair	Champaign, Ill	University of Illinois
C. E. Paulus	Chicago	University of Chicago
C. R. W. Kegley	Chicago	Hospitals and Professional Schools
C. A. Naumann	Evanston	Northwestern University
J. M. Uber	Macomb	State Teachers College
C. I. Empson	Decatur	James Millikin University
W. L Wilson	Peoria	Bradley Institute
O. G. Beckstrand	Rockford	Rockford College
D. R. Kabele	Wilmette	National College

Indiana Synod:

H. C. Stolldorf	Lafayette, Ind.	Purdue University
H. A. Kunkle	Muncie	State Teachers College
A. K. Trout	Indianapolis	Butler University
I. W. Gernert	Nashville, Tenn.	All Schools in Nashville

Iowa Synod:

W. S. Dysinger ....Iowa City, Iowa ....Iowa State University
J. J. Gent ....Cedar Rapids ....Coe College
J. A. Miller ....Davenport ....Palmer School
A. J. Beil......................Des Moines ....Drake University
R. M. Badger ....Dubuque ....Dubuque University
W. F. Rex ....Fairfield ....Parsons College
A. B. Schwertz ....Sioux City ....Morningside College

Kansas Synod:

C. A. Puls ....Lawrence, Kansas ....Kansas University
W. J. Boldt ....Emporia ....S. T. C. & Emporia
                                                                        College
A. M. Hahn ....Hays ....State Teachers College
B. R. Lantz..................Salina ....Wesleyan College
C. L. Stager ....Topeka ....Topeka College
E. E. Stauffer ....Wichita ....Wichita College

Maryland Synod:

R. D. Clare ....Baltimore, Md. ....Goucher College and
                                                                        Johns Hopkins
O. F. Blackwelder.......Baltimore ....Johns Hopkins
W. A. Wade ....Baltimore ....State Teachers College
A. J. Traver ....Frederick ....Hood College
W. V. Simon.................Frostburg ....State Teachers College
H. R. Spangler ....Lutherville ....Maryland College for
                                                                        Women
Paul Quay ....Westminster ....Western Maryland Col-
                                                                        lege
S. H. Kornmann ....Washington, D. C. ....University of Md. (Col-
                                                                        lege Pk.)
C. C. Rasmussen ....Washington, D. C............George Washington Uni-
                                                                        versity
Frances Dysinger ....Washington, D. C............Executive Secretary of
                                                                        Inner Mission Society.
                                                                        (Director of Metro-
                                                                        politan Student Work).

Michigan Synod:

H. O. Yoder ....Ann Arbor, Mich. ....University of Michigan
H. J. Fenning ....Battle Creek ....Battle Creek College
F. H. Bloch ....Kalamazoo ....State Teachers College,
                                                                        Kalamazoo College

Nebraska Synod:

G. K. Rubrecht ....Lincoln, Nebr. ....University of Nebraska
W. C. Heidenreich ......Wayne ....State Teachers College
W. H. Traub ....Omaha ....Omaha University

New York Synod:

F. W. Schaeffer ....New Britain Conn. ....State Teachers College
B. Mehrtens ....New Haven ....Yale University
G. R. Seltzer ....Hartford ....Hartford Foundation

N. D. Goehring ....Boston, Mass. ....Harvard University, M. I. T., all Colleges in Boston area

A. H. Holthusen ....New Brunswick, N. J.......Rutgers and N. J. College for Women

C. E. Frontz ....Albany, N. Y. ....State Teachers College

H. J. Pflum ....Buffalo ....State Teachers College and Buffalo University

S. M. Paulson ....Brooklyn ....Pratt Institute

C. E. Eichner ....Elmira ....Elmira College

W. M. Horn ....Ithaca ....Cornell University

A. Steimle ....New York ....Columbia University

P. E. Scherer ....New York ....New York University

R. J. Van Deusen ....Oneonta ....State Teachers College

F. J. Baum ....Poughkeepsie ....Vassar College

H. D. Shimer ....Schenectady.......................Union University

E. L. Keller ....Syracuse ....Syracuse University

F. R. Knubel ....Rochester ....Rochester University and other colleges

A. W. Baker ....Troy ....Rensselaer Polytechnic and Russel Sage College

North Carolina Synod:

H. A. Schroder ....Durham, N. C. ....Duke University and University of North Carolina

A. J. Yount ....Boone ....State Teachers College

J. F. Crigler ....Charlotte ....Queens College

E. A. Shenk ....Greensboro ....N. C. College for Women

S. W. Hahn ....Winston-Salem ....Salem College

R. B. Peery ....Raleigh ....State College

M. L. Stirewalt ....Salisbury ....Catawba College

Northwest Synod:

C. L. Grant ....St. Paul, Minn. ....Macalester College

C. J. Rockey ....Madison, Wis. ....University of Wisconsin

J. F. Fedders ....Milwaukee ....State Teachers College and Downer

A. A. Zinck ....Milwaukee ....Marquette University

E. R. Wicklund ....Oshkosh ....State Teachers College

R. R. Doering ....Platteville ....State Teachers College

D. E. Bosserman ....Appleton ....Lawrence College

C. F. Schneider ....Beloit ....Beloit College

A. A. Hahn ....Waukesha ....Carroll College

Joseph Stump ....La Crosse ....State Teachers College

Ohio Synod:

Louis A. Sittler ....Columbus, Ohio ....State University of Ohio

F. D. Daubenbis ....Oxford ....Miami University and Western College for Women

W. L. Harmony ....Ada ....Ohio Northern University

F. C. Fry ....Akron ....Akron University
S. D. Meyers ....Alliance ....Mt. Union College
A. H. Smith ....Ashland ....Ashland College
D. T. Holland ....Bowling Green ....State Teachers College
H. L. Meister ....Cincinnati ....Univ. of Cincinnati
Joseph Sittler, Jr. ....Cleveland ....Western Reserve & Case
C. L. Venable ....Dayton ....Dayton University
B. F. Hofer ....Defiance ....Defiance College
H. R. Merle ....Delaware ....Ohio Wesleyan
H. A. Sayles ....Elyria ....Oberlin
H. Ward Grieb ....Findlay ....Findlay College
M. W. Wappner ....Kent ....State Teachers College
W. L. Spielman ....Marietta ....Marietta College
W. O. Kantner ....Tiffin ....Heidelberg College
R. G. Schulz ....Toledo ....Toledo University
P. S. Kelly ....Wooster ....Wooster College
F. C. Rambow ....Newark ....Denison (Granville)

Pacific Synod:
F. S. Beistel ....Eugene, Oregon ....University of Oregon
W. E. Brinkman ....Portland ....Reed College
O. A. Bremer ....Seattle, Wash. ....Univ. of Washington

PENNSYLVANIA SYNODS:

Allegheny Synod:
E. L. Manges..................Huntington, Pa. ....Juniata College

East Pennsylvania:
U. E. Apple ....Annville ....Lebanon Valley College
A. C. Kanzinger ....Ardmore ....Haverford College
P. W. Dieckman ....Easton ....Lafayette College
R. H. Gearhart ....Philadelphia ....University of Pennsyl-
                                                                       vania and other col-
                                                                       leges in Philadelphia,
                                                                       Princeton University
L. W. Evans ....West Chester ....State Teachers College
S. W. Herman ....Harrisburg ....Hospital Schools

Ministerium of Pennsylvania:
W. C. Schaeffer ....Allentown Pa. ....Cedar Crest College
G. F. Gehr ....Bethlehem ....Lehigh University and
                                                                       Moravian Colleges
M. A. Kurtz ....Bethlehem ....Lehigh University
H. A. Weaver ....Chester ....Pennsylvania Military
                                                                       Academy
W. O. Fegeley ....Collegeville ....Ursinus College
R. B. Lynch ....Kutztown ....State Teachers College
James Harrison ....Lancaster ....Franklin and Marshall
P. J. Henry ....Millersville ....State Teachers College
L. S. Sweitzer ....Reading ....Albright College
J. S. Kistler ....Stroudsburg ....State Teachers College

Pittsburgh Synod:

J. K. Rizer........................Clarion, Pa. ....State Teachers College
A. J. Pfohl ....Indiana ....State Teachers College
R. A. Kline ....Meadville ....Alleghany College
R. C. Lauffenberger......Prospect ....S. T. C. at Slippery Rock
Reginald Dozer ....Pittsburgh ....University of Pittsburgh
                                                                   and Carnegie Tech.
H. B. Ernest ....Washington ....Washington and Jeffer-
                                                                   son College

Susquehanna Synod:

J. T. Harkins ....State College ....Pennsylvania State Col-
                                                                   lege
N. S. Wolf ....Bloomsburg ....State Teachers College
W. F. Brown ....Danville ....Hospital Schools
R. B. McGiffin ....Lewisburg ....Bucknell University
C. H. Stein ....Lock Haven ....State Teachers College

West Pennsylvania Synod:

W. W. Barkley ....Shippensburg ....State Teachers College
A. R. Steck ....Carlisle ....Dickinson College
C. A. Neale ....Chambersburg ....Wilson College and Penn
                                                                   Hall
H. Anstadt ....Chambersburg ....Wilson College and Penn
                                                                   Hall

Rocky Mountain Synod:

W. A. Voss ....Boulder, Colo. ....University of Colorado
R. B. Wolf ....Colorado Springs ....Colorado College
E. W. Harner ....Denver ....Denver University,
                                                                   School of Mines
A. O. Frank ....Albuquerque, N. M.........University of New
                                                                   Mexico
H. S. Lawrence ....Laramie, Wyoming ....University of Wyoming

South Carolina Synod:

P. D. Brown ....Columbia, S. C. ....University of South
                                                                   Carolina
C. A. Freed ....Columbia ....Columbia College
G. J. Gongaware ....Charleston ....Citadel, College of
                                                                   Charleston
B. M. Clark ....Walhalla ....Clemson College
J. E. Stockman ....Greenville ....Furman and Greenville
                                                                   Colleges
C. B. Caughman ....Rock Hill ....Winthrop College
F. G. Morgan ....Spartanburg ....Converse and Wofford
                                                                   Colleges

Virginia Synod:

D. W. Zipperer ....Blacksburg, Va..................Virginia Polytechnic
M. L. Minnich ....Harrisonburg ....State Teachers College

R. L. Markley ....Lynchburg ....Lynchburg, Randolph
                                                      Macon, Sweet Briar
                                                      Colleges
Lewis Koon ....Radford ....State Teachers College
C. M. Teufel ....Staunton ....Staunton Military, Mary
                                                      Baldwin
J. H. Fray ....Shepherdstown, W. Va...Shepherd College
S. C. Ballentine ....Bristol, Tenn. ....King, Sullins, Intermont
                                                      Colleges
A. M. Huffman ....Knoxville ....University of Tennessee
J. J. Scherer ....Richmond ....All Schools
J. L. Sieber ....Roanoke ....Hollins College

West Virginia Synod:

W. R. Hashinger ....Morgantown. W. Va. ....University of W. Va.
W. P. Cline ....Fairmont ....Fairmont College
C. E. Butler ....Huntington ....Marshall College

Canada Synod:

T. S. Rees ....Winnipeg, Manitoba ......University of Manitoba
N. Willison ....Hamilton, Ont. ....MacMaster and Normal
                                                      College

Other Lutheran Pastors Who Work With Students

The *Augustana* Synod has continued to co-operate with us in work with students. Students of that synod are among the most devoted in almost every student group. To two student centers, Minneapolis, Minn., and Manhattan, Kansas, grants are made from our Board. At Manhattan, the Rev. Armour Edberg, pastor, a new church plant has been dedicated. The fine personal work of Pastor C. A. Wendell, at the University of Minnesota, is well known. At Los Angeles, Cal.; Boulder, Col.; Des Moines, Ia.; and Lincoln, Nebr., the work of the Augustana pastors is co-ordinated with that of pastors of the United Lutheran Church.

Thirteen pastors of the Augustana Synod are rendering valuable service in the student field at the following places:

A. P. G. Anderson ......Los Angeles, Calif. ....University of Southern
                                                      California
J. S. Benson ....Boulder, Colo. ....University of Colorado
R. R. Oliver ....Moscow, Idaho ....University of Idaho
A. O. Hedstrom ....Bloomington, Ill. ....State Teachers College
E. W. Magnusson ....DeKalb, Ill...........................State Teachers College
P. A. Johnson ....Galesburg, Ill....................Knox College
E. F. Bergren ....Des Moines, Iowa ....Drake University
A. Edberg ....Manhattan, Kans. ....State College
A. O. Hjelm ....Worcester, Mass. ....Worcester, Polytechnic
O. H. Bostrom ....Marquette, Mich................State Teachers College
C. A. Wendell ....Minneapolis, Minn........... University of Minnesota
G. A. Elliott ....Lincoln, Nebr. ....University of Nebraska
E. A. Larson ....Tacoma, Wash. ....College of Puget Sound

Seventeen pastors of the *American* Lutheran Church are listed as student pastors. With the Commission on Student Work, through its chairman, the

Rev. Paul Bierstedt, of Columbus, Ohio, the student secretaries of our Board co-operate.

Twenty-eight pastors of the *Norwegian* Lutheran Church care for the spiritual welfare of Lutheran students, particularly in colleges and universities of the Northwest.

Seventy-five pastors of the *Missouri Synod* serve students, some of them at the same points where we are working. At other points there is only the Missouri Lutheran pastor, as for example, at the universities of Virginia, Alabama, Indiana, Missouri, and Arizona.

4. Co-operative Activities and Contacts

Without the willing and valued co-operation of the synods, boards, and auxiliary organizations of the Church, work with students of the Church would be hampered.

Co-operation With Synods

The Board of Education several years ago requested the synods of the United Lutheran Church to appoint a standing committee on student work. Through such a committee, synod may become directly acquainted with the student problems on its own territory; and through it the Board may be kept informed of changes and problems affecting students. With such a committee, the secretaries of the Board try to keep in close touch both through correspondence and during visits made to institutions on the territory of synod. The following synods have committees on student work which in most instances have been functioning satisfactorily:

Illinois	Nebraska	Pennsylvania Ministerium
Maryland	New York	
Michigan	Ohio	East Pennsylvania
Northwest	West Virginia	Susquehanna

The *Synod of Ohio* and the Board have worked out close co-operation. The Ohio Synod Student Committee has immediate oversight of work being done among students on its territory. The synod and the Board contribute equal amounts to the expense of this work. All policies and programs for the work on synod territory and in local student centers are determined jointly by the committee of synod and the secretaries of the Board. By this plan it has been possible to render more unified and effective service to students on the territory of the Ohio Synod.

The Board of Education of the United Lutheran Church co-operates with the *New York Synod* in work among students through its Board of Education. For the work among students in Greater Boston, the Board of Education of the United Lutheran Church makes an annual financial grant. For the work among students in Metropolitan New York, the Board of Education has, this past year, given the services of one of its secretaries,

Miss Winston, who has spent at least half of the academic year in that field. At a meeting of the Board of Education of the New York Synod, in December, 1931, the following action was taken: "It is the sentiment of this Board that a full-time student pastor be employed in the Metropolitan area (New York) as soon as funds become available for this purpose."

With the *Synod of North Carolina* the Board of Education shares in the directing and financing of work among students in two important places, the University of North Carolina and Duke University.

It is a source of gratification to the Board that synods are becoming more and more conscious of their responsibility for student members of the Church. Partially as the result of the emphasis placed upon the responsibility of the Church to her students, thirteen synods are making regular grants to congregations doing work among students to the amount of $15,317 annually, as reported to Mr. Harry.

Co-operation With Boards

The following principles of co-operative work at educational centers have been agreed upon between the *Board of American Missions and the Board of Education*:

I. Regarding Pastors of Churches in Educational Centers—

Where a portion of the salary of a pastor of churches in an educational center is paid by the Board of Education and the Board of American Missions, the president of the synod and the Synodical Mission Committee are requested

(a) to secure the advice of the said Boards in suggesting candidates for such parishes.

(b) to secure the advice of the Board of Education before seeking the approval of the Board of American Missions.

II. Regarding the Removal of Men Doing Unsatisfactory Work—

(a) All constitutional provisions, both of the synod and the congregation, shall be carefully observed in seeking such a change of pastorate.

(b) The first step in such action shall be a conference of representatives of the Board of American Missions and the Board of Education.

(c) Out of such conference a committee shall be appointed to meet with the president of the synod, who shall arrange for a consultation that shall include the pastor concerned, representatives of the Boards, and the synodical authorities.

(d) If such conference, or conferences, fail to secure the necessary readjustment, then the Boards shall withdraw their support from the field.

III. Method of Work—

Inasmuch as the care of Lutheran students is an integral part of the responsibility of a Lutheran congregation in a community where there are

Lutheran students, the policy and program of the local mission, set up by the pastor, the church council, and the synodical authorities, must be approved by representatives of both the Board of American Missions and the Board of Education.

In twenty-three congregations in educational centers located in thirteen different synods, the Board of Education is directly interested with the Board of American Missions. The latter Board has $155,312 in loans to these congregations, and during the past fiscal year granted them $5,027.50 for interest charges and donations and $13,520 on pastors' salaries. The Board of Education granted to these congregations the past fiscal year as aids in working with students, a total of $9,871.66.

The Board of Deaconess Work by a definite action asked the Board of Education to assist in presenting the claims of the female diaconate to women students. Through conferences and correspondence with Dr. Foster U. Gift and the deaconesses, eight student centers in North Carolina, South Carolina, and Virginia were visited by Sister Pearle Lyerly, of the Church of the Advent, New York City; and two teachers colleges in Pennsylvania were visited by Sister Anna Ebert, directing sister of the Philadelphia Motherhouse. Both deaconesses received enthusiastic hearings. Such visits will be continued in the future.

Co-operation With Agencies

With the *Women's Missionary Society of the United Lutheran Church in America,* the Board of Education has, since its organization, maintained close co-operation. Two women, appointed by and from the Executive Board of the Women's Missionary Society, are valued advisory members of the Board of Education and of the Committee on Student Work. The Executive Board of the W. M. S. budgets annually a generous amount of money for work among women students in particular. The Women's Missionary Society of the United Lutheran Synod of New York, and that of the Ministerium of Pennsylvania, carry a large share of this amount because of the large number of women students in their respective areas.

The United Lutheran Church has the distinction of being the first Church which, through one staff agency, has brought to college women the complete challenge of the Church. The Executive Board of the Women's Missionary Society, in 1918, saw the advantages of doing its promotional and recruiting work among young women in college campuses as far as possible through a secretary for women students on the staff of the Board of Education. With that understanding, the original grant was made to the Board. The women secretaries of the Board have always kept this purpose in mind in their visits to college and university campuses, to professional schools and to hospital training schools.

This close relationship is indicated by the fact that in 1922 the Executive Board of the Women's Missionary Society appointed Miss Markley to the

Candidate Committee, and since 1924 she has been chairman of the committee. This candidate committee is charged with finding the young women who are qualified to fill specific positions under the various Boards of the Church. By this committee young women are recommended through the Executive Board of the W. M. S. for appointments by the Board of American Missions and by the Board of Foreign Missions. The chairmanship of this committee demands an immense amount of correspondence, in addition to frequent personal interviews, and to regular committee meetings.

Requirements, educational and professional, for successful Christian service are steadily advancing. Our women workers must be sought among students or recent graduates. A review of appointments over a series of years shows that our women missionaries have received their undergraduate training in Lutheran colleges, in other denominational colleges, as well as in state colleges and universities. Professional or graduate work is almost always from necessity taken at non-Lutheran institutions.

Miss Markley, as one of the eight members ex-officio, is a member of the Literature Committee of the Women's Missionary Society and of its sub-committee on manuscripts. This literature committee, through regular meetings and correspondence, is the educational agency of the Women's Missionary Society.

Miss Winston maintains a close relationship with the secretary for young women. She functions especially through the sub-committee on literature for young women. Both she and Miss Markley have been on the committees of arrangements for the biennial congresses of the young women of the United Lutheran Church.

Both Miss Markley and Miss Winston are called upon as speakers for missionary conventions and conferences, thirteen such having been attended during the biennium, exclusive of the biennial conventions. On such occasions the essential relations of Christian higher education and the progress of the Church both at home and abroad is stressed.

A student secretary in the Women's Missionary Society of the synods (and conferences) is the direct personal connection which the Board has with the synodical groups of missionary women. The office is in regular touch, through correspondence and personal interviews, with seventy such women in every part of our Church. These student secretaries, since 1919, have been getting the student census from the congregations of their respective synods. During the past academic year, 1,404 congregations, about 35 per cent of all U. L. C. congregations have reported 7,345 student members; of these 3,625 were women and 3,720 were men. These names are valuable both to student pastors and to the staff secretaries in making contacts with students. This means of uniting the home congregation with the college town congregation through the Board is effective in helping make the Church a vital and personal factor in the lives of the students. The taking of the census in the local congregation helps arouse interest not only in students but in the recent college graduates who should be assuming responsibilities in congregational activities. The student secretaries and the census taking have been real educative factors not only in bringing to the local constituency the general work of the Board but also in facing questions pertinent especially to the higher education of the young women of the Church.

With the *Luther League,* the Board during the biennium has begun a co-operative plan in the field of recruiting and Christian guidance. Names of high school boys and girls, who are planning to go on to college and who are looking forward to the gospel ministry or full-time Christian service, are reported to the student secretaries of the Board for correspondence and for future contacts. Some printed material in the field of Christian guidance is being put out jointly by the Board and the Luther League.

Mr. Harry has continued his intimate connection with the Luther League by acting as editor of the *Topics Quarterly,* and as chairman of the Literature Committee.

Reports from student pastors show that in a considerable number of places the Luther League is the organization of the local congregation through which the work with students is done. In an appreciable number of places the Luther League Topics have formed the basis for the study and discussions of student groups.

Co-operation at Student Centers

At five places student work is carried on through joint committees representing some general bodies of Lutherans. Our Board makes a grant at each of these points and has part in the general direction of the work.

At the *University of Michigan* a joint committee consisting of members of the congregation of the United Lutheran Church and members of the congregation of the American Lutheran Church has immediate oversight over the work done with students. The United Lutheran congregation is small. The American Lutheran congregation is large and has an unusually fine equipment for student work. Agreement has been reached by which the Parish House of the American Church is the student center for our work, and the pastor of the United Lutheran Church directs the student work. He also has an office on the campus in Lane Hall, where other university workers with students have headquarters.

At the *State Teachers' College at Cedar Falls, Iowa,* a Martin Luther Foundation has been established which is supported by grants from the Iowa district of the American Lutheran Church, from our Board through the Iowa Synod (U. L. C. A.), from membership fees in the Foundation, from private donations, and from the rental of rooms in the student home, which the Foundation owns and operates. The pastor in charge is a member of the American Lutheran Church.

At the *University of Nebraska* there is a joint committee on work with students whose budget is balanced by grants from the English Nebraska and German Nebraska Synods of the U. L. C. A., from the Danish Synod and from the Augustana Synod, as well as from our Board. The committee, composed of pastors and laymen, employs a secretary-fellow, who receives the equivalent of a university fellowship from the committee, and makes the initial contacts with students, links them with congregations of our synods and directs the activities of the Lutheran Student Association.

In *Oregon* some years ago, pastors and laymen formed the Oregon Lutheran Student Service Association. This association is organized somewhat like an Inner Missionary Society, providing for individual memberships and participation by corporate groups. The Rev. William Schoeller, of the American Lutheran Church, has been the executive secretary from the outset, and has done very valuable work among the Lutheran students at the three state institutions in the Willamette Valley: The State University at Eugene, the State College at Corvallis, and the State Teachers College at Monmouth. The association receives grants from our Board, the American Lutheran Church, the Norwegian Lutheran Church and the Augustana Synod.

At *Los Angeles, California,* during the year just passed, a joint committee for student work has been organized consisting of members of the United Lutheran Church and of the Augustana Synod. Our Board contributes to its budget, and up to the present time has carried the major portion of it. The committee is served by an executive secretary, Miss Muriel Bixby, a member of the United Lutheran congregation in Hollywood, the Rev. G. J. Dorn, D.D., pastor. Pastors of the United Lutheran Church and of the Augustana Synod work directly with students on the campuses of the various universities and colleges of the Los Angeles area. The committee hopes to interest other synodical groups, and to become a thoroughly representative committee for Lutheran student work in this area.

Co-operation With the Lutheran Student Association of America

This is a nation-wide association of Lutheran students. Students from practically every general Lutheran body are active in the association, although it has no direct affiliation or relation to any synod. The work of the L. S. A. A. is directed by a National Council made up of the officers of the seven regions into which it has been divided. Secretary Harry has been one of the advisors of the council since the formation of the association, ten years ago.

The president of the L. S. A. A. is Mr. Eugene Olson of Iowa State College. The *American Lutheran Student,* the official paper, has been issued three times a year during the biennium, under Editor Norris Halvorsen, of Luther Seminary, St. Paul.

The L. S. A. A. has continued its assistance to the Theological Seminary in Leningrad, Russia, through the National Lutheran Council, by gifts amounting to about one thousand dollars during the biennium. The annual graduate scholarship, amounting to $150 for a Lutheran student in India, has been continued. The holder of this scholarship in a university in India is not always a student of the United Lutheran Church in India, but the scholarship is administered by the faculty of our Andhra Christian College.

During the biennium, L. S. A. A. Conferences have been held through the regional organizations in the following places:

North Atlantic—Mt. Airy Seminary and Muhlenberg College.
Southeast—University of South Carolina and Newberry College.
Ohio Valley—Capital University and University of West Virginia.
Mississippi Valley—Iowa State Teachers College and Iowa State University.
Southwest—Kansas State College and University of Nebraska.
North Central—State Teachers College, St. Cloud, Minnesota, and Gustavus Adolphus College.
Pacific Northwest—Washington State College and College of Puget Sound.

Metropolitan conferences of L. S. A. A. groups were held in New York City in 1931 and 1932, and in Evanston, Illinois, in 1931. These conferences are concrete evidence of a feeling among students, faculty, and student pastors, that the seven regions of the L. S. A. A. as now constituted are geographically too large for the continuance of successful conferences.

Secretaries of the Board of Education have, by invitation, been present and on the program of all Regional Conferences except those in the North Central and Pacific Northwest regions.

The budget of the L. S. A. A. is met by student contributions. Our Board of Education has helped with small deficits which have occurred, particularly in connection with the publication of *The American Lutheran Student* which is distributed without charge to members of the L. S. A. A. who desire it.

More than a thousand students have attended the various L. S. A. A. Conferences during the biennium as guests of the Lutheran students on the campuses named. No Lutheran fellowship of the present is doing more to help the future leaders of the Lutheran Church of America to understand one another, and so to prepare the way for a united witness for Christ and His Word by the Lutheran Church.

5. Items of Interest

Conference on Christian Culture in Our Church Colleges

On the suggestion of the staff of the Student Division, the Board, in December, 1930, invited to a two-day conference the academic deans, the deans of men, deans of women, professors of Bible, and professors of Religious Education of all our United Lutheran Colleges. All faculties, save that of Saskatoon, were represented in the thirty-five men and women who accepted the invitation. The main theme—noted above—was introduced in its various divisions in a fifteen-minute talk by a speaker chosen in advance; the topic was then thrown open for discussion.

In this Conference, for the first time, the faculty men and women of our various Church colleges met to discuss the common problem which is of prime importance to the whole educational system of our Church. Something of the value of the conference may be gained by the Report of the Finding Committee:

1. The members of the Conference appreciate heartily the privilege extended them by the Board of Education. It is believed that important values arising out of the enjoyable fellowship and stimulating discussions will be reflected in the personal attitudes and campus work of the participants.

2. A continuation of the Conference plan with more extended and specialized program is desired.

3. An increased conviction of the crucial importance of the church college in the continuing life of the church has resulted.

4. There has come a renewed sense of responsibility for the genuinely Christian culture of youth on Lutheran campuses.

5. There is apparent a wholesome unity of purpose regarding the main goal of Christian culture, while there is an equally wholesome divergence of opinion as to the theoretical and practical solution of the problems involved.

6. There is a necessity for ascertaining the religious status of the student as he comes to college, and this factor should guide the program of his culture.

7. The procedures for the Christian culture of students will be of both personal and individual and social or group nature.

8. The spiritual status of many present-day students necessitates a systematic assistance toward the attainment of a more vital, moral and religious life, and a more comprehensive intellectual grasp of Christian truth.

9. In the presentation of religious truth a persuasive positive approach is desired.

10. There is to be a recognition of the distinctive character of the Lutheran college, although a too high degree of uniformity is not to be sought.

11. In a majority of Lutheran colleges the expansion of curricular work in Bible, religion, and Religious Education appears to be desirable.

12. There is a necessity for the increasing co-operation between the colleges and the local churches.

13. Dignified, beautiful, and reverent services of worship are essential to the Christian program on the campus. To this end properly appointed chapel buildings are sorely needed at many of our colleges.

14. There is an earnest concern to meet the proper expectation of the Church for a well-trained lay and professional leadership.

15. It is to be recognized that Christian culture is the co-operative task of every member of the faculty and administrative staff, and its effectiveness rests upon the life and teachings of all.

16. Students should have a vital share in the control of campus life as a part of their Christian culture.

17. It is imperative that the Christian principles shall be manifested in all departments of the college life and activity.

18. The social program of the college should contribute to the development of skill in the social graces and the ability to meet the situations of polite society with ease.

19. The spiritual use of the increasing margin of leisure time suggests that appreciation and expression in the field of fine arts deserves attention.

20. There is reason for encouragement in the reports of Christian activity on the part of students on Lutheran campuses. The vital place of this extra curricular activity, when properly directed, is to be recognized.

21. The Lutheran college will find its ultimate goal in the affirmation of its historic heritage—a Christ-centered faith and life.

Christian Guidance and Recruiting

This fundamental phase of the work of the Board is indicated in the By-Laws: "to discover, develop, and direct future leaders of the Church and to secure an adequate ministry." The secretaries have always been actively interested in Christian guidance and recruiting. Many interviews and much correspondence with students relate to this phase of the work of the staff. The enlistment of young women for full-time Christian service under the Boards of American Missions and Foreign Missions is done by co-operative arrangements through the Executive Board of the Women's Missionary Society. Young women desirous of serving in parishes are directed to the diaconate or if properly qualified are put in touch with pastors and presidents of synods. To the work of Christian guidance the Luther League is giving assistance through its life service department. Enlisting young women for Christian service, and helping men hear the call to the Gospel Ministry, will be a continuing responsibility for the secretaries.

Service to Students in Form of Scholarships

Many Boards of Education have a large fund for scholarships and loans for use by students. Our Board has one slowly growing fund for the use of women students. This past biennium five young women have received varying amounts: one for graduate study preparatory to going to the foreign field; one each at Carthage, Bethany, and Wittenberg; one at a State Teachers College in Pennsylvania. The regulations governing this fund are those presented by the Board and adopted by the Church in 1930. Young women who do not go into full-time Christian service repay all money received from this fund.

Another important, but equally slowly growing fund, is that of the Permanent Ministerial Education Fund. By agreement with the California Synod, the Board has been aiding the students for the ministry from that synod. Their transportation expenses have been paid to Fremont, Nebraska, where they attended Midland College and Western Seminary. During the biennium, we have aided four students in this manner.

Publications

During the biennium the Board has published and distributed, without charge, three books for guiding the discussions of students on our various campuses.

Jesus the Unique—Prepared by our pastor at the University of Pennsylvania, the Rev. R. H. Gearhart, Jr. It consists of an outline for each topic with questions to open the discussion and scripture references.

Facing the Faith—Prepared by the American Lutheran Pastor, at Ohio State University, the Rev. Paul E. Bierstedt. This booklet was published jointly by our Board and the Students' Service Commission of the Joint Synod of Ohio just before the merger of the Joint Synod of Ohio with other synods forming the American Lutheran Church. Each topic is presented in two brief paragraphs as a problem, followed by helpful references and questions for discussion.

How—Prepared by the Rev. C. P. Harry, secretary of the Board. There are five studies, consisting of questions for general discuussion, Bible notes, other references, and several pages of suggestions in which various aspects of the topic are briefly considered to stimulate discussion.

The Student Division has continued to use, with good results, material prepared for student work in earlier years. The following folders have been especially useful during the past biennium:

> *"The Lutheran Church and Modern Religious Life," "Making Life Count,"* and *"Personal Work,"* by C. P. Harry.

> *"At College,"* by W. S. Dysinger, our pastor at Iowa State University.

> *"What To Do"*—a 22-page booklet intended to help students to organize and carry on Christian work on the campus.

> *"Helping the Student"*—a 15-page booklet, prepared especially for pastors and congregational student committees, showing how they may help the students in developing Christian activities.

The last two have been prepared by the secretaries of the Student Division. Two folders on the ministry have been prepared and widely distributed:

"Would You Do It Again," by George W. Nicely, D.D.

"Why I Became a Minister"—Brief statements by the following well-known pastors of the United Lutheran Church: Paul E. Scherer, Oscar T. Blackwelder, Ross H. Stover, Norman D. Goehring, Amos J. Traver.

Service Bulletin

During the biennium, issues of the *Service Bulletin* have been prepared by the secretaries of the Student Division and mailed to all pastors working with students, presidents of synods, presidents of our own colleges and seminaries, members of the Board, members of synodical student committees, officers of the Lutheran Student Association of America, and a selected list of those interested in student work throughout the Church. The mailing list includes about 350 names.

The Service Bulletin seeks to bring the news of the student field to all the pastors and to others interested in it, outlines work which should be done and methods of doing it for the season following each issue, calls attention to important books for student workers, and reviews them briefly. The *Service Bulletin* is also a means of sharing methods of work successful in one place with our workers in other fields. Many of the issues contain special articles on outstanding features of the work or problems immediately pressing. For example, in the November, 1930, issue, Secretary Harry contributed an article on the vital issue we face today in seeking to present and develop a positive Christian faith in a world which neglects or denies the Word of God. In the September, 1931 issue there is an article on guest membership, by our pastor in Philadelphia, the Rev. R. H. Gearhart, Jr.

Conference of Church Workers

The third tri-ennial meeting of the conference of Church workers in universities and colleges, held January, 1931, with more than 200 registered delegates, was attended by Miss Markley. The following statement appeared on the program: "For a number of years, leaders of youth have become perplexed concerning their religious message to young people. This conference is set to state clearly the reality of the spiritual, and to open our eyes to the real trends in scientific and social thought." It was left for the scientist, Dr. Edmund S. Conklin, to point out that perplexity concerning a religious message is primarily due to absence of a religious experience. Of this conference, the Rev. R. H. Gearhart, Jr., pastor for Lutheran Students in Philadelphia, was elected president.

Student Conferences

Only two *Christian Association Summer Conferences* have been attended: Silver Bay (Y. W.) by Miss Winston, and Forest Park (Y. W. and Y. M.)

by Miss Winston and Mr. Harry. Miss Winston, as chairman of a sub-committee of the Federated Student Committee (composed of all women working among students under the auspices of Church Boards, Y. W. C. A., and Student Volunteers), procured data indicating a decided tendency on the part of the various Churches to provide adequate courses for their students with other young people in their own summer conferences. Students seem to be attending these Church conferences in increasing numbers, especially where they function as Leadership Training Camps, like the Lutheran Camp at Biglerville.

The staff was represented at the important *National Student-Faculty Conference*—the first of its kind—held in Detroit in January, 1931, by Miss Winston and Mr. Harry. This conference marks a definite advance in the integration of all educational processes in academic and religious life.

At the *Eleventh Quadrennial Convention* of the *Student Volunteer Movement* held in Buffalo, in the holiday season of 1931-32, Miss Markley represented the staff. About 2,000 students, missionaries and church workers were present, as over against the 4,000 hoped for and 6,000 at Indianapolis in 1923. There was an excellent balance between public platform addresses and discussion lead groups from 100 to 200. There was a decided turn toward a more evangelical point of view than evidenced at the two previous quadrennial conventions. The Lutheran group came from seven United Lutheran, six other Lutheran institutions, and eleven non-Lutheran colleges and universities. Of the total sixty, ten men and five women students are directly considering missionary service. A student dinner was arranged under the auspices of the Buffalo Lutheran Student Association. A service was held in Holy Trinity Church, the Rev. H. J. Pflum, D.D., pastor, with Secretaries Koller, Thomas, Fry; four missionaries from Japan, one from India, one from Africa, and one from Persia, in the program.

6. Problems in Ministering to Students

Time Pressures. It is becoming increasingly difficult to work with students in large groups. This is due in part to time pressures. Colleges have raised academic standards and students are worked harder. With elective courses becoming more general, students' time is more broken up and it is more difficult to gather groups, except for a few moments at lunch. Increasing numbers of students leave the college campus over the week-end. This makes it more difficult for pastors to serve them on Sundays. We are seeking to develop methods by which pastors will still be able to care for students under these new conditions. Many students must earn the money to pay at least in part for their college education. An earnest student desiring to participate fully in college life, and compelled to earn much of his own way, is hard pressed for time. To many religion seems to offer the least tangible returns, and to represent the least loss if neglected for a while. The Church, too, is left out in favor of more pressing interests.

Inadequate Training. This under-valuation of religion results in part from the fact that for the prospective college student the present parish educational program fails to provide adequate situations and techniques which are germinal of genuine Christian experience, and which correlate vital religion and practical daily living. Christian behavior and thought patterns as well as personal responsibility and initiative are not sufficiently established, and, therefore, tend to disintegrate in new situations resulting in lax living, mental confusion and religious doubt.

At college these new situations involve the replacement of stabilizing home influences by abnormal living conditions, personal isolation, and crowd pressures with the consequent necessity of choice of friends, and of initiative in the use of time, amusements and opportunity. In the expanding and developing thought areas of college, often dominated by agnostic, mechanistic or humanistic philosophies which leave Christ out, it is difficult for the student to sustain and develop Christian living in keeping with his intellectual attainment. Not sufficiently established in the faith before coming to college, many students go down in doubt and confusion, and are lost to the Church in spite of the best efforts of the Church near the campus. At the same time this same break-up of thought and behavior patterns on the campus affords the Church her great opportunity. Many students have found a real foundation for their faith and genuine Christian living through the ministry of our pastors in university and college centers.

Co-operation. Work with students is often hampered by the unsystematic way in which the Church has provided for the care of her students in the past, or by the failure of some Lutheran Church groups to co-operate in this ministry. The local pastor and congregation is primarily responsible for the welfare of Lutheran students attending the college within the bounds of the parish, and the synod should assume or share that responsibility when the local congregation is unable to carry it alone.

Yet there are groups of our students, in some cases in important institutions, in towns where there is *no Lutheran or United Lutheran congregation.* A secretary of the Board, or the nearest pastor for students, makes occasional visits to such groups. In some cases the groups have carried on as Lutheran Student Associations. At Cornell, such a student association became the nucleus for the present congregation.

At several important places there is *no church edifice.* At some points service is held only on alternate Sundays. This is an inadequate arrangement, especially when at the same points other denominations have well-equipped churches and regular services. Yet in many of these instances our students have shown fine loyalty, and our pastors have worked hard to serve them.

The Church needs no extravagant houses of worship but it does need *suitable and churchly edifices* if it is to develop reverence in worship and give proper Christian training and ideals. Sometimes the church is located so that it is difficult to make any appeal to the students to attend. In some places relocation and rebuilding has shown marked good results.

A student group is not strengthened when several congregations make counter-efforts to attract and serve it. While students naturally have liberty in choosing their church home, pastors and *congregations should co-operate and agree on program and leadership.*

Strange as it may seem, it is possible for a *pastor* over a period of years *to fail to see his opportunity* for service to students. Occasionally congregations have called pastors who lack personal qualifications to serve young people and students. The inevitable result is a growing chasm between the campus and the Church and the loss of faculty as well as students.

In states where there are several synods, one synod or one congregation cannot deal adequately with a large group of students coming from congregations of the different synods. In one such state institution the advancement of good work among students has waited the necessary financial *co-operation of all the synods* concerned. But, because the congregation necessarily belonged to one of the synods, it has been impossible to arouse the interest of the others in the situation sufficiently to secure this co-operation. On the other hand, in a metropolitan area in the same state, the co-operation of two of the synods has made possible an outstanding place of work with students.

In several great middle western states *co-operation of various general Lutheran bodies* whose students attend the state institutions, has been ineffective or entirely lacking. In such places our student work is compared unfavorably with the work of foundations of other Churches with their imposing buildings and salaried staff. Our students have not been attracted because work with Lutheran students appears weak by contrast, divided and sometimes even hostile. Nevertheless, the relative proportion of our students reached in spite of these handicaps makes a direct challenge to the Lutherans of America to effect better co-operation at least in this important field.

In *large metropolitan centers* like Boston, New York, Philadelphia, Los Angeles, the problem is to integrate for effective service, groups of students on many campuses, several congregations in co-operation with the synods involved, and the Board of Education. In two of these centers, Boston and Philadelphia, the problem is being solved with vigor and success.

III. PROMOTION AND PUBLICITY

Practically all the work of the Board and of its staff has some promotional or publicity value in the field of Christian higher education: in the individual parishes; among students in all kinds of institutions of higher learning; for our own colleges and seminaries; and in behalf of the United Lutheran Church to the general public. A few avenues of influence not previously referred to may properly be mentioned here.

1. Co-operative Contacts

With the Lutheran Augustana Synod of North America

The Rev. G. A. Brandelle, D.D., president of the Augustana Synod, continues a valued advisory member of our Board. This synod has continued its co-operation in work with Lutheran students at non-Lutheran institutions by contributing a total of $4,400 during the biennium.

With the Suomi Synod

In accordance with the action of the Church in the 1930 Convention with regard to seeking "all possible co-operation with the Suomi Synod," the Board authorized its executive secretary to ascertain what this Board might do. Upon invitation from the president of Suomi College and Seminary, a visit was made to that institution. Addresses were delivered to the college students, seminary students, and extended conferences held with President Wargelin, of the college, and President Haapenen of the synod.

Several years ago this Board paid the salary of a teacher in the Theological Seminary. Because of certain conditions within the synod this arrangement ceased. The Board will look with favor upon the renewal of this co-operative plan when the Suomi Synod desires to initiate it.

A distinct piece of service was rendered Suomi College by having our colleges agree to admit the outstanding students from that college without examination. Carthage and Wittenberg have had students from Suomi and find that they have done satisfactory work and are of a desirable type.

With the Icelandic Synod

This Board co-operates with the Icelandic Synod by giving the Jon Bjarnason Academy, located at Winnipeg, Canada, an annual grant. The institution was visited by the executive secretary and extended conferences were held with the officials. The inspector of Secondary Schools in Manitoba has highly commended the institution both for its successful work in academic instruction and for the wholesome atmosphere which prevails. He would greatly regret the closing of the institution, "if such step became necessary, due to financial stress or for other reasons."

With the National Lutheran Educational Conference

The executive secretary of our Board has been secretary of this Conference for the past three years and renders important service in planning for the annual meeting and preparing and distributing the proceedings. In addition, he directs the Teachers' Bureau for the Conference in which Lutheran men and women with a Master's or Doctor's degree may register. Their names and qualifications are then sent to all the institutions enrolled in the Conference. In this manner, and also through private correspondence, the office has enabled Lutheran institutions to obtain valuable teachers.

With the Council of Church Boards of Education

This is a co-ordinating agency of more than twenty Protestant Church Boards of Education. During the biennium all members of the staff served on such important committees as the executive committee, college committee, university committee; and in addition, Miss Markley was vice-president, 1930-31, and the executive secretary was president in 1931-32.

2. Promotional Activities

The Day of Prayer for Students in Colleges and Seminaries

Prior to the Reformation Seasons, the Board sent to all pastors packets containing two large posters and folders with the following titles: "The Work of the Board of Education;" "A Catechism on Higher Education;" "Why I became a Minister;" "Would You Do It Again?" by Dr. G. W. Nicely; and "Luther's Contribution to Education," by Dr. R. B. Peery. About 215,000 pieces of these folders were sent gratis to the pastors at their request—about twelve and one-half per cent of all United Lutheran pastors. These pastors were distributed in thirty-five states, including Canada, and twenty-five synods.

Articles Published

An informed Church is generally a responsive Church. Definite efforts are made to keep the Church aware of the educational situation in our institutions and of educational problems confronting the Church. The many articles prepared by the staff have appeared in *The Lutheran, The Parish School, Lutheran Woman's Work, New York Women's Missionary Society Bulletin, The News Bulletin of the National Lutheran Council, The American Lutheran Student, The Bond,* and *Christian Education.*

Service to Local Parishes

While the printed word is a valable medium for the transmission of inspiration, the spoken word is a more effective means. During the biennium, the staff has been in an average of more than one different church a Sunday, speaking at the Church service, the Sunday school, and Young Peoples' organizations. In these addresses the secretaries tell the story of the work of the Board and show how it is co-ordinated with the work of other Boards and agencies and its vital significance in the development of the Church.

Conferences and Conventions

By the very size of the Church it is impossible for the staff of any Board to reach during a biennium all congregations, but it is possible to reach a large portion of the Church through attendance at conferences and conventions. The Board's staff and representatives have visited nineteen different synods, four synodical conferences, twenty-two missionary conventions, four Luther League conventions, six summer schools, nineteen student conferences, and sixteen national educational conferences.

IV. SEARCH AND RESEARCH

"It shall have authority to prepare general surveys of educational standards; to investigate any phase of educational work, and make recommendations to institutions and synods."—(Constitution—Article VIII.)

The projects for special study this biennium have grown out of the recurring and continuing problems of importance in the very life of the Church—the enlistment of the finest type of young men for the Ministry, the religious atmosphere and life at our Church colleges, and the program of education for every member of the Church—young and old.

1. Ministerial Candidates and Education

The object of this Board shall be—"stimulate the supply of candidates for the ministry, to administer the work of ministerial education for co-operating synods."

One of the important features of the work of the Board of Education has always been seeking out and helping young men to prepare for the Holy Ministry. It is gratifying to observe how eager and effective the work of our synods and seminaries has been in this field. The responsibility of maintaining the Church's ministry rests particularly upon the local pastor and the synod. However, the United Lutheran Church is one Church. No synod is composed solely of pastors who were reared and educated on its own territory. Men come to our seminaries from all parts of the Church and graduates of our seminaries move freely from synod to synod. There is, therefore, an important place for the work of the Board of Education in co-ordinating and rendering most effective the work of the synods and seminaries.

With a view to functioning in this field more adequately, during the biennium of 1928-1930, careful detailed study was made of the methods used by the various synods in granting financial aids to pre-ministerial students. The result of the study was the presentation to the United Lutheran Church Convention in 1930, of a Church Scholarship Plan. (Minutes of Seventh Biennial Convention, pp. 352-367.) The following resolution was passed:

"That the uniform plan of giving grants to students by synods, as prepared by the secretarial staff of the Board of Education, be approved by the United Lutheran Church in America, and recommended for adoption by the respective synods, with such modifications as may be deemed wise to fit the conditions of the various synods, so that this work of the Church may be continued on a more efficient and effective basis." (Minutes of 1930 Convention, p. 396).

It was further moved:

"That the Board of Education be requested to study the question still further and to bring up at the Convention, two years hence, any additional suggestions that seem to be wise and good for the guidance of synodical boards of ministerial education." (Minutes of 1930 Convention, p. 407).

Up to July 1, 1932, *twelve* synods have reported concerning their action relative to the Church Scholarship Plan: *one* has not considered it because it had recently worked out a new plan for itself; *eleven* have accepted or are considering it with favor in the proper committee of synod.

The synods reporting have indicated that in the year 1931 the amount devoted to ministerial education through individual student grants or Church Scholarships amounted to $123,998.

For growing effectiveness in finding, enlisting and assisting young men as candidates for the gospel ministry, the Board of Education has taken action requesting every synod of the United Lutheran Church to appoint a standing committee on the ministry or so to arrange their present boards or committees relating to the work of the ministry that it may be possible through the Board of Education to co-ordinate and develop this work according to the needs of the Church. The Board has suggested to the synods that the functions of the Standing Committee on the Ministry should be:

1. To undertake an educational program by which the parents and boys of the Church would know what the functions of the Ministry are, what preparation is required, and how the Church is ready to aid those who seek to make this preparation.

2. Definitely to seek out boys qualified for the ministry and to enroll them in proper preparation for this office. Both these functions would be carried out through the issuing of printed matter, conferences and personal work.

3. To direct young men willing to prepare themselves for the ministry, so that they would have the best general preparation; and those especially qualified for service in particular fields, it would direct in such specializations.

4. In addition, to study constantly the needs of the synod in order to direct men to make such special preparations as might be needed, and for which they might be qualified, so that the Church might have a well-balanced and sufficient supply of ministers for the pastorate and other special fields of work.

5. In all these activities to cultivate the closest possible contact and co-operation with the college and seminary representatives to whom special responsibilities in the recruiting and directing of young men for the ministry may be committed.

6. Finally, to carry out the Church Scholarship Plan, ministerial education aid, on the territory of synod and in connection with the seminaries or colleges to which the synod's students would go.

On its part the Board of Education is prepared, through its Student Division, to co-operate with synodical committees on the ministry in preparing printed matter, in stimulating the recruiting of men for the ministry, and in presenting the needs of the whole Church for pastors; and **to** co-ordinate the work of the synodical committees on the ministry.

Eight synods have taken favorable action and appointed such a standing committee on the ministry. Other synods have informed the Board that they favor the plan but believe that they can co-operate through their present agencies in the work suggested. **(See Recommendation 1).**

2. Religious Life At Our Church Colleges

The Board authorized the study of the religious life of students in the colleges of our Church, and accordingly a "Questionnaire on Religious Life of Students in the Colleges of the United Lutheran Church as Expressed in Curricula and Extra Curricula Activities," was sent to the fourteen colleges. The purpose of this study was to ascertain the changes which had taken place, so far as they could be quantitatively ascertained since the period of the survey of higher education. It is with considerable pleasure that we report the following evidences of distinct development in the religious activities at our colleges.

Religious Courses

In 1928 the thirteen four-year colleges offered sixty-seven courses in religion and related subjects. In 1930-31, these same colleges offered one hundred twenty-two courses in Bible and religious education alone. This is an increase of 82 per cent. If we were to include related subjects, the increase would be more than 100 per cent.

Some of these subjects are: Old Testament; New Testament; Bible History; Life of Christ; Between the Testaments; Christianity as History; Apostolic Age; Bible Survey; Christian Doctrine; Christianity and Modern Thought; Lutheran Fundamentals; Christian Sociology; History of Religious Education; Principles of Religious Education; Catechetics; the Sunday school—its organization and administration; Curriculum and Program of Religious Education, and Christian Ethics.

These departments of Bible and religious education have increased in size and professional rating. When new teachers are secured, they are selected on the basis of scholastic ability and training, and Christian character.

The colleges are increasing the number of hours of religious study required for graduation. It is not implied that students will necessarily become more religious through the taking of subjects, but it is asserted that no student can graduate at one of our colleges, after taking two or more courses in some religious subject, without having received some very definite and positive impression of the significance of religion in general and of Christianity in particular.

Religious Activities and Organizations

Courses are not the only means whereby our colleges develop the religious life of the students. There are various organizations and student activities such as Luther League, Student Volunteers, Lutheran Student Association,

Young Men's Christian Association, Young Women's Christian Association, Ministerial Association, Mission Study Groups, Bible Study Groups, Gospel Teams, and last but not least, chapel.

Daily chapel is maintained at all the colleges except one which has it weekly. Attendance is compulsory with one exception. The chapel services have singing, Bible reading, prayer, and an address on some topic of religion, ethics, social or political import. Generally, the address is an application of the Gospel of Christ to the particular topic. The cause of missions, the challenge of the ministry and other professions, and many other moral and religious subjects are presented. The effect of this experience of having faculties and students think together on these great subjects is often most dynamic. Some think of the chapel service as the most powerful twenty minutes of the day's work.

On Sunday the students attend church services somewhere in the community. Many of them participate in some form of Sunday school or other religious organization work. At one of the colleges there are five teams who visit communities presenting in song and address the Gospel message. And during the week there are the meetings of the various student organizations mentioned above.

Religion All Day Long

It is suggested that perhaps the most potent religious influence of our colleges may be found in the contacts of students and professors in the classrooms and in private conference. Most of the courses offer opportunity for Christian interpretation. Many students testify that their lives have been greatly changed by the Christian influence of a professor of mathematics, or of history, or of philosophy, or of languages, or of biology.

The colleges are recognizing this fact and are increasing the number of student advisors. The scope of their work and responsibilities is increased. In this way there is the sincere attempt to let the college function in *loco parentis*.

The study of the religious life at our colleges reveals that they are providing, to an increasing degree, for the religious guidance and development of the students. These provisions are receiving increasingly primary consideration, and are not matters of incidental occurrence.

3. Correlated Educational Program

According to the action of the United Lutheran Church, in Convention at Milwaukee, the Parish and Church School Board was instructed to gather from the various Boards and agencies of the Church, "all possible information pertaining to the educational program of the parish," "it being understood that in the formulation of the plan, the Board of Education, through a special committee. shall furnish all possible information concerning policies, programs and curricula of the higher educational institutions of the United

Lutheran Church in America as they affect the educational program of the parish." The request for the information needed from the Board of Education was received from the Parish and Church School Board, in May, 1932. On the basis of their request, questionnaires were immediately formulated in the office of the Board of Education and sent to the colleges and seminaries. Commencement activities made it difficult for the institutions to send prompt replies. Due to the amount of time that necessarily has been consumed by the Parish and Church School Board in gathering data and putting it into proper form, it is impossible for the Board of Education to present, at the 1932 Convention of the Church, "an inclusive educational plan for the Church which will include the educational plan for the parish as formulated by the Parish and Church School Board." (Minutes of the 1930 Convention.)

V.   ADMINISTRATION

1.   Board Personnel

The following constituted the officers and membership of the Board for the biennium:

Officers:
    President—Rev. H. R. Gold, D.D.
    Vice-President—Professor Hugo C. M. Wendel, Ph.D.
    Secretary—Rev. Gould Wickey, Ph. D., D.D.
    Treasurer—Thomas P. Hickman.

Members:
    Terms expiring 1932—Rev. C. H. Stein, D.D., Rev. G. M. Diffenderfer, D. D., Mr. J. H. Dingle, Mr. C. J. Driever, Rev. Paul H. Krauss, D.D., Prof. Ralph D. Owen, Ph.D., Prof. Hugo C. M. Wendel, Ph.D.

    Terms expiring 1934—The Rev. E. C. Herman, D.D., Dean Adelaide Burge, Mr. W. J. Showalter, Sc.D., LL.D., Hon. Charles Steele, Rev. A. A. Zinck, D.D., S.T.D., Rev. H. H. Bagger, Rev. M. L. Stirewalt, D.D.

    Terms expiring 1936—Henry W. Bikle, Esq., LL.D., Rev. H. J. Black, D.D., Rev. H. R. Gold, D.D., Rev. F. K. Fretz, Ph.D., D.D., Rev. W. H. Greever, D.D., Mr. Frederick Henrich, Prof. R. S. Saby, Ph.D.

    The Rev. C. H. Stein, D.D., was elected by the Executive Board to fill the unexpired term of the Rev. C. R. Bowers, D.D., who resigned during the biennium.

Advisory Members:
    Rev. G. A. Brandelle, D.D., Mrs. C. E. Gardner, Mrs. A. Pohlman.

Committees:
    Executive—The officers, together with the Rev. E. C. Herman, D.D., Mr. W. J. Showalter, Sc.D., LL.D., and Prof. Ralph D. Owen, Ph.D.

Institutions—Rev. A. A. Zinck, D.D., S.T.D., Rev. H. H. Bagger, Rev. M. L. Stirewalt, D.D., Rev. H. J. Black, D.D.

Student Work—Rev. Paul H. Krauss, D.D., Rev. G. M. Diffenderfer, D.D., Rev. W. H. Greever, D.D., Rev. C. H. Stein, D.D., Dean Adelaide Burge, Mrs. A. Pohlman, Mrs. C. E. Gardner.

Public Relations—Mr. W. J. Showalter, ScD., LL.D., Rev. E. C. Herman, D.D., Hon. Charles Steele.

Research—Prof. Hugo C. M. Wendel, Ph.D., Professor R. S. Saby, Ph.D., Prof. Ralph D. Owen, Ph.D., Rev. F. K. Fretz, Ph.D., D.D.

Investments—Mr. H. W. Bikle, LL.D., Mr. C. J. Driever, Mr. J. H. Dingle, Mr. Frederick Henrich.

2. Board Nominations

The nominations of the Board for the terms which expire at this Convention are the following:

Clergy	Synod
*Rev. G. M. Diffenderfer, D.D., Carlisle, Pa.	Maryland Synod
*Rev. P. H. Krauss, D.D., Ft. Wayne, Ind.	Michigan Synod
*Rev. C. H. Stein, D.D., Lock Haven, Pa.	Susquehanna Synod
Rev. W. H. Traub, D.D., Omaha, Nebr.	Nebraska Synod

Lay	
Mr. L. C. Hassinger, Bristol, Va.	Virginia Synod
Mr. C. J. Driever, Chicago, Ill.	Illinois Synod
*Prof. R. D. Owen, Ph.D., Philadelphia, Pa.	East Pennsylvania Synod

*Nominated to succeed himself.

3. Our Budget Problem

The expenditures of the Board were reduced from $135,000 in 1930-31 to $112,000 in 1931-32. The budget for the ensuing year has been prepared on the basis of an expected income of $100,000, allotting 55 per cent in grants to colleges and seminaries, 15 per cent to student centers, and 30 per cent to cover the service rendered to the institutions and the student centers in printing, travel, salaries, and also to include all administrative expenses.

This will mean a tremendous reduction in all grants and expenses. The Board has already reduced the salaries of the staff from ten to sixteen and two-thirds per cent. Our institutions and student centers are constantly urging larger grants and greater assistance. Lacking the income from apportionment, our only hope is that friends who see the vital importance of our work and the significant contributions which Christian higher education makes to the Church and civilization, will come to our aid with part of that with which they have been blessed.

VI. CONCLUSION AND RECOMMENDATIONS

The Board of Education recognizes the unfailing help of the great Head of the Church. We look with satisfaction upon the definite functioning of the survey in the life of the colleges and upon the increased service being rendered by the secretaries, both to the institutions and to the Church.

We face the future with the consciousness that we are living in a period of great opportunity for the cause of Christian higher education. Youth are seeking answers to their questions and hearing eagerly and sympathetically those who speak with conviction and experience. The great scientists of the day are declaring for the reality of a controlling power which is akin to our individual minds. The universe shows that there is "something else besides cyclonic storms of energy or dust-wreath swirls of matter." Our student pastors and the faculties of our colleges and seminaries are presenting the type of message which will satisfy the student mind, strengthen the character, and develop calmness of spirit. We pray for strength and wisdom to fulfill the responsibilities involved in such an opportunity.

The following recommendations are presented for your prayerful consideration:

1. *Synodical Committees on the Ministry*

Resolved, That every synod of the United Lutheran Church be requested to appoint a Standing Committee on the Ministry or so to arrange their present committees (or boards) relating to the work of the ministry that it may be possible, through the Board of Education, to co-ordinate and develop this work according to the needs of the Church.

2. *The Comprehensive Educational Plan for the Church*

Resolved, That the Board of Education be instructed to prepare and report to the next Convention a comprehensive educational plan for the Church which will include the educational program for the parish as formulated by the Parish and Church School Board.

Signed:

HOWARD R. GOLD, *President,*
GOULD WICKEY, *Secretary.*

REPORT OF THE TREASURER OF THE BOARD OF EDUCATION

CASH ACCOUNTS BY FUNDS
July 1, 1930, to June 30, 1931
GENERAL FUND

Balance, July 1, 1930 .... $13,169.75

RECEIPTS

Apportionment, United Lutheran Church $120,750.00
Women's Missionary Society 3,000.00
Contributions from Synods, etc. 4,823.16

Interest on Bank Balance 66.32
Refunds and Miscellaneous 179.86
                                                                                                  ——————— 128,819.34
                                                                                                  ————————
                                                                                                  $141,989.09

DISBURSEMENTS

Salaries:
   Secretaries $17,499.96
   Clerical 2,057.11
Services 223.46
Travel:
   Secretaries 5,316.66
   Board 1,315.31
Rent:
   Office 1,500.00
   Residence 1,200.00
Stationery 328.14
Equipment and Furniture 288.51
Telephone and Telegraph 368.63
Postage and Mailing 944.77
Printing and Publicity 2,913.61
Magazines and Books 189.21
Advertising 85.20
Legal and Auditing 233.64
Dues and Fees 750.34
Conferences 2,200.97
Miscellaneous 91.50
Grants, Seminaries and Colleges:
   Southern Seminary, Budget $2,499.96
   Chicago Seminary, Budget 2,499.96
   Chicago Seminary, Special 3.31
   Breklum-Kropp Seminary, Budget 6,000.00
   Breklum-Kropp Seminary, Special 1,590.00
   Hartwick Seminary, Budget 1,200.00
   Martin Luther Seminary, Budget 1,500.00
   Pacific Seminary, Budget 2,499.96
   Philadelphia Seminary, Special 9.31
   Northwestern Seminary, Special 5.00
   Saskatoon College and Seminary, Budget 6,999.96
   Saskatoon College and Seminary, Special 51.00
   Waterloo College and Seminary, Budget.... 4,999.92
   Midland College and Western Seminary,
     Budget 12,000.00
   Midland College and Western Seminary,
     Special 2,000.00
   Newberry College, Budget 5,400.00
   Roanoke College, Budget 3,499.92
   Wagner College, Budget 2,499.96
   Susquehanna University, Budget 3,000.00
   Thiel College, Budget 2,499.96
   Lenoir Rhyne, Budget 3,499.92
   Gettysburg College, Budget 1,200.00
   Wittenberg College, Budget 1,200.00
   Muhlenberg College, Budget 1,200.00

Hartwick College, Budget	999.96	
Marion Junior College, Budget	999.96	
Collegiate Institute, Budget	499.92	
Jon Bjarnason Academy and College, Budget	1,999.92	
		$72,357.90
Budgets	68,699.28	
Specials	3,658.62	
	$72,357.90	

Grants, Student Centers (Budget) :

California, Berkeley	$500.00
California, Los Angeles	500.00
Colorado, University	500.00
Illinois, University	733.32
Illinois, Northwestern	500.00
Illinois, Chicago U.	500.00
Illinois, Chicago City	600.00
Illinois, Macomb S. T. C.	50.00
Indiana, Purdue	400.00
Iowa, University	500.00
Iowa, Cedar Falls S. T. C.	100.00
Kansas, University	400.00
Kansas, State College	300.00
Michigan, University	600.00
Michigan, Kalamazoo, S. T. C.	100.00
Minnesota, University	1,000.00
Nebraska, University	600.00
Nebraska, Grace Church (Lincoln)............	500.00
New York Synod Student Work, Boston Area	2,799.96
New York City Metropolitan Area	915.85
North Carolina, University	112.50
North Carolina, State College	33.33
North Carolina, Duke University	100.00
North Carolina, College for Women	50.00
North Carolina, Boone S. T. C.	25.00
Ohio Synod Student Work	183.00
Oregon, University	300.00
Oregon, L. S. A. A.	1,000.00
Pennsylvania, Philadelphia Area	3,000.00
Pennsylvania, State College	800.00
Pennsylvania, West Chester S. T. C.............	800.00
South Carolina, State College	150.00
South Carolina, College for Women	500.00
Virginia, V. P. I.	116.66
Washington University	800.00
Washington, D. C., Metropolitan Area....	50.00
West Virginia, University	600.00
Wisconsin, University	2,000.00
Wyoming, University	250.00
Lutheran Student Association	500.00
Miscellaneous Points	91.14
	$23,560.76

Deficit—Annuities 537.96
Deficit—Breklum-Kropp Student Aid 1,032.82
—————$134,996.46

Balance on Hand, June 30, 1931 ....**$6,992.63

SCHOLARSHIP AND LOAN FUND FOR WOMEN

	Income	Principal Fund Cash	Investments
Balance, July 1, 1930	$143.88	$1,584.61	$5,907.18

RECEIPTS
Income on Investments	318.80	
Gifts and Contributions	200.00	
Transferred from Principal Fund	584.61	584.61
	$1,247.29	$1,000.00

DISBURSEMENTS
Loaned to Women $800.00

Balance, June 30, 1931 .... $447.29 $1,000.00 $5,907.18

CALIFORNIA COLLEGE
Balance, July 1, 1930 and June 30, 1931 .... $60.00

LUTHERAN WOMEN'S COLLEGE
Balance, July 1, 1930 .... $1,993.65

DISBURSEMENTS
Transferred to Grace College $1,993.65

Balance, June 30, 1931 .... None

BREKLUM-KROPP STUDENT AID FUND
Balance, July 1, 1930 .... None

RECEIPTS
Gifts and Contributions $120.33

DISBURSEMENTS
Loaned to Students $1,153.15
Deficit to General Fund 1,032.82
——————— $120.33

Balance, June 30, 1931 .... None

ANNUITY FUND

	Income	Principal Fund Cash	Investments
Balance, July 1, 1930		$458.13	$61,286.70

**Includes $476.57 advanced traveling expenses.

RECEIPTS

Bequests, Bonds and Notes			$10,000.00
Bequests, Cash		$500.00	
Income on Investments	$3,761.22		
Deficit (from General Fund)	537.96		
	$4,299.18	$958.13	

DISBURSEMENTS

Paid to Annuitants	$4,285.15		
Investment for Principal Fund		$668.75	$668.75
Balance, June 30, 1931	$14.03	$289.38	$71,955.45

PERMANENT MINISTERIAL EDUCATION FUND

		Principal Fund	
	Income	Cash	Investments
Balance, July 1, 1930	$231.44	$480.97	$7,425.00

RECEIPTS

Bequest		$373.20	
Income on Investments	$494.21		
	$725.65	$854.17	

DISBURSEMENTS

Transportation Paid	$635.00		
Investment for Principal Fund		$73.75	$73.75
Balance, June 30, 1931	$90.65	$780.42	$7,498.75

INVESTMENTS

ANNUITY FUND

Bonds:	Book Values
$8,000 Altoona & Logan Valley Elec. Rwy. 4½s, 1933	$6,400.00
5,000 Appalachian Electric Power Co. 5s, 1956	4,950.00
2,000 Associated Gas and Electric 5½s, 1938	2,000.00
4,000 Baltimore and Ohio R. R., S. W. Div. 5s, 1950.	4,055.00
2,000 Baltimore and Ohio R. R. 5s, 1948....................	1,975.00
6,500 Bell Telephone Co. of Pa. 5s, 1948.....................	6,395.00
1,000 Burlington Realty Trust 5½s, 1935 (Boston Parcel Post Station)	980.00
1,000 Chelsea Hotel Co. 6s, 1945	1,000.00
1,000 Chesapeake & Ohio R. R. 5s, 1935	969.67
3,000 Georgia Power Co. 5s, 1967	2,943.75
2,000 Lackawanna & Wyoming Valley R. R. 5s, 1951.	1,935.00
1,000 Minnesota Power and Light 5s.	1,000.00
1,000 Pennsylvania R. R. Equipment 5s, 1934............	992.26
2,000 Pennsylvania R. R. Equipment 5s, 1935............	1,965.60
3,000 Pennsylvania R. R. Equipment 5s, 1938............	2,974.80
1,000 Phila. Electric Co. 5½s, 1947	1,030.00
4,600 Phila. Electric Co. 5s, 1966	4,574.37
3,500 Phila. Electric Power Co. 5½s, 1972	3,631.25
2,000 Phila. Suburban Water Co. 5s, 1955	1,955.00

5,000 Quaker City Tank Line Equipment 5½s, 1934	5,000.00	
4,000 United Post Offices Corporation 5½s. 1935	4,000.00	
2,500 Washington Gas Light Company Gen'l Mortgage 5s	2,668.75	

Stocks:
13 shares Western Union Telegraph Co.	1,560.00	

Ground Rents:
Ground rent on 1019—15th St., N. W., Washington, D. C., 6%	7,000.00	
		$71,955.45

SCHOLARSHIP AND LOAN FUND FOR WOMEN

Bonds:
$1,000 Associated Gas and Electric Co. 5½s, 1938	$1,000.00	
1,000 Chesapeake & Ohio R. R. 5s, 1935	969.68	
1,000 Lackawanna & Wyoming Valley R. R. Co. 5s, 1951	967.50	
3,000 Westmoreland Water Co. 5s, 1952	2,970.00	
		5,907.18
		$77,862.63

PERMANENT MINISTERIAL EDUCATION FUND

Bonds:
$1,000 Appalachian Electric Power Co. 5s. 1956	$990.00	
500 Fort Spring Magisterial Dist., Greenbrier Co., State of West Virginia Road Bonds, 5s, 1936	500.00	
1,000 Illinois Post Office Bldg. Corp, Chicago Ave. Station—Post Office 5½s, 1932	1,000.00	
2,000 Lackawanna & Wyoming Valley R. R. 5s, 1951	1,935.00	
1,000 Phila. Electric Power Co. 5½s, 1972	1,022.50	
1,000 Phila. Suburban Water Co. 5s, 1955	977.50	
1,000 Washington Gas Light Co. Gen'l Mortgage 5s	1,073.75	
		$7,498.75
		$85,361.38

BALANCE SHEET

June 30, 1932

ASSETS

Cash in Bank	$4,850.55	
Investments at ledger values (as annexed)	88,491.94	
Furniture and Office Equipment	2,260.02	
		$95,602.51

FUNDS

General Fund	$6,358.59
Annuity Fund	70,244.83
Endowment Fund	1,000.00
Permanent Ministerial Education Fund	10,779.17

Scholarship and Loan Fund for Women 7,159.92
California College Fund 60.00
                                                                                    $95,602.51

CASH ACCOUNTS BY FUNDS

July 1, 1931, *to June* 30, 1932

GENERAL FUND

Balance, July 1, 1931 .... $6,516.06

RECEIPTS
Apportionment, United Lutheran Church $103,450.00
Women's Missionary Society 3,000.00
Augustana Synod 1,700.00
Gifts and Contributions 255.59
Refunds, Interest, etc. 731.86
Transfer from Permanent Ministerial Education Fund.. 311.00
                                                                                    109,448.45

                                                                                    $115,964.51

DISBURSEMENTS
Administration:
Secretaries Salaries $1,395.85
Clerical Salaries 729.86
Services 103.20
Secretaries Travel 11.86
Board Travel 998.28
Stationery and Supplies 377.07
Equipment and Furniture 377.13
Telephone and Telegraph 114.15
Postage and Mailing 158.99
Printing and Publication 2.39
Magazines and Books 51.00
Insurance 64.00
Rent 2,100.00
Auditing 290.85

                                                                                    $6,774.63

Institutions:
  Salaries $2,479.85
  Expenses 501.55
                                                                          2,981.40

Student Service:
  Salaries $8,666.42
  Expenses 3,916.44
                                                                          12,582.86

Promotion:
  Salaries $5,053.64
  Expenses 4,121.32
                                                                          9,174.96

Grants, Seminaries and Colleges:
(Budget)

Southern Seminary	$2,374.98
Chicago Seminary	2,374.98
Breklum-Kropp Seminary	1,500.00
Hartwick Seminary	1,140.00
Martin Luther Seminary	1,425.00
Pacific Seminary	2,374.98
Saskatoon College and Seminary	6,999.96
Waterloo College and Seminary	4,999.92
Midland College and Western Seminary	10,275.00
Newberry College	4,560.00
Roanoke College	2,850.00
Wagner College	1,425.00
Susquehanna University	2,850.00
Thiel College	2,850.00
Lenoir Rhyne	2,850.00
Gettysburg College	499.98*
Wittenberg College	949.98
Muhlenberg College	499.98*
Carthage College	949.98
Hartwick College	949.98
Marion Junior College	949.98
Jon Bjarnason Academy and College	1,899.96
	$57,549.66

Grants, Student Centers (Budget):

California, Berkeley	$462.50
California, Los Angeles	475.00
Colorado, University	462.50
Idaho, University	29.15
Illinois, University	760.00
Illinois, Northwestern	362.50
Illinois, Chicago U.	475.00
Illinois, Chicago City	570.00
Illinois, Macomb S. T. C.	45.00
Indiana, Purdue	380.00
Iowa, University	475.00
Iowa, Cedar Falls S. T. C.	95.00
Kansas, University	285.00
Kansas, State College	217.50
Kansas, Emporia	41.00
Michigan, University	540.00
Michigan, Kalamazoo S. T. C.	47.50
Minnesota, University	925.00
Nebraska, University	462.50
Nebraska, Grace Church (Lincoln)	380.00
New York Synod Student Work Boston Area	2,659.98
New York City Metropolitan Area	290.15
North Carolina, University	285.00
North Carolina, State College	285.00
North Carolina, Duke University	215.00

*Released half year's grant in favor of Canadian institutions.

North Carolina, College for Women 25.00
North Carolina, Boone S. T. C. 25.00
Ohio Synod Student Work 665.00
Oregon, University 190.00
Oregon, L. S. A. A. 950.00
Pennsylvania, Philadelphia Area 2,850.00
Pennsylvania, State College 730.00
Pennsylvania, West Chester S. T. C. 760.00
Pennsylvania, Slippery Rock S. T. C. 25.00
South Carolina, State College 151.60
South Carolina, College for Women 391.66
Virginia, V. P. I. 332.50
Washington, University 760.00
Washington, D. C., Metropolitan Area......   50.00
West Virginia, University 570.00
Wisconsin, University 1,900.00
Wyoming, University 237.50
Canada, Saskatoon 25.00
Lutheran Student Association 450.00
Miscellaneous Points 35.00
                                                        ——————— $22,348.54
Transfer to Annuity Fund 453.89
                                                        ——————— 111,865.94

Balance on Hand, June 30, 1932 .... $4,098.57

SCHOLARSHIP AND LOAN FUND FOR WOMEN

| | | Principal Fund | |
	Income	Cash	Investments
Balance, July 1, 1931	$447.29	$1,000.00	$5,907.18

RECEIPTS

Income on Investments	$397.95		
Principal Fund		$245.24	
	$845.24	$1,245.24	

DISBURSEMENTS

Investment for Principal		$1,000.00	$1,007.50
To Students	$590.00		
Accrued Interest on Investment	10.00		
To Principal Fund	245.24		
	$845.24		
Balance, June 30, 1932	....	$245.24	$6,914.68

CALIFORNIA COLLEGE

Balance, July 1, 1931 and June 30, 1932 .... $60.00

ANNUITY FUND

| | | Principal Fund | |
	Income	Cash	Investments
Balance, July 1, 1931	$14.03	$289.38	$71,955.45

RECEIPTS

Income on Investments	$3,852.00		
Annuity Purchased		$500.00	
Securities Sold or Matured		4,530.00	4,530.00
Securities Transferred		2,668.75	2,668.75
Transfer from General Fund	453.89		
	$4,319.92	$7,988.13	$64,756.70

DISBURSEMENTS

Paid to Annuitants	$4,285.51		
Accrued Interest on Securities Purchased	34.41		
Investment for Principal Fund		5,111.81	5,111.81
Transfer to Permanent Ministerial Education Fund		2,500.00	
	$4,319.92	$7,611.81	
Balance, June 30, 1932	....	$376.32	$69,868.51

PERMANENT MINISTERIAL EDUCATION FUND

		Principal Fund	
	Income	Cash	Investments
Balance, July 1, 1931	$90.65	$780.42	$7,498.75

RECEIPTS

Income on Investments	$447.00		
Refund	5.50		
Transfer from Annuity Fund		2,500.00	
	$543.15	$3,280.42	

DISBURSEMENTS

To Students	$227.50		
Investment for Principal Fund		$3,210.00	$3,210.00
Accrued Interest on Investment	4.65		
To General Fund	311.00		
	$543.15		
Balance, June 30, 1932	....	$70.42	$10,708.75

ENDOWMENT FUND

	Principal Fund
Balance, July 1, 1931	....

RECEIPTS

Note—Lutheran College and Seminary, Saskatoon (Secured by $1,000.00 Liberty Loan, 4th, 4¼s	$1,000.00
	$1,000.00

DISBURSEMENTS

None	....
Balance, June 30, 1932	$1,000.00

INVESTMENTS
ANNUITY FUND

Bonds: Book Values

$8,000 Altoona and Logan Valley Elec. Rwy. 4½s, 1933	6,400.00
5,000 Appalachian Electric Power Co. 5s, 1956	4,950.00
2,000 Associated Gas & Electric Co. 5½s, 1938	2,000.00
4,000 Baltimore and Ohio Railroad, S. W. Div. 5s, 1950	4,055.00
2,000 Baltimore and Ohio Railroad 5s, 1948	1,975.00
6,500 Bell Telephone Co. of Penna. 5s, 1948	6,395.00
1,000 Burlington Realty Trust 5½s, 1935 (Boston Parcel Post Station)	980.00
1,000 Chelsea Hotel Co. 6s, 1945	1,000.00
1,000 Chesapeake and Ohio R. R. 5s, 1935	969.67
3,000 Georgia Power Co. 5s, 1967	2,943.75
2,000 Lackawanna and Wyoming Valley R. R. 5s, 1951	1,935.00
3,500 Liberty Loan Fourth 4¼s, 1938	3,587.81
1,000 Minnesota Power and Light 5s, 1955	1,000.00
1,000 Penna. R. R. Equipment 5s, 1934	992.26
2,000 Penna. R. R. Equipment 5s, 1935	1,965.60
3,000 Penna. R. R. Equipment 5s, 1938	2,974.80
4,600 Philadelphia Electric Co. 5s, 1966	4,574.37
3,500 Philadelphia Electric Power Co., 5½s, 1972	3,631.25
2,000 Philadelphia Suburban Water Co. 5s, 1955	1,955.00
5,000 Quaker City Tank Line Equipment, 5½s, 1934	5,000.00
4,000 United Post Office Corp. 5½s, 1935	4,000.00
1,500 Western Electric 5s, 1944	1,524.00

Stocks:

13 shares Western Union Telegraph Co.	1,560.00

Ground Rent:

1019—15th Street, N. W., Washington, D. C., 6 per cent	3,500.00

$69,868.51

SCHOLARSHIP AND LOAN FUND FOR WOMEN
Bonds:

$1,000 Associated Gas and Electric Co. 5½s, 1938	$1,000.00
1,000 Chesapeake and Ohio R. R. 5s, 1935	969.68
1,000 Lackawanna and Wyoming R. R. Co. 5s, 1951	967.50
3,000 Westmoreland Water Co. 5s, 1952	2,970.00
1,000 Western Electric 5s, 1944	1,007.50

$6,914.68

PERMANENT MINISTERIAL EDUCATION FUND
Bonds:

$1,000 Appalachian Electric Power Co. 5s, 1956	$990.00
500 Fort Spring Magisterial Dist., Greenbrier Co., State of West Virginia, Road Bonds, 5s, 1936	500.00
1,000 Illinois Post Office Bldg. Corp., Chicago Ave. Station Post Office 5½s, 1932	1,000.00

2,000 Lackawanna and Wyoming Valley R. R. 5s.
    1951 .... 1,935.00
1,000 Philadelphia Electric Power Co. 5½s, 1972 .... 1,022.50
1,000 Philadelphia Suburban Water Co. 5s, 1955.... 977.50
4,000 Washington Gas Light Co., Gen'l Mtge. 5s,
    1960 .... 4,283.75
                                       $10,708.75

ENDOWMENT FUND

$1,000 Note of Lutheran College and Seminary, Saskatoon,
    (Secured by $1,000 Liberty Loan Fourth 4¼s)............ $1,000.00

                                   $88,491.94

Respectfully submitted,
THOS. P. HICKMAN,
Treasurer.

Philadelphia, Pa.,
August 1, 1932.

We have audited the books of account of the Treasurer of the Board of Education of The United Lutheran Church in America, for the biennium beginning July 1, 1930 and ending June 30, 1932, and we hereby certify that in our opinion the foregoing statements of cash receipts and disbursements for the year ended June 30, 1931, and cash receipts and disbursements for the year ended June 30, 1932, together with balance sheet as of June 30, 1932, and the other statements transmitted herewith, are true and correct.

TAIT, WALKER AND BAKER,
Accountants and Auditors.

Dr. Gold introduced Mr. C. M. Distler, who addressed the Convention. The following Secretaries of the Board of Education then addressed the Convention: Miss Mildred Winston, the Rev. C. P. Harry, Dr. Mary E. Markley and the Rev. Gould Wickey.

Recommendation 1 was adopted.

Recommendation 2 was withdrawn by the President of the Board of Education because this matter was already covered by the action of the Convention on item IV, B, 7 (b) of the Executive Board's report.

It was moved and carried that the report of the auditors be accepted.

The report of the Committee on Plan of Apportionment was taken up as an item of unfinished business.

It was moved and carried that all the items in the proposed plan, together with the entire report, be referred to the synods for consideration at their next annual session, their actions thereupon to be reported to this Committee on Plan of Apportionment, which shall make recommendation to the next meeting of The United Lutheran Church in America.

The Rev. E. B. Burgess, Chairman of the Commission on Survey of Canadian Synods, addressed the Convention.

At twelve o'clock the Convention adjourned with prayer by the Rev. A. R. Wentz.

FOURTH SESSION

BENJAMIN FRANKLIN HOTEL.

Philadelphia, Pennsylvania.

Friday, October 14, 1932, 2.00 P. M.

Devotions were conducted by the Rev. W. A. Reiser, and the President called the Convention to order.

The election of a Secretary, which was a special order for this time, was by common consent postponed until after the hearing of the report of the Committee of Reference and Counsel.

The report of the Committee of Reference and Counsel was presented by the Rev. H. Brezing, Chairman of the Committee.

Report of the Committee of Reference and Counsel

1. Your Committee of Reference and Counsel being advised that the American Lutheran Church is at present assembled in convention at Fond du Lac, Wis., brings this fact officially to the attention of the United Lutheran Church and recommends the appointment of the Rev. Charles M. Jacobs to convey to the American Lutheran Church the greetings of this body.

2. A cablegram from Liberia reads: "Greeting to convention. Present crisis in Liberia calls for your continued sympathetic co-operation on behalf of church and mission. (Signed) Heilman." Your Committee recommends that we recognize this thoughtful greeting of our missionaries and instruct the President of the Board of Foreign Missions to assure them that the Church is going forward prayerfully and courageously with her missionary program.

3. The Rev. K. K. Olafson, President of the Icelandic Lutheran Synod, conveys by letter the greetings of his Synod to our body, expressing at the

same time appreciation for our work and for our sympathetic attitude toward the Icelandic Synod. We recommend that this communication be answered by our Secretary with assurances of hearty reciprocation of the greetings and felicitations.

4. The Luther League of the State of New York telegraphs greetings to the Convention. We recommend that the Chairman of the Committee on Associations of Young People be asked to acknowledge this greeting, assuring the Luther League of New York that we look with confidence to the young Christians of today in the expectation that they will carry on effectively the work of the Church tomorrow.

5. The Rev. L. L. Uhl, pioneer missionary of the Lutheran Church in India is present. We recommend that he be given an opportunity to address the Convention for five minutes in connection with the discussion of the report of the Board of Foreign Missions.

6. The Rev. E. W. Harner, Denver, Colo., asks permission to tell the Convention concerning the work of the National Lutheran Sanatorium for the tubercular. We recommend that five minutes be given him during the discussion period of the report of the Inner Mission Board.

7. Your Committee has received a request from the delegation of the Illinois and of the Wartburg Synod to recommend an appropriation of $5,000 for an exhibit in the Century of Progress Exposition to be held in Chicago next year. The Committee recommends that this request be referred to the Executive Board with power to act.

8. The Rev. G. A. Brandelle, representing the Augustana Synod, and the Rev. T. A. Kantonen, representing the Suomi Synod, are present to extend greetings. We recommend that the Convention hear them as the first order of business this afternoon.

9. Upon representations made to your Committee, we recommend that the report of the Representative to the American Bible Society be moved forward to this afternoon, and that our representative yield his time for presentation to Secretary G. W. Brown, of the American Bible Society, who is present on the floor of the Convention.

10. At the suggestion of the Committee on President's Report, we recommend that the presentation of its report be set for Monday afternoon immediately following the report of the Committee on Evangelism.

Item 1. The recommendation was adopted. The Rev. C. M. Jacobs was asked to prepare and send a greeting to the American

Lutheran Church now convened at Fond du Lac, Wis. Dr. Jacobs afterwards reported that the following greetings were sent:

"The United Lutheran Church in America, in convention assembled at Philadelphia, to the American Lutheran Church, assembled at Fond du Lac, Wis., sends greetings in Christ Jesus, our Lord.

"We render thanks to God for every consolidation of Lutheran Church bodies which furthers the cause of Jesus Christ and the progress of His Kingdom. We recognize in the American Lutheran Church a body so formed, which holds the same faith and subscribes the same Confessions as do we ourselves. We pray that the time may come when a fundamental unity of faith may break down all the barriers and destroy all the misunderstandings which now separate the Lutheran Church bodies of America and produce one great Church that will witness to all men the power of the Holy Spirit, through God's Word, to bring together those who are now apart. And we invoke God's blessing upon all labors, whether yours or ours, that are directed to this end."

Item 2. The recommendation was adopted. The Rev. S. W. Herman, President of the Board of Foreign Missions, was requested to respond to the greeting from Liberia.

Item 3. The recommendation was adopted and the Secretary was instructed to send greetings to the Icelandic Synod and to express our appreciation of the close relationship between our Church and the Icelandic Synod.

Item 4. The recommendation was adopted and the Chairman of the Committee on Associations of Young People was asked to acknowledge these greetings.

Item 5. The recommendation was adopted.

Item 6. The recommendation was adopted.

Item 7. The recommendation was adopted.

Item 8. The recommendation was adopted.

Item 9. The recommendation was adopted.

Item 10. The recommendation was adopted.

The Rev. G. A. Brandelle, President of the Augustana Synod, was then introduced and addressed the Convention. The Rev. L. S. Keyser responded to the address of Dr. Brandelle.

The Rev. T. A. Kantonen, representative of the Suomi Synod, was introduced and addressed the Convention. The Rev. H. R. Gold responded to the address of the Rev. Mr. Kantonen.

The Rev. H. C. Alleman presented the report of the Representative on the Advisory Committee of the American Bible

Society, and introduced the Rev. G. W. Brown, 'one of the General Secretaries of the American Bible Society, who addressed the Convention.

REPORT OF REPRESENTATIVE IN THE ADVISORY BOARD OF THE AMERICAN BIBLE SOCIETY

(For action on the recommendation in this report see p. 172.)

Your representative in the Advisory Board of the American Bible Society herewith submits his sixth biennial report.

Two meetings of the Board were held during our biennium. Your representative was present at the meeting, December 1, 1930, while Dr. E. B. Burgess represented the Church at the meeting, December 2, 1931. Full reports of these meetings were made in *The Lutheran.* It is necessary here only to call attention to the fact that the chief function of the Board is to consider the recommendations of the secretaries and the treasurer of the Society, and to submit its findings to the Board of Managers, with whom it is invited to sit throughout their consideration. The annual budget of the Society is over a million dollars. The Society has realized approximately a quarter of that amount from invested funds and rentals, about $200,000 from individual gifts and annuities, and upwards of $375,000 from sales. For the balance of $225,000 it must look to the Churches. In 1930, the Churches contributed $184,550, while 1931 showed a shrinkage to $166,048.

After an all-day meeting, December 2, 1931, the Advisory Council unanimously adopted the following resolutions and requested their reference to the several Churches:

The Advisory Council of the American Bible Society, made up of the officially appointed representatives of twenty-three different denominations holding to the evangelical faith, has listened with great interest to the story of the work done by the Society which, during the year 1930, carried on work in 285 languages and dialects and distributed more than twelve million Bibles, Testaments and Portions.

The translation, publication and distribution of the Scriptures is the common task of all the churches, for which no one denomination has either the resources or equipment. The churches of America, therefore, have entrusted the American Bible Society with the major task of providing the Scriptures for the fulfillment of this mission. All the denominations alike are dependent upon and make constant 'use of the work done by the American Bible Society. The prosecution of their missionary work would be severely handicapped without its invaluable assistance.

Since this is the common responsibility of all the churches, the agency approved by them as worthy should be supported in a manner adequate to the need and the opportunity. The Society is a national institution with an organization that is world-wide. To do its work effectively it must have the consistent and adequate support of all the churches. We as a Council recommend, therefore, to the Board and Officers of the Society that an approach be made to all the denominations here represented to secure continued co-operation and definite commitments on the part of all for the support and extension of this great work.

The methods that are most helpful in furnishing a substantial basis are: giving the Society a place in the denominational budget on a percentage basis; the voting of a specific sum by some boards of the denomination; or an annual offering on a fixed date. We pledge ourselves as representatives of our different churches to co-operate with the Society in every way possible in bringing these methods before our official bodies and urging upon them this duty.

We heartily endorse the way in which the work of the Society is administered, for it commends itself as conservative in financing and yet going forward unhesitatingly with plans for more and better work. We are greatly impressed with the sound basis provided for the protection of annuities, and we commend the administration for the wisdom and prudence thus manifested. We shall recommend this as a satisfying way to help extend the Kingdom and at the same time provide an income for old age.

We rejoice in the evidence submitted today that the management is alive to the importance not only of the distribution of the Scriptures but of getting men to read the Word. The various methods set forth before us we commend to the pastors of our churches as suggestions and helpful in the fulfilling of their own programs of work.

Though the Society has felt the pinch of the depression and consequently of reduced income, yet neither the quality nor extent of its work has been seriously affected. The loss of financial income is often a blessing in disguise when it leads to the development of other resources.

We wish to assure the Board and Secretaries that we regard their work as ours, and that they will have our continued sympathy, prayers, and earnest co-operation in the extension of the Kingdom of our Lord and Saviour Jesus Christ through the translation, publication and distribution of the Scriptures.

Yours in the fellowship and service of God in Christ,

Your representative recommends that the United Lutheran Church continue its representation in the Advisory Board of the American Bible Society.

Respectfully submitted,

HERBERT C. ALLEMAN.

The recommendation was adopted.

Committee of Tellers No. 1 was instructed to pass ballots for the election of a Secretary. The Rev. E. B. Burgess asked that the delegates refrain from voting for him as Secretary.

On motion the report of the Board of Ministerial Pensions and Relief was made a special order for five o'clock this afternoon.

The report of the Committee on Army and Navy Work was presented by the Rev. Wm. Freas, Secretary of the Committee.

REPORT OF THE COMMITTEE ON ARMY AND NAVY WORK

(For action on the recommendations in this report see p. 175.)

Your Committee on Army and Navy work carried over the organization of the previous biennium. The expense of meetings of the Committee was thus saved to the Church.

The committee has functioned through the Executive Committee composed of:

> Reverend Charles Trexler, D.D., *Chairman.*
> Reverend Wm. Freas, D.D., *Secretary.*
> Mr. Charles H. Dahmer.

This committee has held a number of meetings and considered applications for Chaplaincy and submitted plans to the members of the committee.

During the previous biennium practically all Lutheran applications for appointment to the Chaplaincy came to your committee. During this biennium, however, the National Lutheran Council, through its Executive Director, the Reverend Ralph H. Long, D.D., has become interested in this matter and applications for appointment to the Chaplaincy from members of other general bodies have gone to the National Lutheran Council for approval.

I. REGULAR CHAPLAINS

During the biennium two pastors of The United Lutheran Church in America have been appointed as regular army Chaplains. Both of these men have had the approval of your committee. In addition five applications for Chaplaincy appointment, three to the Army and two to the Navy have had the consideration and approval of the committee. Of these men two have been rejected because of failure in physical examination. One has been dropped by the Navy department from further consideration. Two applications still remain on file pending possible appointment.

There are at present nine Lutheran Chaplains serving in the Army, six of whom are members of The United Lutheran Church in America. There are four Lutheran Chaplains in the Navy, one of them a member of The United Lutheran Church in America.

II. RESERVE CHAPLAINS

Your committee has considered applications of three men for appointment in the Chaplains Reserve Corps of Army or Navy. These men have been approved by your committee and appointed as Reserve Chaplains. To the best of our knowledge there are at this time ninety-two Lutheran pastors who are members of the Chaplains Reserve. Fifty-six of this number are members of The United Lutheran Church in America. It is desirable that properly qualified pastors seek appointment in the Reserve Corps in either the Army or Navy.

III. CONTACTS WITH CHAPLAINS

The Chaplains by the very nature of their service are cut off to a large degree from fellowship with the Church. In the effort to remedy this isolation your committee has initiated regular correspondence with the Chaplains now in service. That this contact is deeply appreciated is very evident through the letters which have come to us from our Chaplains. In addition an effort is being made that the synods which have upon their clerical roll a Chaplain may maintain a closer contact with the Chaplains. Your committee has suggested that presidents of synods, or one appointed for the purpose, keep in touch with the Chaplains by correspondence, and that the Chaplains be urged to follow the same course with their synodical officers. Synods have been urged to give such assistance as possible to Chaplains in their religious work in their camp or post to which they are assigned. It has been further suggested that Chaplains be asked to inform their synods concerning the activities of their work. Wherever it may be possible, synodical financial assistance is urged for Chaplains work. Some synods make constitutional provision for such assistance.

IV. GENERAL ITEMS

There still remain many small posts and camps to which men in service are assigned for whom no provision for religious service is made. Many of these posts are located where we have no congregations. There are others, however, in which local pastors have interested themselves in the welfare of the man. This service might well be enlarged to include all pastors where it is possible for us to render a service in the name of the Church.

Chaplain St. Clair still continues as Civilian Chaplain at the Speedwell Hospital near Chicago, Illinois. His support has been very meager, as certain sources of revenue have failed. He still continues to do a fine piece of work among the thousands of men who are in the hospital.

RECOMMENDATIONS

1. *Resolved,* That this Convention suggest to the synods upon whose roll the name of a Chaplain is found that they make every effort to maintain a closer contact with the Chaplain and to render such assistance to him in his religious work as may be possible.

2. *Resolved,* That we suggest to synods that a place be provided upon the program of their annual conventions for the presentation of the work of Chaplains, and that if possible one of our Lutheran Chaplains be invited to speak to the convention of synod.

3. *Resolved,* That we request the Lutheran Publication House to supply to our Chaplains Sunday school literature without charge. [Amended by the Convention, see p. 175.]

Respectfully submitted,

CHARLES TREXLER, *Chairman.*

WM. FREAS, *Secretary,*

Dr. Freas introduced Major John Hall, Lutheran Chaplain, who addressed the Convention.

The recommendations of the Committee were then taken up.

Recommendations 1 and 2 were adopted.

On motion recommendation 3 was amended by striking out the words "Lutheran Publication House" and inserting the words "The Lutheran Church Book and Literature Society." On further motion the recommendation was amended by inserting the words "and other Church" after the words "Sunday School." The amended recommendation is as follows:

> "*Resolved,* That we request the Lutheran Church Book and Literature Society to supply to our Chaplains Sunday school and other Church literature without charge."

The amended recommendation was adopted.

Committee of Tellers No. 1 reported that there was no election in the balloting for Secretary. The Committee was instructed again to pass ballots for the election of a Secretary.

At four o'clock, the time appointed for the special order of business, the Secretary presented the item of the Executive Board's report concerning the Training of Ministers and Teachers (II, 9) as contained in the Supplemental Report of the Executive Board, Item "A".

The Convention proceeded to consider the recommendations connected with the report. It was moved to adopt I. Discussion of this motion continued until five o'clock, the time appointed for the consideration of the report of the Board of Ministerial Pensions and Relief as a special order.

The President called for the report of the Committee of Tellers No. 1 on the election of a Secretary. The Committee reported that the Rev. W. H. Greever received 351 votes out of a total of 424 votes cast. The President declared Dr. Greever electd Secretary of The United Lutheran Church in America. Dr. Greever was called to the platform and presented to the Convention.

The report of the Board of Ministerial Pensions and Relief was presented by Mr. Paul Myers, President of the Board.

THE REPORT OF THE BOARD OF MINISTERIAL PENSIONS AND RELIEF

(For action on the changes in rules proposed in this report see p. 192.)
(For action on the Treasurer's report see pp. 192, 228, 388.)

During the past biennium in addition to its routine duties, the Board has concerned itself with conserving its endowment and the collection of unpaid subscriptions to the Campaign Fund.

The Treasurer's Report will reveal that even in these days of changing values, the Endowment Fund is practically intact, for which it gives devout thanks to Almighty God and records its high appreciation of its Finance Committee.

Of the campaign subscriptions it has collected (July 1, 1932) $3,198,305, or 76½ per cent, $198,305 of this amount being paid during the past biennium. Not all that was to be desired, but possibly not so bad in these days of economic distress. The total subscription was $4,178,065.

The status by synods follows:

Synod	Quota	Subscription	Paid 7/1/32
Pennsylvania Ministerium	$844,446	$849,220	$671,647.13
United Synod of New York	644,916	660,177	541,868.30
Pittsburgh	301,038	341,509	250,909.14
Ohio	273,306	345,000	263,171.99
West Pennsylvania	209,388	191,023	152,767.89
East Pennsylvania	202,992	285,364	206,870.30
Maryland	184,302	222,487	178,401.96
Susquehanna	160,416	128,626	87,837.67
Illinois	136,866	172,903	115,586.30
Alleghany	128,706	140,563	99,164.63
Northwest	102,540	114,200	71,160.78
North Carolina	99,858	84,214	52,712.32
Canada	84,726	45,604	39,277.70
South Carolina	82,212	55,028	36,527.06
Virginia	65,868	67,939	50,507.72
German Nebraska	53,220	26,953	23,907.92
Michigan	52,770	54,169	37,916.71
Indiana	51,156	48,492	41,354.19
Nebraska	49,410	54,842	42,770.18
Wartburg	46,590	27,600	24,803.63
Slovak Zion	32,478	1,710	2,079.45
Kansas	31,368	35,160	24,635.95
Iowa	30,012	26,500	17,720.70
Manitoba	29,748	3,000	3,315.55
California	28,938	31,924	22,213.00
West Virginia	21,480	28,273	21,214.55
**Georgia	21,660	22,975	20,038.71
Texas	18,096	11,810	9,750.44
Pacific	12,372	19,116	12,209.99
Rocky Mountain	8,880	12,968	8,826.11
Nova Scotia	7,458	7,902	6,654.41
**Florida	5,000	4,988	968.26

Mississippi	2,214	3,225	1,676.77
United Lutheran Publication House		50,000	50,000.00
Porto Rico		2,601	1,000.00
Miscellaneous			6,838.44
Total	$4,024,430	$4,178,065	$3,198,305.85

**NOTE: Florida Synod formed after Campaign.

During the post-Easter season of 1931 the Board conducted a clean-up appeal, which while not as successful financially as was hoped, revealed many interesting things, viz.:

Thousands of our people are without employment.

Many of our churches had their funds in neighborhood banks which closed their doors.

In many instances, money which should have been forwarded to the Board of Pensions was deposited in these banks.

Many churches, taking advantage of the Board's offer to do the collecting of unpaid pledges *after* the clean-up appeal, sent in the names of delinquents without conducting the appeal.

Many churches, when they had paid their quota but not their subscription, refused to do more.

While not aggressively going after delinquent subscriptions at present because of the times, it is the purpose of the Board to aggressively prosecute its work in the better days ahead.

STATISTICS

Since our last report the following additions and deductions have been made in the roll:

ADDITIONS

Ministers	116
Widows	63
Children	70
Missionaries	1
Total	250

DEDUCTIONS

Ministers	52
Widows	42
Children	41
Missionaries	2
Total	137

Several applications for relief came to the Board during the past biennium which grew out of the times, but because of the rules under which the Board operates, they could not be granted.

During the biennium forty-three Special Grants were made, amounting to $2,950.00.

The roll by synods is as follows:

Synod	Retired	Disabled	Widows	Children	Missionaries	Pension	Relief
Alleghany	7	....	10	....		$5,800	$250
California	12	4	8	4		9,000	650
Canada	11	2	14	2		9,500	740
East Pennsylvania	14	2	35*	8		17,300	580
Florida	2	....	1	2		1,200	100
Georgia	....	2	8*	1		3,250	240
German Nebraska	11	2	14	7		9,750	330
Illinois	10	3	24**	20		13,400	1,280
Indiana	4	....	7*	1		3,750	450
Iowa	1	....	3	....		1,300	......
Kansas	2	1	10	3		4,350	350
Manitoba	4	4	4	11		4,950	750
Maryland	10	3	31*	1		14,550	800
Michigan	5	1	17	2		7,600	160
Mississippi	1	....	....	....		400	......
Nebraska	5	....	8	1		4,450	100
New York	25	6	76**	19		36,150	3,190
North Carolina	11	....	20	3		10,550	1,240
Northwest	3	....	5	1		2,750	80
Nova Scotia	....	....	....	....		....	......
Ohio	23	3	40	17	1	23,650	1,500
Pacific	4	2	5	1		3,950	500
Pennsylvania Min.	19	8	59	11		29,050	1,860
Pittsburgh	15	2	35*	4	2	18,300	670
Rocky Mountain	5	....	2	1		2,650	350
Slovak Zion	1	2	....	6		1,500	......
South Carolina	5	2	17	5		8,150	940
Susquehanna	8	1	16	....		8,400	560
Texas	2	1	5	3		2,850	630
Virginia	12	3	15	9		10,950	400
Wartburg	5	1	5	....		3,900	550
West Pennsylvania	10	3	31	10		15,000	1,270
West Virginia	1	....	4	4		1,800	......
Specials (3)	....	....	....	....	....	800	......
Total 1932	248	58	529	157	3	$290,950	$20,520
Total 1930	208	42	510	131	5	$261,750	$17,820

NOTE: * Includes Unmarried Daughter of Clergyman.

It was the program of the Board to increase pensions as its income would permit. The sources of income available for pensions are first, income from endowment, and second, the apportionment from the Church.

Considering the distressing times through which we are passing, the income from the endowment has met our expectations—4½ per cent net.

The Church, however, having paid only 53 per cent of its apportionment, reduces the income available to the Board from this source to a point where increase of pensions is out of the question at this time.

For detailed analysis of this matter see the Treasurer's Report.

Professor Christian Boettcher

The Milwaukee Convention referred to this Board and the Board of Education the case of Professor Boettcher of Kropp, Germany.

The Board of Education, the German Conference and the Committee on German Interests have petitioned this Board in his behalf.

Professor Boettcher is a layman, not a member of the United Lutheran Church and therefore does not come within the purview of the rules under which this Board operates.

However, in view of the fact that a considerable portion of the Church seems to think that he should have some consideration, the Board has voted him an annual grant of $100 which may be increased to $150 in an emergency.

This action should have the approval of the Church.

Annuity Bonds and Bequests

During the biennium 7 bonds amounting to $5,300 have been sold, and 16 bequests have been received amounting to $19,590.

The attention of the Church is directed to the fact that the Board issues annuity bonds at a liberal rate of interest and pastors and attorneys are asked to call the attention of their parishoners to these bonds and to suggest the Board of Ministerial Pensions and Relief as an institution worthy of remembrance in their wills.

Women's Missionary Society

The Board herewith records its high appreciation of the $5,000 annual appropriation from the Women's Missionary Society and of the faithful attendance of its two members who attend its meetings in an advisory capacity.

At the request of the Society, its gifts are placed in the Endowment Fund rather than in the Operating Fund as heretofore.

Nominations

At this Convention the terms of the following members expire:

Mr. Peter P. Hagan.
Mr. J. Elsie Miller.
Paul F. Myers, Esq.
Mr. William F. Schneider.
Mr. A. F. Sittloh.

The Board places in nomination the following:

Paul F. Myers, Esq., Washington, D. C. (Maryland Synod).
Mr. Albert F. Sittloh, Richmond, Ind. (Indiana Synod).
Mr. J. C. Rovensky, New York City, N. Y. (New York Synod).
Mr. Belding B. Slifer, Jenkintown, Pa. (East Pennsylvania Synod).
Mr. Daniel F. Yost, Norristown, Pa. (Ministerium of Pennsylvania).

Rules

The Board submits the following changes in its rules for adoption:

Pensions, Rule No. 1—now reads:

"Ministers of The United Lutheran Church in America, who are sixty-five years of age, or older, and who are in good and regular standing in the synods to which they belong, shall, on retirement, be eligible to a minimum pension of $400 per annum, provided they shall have served at least 20 years in synods of the United Lutheran Church."

The following addition is submitted:

"Provided further, that ministers coming into the United Lutheran Church from other evangelical churches, in order to qualify for a pension, must serve in one of its constituent synods at least ten years and must have served for an equal number of years in the Communions from which they come."

PENSIONS, RULE No. 5—now reads:

"Widows of ordained clergymen of the United Lutheran Church, whatever their time of service, shall be granted an annual pension of $300, except that, if the husband be retired at the time of death, the marriage must have taken place at least five years before his retirement; and that widows of men transferred from other Communions shall not be eligible to the pension unless the husband has served at least three years in the United Lutheran Church. Widows pensions cease on remarriage. Membership in a congregation of the United Lutheran Church is required, unless for reasons approved by the Executive Committee."

Permission is asked to change the words "five years" in the fourth line to "ten years."

The rule then to read:

"Widows of ordained clergymen of the United Lutheran Church, whatever their time of service, shall be granted an annual pension of $300, except that, if the husband be retired at the time of death, the marriage must have taken place at least ten years before his retirement; and that widows of men transferred from other Communions shall not be eligible to the pension unless the husband has served at least three years in the United Lutheran Church. Widows pensions cease on remarriage. Membership in a congregation of the United Lutheran Church is required, unless for reasons approved by the Executive Committee."

PENSIONS, RULE No. 3—now reads:

"In exceptional cases these conditions, other than retirement, may be waived by unanimous vote of the Executive Committee."

Permission is asked to substitute the word "Board" for "Executive Committee."

The rule then to read:

"In exceptional cases these conditions, other than retirement, may be waived by unanimous vote of the Board."

The rule then to be transferred to the end of all rules.

GENERAL RULE No. 4—reads as follows:

"A statement on a blank provided by the Board, shall be required in June of each year of all on the Roll, to the effect that they are still eligible to Pensions."

Permission is asked to eliminate this rule for two reasons, viz:

(a) Ample provision is made in Rules No. 1 to No. 8 under Pensions, and Rule No. 7 under General Rules.

(b) It has never been put into effect in the Board's history.

GENERAL RULES NO. 8 AND NO. 9—read as follows:

"8. Legacies or trust funds shall be invested in accordance with the laws of Pennsylvania governing such funds, and shall be made under the supervision of the Board."

"9. The Treasurer shall be the custodian of all the securities of the Board, which shall be in as far as possible, registered in the name of the Board. The Treasurer shall give satisfactory surety in such sum as may from time to time be determined by the Board. The President shall sign checks in the absence of the Treasurer at the Treasurer's request. The President shall also have access to the vault."

Permission is asked to transfer these rules to their proper place in the by-laws of the Board under the duties of the Treasurer, the last sentence in Rule No. 9 to be eliminated owing to the action of the Board at its meeting November 22, 1928, viz.:

Resolved

"That in the event of the death of the Treasurer of the Board, the President and the Finance Committee shall have the right of immediate access to the Safe Deposit Box, provided that the Executor of the Estate of the Treasurer is present upon the opening of the box and such Executor shall be entitled to a receipt for the contents thereof upon turning over the same to the successor of the late Treasurer after said successor has given bond as such; and further provided that neither the President of the Board nor the Finance Committee or any member thereof shall be permitted to remove from the Safe Deposit Box of the Board any of the securities or monies therein belonging to said Board and that the same shall not be turned over to the custody of the successor of the deceased Treasurer until said successor shall be elected as such and has given a corporate security bond astisfactory to the Executive Committee for such an amount as said committee may determine to be necessary but in no event for less than $250,000."

It was the intention of the Board when the campaign was successfully completed to pay pensions as follows: Retired and Disabled Clergymen and Missionaries $600, Widows of Clergymen $400, dependent Children of Clergymen to the age of 16 years, $100.

The Board now asks permission to change the amount to be paid to widows to $300 for two reasons, viz.:

1. Widows often engage in employment.

2. Other church pension systems pay to the widow 50 per cent of the amount paid to retired clergymen.

Respectfully submitted,
HARRY HODGES, Executive Secretary.

REPORT OF THE TREASURER OF THE BOARD OF MINISTERIAL PENSIONS AND RELIEF

BALANCE SHEET
June 30, 1932
ASSETS

Cash in Bank and on Hand	$159,208.83	
Cash in Closed Institutions	98,730.63	
		$257,939.46
Investments at Ledger Values:		
U. S. Liberty Loan Bonds	$10,504.12	
Other Bonds	1,128,804.30	
		1,139,308.42
Adjusted War Service Certificate		1.00
Mortgages		1,696,465.00
Real Estate		402,777.88
Accounts Receivable		1,283.65
Furniture and Fixtures		1,831.39
Total Assets		$3,499,606.80

LIABILITIES AND FUNDS

Annuities		$85,450.00
Funds:		
Endowment	$3,404,511.05	
General	9,645.75	
		3,414,156.80
Total Liabilities and Funds		$3,499,606.80

STATEMENT OF RECEIPTS AND DISBURSEMENTS
July 1, 1930, to June 30, 1931

	Endowment Fund	General Fund
Balances on Hand, July 1, 1930	$176,963.94	$24,525.33
Receipts:		
Campaign for Endowment Fund	308,972.42	
United Lutheran Church Apportionment	....	162,150.00
Women's Missionary Society	5,000.00	
Bequests	8,392.00	
Donations:		
General	1,637.00	1,054.77
Relief	....	3,964.10
Interest:		
On Bank Balances	....	3,357.65
On Investments	....	163,253.04
Annuity Contracts Sold	1,800.00	
Mortgages Paid in full or on account	30,500.00	
	$533,265.36	$358,304.89

Disbursements:		
Pensions and Relief:		
Retired Ministers		$95,008.23
Disabled Ministers		21,315.87

Widows and Mothers of Ministers..		163,833.28
Children of Ministers		5,480.08
Missionaries		1,699.82
Annuity Interest		5,708.70
Salary of Executive Secretary...		3,600.00
Salary of Office Secretary..		1,820.00
Traveling Expenses of Executive Secretary....................................		840.00
Expenses of Treasurer and Other Board Members......................		4,380.56
Printing and Stationery...		674.30
Office Supplies and Expense..		1,572.55
Rental of Office		765.00
Auditing		450.00
Campaign Expenses	$5,621.95	....
Equipment Purchased		91.00
Investments Purchased, Bonds................................	276,963.79	....
	$282,585.74	$307,239.39
Balances on hand, June 30, 1931...................................	250,679.62	51,065.50
	$533,265.36	$358,304.89

STATEMENT OF RECEIPTS AND DISBURSEMENTS
July 1, 1931, to June 30, 1932

	Endowment Fund	General Fund
Balances on Hand, July 1, 1931...................................	$250,679.62	$51,065.50
Receipts:		
Campaign for Endowment Fund................................	68,147.01	....
United Lutheran Church Apportionment..............	....	138,650.00
Women's Missionary Society	5,000.00	....
Bequests	4,195.00	500.00
Donations:		
General	369.66	910.20
Relief		3,628.30
Interest:		
On Bank Balances	....	3,092.42
On Investments..	....	158,691.59
Annuity Contracts Sold......................................	2,500.00	....
Mortgages Paid in Full or on Account..................	99,187.00	....
Real Estate Sold	18,700.00	....
Rents Received	....	14,637.33
Investments Sold and Retired	6,000.00	....
	$454,778.29	$371,175.34

Disbursements:		
Pensions and Relief:		
Retired Ministers		$105,307.23
Disabled Ministers		22,668.90
Widows and Mothers of Ministers................................		167,179.98
Children of Ministers		7,085.60
Missionaries		1,866.48
Annuity Interest		5,671.99
Salary of Executive Secretary.................................		3,600.00
Salary of Office Secretary		1,820.00

Traveling Expenses of Executive Secretary.................................... 1,134.71
Expenses of Treasurer and Other Board Members........................ 4,380.80
Printing and Stationery ....~............. 601.30
Office Supplies and Expenses.................................... .... 1,224.39
Foreclosure Costs of Real Estate............................ $21,667.51
· Rental of Office 765.00
Auditing 597.29
Campaign Expenses 288.16
Equipment Purchased 43.90
Investments Purchased —Bonds.............................. 182,552.50 ....
Real Estate Expenses:
   Legal Expense 10,875.00
   Appraisal Fees 3,850.00
   Taxes, Repairs and Commissions on Rents, etc. 24,833.43

                                                  $204,508.17 $363,506.00
Balances on Hand, June 30, 1932................................... 250,270.12   7,669.34

                                                  $454,778.29 $371,175.34

BONDS OWNED, ENDOWMENT FUND
June 30, 1932

		Value As Carried on Books
U. S. Government Obligations:		
$10,950	U. S. Fourth Liberty Loan 4¼s, 1933-38........................	$10,504.12
Other Bonds:		
$25,000	American Telephone and Telegraph 5½s, 1943..............	27,312.50
25,000	American Telephone and Telegraph 5s, 1965....................	25,175.00
50,000	Appalachian Electric Power 5s, 1956................................	49,987.50
50,000	Atchison, Topeka & Santa Fe 4s, 1995.............................	48,321.25
25,000	Baltimore & Ohio Railroad 5s, 1995...............................	25,515.00
5,000	Bell Telephone Company 5s, 1960......................	5,041.25
50,000	Buffalo, Rochester & Pittsburgh Cons. 4½s, 1957........	47,250.00
25,000	Canadian Pacific R. R. Equip. Trust 5s, 1944....................	25,375.00
25,000	Carolina Power and Light Co. 5s, 1956...........................	25,175.00
5,000	Central District Telephone Co. 5s, 1943.......................	4,875.00
25,000	Chesapeake & Ohio R. R. Equipment 4½s, 1940............	24,900.33
25,000	Chesapeake & Ohio R. R. General 4½s, 1992.................	26,312.50
6,000	Chicago, Indianapolis & Louisville 5s, 1966.....................	6,000.00
25,000	Chicago & Northwestern 4¾s, 1949..........................	24,925.00
50,000	Consolidated Gas of New York 5½s, 1945........................	53,557.50
1,000	Dairy Operators Company 6s, 1941.................................	1,000.00
1,000	Des Moines City Railway Company 5s, 1936...................	950.00
50,000	Georgia Power Company 5s, 1967....................................	49,987.50
25,000	Harbour Commission of Montreal, The, 5s, 1969............	25,412.50
1,000	Howard Gas & Coal Company 6s, 1937.............................	1,000.00
5,000	Lehigh Valley Railroad Company 5s, 2003.....................	5,110.00
10,000	Montreal Metropolitan Commission, The, 4½s, 1953..	9,262.50
50,000	New York Central Railway Company 4½s, 2013..........	49,531.25
50,000	New York, Chicago & St. Louis 4½s, 1978.....................	48,870.00
10,000	Ottawa, City of, 4½s, 1954..	9,309.96
1,000	Pacific Telephone and Telegraph Co. 5s, 1937..............	1,000.00

25,000	Pennsylvania Co. Secured 4¾s, 1963	24,675.00
25,000	Pennsylvania Railroad Deb. 4½s, 1970	23,812.50
5,000	Pennsylvania Railroad Mortgage Bond 4½s, 1965	5,000.00
25,000	Pere Marquette Equipment 4½s, 1942	24,885.22
25,000	Pere Marquette Railway 1st Mortgage 4½s, 1980	24,937.50
10,000	Philadelphia, City of, 4s, 1947	8,456.81
15,000	Philadelphia, City of, 4s, 1953	12,174.90
75,000	Philadelphia, City of, 4¼s, 1977-2047	67,296.87
25,000	Philadelphia, City of, 4¼s, 1978-2048	20,112.71
25,000	Philadelphia Company 5s, 1967	24,675.00
49,000	Philadelphia Electric Power Co. 5½s, 1972	50,477.50
24,500	Philadelphia Rapid Transit Co. 6s, 1944	24,500.00
5,000	Pittsburgh, Cincinnati & St. Louis 5s, 1975	4,985.00
20,000	Province of Alberta, Canada, 5s, 1959	19,775.00
10,000	Province of Manitoba, Canada, 5s, 1959	9,937.50
25,000	Province of Ontario, Canada, 5s, 1960	25,750.00
25,000	Province of Saskatchewan, Canada, 5s, 1959	25,112.50
25,000	Southern Pacific Railroad 4½s, 1969	24,281.25
25,000	Southern Pacific, Oregon Lines, 4½s, 1977	24,375.00
2,000	Tennessee Power Company 5s, 1962	1,600.00
25,000	Texas Corporation Conv. 5s, 1944	25,312.50
25,000	Virginia Power Company 5s, 1942	25,515.00
10,000	Walnut Street Trust Building 6s, 1932	10,000.00

$1,139,308.42

BOARD OF MINISTERIAL PENSIONS AND RELIEF
ENDOWMENT FUND
Mortgages Owned, June 30, 1932, in Safe Deposit Box

No.	Premises	Amount
1	522 Godfrey Avenue	$3,000.00
2	528 Godfrey Avenue	2,500.00
3	532 Godfrey Avenue	3,500.00
4	538 Godfrey Avenue	3,000.00
5	542 Godfrey Avenue	3,000.00
6	544 Godfrey Avenue	3,000.00
7	2762 N. Ringgold Street	1,800.00
10	3102 N. 27th Street	2,500.00
11	2356 N. 15th Street	2,200.00
12	599 E. Cheltenham Avenue	3,900.00
16	1329 65th Avenue, North	6,500.00
17	3022 "B" Street	2,200.00
19	723 Rhawn Street	3,000.00
20	NEs Afton Street, 300 ft. 1¼ in. NW Bustleton Avenue (2235 Afton)	3,000.00
22	NWs Claridge Street, 150 ft. SW Faunce Street (No. 7530)	3,500.00
28	5708 Virginian Road	6,000.00
29	8514 Cypress Avenue	9,000.00
32	1133 Faunce Street	2,500.00
34	SEs High School Road 140 ft. NE Marvin Road, Elkins Park, Pa.	9,000.00
35	3357 St. Vincent Street	4,000.00
37	Ns Chelten Avenue, 149 ft. 0—⅝ in. E. Old York Road..	4,950.00
42	Lot No. 74 Penrose Homestead, Elkins Park, Pa.	7,000.00

No.	Premises	Amount
45	78 E. Bringhurst Street	4,500.00
47	423 Passmore Street	2,500.00
48	425 Passmore Street	3,000.00
49	427 Passmore Street	3,000.00
50	2836 N. 27th Street	1,500.00
53	312 Chandler Street	4,000.00
54	8431 High School Road, Elkins Park, Pa.	3,000.00
55	8435 High School Road, Elkins Park, Pa.	3,000.00
59	3310 St. Vincent Street	3,600.00
62	SWs St. Vincent Street, 285 ft. 6 in. SE, Summerdale Avenue	3,000.00
63	514 Chelten Avenue	15,000.00
65	1421 W. Westmoreland Street	8,000.00
69	7248 Tabor Street	3,500.00
72	NWs Cadwalader Ave., 125 ft. NE, Waring Road	12,000.00
74	117 York Road, Hatboro, Pa.	8,000.00
75	115 York Road, Hatboro, Pa.	8,000.00
77	4277 Leidy Avenue	3,000.00
79	Weisel Road lead. from Limekiln Pike to Bristol Road, Warrington Twp.	6,000.00
80	3320 St. Vincent Street	3,800.00
81	6221 Hasbrook Street	3,000.00
82	473 Devereaux Street	3,500.00
84	5949 Elsinore Street	3,000.00
85	5957 Elsinore Street	3,000.00
86	5961 Elsinore Street	3,000.00
89	NWs Sumac Street, 217 ft. 8⅞ in. NE cor. Righter and Sumac	25,000.00
90	3401 N. 16th Street	19,600.00
91	7531 Lawndale Avenue	3,000.00
92	Es 5th Street and Ss Spencer Streets	12,400.00
94	6888 N. 20th Street	6,000.00
95	3337 St. Vincent Street	3,800.00
96	305 Corinthian Avenue, Overlook Hill, Willow Grove, Pa.	3,000.00
97	SW cor. Jenkintown and Evergreen Roads, Jenkintown, Pa.	12,000.00
101	3459 Princeton Avenue	500.00
102	7214 Frankford Avenue	8,000.00
103	337 Hellerman Street	4,000.00
104	148-150 W. Girard Avenue	11,500.00
105	NE cor. 5th and Fern Streets (6041 N. 5th)	14,500.00
106	SEs Haines Street, 87 ft. SW of Rodney Street	30,000.00
107	7215 Oak Avenue	2,500.00
108	143 W. Wyoming Avenue	6,500.00
109	5345 Bellfield Avenue	3,000.00
111	206 W. Widener Street	3,000.00
112	4015 Teesdale Street	3,200.00
113	4017 Teesdale Street	3,200.00
114	4033 Teesdale Street	3,200.00
115	4035 Teesdale Street	3,200.00
116	4037 Teesdale Street	3,200.00
117	4039 Teesdale Street	3,200.00
118	4041 Teesdale Street	3,200.00

No.	Premises	Amount
120	4061 Teesdale Street	3,200.00
121	4045 Teesdale Street	3,200.00
122	4047 Teesdale Street	3,200.00
123	4049 Teesdale Street	3,200.00
124	4051 Teesdale Street	3,200.00
125	4053 Teesdale Street	3,200.00
126	4055 Teesdale Street	3,200.00
127	4057 Teesdale Street	3,200.00
128	4063 Teesdale Street	3,600.00
129	1622 W. Erie Avenue	12,000.00
130	184 W. Fern Street	3,000.00
131	258 W. Linton Street	3,000.00
132	223 W. Widener Street	3,000.00
134	609 Godfrey Avenue	3,250.00
135	611 Godfrey Avenue	3,400.00
136	613 Godfrey Avenue	3,425.00
137	615 Godfrey Avenue	3,250.00
138	617 Godfrey Avenue	3,500.00
139	619 Godfrey Avenue	3,500.00
141	623 Godfrey Avenue	3,400.00
145	631 Godfrey Avenue	3,200.00
160	Waverly Road, 224.66 ft. NW Mill Road	25,000.00
162	531 E. Godfrey Avenue	3,000.00
164	2445 W. Columbia Avenue	5,000.00
165	6529 Rising Sun Avenue	9,000.00
167	218 W. Linton Street	3,000.00
168	230 Linton Street	2,500.00
169	243 W. Widener Street	3,000.00
170	226 W. Widener Street	2,900.00
171	1004 66th Avenue, North	15,000.00
172	517 Ryers Avenue	3,500.00
173	2514 W. Somerset Street	3,000.00
174	5415 Tacoma Street	4,000.00
175	2915 N. 22nd Street	10,000.00
178	7611 Verree Avenue	3,600.00
179	22-24 Park Avenue, Upper Darby, Pa.	20,000.00
180	4704 N. Lawrence Street	3,000.00
181	6032 N. Phillip Street	3,000.00
182	232 Linton Street	3,000.00
183	240 W. Widener Street	3,000.00
184	229 W. Widener Street	2,900.00
185	208 Linton Street	3,000.00
186	620 Levick Street	5,000.00
187	3429 Englewood Street	3,500.00
188	3353 St. Vincent Street	3,800.00
189	5901 Belden Street	10,000.00
191	7116 Old York Road	12,000.00
192	2505 N. 18th Street	3,000.00
194	2612 W. Lehigh Avenue	10,000.00
195	4058 Teesdale Street	3,200.00
197	4010 Teesdale Street	3,200.00
198	4012 Teesdale Street	3,200.00
199	4014 Teesdale Street	3,200.00
201	4034 Teesdale Street	3,200.00

No.	Premises	Amount
202	4038 Teesdale Street	3,200.00
204	4042 Teesdale Street	3,200.00
205	4044 Teesdale Street	3,200.00
206	4046 Teesdale Street	3,200.00
207	4048 Teesdale Street	3,200.00
208	4050 Teesdale Street	3,200.00
210	4056 Teesdale Street	3,200.00
211	4054 Teesdale Street	3,200.00
212	2919 Hale Street	3,300.00
213	2921 Hale Street	3,300.00
214	2917 Hale Street	3,300.00
215	2925 Hale Street	3,300.00
216	2923 Hale Street	3,300.00
218	5952 Elsinore Street	3,000.00
220	2009 Norris Street	3,000.00
224	2862 N. Stillman Street	1,400.00
226	2605 N. Douglass Street	2,200.00
227	622 E. Brill Street	3,000.00
229	6429 Lawndale Avenue	1,500.00
230	3436 Englewood Street	3,500.00
233	924 W. Rockland Street	4,000.00
234	5300 Wayne Avenue	18,000.00
235	2642 Germantown Avenue	15,000.00
236	263 Linton Street	2,000.00
249	Broad and Erie Avenue	500,000.00
250	610 E. Brill Street	3,000.00
251	SW cor. Rhawn and Ridgeway Streets	4,900.00
252	2759 N. Croskey Street	2,500.00
253	616 E. Brill Street	3,000.00
256	1031 Pleasant Street	1,100.00
257	3427 Princeton Avenue	3,950.00
259	3425 Princeton Avenue	3,750.00
260	36 Robbins Avenue	3,500.00
261	3228 N. Carlisle Street	3,000.00
263	626 E. Brill Street	2,500.00
264	6058 Beechwood Street	3,000.00
265	6056 Beechwood Street	3,000.00
266	6054 Beechwood Street	3,000.00
269	224 Forest Avenue, Narberth	5,000.00
272	2404 N. 26th Street	2,000.00
274	5127 Sheldon Street	2,000.00
275	7526 Tabor Avenue	2,500.00
276	3451 Princeton Avenue	4,000.00
277	2764 N. 22nd Street	2,000.00
278	3300-02 Kensington Avenue	15,000.00
279	461-63 E. Girard Avenue	3,000.00
280	2248 W. Huntingdon Street	2,000.00
281	6064 N. 21st Street	5,500.00
282	3435 Princeton Avenue	3,800.00
283	3445 Princeton Avenue	3,750.00
284	SEs Easton Road and SWs Toxony Avenue	14,000.00
285	656 E. Brill Street	3,000.00
289	535 E. Church Road, Elkins Park, Pa.	9,000.00
290	537 E. Church Road, Elkins Park, Pa.	9,600.00

No.	Premises	Amount
291	Lot No. 25, Penrose Homestead (308 Marion Road)	12,000.00
292	6520 N. 16th Street	5,500.00
293	6167 Oakley Street	5,000.00
294	3470 Bowman Street	5,500.00
295	3430 Midvale Avenue	5,200.00
296	2002 Haines Street	5,000.00
297	614 Boyer Road, Rowland Park	5,000.00
298	401 Sanger (Sentner) Street	4,600.00
300	600 E. Brill Street	4,500.00
302	4239 Cottman Street	4,000.00
303	4237 Cottman Street	4,000.00
304	4235 Cottman Street	4,000.00
305	5949 Bingham Street	3,500.00
306	5923 Bingham Street	3,500.00
307	5917 Bingham Street	3,500.00
308	555½ Cheltenham Avenue	3,500.00
309	5340 Germantown Avenue	18,000.00
310	213 Evergreen Road, Jenkintown Manor, Pa.	11,000.00
311	NWs Ogontz Ave. 150.28 ft. SW Manor Road (8240 Ogontz Avenue)	9,000.00
312	5900-02-04 Kemble Avenue	9,000.00
313	6236 Hasbrook Avenue	8,000.00
314	2853-55 Oakdale Street	7,040.00
315	600 E. Woodlawn Avenue	6,000.00
316	N.W. cor. Buxmont Street and Overhill Road	6,000.00
317	S.W. cor. Wellington Road and Sunset Avenue, Jenkintown, Pa.	35.000.00
319	2004 Haines Street	5,000.00
320	3443 Princeton Avenue	3,500.00
322	614 E. Brill Street	3,000.00
324	532 Fanshaw Street	3,300.00
326	4225 Cottman Street	4,000.00
327	711 Chelten Avenue	18,000.00
328	1310 Butler Street	4,000.00
329	231-33 Coulter Street	12,000.00
330	2226 N. 13th Street	4,500.00
331	4221 Cottman Street	4,000.00
332	4630 N. 5th Street	9,000.00
333	2208-10 Hunting Park Avenue	8,000.00
334	5961 Bingham Street	3,000.00
335	5900 N. 21st Street	7,500.00
336	213 Church Road, Elkins Park, Pa.	6,000.00
337	755 E. Herkness Street	4,000.00
338	N.E. cor. 16th and McKean Streets	7,500.00
339	4217 Stirling Street	3,000.00
340	4215 Stirling Street	3,000.00
341	4209 Stirling Street	3,000.00

$1,692,165.00

Participating Trust Certificates Property in Park County, Montana. 6 per cent ... 800.00

Wm. Hoppe, 17 W. 106th Street, New York, N. Y. ... 3,500.00

Total Mortgages Owned ... $1,696,465.00

Respectfully submitted,
PETER P. HAGAN, *Treasurer.*

Philadelphia, Pa., July 23, 1932.

We have audited the accounts of the Treasurer of the Board of Ministerial Pensions and Relief of The United Lutheran Church in America, for the biennium beginning July 1, 1930, and ending June 30, 1932; we have also examined the mortgages owned by this Board as of June 30, 1932, and we hereby certify that the foregoing statements:

Balance Sheet, at June 30, 1932

Statement of Receipts and Disbursements for the year ending June 30, 1931

Statement of Receipts and Disbursements for the year ending June 30, 1932

Bonds Owned (Endowment Fund) at June 30, 1932

Mortgages Owned, at June 30, 1932

are in accordance with the books of account, and are true and correct.

TAIT, WALKER & BAKER,
Accountants and Auditors.

SUPPLEMENTAL REPORT OF THE TREASURER OF THE BOARD OF MINISTERIAL PENSIONS AND RELIEF

REAL ESTATE OWNED

October 1, 1932

	Mortgage	Appraisals 1930	1932	Cost	Monthly Rental
32 E. Armat Street	$20,000	$30,000	$28,000	$21,285.13	$50.00
1221 Atlantic Street	2,500	2,500	1,000	2,566.43	vacant
3031 N. Bonsall Street ...	2,000	2,000	2,000	2,000.00	20.00
602 Brill Street	3,000	4,000	3,500	3,302.12	30.00
612 Brill Street	3,000	4,000	3,500	3,256.67	30.00
618 Brill Street	3,000	4,000	3,500	3,273.03	30.00
658 Brill Street	3,000	4,000	3,500	3,147.31	30.00
917 Chandler Street	3,500	4,800	3,500	3,665.48	30.00
6631 Chew Street	8,000	7,500	6,500	8,252.83	25.00
6633 Chew Street	8,000	7,500	6,500	8,489.35	53.00
2252 N. Corlies Street ...	2,500	2,500	2,800	2,668.51	23.00
300-04 So. Easton Road .	15,000	20,000	15,000	15,591.95	127.00
931 Edgeley Street	1,500	2,000	1,800	1,758.83	20.00
2204 N. 18th Street	3,500	6,000	4,000	3,607.81	35.00
5945 Elsinore Street	3,000	3,800	3,800	3,399.62	30.00
5959 Elsinore Street	3,000	3,800	3,800	3,391.19	30.00
2311 N. Garnet Street ...	2,200	2,400	2,000	2,486.05	25.00
2355 N. Garnet Street ...	2,000	2,400	2,000	2,174.67	25.00
2040-42-44-46 German-town Avenue	10,000	10,000	5,000 Ground Val.	10,566.21	vacant
601 Godfrey Avenue	4,000	4,800	4,500	4,288.52	35.00
621 Godfrey Avenue	3.500	4,500	3,500	3,601.29	32.50
625 Godfrey Avenue	3,500	4,500	3,500	3,736.42	32.50
627 Godfrey Avenue	3,500	4,500	3,500	3,601.29	32.50
629 Godfrey Avenue	3,500	4,500	3,500	3,601.29	32.50
633 Godfrey Avenue	3,500	4,500	3,500	3,601.29	32.50

	Mortgage	Appraisals 1930	1932	Cost	Monthly Rental
635 Godfrey Avenue	3,500	4,500	3,500	3,736.42	32.50
637 Godfrey Avenue	3,500	4,500	3,500	3,736.42	32.50
639 Godfrey Avenue	3,500	4,500	3,500	3,601.29	32.50
641 Godfrey Avenue	3,500	4,500	3,500	3,736.42	32.50
643 Godfrey Avenue	3,500	4,500	3,500	3,601.29	32.50
645 Godfrey Avenue	3,500	4,500	3,500	3,601.29	32.50
647 Godfrey Avenue	3,500	4,500	3,500	3,736.42	32.50
649 Godfrey Avenue	3,500	4,500	3,500	3,736.42	32.50
651 Godfrey Avenue	3,500	4,500	3,500	3,736.42	32.50
653 Godfrey Avenue	3,500	4,500	3,500	3,736.42	32.50
655 Godfrey Avenue	3,500	4,500	3,500	3,736.42	32.50
657 Godfrey Avenue	3,500	4,500	3,500	3,736.42	32.50
659 Godfrey Avenue	4,000	4,500	3,500	4,268.49	35.00
1411 Hunting Park Ave. ..	12,000	....	12,000	12,575.74	110.00
1939 Independence Street.	3,500	4,200	3,500	3,756.53	30.00
2943-45 Kensington Ave. .	20,000	30,000	28,000	20,801.55	vacant
1210 Limekiln Pike	15,000	20,000	15,000	15,042.10	50.00
8237 Manor Road	9,000	11,500	10,000	9,575.50	65.00
Overhill Rd. and Buxmont	7,500	10,000	8,500	7,932.36	50.00
6128 Palmetto Street	2,500	3,200	3,000	2,810.21	25.00
7308 Palmetto Street	2,500	3,500	2,800	2,703.36	25.00
20 Queen Lane	10,000	10,000	9,000	10,880.44	107.00
2843 Ringold Street	2,200	2,600	2,200	2,485.49	25.00
6407 Rising Sun Avenue ..	5,500	8,500	7,300	6,355.49	47.50
6506-08 Rising Sun Ave.	8,000	11,000	11,000	8,689.36	vacant
2531 W. Seltzer Street ..	2,500	2,800	2,500	2,813.93	22.00
435 Sentner Street	5,000	6,000	6,000	5,342.09	55.00
1942 Spencer Street	3,500	5,500	3,500	3,782.27	40.00
2124 Spencer Street	2,000	3,500	2,800	2,160.96	20.00
1111 Stratford Avenue ...	12,000	12,000	8,500	13,080.59	vacant
5809-11 Torresdale Ave..	40,000	60,000	30,000	40,334.50	175.00
2231 N. Uber Street	3,500	4,000	3,500	3,565.86	30.00
525 E. Vankirk Street ...	4,200	6,000	5,400	4,388.02	40.00
5528 Wayne Avenue	45,000	....	50,000	47,687.10	585.00
Above Real Estate acquired by foreclosure to 7/1/32	$381,600	$485,300	$393,900	$402,776.88	
Following Real Estate acquired July 1 to Oct. 1, 1932					
707 Chelten Avenue	18,000	30,000	18,000	18,245.55	100.00
2917 Hale Street	3,300	4,000	3,750	3,421.37	30.00
2919 Hale Street	3,300	4,000	3,750	3,421.37	30.00
2921 Hale Street	3,300	4,000	3,750	3,421.37	30.00
2923 Hale Street	3,300	4,000	3,750	3,421.37	30.00
2925 Hale Street	3,300	4,000	3,750	3,421.37	30.00
4277 Leidy Avenue	3,000	4,000	3,700	3,106.66	vacant
153 Sumac Street and ⎰ 214-24 Kalos Street ⎱ ..	25,000	30,000	18,000	28,448.84	100.00
227 W. Widener Street ..	2,900	4,000	3,800	2,957.02	30.00
	$447,000	$573,300	$455,950	$472,641.80	$3,117.00

Mr. Harry Hodges, Executive Secretary of the Board, explained the recommendations contained in the report.

On motion it was decided to approve the action of the Board of Ministerial Pensions and Relief in granting aid to Prof. Christian Boettcher.

On motion the proposed changes in rules on the granting of pensions and relief were referred to the Executive Board with power to act.

The Rev. F. Noeldeke, on behalf of the Kropp men in the United Lutheran Church, thanked the Convention for the action in the case of Prof. Boettcher.

The report of the Treasurer of the Board was taken up for consideration. It was moved that the entire report of the Treasurer with the auditors' report be referred to the Commission on Investments for investigation and report to the Executive Board.

Mr. E. M. Rabenold, speaking in favor of the motion, was, on motion, granted an indefinite extension of time. During the consideration of this motion it was moved and carried that this matter be postponed until tomorrow morning, after the report of the Commission on Investments, and that the report of the Commission on Investments be made a special order for ten o'clock.

At six o'clock the Convention adjourned with prayer by the Rev. W. A. Reiser.

Friday Evening

A service was held at Zion-St. Michael's Church. The Rev. E. H. Delk presided and conducted the service. The Hon. Claude T. Reno delivered an address in recognition of the bicentennial of the birth of George Washington. The Rev. G. A. Brandelle delivered an address in recognition of the tricentennial of the death of Gustavus Adolphus.

FIFTH SESSION

Benjamin Franklin Hotel.
Philadelphia, Pennsylvania.
Saturday, October 15, 1932, 8.45 A. M.

Matins were conducted by the Rev. A. Steimle.

The Convention was called to order by the President.

The Minutes of the Third and Fourth Sessions were read by the Secretary and declared approved.

The Secretary reported on the roll of delegates as follows:

Number of delegates elected:
Clergymen, 276; Laymen, 275. Total—551.
Number of delegates in attendance:
Clergymen, 275; Laymen, 260. Total—535.
Twenty-five synods have one hundred per cent attendance of their delegations.
One clergyman and fifteen laymen are absent. Two synods have one delegate absent; five synods have two delegates absent; one synod has four delegates absent.
Two delegates from the Andhra Evangelical Lutheran Church in India and one delegate from the Japan Church are present.

On motion the associate delegates, the Rev. G. A. Rupley and the Rev. F. L. Coleman, of the Andhra Evangelical Lutheran Church, and the Rev. L. S. G. Miller, of the Japan Church, were given a seat and a voice in the Convention.

It was moved and carried that the proposed amendments to the By-Laws, Section V, C, Items 11 and 12, which were presented on Friday, be adopted.

The Rev. W. A. Wade, Chairman of the Nominating Committee, reported nominations as follows:

For the *Executive Board*:
Rev. E. B. Burgess, Rev. E. P. Pfatteicher, Rev. A. Steimle, William E. Hirt, Robbin B. Wolf, John L. Zimmerman, Rev. J. M. Bramkamp, Rev. E. W. Harner, Rev. J. S. Simon, Peter P. Hagan, J. W. Jouno, William H. Menges.

The President declared the nominations closed.

For the *Commission of Adjudication*:

Rev. Luther Kuhlman, Rev. W. F. Rangeler, C. M. Efird, Rev. B. R. Lantz, Rev. H. Offermann, F. B. Wickersham.

The President declared the nominations closed.

For the *Committee on Church Papers*:

Rev. M. R. Hamsher, Rev. E. P. Pfatteicher, Henry Streibert, Rev. F. A. Bowers, Rev. D. B. Young, C. W. Howe.

The President declared the nominations closed.

The Rev. J. L. Sieber, Chairman of the Nominating Committee, reported the nominations for members of the *Executive Committee of the Laymen's Movement* as follows:

H. J. Albrecht, J. L. Clark, Peter P. Hagan, Henry W. Harter, E. G. Hoover, J. P. Hovland, E. Clarence Miller, Harvey C. Miller, George E. Neff, John L. Zimmerman, M. H. Buehler, J. Milton Deck, Walter J. Johnson, John C. Lynch, E. Harry Schirmer, Burton C. Simon, Charles Steele, F. H. Wefer, H. T. Wentz, H. E. Young.

The President declared the nominations closed.

The report of the Inner Mission Board was presented by Mr. Carl M. Distler, President of the Board.

REPORT OF THE INNER MISSION BOARD

(For action on the recommendations in this report see. p. 229.)

The Inner Mission work of the Church presents the challenge of a great undone task. It is a call to every member of the Church to be a missionary. It is following the example of Jesus who was "a person going about doing good." It was natural for Him to do good. This same constant doing of good must be realized in the life of each member of the Church. Each one can be busy always in merciful work. With the work goes always the Word. It is proclaimed not only by the pastor but by each member of the Church as a part of his Christian activity. The congregation is responsible for the need, helplessness and trouble in its own community. In meeting this challenge the Church has but taken its first short steps. There are many individuals and congregations busy in merciful work. It is, however, largely uncorrelated and inadequate. Confusion exists particularly as between the Church and informal groups of Christian people.

Here is being done the great work of inspiring the Church to a truer understanding of its privilege of service. Each member of the Church must come to know more truly the joy of service to needy and unfortunate, lonely and erring. It is in this field of activity that we find the possibility of co-operation with other Lutheran general bodies and the members thereof. Already much progress has been made in this co-operation, and the possibilities of such co-operation are endless.

Your Board, appointed for the purpose of stimulating the merciful work of the Church, herewith respectfully submits this report.

I. Organization

At the Milwaukee Convention of the Church the following were elected to membership in the Board: Reverend G. H. Bechtold, Reverend H. Brezing, D.D., Reverend P. D. Brown, D.D., Carl M. Distler, Esq., and Mr. T. C. Rohrbaugh. With the election of these new members an entire change in the personnel of the Board has occurred.

The other members of the Board whose terms of office held over are: Reverend H. Brueckner, D.D., Reverend F. B. Clausen, D.D.; Reverend J. F Fedders, D.D., Reverend S. E. Greenawalt, D.D., Reverend R. E. Kern, Reverend J. J. Scherer, Jr., D.D., Mr. Robert F. Bowe, Mr. A. H. Durboraw, Mr. T. P. Hickman and H. C. Hoffman, M.D.

The following officers were elected for each year of the biennium:

President—Carl M. Distler, Esq.
Vice-President—Reverend F. B. Clausen, D.D.
Secretary and Treasurer—Reverend Wm. Freas, D.D.

It is proper that here due appreciation should be expressed of the faithful service of the Reverend E. F. Bachmann, D.D., who for eleven of the first twelve years of the merger had served as president of the Board. Under his leadership policies were developed and activity begun.

The Board is under the necessity of recording the death of one of its valued members, the Reverend J. S. Schantz, who was called to his reward on Thursday, March 26, 1931. Pastor Schantz was for many years in charge of the Hospice for Young Men in Philadelphia. He directed the work of the Philadelphia Settlement, leading in a large growth in its work, and was responsible for the organization of the work of the Artman Home, near Philadelphia. The members of the Board were deeply grieved by the passing of Brother Schantz, and adopted a fitting tribute to him, recognizing his long and faithful Inner Mission work. To fill the unexpired term of Pastor Schantz, the Board nominated the Reverend Rufus E. Kern of

Hamburg, Pa., to the Executive Board of the Church, which Board elected Pastor Kern to membership in the Inner Mission Board.

II. The Regular Work of the Board

The regular work of the Board naturally falls into three phases of activity which are called Congregational, Institutional and Educational.

1. *Congregational Activities.*

(a)   In the effort to realize the ideal of every member of the congregation busy in merciful work, a number of plans for Inner Mission activities have been submitted to Synodical Inner Mission Committees through which the Board does its work.   Important among these suggestions has been the plan to provide religious care for those who are in the many institutions other than those of the Church.   In this service evangelism of necessity has the important place.   The preaching of the Gospel is the very essence of Inner Mission work.   Here is the great difference from social service and welfare work.   Reports from Synodical Committees indicate that in many places this need is now being largely met.   Pastors are regular Chaplains in a number of instances.   At many more institutions our pastors and groups of people from our congregations are conducting regular religious services. In addition to religious services, social and recreational work is being carried on regularly.   It is the cause of real gratification that this practice is now being so generally followed.

(b)   Unemployment.   At the Milwaukee Convention of the Church a recommendation upon unemployment was adopted as follows:

"*Resolved,* That the United Lutheran Church urge every congregation directly affected by unemployment to appoint a special committee to assist its members in finding work and to co-operate with other religious and secular agencies of their community for relief of the situation in general."

To make this resolution of the Church effective, the following plan was submitted to our congregations through Synodical Inner Mission Committees. To meet the needs arising from unemployment let each congregation appoint a committee on relief.   The committee should be organized and work upon the basis of the following plan.   Conditions may make it wise to modify this plan to meet local circumstances.

"1.   The committee should represent the Church Council and various organizations of the congregations and comprise men and women, young people, wage-earners and employees. The number should be from five upwards according to the size and needs of the congregation.

"2.   The officers of the committee should act as an Executive Council, passing finally upon all recommendations for financial and other aid submitted by members of the committee.

"3. Wherever found necessary, a fund shall be created by outright gifts, or by subscriptions, the return of which shall be guaranteed by the congregation, to extend loans for three to six months to unemployed members of the Church who have been in good standing at least one year before the application for relief, and to be repaid without interest.

"4. The pastor should be an advisor of both the applicant and the committee, and should therefore not be a voting member of the committee.

"5. Applications by others than members in good standing for financial assistance by the congregation shall be granted only when the needs of regular members in distress have been met and when a careful investigation of the applicant's condition shall warrant it.

" 'If any provide not for his own, and especially for those of his own house, he hath denied the faith, and is worse than an infidel.'— I Tim. 5, 8.

" 'As we have, therefore, opportunity, let us do good unto all men, especially to them who are of the household of faith.' "—Gal. 6, 10.

Very often it will be found wise to supply food, clothing, fuel, etc., rather than money. In such work many can have a part. Opportunities for personal service will be numerous. Co-operation with local agencies will often make possible a larger service. Always Christian motives and methods should be used.

Reports from Synodical Committees indicate that our congregations generally have busied themselves in doing all possible in the relief of the distress caused by unemployment. In a number of instances congregations have adopted a well conceived plan and have carried on a most effective service. In many other instances in addition to the work done directly by the congregation there has been a close co-operation with local agencies which have been concerned with this matter. The Church will find evidence of a real life in its members in this application of religious principles into practice. There can be no letting down in this activity. We must carry on lovingly and patiently to bring all relief possible to those in need. **(See Resolutions 1 and 2.)**

(c) In addition items were sent to Synodical Inner Mission Committees for the development of Inner Mission work upon the territory and in the congregations of their synods.

I. For the guidance of Synodical Inner Mission Committees.

1. That where a synod has a Mission Committee in charge of both Home and Inner Mission work that a separate Board or Committee for each be established, if necessary by an amendment to the synodical constitution.
2. That in the effort to give a degree of permanence to Inner Mission Boards or Committees that we respectfully urge upon our synods, such boards or committees, either continuous or with rotating member-

ship. That such committee should have at least one member from each conference of the synod.

3. That an adequate appropriation for such Inner Mission Board or Committee be made by the synod to cover the traveling expenses of meetings of this committee and the necessary postage and stationery.

4. That we emphasize the importance of an Inner Mission Committee in each congregation. We have suggested that the pastor and one member of the Church Council and each of the organizations of the congregation form this committee. That when work is done by a different organization of the Church an effort be made to coordinate it through this committee so that there will be no duplication of the work.

II. For the guidance of the congregations.

Many of our congregations are engaged in doing Inner Mission work in their communities and are being blessed in it. Often it is not called Inner Mission work nor thought of as such. Other congregations may have this same blessing. We suggest the following items for consideration and action by synods, Synodical Inner Mission Committees and congregations.

1. Social agencies of state, county and city are making such rapid progress in the advancement of their work that there is danger of the Church losing this possibility of expressing her religious life. It is often necessary to work with established agencies in the relief of the poor and distressed. It is important that we shall strive to impress the Christian standpoint of all service, and to have this attitude recognized by them.

2. It is necessary that the congregation appreciate that it is responsible for the needy families and individuals among its own members and in the community. Plans for their relief should be made constantly.

3. That the pastor with his Inner Mission Committee seek out the poor and needy. While many are doing such work yet it is surprising to discover how many are in need of its ministrations. Many of the most worthy hide their need and will not seek help from the Church to which they may rightly turn. Experience in many places has demonstrated this truth. We suggest that relief work include among other things efforts to maintain the integrity of the family, provide shelter, food and clothing, concern about the health, particularly about the children, and when necessary the rehabilitation of the home so that it may again become united and self-sustaining.

4. Establish or stimulate a relief fund through alms boxes in the Church auditorium, some special funds, or other means that may fit into the particular work of each congregation. Many people are thankful for blessings which they have received, and would welcome the opportunity of expressing this thankfulness by helping others.

Two books are suggested for reading in connection with the above suggestions. "The Vestrymen," by C. P. Swank, D.D., and "The Art of Helping People Out of Trouble" by Karl de Schweinitz. **(See Resolution 3.)**

(d) The latest plan passed on to our congregations through our Synodical Inner Mission Committees has been the plan for a Preaching Mission. It has already met a sympathetic response. The object in view is the stimulation of the spiritual life of its members, the recalling of the lukewarm and erring, the gathering in of new people so that all might unite in a fuller and more complete service of mercy in their own communities. A general committee, under the pastor's direction, shall be in charge. It is thought best to seek a pastor of another congregation to preach. The teachings of the Lutheran Church should be explained. Christian practice and activity should be urged. The Gospel application will be made. Prayer groups should be formed. The whole congregation should pray for the Mission at an indicated time each day.

The general committee will make all plans and meet with district committees as necessary. Constant and faithful preparation is most essential.

The plan includes the organizing of the community in sections with committees responsible for each; visitation by the committee in each district to seek the unchurched and lapsed; tell of the services arranged; urge attendance by those they visit.

Much is hoped for as the result of the conducting of Preaching Missions.

(e) As a further matter concerning the congregation a study is being made of Child and Family Welfare which will lead to suggestions for activty by the congregations in their own communities. This study is being made by our Congregational Committee.

2. *Institutional*

(a) The Milwaukee Convention of the Church approved the classification of institutions in which all institutions of mercy of a similar character were brought under the same heading. It is well-known that about half of the institutions of mercy in which the people of The United Lutheran Church in America are concerned are operated in co-operation with Lutherans of other general bodies. A surprisingly big work is done by such institutions and agencies of mercy. Many of them have been active for many years in this service, but others are of more recent origin. The effort is being made to present a clearer picture of our institutional work through co-operation with the Statistical and Year Book Committee of the Church and the National Lutheran Council. A number of conferences have been held with the former committee and its representatives, and the effort to present the institutional situation of our Church more adequately is going forward. Final results cannot yet be reported, but steps are being taken in the direction of a more adequate display of institutional work. In reply to the request of the General Inner Mission Conference, the National Lutheran Council has initiated a survey of Inner Mission institutions and the Church, to discover the needs and opportunities for this kind of work. Your Board has given its full approval to this survey, and is lending its co-operation to it.

The general bodies of The Lutheran Church in America support and manage about 400 institutions and agencies of mercy. They bring the contact of the Church each year to about 850,000 people, and are responsible for an annual outlay of more than eight and a half million dollars. Of these institutions the U. L. C. A. supports and controls directly or is associated with members of other Lutheran bodies in the support and control of 104 institutions. This institutional work of the U. L. C. A. activity brings a Christian contact with at least 250,000 people each year. The Church contributes for this work over three and a half million dollars each year.

In addition to the institutional work many congregations are doing Inner Mission work for which figures are not available. It is, however, a conservative estimate that the Inner Mission activities of the Church in institution, society and congregation touch a half million souls each year, and that the Church contributes more than four million dollars for the support of its Inner Mission activities.

(b) For some time there has been a demand for a model constitution for Inner Mission societies. After a study of the constitutions of existing societies such a model constitution has been prepared and is available for those who may be able to use it. It is hoped that in many places in the Church plans for the establishment of Inner Mission societies will be made, and that activity of these societies in which the congregations of the city or town may have a share will go rapidly forward.

(c) New Institutions.

The following new institutions and agencies have been established during the biennium: an Inner Mission Society in Los Angeles, California, this Society has arranged for the purchase of property to be used as a Hospice; an Inner Mission Society in Saginaw, Michigan; an Inner Mission Society in Detroit, Michigan. The last name is a reorganization, now open to members of the U. L. C A. The Toledo Inner Mission Society now includes members of the U. L. C. A.

3. *Educational.*

(a) The Training of Workers. One of the great problems of the Church is the adequate training of workers for its Inner Mission work and also for secular social work. Negotiations are in progress with one of our Lutheran colleges, looking forward to the establishment of courses leading to a diploma which will be recognized everywhere in social work. A serious difficulty is the arranging for field work in connection with such a course, which is required as a necessary part of the training of such workers.

Trained workers are needed to be leaders in the Inner Mission work of our Church. It is always difficult to find such workers when they are needed. It has, however, become obvious that we must train workers who shall have such a stand in the field of social and welfare work that they shall be recognized in this field. There is slowly developing a very definite feeling that there is something missing in social work as it is conducted today. The suspicion is beginning to occur to some that it is religion which is needed. If we could train our Lutheran young people in our own schools for this work it will be possible for them to take positions of leadership in social work.

(b)   Closely associated with the above is the investigation now going on of establshed schools for social work. Your Board expects to recommend at least one school to those of our young people who desire to prepare themselves for social work.

(c)   The following suggestions have been made for Synodical Inner Mission Committees. Outline studies on the Inner Mission for five Inner Mission study hours are in preparation and the effort will be made to have those outlines used for study by congregational groups. Efforts to arrange conferences, at which Inner Mission work may be discussed, are under way.

(d)   The Church has set aside the month of June as Inner Mission month. In the effort to be helpful to our pastors and congregations in the proper observance of this month, sermon outlines and illustrative material have been sent to all the pastors of the Church. Articles have appeared in *The Lutheran*. Many letters of real appreciation indicate that this has been a helpful service to our congregations.

(e)   Four topics for study in the Luther League have been or are in process of preparation. They have aroused real interest in Inner Mission work, and have brought many requests to the office of the Board.

(f)   The General Inner Mission Conference has met and discussed many Inner Mission problems. This is a free conference group at which members from many of our general bodies are present. It has proven to be helpful each year and stimulating to those in attendance. In addition, a larger number of Lutherans have been interested in and attending the Annual Conferences on Social Work to which social leaders from all over the country come. In connection with these conferences an arresting exhibit of Lutheran activity has been made, and the Lutherans present at the conference have met for discussion.

(g)   A new series of "A Message for the Day," edited and distributed by the Board, is in course of preparation. The subscription list now numbers about 8,500. The "Message" has proven to be of real value. It has been a blessing to those who have received it, and many evidences of appreciation for it have been received.

III.   SPECIAL ACTIVITIES OF THE BOARD

1. Work for the Deaf. Work for the deaf has been carried on at seventeen different points throughout the Church by two full-time and one volunteer missionary. Over 200 services a year have been conducted with an attendance of somewhat over 3,000. Communion services have been held. Pastor Kaercher, a deaf-mute, a graduate of Gallaudet College and the Philadelphia Seminary, works under the direction of the Board of Inner Missions of the Ministeriuum of Pennsylvania, upon whose territory this work is done. In addition to nine regular points, he does much personal work in many towns of Eastern Pennsylvania and Western New Jersey.

In Kansas and adjacent states Pastor Sibberson, a hearing and speaking man, carries on a service to deaf-mutes at seven regular points.

New activities have been added in the biennium. Gallaudet College, in Washington, has been regularly visited by one of our missionaries. A group of negroes in New York has been gathered together and met regularly by one of the pastors to the deaf. The glove for the use of blind deaf has been widely distributed, Germany and Switzerland having been added to the seven foreign countries from which requests have come, in addition to many of our own States.

2. Immigrant and Seamen's Work. In November of 1931, Secretary E. A. Sievert, who has served the Board faithfully since January, 1925 as Secretary for Immigrant and Seamen's Work, felt called upon to resign because of the large decrease in immigration. He accepted a call to become pastor of Christ Lutheran Church in Ridgefield Park, N. J. The Board felt constrained, with much regret, to accept the resignation of Secretary Sievert. As, however, the need for some work remained, negotiations were opened with Secretary Sievert and Christ Church by which an arrangement has been made for part-time service by Pastor Sievert in this same capacity. He has continued giving a portion of his time to this work and has carried it on most effectively. The work has proven to be greater than anticipated, due to the large number of aliens returning to the countries of their origin.

There follows a detailed report of Immigrant and Seamen's Work.

(a) Port of New York. Ever since the immigrant work was entrusted to your Board, Port Work for Immigrants in the Port of New York has been carried on in co-operation with the Lutheran Emigrant House Association. This organization has a record of over sixty years of service in port work for immigrants in the harbor of New York. The co-operative arrangement with this association has been a most happy one. It has not only avoided duplication of work and workers, but it has also saved money for the Church. Through this arrangement the Secretary for Immigrant Work became the pastor of the Lutheran Emigrant House Association and thus has the direct supervision of the work.

Through this co-operation it is possible to meet all incoming steamers and to assist immigrants in every way. The field of activities is on board the steamers, at the piers, the railroad stations and Ellis Island. Frequently lodging or work, or both, are found for the immigrant that applies for this assistance.

It was possible during the biennium beginning April 1, 1930 and ending March 31, 1932, for the workers to make 333 visits to ships and piers to render assistance to 2,612 passengers at the piers, on the boats and at railroad stations. In addition, 2,436 immigrants have been served at the office of the Emigrant House Association of New York, of which Pastor Sievert is also pastor, and with which organization the Board is co-operating in immigrant work. The total served in the Port of New York is, therefore, 5,048.

Since the beginning of this year, developments at Ellis Island in the deportation division, re-entry permit department, and the law office, have made it necessary to keep a worker there quite regularly. Our work is chiefly among those foreigners who are to be deported—many of whom are destitute and among whom are many Lutherans. It was possible, by the arrangements made, to render much appreciated and helpful service in the first five months of 1932 in 598 cases. This service rendered in the name of the Church does much to create a friendlier spirit toward the Church.

(b) Other Ports in the United States. Other ports have been kept in mind by your Board, and the investigations made are kept on file for future use. That nothing has been undertaken is due largely to the fact that the local constituency of The United Lutheran Church in America in these ports is too weak to support such port work alone, and that your Board was not in position financially to undertake it. The one port which makes an exception is the port of Philadelphia, where the port work both for immigrants and seamen is adequately taken care of by the Inner Mission Board of the Ministerium of Pennsylvania.

(c) Canadian Ports. The splendid work that had developed in these ports has, through the curtailment of immigration, entered upon a period of repose. Our immigrant pastors have been released for part-time in other work. In Montreal the Canada synod has undertaken a home mission project and entrusted it temporarily to the immigrant pastor. Although in the year ending March 31, 1931, 8,707 Lutheran immigrants entered the port of Montreal, the number decreased gradually so that but 1,500 entered in the year ending March 31, 1932.

In Winnipeg the Manitoba Synod launched out into city mission work with considerable success, and enlisted the services of the immigrant pastor for this purpose. Nevertheless it was possible to minister adequately to many of the Lutherans who still entered western Canada during the past biennium.

(d) Foreign Contacts. Contacts with foreign ports have been continued. The main ones are with those of the ports of Hamburg and Bremen. These mission pastors gather and send names of immigrants to us, thus enabling our workers to meet them on arrival. These mission pastors likewise receive from us the names of those who are deported from Ellis Island and Canadian ports for foreign ports, which enables the missions in Hamburg and Bremen and other ports to meet these unfortunates and assist them to reach their homes before they are stranded.

Those who are deported are those who have overstayed their time allowed when entering this country; aliens who have become public charges; and those who voluntarily present themselves to the authorities requesting to be sent home.

There has been a large increase in the emigration of aliens until the number leaving the United States to return to the country of origin is seven times the number entering this country as immigrants.

Some of the other outstanding contacts abroad are: "Das Deutsche Auslands Institute," in Stuttgart; The City Missionary Bock in Nuerenberg, "Der Evangelische Haupt-Verein fuer Deutsche Ansiedler und Auswanderer," in Berlin, and other smaller agencies from whom we hear occasionally.

(e) Follow-up Work. Our follow-up work, which we always considered, and still do consider, one of the most important branches of our work, has received a considerable set-back through the fact that immigration has been curtailed to less than 5 per cent of the regular quota allotments to the various Transatlantic countries. Consequently, we cannot report as favorably in this branch of our work as heretofore. Nevertheless it was possible to send out 8,534 names and addresses of those who have entered the port of New York during the past biennium. A similar service has been rendered by the immigrant pastor at Montreal for the immigrants entering Canada. The ratio of the number of returns received on these addresses per month was the same as when many hundreds were sent out each month, namely, about one to three. By reason of the small number that entered we were enabled more readily to get into personal contact with them and gather information from the newcomers as to their religious status.

(f) Seamen's Work. Even though regular immigration has considerably decreased, there is one class that still comes and goes in hardly decreased numbers with every ship that enters and leaves port—the seaman. His stay on shore is at most sixty days. During this time he must be cared for. The bulk of the seamen from the Scandinavian countries and Germany are Lutheran. The Lutheran Church has a duty toward these men who give up so much of comfort and who by circumstances are compelled to lead a hard and trying existence in the service of the rest of humanity.

Seamen's work has been adequately carried on in Hoboken, N. J., and in Philadelphia, Pa., for some time. But owing to the lack of funds your Board was in no position to undertake this so necessary work in those ports (Houston, Texas; Los Angeles and San Francisco, California; Seattle, Washington; Vancover, B. C.; Baltimore, Md., and the chief Lake Ports) investigated by the Secretary for Immigrant and Seamen's Work, and found ripe for such undertaking. Even the Harbor of New York, though much is being done by various denominations and other organizations, is by no means covered, and the Manhattan and Brooklyn sides of the harbor are sorely in need of work for seamen by the Lutheran Church. When will the Church avail herself of the opportunities at her door?

3. *Work for Mountain Children.*

(a) The work of the Konnarock Training School, supported by the Women's Missionary Society and operated by them through the Inner Mission Board, has been carried on during the biennium with marked success. An average of thirty-two girls has been in attendance at the school. An important development of the biennium was the appointment of a nurse to organize health work in the school and community. An unusual piece of work has developed under her guidance, which has been of inestimable value to the community. It has been the means of opening the hearts of many of the mountain perents to the Gospel. The regular educational and vocational work of the school is capably carried on under a corps of teachers led by Miss Helen Dyer as superintendent. Some Daily Vacation Bible Schools have been operated at various points of the mountains under the general direction of the school but with volunteer workers from over the country. The work has brought a real blessing to the people of the mountains in Southwest Virginia.

The school includes a fine dormitory, in which a chapel and schools are also located; barn and outbuildings, pedigreed live stock, protected water rights, etc. The school represents an outlay of $45,000 and an annual budget of $11,000.

The Board in control consists of: Mrs. G. W. McClanahan, Mr. G. B. Morehead, Mr. E. F. Schmidt, Mrs. S. R. Kepner, Miss Flora Prince, Mr. H. L. Bonham, Mrs. W. F. Morehead, Reverend J. J. Scherer, Jr., D.D., Mr. L. C. Hassinger.

The officers of the Board are: Chairman, Reverend J. J. Scherer, Jr., D.D.; Vice-Chairman, Mrs. W. F. Morehead; Treasurer, Mr. L. C Hassinger; Secretary, Mrs. S. R. Kepner.

(b) Following long negotiations, the Iron Mountain Lutheran School has begun its work for boys. The school is located at Konnarock, Virginia. It is supported by the Brotherhood and operated by them through the Inner Mission Board. In this connection a new effort was made for the domestication of the Inner Mission Board in the State of Virginia. It was found that this was legally impossible. The original plan was to conduct the work of the Konnarock Training School for girls and the Iron Mountain Lutheran School for boys under one Board. To this plan both the Women's Missionary Society and the Brotherhood had given their assent. It was, however, found that the difficulties were so many that it would be better to have separate Boards for the two schools. That of the Iron Mountain Lutheran School has now been incorporated under the corporation laws of the State of Virginia and has organized for work. The Reverend C. L. Miller was named as Superintendent of the Iron Mountain Lutheran School, with the approval of the Inner Mission Board. Fifteen boys are at present at the school receiving in addition to a religious and academic training, vocational training in farming, dairying, fruit raising and similar activities. The operation of the school consummates plans which were in preparation over a period of years, and opens a well-balanced activity by the Church for the children of the Southern mountains. It should prove to be a real joy for the men of the church as has the similar work for the women.

The property secured is a fully equipped farm with about eight buildings.

One was a hotel, now a dormitory. Several houses, a barn, store and church are included. The purchase price is about $26,000. The members of the Board of the Iron Mountain Lutheran School are: Mr. H. E. Isenhour, Mr. L. C. Hassinger, Dr. S. J. McDowell, Mr. W. B. Keller, Dr. J. W. Kapp, Dr. J. J. Scherer, Jr., Mr. T. P. Hickman, Dr. H. C. Hoffman, Mr. T. C. Rohrbaugh, H. L. Bonham, Rev. R. Homer Anderson.

The officers of the Board are: President, Mr. H. E. Isenhour; Vice-President, Mr. L. C. Hassinger; Secretary, Mr. W. B. Keller; Treasurer, Mr. H. L. Bonham.

(c) It was found desirable for the Synod of Virginia to place a pastor at Konnarock. The plan is for this pastor to serve the people of the Southern Mountains, seeking to carry his ministry into a slowly increasing territory and heading up the development of mountain work in more of the mountain communities. Such a pastor has not yet been secured, but the Reverend C. W. Cassell has been appointed as supply. He is now carrying on his work under the direction of the Virginia Synod with the support of the Inner Mission Board.

IV. General Matters

1. Memorial on Immigrant Work from the Nova Scotia Synod. The following memorial from the Nova Scotia Synod was referred to the Inner Mission Board by the Milwaukee Convention:

That synod memorialize the United Lutheran Church on the question of Lutheran immigrant work at the port of Halifax.

May we further connect this memorial with the action of the Executive Board of the United Lutheran Church relative to the seeking for co-operation of other general Lutheran bodies in immigrant work.

The memorial refers to regular service to immigrants on boats touching at the point of Halifax. Our answer is that the immigrant pastor of Montreal goes to Halifax for this purpose occasionally; that almost without exception immigrants touching at Halifax proceed to Montreal, where they are met by the Immigrant Pastor; that the local Lutheran pastor in Halifax meets such boats as his work permits, and that the Board has called the attention of the Inner Mission Committee of the Canada Synod to this matter (Immigrant Work at Montreal is under the direction of this Committee), urging that as possible and necessary more ships should be met at Halifax.

Co-operation with other Lutheran general bodies is in operation and other co-operations have been sought as need required.

2. A member of the Board, the Reverend G. H. Bechtold, was invited by President Hoover to attend the White House conference on Child Welfare and Protection in Washington, D. C., November 19 to 22, 1930. He reported that the conference brought together social workers from every corner of our country. The conference was organized into four departments—Medical

Service, Public Health and Organization, Education and Training, and the Handicapped Child. The outstanding impression was that the Church, as an agency that has not only done pioneer work in the field but that is continuing to function, was continually ignored. It is desirable that the Church take the material developed by the conference, much of it invaluable, and translate it into a dynamic that will lead the Church into larger fields of service to the needy and to an intensive training of its own people for public and private service.

3. Following negotiations, the Inner Mission Board agreed to membership in the International Federation on Inner Mission and the Diaconate. The Board has been represented at the meetings of this federation by Dr. Brueckner in 1929 and by Dr. Samuel Trexler in 1930 at Upsala, Sweden. These brethren have brought interesting reports of the conference, and have commended most highly the spirit animating them and the activity which they represent. Of the 1930 conference our representative says:

"One of the noteworthy things of the meeting was the inspiration of a Christian character which it brought. It indicated a united Christendom in the doing of works of mercy. Seventeen countries were represented. The opportunity was given to become acquainted with the workers in the countries of Europe. The most vital personality was Archbishop Soderblom. A large contribution to the conference was given by the personality of Dr. Steinweg. The problems discussed at the conference grew out of the European situation as a background, but had the same fundamental basis as our own. It has been revealed by the conference that it is very difficult to serve in these days. Sometimes, however, to be served is more difficult. The greatest problem before the meeting was the problem of Russia, upon which certain of the members of the conference spoke with great authority."

4. Finances. In common with all the activities of the Church, the Board has felt the financial pressure. In an effort to meet the situation adequately there has been a general reduction in the salaries paid by the Board of at least 10 per cent. In addition a strict budget has been drawn, limited to absolutely essential expenditures, and these reduced just as far as possible. To balance the budget on the very meager and limited allowance provided, your Board has been compelled to cut its expenses to the very bone, sometimes removing even a part of the bone. That much necessary work has been abandoned or not undertaken because of financial inability is abundantly evident. The work of the Board has been seriously handicapped, and the realization of its objectives delayed by reason thereof. Your Board pleads for a budget proportion which will enable it to do the work which it can and should be doing, all of which will redound to the honor and glory of the Church. It is the hope of the Board that a more adequate financial provision will make possible the initiation of new work under the authority given to the Board by the Milwaukee Convention to initiate local activities.

5. Feeling the necessity of a real study of the Inner Mission field of the

Church, the Board has initiated such a study. This includes a survey of the work already done and planned by the Board as well as the untouched work in the Inner Mission field generally. Such a survey will be of great help in planning an adequate program for congregations, synods and institutions of the Church and developing a deeper interest in and a wider application of Inner Mission ideals.

V. Inner Mission Institutions and Agencies

In the following classification of institutions and agencies about half of them are conducted without the control of the Church or any of its parts but in association with Lutherans of other General Bodies. Those institutions or agencies which are so operated are marked in the following list with an asterisk. Those which have no asterisk before them are under full control of The United Lutheran Church in America, one or more of its synods, groups of individuals, all of whom are members of the U. L. C. A.

1. *Classification of Inner Mission Institutions and Agencies.*

Unless otherwise noted the institutions and agencies on the following list are owned, controlled and supported entirely by The United Lutheran Church in America, one or more of its constituent synods, one or more of its congregations, or by associations within constituent synods.

(Intersynodical—with one or more other Lutheran General Bodies.)

(Non-Synodical—self-perpetuating Board of Managers, majority Lutheran with full control.)

Date of Founding
I. *General Inner Mission Board*

1918   1. Inner Mission Board of The United Lutheran Church in America, Inc.
      (a) Work for the Deaf (with Ministerium of Pennsylvania and Kansas Synod).
      (b) Seamen's and Immigrant Work (with Lutheran Emigrant House Association and Canada and Manitoba Synods).
      (c) Konnarock Training School (with Women's Missionary Society).
      (d) Iron Mountain Lutheran School (with The Brotherhood).

II. *Synodical Inner Mission Board*

1923   1. Board of Inner Missions of the Evangelical Lutheran Ministerium of Pennsylvania and the Adjacent States.

A. Activities of Board
1899   (a) City Mission, Philadelphia, Pa.
1908   (b) Lutheran Seamen's and Immigrant Mission, Philadelphia, Pa.
1922   (c) Lutheran Children's Bureau, Philadelphia, Pa.
1922   (d) Lutheran Bureau, Philadelphia, Pa.
1925   (e) Mission to the Deaf.
1929   (f) Mission to the Blind.

B. Other Inner Mission Institutions and Agencies on the
Territory of the Ministerium of Pennsylvania

1859 (a) Orphans' Home and Asylum for the Aged and Infirm of the Evangelical Lutheran Church at Germantown, Philadelphia, Pa.
1884 (b) Mary J. Drexel Home and Philadelphia Motherhouse of Deaconesses, Philadelphia, Pa.
1897 (c) The Lutheran Orphans Home in Berks County, Topton, Pa.
1905 (d) The Inner Mission Society of the Evangelical Lutheran Church of Philadelphia, Pa.
1905 (e) The Luther Hospice for Young Men, Philadelphia, Pa.
1905 (f) The Lutheran Settlement, Philadelphia, Pa.
*1906 (g) Kensington Dispensary for the Treatment of Tuberculosis, Philadelphia, Pa. (Non-synodical).
*1908 (h) Tabor Home for Children, Doylestown, Pa. (Non-synodical).
*1908 (i) Good Shepherd Home, Allentown, Pa. (Non-synodical).
*1913 (j) River Crest Preventorium of Kensington Dispensary, Mont Clare, Pa. (Non-synodical).
1915 (k) Artman Home for Lutherans, Ambler, Pa.
1920 (l) Tryon Hall, Philadelphia, Pa.
1923 (m) The Lutheran Inner Mission Society of Trenton, N. J., and vicinity.
? (n) The Lutheran Inner Mission Society of Reading and vicinity (Intersynodical).

C. "The Institution of Protestant Deaconesses,"
Pittsburgh Synod

* (a) Passavant Hospital, Pittsburgh, Pa. (Intersynodical).
(b) Memorial Homes for Epileptics, Rochester, Pa. (Intersynodical).
(c) Orphans' Home and Farm School, Zelienople, Pa.

III. *Children's Homes*

*1806 1. Emaus Orphan House, Middletown, Pa. (Non-synodical).
1852 2. Orphans' Home and Farm School, Zelienople, Pa.
1859 3. Orphans' Home (and Asylum for the Aged) at Germantown, Philadelphia, Pa.
1864 4. Evangelical Lutheran St. John's Orphan Home, Buffalo, N. Y.
*1866 5. Wartburg Orphans' Farm School of the Evangelical Lutheran Church, Mt. Vernon, N. Y. (Intersynodical).
1868 6. Tressler Orphans' Home, Loysville, Pa.
1886 7. Tabitha Home (also Old Peoples' Home), Lincoln, Nebr.
1888 8. The Lutheran Orphan Home of the South, Salem, Va.
1897 9. The Lutheran Orphans' Home in Berks County, Pa., Topton, Pa.
1903 10. Oesterlen Orphans' Home, Springfield. Ohio.
1904 11. Nachusa Lutheran Orphanage, Nachusa, Ill.
1904 12. Kinderfreund, Jersey City, N. J. (also Old Peoples' Home).
1908 13. Ebenezer, (Orphanage for Girls), Frederiksted, Virgin Islands. (Board of American Missions).
*1908 14. Good Shepherd Home, Allentown, Pa. (Nonsynodical).
*1908 15. Tabor Home for Children, Doylestown, Pa. (Non-Synodical).
*1914 16. Inner Mission Center, Brooklyn, N. Y., Second Street (Non-Synodical).
*1919 17. Children's Receiving Home, Maywood, Ill. (Intersynodical).
*1919 18. Children's Receiving Home, St. Paul, Minn. (Intersynodical).
1920 19. Bethesda Home, Meadville, Pa.
*1924 20. Inner Mission Center, Brooklyn. N. Y. (Intersynodical).

IV. *Fresh Air Camps and Homes*

*1922   1. Wilbur J. Herrlich Memorial Home, Towners, N. Y. (New York Inner Mission Society).
*   2. Jolly Acres (Baltimore Inner Mission Society).
*   3. Fresh Air Home (Lutheran Welfare Society, Minneapolis, Minn.)
*   4. Summer Camp (Pittsburgh Inner Mission Society).

V. *Homes for Problem Children*

1920   1. Bethesda Home, Meadville, Pa.
1927   2. Williams-Henson Home for Boys, Knoxville, Tenn.
*1928   3. Bethany Home, Milwaukee, Wis. (Intersynodical).

VI. *Old Peoples' Homes*

1859   1. Asylum for the Aged and Infirm of the Evangelical Lutheran Church of Germantown, Philadelphia, Pa. (Also Orphans' Home).
1888   2. Tabitha Home, Lincoln, Nebr. (also Orphans' Home).
1888   3. Mary J. Drexel Home, Philadelphia, Pa. (also Deaconess Mother-house).
1890   4. National Lutheran Home for the Aged, Washington, D. C.
1896   5. Lutheran Church Home for the Aged and Infirm of Buffalo and Erie Co., N. Y.
1896   6. The Francke Home, Charleston, S. C.
*1897   7. Mary Louise Heins Home for the Aged and Infirm, Mt. Vernon, N. Y. (Intersynodical).
1904   8. Kinderfreund, Jersey City, N. J.
1905   9. Old Peoples' Home of the Pittsburgh Synod, Zelienople, Pa.
1906   10. Lutheran Home for the Aged, Erie, Pa.
1906   11. Feghtly Lutheran Home, Tippecanoe City, Ohio.
*1908   12. Good Shepherd Home, Allentown, Pa. (Non-synodical).
1911   13. Lowman Home for the Aged and Helpless, White Rock, S. C.
1918   14. Lutheran Home for the Aged, Southbury, Conn.
1919   15. The Lutheran Church Home for the Aged and Infirm of Central, N. Y., Clinton, N. Y.
1927   16. The Louisville Lutheran Home, Jeffersonville, Ky.
1930   17. The Mulberry Lutheran Home for the Aged, Mulberry, Ind.
      18. Los Angeles, Los Angeles, Calif.

VII. *Homes for Dependents, Destitute and Helpless*

*1908   1. Good Shepherd Home, Allentown, Pa. (Non-synodical).
1911   2. Lowman Home for the Aged and Helpless, White Rock, S. C.

VIII. *Homes for Epileptics*

*1895   1. Passavant Memorial Homes for the care of Epileptics, Rochester, Pa. (Intersynodical).
1911   2. Lowman Home for the Aged and Helpless, White Rock, S. C.

IX. *Hospitals*

*1849   1. Passavant Hospital, Pittsburgh, Pa. (Intersynodical).
1890   2. Children's Hospital of Mary J. Drexel Home, Philadelphia, Pa.
1895   3. Women's and Children's Hospital, Guntur, India (Board of Foreign Missions).
*1898   4. The California Hospital (Lutheran), Los Angeles, Calif. (Intersynodical).

*1898 5. Robinwood Hospital, Toledo, Ohio (Intersynodical).
*1898 6. Lutheran Hospital of Manhattan, New York City (Non-synodical).
1910 7. Women's and Children's Hospital, Chirala, India (Board of Foreign Missions).
1911 8. Women's and Children's Hospital, Rajahmundry, India (Board of Foreign Missions).
1916 9. General, Rentichintala, India (Board of Foreign Missions).
1922 10. General Hospital, Tarlupad, India (Board of Foreign Missions).
1925 11. General Nidadavole, India (Board of Foreign Missions).
1926 12. General Hospital, Zorzor, Africa (Board of Foreign Missions).
1927 13. National Lutheran Sanatarium, Albuquerque, New Mexico.
1928 14. Lutheran Hospital Reuss Memorial, Cuero, Texas.
*1928 15. St. Luke's Lutheran Hospital, Milwaukee, Wis. (Intersynodical).
? 16. Muhlenberg, Monrovia, Liberia, Africa (Board of Foreign Missions).
? 17. General, Tsingtao, China (Board of Foreign Missions).

X. *Seamen's and Immigrants Missions*
*1869 1. Lutheran Emigrant House Association of New York (Non-synodical).
*1907 2. Seamen's Mission, Hoboken, N. J. (Non-synodical).
1908 3. Seamen's and Immigrant Mission of the Ministerium of Pennsylvania for Philadelphia, Pa.

XI. *Hospices*
1905 1. The Luther Hospice for Young Men, PPhiladelphia, Pa.
*1917 2. Lutheran Hospice for Girls, Baltimore, Md. (Intersynodical).
*1918 3. Cotta Home for Young Women, Pittsburgh, Pa. (Intersynodical).
*1919 4. Trabert Hall (for Young Women), Minneapolis, Minn. (Inter-synodical).
1920 5. Tryon Hall (for Young Women), Philadelphia, Pa.
1921 6. The Lutheran Hospice for Girls, Akron, Ohio.
*1921 7. Lutheran Hospice for Girls, Milwaukee, Wis. ((Intersynodical).
1924 8. United Lutheran Church Girls Club, Chicago, Ill.
1925 9. State Luther League Hospice, Omaha. Nebr.
1928 10. Lutheran Hospice for Girls, Reading, Pa.
   11. Hospice, Los Angeles, Calif.

XII. *Settlements*
1890 1. St. John's Lutheran Settlement House, Knoxville, Tenn.
1905 2. The Lutheran Settlement, Philadelphia, Pa.
*1914 3. The Luther House, Minneapolis, Minn. (Intersynodical).
   4. Martin Luther Neighborhood House, Philadelphia, Pa

XIII. *Miscellaneous Institutions and Agencies*
1899 1. City Mission, Philadelphia, Pa.
1904 2. Queen Louise Home (for sick and neglected babies), Frederik-sted, St. Croix, Virgin Islands (Board of American Missions).
*1906 3. Kensington Dispensary for the Treatment of Tuberculosis, Philadelphia, Pa. (Non-synodical).
1907 4. Queen Louise Home, (for sick and neglected babies), Christen-sted, St. Croix, Virgin Islands (Board of American Missions).
*1913 5. River Crest Preventorium of Kensington Dispensary, Mont Clare, Pa. (Non-synodical).

*1915 6. Artman Home for Lutherans, Ambler, Pa. (Non-synodical).
 1922 7. Lutheran Children's Bureau, Philadelphia, Pa.
 1922 8. Lutheran Bureau, Philadelphia, Pa.
*1922 9. Wilbur J. Herrlich Memorial Farm, Towners, N. Y. (Inter-
        synodical)
*1924 10. Inner Mission Center, Brooklyn, N. Y. (Intersynodical).
*1930 11. Inner Mission—Social Service Branch, Pittsburgh, Pa. (Inter-
        synodical).

XIV. *Inner Mission Societies*
 1902 1. The Inner Mission Society of the Evangelical Lutheran Church,
        Philadelphia, Pa.
*1905 2. The Lutheran Welfare Society in the Twin Cities, Minn. (Inter-
        synodical).
*1907 3. The Lutheran Inner Mission Society of Pittsburgh, Pa. (Inter-
        synodical).
*1907 4. The Inner Mission Society of the Evangelical Lutheran Church
        in New York City (Intersynodical)
*1909 5. The Inner Mission and Rescue Society, Brooklyn, N. Y. (Non-
        synodical).
*1910 6. The Inner Mission Society of the Evangelical Lutheran Church
        in Brooklyn, N. Y. and vicinity (Intersynodical).
*1914 7. The Inner Mission Society of the Evangelical Lutheran Church
        of Baltimore, Md. and vicinity (Intersynodical).
 1917 8. The Inner Mission Society of the State of Connecticut.
 1917 9. The Inner Mission Society of the Chicago Area, Chicago, Ill.
 1917 10. The Inner Mission Society of Washington, D. C.
*1921 11. The Milwaukee Inner Mission Society of the Evangelical Lu-
        theran Church, Milwaukee, Wis. (Intersynodical).
 1923 12. The Inner Mission Society, Trenton, N. J.
    ? 13. The Inner Mission Society, Charleston, S. C.
 * ? 14. The Inner Mission Society of the Evangelical Lutheran Church
        of Reading, Pa., and vicinity (Intersynodical).
       15. The Inner Mission Society of Saginaw, Mich.
       16. The Inner Mission Society of Detroit, Mich.
       17. The Inner Mission Society of Los Angeles, Calif.
 *   18. The Lutheran Inner Mission Society, Mandan, North Dakota
        (Intersynodical).
 *   19. Lutheran Welfare Society, Portland, Oregon (Intersynodical).
 *   20. Lutheran Welfare Society, Seattle, Washington (Intersynodical).
 *   21. Lutheran Welfare Society, Tacoma, Washington (Inter-
        synodical).
 *   22. Lutheran Inner Mission Society, Toledo, Ohio (Non-synodical).
       23. Lutheran Women's Inner Mission League of Wheeling, W. Va.

XV. *Deaconess Motherhouses*
 1884 1. Philadelphia Motherhouse for Deaconesses, Philadelphia, Pa.
 1895 2. The Lutheran Deaconess Motherhouse and Training School,
        Baltimore, Md.

2. *Reports for Institutions.*
According to constitutional requirement the Inner Mission Board hereto-
fore has presented reports from the institutions and agencies listed above.
In the interest of economy of space decision was made by the Board to give

a summary only of each class of institution instead of individual reports. This summary follows:

(a) Children's Homes.

The members of The United Lutheran Church in America are interested in twenty children's homes. In these homes 1,910 children are cared for at an expenditure of about $750,000, the average cost of the care for each child is slightly less than $400. Of these homes, twelve may be classed as those of The United Lutheran Church in America, eight being inter-synodical or non-synodical. In the list there are fifteen homes which care for orphans, half-orphans, and in a few instances children with both parents living. Two of them are receiving homes for the temporary care of children. Two are Inner Mission centers where provision is also made for temporary care. Of these homes one is operated and supported by the Board of American Missions in the Virgin Islands. Twenty-four of our synods have an interest in the support and control of these homes. There is no children's home for The United Lutheran Church in America west of Lincoln, Nebraska.

(b) Fresh Air Camps and Homes.

Four such camps are in operation, caring for 1,304 children at a cost of $31,000. The average cost for each child, almost without exception a two weeks' vacation in the summer time, is $24. All are intersynodical or non-synodical and are operated by Inner Mission Societies.

(c) Homes for Problem Children.

Of these homes two are of The United Lutheran Church in America and one is inter-synodical. The members of three synods are interested in their support and control. 167 children are cared for at an annual outlay of slightly over $60,000 or an average of $367 for each child. These homes receive children who are delinquent and might soon come into juvenile courts, and attempt to rehabilitate them. The success of their work has been great.

(d) Old Peoples' Homes.

Of the eighteen homes for old people, sixteen are classed as United Lutheran Church in America and two as intersynodical or non-synodical. 558 old people are cared for at an outlay of about $250,000 a year. The average cost of the care of each old person is $438. Admission fees in these homes range from $250 to $1,000. In very exceptional cases all of them waive this requirement and admit a person even if there is no money at all. For this class of institution there are more requests for admission than for any others. Three of these institutions (National Home for the Aged. Washington, D. C.; Tabitha Home, Lincoln, Nebraska, and Lowman Home, White Rock, S. C.), are in part supported from the budget of The United Lutheran Church in America. Except for these three, nineteen synods are represented in the control and support of homes for old people.

(e) Homes for Dependents, Destitute and Helpless.

There are two such institutions both of which do a varied work so that they must also be included in Children's Homes, Old Peoples' Homes and Homes for Epileptics. One of these is of The United Lutheran Church in America and the other non-synodical. Seventy persons are cared for as dependents, etc., at an estimated outlay of $26,000, making the average cost per person $376. Two synods are represented in the management and support of these institutions.

(f)   Homes for Epileptics.

There are two such homes, one of The United Lutheran Church in America and one intersynodical. In one of these institutions (the Passavant Memorial Home for Epileptics, Rochester, Pa.) 185 epileptics are tenderly cared for at an annual outlay of $37,000, the cost per person being about $200. Figures for the other home are impossible as it also does work for the aged and dependent.

(g)   Hospitals.

Of the seventeen hospitals listed, thirteen are of The United Lutheran Church in America and five intersynodical. Eight of the thirteen U. L. C. A. hospitals are operated by the Board of Foreign Missions in connection with its work abroad and reported by that Board. Eight synods are represented in the support and control of the remaining nine hospitals. Somewhat over 23,000 patients are cared for each year at an annual outlay of about $1,570,000 in the hospitals in this country. The work of the hospitals is the means of bringing many people into vital contact with the Church.

(h)   Seamen's and Immigrant Missions.

Of the three such missions one is of the U. L. C. A. and two non-synodical. Two synods are represented in their control and support. 1,223 persons were served at an annual outlay of about $47,000. In addition, many seamen were met by the missionaries and came into contact with them in reading rooms and dormitories provided. Many seamen are discharged from their ships in our country and have become a heavy charge upon the facilities of our seamen's mission. The report of immigrant work is included under the proper heading in the report of the Board.

(i)   Hospices.

Of the eleven hospices listed above one has just been purchased and no report upon it is available. Of the remaining ten, six are of the U. L. C. A. and four intersynodical. 1,222 persons were cared for at an annual outlay of slightly over $100,000. The hospices are operated by individuals, congregations, groups of individuals outside the congregations, and Inner Mission Societies. Ten of the synods of our Church are interested in this safeguarding of our young people who come to our larger cities and towns.

(j)   Settlements.

Of the four settlements one of them is really a general mission work among foreign people. The remaining three care for 716 people at a cost of about $7,000 per year. These figures do not adequately present the work which the settlements do in the poorer sections of our cities where they gather together the children and older folks and render them a Christian service of great importance.

(k)   Miscellaneous Institutions and Agencies.

Of such institutions, eleven in number, five are of the U. L. C. A. and six are intersynodical or non-synodical. Two of the United Lutheran Church institutions are operated by the Board of American Missions in the Virgin Islands. Two synods are represented in their management and support of those in this country. 1,304 persons were served at an annual outlay of about $140,000. In addition the Board of American Missions reports on the institutions in the Virgin Islands. The activities of these institutions are so diverse that it is difficult to present an adequate picture of them.

(1) Inner Mission Societies.

Among the important activities in the Inner Mission field is the work of the Inner Mission Societies. Of the twenty-three listed, one has been organized very recently and no figures are available. These societies employ 220 full-time workers and many volunteers. Their activities reach into hospitals, institutions of mercy, asylums, penal institutions, congregations, private homes and the unchurched. They maintain contacts with city, county and state social and welfare agencies. They represent the Church in many places and bring those who are found into contact with congregations. Workers of these societies have come into touch with at least 400,000 persons each year and have expended about $475,000 in their work. Ten of our synods are interested through their members in their activities.

(m) Deaconess Motherhouses.

Although they will be reported upon in another place in the Bulletin it is fitting to mention that there are two Deaconess Motherhouses in which the members of the U. L. C. A. are interested. 155 Deaconesses are members of the families of these two motherhouses. Fifty probationers are in course of training. In quite a number of our Inner Mission Institutions and Agencies, deaconesses are either leaders or workers. Their efficient service has helped to make effective the Inner Mission activities of the Church.

VI. TREASURER'S REPORT

STATEMENT OF RECEIPTS AND DISBURSEMENTS
July 1, 1930 to June 30, 1931

RECEIPTS

	General	Mountain	Immigrant	Deaf
Apportionment	$10,070.20	$693.22	$7,783.24	$2,153.34
Loans from Bank	1,000.00			
"Message" Subscriptions	994.76			
Literature Sales	13.05			
Contributions	102.19	248.30		85.00
Contributions for Others	5.17			
Women's Missionary Society		10,499.94		
Total Receipts	$12,185.37	$11,441.46	$7,783.24	$2,238.34

DISBURSEMENTS

	General	Mountain	Immigrant	Deaf
Salaries of Secretaries	$3,999.96		$2,800.00	
Salaries of Clerks	1,455.00		1,325.00	
Salaries of Pastors			3,535.80	$2,236.63
Traveling Expense: Secretaries	3,001.02		319.03	
Expenses—Board	959.16	$68.75		
Maintenance Contribution Lutheran Church House	775.75			
Office Expenses	1,009.97		99.61	
Interest on Bank Loans	49.11			
William-Henson Home	200.00			
Literature Printing	90.68			
Contributions for Others	5.17			

School Expenses:

Salaries	3,325.00
Other	6,258.28
Iron Mountain (Traveling)	33.71

Total Disbursements	$11,545.82	$9,685.74	$8,079.44	$2,236.63

SUMMARY OF CASH IN BANK
July 1, 1930 to June 30. 1931

	General	Mountain Work	Immigrant Work	Deaf Work	Total
Balance, July 1, 1930	$430.14*	$235.94	$1,030.23	$213.47*	$622.56
Receipts	12,185.37	11,441.46	7,783.24	2,238.34	33,648.41**
	11,755.23	11,677.40	8,813.47	2,024.87	34,270.97
Disbursements	11,545.82	9,685.74	8,079.44	2,236.63	31,547.63
	209.41	1,991.66	734.03	211.76*	2,723.34
Transfers	318.13*	73.86*	23.02	415.01	
Balance, June 30, 1931	$108.72*	$1,917.80	$711.01	$203.25	$2,723.34**

*Deficit.

**Includes receipts from June Apportionment and Women's Missionary Society in the sum of $2,716.66 received in July.

STATEMENT OF RECEIPTS AND DISBURSEMENTS
July 1, 1931 to June 30, 1932

RECEIPTS

	General	Mountain	Immigrant	Deaf
Apportionment	$10,603.41	$1,178.65	$4,166.19	$1,807.75
Loans	17,125.01			
"Message" Subscriptions	1,001.01			
Literature Sales	8.95			
Contributions	128.32	474.43	100.00	80.00
Contributions—Travel	226.75			
Contributions—Others	5.50			
Women's Missionary Society		10,999.92		
Refunds and Adjustments	4.10	62.00	100.00	
Total Receipts	$29,103.05	$12,715.00	$4,366.19	$1,887.75

DISBURSEMENTS

	General	Mountain	Immigrant	Deaf
Salaries—Secretaries	$3,799.98		$2,120.00	
Salaries—Clerks	1,486.00		1,213.00	
Salaries—Pastors			1,367.50	$2,658.29
Travel—Secretaries	2,933.68		208.66	

Travel—Executive Committee	88.37	
Travel—Boards	22.00	
Expenses—Boards	763.15	8.25
Maintenance Contribution Lu-		
theran Church House	907.03	
Office Expenses	1,241.86	228.50
Literature—Printing	567.41	
Literature—Purchased	6.00	
William-Henson Home	492.52	
Loans Repaid	17,220.00	
Contributions—Others	5.50	53.00
School Expenses:		
Salaries		7,440.00
Other Expenses		4,274.05
Health Work		999.96

Total Disbursements	$29,533.50	$12,775.26	$5,137.66	$2,658.29

SUMMARY OF CASH IN BANK
July 1, 1931 to June 30, 1932

	General	Mountain Work	Immigrant Work	Deaf Work	Total
Balance, July 1, 1931	$108.72*	$1,917.80	$711.01	$203.25	$2,723.34
Receipts	29,103.05	12,715.00	4,366.19	1,887.75	48,071.99
	28,994.33	14,632.80	5,077.20	2,091.00	50,795.33
Disbursements	29,533.50	12,775.26	5,137.66	2,658.29	50,104.71
	539.17*	1,857.54	60.46*	567.29*	690.62
Transfers	570.51	815.59*	258.38*	503.46	
Balance, June 30, 1932	$31.34	$1,041.95	$318.84*	$63.83*	$690.62

*Deficit.

BALANCE SHEET
June 30, 1932

ASSETS

Cash in Bank	$690.62
Petty Cash Funds and Stamps	57.25
Cash on Hand (Undeposited Checks)	10.00
Advances—Traveling Expenses	10.14
Inventory of Salable Literature, at Estimated Value	100.00
Furniture and Fixtures, at Estimated Value	225.00
Total Assets	$1,093.01

LIABILITIES AND FUNDS

Notes Payable—Bank	$1,000.00
Unpaid Vouchers	3,992.61

Funds:
General $3,272.75*
Mountain Work 125.29
Immigrant Work 688.31*
Deaf Work 63.83

Total Funds 3,899.60*

Total Liabilities and Funds $1,093.01

Respectfully submitted,
WM. FREAS, *Treasurer.*

Philadelphia, Pa., August 4, 1932.
We have audited the books of account of the Treasurer of the Inner Mission Board of The United Lutheran Church in America, for the biennium beginning July 1, 1930 and ending June 30, 1932, and we hereby certify that, in our opinion, the foregoing statements of Cash Receipts and Disbursements for the years ended June 30, 1391 and June 30, 1932, and the Balance Sheet as of June 30, 1932, are in accordance with the books of account, and are true and correct.

TAIT, WALKER & BAKER,
Accountants and Auditors.

RECOMMENDATIONS

1. *Resolved,* That we express our joy at the fine response of our congregations to the relief of distress caused by unemployment.
2. *Resolved,* That we urge upon our congregations that they continue their efforts to relieve the distress of our members and communities, not only the distress that now exists but also that which is in prospect.
3. *Resolved,* That we commend to our congregations and people a deeper interest in Inner Mission work in their communities, and request them to adopt a plan for a fuller service and to work towards its fulfillment.
4. *Resolved,* That we express our gratitude for the splendid service rendered by our Institutions of Mercy and Inner Mission Societies, and commend them to the interest and whole-hearted support of our church.

Respectfully submitted, for the Board,
CARL M. DISTLER, *President.*
WM. FREAS, *Executive Secretary,*

Mr. Distler introduced the Rev. Wm. Freas, Executive Secretary and Treasurer of the Board, who addressed the Convention. Dr. Freas introduced the Rev. E. A. Sievert, Secretary for Immigrant Work, and Miss Amelia D. Kemp, Executive Secretary of the Women's Missionary Society, who addressed the Convention.

The Rev. G. H. Bechtold, a member of the Board, introduced Mrs. R. C. Young and Miss Martha Bauerle, two deaf mutes, who "sang" "Nearer My God To Thee" in the sign language, and Miss Grace Pearl, a blind, deaf mute, who recited one of her own poems.

The consideration of the report of the Inner Mission Board was interrupted at this time because of the special order.

The report of the Commission on Investments as printed in the Bulletin, together with the Supplemental Report, was presented by Dr. E. Clarence Miller, Chairman of the Commission.

REPORT OF THE COMMISSION ON INVESTMENTS

(For action on the recommendation in this report see p. 228.)

In accordance with the action of the Church at its 1930 Convention authorizing the formation of an Investment Commission, individuals elected by the Executive Board and by other boards and agencies were called together by President F. H. Knubel, on March 20, 1931, at the Church House in New York City, for the purpose of carrying out the recommendations of the Church. It was deemed wise to effect only a temporary organization at that time. Accordingly, President F. H. Knubel was elected temporary chairman and Dr. Gould Wickey temporary secretary. Five meetings were held during the biennium. The following report is submitted for the information of the Church and as a record of the progress made.

1. CLARIFICATION OF POINTS IN RECOMMENDATIONS ADOPTED IN 1930. *The Relationship of Recommendation 7 to Recommendation 5.*

President Knubel was asked to rule on the relationship of Recommendation 7 to Recommendation 5 as found in the 1930 Minutes (page 337). President Knubel submitted the following decision which will stand as authoritative unless reversed by the Church:

A careful examination of the report and especially the recommendations of the Commission on Method of Investing Endowment Funds reveals that in Recommendation 5 we have a *general* statement concerning "a plan" and in Recommendation 7 a *specific* provision which must be included in "such plan." The importance to the general plan of this specific item becomes manifest when one recognizes that Recommendation 6 is so worded as to be exactly parallel with Recommendation 7. Recommendation 6 is another *specific* provision which must be included in "such plan." In other words, the requirement for the merging of all funds (Recommendation 7) is of equal importance with the requirement that all funds shall be committed for safekeeping with banks and/or trust companies (Recommendation 6). The relationship of Recommendation 7 to Recommendation 5 is therefore the specification of something vitally essential to the general plan, without which the general plan cannot be devised.

This view is upheld by a realization of the fact that the debate at the Milwaukee Convention was focalized upon the provision in Recommendation 7. It is upheld also by the Commission's own emphasis in its report that "best results" would be achieved by the merging of all funds, and by the Commission's elaboration of six reasons in favor of this merging.

On the other hand and although the Commission is not fulfilling its instructions unless it plans now and definitely for a merger of funds, nevertheless its responsibility under Recommendation 5 will not have been fulfilled unless it also plans to bring under its supervision "all" funds even before they are ready for merging. The words "as soon as practicable" manifestly refer to the words immediately following, "to perfect and put into operation a plan" and not to the more remote words "bringing under its supervision, etc."

This view is upheld by the original purposes in mind when the idea of a commission was proposed and by the frequent repetition in the report of the phrase "all funds." It is upheld also by the statements in the Commission's introductory item 7 of its report.

Any arrangement in the plan concerning funds not immediately to be merged must, however, be definitely regarded as temporary in its character and as merely preparatory to the inclusion of such funds also in the merged fund. To complete this ruling the introductory item 8, previously mentioned, must be given weight. It is clear from that item that the preparatory "supervision" of unmerged funds involves "the working out of all details with each endowed agency or with its duly authorized committee in order that due attention may be given to special situations." In other words, the "supervision" becomes in reality an advisory or a consultative supervision.

Miscellaneous

All boards and agencies with more than $25,000 invested funds must elect an official representative to membership on the Commission.

Boards and agencies having less than $25,000 invested funds may select representatives, but they shall not be members of the Commission.

All representatives must be members of the boards.

Endowed Lutheran institutions may come in upon vote of the Commission.

The phrase in Recommendation 5, "any other funds that they may have for investment," does not refer to funds held by any board or agency for temporary investment such as temporary surplus funds. However, other temporary funds were noted, such as building funds, annuity funds and unrestricted gifts, which may be restricted by the boards or agencies, for which the rules and regulations of the Commission should make provision.

Boards with temporary funds may seek the advice of the Commission with regard to such investments, if so desired.

In Recommendation 12, the "proper legal advice" referred to is that of the respective boards and agencies.

2. LEGAL OPINION ON THE GENERAL PROJECT

Your commission deemed it advisable to consult legal advice with regard to the whole subject as approved at the 1930 Convention. The following is the complete statement of Attorneys Ralph L. Smith, Pittsburgh, Pa., and William H. Earnest, Harrisburg:

To the Investment Commission of the United Lutheran Church,
New York City.
DEAR SIRS:

On May 6, 1931, Robbin B. Wolf, Esq., notified us that we were appointed attorneys "to render an opinion to the Investment Commission of The United Lutheran Church in America as to the legality of the plan adopted at the Milwaukee Convention of the United Lutheran Church for the Investment of Trust Funds of the Boards of the Church and such other institutions as may care to co-operate," and referred to pages 335 to 338 of the minutes of the Milwaukee Convention.

We have been giving the matter consideration but have been handicapped by the fact that there seems to be no precedents that we have thus far found to guide us in our conclusions.

With respect to the legality of the general plan suggested in the Report of the Investment Commission to the Milwaukee Convention, three questions merit attention.

  I. Have the several incorporated boards of the United Lutheran Church the legal right to invest their funds through the agency of a single Investment Commission as proposed?

 II. Has The United Lutheran Church in America the legal right to control the investment of such funds in the manner proposed?

III. Does such method of pooling the funds of the several boards for investment constitute a merger of the funds in a legal sense, and, if so, is such a merger of funds a lawful exercise of the power of the boards owning the funds?

I.

We have examined the various charters, constitutions and by-laws of the corporate bodies whose funds are to be controlled or invested. Some have one provision relative to investments and some another, and some none at all. If the proposed plan is to be followed all should be uniform and proper legal steps be taken to amend the by-laws or constitutions, as the case may be, by inserting in them the specific power to invest their funds through the Investment Commission of the United Lutheran Church.

We understand that the several boards shall turn over to certain depositories to be named, the funds which they have for investment. We, therefore, believe that the by-laws of the boards should contain a provision somewhat as follows:

"The funds for investment belonging to the Board shall be remitted to such depository as may be designated by the Investment Commission of The United Lutheran Church in America for investment under the direction of said Investment Commission, in accordance with the rules and regulations thereof."

In accordance with this thought we make the following suggestions:

1. The Board of American Missions of The United Lutheran Church in America, incorporated under the laws of Pennsylvania by the Court of Common Pleas of York County, Pennsylvania.

(a) In the charter of this corporation the yearly income thereof is limited to $50,000. This provision of the charter should be amended to read as follows:

"The yearly income of said corporation, other than that derived from real estate, shall not exceed the amount limited by law."

(b) Amend by-laws by adopting provision substantially as hereinbefore indicated.

2. The Board of Foreign Missions of The United Lutheran Church, Inc., chartered under the laws of the State of Maryland.

(a) Section 4 of Article V of the by-laws governing the duties of the financial department should be eliminated and a provision such as we have heretofore suggested adopted in its stead.

(b) We suggest that the plan on page 18 of the Handbook submitted to us, relating to annuity gifts, be discontinued.

3. The Board of Ministerial Pensions and Relief of The United Lutheran Church in America, chartered by the Common Pleas Court of Philadelphia, Pennsylvania.

(a) Article IX of the by-laws providing for investment by the Board should be eliminated and a provision substantially as noted heretofore be adopted in its stead.

4. The Board of Education of The United Lutheran Church in America, chartered under the laws of the State of New York.

(a) Section II of Article III of the by-laws should be eliminated and a provision substantially as noted heretofore be adopted in its stead.

5. The Board of Publication of The United Lutheran Church in America, incorporated by the Common Pleas Court at Philadelphia, Pennsylvania.

(a) There is some question in our minds whether Section Eight of the charter is not too broad in requiring all profits and earnings of the corporation to be appropriated to purposes other than for the use of the Board itself. If the present provisions were strictly followed there might be no funds to invest, nor reserve for profit and loss.

(b) If Section Eight of the charter is amended so as to leave funds in the control of the Board for investment purposes, then the by-laws should be amended by inserting therein a provision substantially as noted heretofore.

6. The Women's Missionary Society of The United Lutheran Church in America, chartered by the Court of Common Pleas of Allegheny County, Pennsylvania.

(a) Following Section 5 of Article IV of the Constitution, we would suggest that another section be added substantially as heretofore suggested.

If the foregoing suggestions are followed, we are of opinion that there is no legal objection to the several boards turning over their funds for investment as proposed under direction of the Investment Commission of the United Lutheran Church.

II.

With respect to the legal right of The United Lutheran Church in America to create or appoint an agency or commission to control investment of the funds of the several boards, its charter appears to be comprehensive enough to include such power unless there be statutory prohibitions or regulations in the laws of the State of New York which provide to the contrary. We have not had opportunity to investigate this phase of the question, but the provisions of Section 15 of Chapter 53 of the laws of 1909, as amended by act approved May 6, 1918, a copy of which was sent to us, appear to grant ample power in the premises.

III.

With respect to the legality of the several boards pooling their funds for investment purposes in the manner proposed, care must be taken to avoid anything which might be attacked as a diversion of the property of the several boards from the original purposes for which the property was acquired. If the proposed plan of investment involved the relinquishment by the boards of their ownership of their funds, and the merging thereof in a fund owned by the United Lutheran Church, we are opinion that it would not be lawful. The merger of the several synods into the United Lutheran Church has been upheld by the Supreme Court of Pennsylvania in the case of

Nagle, v. Miller, 275 *Pa.* 157, but the opinion was based, in part, upon the proposition that the merger did not constitute a diversion of property from the purpose for which it was acquired.

As we understand the plan of the Investment Commission, each board will receive back from the depository a Certificate of Interest or Ownership proportionate to its share of the entire pool, and each board would continue to own an undivided interest in each investment made in the same proportion. We believe this would be a pooling of funds which would be permissable, and that it is improperly called a "merger" of funds in paragraph 6 of the Commission's Report to the Milwaukee Convention, and would suggest that it be referred to as a pooling of funds instead of a merger. We believe that this would not change the fact that each board would have an individual interest in each investment corresponding to its proportionate interest in the whole fund. It would be similar to the method used by trust companies when they invest in one mortgage the funds belonging to a number of minors for whom they are guardian. In our opinion, the plan of the Investment Commission is similar and there would appear to be no legal objection to the several boards adopting this method of investing their funds.

Our advice applies to funds "unrestricted as to investment," as referred to in Recommendation 6 on page 335 of the minutes of the Milwaukee Convention. Where a board has funds given to it by will or deed of trust containing directions how the funds are to be kept and invested, it would, of course, be impossible for the donee to change the terms of the donations or vary from the directions laid down.

In view of the fact that the details of the investment plan through depositories have not been given us, we can give an opinion only on the general features of the plan as hereinbefore mentioned. We can readily understand that there will be certain difficulties, both legal and practical, in putting the plan into effect, because of the nature of the present investments of the several boards, the varying amounts of income arising therefrom, and other matters of similar nature. Consideration will have to be given to the fact that legal title to all investments must apparently be placed in the depositories. We feel, however, that these matters are not before us at the present time and that we have been asked for an opinion merely upon the legality of the general plan.

Respectfully submitted,
(Signed)   RALPH L. SMITH.
WM. H. EARNEST.

June 11, 1931.

3. THE RULES AND REGULATIONS OF THE INVESTMENT COMMISSION

The following constitutes the Rules and Regulations of the Investment Commission as adopted thereby, approved by the Executive Board, and declared by Attorneys Earnest and Smith as being not in conflict with the legal opinion rendered by them with regard to the legal status of the Investment Commission:

I. *Meetings*

Regular meetings of the entire Commission shall be held at least once a year, the time and place to be agreed upon by the members of the Commission.

Special meetings may be called by the chairman and must be called upon the written request of three members.

Ten days' notice must be given of all meetings.

II. *Officers*

The officers of the Commission shall be a chairman and a secretary. Each shall hold office for one year, or until his successor is elected and qualifies.

III. *Duties of Officers*

The chairman of the Commission shall preside at the meetings of the Commission and shall in general perform such duties as are incident to his office or prescribed by the Commission.

The secretary shall keep the minutes of the proceedings of the Commission. He shall see that proper notice of all meetings is sent and shall perform such other duties as may be prescribed from time to time by the Commission, the Executive Committee and/or the chairman.

IV. *Committees*

There shall be an Executive Committee consisting of the chairman of the Commission and four (4) members elected annually by the Commission from its membership. The Executive Committee shall elect its own chairman.

Other committees may be elected or appointed as may from time to time be decided upon by the Commission.

V. *Executive Committee*

The Executive Committee shall hold meetings at such times as it may determine. It shall have supervision of all investments coming under the jurisdiction of the Commission, subject to rules and regulations adopted by the Commission from time to time.

It shall keep minutes of its proceedings, mailing copies to all members of the Commission, and report fully to each meeting of the Commission.

A majority of the Committee shall constitute a quorum but no action of the committee shall be binding without the affirmative vote of three of its members.

The approval of three members of the Executive Committee shall constitute the necessary authority for the purchase or sale of securities. The certification of the chairman of the committee shall be evidence of such approval.

The chairman of the Commission shall have the power to fill from the membership of the Commission temporary vacancies in the Executive Committee.

VI. *Appointment of Depository*

The Commission, under contract approved by counsel, shall designate a depository, or depositories, to receive and hold for safe-keeping all endowment and trust funds and permanent investments, the depository or depositories to collect the income from investments and to make such changes in such investments from time to time as shall be duly authorized.

The depository or depositories shall furnish such statements as the Commission or its Executive Committee shall direct.

The depository or depositories shall receive such fees and/or commissions for service as said Commission shall arrange.

No endowment or trust funds or investments shall be withdrawn from any depository nor shall any change of depository or depositories be made except upon action of the Commission.

VII. *Custody and Care of Funds*

When the Commission shall have become duly organized and a depository or depositories shall have been appointed, all of the boards and agencies of the Church shall be notified; thereafter all endowment or trust funds received by such boards and agencies shall be delivered into the custody of a designated depository to be held for the accounts of the several depositing boards or agencies, and administered by the Commission.

In order that all boards and agencies may have a reasonable opportunity to determine the time for transferring their present endowment and trust funds and permanent investments to the depository or depositories designated by the Commission, that the largest values may be realized on securities now owned by them, October 1, 1936, is hereby fixed as the ultimate time for the transfer of all such funds; but for good cause shown by any board or agency, this time may be extended as to it. The funds so transferred must be in cash or in securities acceptable to the Commission at their market values.

As investments representing the funds not pooled are converted into cash, the proceeds must be promptly deposited with the depository designated by the Commission. The depository shall issue to each board, agency, or other institution a receipt showing the amount deposited and promptly advise the chairman of the Commission.

Until such transfers are completed the Commission is to exercise advisory and consultative supervision of all such funds but the decision of the board or agency shall prevail.

Any board or agency may, with the consent of the Commission, withhold from deposit in such designated depository any funds or assets which by reason of their form or because of limiting conditions in the instrument of gift cannot or should not be so deposited, or the immediate deposit of which should for good reason be delayed.

VIII. *Distribution of Income*

The net income derived from the funds invested shall be distributed monthly to the boards and agencies of the Church whose endowment and trust funds and permanent investments are administered by the Commission in the proportion of their interest in said fund as shown by the total amount of their deposits. The fiscal year shall be identical with that of The United Lutheran Church.

IX. *Adjustment of Profit and Loss*

All profits derived from the sale or payment of investments shall be credited to a reserve fund; and all losses incurred on the investments shall be charged against such reserve fund. If the reserve fund is insufficient to absorb incurred losses, the deficiency shall be charged against income. Accumulated reserve may be invested or may be distributed pro rata from time to time on order of the Commission.

X. *Investments*

In the investment of endowment and trust funds, the Commission shall consider first, safety of principal; and second, income return.

Investments made by the Commission shall be restricted to the following: U. S. Government, state and municipal securities; high grade corporate bonds and notes, certificates of indebtedness and equipment trust obligations; and first mortgages on approved real estate of a residential character, occupied by the owner.

XI. *Mortgages*

The amount of funds to be invested in mortgages in any one community shall be subject to limitation by the Commission.

Before any mortgage loan shall be accepted and approved by the Executive Committee, an appraisal of the real estate offered as security shall be made by a local committee, together with a bank or trust company, or real estate expert of the community wherein the property is located, all of these to be appointed by the Executive Committee.

Five years shall be the maximum term of mortgage loans and any such loans shall be reinvestigated before a renewal is granted.

XII. *Quorum*

A majority of the members of the Commission shall constitute a quorum for the transaction of business.

XIII. *Amendments*

These rules and regulations may be amended at any meeting by a majority of the entire Commission, subject to the approval of the Church or ad interim of the Executive Board of The United Lutheran Church in America.

4. THE PERMANENT ORGANIZATION

The officers and personnel of the Commission as at present constituted is as follows:

The Members:
(a) *As elected by the Executive Board.*
        W. H. Stackel, Rochester, N. Y.
        W. G. Semisch, Jenkintown, Pa.
        S. F. Telleen, Ridgewood, N. J.
        R. B. Wolf, Esq., Pittsburgh, Pa.
(b) *As ex-officio.*
        Rev. F. H. Knubel, D.D., LL.D.
        E. Clarence Miller, LL.D.
(c) *As elected by their respective Board or Agency.*
        Miss Flora Prince, the Women's Missionary Society.
        Rev. S. W. Herman, D.D., the Board of Foreign Missions.
        Grant Hultberg, D.C.L., the Board of American Missions.
        Hon. Charles Steele, the Board of Education.
        Peter P. Hagan, the Board of Ministerial Pensions and Relief.

The Officers and Executive Committee:
Chairman, Dr. E. Clarence Miller.
Secretary, Dr. Grant Hultberg.
The Executive Committee, in addition to Chairman Miller:
        Mr. S. F. Telleen.
        Mr. Wm. H. Stackel.
        Mr. Wm. G. Semisch.
        Rev. S. W. Herman, D.D.

5. CONCLUSION AND RECOMMENDATION

All boards and agencies were notified of the permanent organization of the Commission, sent a copy of the Rules and Regulations and also the legal opinion expressed by Attorneys Earnest and Smith regarding the general plan as adopted by the Church in 1930 and the specific Rules and Regulations. The attention of these boards and agencies was called to the action of the Church which reads as follows:

"That all Boards and Agencies are hereby instructed under proper legal advice to co-operate with the Commission in perfecting these plans and putting them into operation as soon as practicable and to conform their by-laws to the procedure herein outlined." (Minutes of 1930 Convention, p. 338.)

They were asked to report to the Commission before October 1, 1932, the action taken at their next meeting.

We submit the following recommendation for the action of the Church:

That the term "merge" and/or its derivatives, found in the Report of the Committee on Investment of Endowments as adopted at Milwaukee (see pp. 335-338), be changed to "pool" and/or its derivatives.

E. CLARENCE MILLER, *Chairman.*

GRANT HULTBERG, *Secretary.*

SUPPLEMENTAL REPORT OF THE COMMISSION ON INVESTMENTS

(For action on this report see p. 228.)

As indicated in the original report, the Commission formulated its rules and regulations in accordance with the directions given by the Milwaukee Convention in 1930. Since the printed report was prepared, the rules and regulations have been submitted to the various boards which, in turn, have referred them to counsel for legal advice. Several boards have reported on the legal advice thus obtained, and in every instance, this advice of counsel has been against the full and complete participation in the plan as presented in the rules and regulations.

Your Commission therefore recommends that the United Lutheran Church now authorize the Commission to formulate rules and regulations on the basis of a plan that will permit it, until otherwise ordered, to operate in an advisory capacity with boards and agencies in the care and investment of endowment and/or trust funds, and in the selection of depositories and similar agencies for the care and custody of such funds.

The formulation of such a plan and rules shall be begun at once by the Commission, which shall seek the advice and co-operation of the boards and agencies interested, and when such plan and rules shall have been adopted by the Commission, they shall be submitted to the Executive Board of the United Lutheran Church for its approval.

If, and when the Executive Board gives its approval, the aforesaid plan and rules shall be submitted to the boards and agencies for their approval and co-operation in making them operative for the care, custody and investment of their endowment and/or trust funds.

Respectfully submitted,

E. CLARENCE MILLER, *Chairman.*

GRANT HULTBERG, *Secretary.*

The recommendation of the Commission "That the term 'merge' and/or its derivatives, found in the Report of the Committee on Investment of Endowments as adopted at Milwaukee (see pp. 335-338), be changed to 'pool' and/or its derivatives," was taken under consideration. It was moved and seconded to rescind the action of the Milwaukee Convention (1930) in adopting the recommendations 1 to 12 presented by the Commission on Investments. The motion was carried.

The recommendations presented to the Milwaukee Convention were thus brought under consideration.

It was moved and seconded to adopt them.

It was moved and carried that the original recommendations be amended by the substitution of the word "pool" and/or its derivatives for the word "merge" and/or its derivatives wherever the latter word or its derivatives occur in the recommendations.

Other motions to amend were lost. After extended discussion the previous question was moved and carried. The motion to adopt the recommendations to the Milwaukee Convention as amended by the Philadelphia Convention was put and carried.

On motion the Supplemental Report of the Commission on Investments was adopted as presented.

The special order for this time was the item concerning the reports of the Treasurer and the auditors of the Board of Ministerial Pensions and Relief, a motion pending at the time of adjournment of the last session, namely, "That the entire report of the Treasurer, with the auditors' report, be referred to the Commission on Investments for investigation and report to the Executive Board."

It was moved and seconded as an amendment to the pending motion "That such Commission on Investments be requested to present at least a preliminary report of its findings to this Convention under a special order to be set for Tuesday morning, October 18, at 10 o'clock. The motion was carried. The original motion as amended was carried.

Consideration of the report of the Inner Mission Board was continued. The Rev. Wm. Freas introduced the Rev. E. F.

Kaercher, who repeated the Twenty-third Psalm in the sign language of deaf mutes.

Dr. Freas introduced Mr. H. E. Isenhour and the Rev. E. Walter, who spoke of the several aspects of Inner Mission work. The Rev. E. W. Harner spoke to the Convention concerning the Lutheran Sanatorium at Albuquerque, N. M., and presented the following resolution in behalf of the Sanatorium:

> *Whereas,* The Rocky Mountain Synod of The United Lutheran Church in America, by establishing the National Lutheran Sanatorium, for the care of the tuberculous, in Albuquerque, New Mexico, is rendering a great humanitarian service in the cause of Christ and humanity, and
>
> *Whereas,* The board of directors of the sanatorium desires to provide more adequately for the many worthy demands for help made upon the institution, therefore,
>
> *Be It Resolved,* That The United Lutheran Church in America, now in session in Philadelphia, Pa., express its appreciation of the work being done and commend the work of the institution to the individual members of the Church and friends of humanity everywhere.

The resolution was adopted.

Recommendations 1, 2, 3, and 4 of the Inner Mission Board were adopted.

It was moved and carried that the report of the auditors be accepted.

The report of the National Lutheran Home for the Aged was presented by the Rev. John Weidley, President of the Board of Directors.

REPORT OF THE NATIONAL LUTHERAN HOME FOR THE AGED

(For action on the recommendation in this report see p. 239.)

At its 1928 Convention, held in Erie, Pennsylvania, The United Lutheran Church in America approved an understanding, reached previously between its officers and representatives of the National Lutheran Home for the Aged, wherein it was acknowledged that "The present direct relationship of the institution to the Church is recognized as a distinct and temporary exception to the policy of the Church concerning institutions of mercy" and it was agreed that The United Lutheran Church in America would, for the present, continue to elect the Board of the Home for the Aged and include it in its budget, but that "The institution will aim to secure the direct support of the constituent synods of the Church" and "This entire action is to be reviewed within the period of ten years." The convention further declared that "The Church requests particularly the following synods to give earnest consideration to the appeal: Maryland, West Pennsylvania, East Pennsylvania, Susquehanna of Central Pennsylvania, Alleghany, West Virginia." (1928 Minutes, U. L. C., page 64.)

In conformity with the policies and plans above outlined, the president of the National Lutheran Home for the Aged requested the presidents of the above-named synods each to appoint one clergyman and one layman from his synod to meet with those appointed from the others of those synods and with the Executive Committee of the Home for the Aged in a conference to consider and report to their principals on the action necessary to be taken to consummate such a change in the control and support of the home. Each of the six synods thus invited, namely, Maryland, West Pennsylvania, East Pennsylvania, Susquehanna of Central Pennsylvania, Alleghany and West Virginia, appointed such representatives and these met in conference with the Executive Committee of the Home for the Aged on October 20, 1931. At that conference it was unanimously agreed by all present that the representatives from each of the six synods represented would recommend to his or their synod that it place The National Lutheran Home for the Aged on its budget at its next convention for a per capita apportionment of ten cents, that it agree to accept representation on the Board of Trustees of the home through one clerical and one lay member and that it elect such trustees at its next convention to take office upon the expiration of the terms of the then members of the board of the home for such term as should subsequently be determined when the necessary amendments to the by-laws of the home should be determined. A uniform report of this conference, its conclusions and recommendations, was drawn up and this uniform report was presented to each of the named six synods at its next convention, with the hope that they would all accept the plan without qualification and that the transfer of control and support from The United Lutheran Church in America to the named six synods could be made immediately after the 1932 convention of The United Lutheran Church in America. This hope cannot be realized and the consummation of the plan has been delayed, as will be shown.

At their respective conventions, held in the Spring of 1932, the Synods of Maryland and West Virginia accepted the recommendations of the uniform report, placed the Home for the Aged on their respective budgets for the per capita of ten cents asked, and elected their representatives on its Board of Trustees, all this conditioned only on the plan becoming operative. The Synod of East Pennsylvania elected its trustees for the board of the home and placed the home on its budget for the required per capita of ten cents, with the proviso, however, that this action should be effective only in the event that all of the six named synods should agree to co-operate equally per capita in the plan and that preference in admission into the home should be given to applicants from contributing synods. The Synod of West Pennsylvania voted to co-operate with the other five named contiguous synods in the support of the home, but neither placed the home on its budget nor elected any representatives on its Board of Trustees. The Susquehanna Synod of Central Pennsylvania elected trustees to serve on the board of the home, but did not accept the recommendation for a per capita of ten cents on its budget, appropriating instead $250 for the one year of 1932. The Alleghany Synod adopted the recommendations of the uniform report, but with a limitation of one year on the term of the trustees elected.

From the above it will be seen that it will be impossible to place the proposed plan of transfer in operation this Fall. The Synod of East Pennsylvania, for instance, conditioned its acceptance of the plan upon all of the six named synods co-operating equally per capita in the support of the home, while the Susquehanna Synod of Central Pennsylvania rejected the recommendation for a ten cent per capita and appropriated a flat $250 for one year and the West Pennsylvania Synod made no appropriation whatever, either per capita or in fixed amount, for the support of the home and elected no trustees to serve on its board. The plan must be adopted in one form, by all of the synods which propose to enter into it, before it can become operative. It will be resubmitted to all of the six named synods at their next conventions and every effort made, by further conference between their representatives and those of the Home for the Aged, to secure uniform acceptances, which will permit the proposed plan to become operative.

Meanwhile, the Board of Trustees of the National Lutheran Home for the Aged recommends as follows:

That, whereas the present By-Laws of the National Lutheran Home for the Aged provide that no amendment of certain sections thereof shall become effective until reported to and ratified by The United Lutheran Church in America, in order that the transfer of the control and support of said home from The United Lutheran Church in America to consenting contiguous synods may be made effective as soon as it can be satisfactorily arranged and need not be delayed, after such arrangement, by the necessity of awaiting the next convention of The United Lutheran Church in America thereafter for report to and ratification by such convention of the necessary amendments to the By-Laws of the Home for the Aged, the Executive Board of The United Lutheran Church in America be empowered to receive the report and to ratify in the name of The United Lutheran Church in America any amendments to said By-Laws of The National Lutheran Home for the Aged which may require such report to and ratification thereof by The United Lutheran Church in America to make them effective.

The board nominates for the next biennium the following members: Rev. Henry Anstadt, D.D.; Rev. Oscar F. Blackwelder, D.D.; Rev. J. L. Frantz; Rev. J. E. Harms, D.D.; Rev. J. T. Huddle, D.D.; Rev. Richard Schmidt, D.D.; Rev. H. E. Snyder, Rev. F. R. Wagner, D.D.; Rev. John Weidley, D.D.; L. Russell Alden, Esq.; W. K. Butler, M.D.; F E. Cunningham, Esq.;

Harry T. Domer, Litt.D.; W. H. Finckel, Esq.; Mr. John H. Jones; Mr. F. W. Kakel; Mr. H. L. Snyder.

Respectfully submitted, for the Board,

JOHN WEIDLEY, President.

REPORT OF THE TREASURER OF THE
NATIONAL LUTHERAN HOME FOR THE AGED
BALANCE SHEET
June 30, 1931
ASSETS:

Cash in banks:

Columbia National Bank	$ 1,549.57	
National Savings and Trust Company	2,766.94	
American Security and Trust Company	10,499.17	
Washington Loan and Trust Company	318.23	
		$ 15,133.91
Securities at par values, as annexed		104,175.00

Real Estate:

National Lutheran Home Property, Washington, D. C.	$ 27,598.00	
Square 4120 and 4124	11,871.48	
Main Building	91,555.64	
Farmer's cottage and barn	5,000.00	
Grundy County Tract, Tennessee	200.00	
		136,225.12
		$255,534.03

FUNDS:

Trust funds	$ 43,629.54	
Annuity funds	19,833.34	
Legacy fund	9,091.77	
New building fund	91,955.64	
Maryland Synod building fund	45,578.59	
Endowment fund	1,108.00	
General fund loan account	100.00	
Admission fee fund	250.00	
General funds	43,987.15	
		$255,534.03

BALANCE SHEET
June 30, 1932
ASSETS:

Cash in banks:

American Security and Trust Company	$ 4,930.28	
Columbia National Bank	2,411.04	
National Savings and Trust Company	2,370.04	
Washington Loan and Trust Company	318.23	
		$ 10,029.59
Securities at Ledger Values		125,888.75

Real Estate at Ledger Values:

National Lutheran Home Property, Washington, D. C.	$ 27,598.00	

Squares 4120 and 4124, Washington, D. C.	11,871.48
Main Building	91,555.64
Farmer's cottage and barn	5,000.00
Grundy County Tract, Tennessee	200.00

136,225.12

$272,143.46

FUNDS:

General fund	$133,099.17
Annuity fund	19,833.34
Endowment fund	6,524.37
Maryland Synod building fund	50,458.65
Legacy fund	10,800.00
New building fund	400.00
General fund loan account	100.00
Admission fee fund	250.00
Trust funds	50,677.93

$272,143.46

CASH RECEIPTS AND DISBURSEMENTS
For the year ended June 30, 1931

Receipts	General Fund	Legacies	Trust Fund	Maryland Synod Building Fund	Endowment Fund
United Lutheran Church	$10,298.32				
Admission fees	2,000.00				
Sale of farm products	65.05				
Miscellaneous	866.29				
Insurance	1,097.26				
Legacies		$1,603.15			$ 108.00
Income from securities	4,192.42				
"Home News" receipts	87.93				
Donations	526.86			$ 578.59	
Bonds matured			$5,700.00		
Received from inmates			3,338.64		
Total receipts	$19,134.13	$1,603.15	$9,038.64	$ 578.59	$ 108.00

Disbursements		
Board of Lady Managers for domestic expenses	$ 7,150.00	
Farm labor and expense	2,517.41	
Gas, fuel, electricity	2,011.43	
Engineers' wages	963.50	
Medical and nursing	2,020.83	
Religious services	290.00	
Funeral expenses	1,222.20	
Repairs to building, plumbing, etc.	2,384.09	
Executive expenses	1,255.66	
Taxes and water rent	255.69	
Auto and repairs	645.80	
Interest	3,555.34	
"Home News" expenses	313.35	
Miscellaneous	1,353.51	
Legacies (purchase of securities)		$ 611.38
Total disbursements	$25,938.81	$ 611.38

Excess or deficiency of cash receipts	$ 6,804.68	*$ 991.77	$9,038.64	$ 578.59	$ 108.00

* Deficit,

CASH RECEIPTS AND DISBURSEMENTS

For the year ended June 30, 1932

Receipts:	General Fund	Legacies	Trust Fund	Maryland Synod Building Fund	Endowment Fund	Annuity Fund
United Lutheran Church	$ 9,090.00					
Admission fees	1,989.60					
Sale of farm products	15.00					
Ford truck	4.75					
Legacies		$ 639.63				
Income from securities	3,852.10			$ 4,753.57	$ 5,321.37	
"Home News" receipts	70.51					
Donations	1,109.41			422.84	95.00	
Bond matured						
Miscellaneous	1,814.45		$ 499.76			
Received from inmates			1,238.63			
Payments on notes				20,050.00		$ 350.00
Street condemnation	609.87					
Total Receipts	$18,555.69	$ 639.63	$ 1,738.39	$25,226.41	$ 5,416.37	$ 350.00

Disbursements:

	General Fund
Board of Lady Managers	$ 6,500.00
Farm labor and expense	1,945.94
Gas, fuel and electricity	2,234.72
Engineer's salary	1,006.40
Medical and nursing	1,204.70
Religious services	20.00
Building repairs	2,159.96
Funeral expenses	628.26
Interest	3,638.72
Executive expenses	1,257.70

Deaconess' services	400.00				
"Home News" expenses	176.51				
Auto expenses	80.00				
Taxes	246.43				
Professional services	450.00				
Miscellaneous	437.24				
Plumbing	244.13			$25,013.44		$5,135.94
				296.35	
Securities purchased					$3,954.37
Accrued interest on securities purchased					
Total Disbursements	$22,630.71			$25,309.79	$3,954.37	$5,135.94
Excess or deficiency of Cash Receipts	$ 4,075.02*	$ 639.63	$ 1,738.39	$ 83.38*	$ 1,462.00	$ 4,785.94*

* Deficit.

SUMMARY OF CASH

Cash in banks, July 1, 1930		$11,221.59
Receipts	$24,762.51	
Bonds matured	5,700.00	
		30,462.51
		$41,684.10
Disbursements	25,938.81	
Securities purchased	611.38	
		26,550.19
Balance, June 30, 1931		$15,133.91

Cash in banks, July 1, 1931		$15,133.91
Receipts	$25,065.73	
Legacies	5,961.00	
Bond matured	499.76	
Payments on notes	20,400.00	
		51,926.49
		$67,060.40
Disbursements	22,630.71	
Securities purchased	34,103.75	
Accrued interest on securities purchased	296.35	
		57,030.81
Balance, June 30, 1932		$10,029.59

SECURITIES OWNED
June 30, 1932
Trust Fund

		Value as Carried on Ledger
Bonds:		
$ 2,000	Washington Gas Light Co. Series "A" 6s, 1933	$ 2,000.00
5,000	Washington Ry. and Electric Co. 4s, 1951....	5,000.00
10,000	Capital Traction Co. 5s, 1947.............................	10,000.00
5,000	Washington Ry. and Electric Co. 4s, 1951......	5,000.00
600	United Rys. and Electric Co. 5s, 1936............	60.00
1,000	Maryland Electric Rys. Co. 5s, 1933...............	800.00
50	Liberty Loan 3½s, 1947.....................................	50.00
450	Liberty Loan 4th 4¼s	450.00
500	Island Oil and Transport Corporation 8 per cent (Certificate of Deposit)	500.00
1,000	Potomac Electric Power Co. 5s, 1936................	1,000.00

Stocks:		
Shares		
30	Drovers and Mechanics National Bank, York, Penna.	300.00
1	Codorus Canning Co., Penna.	100.00
4	Codorus National Bank of Jefferson...................	400.00
16	American Telephone and Telegraph Co.	1,600.00

11   Union National Bank, Westminster, Md. 275.00
5   Capital Traction Co., Washington, D. C. 500.00

Notes:
Number
   4   Promissory Notes of Rose J. Waggamen for
      $500 each at 6 per cent, secured by first deed
      of trust on Lot 10, Square 3956, 1309 Frank-
      lin Street, N. E., Washington, D. C.............   2,000.00
   1   Promissory Note of The Broadmoor Corpora-
      tion at 6 per cent, Parcel 56/50, Washing-
      ton, D. C. 5,000.00*
   1   Joint and Several Promissory Note of George
      W. Rohrer and Irene McGraw Rohrer at 6
      per cent (unsecured) 4,800.00
                                      ——— $ 39,835.00

LEGACIES

Bonds:
1,000   United Rys. & Elec. Co. of Baltimore 4s, 1949..$ 1,000.00
  500   Fort Spring Magisterial District Road Bonds,
        Greenbrier County, W. Va., 1934.....................   500.00
Stocks:
Shares
  10   Drovers and Mechanics National Bank, York,
       Penna. 100.00
   5   American Telephone and Telegraph Co..............   500.00
  40   Summers Fertilizer Co., Inc. 8 per cent Pref.....   2,800.00

Notes:
Number
   5   Promissory Notes of Howard A. Schladt for
      $1,000 each at 6 per cent, secured by Lot 4,
      Square 2138, Washington, D. C. 5,000.00*
   3   Promissory Notes of Rogers M. Fred at 6 per
      cent, secured by first deed of trust on parts
      of Lots 273-74-75, Square 2589, Washing-
      ton, D. C. (Balance) 900.00
                                      ——— $10,800.00

ENDOWMENT FUND

Bonds:
$1,000   Washington Gas Light Co. Series "A" 6s, 1933   1,000.00
  2,000   Pennsylvania Power Co. 1st Mtge. 5s, 1956....   1,900.00
  2,000   U. S. Fourth Liberty Loan 4¼s, 1933-38........   2,054.37
                                      ——— $ 4,954.37

GENERAL FUND LOAN ACCOUNT

Stock:
Shares
   1   American Telephone and Telegraph Co. 100.00

ADMISSION FEE FUND

Bonds:
$250   U. S. Fourth Liberty Loan 4¼s, 1933-38...........................   250.00

NEW BUILDING FUND

Stock:
Shares

4   Baltimore and Ohio Railroad Co., Common............................   400.00

ANNUITY FUND

Bonds:
$3,000   Washington Gas Light Co. Series "A" 6s, 1933 $3,000.00
  5,000   U. S. Fourth Liberty Loan 4¼s, 1933-38..........   5,135.94

Stock:
Shares

8   American Telephone and Telegraph Co............   800.00

Notes:
Number

4   Promissory Notes of Bryce G. Payne at 6½ per
      cent, secured by parts of Lots 14 and 15,
      Square 2528, Washington, D. C......................   2,500.00*

5   Promissory Notes of Harry Wardman and
      Thomas P. Bones, for $1,000 each, at 6 per
      cent, secured by Lots 14, 15 and 16 and parts
      of Lots 17 and 3, Square 219, Washington,
      D. C. 5,000.00*

7   Promissory Notes of Rogers M. Fred for $500
      each at 6 per cent, secured by first deed of
      trust on parts of Lots 273-74-75, Square
      2589, Washington, D. C. (Balance) 3,150.00
                                                                    ————— $ 19,585.94

MARYLAND SYNOD BUILDING FUND

Bonds:
$15,000   Washington Gas Light Co. Series "A" 6s,
           1933 ....$15,000.00
  5,000   Capital Traction Co. 1st Mtge. 5s, 1947........   5,000.00
  4,000   Commonwealth Water Co. of New Jersey
           1st Mtge. Series "A" 5½s, 1947....................   3,800.00
  3,000   Pennsylvania Power Co. 1st Mtge. 5s, 1956 ...   2,850.00
  5,000   Washington Gas Light Co. Gold Notes 4½s,
           1933 ....   4,831.25
  1,000   U. S. Fourth Liberty Loan 4¼s, 1933-38........   1,027.19
  4,000   Federal Land Bank of Louisville 5s, 1941....   3,750.00
  4,000   Federal Land Bank 5s, 1941—
           Wichita, $2,000
           Baltimore, $2,000 ....   3,755.00

Notes:
Number

1   Promissory Note of Rogers M. Fred at 6 per
      cent, secured by first deed of trust on parts
      of Lots 273-74-75, Square 2589, Washing-
      ton, D. C. (Balance) 450.00

6   Promissory Notes of A. Joseph Howar for
      $250 each at 6 per cent, Lot 20 and part of
      Lot 19, Square 529, Washington, D. C........   1,500.00

10 Promissory Notes of Archie L. Straub for
     $500 each at 6 per cent, Lot 72, Square 622,
     Washington, D. C. (Balance) 5,000.00*

Stock:
Shares
  30 Potomac Electric Power Co. 5½ per cent Pre-
       ferred Series of 1927 .... 3,000.00
                                                                    ———— $ 49,963.44

                                                                         $125,888.75

* In the possession of Swartzell, Rheem and Hensey Co., Trustees in Bankruptcy.

                     Respectfully submitted,
                              HARRY T. DOMER, *Treasurer.*

                                   Philadelphia, Pa., August 3, 1932.
We have audited the books of account of the National Lutheran Home
for the Aged for the biennium beginning July 1, 1930 and ending June 30,
1932, and we hereby certify that in our opinion, the foregoing statements
submitted by its treasurer, are true and correct.
                     TAIT, WALKER & BAKER,
                                   Accountants and Auditors.

The recommendation was adopted.

It was moved and carried that the report of the auditors be
accepted.

The report of the Board of Deaconess Work was presented by
the Rev. W. A. Wade, President of the Board.

REPORT OF THE BOARD OF DEACONESS WORK

(For action on the resolutions in this report see p. 252.)

The Board of Deaconess Work herewith presents its eighth biennial
report to The United Lutheran Church in America.

I. *General*

REORGANIZATION

The Board of Deaconess Work met in the Mary J. Drexel Home and
Motherhouse of Deaconesses, Philadelphia, October 23, 1930, in regular
quarterly session, and also for the biennial reorganization of the board.
The following new members, elected at the Milwaukee Convention, were
presented: The Rev. C. T. Benze, D.D., the Rev. Allen L. Benner, D.D.,
the Rev. L. A. Thomas, D.D., Frederick J. Singley, Esq., and Mr. E. S.
Gerberich. The following officers were elected: The Rev. William A.
Wade, D.D., president; the Rev. U. S. G. Rupp, D.D., vice-president;
the Rev. Foster U. Gift, D.D., secretary; Mr. Pearre E. Crowl, treasurer.

REASONS FOR ENCOURAGEMENT AND HOPEFULNESS

It is with deep gratitude to Almighty God that we are able to report
substantial progress in the Deaconess Work during the past biennium. Gen-

eral interest in the work has been manifest in various ways throughout the Church. That the future outlook is brighter is evidenced by the fact of a larger number of candidates and a larger number of consecrations in both of our Motherhouses than during any previous biennium in the history of the institutions. This is most gratifying to the members of the board and to those who have dedicated their lives to the high calling of the diaconate. **(See Resolution No. 1.)**

PRESENTATION OF DEACONESS CAUSE

The cause has been presented by the pastors of the Motherhouses, by members of the board, by deaconesses and many others at various synodical and conference conventions, educational institutions and young people's gatherings. The Women's Missionary Society has co-operated most heartily, and deaconess secretaries have been appointed in both conference and synodical societies. The Luther League has rendered valuable service in the effort to enlist young women for the ministry of mercy. The cause of Deaconess Work has a place annually among the topics of the Luther League, and through its department of life-service the work is stressed. **(See Resolution No. 4.)**

SEPTUAGESIMA SUNDAY

The United Lutheran Church has designated *Septuagesima Sunday* as the day for this cause to be presented annually by all of our pastors. While there are many ways in which information may be conveyed effectually concerning this important cause, there is perhaps none more effectual than this. If the pastor includes an appeal in the presentation of the Gospel lesson on Sunday morning, and the superintendent of the church school and the teachers of young women's classes and the leader of the Luther League meeting all stress the joy and blessing of this phase of life-service, many young women may be interested in devoting their lives to it. **(See Resolution No. 5.)**

NECESSARY VACANCY FILLED

Because of conflicting duties on the regular board meeting days, it became necessary for the Rev. C. T. Benze, D.D., to resign as member of the board. Dr. Benze and all members of the board regretted this very much. The Rev. J. J. Schindel, D.D., was nominated by the board to fill the vacancy, and he was elected by the Executive Board. The board is happy to have Dr. Schindel whose experience and advice are most valuable.

RECOGNITION AND APPRECIATION OF SERVICE

The present senior member of the board, in time of continuous service, is the efficient treasurer, Mr. Pearre E. Crowl, who retires with this convention after twelve years of faithful and efficient service. Having been a bookkeeper, an accountant and a builder before his retirement some years ago, Mr. Crowl has been of invaluable service to the board in various ways.

Public recognition of this was made at the service of installation and consecration at the Baltimore Motherhouse, on the evening of June 23, 1932.

At the regular board meeting on June 23, 1932, and again at the public service that evening, due recognition was given to the distinguished service of the retiring head sister, Sister Sophia Jepson, who has completed almost thirty years of efficient leadership in the institution. The pastor, the Rev. Foster U. Gift, D.D., and the training sister, Sister Edna Hill, having completed ten years of most successful work in the institution, were commended most highly.

Dr. Charles E. Hay, Pastor Emeritus

The Rev. Charles E. Hay, D.D., after having completed twenty-five years of distinguished service as pastor of the Baltimore Motherhouse, retired from active service and was made pastor emeritus on June 1, 1929. Dr. Hay's illness has extended through several years, and while he is able to sit up a while each day, his weakness gradually increases. His genuine, child-like faith in our loving heavenly Father continues, and during his brighter periods he finds great joy in communion with the Father of comfort and saving grace, and in hearing of the continued progress in the work to which he has devoted so much of his useful life.

Board Nominations

The following members, having completed their first term of six years, have been renominated by the board for a second term: The Rev. George N. Lauffer, D.D., the Rev. William A. Wade, D.D., Mr. I. Searles Runyon and Edgar W. Young, Esq. Mr. Harry R. Hagerty was nominated in place of Mr. Crowl, who by constitutional limitation is ineligible for re-election.

II. Report of the Baltimore Motherhouse

At the present time there are fifty-six consecrated sisters and twenty-one probationers connected with the Baltimore Motherhouse. Of this number thirty are serving as parish deaconesses, thirteen are working in ten institutions of the Church of an inner mission character, one is a missionary in Africa and three are engaged in private nursing. In addition to these, forty-four centers in which our sisters are "serving for Jesus' sake" the Motherhouse conducts a Christian kindergarten, a very successful weekday church school and every Tuesday afternoon during the school year the entire student body is engaged in practical work, largely under the direction of the Baltimore Inner Mission Society.

Consecration Services

On June 25, 1931, Sisters Vernetta Kunkel, Anna Melville, Ruth Paris, Chloe Sibold and Marie Stork were solemnly consecrated as deaconesses. On June 23, 1932, Sister Evelyn Lukens was admitted to full fellowship in the Sisterhood by consecration.

THE TRIENNIAL HOMECOMING

The third Triennial Homecoming, held in June, 1932, will long be remembered as a very happy event. Considered in all its aspects it will probably stand out in the future as the most notable of the three. This custom of having all the consecrated sisters return to the Motherhouse once in three years for two weeks of study and fellowship has resulted in a marked enrichment of the life of the Sisterhood.

ELECTION OF NEW HEAD SISTER

At the meeting of the board in February, 1932, Sister Sophia Jepson asked to be relieved of the duties of head sister, an office which she has filled for almost thirtty years with unusual devotion and success. Her request was granted with deep regret and by unanimous action of the board she was elected to the office of Head Sister Emeritus.

After much thought and prayerful deliberation, at the board meeting in April, 1932, Sister Martha Hansen was chosen as Sister Sophia's successor. Sister Martha came to the Motherhouse in 1920 and in 1922 was assigned as Sister-in-Charge of the Lutheran Settlement in Philadelphia. During the past ten years she has filled this position at the Settlement with marked ability and success, revealing qualifications which peculiarly fit her for executive responsibilities. Her academic background includes a general public school education, a complete business course and some special training at the University of Wisconsin, located at her home in Madison. In the judgment of the board and the Sisterhood she is well fitted for the position to which she has been called.

DEDICATION OF THE ANNEX

At its meeting in January, 1931, the board authorized the purchase of a plot of ground to the east of the property now owned by the Motherhouse. The newly acquired land has a frontage on Warwick Avenue of 419 feet, with an average depth of 170 feet, and was formerly a part of the estate of the late LeRoy White, which was bequeathed by him to an order of Episcopal Sisters. The purchase included a large frame schoolhouse with an adjoining four-room cottage facing on Warwick Avenue. Moreover, the purchase price of this valuable property was only $10,000, although its assessed value for taxable purposes was $16,800. In the judgment of the board the acquisition of this property was very fortunate both for the protection of the Motherhouse grounds and also for any future expansion. In the fall of 1931 the steadily increasing number of candidates and special students compelled the board to face the question of retrenching or providing additional dormitory facilities. The problem was solved by authorizing the remodeling of the buildings on the newly purchased property so as to provide room for fifteen additional students, office and bedroom for the sister-in-charge, bathroom facilities and a social hall, all of which was done at the total cost of only about $6,000. The purchase and remodeling of these buildings, however, was made possible only because of several special bequests which came to the Motherhouse recently. The annex was solemnly dedicated on June 23, 1932.

THE TRAINING SCHOOL

Including candidates and probationers the total number of young women enrolled in the Training School for 1931-32 was forty-six. The total number for 1930-31 was thirty-six and for the previous year thirty-three. Including those who have pursued the special courses for Christian workers, the Baltimore Motherhouse has trained a total of over five hundred young women for service in the Church. Of this number seventy-seven are deaconesses, twelve are missionaries or the wives of missionaries, at least sixty are engaged in full-time Christian service in parishes or institutions of the Church, about fifty have married ministers and surely most of the others are exerting a leavening influence which is greatly enriching the life of the entire Church. And what does it cost the Church to carry on this extensive work through the Baltimore Motherhouse? During the past seven years the average annual amount received from The United Lutheran Church in America has been less than $25,000, which indicates clearly that the Baltimore Motherhouse is rendering a splendid service to the Church at a minimum financial outlay.

III. *Report of the Philadelphia Motherhouse*

In the present intensified conflict of spiritual and carnal forces the true deaconess fills a place of unusual importance. She is a public representative of the Church. By her garb she attracts the attention even of the indifferent and hostile showing that Christ still has followers with the courage to confess Him wherever they go. By her ministry of mercy extended to the needy without distinction of race or creed, she proves that obedience to Christ is the greatest bond of brotherhood in the world. By her service without wages, she is a standing reproof of the greed which causes envy and strife between individuals, classes and nations. The deaconess, a trained, full-time, consecrated worker, receiving only her maintenance, is therefore making one of the most effective contributions to the Church's witness-bearing mission in the world.

OUR SISTERS AND THEIR WORK

The Philadelphia Motherhouse has 109 sisters, of whom eighty-eight are consecrated deaconesses and twenty-one probationers. Of these, thirty-six are in the service thirty years or more; twelve over forty years; one of these more than sixty years and thirty-two are with us less than ten years. Retired are seven; on leave of absence, two; leaving ninety-nine in active service. These are stationed at the Motherhouse and its three departments, the Mary J. Drexel Home for the Aged, with fifty-two men and women; the Children's Hospital with 2,130 patients and 30,495 dispensary visits during the biennium; and the Lankenau School for Girls and Kindergarten. Our sisters are also serving the Lankenau hospital, where during the biennium, 8,525 patients were admitted and 52,405 visits were made to the dispensary; the Kensington Dispensary for the Treatment of Tuberculosis with 950 patients and its preventorium, "River Crest," near Phoenixville, Pa., where the health of 608 children was built up during 1930 and 1931. The Tabor Home has a family of eighty boys and girls from broken-up families in charge of our sisters, and the Lutheran Home in Erie, Pa., about forty-five aged men and women. The Inner Mission Society of Berks County and its Hospice for Women in Reading, Pa., are served by our sisters; likewise seven congregations in Philadelphia, Easton and Erie, and New York, Brooklyn, and New Haven, Conn. Two of our deaconesses are visiting regularly in the Philadelphia County Prison. All these various fields of labor bring our sisters into direct contact with tens of thousands of persons every year and enable them to extend their influence far beyond the borders of our Lutheran Church.

THREE MAJOR PROBLEMS

The Philadelphia Motherhouse faces three major problems, in the solution of which it must solicit a larger co-operation of the United Lutheran Church.

1. The immediate need of a larger number of well qualified young women for the diaconate. The call of the Church's congregations and especially of her institutions for more sisters than we can furnish has frequently been brought to the attention of the Church; but now the situation is becoming more acute. Despite the fact that thirty young women have been added during the past decade, the net gain in numbers has been small because of losses natural in any organization. It takes years of training and experience to qualify for leading positions and for certain highly specialized work. The Motherhouse gladly gives that training, not merely in a practical way, but by sending some of the sisters to other schools. We now have five with academic degrees and two others who are graduates of the college of pharmacy. But we very much need also one or more high-grade experienced teachers, dieticians, social workers and graduates in religious education to fill such professional positions as deaconesses. We ask pastors and others to bring this immediate need to the attention of truly consecrated young women who have such training.

2. Our Lankenau School for Girls. This is the only school in this country conducted by deaconesses and the only boarding school in the Lutheran Church in this country for girls from the age of six years upward. Membership in the Association of Colleges and Secondary Schools of the Middle Atlantic States is evidence of the high standard of its high school department. Religious instruction and other character building influences have created a life-long loyalty among most of the former students. The

present economic situation, however, has made the school an additional drain on the resources of the Motherhouse which must apply the income from the endowment primarily to the support of the Mary J. Drexel Home for the Aged and the maintenance of deaconesses. A capacity enrollment of resident pupils would turn the Lankenau School into a source of income and would wipe out a large part of the deficit annually incurred by the Motherhouse during recent years. Will not the pastors of the United Lutheran Church bring the Lankenau School with its unique advantages to the attention of parents planning to send their daughters to a private school?

3. Balancing the budget. A summary of the treasurer's reports for the past biennium reveals the problem:

Receipts

	1930	1931
From stations served by Sisters	$11,264.32	$10,142.43
Entrance fees to the Home for Aged	5,850.00	5,117.50
Children's Hospital	25,265.84	16,147.47
Income from investments	33,513.51	30,825.62
Miscellaneous	5,695.27	5,061.88
Total	$81,588.94	$67,294.90

Expenses

	1930	1931
Deaconess account	$20,241.73	$18,375.30
Salaries	9,720.04	9,720.04
Wages	22,380.13	23,990.84
Household supplies	18,759.75	17,230.88
Repairs and improvements	10,105.58	7,570.72
Miscellaneous	24,128.08	26,253.11
Total	$105,335.31	$93,140.89
Deficit	$ 23,746.37	$25,845.99

	1930	1931
These deficits were reduced by United Lutheran Church on apportionment	$ 2,000.00	$ 3,000.00
Friends of Children Donation Day	5,000.00	10,014.42
Miscellaneous gifts		60.50
	7,000.00	13,074.92
Net deficit	$ 16,746.37	$12,771.07

The Philadelphia Motherhouse is deeply grateful to the United Lutheran Church for the annual appropriation of $5,000 toward its deaconess department, and to the congregations and friends contributing toward the support of the Children's Hospital. Without such help our deficits would by this time have seriously endangered this institution which in former years never asked for financial assistance, but now is in the position foreseen by its founder, John D. Lankenau. In a note written in January, 1896, and only discovered recently, he makes an appeal to his fellow citizens, closing with the words which we must pass on to the Church today: "I hope that the Philadelphia public will in the future contribute liberally to this worthy establishment, for it truly deserves it."

IV. *Resolutions Submitted by the Board*

1. That the United Lutheran Church rejoices in the ever-increasing interest in the diaconate as expressed in the larger number of candidates and the larger number of investitures in our two Motherhouses during the past biennium.

2. That the Church records its appreciation of the splendid service rendered by our deaconesses, and of their consecration, devotion and willingness to enter upon the loving service of the ministry of mercy wherever and whenever called.

3. That we commend to the Church the value of deaconess service both in the parish and institutions of the Church, and that we bespeak for this cause the hearty support of our pastors, our congregations and the official representatives of the various agencies of the Church.

4. That parents, pastors, Church school superintendents, teachers of young women's classes and leaders of young people's organizations be urged to make frequent reference to this helpful ministry, and bring to the attention of young women the larger opportunities thus offered for blessed Christian life-service.

5. That we again request our pastors to present the Deaconess Cause to their congregations on *Septuagesima Sunday* with the appeal for young women to consider the high calling of the diaconate.

6. That we commend the Annuity Bond Plan of the Board of Deaconess Work, the proceeds of which are to be used eventually for the support of the aged sisters.

WILLIAM A. WADE,
President of the Board.
FOSTER U. GIFT,
Secretary of the Board.

REPORT OF THE TREASURER OF THE BOARD OF DEACONESS WORK

BALANCE SHEET, June 30, 1932

ASSETS:

Cash in bank:

New Building Fund	$ 4,545.35
Endowment Fund	4,706.36
Annuity Fund	530.83

General Fund (bank overdraft)	—1,359.74	
Petty cash, Imprest Funds	439.60	
		$ 8,862.40
Ground Rents Owned		27,100.00

Real estate, buildings, etc., at ledger values:

Motherhouse, North and Thomas Aves., Baltimore, Md.	$271,597.00	
Properties at 1901 and 1905 Thomas Ave., Baltimore, Md.	17,210.00	
Property at 1908 Warwick Ave., Baltimore, Md.....	22,105.12	
		310,912.12
Lorraine Park Cemetery Burial Lot		600.00
		$347,474.52

FUNDS:

General fund	$308,591.98	
Annuity fund	27,630.83	
New building fund	6,545.35	
Endowment fund	4,706.36	
		$347,474.52

CASH RECEIPTS AND DISBURSEMENTS

July 1, 1931, to June 30, 1932
GENERAL FUND

Balance, July 1, 1931	$ 3,453.39	
Petty cash, imprest funds	947.94	

RECEIPTS:

United Lutheran Church $24,700.00		

Synods:

New York and New England Synod $113.50		
German Nebraska Synod 4.50		
	118.00	
Tuition	3,187.50	
Kindergarten	322.00	
Nursing	95.00	
Stations	8,483.94	
Miscellaneous	149.73	
Discounts earned	225.40	
Interest on bank deposits	44.98	
Property fund	2,000.00	
Transfer from annuity fund	162.07	
Loan repaid	600.00	
Monument fund	185.70	
		40,274.32
		$44,675.65

DISBURSEMENTS:

Book Fund ....$	978.45	
Incidental fund	50.00	
Lectures and instructions	1,007.00	
Water rents	124.57	

Board expenses	474.16
Pastors' salaries	4,000.00
Pastors' traveling expenses	232.19
Pastors' office expenses	839.31
Sisters' quarterly allowances	4,811.25
Sisters' traveling expenses	305.10
Sisters' personal expenses	3,306.84
Household expenses	6,125.00
Engineer	900.00
Labor	528.00
Grounds and stock	835.50
Domestic help	3,175.00
Wearing apparel	1,459.25
Monument fund	640.00
Vacation allowances	1,375.00
1908 Warwick Avenue	494.81
Telephone and telegraph	240.28
Printing and stationery	1,083.47
Repairs and supplies	681.70
Gas and electricity	716.20
Coal	1,093.07
Insurance	590.28
Doctor, dentist, etc.	696.85
Improvements	5,305.12
Auditing	110.00
Miscellaneous, including photos, carfares, kindergarten, postage, etc.	776.39
Permits	141.00

	$43,095.79
Mary J. Drexel Home and Philadelphia Motherhouse for Deaconesses	2,500.00

45,595.79

Bank overdraft, June 30, 1932	—1,359.74
Petty cash, imprest funds	439.60

—920.14

$44,675.65

CASH RECEIPTS AND DISBURSEMENTS

July 1, 1930, to June 30, 1931
GENERAL FUND

Balance, July 1, 1930 .... $ 8,623.03

RECEIPTS:

United Lutheran Church $28,980.00

Synods:

United Synod of New York	$ 93.10	
Ohio	5.00	
Michigan	10.00	
East Pennsylvania	119.00	
Pittsburgh	7.57	
		234.67
Tuition		4,693.00
Kindergarten		358.75

Nursing	130.00
Stations	8,685.83
Miscellaneous	119.95
Discounts earned	98.44
Interest on deposits	73.43
Annuity fund	1,641.50
Monument fund	59.50
Property fund	1,000.00
Rentals received	40.00
	46,115.07
	$54,738.10

DISBURSEMENTS:

Book fund	$ 566.07
Lectures and instruction	830.05
Expenses—1901 Thomas Avenue	458.00
Expenses—1905 Thomas Avenue	453.00
Annuity bond interest	1,436.00
Board expenses	245.62
Pastors' salaries	4,000.00
Pastors' traveling expense	318.73
Pastors' office expense	168.80
Sisters' quarterly allowance	4,641.25
Sisters' personal expenses	3,075.25
Household expenses	6,323.82
Engineer	900.00
Labor	528.00
Grounds and stock	29.72
Domestic help	3,025.00
1908 Warwick Ave. (on account of purchase)	2,259.91
Wearing apparel and dry goods	1,649.82
Vacation allowances	1,450.00
Painting	4,351.58
Repairs	5,414.10
Coal	1,149.64
Gas and electricity	708.15
Clerical help	651.00
Telephone	125.74
Farm and garden supplies	539.75
Printing and stationery	746.14
Hospital and medical expense	951.07
Insurance	616.53
Postage	98.58
Water rent	80.84
Miscellaneous travel	96.12
Auditing	145.00
Miscellaneous expense	251.43

Total disbursements for Motherhouse	$48,284.71
Mary J. Drexel Home and Philadelphia Motherhouse for Deaconesses	3,000.00
	$ 51,284.71
Balance in bank, June 30, 1931	3,453.39
	$54,738.10

SUMMARY OF FUNDS
June 30, 1931

	General Fund	New Building Fund	Endowment Fund	Annuity Fund
Balance, July 1, 1930 ....$	8,623.03	$8,857.78	$4,062.14	$330.83
Receipts:				
United Lutheran Church in America	28,980.00			
Synods	234.67			
Miscellaneous	14,159.40			
Annuity fund (income from ground rents)	1,641.50			
Monument fund	59.50			
Property fund (loan)	1,000.00			
Rent received	40.00			
Legacies		139.35		
Interest ....á............		379.70	186.50	
Subscriptions			255.45	
	$54,738.10	$9,376.83	$4,504.09	$330.83
Disbursements:				
Expenses—Baltimore Mother-house ....$	44,588.80			
Mary J. Drexel Home and Philadelphia Motherhouse for deaconesses	3,000.00			
Interest on annuity bonds	1,436.00			
Purchase — 1908 Warwick Ave., Baltimore, Md.	2,259.91			
Loan to general fund		$1,000.00		
Purchase — 1908 Warwick Ave., Baltimore, Md.		8,000.00		
Balance, June 30, 1931	3,453.39	376.83	$4,504.09	$330.83
	$54,738.10	$9,376.83	$4,504.09	$330.83

SUMMARY OF FUNDS
June 30, 1932

	General Fund	New Building Fund	Endowment Fund	Annuity Fund
Balance, July 1, 1931 ....$	3,453.39	$ 376.83	$4,504.09	$ 330.83
Petty cash, imprest funds	947.94			
Receipts:				
United Lutheran Church	24,700.00			
Synods	118.00			
Miscellaneous	12,463.57			
Income from ground rents				1,641.50
Monument fund	185.70			
Property fund (loan)	2,000.00			
Legacies and gifts		6,040.00		
Interest bank deposits..................	44.98	75.90	182.27	
Subscriptions		52.62	20.00	

Annuities				800.00
Transfer from annuity fund	162.07			
Loan repaid	600.00			
	$44,675.65	$6,545.35	$4,706.36	$2,772.33

Disbursements:

Expenses, Baltimore Mother-house $42,600.98				
Mary J. Drexel Home and Philadelphia Motherhouse for Deaconesses	2,500.00			
Interest on annuity bonds				$1,479.43
Loan to general fund....................		$2,000.00		
Refund temporary loan from general fund				600.00
Transfer to general fund				162.07
Expenses 1908 Warwick Ave.....	494.81			
Balance, June 30, 1932	—920.14	4,545.35	4,706.36	530.83
	$44,675.65	$6,545.35	$4,706.36	$2,772.33

Respectfully submitted,
PEARRE E. CROWL, *Treasurer.*

GROUND RENTS OWNED
June 30, 1932

Property	Amount
2002 E. 30th Street	$ 2,100.00
3007 Wayne Avenue	1,300.00
2430 Liberty Heights Avenue	1,500.00
5301 Midwood Avenue	1,000.00
344 North Hilton Street	1,200.00
247 North Payson Street	1,000.00
3810 Plateau Avenue	1,400.00
819 S. Elwood Avenue	600.00
2019 W. North Avenue	1,333.33
4504 Wakefield Road	1,500.00
4506 Wakefield Road	1,500.00
4508 Wakefield Road	1,500.00
38 S. Calverton Road	1,200.00
40 S. Calverton Road	1,400.00
3703 Woodbine Avenue	1,500.00
46 Prospect Avenue	1,500.00
53 Prospect Avenue	1,500.00
20 Prospect Avenue	1,400.00
1740 Moreland Avenue	1,166.67
5309 St. George's Avenue	1,600.00
	$27,100.00

Philadelphia, Pa., July 30, 1932.
We have audited the books of account of the Board of Deaconess Work of The United Lutheran Church in America, for the biennium beginning July

1, 1930, and ending June 30, 1932, and we hereby certify that in our opinion, the foregoing: Balance sheet, as of June 30, 1932, and the statements of cash receipts and disbursements for the two years included in the audit, are true and correct.

TAIT, WALKER & BAKER,

Accountants and Auditors.

Dr. Wade introduced the Rev. F. U. Gift and the Rev. E. F. Bachmann, who addressed the Convention. Dr. Bachmann presented Sister Magdalene von Bracht and Sister Anna Ebert to the Convention.

Resolutions 1, 2, 3, 4, 5 and 6 were adopted.

It was moved and carried that the report of the auditors be accepted.

Moved and carried, that, without being a special order, the item in the report of the Executive Board concerning the Training of Ministers and Teachers (II, 9) as presented in Item "A" of the Supplemental Report of the Executive Board, be put on the order of business after the report of the Board of Foreign Missions on Monday.

At twelve o'clock the Convention adjourned with prayer by the Rev. A. Steimle.

Saturday Afternoon

For the entertainment of the delegates and visitors to the Convention, the Philadelphia Committee on Arrangements provided a pilgrimage to Valley Forge and to Augustus Church at the Trappe. In addition to two large sight-seeing buses, one hundred and sixty-two cars were in the line of procession.

At the Trappe the delegates and visitors disembarked and visited the grave of Henry Melchior Muhlenberg, and the old Augustus Lutheran Church. The Rev. F. H. Knubel placed a wreath upon Muhlenberg's grave. The Rev. A. R. Wentz, speaking from the pulpit of Augustus Lutheran Church, addressed the assemblage on the subject, "Muhlenberg and Washington Speak."

The pilgrimage returned to the city by way of the Lutheran Theological Seminary at Mt. Airy.

Sunday Afternoon

On Sunday afternoon, October 16, at two-thirty o'clock, Choral Vespers were conducted in the new Philadelphia Convention Hall, under the auspices of the local Committee on Arrangements. The service began at two-thirty o'clock with a half-hour organ prelude by Mr. Frederick C. Rauser. The order of Vespers was conducted by the Rev. J. J. Schindel. Mr. Harold P. Lewars presided at the organ. Mr. Rauser conducted a choir of seven hundred and fifty in the singing of Palestrina's "Thee We Adore, O Christ." Mr. Lewars conducted the choir in the rendition of John Sebastian Bach's Reformation Cantata, "A Stronghold Sure."

The address was delivered by the Rev. R. E. Tulloss, President of Wittenberg College, on the subject, "Releasing a Living Message."

It was estimated that twelve thousand people were in attendance.

SIXTH SESSION

Benjamin Franklin Hotel.
Philadelphia, Pennsylvania.
Monday, October 17, 1932, 8.45 A. M.

Matins were conducted by the Rev. P. E. Monroe.

The Convention was called to order by the President.

The Minutes of the Fifth Session were read by the Secretary and declared approved.

The Rev. A. A. Zinck, Chairman of the Nominating Committee, reported nominations as follows:

For the *Board of Foreign Missions*:

Rev. Robert D. Clare, Rev. C. A. Dennig, Rev. S. W. Herman, Rev. S. T. Nicholas, John J. Bruns, Charles H. Dahmer, Claude L. Peterman, Rev. H. H. Beidleman, Rev. A. H. Keck, Rev. P. W. Roth, Rev. L. A. Thomas, C. W. Fuhr, A. H. Reu, C. S. Stine.

The President declared the nominations closed.

For the *Board of American Missions*:

Rev. F. O. Evers, Rev. L. H. Larimer, Rev. H. J. Pflum, Rev. L. W. Steckel, Horace W. Bikle, Henry F. Heuer, John A. Hoober, Rev. T. K. Finck, Rev. C. E. Frontz, Rev. C. E. Gardner, Rev. D. D. Kistler, J. K. Jensen, J. Martsolf, E. H. Schirmer.

. The President declared the nominations closed.

For the *Board of Northwestern Missions*:

Rev. F. O. Evers, Rev. L. H. Larimer, Rev. H. J. Pflum, Rev. L. W. Steckel, Horace W. Bikle, Henry F. Heuer, John A. Hoober, Rev. T. K. Finck, Rev. C. E. Frontz, Rev. C. E. Gardner, Rev. D. D. Kistler, J. K. Jensen, J. Martsolf, E. H. Schirmer.

The President declared the nominations closed.

For the *Immigrants Mission Board*:

Rev. F. O. Evers, Rev. L. H. Larimer, Horace W. Bikle, Henry F. Heuer, Rev. C. E. Frontz, Rev. C. E. Gardner, J. K. Jensen, J. Martsolf.

The President declared the nominations closed.

For the *West Indies Mission Board*:

Rev. F. O. Evers, Rev. L. H. Larimer, Rev. H. J. Pflum, Rev. L. W. Steckel, Horace W. Bikle, Henry F. Heuer, John A. Hoober, Rev. T. K. Finck, Rev. C. E. Frontz, Rev. C. E. Gardner, Rev. D. D. Kistler, J. K. Jensen, J. Martsolf, E. H. Schirmer.

The President declared the nominations closed.

For the *Board of Education*:

Rev. G. M. Diffenderfer, Rev. P. H. Krauss, Rev. C. H. Stein, Rev. W. H. Traub, C. J. Driever, L. C. Hassinger, Ralph D. Owen, Rev. H. F. Miller, Rev. E. S. Rudisill, Rev. H. T. Weiskotten, Rev. A. R. Wentz, W. B. Ahlgren, W. A. Granville, Edwin W. Herrmann.

The President declared the nominations closed.

For the *Inner Mission Board*:

Rev. S. E. Greenawalt, Rev. Harold S. Miller, Rev. J. L. Sieber, Robert F. Bowe, H. C. Hoffman, Rev. F. M. Brown, Rev. D. A. Davy, Rev. I. R. Ladd, H. E. Isenhour, S. E. Long.

The President declared the nominations closed.

For the *Board of Publication*:

Rev. Henry Anstadt, Rev. Harry F. Baughman, Rev. John W. Horine, Rev. Russell D. Snyder, Charles Baum, M. P. Moller, Jr., Claude T. Reno, Rev. F. C. Fry, Rev. A. B. Leamer, Rev. J. B. Moose, Rev. Paul E. Scherer, E. F. Eilert, J. G. Kurzenknabe, D. Smith.

The President declared the nominations closed.

For the *Board of Ministerial Pensions and Relief*:

Paul F. Myers, Joseph C. Rovensky, Albert F. Sittloh, Belding B. Slifer, D. F. Yost, M. H. Buehler, G. Hemsing, A. W. Sandrock, O. R. Sardeson, F. Seiberling.

The President declared the nominations closed.

For the *Parish and Church School Board*:

Rev. J. D. M. Brown, Rev. M. Hadwin Fischer, Rev. F. R. Knubel, George M. Jones, Rev. J. H. Dressler, Rev. E. E. Flack, Rev. A. J. Traver, E. Keister.

The President declared the nominations closed.

For the *Board of Deaconess Work*:

Rev. George N. Lauffer, Rev. William A. Wade, Harry R. Hagerty, I. Searles Runyon, Edgar W. Young, Rev. H. A. Bosch, Rev. C. J. Shealy, J. M. Deck, H. B. Gerhardt, I. A. Schaffer.

The President declared the nominations closed.

For the *Board of the National Lutheran Home for the Aged*:

Rev. Henry Anstadt, Rev. Oscar F. Blackwelder, Rev. J. L. Frantz, Rev. J. E. Harms, Rev. John T. Huddle, Rev. Richard Schmidt, Rev. H. E. Snyder, Rev. F. R. Wagner, Rev. John Weidley, L. Russell Alden, W. K. Butler, F. E. Cunningham, H. T. Domer, W. H. Finckel, F. W. Kakel, Harry L. Snyder, Rev. J. L. Hoffman, Rev. C. G. Leatherman, Rev. P. Lucas, Rev. R. B. McGiffin, Rev. H. C. Michael, Rev. S. T. Nicholas, Rev. S. Snyder, Rev. W. A. Wade, Rev. C. E. Walter, D. P. Deatrick, H. A. Fritsch, T. P. Hickman, I. N. Hoover, S. Z. Miller, A. R. Nissly, J. E. Reisner, M. L. Yarrison.

The President declared the nominations closed.

The report of the Board of Foreign Missions was presented by the Rev. S. W. Herman, President of the Board.

REPORT OF THE BOARD OF FOREIGN MISSIONS

(For action on the recommendations in this report see p. 293.)

The Board of Foreign Missions submits herewith to the United Lutheran Church its Eighth Biennial Report. In making this report your Board is giving you a summary of what has been done during the last two years. The report will be made according to the departments of work touching, therefore, the work in the fields and the work at home.

The Board is conscious that Foreign Missions is not alone its task, but that of the whole Church, and that as an activity of our Church foreign mission service is great or little as the Church stands back of those to whom it has entrusted the work. The interest and support of the Church are vital.

In looking over the work, particularly of this last year, we are struck with the growing opportunities in the mission fields on the one hand and the decreasing income at home. The lack of funds to carry on the wonderful missions we now have is most distressing. We are face to face with the fact that the Foreign Mission activities of the United Lutheran Church must either be taken more seriously or the Church will be compelled to reduce its mission fields built up at a great cost of lives and money. The biennium, however, in spite of what may be ahead, has some encouraging things to report.

A Balanced Budget

In reporting some of the things accomplished this biennium we should not miss the fact of a balanced budget when so few Foreign Boards during these years of depression have balanced their budgets. For the next biennium the Board has been compelled to cut the budget both at home and abroad. During the biennium our apportionment fell off ten per cent, our contributions from special gifts nine per cent, and from co-operating synods thirty per cent. The Board was compelled to reduce its budget. This will effect all fields and all work here at home. No report would be true if this was not brought to your attention. The Board cannot spend more than it receives.

The Debt

Full figures of a financial character will be found in the Treasurer's report, but we should say this in our introduction. The debt is gradually growing less. Three and a half years ago it was $443,000. Today, in spite of the last two years, it is $192,000. Many foreign mission debts are growing, ours is decreasing. During the last biennium we received $51,000. Our present bank indebtedness is $35,000. It is not the intention of the Board to continue this Epiphany appeal for the debt, but to place the whole cause of missions before the Church during Epiphany, believing that with an increase of receipts will come a clearing away of the debt. **(See Resolution 1.)**

Co-operating Organizations

We want to report to the convention, in the heartiest manner and with the greatest appreciation, the co-operation of the Women's Missionary Society. It continually manifests its desire to help in every way both with missionaries and money.

The Society sends its money through the General Board and all missionaries are commissioned and work under the authority of the General Board on which the Society has two representatives. During the biennium, the Women's Board contributed through us $439,511.41. This in addition to the General Board's expenditure.

We are profoundly grateful for the help of that great auxiliary, the Women's Missionary Society.

However, the Board wishes to repeat what it said last year, that in its estimation the best service in missions cannot be done until the idea of separate women's work and men's work is eliminated and there be but one Board of management and control on which the women shall have a fair representation. **(See Resolution 11.)**

The Luther League, always missionary, has continued its co-operation, and this biennium will erect, at a cost of $15,000, a new building at the seminary in Tokyo, Japan.

Co-operating Synods

Three general bodies or synods co-operate with us. *Augustana in India.* This biennium the Augustana Synod contributed to the general work in India $16,202.96, and the Women's Society contributed perhaps $30,000 through the Women's Board. This was given mostly for building. Augustana Synod has two representatives and one full member on the Board. *The Danish Synod* co-operates with us in Japan and contributed $12,801.99. This synod has two representatives on the Board. *The Icelandic Synod* co-operates also in Japan, and has recently elected a representative. During the biennium it contributed $2,400. The co-operation of these synods is greatly appreciated, and is of great value not only in a financial way, but in a spiritual way.

New Missionaries

One of our great regrets is the fact that with reduced income we have not been able to increase as we would like the number of our missionaries. Without money we cannot send more missionaries, as every new missionary effects the entire budget.

However, during the biennium we have sent Dr. C. K. Lippard, who had resigned, with his wife to Japan. Rev. Leon E. L. Irschick, who had resigned, with his wife and family, has been returned to India. Rev. Dr. E. Neudoerffer, who was once a missionary to India, with his wife, has been returned to India. Dr. Lippard and Dr. Neudoerffer are practically new missionaries, as they have been in America over five years.

Other missionaries who have been sent out are: Rev. and Mrs. Ralph Sell to China, Rev. and Mrs. John C. Peery to India, Mrs. William Matzat to China, Mrs. J. D. Curran to Africa, Miss Jessie Mae Cronk to India, Miss Christie Eleanor Zimmerman to India, Dr. James A. Bradley to India (resigned), and W. Henry Gauger to India (resigned). In addition, two short-term missionaries were sent to take the place of missionaries on furlough—Rev. K. R. Jensen to the Argentine and Rev. Paul M. Counts to British Guiana.

Deaths

Under the report of the fields in which they served record will be given of missionaries who died while in service. Rev. J. D. Curran in Africa and Rev. William Matzat in China and Rev. Harry Goedeke in India. They were strong men and good missionaries, and the Board desires to bear witness to their fine service and worth as missionaries of the Church. At home, Miss Ellen B. Schuff, a retired missionary, passed away.

Missionaries on Furlough

Every effort is made under the department of Home Base to care for our missionaries on furlough. On the arrival of our missionaries they are met by a representative of the Board and given every attention. This service is greatly appreciated. In New York, the representative is Rev. E. R. Jaxheimer; in San Francisco, Rev. E. A. Trabert, D.D., and when missionaries come by way of Vancouver or Seattle the pastors of the city are asked to meet them.

It should be reported here with appreciation that during the biennium two homes or houses have been arranged for missionaries on furlough. One is in Baltimore, at 2900 Woodland Avenue, by the women of the Maryland Women's Missionary Society, and one in Mt. Airy, by the Women's Missionary Society of the Ministerium of Pennsylvania. This, with a double house maintained by the Women's Missionary Society of Ohio, makes available four homes for missionaries on furlough. The Board pays rent to the missionaries living in these homes, except that of Maryland, because they belong to the Women's Missionary Society and must be kept up. They are a wonderful help in having our missionaries live in comfort near to church centers and institutions, and are greatly appreciated by the Board.

Andhra Christian College

Andhra Christian College is considered in the part of this report referring to India. It also appears in the Treasurer's report. In addition it involves many questions of administration.

So in a sense it has become a larger matter than any one section of this report covers.

We would, therefore, like to present in a few papagraphs the present situation regarding the proposed United Andhra Christian College.

There has been contributed for Andhra Christian College $277,432.48. Of this total sum $19,992 has been given at the request of the mission for temporary and movable equipment to the College at Guntur, which now bears the name of Andhra Christian College.

While no definite division of the money contributed has been made, yet at the request of the Mission the interest on $150,000 is given to the College, as it is now conducted, for maintenance. The remainder of the money is held for buildings and interest is added to the principal so held each year. The total amount now on hand is $257,440.48.

During the years of the Board's deepest financial troubles some of this money was borrowed to conduct the work of the Board. This is being returned rapidly—$30,000 in the last year. And it would be possible to send out to India, if so required, the amount that would naturally go for buildings.

The matter of location and the participation of the other Foreign Boards remains undecided, no matter how hard we have pressed for final action. In the mission there is apparently no unanimity of opinion as to location, and the other Foreign Boards when approached in person, say that they do not have the money at present to co-operate. However, your Board has gone ahead and terms of agreement on which we might come together have been formulated. These terms of agreement and the sending of them to the other Boards have been approved by the Executive Board of the U. L. C. A. At present they are in the hands of the Mission in India. We are waiting the Mission's reaction before presenting them to the other Boards.

Looking Forward

Your Board, in its report, in spite of times of depression, reduced income, and shortage of missionaries is not dismayed nor discouraged. We are trying to meet conditions as they are and at the same time we are looking to a better day.

HOME BASE

This department's work, as indicated in our report, is mainly given to the cultivation of the Home Church and the care of missionaries on furlough.

The travel arrangements for our missionaries to and from their fields of labor demands the careful consideration of the department of Home Base and Travel Committees of the Missions. When its cost is considered, amounting to about $40,000 a year, and the comfort and health of the missionaries, quite a serious piece of work is undertaken and done.

The most important problem of the Home Base Department is to see to the general health of all prospective missionaries and also that of returned missionaries and those to be sent back after their furloughs at home. Through the Diagnostic Clinic of Johns Hopkins Hospital, there has, during the last biennium, been great improvement in handling all health problems. In the various foreign fields the setting up of health committees, under which all missionaries are periodically examined physically, has been found most beneficial in keeping up good health conditions among our missionary force.

Quite a considerable work and much correspondence are involved in the conduct of this department. About thirty-five missionaries, including their families, must be sent out each year and welcomed home, concerning whose health and physical fitness the Board must be assured. Besides all this, the location of missionaries while at home calls for a good bit of assistance to see that they carry out the directions of the Diagnostic Clinic and make the best use of their furloughs personally and in the interest of the cause they represent.

DEPARTMENT OF SPECIAL GIFTS

We wish to acknowledge our gratitude to congregations, societies and individuals who have so faithfully kept up their support during these past two years. Some patrons have been compelled by force of circumstances to ask for cancellation. As a result the total receipts show a decrease of nine per cent over the former biennium. The figures at the end of June, 1932, indicate that seven less missionaries and seventy-three fewer native workers are now supported as compared with June, 1930. On the other hand, the list of parishes abroad has increased by twenty-one. These were secured during the early part of the biennium. In the matter of the proteges, your Board has voted to assign workers by name as well as by number. This plan stimulates interest with its personal touch.

In addition to securing the support of parishes abroad, this department has endeavored to see that correspondence between the field and the patron is carried on regularly.

The Board believes that close contact with the work is a great educational force in the home church. A project will quicken interest where other methods fail. The more missionaries keep up their part of the task, the more the supporters are encouraged. Of late, in spite of many pressing responsibilities, the missionaries have been forwarding descriptions for the patrons. Frequently kodak pictures of the congregation and school and other scenes of interest are sent. These are most acceptable, and encourage the supporters in continuing their co-operation. On numerous occasions missionaries have forwarded descriptions but as no reply was received from the patron they did not know whether the material had reached its destination or not. As a result, one Mission Council recently urged the Board to request the patrons to acknowledge receipt of correspondence as often as received. In his communications the patron is at liberty to ask for additional facts and other information.

Upon the suggestion of the department, quite a number of Sunday schools have secured large world missionary maps which were hung in some prominent place. On this map ribbons were attached which reached from the town where the patrons reside to the field supported. This constant reminder has materially aided in sustaining interest.

CONGREGATIONS SUPPORTING MISSIONARIES

Supporters	Pastors	Missionary	Field
Allentown, Pa., Christ's	G. H. Kinard	H. H. Moyer	India
Ashland, Ohio, Trinity	A. H. Smith	J. M. Armbruster	Argentine
Baltimore, Md., Second Eng.	J. E. Grubb	L. W. Slifer	India
Baltimore, Md., St. Mark's	R. D. Clare	I. Cannaday	India
Baltimore, Md., St. Paul's	J. B. Rupley	Jacob R. Jensen, M. D.	Africa
Boyertown, Pa., St. John's	D. F. Longacre	C. E. Swavely	India
Brooklyn, N. Y., Redeemer	H. T. Weiskotten	A. F. A. Neudoerffer	India
Buffalo, N. Y., Holy Trinity	H. J. Pflum	Ernst Neudoerffer	India
Canton, Ohio, Trinity	Earl C. Herman	A. C. Knudten	Japan
Canton, Ohio, Trinity	Earl C. Herman	George Rupley	India
Canton, Ohio, Trinity	Earl C. Herman	Harvey J. Currens	Africa
Chambersburg, Pa., First	Henry Anstadt	James W. Miller	Africa
Charleston, S. C., St. Andrews	Chas. B. Foelsch	C. K. Lippard	Japan
Dayton, Ohio, First	Chas. L. Venable	G. R. Schillinger	Japan
Dayton, Ohio, First	Chas. L. Venable	Victor McCauley	India
Ft. Wayne, Ind., Trinity	Paul H. Krauss	Luther A. Gotwald	India
Ft. Wayne, Ind., Trinity	Paul H. Krauss	J. I. Haltiwanger	Africa
Greensburg, Pa., Zion		August Schmitthenner	India
Greensburg, Pa., First	Chas. W. Shindler	Geo. K. Gesler	Africa
Hanover, Pa., St. Matthew's	Harry H. Beidleman	J. C. Peery, Jr.	India
Hanover, Pa., St. Mark's	John S. Tome	Theo. Scholz	China
Harrisburg, Pa., Memorial	L. C. Manges	R. W. Sell	China
Harrisburg, Pa., Zion	S. W. Herman	R. M. Dunkelberger	India

Harrisburg, Pa., Zion............S. W. Herman............L. Grady Cooper........ ...... China
Harrisburg, Pa., Zion............S. W. Herman............John K. Linn.................Japan
Hummelstown, Pa., Zion........C. G. Leatherman........P. O. Machetzki.............Argentine
Huntingdon, Pa., St. James....Edmund L. Manges....Geo. K. Gulck, M. D....... Africa
Johnstown, Pa., First............G. W. Nicely...........A. J. Stirewalt.................Japan
Lititz, Pa. St. Paul's............J. Harold Mumper....Rajah Manikam..................India
Mansfield, Ohio, First............H. C. Roehner............C. E. Norman.....................Japan
Mansfield, Ohio, First............H. C. Roehner............J. C. Finefrock.................India
New York State Luther
  League ....Rev. F. W. Heins...........Japan
Oregon, Ill., St. Paul's............J. E. Dale.................Mrs. Wm. Matzat...........China
Perkasie, Pa., Hilltown
  Parish ....Chas. F. Brobst.........Chas. H. Reinbrecht.......China
Phila., Pa., Nativity..............J. C. Fisher...............H. H. Sipes.......................India
Phila., Pa., St. John's............K. P. Otten..............W. Theo. Benze................India
Phila., Pa., Tabernacle........Wm. J. Miller....…....M. L. Dolbeer...................India
Phila., Pa. Temple.............A. Pohlman.............N. R. Sloan, M. D........Africa
Pittsburgh, Pa., First Eng....A. J. Holl..................Fred L. Coleman.............India
Pittsburgh, Pa., Mt. Zion......G. Elmer Swoyer.......J. Arthur Linn................Japan
Reading, Pa., Trinity............Herman F. Miller......Edward T. Horn.............Japan
Richmond, Va., First............J. J. Scherer..............Robert S. Oberly.............Africa
Rochester, Pa., Grace............H. Reed Shepfer........Edmund G. Wood.............India
Rockford, Ill., Trinity............H. M. Bannen............C. W. Hepner.................Japan
Rockford, Ill., Trinity............H. M. Bannen....…...V. Ch. John.....................India
Shelby, Ohio First.................D. Bruce Young.......P. P. Anspach............ .... China
Shippensburg, Pa.,
  Memorial ....W. W. Barkley..........J. Roy Strock.................India
Toledo, Ohio, Glenwood..........A. E. Bell..................Virgil E. Zigler, M. D..... India
Washington, D. C., Keller
  Memorial ....Samuel T. Nicholas....F. C. Burger..................India
Wilkinsburg, Pa., Calvary......Albert W. Stein-
                          furth ....David Day Dagle.........Africa
Wilmington, Del....................Dr. C. S. Stine............Ray Cunningham.............India
Winchester, Va., Grace........L. A. Thomas........ ....L. S. G. Miller.................Japan
York, Pa., Zion....................W. R. Sammel...........J. Russell Fink.................India
York, Pa., St. Matthew's........J. R. Baker ....Harry Heilman..................Africa

CONGREGATIONS SUPPORTING PARISHES ABROAD AT $500 OR MORE

Supporter	Pastor	Parish Abroad	Field
Allentown, Pa., St. John's....W. C. Schaeffer, Jr...Tanuku Station.................			India
Buffalo, N. Y., Redeemer......J. Sahner Blank.........Kyoto			Japan
Carlisle, Pa., First Cong. and S. S....................A. R. Steck............Attota, Tenali..............			India
Greensburg, Pa., S. S. Assn., Greensburg Conference..Tallapudi Station.............			India
Harrisburg, Pa., Augsburg S. S...................A. M. Stamets............Gurzala, Palnad...............			India
Harrisburg, Pa., Bethle- hem Ch..............................E. Martin Grove........Tunduru, Narsapur.........			India
Johnstown, Pa., Moxham S. S...................H. M. Michael........Blind Sch., Rentich- intala Palnad...............			India
Lancaster Pa., Grace S. S....A. L. Benner.............Chinnayagudem, Talla- pudi			India
Lewistown, Pa., St. John's.... ....Tai Tung Chen.................			China
State Luther League, N. C..Pidugarala, Palnad.........			India
Norristown, Pa., Holy Trinity ....P. L. Yount...............Chirala Station, Bapatla			India
Phila., Pa., Bethel Ch............J. E. Rudisill...............Higher Elementary Sch., Sattenapalli.........			India
Phila., Pa., Holy Com- munion Ch.............................J. Henry Harms.........Fukushima, Osaka...........			Japan
Phila., Pa., St. Matthew's Ch..............................T. Benton Peery....Kobe Station.................			Japan
Philadelphia, Pa., Messiah......R. H. Stover.........Saga Rural......................			Japan
		Elur	
		Tai Tou............................	
Pottsville, Pa., Trinity Ch.....E. W. Weber.............Saga			Japan
Springfield, Ohio, Students Wittenberg College........................... ......Kiaochow Bible Sch., "Wittenberg in China"			China

Warren, Pa. First Ch.	C. A. Dennig..............	Minamata	Japan
Wilkinsburg, Pa., Calvary......	A. W. Steinfurth......	San Martin	Argentine
		Yenagoni	India
		Honjo	Japan
		Hsueh Chia Tao.................	China
Zanesville, O..............................	W. M. Hackenberg....	Polavaram Agency............	India
		Li Tsun.................................	China
		Teh	Africa

(A complete list of supporters of Parishes is available in the 7th Edition of the Parish Abroad booklet.)

LITERATURE

It is gratifying to observe how seriously the synodical committees on Foreign Missions are taking the matter of the missionary education of the churches and how often they urge subscriptions for the monthly missionary magazines of the Board, "The Foreign Missionary," and "Der Missionsbote," and also the use of the Board's stereopticon slides and lectures, as well as other methods of missionary education.

Dr. Paul C. Burgdorf, of Baltimore, has ably edited "Der Missionsbote," since January, 1931, inserting many appropriate pictures and articles, which have improved its appearance and enhanced its value. Pastors of German and German-English congregations should do all they can to increase the circulation of this magazine, which is also used by the Literature Department of the Women's Missionary Society for the publication of its monthly programs in German.

"The Foreign Missionary," edited by Secretary Dr. George Drach, which celebrated its golden jubilee in 1930, is indispensable for all who wish to keep in constant touch with the work and workers in all our foreign fields. "The Foreign Missionary" has a circulation of six thousand copies, "Der Missionsbote" twenty-five hundred copies.

Stereopticon Lectures—During certain seasons of the Church year as many as an average of one lecture with slides a day has been sent out from the office of the Board of Foreign Missions for use in all parts of our country, in Canada and in the West Indies. These lectures with slides are kept up to date by missionaries on furlough, and offer as effective a means of missionary education and inspiration as can be devised.

Motion Pictures—During the biennium motion pictures have been taken by our missionaries in Argentine, Japan, India, Liberia, China and Africa, which graphically depict the various kinds of mission work and incidentally the interesting habits and customs of the native people. For the present their use is restricted to the Board and missionaries on furlough. The Board hopes, however, to organize this department so that the films may be made available for those who can arrange to secure a projector and screen to show them.

Occasional Literature—The annual report of the Mission and the Board will be published this year in an abbreviated form to reduce expenses and few occasional pamphlets and leaflets are being published at present because of the reduced budget of the Board.

INDIA

MISSIONARIES

Name	Residence	Arrival
Rev. L. L. Uhl, D.D.	Emeritus	1873
Miss Agnes I. Schade	Emeritus	1890
Miss Katherine Fahs	Emeritus	1894
Miss Mary Baer, M.D.	Chirala	1895
Miss Annie E. Sanford	Furlough	1895
Rev. Dr. S. C. Burger	Furlough	1898
Rev. Dr. and Mrs. Victor McCauley	Tenali	1898
Rev. Dr. and Mrs. E. Neudoerffer	Luthergiri	1900
Miss Emilie L. Weiskotten	Rajahmundry	1900
Rev. Dr. and Mrs. Isaac Cannaday	Guntur	1902
Rev. Dr. and Mrs. J. Roy Strock	College, Guntur	1908
Miss Jessie S. Thomas	Guntur	1908
Miss Betty A. Nilsson, M. D.	Furlough	1908
Rev. Dr. and Mrs. R. M. Dunkelberger	Rajahmundry	1909
Rev. and Mrs. J. C. Finefrock	Tanuku	1911
Miss Agatha Tatge	Rajahmundry	1911
Rev. and Mrs. A. F. A. Neudoerffer	Tallapudi	1912
Rev. G. R. Haaf	Retired	1912
Rev. and Mrs. T. A. Holmer	Dowlaishwaram	1912
Miss Florence M. Welty	Guntur	1912
Miss Mary S. Borthwick	Samulkot	1912
Rev. Dr. and Mrs. H. H. Sipes	High School, Guntur	1913
Miss Louise A. Miller	Repalle	1913
Rev. and Mrs. Fred L. Coleman	Theol. Sem., Madras	1914
Rev. Dr. and Mrs. J. E. Graefe	Furlough	1915
Rev. and Mrs. George A. Rupley	Furlough	1915
Miss Charlotte B. Hollerbach	Rajahmundry	1915
Miss Hilma Levine	Guntur	1915
Miss Agnes C. Christenson	Bhimawaram	1915
Rev. and Mrs. Harry Goedeke	Rentichintala	1919
Miss Emma K. Baer	Chirala	1919
Rev. and Mrs. J. R. Fink	Sattenapalle	1921
Rev. and Mrs. H. H. Moyer	Bhimawaram	1921
Rev. and Mrs. A. F. A. Schmitthenner	Peddapur	1921
Rev. and Mrs. L. A. Gotwald	Chirala	1921
Rev. and Mrs. M. L Dolbeer	Narasaravupet	1921
Miss Lilith Schwab	Narasaravupet	1921
Miss Alice J. Nickel	Furlough	1921
Miss Selma Anderson	Rajahmundry	1921
Miss Metta K. Blair	Rajahmundry	1921
Miss Pauline Whitteker	Samulkot	1921
Miss Maida S. Meissner	Rajahmundry	1921
Miss Edna Engle	Furlough	1921
Rev. and Mrs. Clarence H. Swavely	Tarlupad	1922
Rev. and Mrs. Leon L. Irschick	Furlough	1922
Miss Clara Leaman	Rentichintala	1923
Miss Verna Lofgren	Rentichintala	1923
Miss Lottie Martin	Guntur	1923
Miss Edith Eykamp	Rajahmundry	1924
Miss Emma Johnson	Tenali	1924
Rev. and Mrs. W. Theodore Benze	Furlough	1925
Mr. and Mrs. R. L. Cunningham	Furlough	1925

Name	Residence	Arrival
Rev. and Mrs. L. W. Slifer	Repalle	1925
Miss Arline Beal, M. D.	Furlough	1925
Miss Frances M. Segner	Guntur	1927
Dr. and Mrs. Virgil E. Zigler	Rentichintala	1928
Miss Nellie S. Cassell, M. D.	Guntur	1928
Miss Grace L. Moyer, M. D.	Rajahmundry	1928
Miss Mabel H. Meyer	Chirala	1928
Miss Hilda M. Kaercher	Rajahmundry	1928
Rev. and Mrs. E. G. Wood	Guntur	1929
Miss Susan Glatz	Kodaikanal	1929
Miss Ada Kron	Bhimawaram	1929
Miss Christie Zimmerman	Repalle	1930
Miss Jessie Mae Cronk	Rajahmundry	1930
Rev. and Mrs. J. C. Peery, Jr.	Peddapur	1931
Miss Barbara De Remer, M. D.	Under appointment	1932
Miss Amelia L. Brosius	Under appointment	1932

Those who resigned during the biennium are:

Mr. and Mrs. William Bembower	Resigned	1911
Rev. and Mrs. Oscar V. Werner	Resigned	1911
Rev. and Mrs. Fred J. Fiedler	Resigned	1921
Rev. and Mrs. Carl B. Caughman	Resigned	1922
Dr. and Mrs. James Bradley	Resigned	1930
Dr. and Mrs. Gauger	Resigned	1931

At the close of this biennium missionaries in active service number: 26 ordained, 2 unordained missionaries, 26 wives, 38 single women; total missionaries 92. There are three emeritus missionaries, twelve have resigned and two died. (Rev. Harry Goedeke on July 7, 1932, at Rentichintala, and Miss Ellen B. Schuff on January 14, 1932, at Los Angeles, California.)

OUR CENTER OF INTEREST

The Far East is attracting more and more attention with the passing years. Americans know more about India, Japan and China today than they ever did. Daily papers and magazines mention and describe affairs and movements and men of these countries in practically every issue. Our interest in this connection, however, is not with the political situation in India or with the influence of Gandhi or any other person or party on the land or the government of India or on the lives of Indians; but our interest here centers on what has occurred in our mission field in the Andhra or Telugu country of South India and how much progress the Church of Jesus Christ is making there.

More Sudras Are Coming—Without question the most significant feature of our India mission work is the increasing number of middle class people, called Sudras, who are coming in to the Christian Church. Hitherto our mission work has been among the outcaste people and when the Evangelical Lutheran Church in the Andhra country was organized in 1927 and enrolled as an advisory synod of The United Lutheran Church in America, the number of Sudra converts was comparatively small. If the movement which has recently increased so rapidly keeps up and swells to ever larger proportions, as it has every appearance of doing, not many more years will elapse before the Lutheran Church in our India mission field will become predominantly Sudra. The same may be said of a number of other mission fields in South India. The significance of this movement for the entire country can scarcely be overestimated. One of our Indian Lutheran pastors, Rev. R. D. P. Augustus, on the basis of recent experiences on a visit to a number of villages in several taluks or counties draws the following conclusions:

"1. The Church today has an unexampled opportunity to evangelize these taluks and others around.
"2. The eagerness of the high castes and Sudra castes, to hear of Jesus and know more of Him, is very remarkable.
"3. The way they are coming forward to confess His name and receive baptism publicly, is an unquestionable work of the Holy Spirit.
"4. It looks as if the people of the taluks had opened their doors before the Church as a challenge.
"5. The masses are asking, 'Where is the King and the Saviour born unto us?' They say, as it were, 'We have come to worship Him.'"

Andhra Evangelical Lutheran Church.—To hundred and twenty-five delegates attended the fifth annual convention of the Andhra Evangelical Lutheran Church at Rentichintala on September 23 to October 2, 1931. The lay delegates were unordained Christian workers and members of congregations. The proportion was about six ordained men, including missionaries, to four lay delegates. Twenty-three graduates of the Luthergiri Theological Seminary were ordained. The Church now has seventy-three ordained Indian pastors, and there remain at least forty more charges of from one to ten village congregations in need of pastors. The subjects of discussion and action which received the most attention at the convention were: Stewardship, Work Among Sudras, Young People's Work, Rural Reconstruction.

Relations between the organized mission and the Andhra Church are friendly, frank, mutually helpful and pleasing. The Church has taken over the Bible Training School and Theological Seminary at Luthergiri, the Tuberculosis Sanatorium at Rajahmundry and the extensive work of the 1,500 congregations and 1,000 village parochial schools, together with the evangelization of the non-Christians of all castes and religions. A further installment of transferred work awaits the development of the Church in self-government and self-support. At present the Indian contributions, government grants, fees and other local receipts approximate five-twelfths of the total receipts for all work and workers, not including salaries and allowances of foreign missionaries.

Federation of Evangelical Lutheran Church in India.—The second convention of the Federation of Lutheran Church in India was held at Ranchi, December 28, 1929, to January 2, 1930. One of our missionaries, the Rev. R. M. Dunkelberger, D.D., is president of this all-India body, whose official organ is "The Gospel Witness," edited by Drs. I. Cannaday and R. B. Manikam. Among the items of business and discussion at the present time are: A common liturgy in English for all the Lutheran Churches in India, a Joint Board of Publication, Lutheran Work in Calcutta, Indian Deaconess Homes, the Joint Theological College in Madras, Young People's Work and the National Lutheran Missionary Society. This Federation serves as a unifying force among Lutherans and as a bulkwark against false unionistic movements.

Joint Theological College, Madras.—While our mission has continued and will continue to train men in their own vernacular for the gospel ministry at Luthergiri, who will have to bear the burden of this holy calling in the Andhra Lutheran Church, a selected number of men with B. D. degrees must be educated to become leaders in theological education and pastoral service in view of the development of a self-supporting and self-governing Indian Church. As a consequence arrangements have been made in India to co-operate temporarily in the Joint Theological College at Madras. Others co-operating are the Leipsic mission, the Swedish Church mission, the Tamil Evangelical Lutheran Church, the Andhra Evangelical Lutheran Church, and the Danish Church mission. Each is to contribute Rs. 500 or about $165 a year for running expenses and supports its own theological students. The Leipsic mission, the Danish Church mission and our own mission each now furnish a theological professor. The college is to be governed by a council of appointed representatives of each of the co-operating bodies. Our mission has agreed to co-operate for three years ending June 30, 1934. Our Board has given tentative approval to these arrangements but cannot give full and final sanction until the text of the proposed constitution of this theological college has been worked out. When this has been done the Board will ask for ratification by The United Lutheran Church in America.

Andhra Christian College.—Of all our mission institutions the College is the nearest to self-support, the Indian receipts, including government grants and fees, being $28,000 and the American subsidy $6,000. This is provided by interest on endowment funds in the hands of the Board. Whatever may be the future of the College, the past and present give us abundant cause for thanksgiving and rejoicing. It is now one of the leading Christian colleges in South India, and first among the twelve colleges in the Andhra University in point of student strength, having an enrollment of over 800, of whom 108 are Christians. The faculty numbers forty-four, of whom twenty-three are Christians, eleven being Lutherans. The missionary members of staff are: Dr. J. Roy Strock, principal, and Dr. H. H. Sipes, vice-principal and treasurer.

The problem of making our College in India an inter-mission college or a United Andhra Christian College, is still in the process of solution. Meanwhile we are carrying on at Guntur with recognized success.

Intensive Effort.—The emphasis in our work in India always has been an intensive effort rather than extensive development. As a consequence our India mission is one of the strongest and most flourishing in India and now is the largest Lutheran mission in the world. Among other proposed developments which have great significance for the future are: The co-ordination of all hospital and medical work in the field; a better division of territory for missionary supervision, one step in this direction having been taken by the transfer of headquarters from Tadepalligudem to Tanuku, where a new missionary bungalow has been built; the readjustment of boundary lines between the field of the Canadian Baptist mission and our own in the East Godavery district, concerning which no final agreement has as yet been reached; the sale of the mission printeries at Rajahmundry and Guntur, with future emphasis on other industrial mission work such as carpentry and agriculture for village uplift; renewed emphasis on producing a larger percentage of literacy among native Christians.

Statistics.——The baptized membership of the Andhra Evangelical Lutheran Church in India shows an increase of 4,978 during the year 1931, making the total 154,721. In 1,000 parochial schools there is an enrollment of 34,071 boys and girls. There is an average of one parochial school to every one and one-half congregations. In thirty-nine boarding schools there are 1,822 boys and 1,533 girls, a total of 3,355. The number of Sunday schools is 1,088 with an enrollment of 49,806. In three high schools for boys there are 849 pupils and in the high school for girls at Guntur sixty-two pupils.

The foreign missionaries number ninety-two, including ordained and unordained men, wives of missionaries and single women. There are seventy-two ordained Indian pastors and 2,851 other national workers of all grades.

In eight mission hospitals 5,421 in-patients, and in nine dispensaries 22,206 out-patients were treated.

In regard to the Indian support of the mission work the Joint Statistical Secretary, Rev. J. Russell Fink, writes: "The Church's benevolence in 1931 was $23,500 (Rs. 70,638). This is a decrease but other cash receipts, school grants and hostel grants have increased and they have aided greatly in this time when offerings have dropped because of the financial depression. However, we rejoice over the effort made by local field church councils to increase the Sunday offerings. The figures and facts of our statistical exhibit show how tremendous our burden in India is."

DEATH OF TWO MISSIONARIES

Ellen B. Schuff.—After prolonged illness in the California Lutheran Hospital, Los Angeles, Ellen B. Schuff died on January 14, 1932, aged 57 years, 6 months and 18 days. She first went to India as a woman missionary in 1900 and served continuously in educational and evangelistic work for women and children until 1928, when she retired and made her residence in Los Angeles. Her last assignment in India was at Repalle, where she erected the Girls' Boarding School, of which she had charge. The funeral was held on January 18, 1932, and was attended by a large number of friends and acquaintances. Dr. D. R. Huber, pastor of the First Lutheran Church of Los Angeles, officiated.

Rev. Harry Goedeke.—When Rev. Harry Goedeke went to India as a missionary in 1919, he threw himself into the work with an enthusiastic vigor which was exemplary; and by his side from first to last stood his wife, nee Martha K. Hoener, whose ability as a missionary was recognized by the mission in her appointment to work both at Guntur and Rentichintala. Rev. Mr. Goedeke, during his first term of service, was the treasurer of the mission while it was being reorganized and merged into one mission. He fulfilled the duties of this office as well as the position of district missionary for the Guntur taluk and town work. After his first furlough he went to Rentichintala in 1928, where he died of anæmia on July 7, 1932, having served as a missionary for thirteen years. He reached the age of forty-nine years, nine months and six days. He married Martha K. Hoener on June 11, 1919, the year in which they sailed for India. He was a member of the Third English Lutheran Church, Baltimore, and his wife a member of Grace Lutheran Church, Baltimore. He was graduated from the Baltimore Business College in 1903, and after that for about ten years he rendered efficient service as office secretary of the Board of Foreign Missions of the General Synod in Baltimore, where his interest in foreign missions was developed. He was graduated from Gettysburg Theological Seminary in 1919. Just before sailing he was ordained by the Maryland Synod on September 14, 1919, and eleven days later he was commissioned in Grace Church, Baltimore.

The funeral service was held in Guntur and his remains lie buried there by the side of other men and women who also have given the full measure of their devotion to the Christianization of the Telugus in South India.

JAPAN

MISSIONARIES

Name	Residence	Arrival
Rev. and Mrs. J. M. T. Winther	Kurume	1898
Rev. Dr. and Mrs. A. J. Stirewalt	Tokyo	1905
Rev. Dr. and Mrs. L. S. G. Miller	Furlough	1907
Rev. Dr. and Mrs. C. K. Lippard	Under reappointment	1909
Rev. Dr. and Mrs. Edward T. Horn	Theological Sem., Tokyo	1912
Rev. and Mrs. Charles W. Hepner	Osaka	1912
Miss Martha B. Akard	Kumamoto	1913
Rev. and Mrs. John K. Linn	Theological Sem., Tokyo	1915
Rev. and Mrs. S. O. Thorlaksson	Furlough	1916
Rev. and Mrs. D. G. M. Bach	Kumamoto	1916
Rev. and Mrs. Clarence E. Norman	Furlough	1917
Miss Maude O. Powlas	Ji Ai En, Kumamoto	1918
Miss Annie P. Powlas	Tokyo	1919
Rev. and Mrs. George N. Schillinger	Kyushu Gakuin, Kumamoto	1920
Rev. and Mrs. Arthur C. Knudten	Nagoya	1920

Name	Residence	Arrival
Miss Marion E. Potts	Furlough	1921
Rev. and Mrs. Arthur J. Linn	Moji	1922
Miss Helen Shirk	Hakata-Fukuoka	1922
Rev. and Mrs. F. W. Heins	Saga	1924
Miss Faith Lippard	Ogi	1925
Miss Grace M. Beers	Furlough	1926
Miss Martha B. Harder	Furlough	1926
Miss Mary E. Heltibridle	Ji Ai En, Kumamoto	1927
Miss Maya Winther	Ogi	1927
Miss Helene Harder	Saga	1927

At the close of the biennium the missionaries in active service number: 14 ordained men, 14 wives, 11 single women; Total missionaries 39.

UNHINDERED PROGRESS

Despite many obstacles and the financial depression in Japan the mission work has gone on without interruption or decline. The recently organized Lutheran Church in Japan has expressed its conviction that opportunities for advance are evident on every side. By a formal resolution the first meeting of the Executive Board of the Japan Evangelical Lutheran Church at Ashiya, Tokyo, July 21-24, 1931, said that new places ought to be occupied as soon as possible in Tokyo, Yokohama, Osaka, Kyoto, Kobe, Kagoshima, Tobata and Dairi. The Board was obliged to admonish the mission, however, to incur no financial expenditure which would create a deficit at the end of the fiscal year. Another resolution of the Church emphasizes the need of more extensive rural evangelism inasmuch as the country districts in Japan are practically unevangelized.

The Lutheran Church in Japan.—The first annual convention of the Japan Evangelical Lutheran Church was held on April 17, 1931, in Tokyo. Rev. I. Miura was elected President; Rev. C. W. Hepner, Vice-President; Rev E. T. Horn, D.D., English Recording Secretary; Rev. Hajime Inadomi, Japanese Secretary; and Rev. J. A. Linn, Treasurer. The voting members present included twenty-six Japanese and thirteen missionaries, the associate members three Japanese and seven missionaries. On Tuesday, April 14th, three men were ordained, making the total number of ordained Japanese pastors thirty. Vice-President Hepner, who is also President of the Japan mission, wrote: "The Japanese themselves are committed to the great task of promoting and extending the Kingdom of God, preserving the pure teaching of the Gospel and the right administration of the Sacraments, and directing effectively the united effort of this Church." The Board of Foreign Missions on May 27, 1931, adopted the following minute: "The Board notes with gratification the formal reorganization of the Evangelical Lutheran Church in Japan under the constitution as approved by the Lutheran Church in America at the seventh biennial convention in Milwaukee, Wis., October 10, 1930. We have sincerely prayed that this would be accomplished and rejoice with you in this concrete move, which will greatly strengthen and prosper the work. We pledge our continued co-operation and support, and convey to you our felicitations for the success that has thus far crowned your efforts. We look forward with confidence and eager anticipation to the growth of the Evangelical Lutheran Church in Japan, thus strengthened by the close affiliation of our missionaries with the Japanese brethren.."

Kyushu Gakuin.—The mission Middle School for boys at Kumamoto, Kyushu Gakuin, celebrated its 20th anniversary on October 1-3, 1931. At that time the new buildings were dedicated and opened: The Ritter Memorial Library, for which the Board provided $12,500, the Science Hall, gymnasium and swimming pool, for which $15,000 was raised in Japan. The raising of these funds in Japan was a notable achievement. While other schools of similar grade in various parts of Japan have struggled for an existence and some have been closed, Kyushu Gakuin has advanced to greater prestige and larger usefulness under the efficient direction of the Japanese Principal, Dr. S. Toyama, and the American Dean, Dr. L. S. G. Miller. The enrollment is 650 in all grades.

Kyushu Jogakuin, the girls' middle school, also called the Janice James School for Girls, with an enrollment of 250, graduated its first class on March 18, 1931.

Tokyo Theological Seminary.—The mission in Japan and the Board of Foreign Missions have been greatly encouraged by the pledge of the Luther League of America, to provide $15,000 for the erection of a main building, which includes a chapel, for the use of the Lutheran Theological Seminary at Tokyo. The mission urges the purchase of additional land adjacent to the seminary grounds. During the past year nineteen theological students were enrolled. The multiplication of ordained Japanese pastors insures indigenous growth not only in the cities already occupied but also in surrounding rural territory.

New Buildings.—For the Osaka congregation a lot was purchased and a parsonage built, which temporarily is to be used for church purposes until the Cooper Memorial Chapel can be erected. A chapel has been built at Naogata, parsonage at Shimonoseki and Ebara, and a new church at Omuta.

Statistics.—Thirty-nine missionaries are at work in our Japan Mission, including all ordained men, wives of missionaries and single women. The ordained Japanese pastors number thirty and there are forty-four other national workers in evangelistic and educational work. The baptized membership in twenty-five congregations is 3,359. In seven kindergartens there are 300 pupils. The field contributed last year $13,000. In the theological seminary at Tokyo there are five professors, two missionaries and three Japanese. Over 3,000 pupils attend the twenty-four Sunday schools at the stations and outstations.

CHINA MISSION
MISSIONARIES

Name	Address	Arrival
Rev. and Mrs. P. P. Anspach	Tsingtao	1925
Miss Erva Moody	Tsimo	1925

Name	Residence	Arrival
Miss Elvira Strunk	Furlough	1925
Miss Lydia F. Reich, R. N.	Tsingtao	1927
Rev. and Mrs. C. H. Reinbrecht	Tsingtao	1928
Rev. L. Grady Cooper, Ph.D.	Tsimo	1928
Miss M. Clara Sullivan	Tsimo	1929
Rev. and Mrs. Ralph W. Sell	Tsimo	1931
Miss Mae Leone Rohlfs	Under appointment	
Dr. and Mrs. C. J. Voskamp, former Berlin Missionaries	Retired	1884
Rev. and Mrs. Theo. Scholz, former Berlin Missionaries	Tsingtao	1904
Miss Kate Voget, former Berlin Missionary	Tsingtao	1906
Miss Freda Strecker, former Berlin Missionary	Kiaochow	1908
Mrs. Wm. Matzat, former Berlin Missionary	Tsingtao	1922
Rev. W. Matzat, former Berlin Missionary	Died	

There are sixteen missionaries in active service. Five ordained men, five wives, six single women. Two have been retired, one died, and one is under appointment.

The China Mission, with the present year, enters on its seventh year since its transfer from the Berlin Society to our Board. Our Board agreed to pay for the school and church buildings, the houses and land, a sum of $185,000. To the present time the close of 1932, June 30th, there remains due on the purchase price to the Berlin Society $51,875.

The Mission has at length after many setbacks opened our medical work with much satisfaction and considerable success, though we have not had the needed assistance of an American doctor. The work is in the hands of a Medical Committee, composed of Miss Reich, Mrs. Matzat and Rev. Scholz. A Chinese doctor, Dr. Chang Tung Hsin, a graduate doctor of Shantung Christian University, has been resident physician, and has been assisted by Drs. P. Weischer and Don Lew. Miss Lydia Reich, R. N., has had charge of the nurses. The hospital is a general hospital, and is called The Lutheran Hospital of Tsingtao. It is housed in the old Mission residence, part of which was used as a home of a missionary. It is equipped with five charity beds at 50 cents per day and a limited number of private rooms at $2.50 and $3.00 per day, with a total of twenty beds. The Mission rejoices in the success of the first year, and enters on the second year with high hopes of great usefulness.

The Mission faces a new project. To it attention was called at the meeting of the General Assembly of the United Lutheran Church in China, which is composed of all Lutheran Missions. Our Mission was asked to sponsor and organize a Bible Institute for the training of women teachers and workers. Such a school will make for itself a large place.

Our co-operation has for some years been centered in our Theological

School at Shekow, where our Lutheran Missions have a good Seminary. We have been sending a limited number of men for training and a small contribution for upkeep.

Among the most hopeful organizations of the year past were the Bible Classes for Women in Tsimo and Tsingtao. Of the same helpful character, our Lutheran teachers hold an institute for ten days, which had much influence in promoting our schools and enlarging their usefulness. At the end of the year for two months a Bible Class for Christian and non-Christian women was held regularly, which proved in many ways helpful in acquainting the people with our Christian faith and life.

During the biennium Rev. and Mrs. Ralph Sell came out to reinforce the Mission, Rev. and Mrs. Scholz and Miss Moody returned from furlough, and Miss Strunk came home after her term of six years' service.

The numerical progress in schools and congregations is steady, when conditions, social and political are remembered. Our statistical table shows that under the direction of eighteen missionaries there are 130 national workers, and in the sixty preaching places the baptized members number 1,595, and the communicant members 1,288. Last year there were 259 additions, and inquirers numbering 379; in the congregational Sunday school 1,340 scholars. The field contributions for the year amounted to $2,260.

Death of Missionary Matzat

Willie F. Matzat was born in East Prussia, Germany, July 3, 1893. He was appointed a missionary to China, March 30, 1922, by the Berlin Society, reaching there May 25, 1922.

During the World War he was in the heavy artillery of the German Army. The character of his service seriously affected his nerves, which eventually caused his mental impairment and resulted in his death on September 5, 1930.

He was a man of fine ability, upstanding character, and while in the mission did a noble piece of work. After the work was taken over by our Board from the German Society, he displayed a very fine spirit and did all in his power to help realize the aim of our Board in setting up an American Mission in China. While in America he made many friends wherever he spoke, and enjoyed his visits among our churches. He returned to China, took up his work in his old station at Tsimo, where he died. He is survived by his widow and four children.

Liberia-Africa

missionaries

Name	Residence	Arrival
Mrs. J. D. Curran	Muhlenberg	1912
Sr. Laura E. Gilliland	Phebe Hospital	1915
Mrs. C. E. Buschman	Furlough	1915
Miss Bertha Koenig	Zorzor	1916
Miss Mabel Dysinger	E. V. Day Girls School	1917

Name	*Residence*	*Arrival*
Mr. and Mrs. J. W. Miller	Muhlenberg Boys School	1920
Miss Elsie R. Otto	Zorzor	1920
Mr. and Mrs. I. Ira Haltiwanger	Monrovia	1925
Rev. D. D. Dagle	Sanoyea	1925
Mrs. D. D. Dagle	Furlough	1925
Rev. and Mrs. R. S. Oberly	Zorzor	1925
Rev. and Mrs. H. J. Currens	Zorzor	1927
Rev. and Mrs. Harry Heilman	Neibel Bungalow, Muhlenberg	1927
Jacob R. Jensen, M. D.	Pohlman Bungalow, Muhlenberg	1927
Miss Irene Bloch	Resigned	1928
Rev. Arnold Kaitschuk	Muhlenberg Boys' School	1928
Miss Marie Jensen	Sanoyea	1928
Norman R. Sloan, M. D.	Zorzor	1928
Rev. and Mrs. G. K. Gesler	Muhlenberg Boys' School	1929
George K. Gulck, M. D.	Furlough	1929

The number of missionaries in active service at the end of the biennium is 25; ordained men, 6; unordained men, 5; (doctors, 3; business manager, 1; builder, 1;) wives, 7; single women, 7; resignations, 1.

The republic of Liberia has recently been receiving more than usual attention by the nations of the world. After the published report of the Commission on Slavery and Forced Labor there came a change in the government. Recommendations on reform, prepared by the Commission are now in the hands of the League of Nations, of which Liberia is a member. While our mission has not entered into the politics of the republic, still it is interested in the development of the people, particularly those in the hinterland, of whom there are 1,500,000.

More Liberal Government Policy in the Hinterland

We rejoice that within the last few months the Government has apparently modified its policy. A letter bearing the signature of the President of the Republic was sent to the Mission, granting that body permission to locate for residence its missionaries and evangelists in any village in the interior for the purpose of maintaining day schools and evangelistic centers. Hitherto the Mission was only permitted to maintain a central boarding school in several designated places.

Evangelistic Program and Progress

A very definite evangelistic program has been inaugurated for all the districts including work at the Main Station. More full-time evangelists have been employed, particularly in Zorzor and Sanoyea areas. The Mission reports two hundred and fourteen inquirers for baptism. In quite a number of instances requests have come for visits by evangelists which could not be accepted, due to the limited number of workers. Inquirers and others in some of the larger villages have agreed to erect native houses for teachers' residences and "kitchens" for classes and services if an evangelist teacher will be sent. In one of the stations five workers have been sent to more distant villages while the older pupils in the central school are assisting the remaining workers in carrying on the work of the station and vicinity.

BUILDING ACTIVITIES

Near the close of 1930 the Simon Bungalow at the main station, on the Girls' School side of the St. Paul River was destroyed by fire. This loss was partly met by the completion of the Neibel bungalow on the Boys' School side of the river in 1931. This is a well-constructed building. It is the first of its kind in the Mission. The walls are of rammed earth, plastered with cement both inside and out, giving it the appearance of stucco. Special precautions have been taken against destruction by white ants. The Mission builder is of the opinion that this building will outlast all the rest.

In November, 1931, the Board approved the erection of Day Memorial Church at the Main Station. Funds for this building have been on hand for some time. The local congregation supplied one-fourth cf the required amount. The walls for the church will be made of cement blocks. The interior provides for Lutheran appointments. The Mission has long felt the need for a Church building of this character.

DEATH OF DR. J. D. CURRAN

On September 20, 1930, Dr. Curran met his death. With three other missionaries and seven Africans he was crossing the St. Paul River, when the boat in which they were traveling capsized. All the other passengers were saved, but notwithstanding Dr. Curran's ability as a swimmer and his own physical strength, he succumbed. Dr. Curran was one of the veterans of our Africa field, having given nineteen years of service. At the time of his death he was President of the Mission. Dr. Curran was a strong leader. He was deeply concerned in planting the Church among the multitudes in the hinterland, as his frequent visits into the interior indicate. It was his confidence in the final victory that led the missionaries through many discouraging days and brought them to the optimistic times as recorded in this report. Dr. Curran was a member of the Board of Examiners of the College of Liberia, and the only American missionary to be honored with a degree of Doctor of Divinity by this institution.

The Mission has work in seven stations and 363 towns and half-towns. In addition to the missionaries sixty national workers are engaged in the spread of the Gospel.

There are 250 communicant members in the Church. During the biennium the congregational offerings amounted to $1,102.00.

BRITISH GUIANA

Name	Address	Arrival
Rev. and Mrs. Robert H. Daube	New Amsterdam	1927
Rev. and Mrs. Paul M. Counts	Furlough	(Short Term)

Our Mission in British Guiana has been in charge for the past two years of Rev. and Mrs. Robert H. Daube. They, however, spent a part of this period, from July 28, 1930, to October, 1931, in the United States on a well-earned furlough. During his absence the Rev. and Mrs. Paul M. Counts, former missionaries in Africa, carried on the work. Due to a serious cerebral hemmorhage of Rev. Counts, they were compelled to come to America immediately on the return of Rev. and Mrs. Daube in October.

The question of two missionaries in British Guiana was raised on the general principle that no Mission should have less than two missionaries. A second missionary was deemed necessary for the field, but owing to financial limitations, he could not be sent.

The places in which the Mission operates are the old historic congregation in New Amsterdam, which has an existence of 188 years. The stations within a radius of five miles of New Amsterdam are in the villages of Lochabar, Adelphi, Betsy Ground, Good Manana Land and Mara, in which live East Indians, speaking various Hindu dialects such as Telugu, Tamil, Hindi, Hindustani and Urdu, all able, however, to understand English. This presents a good field for aggressive evangelism. Two East India evangelists and several unpaid workers carry on work among a population of 9,000. In Lochabar, the mother congregation, Ebenezer of New Amsterdam, directs a successful Sunday school at Lochabar, with an enrollment of 130, and the missionary has a Bible Class of forty adults. The need is urgent that this place be provided with a suitable building to carry on the school and organize a church.

The work of the Mission on the Berbice River continues as usual. The five churches and four schools do not make rapid progress, and for the sixteen years of their existence under the few visits, not exceeding four or five times a year, no great progress can be expected. Here if anywhere the work of a second missionary could become fruitful.

Among the Arawak Inuians the congregation and school has held its own, and since the new worker has been placed in charge, all branches of the work have shown marked improvement, as many as fifty members attended the church services on occasions. They are quite willing to erect a new chapel and will supply the timber, if the Board will send a grant of $800.

The New Amsterdam congregation reports a communicant membership of 198 and a baptized enrollment of 350.

Fuller statistics of all our schools and work will be available for our Annual Report. The outlook of the work is hopeful and the annual net budget passed by the Board at its last meeting in May for the new year is, including the missionary salary, $3,553. This is a small amount to keep alive this old historic Church and Mission. The endowment of the Church in the hands of the Trustees of the Government, when the mission was taken over by our Board in 1915 was $20,000 and now is reported as $32,000.

SOUTH AMERICA
ARGENTINE

Name	Address	Arrival
Rev. Paul O. Machetzki, D.D.	Buenos Aires	1922
Rev. and Mrs. John M. Armbruster	Furlough	1924
Miss Corinne Menges	Buenos Aires	1925
Miss Myrtle Wilke	Buenos Aires	1927
Rev. and Mrs. Knud R. Jensen	Resigned—short term	1930

Our Argentine Field has made considerable progress in all spheres. Our national ranks have been filled by the ordination of Mr. Jonas Villaverde, Mr. Dorotea Estrada and Mr. William Holz. Mr. Estrada was trained for the priesthood in the Roman Church, and for five years has been working in our Mission, giving ample evidence of sincerity and acceptance of our Faith. He has for three years had charge of parishes in the Mission in and around Buenos Aires. Mr. Holz, for four years has been head of our Boys' Department and for two years had charge of our Boys' Department, and for two years had charge of our German services in the Viila del Parque Church. Mr. Holz is now at work in the Eldorado field, among our churches, and Mr. Estrada has had charge of our work in and around Buenos Aires. After authorization by the Nebraska Synod, Rev. Machetzki, a member of that synod, ordained Mr. Estrada on the 16th of August, 1931, and Mr. Holz on September 6, 1931, in Buenos Aires. Mr. Villaverde was educated in America at Hamma Divinity, and was ordained on the field by Rev. Armbruster under the authority of the Synod of Ohio.

The most outstanding piece of work in connection with the Argentine Mission was formally begun in April, 1931, when the Board agreed to undertake work in the Province of Misiones, in the Eldorado, the congregations promising to furnish materials and labor for the erection of a central building in the amount of 8,000 pesos, about $2,000. It is gratifying to note that in the five congregational centers there are 789 men and 1,313 women, a total of 2,102 communicants. With these are 52 catechumens and 482 Sunday school children.

The Board approved the Mission's plan of building a church and school center, and authorized work to begin on buildings as soon as title to land can be secured. $6,000 was sanctioned toward the project for land and building fund, as soon as the people made good their promises to help according to agreement.

The purchase of the site at Caseros on which the Mission school and church were located for the last ten years, was made necessary by the bankruptcy of the owner. It was deemed most desirable that our work should not be disturbed and that we should buy the site and buildings thereon. After suitable agreements were arrived at, the Mission determined to buy, and at public auction secure the site, at Pesos 14,700 or about $5,000. The Board sanctioned this purchase, and authorized the Mission to pay off the purchase price out of the rents paid monthly heretofore for the property's use. By careful business planning this property can be paid in full in four or five years. While the growth of the congregation and school is slow, there is every prospect that these institutions in this growing suburb of Buenos Aires will meet with success. The Sunday schools and day schools are flourishing and the congregation has a baptized membership of 100.

The statistics of the Mission show encouraging progress in the biennium. The Sunday schools in the eight centers show 433 scholars; the field contributions amount to 7,499 pesos and young people's organizations are in a flourishing condition.

Our national college and elementary schools show an enrollment of 814 and fees and contributions of 56,922 pesos.

The foreign staff of workers at the close of 1931 number five; two ordained men and three women missionaries. Our national workers number fifty, of whom six are ordained men, five the wives of ministers, eleven men and nine women teachers in secondary schools, and nineteen teachers in elementary schools. Our foreign staff is very small, but is well backed-up by the national workers.

MEETINGS, OFFICERS, BOARD MEMBERS

During the past biennium the Board of Foreign Missions has met regularly every two months with an average attendance of fifteen voting and four co-operating and advisory members. The Board has adopted an amendment to its constitution to be ratified at this biennial convention, which calls for four instead of six Board meetings each year. An amendment to the By-Laws has been adopted to enable the Board to do all of its business at each meeting on one day instead of two days as formerly. **(See Resolution No. 5.)**

The list of Board officers, secretaries and members during the past biennium is as follows:

OFFICERS

President: Rev. Stewart W. Herman, D.D., 121 State St., Harrisburg, Pa.
Vice-President: Rev. George A. Greiss, D.D., 38 S. 8th St., Allentown, Pa.
Recording Secretary: Rev. George Drach, D.D., 18 E. Mt. Vernon Place, Baltimore, Md.
Treasurer: George R. Weitzel, 18 E. Mt. Vernon Place, Baltimore, Md.

SECRETARIES

Rev. Paul W. Koller, D.D.—Executive Secretary (Candidates, Foreign Fields).
Rev. L. B. Wolf, D.D.—Home Base Secretary, Corresponding Secretary for South America and China.
Rev. George Drach, D.D.—Literature Secretary, Corresponding Secretary for India and Japan.
Rev. M. Edwin Thomas, D.D.—Special Gifts Secretary, Corresponding Secretary for Africa.

MEMBERS OF THE BOARD

Terms Expire in 1932

Rev. S. W. Herman, D.D., 121 State St., Harrisburg, Pa.
Rev. J. L. Sieber, D.D., 352 Church Ave., Roanoke, Va.
Rev. Charles A. Dennig, 211 East St., Warren, Pa.
Rev. S. T. Nicholas, D.D., 907 Maryland Ave., N. E., Washington, D. C.,
Mr. William H. Menges, Menges Mills, Pa.
Mr. Martin H. Buehler, 327 Glenn St., Glens Falls. N. Y.
Mr. Charles H. Dahmer, 5th Ave. Bank, 44th St. and 5th Ave., New York City, N. Y.

Terms Expire in 1934

Rev. L. C. Manges, D.D., 1431 Walnut St., Harrisburg, Pa.
Rev. George Greiss, D.D., 38 S. 8th St., Allentown, Pa.
Rev. H. C. Brillhart, D.D., 19 Spruce St., Leetonia, Ohio.
Rev. E. R. Jaxheimer, 8068 87th Rd., Woodhaven, N. Y.
Mr. Paul Van Reed Miller, 642 Widener Bldg., Philadelphia, Pa.
Mr. M. P. Möller, Jr., Hagerstown, Md.
Mr. W. A. Rast, Cameron, S. C.

Terms Expire in 1936

Rev. H. W. Snyder, D.D., 5124 Chevy Chase Parkway, Washington, D. C.
Rev. P. E. Monroe, D.D., Concord, N. C.
Rev. Prof. E. E. Fischer, D.D., 7300 Boyer St., Mt. Airy, Philadelphia, Pa.
Rev. C. M. Snyder, 503 Haws Ave., Norristown, Pa.
Rev. Oscar A. Benson, 7352 Calumet Ave., Chicago, Ill.
Mr. H. Torrey Walker, West Collingswood, N. J.
Mr. Frank Howard, Johnstown, Pa.

CO-OPERATING MEMBERS

Representing the Augustana Synod

Rev. Peter Froeberg, D.D., 81 Hillberg Ave., Brockton, Mass.
Rev. R. F. Thelander, 35 Locust St., Jamestown, N. Y.

Representing the United Danish Church

Rev. J. P. Nielsen, Dana College, Blair, Nebraska.
Rev. M. Jorgensen, 22 Galston Ave., Brooklyn, N. Y.

ADVISORY MEMBERS

Representing the Women's Missionary Society

Miss Flora Prince, 644 Wittenberg Ave., Springfield, Ohio.
Mrs. S. R. Kepner, 122 3rd St., Pottstown, Pa.

NOMINATIONS FOR BOARD MEMBERSHIP

The Board of Foreign Missions at its meeting on May 11, 1932, nominated the following for election at this meeting of the United Lutheran Church:

Rev. S. W. Herman, D.D. (eligible for re-election), East Pennsylvania Synod, 121 State Street, Harrisburg, Pa.
Rev. S. T. Nicholas, D.D. (eligible for re-election), Maryland Synod, 907 Maryland Ave., N. E., Washington, D. C.
Rev. Charles A. Dennig (eligible for re-election), Pittsburgh Synod, Warren, Pa.
Rev. Robert D. Clare, D.D., Maryland Synod, 1900 St. Paul St., Baltimore, Md.

Mr. Charles H. Dahmer (eligible for re-election), United Synod of New York, Scarsdale, N. Y.

Mr. Claude L. Peterman, West Pennsylvania Synod, 253 West Springettsburg Ave., York, Pa.

Mr. John J. Bruns, Maryland Synod, 1920 Park Ave., Baltimore. Md.

We wish to testify to the faithful and valued service rendered by those whose terms have expired and who are ineligible for re-election. Rev. J. L. Sieber, D.D., has been a member for eight years since 1924, when he was elected to fill the unexpired term of the late Dr. M. M. Kinard. Mr. M. H. Buehler has been a member for two full terms since 1920. Mr. William H. Menges has been a member since 1919, when he was elected to fill the unexpired term of the late Mr. Charles A. Kunkel.

RECOMMENDATIONS

The Board of Foreign Missions in deep humility bows before the Great Head of the Church, acknowledging His divine favor and help. Many times during the biennium we had to come to Him as the only source of aid and He has never failed us. Thanks be to God. We pray for His continued blessing, not only upon our Board and work, but upon the whole Church of which we are a part.

1. That the Board of Foreign Missions be permitted to work in churches and Sunday schools for the cancellation of the remainder of the Foreign Mission Debt, without making an appeal or any special emphasis on the debt.

2. That the magazines published by the Board—"The Foreign Missionary" and "Der Missionsbote" be commended to the Church as sources of foreign mission information and inspiration.

3. That we express our deep appreciation to the Augustana Synod for its co-operation in India, and to the United Danish Church and Icelandic Synod for co-operation in Japan.

4. That all congregations in addition to meeting full apportionment be urged to make special foreign mission contributions for assigned purposes such as Foreign Missionaries, Parishes Abroad and Proteges. [Supplemented by the Convention, see p. 293.]

5. That the United Lutheran Church in America ratify the Amendment to Article V, Section 2 of the Constitution of the Board of Foreign Missions to read as follows: "Regular meetings for the transaction of business shall be held every three months at such times and places as the Board may determine."

This amendment changes the word "bi-monthly" to "every three months," and reduces the number of meetings each year from six to four.

STEWART W. HERMAN, *President.*
GEORGE DRACH, *Recording Secretary,*
PAUL W. KOLLER, *Executive Secretary.*

REPORT OF THE TREASURER OF THE BOARD OF FOREIGN MISSIONS

BALANCE SHEET

June 30, 1932

ASSETS

Cash in Banks:

General Fund	$57,740.62	
Investment Fund	12,222.04	
		$69,962.66

Investments at book values, as annexed:
Bonds and Stocks:

Free	$230,001.77	
Pledged as collateral to secure loans payable	68,954.85	
	298,956.62	
Ground Rents, Mortgages and Notes	24,739.88	

Real Estate:

Local Real Estate	$25,251.20		
Philadelphia Real Estate	1,660.64		
Knoxville, Tenn., Real Estate	5,096.10		
Property located at Kodikanal, India	13,000.00		
		45,007.94	
			368,704.44
Accounts Receivable			10,501.59
			$449,168.69

LIABILITIES

Loans Payable to Union Trust Company of Maryland, secured by bonds aggregating at book values, $68,954.85 .... $35,000.00
Unpaid May Draft for India 18,792.29

		53,792.29
		$395,376.40

FUNDS

Trust Funds	$203,106.09
Annuity Funds	86,800.00
Andhra Christian College Fund	257,440.78
Pohlman Fund	1,600.00
Land and Building Fund	13,781.68
Reformation Diamond Jubilee Advance Fund	17,840.64
Kobe Equipment Fund	7,390.43
Women's Missionary Society	59.90
China Famine Relief Fund	91.00
Women's Missionary Society Travel Account	124.00
Mrs. W. Matzat Interest Account	108.75
	$588,343.27

Less Overdraft:
General Fund 192,966.87
                               —————$395,376.40

Note.—The above balance sheet does not include as
Assets, investments in properties in foreign fields,
nor does it include Liabilities incurred in the purchase of such properties.

BALANCE SHEET
June 30, 1931

ASSETS

Cash in banks:
General $77,982.58
Investment Fund 16,285.56
                               ————— $94,268.14

Investments at book values, as annexed:
Bonds and stocks:
Free $194,597.05
Pledged as collateral to secure loans
payable 73,329.26
                       ————— 267,926.31
Ground Rents, Mortgages and Notes 27,639.88
Real Estate:
Local Real Estate $25,251.20
Deposit on Real Estate, Phila., Pa.............. 175.00
Property located at Kodikanal, India.......... 13,000.00
                       ————— 38,426.20
                               ————— 333,992.39

                               $428,260.53

LIABILITIES

Loans Payable to Union Trust Company of Maryland,
secured by bonds aggregating at book values,
$73,329.26 .... $45,000.00
Unpaid May Draft for India 16,505.00
                               ————— 61,505.00

                               $366,755.53

FUNDS

Trust Funds $190,858.21
Annuity Funds 86,452.81
Andhra Christian College Fund 248,779.69
Pohlman Fund 1,600.00
Land and Building Fund 24,093.38
Reformation Diamond Jubilee Advance Fund 19,840.63
Kobe Equipment Fund 6,943.37

                             $578,568.09

Less Overdrafts:
General Fund $211,133.09
Women's Missionary Society 679.47
                                                        ——————— 211,812.56
                                                            ——————$366,755.53

Note.—The above balance sheet does not include as
Assets, investments in properties in foreign fields,
nor does it include liabilities incurred in the purchase of such properties.

RECEIPTS AND DISBURSEMENTS
For the year ended June 30, 1932

RECEIPTS

	General Fund	Women's Missionary Society Fund	Other Funds
United Church on Apportionment $354,000.00			
Women's Missionary Society		$215,485.15	
Augustana Synod	6,292.96		
Danish Synod	4,746.00		
Donations received through Board Treasurer and General Treasurer for General Fund Current Work	102,578.30		
Bequests			$13,178.75
Donations for Specific Funds	10,403.15		5,530.37
Donations for Andhra Christian College			1,141.00
Annuities	5,652.81		6,000.00
Interest on Investments	7,978.13		10,200.09
"The Foreign Missionary" and "Der Missionsbote"	2,967.02		
Interest on Andhra Christian College Endowment Fund	2,680.00		
Rental of Slides	234.50		
Profit on Sale of Bonds	300.00		
Total Fund Receipts for Current Work $497,832.87		$215,485.15	$36,050.21
Donations for Board's Debt	19,354.95		
	$517,187.82	$215,485.15	$36,050.21

SUMMARY OF RECEIPTS

General Fund $497,832.87
Donations for Board's Debt 19,354.95
                                                                            ——————
                                                                            517,187.82
Women's Missionary Society Fund 215,485.15
Other Funds 36,050.21
Sale of Investments or Paid 17,965.00
Payments on Notes Receivable 900.00
Bank Loans Received 115,000.00
Payments on Mortgages 500.00

Payments on Real Estate	14.36
Dorothea Matzat Special	5,244.13
Miscellaneous Receipts	232.75

Total Receipts $908,579.42

DISBURSEMENTS

	General Fund	Women's Missionary Society Fund	Other Funds
Budgets Paid to Missions	$258,659.99	$112,924.76	
Specials Paid to Missions	5,112.03	30,862.51	
Salaries of Missionaries	122,507.53	57,823.85	
Traveling Expenses of Missionaries to and from Fields	32.666.87	9,118.64	
Expenses of Missionaries in Training and on Furlough	3,938.36	316.02	
New Missionaries	800.00		
Gifts to Missionaries and Fields	5,000.24		
Salaries of Secretaries and Treasurer	23,499.97		
Salaries of Clerks, Stenographers, etc.	7,807.00		
Expenses of Secretaries and Treasurer	1,392.15		
Expenses of Board Members	2,396.44		
Expenses of Candidates and Students	105.68		
Outfit Allowances for Missionaries		200.00	
Special Allowances and Pensions	5,626.77		
Disbursements from Specific Funds			$2,514.99
Contributions to Interdenominational Foreign Mission Organizations	2,723.60		
Partial Payment on Purchases of Shantung Mission		3,500.00	14,000.00
"The Foreign Missionary" and "Der Missionsbote"	5,220.39		
Printing Annual Report	1,085.29		
Preparing Stereopticon Slides	62.52		
Publicity	1,028.21		
Moving Pictures	125.00		
Office Supplies and Expenses	1,978.56		
Telephone, Telegraph and Cables	903.05		
Postage and Expressage	443.23		
General Office Expense	265.20		
Auditing	770.09		
Partial Payment Eldorado Property Argentina, S. A.			789.01
Matured Annuities			5,652.81
Advanced against Bequests (Birely Estate)			930.87
Expenses Baltimore Mission House and the "Brown House":			
Repairs	221.55		
Janitor	572.00		
Insurance	85.12		
Water Rent	7.60		
Interest	60.00		

Taxes	177.06		
Miscellaneous Expense	26.00		
Interest on Bank Loans	2,463.15		
Interest on Uninvested Funds of Andhra Christian College	3,575.32		
Interest on Annuities	5,653.22		
Interest on Andhra Christian College Endowment Fund			2,680.00

Total Fund Disbursements for Current Work	$496,959.19	$214,745.78	$26,567.68
Expenses of securing Donations for Board's Debt	2,062.41		
	$449,021.60	$214,745.78	$26,567.68

SUMMARY OF DISBURSEMENTS

General Fund	$499,021.60
Less month of May items paid during month of July, 1932, and included in above total	18,792.29
	480,229.31
Women's Missionary Society Fund	214,745.78
Other Funds	26,567.68
Investments purchased and acquired through Bequest	48,995.31
Bank Loans Repaid	125,000.00
Dorothea Matzat Special	5,244.13
Draft for 1931 Disbursements paid in current period	16,505.00
Advances made (Accounts Receivable)	10,501.59
Expenses advanced in acquiring Knoxville, Tenn., Property	96.10
Real Estate acquired through gift	5,000.00
Total disbursements	$932,884.90

GENERAL SUMMARY

	General Fund	Women's Missionary Society Fund	Other Funds
Fund Receipts for Current Work	$497,832.87	$215,485.15	$36,050.21
Fund Disbursements for Current Work	496,959.19	214,745.78	26,567.68
Excess of funds for Current Work	$873.68	$739.37	$9,482.53

RECEIPTS AND DISBURSEMENTS
For the year ended June 30, 1931

RECEIPTS

	General Fund	Women's Missionary Society Fund	Other Funds
United Church on Apportionment	$414,000.00		
Women's Missionary Society		$224,026.26	

Augustana Synod	9,910.00		
Danish Synod	7,530.99		
Icelandic Synod	1,200.00		
Donations received through Board Treasurer and General Treasurer for General Fund Current Work	118,263.11		
Bequests			$15,612.78
Donations for Specific Funds			1,540.86
Donations for Andhra Christian College			3,811.00
Annuities			1,950.00
Interest on investments	10,886.60		10,484.21
"The Foreign Missionary" and "Der Missionsbote"	3,632.65		
Interest on Andhra Christian College Endowment Fund	2,680.00		
Rental of slides	273.26		
Profit on sales of bonds	20.00		
Total Fund Receipts for Current Work	568,396.61	224,026.26	33,398.85
Donations for Board's debt	35,600.98		
	$603,997.59	$224,026.26	$33,398.85

SUMMARY OF RECEIPTS

General Fund	$568,396.61
Donations for Board's debt	35,600.98
	603,997.59
Women's Missionary Society Fund	224,026.26
Other Funds	33,398.85
Sale of Investments	9,000.00
Payments on Notes Receivable	2,000.00
Bank Loans received	53,500.00
Total Receipts	$925,922.70

DISBURSEMENTS

	General Fund	Women's Missionary Society Fund	Other Funds
Budgets paid to Missions	$314,624.80	$132,572.21	
Specials paid to Missions	2,269.40	35,362.48	
Salaries of Missionaries	133,177.64	61,419.15	
Traveling expenses of Missionaries to and from fields	26,034.41	9,902.37	
Expenses of Missionaries in training and on furlough	10,883.30	540.91	
New Missionaries	1,300.00		
Gifts to Missionaries and Fields	1,996.09		
Salaries of Secretaries and Treasurer	23,499.96		
Salaries of Clerks, Stenographers, etc.	7,975.00		
Expenses of Secretaries and Treasurer	2,100.00		
Expenses of Board Representatives	2,516.42		

Expenses of Candidates and Students	1,041.51		
Outfit allowance for Missionaries		400.00	
Special allowances and pensions	3,394.33		
Disbursements from specific funds			$3,506.77
Contributions to Interdenominational Foreign Mission Organizations	3,329.00		
Partial payment on purchases of Shantung Mission		3,500.00	14,000.00
Payments to Kyushu Gaukuin			12,500.00
"The Foreign Missionary" and "Der Missionsbote"	5,250.15		
Printing Annual Report	1,102.97		
Preparing stereopticon slides	35.10		
Publicity	600.15		
Office Supplies and Expenses	2,363.36		
Telephone, Telegraph and Cables	971.27		
Postage and Expressage	574.12		
General Office Expense	95.80		
Auditing	900.00		

Expenses of Baltimore Mission House
   and the "Brown House":

Repairs	$559.78	
Janitor	572.00	
Water Rents	27.68	
Interest	60.00	
Miscellaneous Expenses	15.66	

	1,235.12		
Interest on Bank Loans	3,327.83		
Interest on Uninvested Funds of Andhra Christian College	4,457.68		
Interest on Annuities	5,618.64		
Interest on Andhra Christian College Endowment Fund			2,680.00
Total Fund Disbursements for Current Work	560,674.05	243,697.12	32,686.77
Expenses of Securing Donations for Board's Debt	2,652.15		
	$563,326.20	$243,697.12	$32,686.77

SUMMARY OF DISBURSEMENTS

General Fund	$563,326.20
Less month of May items paid during month of July, 1931, and included in above total....................	16,505.00
	546,821.20
Women's Missionary Fund	243,697.12
Other Funds	32,686.77
Investments Purchased	33,252.50
Deposit on Mortgage Foreclosure	175.00
Bank Loans Repaid	78,500.00
Total Disbursements	$935,132.59

GENERAL SUMMARY

	General Fund	Women's Missionary Society Fund	Other Funds
Fund Receipts for Current Work	$568,396.61	$224,026.26	$33,398.85
Fund Disbursements for Current Work	560,674.05	243,697.12	32,686.77
Excess or Deficit of Funds for Current Work	$7,722.56	$19,670.86*	$712.08

* Deficit

RECONCILEMENT OF ACCOUNTS

June 30, 1931 and June 30, 1932

	Balances June 30, 1931	Receipts	Disbursements	Transfers Debits	Transfers Credits	Balances June 30, 1932
ASSETS						
Cash	$94,268.14	$908,579.42	$932,884.90			$69,962.66
Investments (Bonds and Stocks)	267,926.31	−17,965.00	−48,995.31			298,956.62
Ground Rents and Mortgages	18,459.88	−500.00			a$1,500.00	16,459.88
Notes Receivable	9,180.00	−900.00				8,280.00
Real Estate	38,426.20	−14.36	−5,096.10	$1,500.00a		45,007.94
Accounts Receivable			10,501.59			10,501.59
	428,260.53	$889,200.06	$868,291.90			$449,168.69
LIABILITIES						
Loans Payable to Bank	$45,000.00	$115,000.00	$125,000.00			$35,000.00
Due on Unpaid Draft	16,505.00		16,505.00		b18,792.29	18,792.29
	$61,505.00	$115,000.00	$141,505.00			53,792.29
	$366,755.53	$774,200.06	$726,786.90	$1,500.00	$20,292.29	$395,376.40
FUNDS						
Dorothea Matzat	$190,858.21	$5,244.13	$5,244.13			$203,106.09
Trust Funds	86,452.81	13,178.75	930.87			86,800.00
Annuity Funds	248,779.69	6,000.00	5,652.81			257,440.78
Andhra Christian College	24,093.38	11,341.09	2,680.00			13,781.68
Land and Building Fund	19,840.63	4,477.31	14,789.01			17,840.64
Reformation Diamond Jubilee	6,943.37	500.00	2,499.99			7,390.43
Kobe Equipment Fund	1,600.00	447.06				1,600.00
Pohlman Fund						91.00
China Famine Relief		106.00	15.00			232.75
Accounts Payable	−679.47*	232.75				59.90
Women's Missionary Society Fund (Overdraft)*	−211,133.09*	215,485.15	214,745.78	18,792.29b		−192,966.87*
General Fund (Overdraft)*		517,187.82	480,229.31			
	$366,755.53	$774,200.06	$726,786.90	$20,292.29	$20,292.29	$395,376.40

RECONCILEMENT OF ACCOUNTS

June 30, 1930 and June 30, 1931

	Balances June 30, 1930	Receipts	Disbursements	Transfers Debits	Transfers Credits	Balances June 30, 1931
ASSETS						
Cash	$103,478.03	$925,922.70	$935,132.59			$94,268.14
Investments (Bonds and Stocks)	$243,673.81	—9,000.00	—33,252.50			267,926.31
Ground Rents and Mortgages	18,459.88					18,459.88
Notes Receivable	11,180.00	—2,000.00				9,180.00
Real Estate	38,251.20		—175.00			38,426.20
	311,564.89					
	$415,042.92	$914,922.70	$901,705.09			$428,260.53
LIABILITIES						
Loans Payable to Bank	70,000.00	53,500.00	78,500.00		$16,505.00	$45,000.00
Due on Unpaid Draft						16,505.00
						61,505.00
	$345,042.92	$861,422.70	$823,205.09		$16,505.00	$366,755.53
FUNDS						
Trust Funds	$185,558.21	$5,300.00				$190,858.21
Annuity Funds	84,502.81	1,950.00				86,452.81
Andhra Christian College Fund	239,844.48	14,295.21	$2,680.00	$2,680.00		248,779.69
Land and Building Fund	40,280.60	10,312.78	26,500.00			24,093.38
Reformation Diamond Jubilee Fund	21,303.63	5.00	1,468.00			19,840.63
Kobe Equipment Fund	5,898.40	1,044.97				6,943.37
Pohlman Fund	1,600.00					1,600.00
China Hospital Fund	1,000.00		1,000.00			
China Famine Relief Fund	344.66	87.90	432.56			
Luther League Educational Building Fund	18.00		18.00			
J. M. Armbruster Fund	105.22	402.99	508.21			
J. C. Finefrock Automobile Fund	80.00		80.00			
Women's Missionary Society Fund (Overdraft)	18,991.39	224,026.26	243,697.12			679.47*
General Fund (Overdraft)	254,484.48*	603,997.59	546,821.20	16,505.00	2,680.00	211,133.09*
	$345,042.92	$861,422.70	$823,205.09	$19,185.00	$19,185.00	$366,755.53

* Deficit

SCHEDULE OF SECURITIES AS OF JUNE 30, 1932

Bonds		Book Values
$1,500	Altoona and Logan Valley Elec. Ry. 4½s, 1933....................	$1,500.00
1,000	American Utilities Co., Series "A." First Ref. 6s, 1945........	1,000.00
3,000	American and Foreign Power Co., Inc., Deb. 5s, 2030........	2,692.50
6,000	Associated Electric Co. 4½s, 1953.....	5,655.00
5,000	Atlantic Coast Line (L. & N. Div.) 4s, 1952.........................	4,293.75
3,000	American Tel. and Tel., Gold Deb. 5s, 1965..........................	3,045.00
2,000	Brooklyn Edison Co., Inc., Gen Series "E" 5s, 1952...............	1,935.00
2,000	Baltimore County, Md., Met. Dist. 4½s, 1956......................	2,073.47
1,000	Baltimore County, Md., Met. Dist. 4½s, 1954......................	1,036.73
4,000	Baltimore and Ohio R. R. Co., 1st, 4s, 1948...........................	3,050.00
3,000	Baltimore and Ohio R. R. Co., Equip. "D" 4½s, 1940...........	2,969.40
2,000	Baltimore and Ohio R. R. Co., S. W. Div. 5s, 1950	1,985.00
4,000	Bonded Mortgage Co. of Baltimore, Series "E" 5½s, 1936.	3,856.00
400	Boro. of Red Lion, Pa. 4½s, 1932.....	400.00
3,620	British Guiana Government (Church Endowment) 5s, 1946.	3,620.00
500	Center Court Apartment, 1st, S. F., 6s, 1936.....	500.00
4,000	Central Illinois Public Service Co. 1st, 4½s, 1967.................	3,790.00
3,000	Central Illinois Public Service Co. 1st, 5s, 1968.....................	2,925.00
1,000	Central Indiana Power Co., 1st, 6s, 1947....	1,000.00
5,000	Central States Electric Corp., Conv. Deb. 5s, 1948...............	4,825.00
1,000	Cespedes Sugar Co., 1st, 7½s. 1939......................................	1,000.00
4,000	Chesapeake and Ohio Ry. Ref. and Improv., Series "B," 4½s. 1995	3,760.00
1,000	Cities Service Co., Conv. Deb., 5s, 1950	1,000.00
3,000	City of Baltimore, Second Conduit Serial Loan of 1924, 4s. 1961	2,902.50
8,000	City of Baltimore, New Sewerage Imp., 4s, 1961.................	7,200.00
5,000	Commonwealth Edison. 1st Mtge, 4s, 1981......................	4,725.00
3,000	Consolidated Gas of Baltimore, Gen'l., 4½s, 1954	2,890.00
3,000	Consolidated Gas, Elec. Lt. and Power Co., 1st Refs., 4s, 1981	2,865.00
2,000	Consolidated Cities Lt. Power and Traction Co., 1st., 5s, 1962	1,659.90
2,000	Continental Bond and Investment Co., 1st Mtge, Series "A," 6s. 1936	2,000.00
3,000	Denmark (Kingdom of), 5½s, 1955	2,985.00
1,000	Detroit Edison Co., 5s, 1933	1,000.00
3,000	Duquesne Gas Corpn., 1st Conv., 6s, 1945	2,925.00
3,000	Detroit Edison Co., Gen'l. and Ref., 4½s, 1961	3,000.00
1,000	Dodge Bros., Inc., Deb., 6s, 1940	702.50
3,000	Electric Power and Light Corpn., Gold Deb., 5s, 2030........	2,790.00
2,500	Electric and Peoples Traction Stock Trust Cert.. 4s. 1945.	2,500.00
1,000	Elk Horn Coal Corpn., Deb., 7s, 1931	1,000.00
1,000	Erie Electric Motor Co., 1st Ref., 5s, 1941	1,000.00
1,500	Federal Mortgage Co., Series "J," 6s, 1940..........................	1,500.00
2,000	Federal Mortgage Co., Series "J," 6s, 1935	2,000.00
5,000	Federated Utilities, Inc., 1st Lien, 5½s, 1957	4,737.50
5,000	Florida East Coast Ry. Co., 1st, 4½s, 1959	3,950.00
4,000	Florida Power and Light Co., 1st, 5s, 1954	3,814.00
3,000	Forty Wall Street Corpn., 1st, 6s, 1958	2,940.00
3,000	Gary Electric and Gas, 1st, 5s, 1934	2,932.50
2,000	Greenwich Water and Gas Co., 1st and Ref., 5s, 1952........	1,820.00

4,500	Hughesville School Ass'n, 1st 5s, 1966	4,500.00
3,000	Houston Lighting and Power 1st and Ref., 4½s, 1981	2,947.50
5,000	Illinois Central R. R. Co., 4¾s, 1966	4,825.00
2,000	Illinois Power and Light Corpn., 1st and Ref., 5s, 1956	1,960.00
2,000	Indiana Ice and Fuel Co., 1st Mtge., 6½s, 1947	2,000.00
4,000	Interstate Power Co.. 5s, 1957	3,900.00
1,000	Johnstown Passenger Rwy. Co., 4s, 1931	1,000.00
3,000	Kentucky Utilities Co., 1st Mtge., 5s, 1961	3,000.00
3,000	Kansas City Power and Light Co., 1st, 4½s, 1961	3,082.50
3,000	Kansas Power and Light Co. (The), 1st and Ref., 6s, 1947	2,737.50
1,000	Lehigh Valley R. R. Co., Gen'l Cons. Mtge., 4s, 2003	1,000.00
19,000	Maryland Electric Rwy. Co., 1st Mtge., 5s, 1933	19,000.00
6,000	Medical Arts Building 5s, 1938	6,000.00
3,000	New York Central R. R., Ref. and Imp., 4½s, 2013	2,992.50
4,000	National Capital Mortgage Co., 1st, 6s, 1939 (Sixteenth Street Highlands of Maryland, Inc.)	4,000.00
500	Nassau and Suffolk Lighting Co., 1st. 5s, 1945	500.00
1,000	National Power and Light Co., Deb. "B," 5s, 2030	606.25
5,000	National Union Mortgage Co., Gold Bond, 6s, 1936	5,000.00
1,000	North Carolina Gas Co., 1st Mtge., S. F.. 6s, 1948	970.00
3,000	North American Co., Deb., 5s. 1961	2,902.50
3,000	New York Central Equipment Trust Co., 4½s, 1942	2,871.36
3,000	New York Edison, 1st and Ref., 5s, 1951	2,910.00
1,000	Oklahoma Railway Co., 1st and Ref., 5s, 1941	1,000.00
3,000	New England Gas and Elec. Ass'n., Conv. 5s, 1950	2,677.50
5,000	Penn Central Light and Power Co., 1st, 4½s, 1976	4,725.00
4,000	People's Light and Power Corpn., 1st, 5½s, 1941	3,880.00
3,000	Philadelphia Co. Secured Series "A." 5s, 1967	3,032.25
1,400	Philadelphia Electric Co., S. F. 1st, 5s, 1966	1,400.00
8,000	Potomac Mortgage Co., 1st Mtge. Coll., 6s, 1935	8,000.00
3,000	Pennsylvania R. R. Co., Gen'l. Mtge., 4¼s, 1981	2,887.50
3,000	Pennsylvania Power and Light Co., 1st Mtge., 4½s, 1981	2,887.50
3,000	Public Service Co. of Northern Illinois, 1st, 4½s, 1981	2,925.00
3,000	Peoples Light, Gas and Coke Co., 1st and Ref., 4s, 1981	2,820.00
2,000	Pennsylvania Electric Co., 1st and Ref., 4s, 1971	1,827.50
2,000	Rawson Realty and Construction Co., Inc., 1st, 5½s., 1938 (Boston Postal Service Station)	2,000.00
1,000	St. Louis County Gas Co., 1st, 5s, 1951	1,000.00
1,000	Scranton Railway Co., Cons. Mtge. 5s, 1932	1,000.00
4,000	Seaboard Air Line, 1st 4s, 1950	3,392.61
3,000	Seaboard Air Line, Seaboard and Roanoke Division, 1st 5s, 1931	3,022.50
1,000	Seventy-Nine Madison Avenue, Corpn., 1st 6s, 1937	1,000.00
3,000	St. George Hotel, 1st Mtg. 5¾s, 1994	945.00
3,000	Southern Pacific Co., Gold 4½s, 1968	2,992.50
4,000	Southwest Missouri R. R. General Ref. 5s, 1931	4,080.00
1,500	Standard Power and Light Corp., Gen'l Deb. 6s, 1957	1,492.50
4,000	Southeastern Power and Light Co. Deb. 6s, 2025	2,700.00
3,000	Safe Harbor Water Power Corp. 4½s, 1979	2,960.00
2,000	Texarkana and Fort Smith Rwy. Co., 1st 5½s. 1950	2,010.00
8,000	United Railways and Electric Co. of Baltimore 4s, 1949	5,760.00
1,000	United Railways and Electric Co. of Baltimore 5s, 1936	1,000.00
1,600	United States Government 1st Liberty Loan 4¼s, 1932-47.	1,600.00

16,450 United States Fourth Liberty Loan 4¼s, 1933-38.................   15,013.40
1,000 United States Rubber Co., 1st and Ref. 5s, 1947 ....   350.00

       Total Value of Bonds $292,836.62

Stocks
Mutual Help Building and Loan Association of Baltimore City,
   Par $100 .... $3,000.00
West Baltimore Building and Loan Association of Baltimore
   City, Par $130 ....   3,120.00

       Total Value of Stocks $6,120.00

       Total Value of Bonds and Stocks $298,956.62

Ground Rents, Mortgages and Notes Receivable
Ground Rents on properties at 920, 924, 1040 and 1042 West
   Fayette Street, Baltimore, Maryland $4,959.88
Mortgage on 2511 N. Calvert St., Baltimore, Md., at 5 per cent.   4,500.00
Mortgage on 5716 Hegerman St.. Philadelphia, Pa., at 6 per cent.   2,500.00
Mortgage on 5849 Woodcrest Ave., Philadelphia, Pa., at 6 per
   cent 4,500.00
Note of L. B. Wolf and Alice B. Wolf, due June 29, 1929, at
   5 per cent 3,100.00
Notes of Charles R. Fisher, guaranteed by C. B.
   Morehead, at 6 per cent, due September 10, 1928
   (extended indefinitely) $2,250.00
      Due September 10, 1929 ....   2,215.00
      Due September 30, 1930 ....   715.00
                                             5,180.00

       Total Ground Rents, Mortgages and Notes Receivable............ $24,739.88

Real Estate
Equity in property at 2900 E. Woodland Ave., Baltimore,
   Maryland $9,251.20
Property at 18 E. Mt. Vernon Place, Baltimore, Maryland.........   16,000.00
Property located at Kodikanal, India 13,000.00
Property located at 1019 S. Randolph St., Philadelphia, Pa.....   1,660.64
Property located at Knoxville, Tennessee 5,096.10

       Total Real Estate $45,007.94

       Total Ground Rents, Mortgages, Notes Receivable and Real
       Estate $69,747.82

SUMMARY

Bonds $292,836.62
Stocks 6,120.00
Real Estate, Mortgages, Ground Rents and Notes 56,747.82
Property located at Kodikanal, India 13,000.00

       Total Book Values $368,704.44

Respectfully submitted,
GEORGE R. WEITZEL, Treasurer.

Philadelphia, Pa., July 19, 1932.

We have audited the books of account of the Board of Foreign Missions of the United Lutheran Church in America, for the biennium beginning July 1, 1930 and ending June 30, 1932, and we hereby certify that, in our opinion, the foregoing Receipts and Disbursements, together with the Balance Sheet and supporting schedules, as submitted by its Treasurer, are true and correct.

TAIT, WALKER & BAKER,
Accountants and Auditors.

Dr. Herman introduced Mr. Geo. R. Weitzel, Treasurer of the Board of Foreign Missions, and the Rev. Paul W. Koller, Executive Secretary of the Board. Dr. Koller presented the following missionaries:

From India: Rev. and Mrs. F. L. Coleman, Rev. George A. Rupley, Rev. and Mrs. Theodore W. Benze, Miss Edna Engle, Miss Mette K. Blair, Miss Amelia L. Brosius, Dr. Barbara E. DeRemer.

From Japan: Rev. L. S. G. Miller, Rev. Clarence E. Norman, Miss Mary Heltibridle, Miss Helene Harder.

From Africa: Rev. and Mrs. Robert S. Oberly, Rev. and Mrs. G. K. Gesler, Miss Elsie R. Otto, Mrs. C. E. Buschman.

From China: Rev. Paul Parker Anspach.

From South America: Miss Myrtle Wilke.

Recommendations 1, 2 and 3 were adopted.

Recommendation 4 was amended by the addition of the following:

"with the understanding that in publishing the list of the congregations complying with this request the board will name all the congregations that make such special supporting contributions."

The recommendation as amended was adopted.

Recommendation 5 was adopted.

The Rev. Paul E. Scherer presented the following resolution:

"Resolved, That the Board of Foreign Missions be instructed to call three or more of our ablest home pastors during a year's leave of absence from their respective parishes, to carry at the board's expense the challenge of missions to our Lutheran people."

On motion the resolution was referred to the Board of Foreign Missions for their consideration and later report.

The Rev. W. A. Wade presented the following resolution:

"Resolved, That we record our thanks to Almighty God for enabling the Church to continue the work of Foreign Missions without the recall of any of our missionaries and at the same time permitting the Board to reduce its indebtedness materially during the past biennium; and

"That we express our appreciation to the Board of Foreign Missions for its splendid service in carrying out the work entrusted to it by the Church; and in their plans for the coming biennium."

The resolution was adopted by a rising vote.

The Rev. L. L. Uhl addressed the Convention on our mission in India.

The Rev. Paul W. Koller presented to the Convention the associate delegates as follows: from the Andhra Evangelical Lutheran Church, the Rev. G. A. Rupley and the Rev. F. L. Coleman; from the Church in Japan, the Rev. L. S. G. Miller. These delegates presented the greetings of their respective bodies. Dr. Koller also presented to the Convention the Rev. C. E. Norman of Japan, Mr. P. Satyanandam, Mr. J. B. Williams and Mr. Hirosuke Ouchi.

Dr. Koller then presented the Rev. L. B. Wolf, retiring Secretary of the Board of Foreign Missions.

It was moved and carried that the report of the auditors be accepted.

The item of the Executive Board's report pertaining to the Training of Ministers and Teachers (II, 9) as contained in the Supplemental Report of the Executive Board, Item "A," was taken under consideration as the item for this place on the program.

It was moved and carried that in view of the lateness of the hour and the importance of the item, this order of business be postponed to a special session to be held at eight o'clock Tuesday evening, at which session this shall be the order of business.

As an item of unfinished business the Convention proceeded to consider the Executive Board's report concerning the Survey of Canadian Synods (III, B) as contained in the Supplemental Report of the Executive Board, Item "B." The Rev. E. B. Burgess presented the recommendations of the Commission on Survey of Canadian Synods.

Recommendations 1, 2, 3, 4, 5, 6, 7 and 8 were adopted.

At twelve o'clock the Convention adjourned with prayer by the Rev. P. E. Monroe.

SEVENTH SESSION

BENJAMIN FRANKLIN HOTEL.
Philadelphia, Pennsylvania.
Monday, October 17, 1932, 2.00 P. M.

Devotions were conducted by the Rev. Mark O. Heller, and the President called the Convention to order.

The report of the Committee of Reference and Counsel was presented by the Rev. H. Brezing, Chairman of the Committee.

Report of the Committee of Reference and Counsel

Your Committee respectfully submits:

1. Greetings have been received as follows:

By cablegram from Rajahmundry, India: "Andhra Lutheran Church Convention sends greetings to Mother Church. Ephesians 3:14-21."

By cablegram from Japan: "Japan Convention greets Philadelphia Convention. II Thessalonians 3:1."

By letter from the American Lutheran Mission in Shantung, China: "Prayerful felicitations and a request to recognize the Rev. P. P. Anspach from the field."

Your Committee assumes that the Rev. Mr. Anspach has all the privileges of visiting missionaries at the Convention and recommends that the communications be referred to the president of the Board of Foreign Missions for suitable reply.

2. Your Committee is happy to note the presence of the Rev. L. W. Boe, President of St. Olaf College, at the Convention. He comes as representative of the Norwegian Lutheran Church of America. We recommend that it be our first order of business this afternoon to hear him, and that at the same time the report of the representative of the Executive Committee of the Lutheran World Convention be moved forward so as to give him an opportunity to speak to the same.

The recommendations in the report were adopted.

As authorized by the action on the recommendation of the Committee of Reference and Counsel, President Knubel called on the Rev. L. W. Boe, who presented the greetings of the Norwegian Lutheran Church of America. The President called upon the Rev. E. A. Trabert, who responded to the greetings of the Norwegian Lutheran Church of America.

The President then called for the report of the Representative of the Executive Committee of the Lutheran World Convention, which was presented by the Rev. L. W. Boe speaking for the Rev. J. A. Morehead.

REPORT OF REPRESENTATIVE OF THE EXECUTIVE COMMITTEE OF THE LUTHERAN WORLD CONVENTION

Due to the illness of Dr. John A. Morehead, president of the Executive Committee of the Lutheran World Convention, it devolves upon the undersigned as the other American member of the Executive Committee to submit report, which under the circumstances must be brief and lacking in that detailed review of the work which otherwise would have characterized it.

On the basis of the resolutions adopted at Copenhagen, the president, Dr. John A. Morehead, has kept in direct contact with the Lutherans in every land and has virtually completed the organization contemplated by the Convention. Through correspondence and personal contact effort has been made to bind the Lutherans of the world together, on the basis of the declarations of faith made both at Eisenach and Copenhagen, for common witness and for common effort in the relief of suffering Lutherans and in support of constructive measures for the advancement of the interests of the Church and the Kingdom.

Living as we still do in the shadows of the Great War, the major portion of the work hitherto is still characterized by what the Germans call "Liebestätigkeit," but as the years go by and the world recovers its balance, it is hoped that the Lutheran World Convention movement will more and more be concerned with forward-looking, constructive plans for the building and strengthening of the Lutheran Church in all lands.

Three major activities have this year engaged the energies of the Executive Committee, *i.e.*:

I. Assisting the suffering Lutheran churches in Europe;

II. Support of the Russian Lutheran Church and especially of the Seminary at Leningrad;

III. The movement of the Lutheran refugees from Harbin, Manchuria, to the State of Santa Catharina in Brazil.

I. The Suffering Lutheran Churches

Lack of means has prevented the Lutheran World Convention from being of assistance in many portions of the Church where a little support would have strengthened the membership materially and would in many cases have laid a solid and substantial foundation, upon the basis of which they could have taken care of matters themselves. The disorganization which came upon many of the churches in minority countries because of the war and the unfavorable economic and other conditions under which they have had to exist and work since, have made many problems acute which otherwise would have been comparatively easy of solution.

Being of assistance involves not merely having the funds necessary to relieve actual distress, but very often is more a question of the committee having the time and means to visit those concerned for the purpose of giving encouragement, counsel and advice as to the proper solution of the problems confronting them. The large correspondence carried on by Dr. Morehead with all parts of the Lutheran world testifies to the need of a central organization to which they can turn in a time of difficulty. Along this line lies the largest opportunity for future service.

II. SUPPORT OF THE RUSSIAN CHURCH AND THE SEMINARY AT LENINGRAD

The support of the Seminary at Leningrad and the Lutheran Church of Russia have for many years constituted the major relief work of the Lutheran World Convention. Increasing difficulties have accumulated around the seminary and those who are carrying on the work of the Church in Russia, at times almost disorganizing the work completely. But due to the loyalty of the leaders, especially Bishops Malmgren and Meyer, and the pastors and congregations of the Church, the work has continued to date and offers practically the only real opportunity for a Protestant Church in Russia today. The seminary at Leningrad is the only Protestant Theological Seminary within the bounds of the Soviet Government. Because of lack of contributions both from America and Europe, not sufficient funds have been at the disposal of the committee to provide the seminary at Leningrad with the regular monthly contributions which are essential and necessary in case they are to continue. Humanly speaking, we may have every reason for giving up the support of the seminary and Church in Russia, because after many years of support there seemingly has been found no permanent solution of their problems. But from a larger standpoint, it is not for us to become discouraged because of lack of results. Our task it is to keep alive the loyal witnesses to the truth and in God's own day will come such permanent results as He deems wise and necessary. Every effort should be put forth to provide adequate support during the balance of the year 1932 and in 1933, so that nothing shall be lacking from this standpoint for the ultimate solution of their problems. The support of the Russian Lutheran Church and its seminary is our primary task today.

III. MOVEMENT OF THE LUTHERAN REFUGEES FROM MANCHURIA
TO BRAZIL

The special problem which has confronted the committee the last year is the moving of the four hundred Lutheran refugees from Manchuria, China, to the State of Santa Catharina in Brazil. Without going into a history of this undertaking, it may be briefly stated that, in the judgment of the president of the Lutheran World Convention, Dr. John A. Morehead, it became absolutely necessary to move the refugees without delay out of Manchuria, to avoid their being sent back into Russia. Every effort was put forth to find a haven of refuge in one of the Lutheran lands, but because of immigration laws and other difficulties the only opening seemed to be in South America, and finally it was decided to transport them to Shanghai, from there to Marseilles, France, and thence to Brazil. The matter of their location in Brazil and the conditions of their settlement there were left in the hands and to the judgment of Professor Friedrich Ulmer, of Erlangen, Germany, with the co-operation and support of Bishop Ihmels, the first vice-president of the Executive Committee. The refugees went on board the S. S. *Porthos* at Shanghai, on May 7, 1932, and landed at Marseilles, France, on June 11th, leaving again on the S. S. *Lipari* from Bordeaux, France, for Brazil, on June 12th. Professor Ulmer, on whose shoulders rested the responsibility of deciding as to the particular place in which they were to settle, decided on the State of Santa Catharina, near the southern boundary, on the border of the State of Rio Grande do Sul. Every care has been taken to provide for the final and satisfactory settlement of the refugees among or neighboring to Lutheran churches in the States of Parana and Santa Catharina. At the present writing it can be reported that they are being settled under the supervision of men selected by the German brethren in Germany.

Dr. Morehead had estimated that the total cost of their transportation and settlement would come to about $56,000, but later figures made it necessary to put the total at $59,000. Not sufficient funds had come in to pay for their transportation at the time they went on board in Shanghai, and the Nansen office at Geneva very kindly put at the disposal of the committee loan of 50,000 Swiss francs, which it will be necessary to repay as early as possible. Throughout in this undertaking the Nansen office of the League of Nations has put at the disposal of the committee its men and means in the furtherance of this objective. This help comes to us because of the unremitting interest in everything that pertains to the Lutheran Church of Graf Moltke, of Copenhagen, Denmark.

When the undersigned took over the responsibility for the office just sufficient funds had come in to pay for their transportation and an immediate call was sent out for $10,000 additional from the Lutheran churches of America and $10,000 from the Lutheran churches in Europe. Because of the difficult economic conditions not sufficient money has come in on the latest call to complete the task. Funds should be raised at once so that this undertaking may be brought to a happy and successful conclusion.

Appended is a report covering the receipts and expenditures of the committee for the years 1930 and 1931. Sufficient funds are not at the disposal of the committee to make it possible to even begin to do in a satisfactory way the work which ought to be done. For the coming year there ought to be raised for the seminary at Leningrad and the support of the Lutheran Church in Russia not less than $25,000. Then there should further be at the disposal of the committee for the suffering churches not less than $10,000.

Since the convention at Copenhagen the amount of money necessary to support the office and the overhead connected with the administration of the office has been provided through the National Lutheran Council. This agreement will expire in January of the coming year. On account of the illness of Dr. Morehead, the future plans for the support of the Lutheran World Convention movement cannot be defined as exactly as desirable at the present time. The Lutheran World Convention Movement as a whole and its work has to that extent been built up around the personality and the experience of Dr. Morehead that vital changes will be found necessary in the organization, in case his illness should make it impossible for him to resume the work again. It is, however, hoped that in the Providence of God, his health will recover so that continued use may be made of his influence and his large experience and many contacts, not only for the benefit of the movement as a whole, but especially in view of the great number of special problems which from time to time are presented to the Lutheran World Convention Committee for solution. His present illness makes it possible in a report to call to the attention of the co-operating Church Bodies the unique and outstanding service which he has contributed ever since he was engaged as one of the commissioners for the National Lutheran Council. Out of the difficulties and distresses of the war, largely as a result of his efforts, has grown a large movement for the strengthening of the Church in the bonds of our common faith and the organization of the Lutherans of the world for common effort. Those of us who have followed Dr. Morehead's leadership and have been with him in the work both here and in Europe can testify to the fact that every dollar entrusted to the committee and disbursed by him has been expended wisely and always with a view to strengthening the people in their confessional standpoint and for the upbuilding of the Lutheran Church.

Since the convention at Eisenach, the participating Church Bodies have annually appropriated and paid for committee expenses a total of about three thousand dollars, apportioned to the respective bodies on a per capita basis. The last year it has been necessary to draw on these funds for relief work, leaving the committee without the necessary means for the meeting this fall. It is our hope and prayer that the usual appropriation will be made this year.

No meeting of the Executive Committee was held during 1931 for reasons of economy. It can, however, not be postponed any longer and this fall it will be necessary for the committee to meet. It is hoped that Dr. Morehead's health will to that extent have improved that it will be possible for him to go along and take part. An invitation has been extended to the committee to meet in Wittenberg, Germany, and later to take part both in Germany and in Sweden in the Gustavus Adolphus celebrations which will take place about the first week in November. The Lutheran World Convention needs the undivided support of its constituent members, especially at this time. The world's misery and troubles are the Church's opportunity.

Out of the distresses of the war this movement was called into existence. It seems as if the way to unity of witnessing and common effort lies in being bound together in common service and common relief of our brethren who are in need. While we are held together by these bonds of love and service, it undoubtedly is God's plan that we shall in that association discover in one another that common faith which we confess and in the consciousness of that unity walk together toward the larger tasks of tomorrow.

The special thanks and appreciation of the Lutheran World Committee are due Drs. Knubel and Long for their kindly help in the administration of the duties of the office during the absence of Dr. Morehead. Miss Sigrid C. Wilson, Dr. Morehead's secretary, also is included because of the many extra burdens and responsibilities she has had to carry during this time.

On behalf of Dr. John A. Morehead,

L. W. BOE,

Member of the Executive Committee,

Lutheran World Convention.

August 9, 1932.

EXHIBIT A
LUTHERAN WORLD CONVENTION
CASH RECEIPTS AND DISBURSEMENTS
From February 1, 1930, *to December* 31, 1930

SUMMARY

Balance—Cash on hand—February 1, 1930...................... $ 2,780.91

RECEIPTS:

For Committee and Operating Expenses (see Schedule I) ....$ 3,535.99

For Executive Office Expenses (see Schedule II).... 11,885.70

For the Relief of Suffering Churches (see Schedule III) 33,361.29

For English Edition of Proceedings of Second Lutheran World Convention (see Schedule IV)........ 376.50

Total receipts from February 1 to December 31, 1930 .... 49,159.48

Total $51,940.39

DISBURSEMENTS:

Committee and Operating Expenses (see Schedule I) ....$ 2,337.26

Executive Office Expense (see Schedule II)............. 9,597.76

Relief of Suffering Churches (see Schedule III)...... 31,121.81

Publishing English Edition of Proceedings of second Lutheran World Convention (see Schedule IV) 661.86

43,718.69

Balance on hand, December 31, 1930................................ $ 8,221.70

SCHEDULE I
FUND FOR COMMITTEE AND OPERATING EXPENSES

February 1, 1930 (Balance) .... $ 2,780.91

RECEIPTS:

United Lutheran Church	$ 1,702.84	
Norwegian Lutheran Church	602.65	
Augustana Synod	433.31	
United Danish Church	34.79	
Joint Synod of Ohio	315.93	
Lutheran Free Church	61.52	
Iowa Synod	278.60	
Icelandic Synod	10.69	
Danish Lutheran Church	27.94	
Interest	67.72	
		3,535.99
		$ 6,316.90

EXPENDITURES:

Traveling expenses, Norway meeting of Executive Committee, etc.	$ 1,316.86	
To Dr. Jorgensen, treasurer, for committee expenses	500.00	
By transfer to Account of English Edition of Book of Second Lutheran World Convention......................	150.00	
News Exchange Bulletin	310.34	
Cablegrams, radiograms, stationery, etc.	60.06	
		2,337.26

Balance, December 31, 1930 .... $ 3,979.64

SCHEDULE II
FUND FOR EXECUTIVE OFFICE

RECEIPTS:

Contributions of the National Lutheran Council	$ 9,917.45	
Individual gifts	1,958.50	
Interest	9.75	
		11,885.70

EXPENDITURES:

Executive salary	$ 5,500.00	
Executive rent allowance	1,100.00	
Secretarial and stenographic service	1,913.00	
Maintenance contribution (rent)	180.00	
Traveling expenses	395.17	
Equipment—Filing cabinet	40.00	
Printing, telephone, telegrams, postage and other miscellaneous items	469.59	
		9,597.76

Balance, December 31, 1930 .... $ 2,287.94

SCHEDULE III
FUND FOR THE RELIEF OF THE SUFFERING CHURCHES

RECEIPTS:

Contributions of the National Lutheran Council......$23,928.94		
Individual gifts from America	510.00	
Remittances from the treasurer of the Lutheran World Convention for transmission to Russia......	7,223.76	
A. Lutherischen Gotteskasten, Hamburg.... $1,450.00		
B. Lutherischen Gotteskasten, Erlangen.... 238.84		
	1,688.84	
Interest	9.75	
		$33,361.29

EXPENDITURES:

Russia $22,421.81		
Russian Refugees	700.00	
Ukrainian Work (Poland)	1,900.00	
India	1,800.00	
Roumania	800.00	
Latvia	750.00	
Holland	500.00	
Austria	500.00	
France	500.00	
Jugoslavia	500.00	
Brazil	500.00	
Switzerland	250.00	
		31,121.81

Balance, December 31, 1930 .... $ 2,239.48

SCHEDULE IV
FUND FOR ACCOUNT OF ENGLISH EDITION OF BOOK OF SECOND LUTHERAN WORLD CONVENTION

RECEIPTS:

From publishing houses and individuals ....$	226.50	
By transfer from Executive and Operating Expense Account	150.00	
		$ 376.50

EXPENDITURES:

Expenses of Dr. Wentz, Editor	6.50	
Printing and binding, etc.	655.36	
		661.86

Deficit, December 31, 1930 .... $ 285.36

EXHIBIT B
LUTHERAN WORLD CONVENTION
CASH RECEIPTS AND DISBURSEMENTS
From January 1, to December 31, 1931

SUMMARY

Balance—Cash on hand, January 1, 1931 .... $ 8,221.70

RECEIPTS:

For Committee and Operating Expenses (see Schedule V) ....$ 3,182.49		
For Executive Office (see Schedule VI)................... 15,015.00		

For the Relief of Suffering Churches (see Schedule VII) 17,913.15
For the Account of English Edition of Book of Second Lutheran World Convention (see Schedule VIII) 285.36
                                                                           —————— 36,396.00

         Total receipts $44,617.70

DISBURSEMENTS:
    Committee and Operating Expenses (see Schedule V) 855.99
    Executive Office Expenses (see Schedule VI)........ 16,570.93
    Relief of Suffering Churches (see Schedule VII).... 20,152.63
                                                                           ——————
         Total 37,579.55

Balance on hand at December 31, 1931... $ 7,038.15

SCHEDULE V
FUND FOR COMMITTEE AND OPERATING EXPENSES
January 1, 1931 (Balance) .... $ 3,979.64

RECEIPTS:
    United Lutheran Church ....$ 1,702.84
    Norwegian Lutheran Church 602.65
    American Lutheran Church 594.53
    United Danish Church 34.79
    Dr. Jorgensen, treasurer 215.52
    Interest 32.16
                                                                           ——————
                                                                                3,182.49

                                                                           $ 7,162.13

EXPENDITURES:
    Traveling expenses ....$ 42.00
    Secretarial service, stationery, postage, etc................ 71.50
    Printing of "Lutheran Churches of the World"........ 457.13
    By transfer to meet deficit on English edition of
        Volume of Second Lutheran World Convention.... 285.36
                                                                           ——————
                                                                                855.99

Balance, December 31, 1931 .... $ 6,306.14

SCHEDULE VI
FUND FOR EXECUTIVE OFFICE
January 1, 1931 (Balance) .... $ 2,287.94

RECEIPTS:
    Contributions of the National Lutheran Council........$13,385.00
    Individual gifts 1,630.00
                                                                           ——————
                                                                                15,015.00

                                                                                17,302.94

EXPENDITURES:

Executive salary	$ 6,000.00	
Executive rent allowance	1,200.00	
Secretarial and stenographic service	2,080.00	
Maintenance contribution (rent)	1,365.70	
Traveling expenses	315.46	
Equipment and furniture—typewriter and desk	148.00	
Printing, telephone, telegrams, postage and other miscellaneous items	354.30	
By transfer to Fund for the Relief of Suffering Churches to meet special emergencies	5,107.47	
		16,570.93

Balance, December 31, 1931 .... $ 732.01

SCHEDULE VII
FUND FOR THE RELIEF OF THE SUFFERING CHURCHES

January 1, 1931, Balance .... $ 2,239.48

RECEIPTS:

Contributions of the National Lutheran Council	$ 5,324.23	
Individual gifts from America	1,953.20	
Remittances from the treasurer of the Lutheran World Convention for transmission to Russia	3,526.44	
Gifts direct from other countries for Russian Relief:		
a. Lutherischen Gotteskasten, Hamburg..$ 450.00		
b. Lutherischen Gotteskasten, Erlangen.. 1,232.81		
c. United Lutheran Church, Australia.... 247.14		
d. Federation Lutheran Churches, India 71.86		
	2,001.81	
By transfer from Executive Office account	5,107.47	
		17,913.15
		$20,152.63

EXPENDITURES:

Russia	$15,282.97	
Russian Refugees	1,947.36	
Ukrainian work (Poland)	1,800.00	
Poland	500.00	
Brazil	500.00	
France	117.30	
Foreign Missions (designated gift for Breklum)....	5.00	
		20,152.63

Balance, December 31, 1931 ....

SCHEDULE VIII
FUND FOR ACCOUNT OF ENGLISH EDITION OF BOOK OF SECOND LUTHERAN WORLD CONVENTION

January 1, 1931, Deficit ....$ 285.36

RECEIPTS:

Account balanced by transfer from Committee and Operating Expense Account 285.36

Balance, December 31, 1931 ....

At the close of his presentation of the work of the Lutheran World Convention, Dr. Boe presented Dr. Morehead personally to the Convention.

The President called for the report of Committee of Tellers No. 1. Mr. H. F. Heuer, Chairman of Committee of Tellers No. 1, reported elections as follows:

For the *Executive Board* each of the following received a majority of the votes cast:

Rev. E. B. Burgess	William E. Hirt
Rev. E. P. Pfatteicher	Robbin B. Wolf
Rev. A. Steimle	John L. Zimmerman

The President declared them elected.

For the *Commission of Adjudication* each of the following received a majority of the votes cast:

Rev. Luther Kuhlman	Rev. W. F. Rangeler
C. M. Efird	

The President declared them elected.

For the *Committee on Church Papers* each of the following received a majority of the votes cast:

Rev. M. R. Hamsher	Rev. E. P. Pfatteicher
Henry Streibert	

The President declared them elected.

For the *Executive Committee of the Laymen's Movement* each of the following received a majority of the votes cast:

H. J. Albrecht	E. G. Hoover
J. L. Clark	E. Clarence Miller
Peter P. Hagan	Harvey C. Miller
Henry W. Harter	George E. Neff
John L. Zimmerman	

The President declared them elected, and stated that one member of the Executive Committee of the Laymen's Movement was yet to be elected.

By unanimous consent it was ordered that the Committee of Tellers No. 1 conduct an election by ballot for one additional member of the Executive Committee of the Laymen's Movement immediately after the close of the afternoon session today.

The report of the Board of American Missions was presented by the Rev. H. W. A. Hanson, Vice-President of the Board.

REPORT OF BOARD OF AMERICAN MISSIONS

(For action on the recommendations in this report see p. 371.)

The Board assists in the maintenance of 682 mission congregations and 78 preaching stations. Its honor roll comprises 524 missionary pastors, teachers and workers in Canada, the United States and the West Indies. They received upwards of 28,000 members.

Fifty-four new missions were organized during the biennium. Forty assumed self-support.

A net gain of 16 per cent in membership is the record of our missions in the West Indies.

Two zones were added to the Lutheran Home Missions Council: Metropolitan New York and Illinois and Adjoining States. Cooperative Lutheran Home Missions have reached an advance stage of Christian comity.

The Board maintains active membership in the Home Missions Council and the International Missionary Council. Through the Home Missions Council it has direct contact with the missionary program, policies and operations of other Protestant denominations. The International Missionary Council is vitally concerned with the Christian approach to the Jews in all parts of the world.

Grateful acknowledgment is made of the unfailing cooperation of synods in meeting the demands for readjustment to the reduced income on apportionment. One of them organized 11 new missions in 1931. Its present objective is one new mission for every month of the year. It had suggested 27 such fields, but only 11 could be organized because of limited funds.

An increasing number of congregations are sponsoring a home missionary. The Church of the Redeemer, Brooklyn, aids in the support of five such pastors.

The Long Island Conference of the United Synod of New York initiated the project of a Children's Mission. Rev. Jesse W. Routte will be the missionary pastor of the first Children's Mission in Jamaica, New York.

The First All West Indian Conference was held in St. Thomas and made a noteworthy record.

Three linguistic groups organized conferences: Slovak, Hungarian and Canadian Finnish.

The first Hungarian Lutheran Church in Canada was dedicated in Windsor, Ontario, July 31, 1932.

The response to the appeal for clothing and supplies for distribution among our Russian brethren in the Canadian Northwest exceeded all previous records.

In these days of new adjustments our force of home missionaries has shown an increasing measure of ability and fidelity. Their impress is evidenced in the lives of people who are drawn, not only to the mission but also to the Master.

The Board's pre-eminent need is an increased Church Extension Fund.

"Speaking of Missions"—this is our constant occupation, our cherished desire.

In his latest book, "A Program for America," Will Durant makes this broad statement, "The drama of Protestantism is reaching its close." Then he asks, "if it were not just as well that this America had never been born."
Here the ends of the earth have met. Forty-six millions of the 122,000,000 people in the United States are counted as communicants of the various churches. Sixteen million children are reckoned in the number of adherents. Our so-called Christian America faces the appalling situation of 60,000,000 souls as a vast home mission field. A parallel situation obtains among the 10,000,000 Canadians. The proportion of the unchurched is a perpetual challenge to home mission effort.
Cities furnish the pattern of American life. They hold the center of the changing scene. Thither young people flock in eager quest. While the trend of population from the city to the country has gained impetus and we ought never under-estimate the importance of rural missions, the march of progress is predominantly city-ward. A new civilization is in the making. Will it be potently Christian? The Church has no right to abate one jot of zeal or faith or effort in Home Missions. This is its immediate duty.

Program of American Missions

The primary aim of the Board of American Missions is to bring the Gospel of Jesus Christ to our fellow Lutherans in North America who are without a church home and the means of grace; to win men and women, Christian or non-Christian, to discipleship of Jesus Christ and to unite them in the fellowship of the Church; to make the Lutheran Church available to those sections which lack its ministry and message; to supply adequate Church leadership where the work of the present Church is limping or halting. It seeks patiently and persistently in the spirit of love to transform competing churches into co-operative churches and gradually to combine them into strong units in order that they in turn become Mother Churches of home missions.
More than five hundred men and women, valiant and loyal, are investing

their lives in this great enterprise. Their history is the story of heroic messengers who brought the Gospel message regardless of the hazards in the way. It is a story of adventure and the stewardship of life. It marks steady advance from the lone pioneer in the days which tried men's souls. Amid variety of methods the purpose is always one, to satisfy the spiritual need of seeking souls.

Many Synods have announced their purpose of strengthening missions already on the roll rather than initiating new missions this year. If this strengthening process gives proof of spiritual advance, it will be amply justified. We must remember, however, that God never writes the word Finis to new conquests in his Kingdom. He modifies our plans and labels as a serial the story which we thought was a complete product.

The Staff

The Board's Staff has been reduced to four full-time workers. This was made imperative by the diminished income from the U. L. C. A. apportionment. Economy is the watch-word. A balanced budget must be maintained. One way out was the discontinuance of the office of General Superintendent. This was followed by no curtailment of the Board's work. The present Staff voluntarily assumed increased duties.

A contributing cause was the expanding activity of the synods through their Home Mission Committees. Too much praise cannot be given for their loyalty and support. Following the Board's example, a number of synods dispensed with their Missionary Superintendents or Field Missionaries. Only in this way could a mounting deficit be avoided.

Tentative provision has been made for the former General Superintendents. Dr. A. D. R. Hancher is the stated supply of the merged congregation at New Market, Virginia Rev. Paul Ludwig is Reiseprediger of the Ministerium of Pennsylvania. Dr. George H. Hillerman carried on the work at Longview, Washington.

The present Staff is constituted as follows: Dr. F. F. Fry, Executive Secretary; Dr. J. F. Seibert, Divisional Secretary of English Missions; Dr. E. A. Tappert, Divisional Secretary of Linguistic Interests; Dr. Z. M. Corbe, Secretary of Finance and Church Extension.

The Board has placed on its records an expression of appreciation of the General Superintendents and their work. They served the Church faithfully for many years. Changing conditions under the Plan of Operation have demonstrated that the synods are doing much of the work formerly entrusted to the General Superintendents. The synods are enlisting and developing men who are more fully informed and taking livelier interest in home missions.

Lutheran Home Missions Council

Two zones were added to the organized work of the Lutheran Home Missions Council--"The Metropolitan District of New York" and "Illinois and

Adjoining States." This makes a total of five zones, including the Northwest, Rocky Mountain and Iowa. The Lutheran bodies participating in the New York area are the American Lutheran Church, Augustana Synod, the Danish Lutheran Church, Missouri Synod, United Norwegian Church, United Danish Church, and United Lutheran Church in America. Meetings are held quarterly. The same constituent group cooperates in the Chicago area with the exception of the Missouri Synod.

The avowed purpose of these Councils is "to foster the spirit of cooperation in home mission work, to encourage intelligent and aggressive prosecution of home mission activities by means of comprehensive surveys which shall be available to all participating bodies, to prevent friction and duplication of effort and to assist in the adjustment of controversies."

The Lutheran Home Missions Council, initiated by the Board of American Missions, met annually since the last convention. Both meetings were held in Chicago the last Thursday in January.

Co-operation Along All Lines

The Board of Education:

The Board of Education assists our Board in the support of pastors at Durham, N. C.; Lafayette, Ind.; University and St. Mark's, Seattle, Wash.; West Chester, Pa.; Boulder, Colo.; Rock Hill and Clemson College, S. C.

The following principles of co-operative work at educational centers were approved by the Board of American Missions and the Board of Education:

Regarding Pastors of Churches in Educational Centers—

Where a portion of the salary of a pastor of churches in an educational center is paid by the Board of Education and the Board of American Missions, the President of the synod and the Synodical Mission Committee are requested

To secure the advice of the said Boards in suggesting candidates for such parishes.

To secure the advice of the Board of Education before seeking the approval of the Board of American Missions.

Regarding the Removal of Men doing unsatisfactory work—

All constitutional provisions, both of the synod and the congregation, shall be carefully observed in seeking such a change of pastorate.

The first step in such action shall be a conference of representatives of the Board of American Missions and the Board of Education.

Out of such conference a committee shall be appointed to meet with the President of the synod who shall arrange for a consultation that shall include the pastor concerned, representatives of the Boards, and the synodical authorities.

If such conference, or conferences, fail to secure the necessary readjustment, then the Boards shall withdraw their support from the field.

Method of Work—

Inasmuch as the care of Lutheran students is an integral part of the responsibility of a Lutheran congregation in a community where there are Lutheran students, the policy and program of the local mission, set up by the pastor, the Church Council, and the synodical authorities, must be approved by representatives of both the Board of American Missions and the Board of Education.

The Board of Foreign Missions:

Recognizing that the missionary cause of the Church is one, the Board has approved missionaries from foreign fields, who were prevented from returning because of health, education or climatic conditions, to serve as missionary pastors of Home Mission parishes.

It cooperated with the Board of Foreign Missions and the Laymen's Movement for Stewardship in planning and successfully carrying out the celebration of the twenty-fifth anniversary of the Laymen's Missionary Movement.

It is united with the Board of Foreign Missions and the Women's Missionary Society in the mission exhibit at the Philadelphia Convention and in presenting free moving pictures of work in Home and Foreign fields.

The Board of Inner Missions:

The Board of American Missions was pleased to take over and carry on Inner Mission work in the West Indies and Rocky Boy Indian Reservation. These types of work include Homes for the Aged, Ebenezer Orphanage, Queen Louise Home, Home for Boys and daily kindergartens in many parishes in the Islands. Its work among sick and neglected children under the direction of a registered nurse is a living illustration of the gospel of love and unselfish devotion. It ministers to the leper colonies at Rio Piedras, Puerto Rico, and Christiansted, St. Croix.

It has continued the grant of part time service to the Rev. Fred W. Kern, Houston, Texas, in caring for Lutheran seamen during their stay in that port.

The Board of Deaconess Work:

The relation of the Deaconess Board to the Board of American Missions is mutually satisfactory. The work of Sister Emma Francis, as matron of Ebenezer Orphanage, and Sister Edith Prince, who heads up a large kindergarten, has the approval of both Boards. These sisters reflect credit upon the Philadelphia Motherhouse. The Board acknowledges its debt of gratitude to the Danish Motherhouse in Copenhagen for the highly efficient service of Sister Maren Knudsen.

The Women's Missionary Society:

The Recording Secretary and Treasurer of the Women's Missionary Society are advisory members of the Board of American Missions. Mrs. A. B. Leamer had served in this capacity at the time of her death. Miss Flora Prince, President; Miss Amelia D. Kemp, Executive Secretary, and Mrs.

Philip M. Rossman were present as invited guests. They were heartily welcome and their participation in the meetings of the Divisional Committees as well as Board sessions proved helpful.

Thirty-six missions are supported by the Society. Among them may be noted the only mission in Alaska, Arizona and Arkansas; Alhambra and Santa Barbara, Calif; Boulder, Pueblo and Barnitz Memorial, Denver, Colo.; West Palm Beach, Florida; Tabor and Westwood, Chicago, Ill.; Gary, Ind.; Trinity, Kansas City, Kansas; Kalamazoo, Mich.; Great Falls, Mont.; Vineland, N. J.; Endicott and St. Albans, N. Y.; Elyria, Ohio; Butler and Messiah, Pittsburgh, Pa.; Rock Hill, S. C.; Nashville, Tenn.; Lynchburg, Va.; Bellingham, Longview and University, Seattle, Wash.; Waukesha, Wis.; Casper and Laramie, Wyo.; Redeemer, Montreal, Que.; Victoria, B. C.; Southern Mountain work at Boone, N. C., and Rocky Boy, Montana.

Students preparing for the ministry of our linguistic groups receive aid from them. All women teachers and workers in the West Indies and at Rocky Boy as well as those who contribute to the progress of our Italian, Hebrew and Southern Mountain work are made possible by their support; acknowledgment is made also of the granting of Church Extension loans, interest donations and special gifts.

The Augustana Synod

The Board is ever mindful of the loyalty of Dr. Alfred Ostrom, former field treasurer and a member of the Augustana Synod. Dr. Ostrom has a longer record of missionary activity in Puerto Rico and the Virgin Islands than any other missionary in that field. He is now on furlough in the States.

Rev. Jesse W. Routte, a graduate of Augustana College and Theological Seminary at Rock Island, has taken up work in Harlem, New York City and Jamaica, Long Island, with the Board's endorsement. He is assistant pastor of the Church of the Transfiguration, New York.

Cordial acknowledgment is made of gifts received in Christmas boxes and assistance in the industrial work of Puerto Rico. The confident hope is expressed for its continuance.

Principles Relating to the Conservation of Causes

The work of the Board of American Missions is a diversified work. It is true the different phases are definitely integrated and interdependent, yet they are distinct. This fact is recognized in the Plan of Operation wherein these different phases are designated as Causes. So distinct are they that the Plan of Operation makes it incumbent upon the Board to recognize these causes in the nominations of the personnel to be elected to the Board.

Under the direction of the Board this work is conducted and carried on by the synods. To aid the synods in the prosecution of the work the Board makes an annual appropriation. The appropriation is made on the basis of the work being done or proposed and contemplated.

A certain amount is budgeted for each synod. It is made in good faith, and if the conditions obtained throughout the year, which existed when the budget was made, it will be paid in full.

Two things must be recognized and remembered by the synods.

First: the budget is made out on the basis of work being done or contemplated.

Second: The total allottment is the sum of the particular and several amounts budgeted for specific work. The total amount does not govern the particular items, but the several and particular items determine the total to be assigned to the synod. Therefore only when the particular work is being done can the synod claim the full amount allocated to it. If any particular phase of activity is abandoned during the year the synod cannot transfer the amount budgeted for that cause to another activity representing another Cause. This particular amount reverts to the Board.

To illustrate: The items representing the work of a given synod total $20,000. The Board has not taken $20,000 and distributed it to meet the particular needs of the synod, but the various activities conducted or proposed require $20,000. The items budgeted aggregate $20,000. Among the items aggregating this total when the budget was made is an item of $5,000 towards the support of a missionary to missionate among the Jews. After six months the synod deems it wise to discontinue this work. It does so. It cannot claim a budgeted balance of $2,500. The unused balance cannot be transferred by the synod to another cause represented in its program. The balance belongs to the Board. It can become available for work being done by the synod through the filing of a proper application requesting the assignment of the amount to a given cause of that synod's work. If this application received the endorsement of the Finance Committee the Board may re-enlist the amount on the Budget of that synod.

Again: Among the items aggregating the $20,000 budgeted to this synod is an item of $1,200 towards the salary of a pastor of the congregation at a given place. The amount is to be paid in monthly installments. The pastor resigns effective June 30th. The vacancy continues for a period of three months. A pastor assumes charge October 1st. The synod has a credit balance of $300. This amount becomes available upon proper application being sent to the Board.

On the other hand, if the congregation reaches the stage of self-sustentation under date of June 30th, the Board may, in its discretion, credit the budgeted balance to the account of this synod. The six hundred dollars not used by the synod is an asset of synod available during the year for such work as the synod may elect.

Policies Approved by the Board

I. Work Among Jews:

The cause of the Evangelization of our Jewish neighbors is a part of the primary obligation of the Church as a whole; accordingly in this phase of the work of The United Lutheran Church in America every pastor and congregation has a duty which cannot be delegated to any department of the Church as a whole or to a group, local or general, but should be recognized and discharged by every congregation as a natural part of its regular parish work.

Whenever, in addition to this congregational activity, it becomes necessary to establish special Jewish Mission stations, they shall be considered as supplemental to such congregational activity and shall be operated according to the following plan of operation:

In order to operate in harmony with the Plan of Operation as approved by the Church, each mission station shall be placed on the budget of the synod to which it is allocated.

Each Mission Station requires the moral and spiritual support of a strong and missionary minded constituency, organized in such manner as adequately to supplement the support granted by the Board of American Missions. As a matter of principle the Board should provide for no other items than the salaries of the Missionary Workers.

This constituency should organize a local committee of pastors and laypersons to have charge of the affairs of the Mission and conduct its business. The personnel of the local committee must be approved by the Board of American Missions and the Synodical Mission Committee.

Regular copies of the Minutes of the local committee shall be forwarded to the Divisional Secretary of Linguistic Interests and the Synodical Mission Committees of the synods cooperating with each particular station.

II. Work Among Italians:

Whereas, the congregation, as the primary body of the Church, is obligated to preach the Gospel to all Nations; therefore every congregation should be impressed with the responsibility to discharge this obligation and through its ministration reach all classes in its vicinity with the Gospel of Christ.

Whereas, there are localities in which reside large numbers of distinctive national characteristics, it is recommended for the effective administration of the Gospel that separate congregations be formed.

That when such organizations are effected, they shall be members of the synod in which they are located, and in preparing the budget, said synod shall be mindful of this work.

III. Work Among Negroes:

Whereas, Since the action taken in 1927 the great shift in the Negro population from the Southern States to the North and West has continued, and

Whereas, There has been no adequate effort on the part of our Church to shepherd these many souls, and on the other hand, unpatriotic and unchristian influences have been active among them, an even greater challenge is presented to our Church to consider the call of Negro evangelization, and

Whereas, the work in Harlem has made marked progress since it was inaugurated, and presents the need for future enlargement,

Therefore, Be It Resolved, That the Board of American Missions declares itself ready to render its assistance in cooperating with the Synod of New York in enlarging the work among Negroes in and around New York City.

In Memoriam

Dr. I. Chantry Hoffman, one of the General Superintendents of the Board since its organization, died suddenly at his home, 319 E. Walnut Lane, Philadelphia, Pa. The following minute was entered upon the records of the Board:

On Memorial Day, 1931, the soul of the Rev. I. Chantry Hoffman, D.D., experienced the full fruition of Christian hope.

After a comparatively brief illness he was called from employment in the kingdom of grace to the enjoyment of the blessedness of the kingdom of glory. He has gone to be with his Lord, in whose presence there is fullness of joy. He has joined that innumerable host of redeemed saints whose constant service is singing the praises of the Lamb, slain from the foundation of the world.

A faithful worker in the vineyard of the Lord has been taken. The voice of a devoted advocate of the cause this Board represents, and is endeavoring to promote, has been stilled. A true believer in the Home Mission Enterprise has been removed from our presence. We cherish his memory and remember his work.

The Board of American Missions, therefore, would record this minute expressive of its recognition and appreciation of the service Doctor Hoffman rendered the Church through his relations with this Board and its predecessors. For more than a quarter of a century he was more or less intimately identified and officially related to the agencies which were charged with the responsibility of making this country of ours Christian. In the fulfillment of the duties connected with this office he manifested consecrated zeal. In the conduct and projection of his work he exhibited sound judgment. In his contact with his brethren and fellow laborers in this great endeavor he displayed a warm sympathy.

We would therefore record our gratitude to God, who called him into his Vineyard and by Whose grace he labored abundantly in the works of his Lord.

At this time also we as a Board would remember most tenderly and affectionately his loved ones. We place them before the Throne of Grace and pray that from day to day they will receive and mark Christ's manifold help and grace.

As we think of the removal of this our fellow worker we cannot put away from our thought the work for which he labored so zealously and to which he was so devoted. Its indispensableness to carry on the unfinished task growing out of the completed work of our Lord comes convincingly before us. Its needs cry aloud.

We therefore pray the Lord of the harvest to thrust forth more laborers into His field. That He would arouse His Church to a deepening realization of the imperativeness of the work we represent, to create a more definite interest in the task given us to do, and beget a more liberal love which will enable us, together with all our fellow Christians, to let loose the forces of our Christian religion with such power that the impact thereof will be felt throughout the entire land, and Christ acknowledged Lord and Redeemer of our Country.

PROFESSOR EDWARD F AKSIM

Professor Edward F. Aksim entered the life immortal on Sunday, October 12, 1930. He was deeply interested in work among Esthonians and had assisted the Board in discovering Esthonian opportunities in the United States and Canada. His survey was so thorough and comprehensive that he was invited twice to come to New York and gather the unchurched Esthonians. On the occasion of his second visit he preached in the Church of the Holy Trinity, New York, to more than 100 Esthonians, including the consul and other officials. At their urgent request he was asked to take charge of this work as a missionary of the Board but declined, owing to impaired health. He was a member of the faculty of Saskatoon College and Seminary and later accepted a call to Waterloo Seminary where he served until the time of his death.

The Board desires to record its high appreciation of Prof. Aksim's sterling qualities and fine scholarship and his missionary zeal among his Lutheran brethren who had come to America from his native land.

DR. BENJAMIN F. HANKEY

Rev. Benjamin F. Hankey, D.D., died suddenly at his home of a heart attack. He had made all preparations for the meeting of the Central Conference of the Pittsburgh Synod which was to have convened that day in Emmanuel Church which he had served as pastor for nearly twenty-five years. When the delegates to the Conference assembled, they held a memorial service. He had been one of our earliest missionaries to Puerto Rico and had served as missionary pastor in San Juan 1899-1900. Twenty years later he revisited the Island. He was an active member of the Board of West Indies Missions and resigned at the time of the merger of the Board of American Missions.

At the time of the Milwaukee Convention, Dr. Hankey had suffered a heart attack. This was followed by another two weeks later. The fatal attack was the third within a month. He is survived by his widow, one daughter and one son; also by one brother and five sisters.

ENGLISH MISSIONS
Dr. J. F. Seibert

English missions are to be found in twenty-nine of the thirty-three synods of The United Lutheran Church in America. They make a large family.

There are three hundred forty-seven parishes and over four hundred congregations. This biennium, particularly, they have had their trials as well as their joys. Pastors and congregations have been hard hit and many, at times, hardly knew which way to turn. Almost every mail brings word of some unexpected situation that has developed because of repeated bank failures or the unemployment of the members. Withal the missionaries have been faithful in preaching the Word and in parish duties. With marked success they have been stressing Evangelism, instructing adult catechetical classes, looking after the thousands of young people gathered in Luther Leagues and making the most of their Brotherhoods and Women's Missionary Societies. They have received upwards of fifteen thousand members, a far greater percentage than the rest of the Church. Despite the gloom a hopeful spirit prevails and pastors and church councils courageously are facing their tasks rejoicing that in these days they can be of service in the upbuilding of the Church.

Self-Supporting

Thirty-seven missions have developed sufficient strength voluntarily to become self-supporting. Under the conditions this is a good record. In a number of instances it has meant real sacrificial giving. It is a joy to note how some of these have desired to relieve the Board of further support in order that others seemingly more worthy than themselves might have sustenance and care. It is interesting to study this list of missions. It reveals, for instance, that seventeen of them were located in what is usually known as the West and twenty in the East and South. If the roll were called it would be noticed that the usual history of the missions has been repeated. Some of these congregations have developed rapidly into self-support. Others have taken a longer time to grow into strength, while a few, and among them some that will be strong, outstanding churches in their several synods, have been supported for years. By contrast with some that have grown to self-support in a few years, others have been slow indeed. Perhaps the Board and the synods concerned, at times have become somewhat discouraged, but now all are happy that these have enrolled as self-supporting units and will increasingly become strong supporters of the Education, Missionary and Charitable programs of the Church. A thoughtful consideration of all the delegates is asked to these missions as they appear in Appendix A.

New Missions

With the Board's decreased income the care of the missions enrolled necessarily has been given the first consideration. Synodical Boards courageously have helped to grapple with the problems. Missionary Superintendents and Field Missionaries have been reduced in number. There has been a consolidation of missions rather than the organization of new ones. Fields white unto harvest could not be entered. Yet there has been no retreat nor has the Board simply marked time. Fields of compelling promise have been entered and work begun, the synods and the Board somehow finding a way with budgeted allottments for their support. Thirty new missions have been started, among which Beaver Dam, Wis.; Mizpah, St. Louis, Mo.; Undercliff, Pa.; North Hollywood, Calif.; Mobile, Ala.; Willow Grove, Pa.; Sweetwater and Longworth, Texas; Wissinoming, Pa.; Laurelton, L. I.; Kokomo, Ind.; Custer City, Okla.; Transfiguration, Rochester, N. Y., and Union, S. C., are some notable examples. Concerning Custer City, Missionary Superintendent McConnell writes: "It is the most extensive, needy, ripe Home Mission field that I have ever contacted." Others write in similar strain. No wonder the Board has gone forward! A complete list of the missions and the synod to which they belong are given under Appendix B.

THE COMMITTEE ON REVIEW

This committee has met periodically. Its function has been to make a study of all missions, especially those that have been on the Board for ten years and upwards and to make recommendations. The results have been stimulating. A new standard has been adopted by which properly to evaluate mission congregations, some of which have been supported for years. In some instances congregations have increased their giving with the resultant of decreased appropriations. In other instances missions have been recommended to the synods as self-sustentation parishes at such salaries as could be paid without mission appropriation, while in still other cases the consolidation of mission congregations into parishes has been recommended. It readily can be seen that the work of this committee, while it is very laborious and means a lot in investigation of source material, has been of great service to the Board and to the Church. It will be continued in the hope that, with the knowledge of the missions gained by patient and somewhat exhaustive study, a more correct diagnosis of all the missions may be possible. The inevitable result will be more and better missions. One result of the study of this committee is that about a dozen of mission parishes with the full cooperation of Synodical Mission authorities no longer receive aid from the Board's treasury.

MISSION CONFERENCES

Conferences of missionaries and of Synodical Boards have been held in practically all the synods where there is a considerable mission program. Subjects of pastoral visitation and Evangelism have been emphasized. In the East Pennsylvania Synod the program was confined to Evangelism. In others the specific work of the mission pastors has received attention. In the Synod of the Northwest the Synodical Board entered very intimately into the problems of the missionary. In the Ministerium of Pennsylvania all missionaries and the Board were dinner guests of the President, the Rev. J. F. Kramlich. Such conferences in which the Board's representatives were present, with marked inspirational benefit, were held this biennium in the Ohio, Pittsburgh, East Pennsylvania, Maryland, United Synod of New York, Illinois, the Synod of Northwest and other synods.

CONGREGATIONS SUPPORTING MISSIONS

First, Altoona, Pa., M. J. Kline, D.D., pastor.
    St. John's, East Juniata, Pa., J. Kaufman, missionary.

Zion, Harrisburg, Pa., S. W. Herman, D.D., pastor.
    Shoop's Colonial Park—St. Paul's, Harrisburg, Pa., Parish, George Miller, missionary.

Memorial, Harrisburg, Pa., L. C. Manges, D.D., pastor.
    First, Valley Junction, Ia., F. C. Maurer, missionary.

Zion, Hummelstown, Pa., C. G. Leatherman, D.D., pastor.
    First, Billings, Mont., H. N. Stoffel, missionary.

Grace, Rochester, Pa., H. R. Shepfer, pastor.
    Holy Trinity, Beaver, Pa., G. L. Ulrich, missionary (1931).
    St. Paul's, Windsor, Ont., Can., John Teutsch, missionary (1932).

Redeemer, Brooklyn, N. Y., H. T. Weiskotten, Ph.D., pastor.
    Bellmore Parish, L. I., Theodore Ressler, missionary.
    Holy Trinity, Brooklyn, N. Y., O. L. Kosmo, missionary.
    Grace, Forest Hills, L. I., C. B. Holand, missionary.
    Jamaica, So.-Rich. Hill Circle Parish, L. I., E. H. Lehr, missionary.
    Epiphany, Laurelton, L. I., C. F. W. Hoppe, D.D., missionary.
    St. Thomas, Locust Manor, L. I., W. F. Frey, missionary.

Trinity, Akron, Ohio, Franklin C. Fry, pastor.
    First Hungarian, Akron, Ohio, Ralph Zimmermann, missionary.

First, Mansfield, Ohio, H. C. Roehner, D.D., pastor.
    Hope, Toledo, Ohio, R. G. Schulz, missionary.

First, Dayton, Ohio, C. L. Venable, pastor.
    North Riverdale, Dayton, Ohio, pastorate vacant.

Trinity, Canton, Ohio, E. C. Herman, D.D., pastor.
    Trinity, Niles, Ohio, J. W. Bressler, missionary.

Keller Memorial, Washington, D. C., S. T. Nicholas, D.D., pastor.
    Grace, Eugene, Oregon, F. S. Beistel, missionary.

Calvary, Wilkinsburg, Pa., A. W. Steinfurth, pastor.
    Advent, Wilkinsburg Manor, Pa., J. E. Slater, missionary.

Mt. Zion, Pittsburgh, Pa., N. S., G. E. Swoyer, pastor.
    Calvary, Arnold, Pa., Paul J. Trout, missionary.

Christ, Chicago, Ill., G. P. Lottich, pastor.
    Westwood, Chicago, Ill., F. L. Schreckenberg, missionary.

North Austin, Chicago, Ill., F. W. Otterbein, pastor.
    Epiphany, Elmhurst, Ill., R. R. Frobenius, missionary.

Covenant, Brooklyn, N. Y., C. H. Hirzel, pastor.
    Christ, Little Neck, L. I., L. F. Gerhart, missionary.

St. Johannis, Reading, Pa., R. H. Ischinger, pastor.
    Field Missionary G. C. Weidenhammer, Manitoba Synod.

Redeemer, Buffalo, N. Y., J. S. Blank, pastor.
    First, Blasdell, N. Y., G. A. Martin, missionary.

Reformation, Rochester, N. Y., F. R. Knubel, pastor.
   Church of the Transfiguration, Rochester, N. Y., E. G. Schaertel,
      missionary.
Miss Julia Wattles, Pittsburgh, Pa.
   Grace, Houston, Texas, W. J. Hoebel, missionary.

In Memoriam

The Board has suffered the loss of a number of successful missionaries by
death. The Rev. F. K. Roof, Jr., of Swansea, South Carolina, had but recently graduated from the Southern Seminary and had entered enthusiastically upon his work as missionary at Swansea. It was a great shock to the
Board to hear of his having drowned, June 30th. A letter of sympathy was
sent to his father, the Rev. F. K. Roof, of New Brookland, South Carolina.

The Rev. George P. Endy, formerly the president of the Synod of Nova
Scotia, had just been installed as pastor at Guelph, Ont., Canada, when word
was received that he suddenly was called home August 16, 1931.

The Rev. J. Nelson Lentz, the Field Missionary for Detroit, closed a successful career, October 6, 1931. He was pre-eminently a church organizer.
His reports of surveys were models. In the course of his life he organized
Grand Forks, N. D.; Spokane, Wash.; Unity and Hope, Chicago; First,
Peoria; Reformation, Luther Memorial, Unity Hope, Augsburg, Nativity
and Resurrection, Detroit, and Trinity, Windsor, Ont., Canada. Some of
these have developed into strong self-supporting churches and the rest are
successful missions. He rests from his labors, but his works do follow him.

Rev. G. Gerlaw Clark, D.D., was a veteran home missionary. Much of
his life was given to mission parishes. The last congregation that he served
was Canon City, Colo. He died at Mayo Hospital, Rochester, Minn., December 19, 1931, after failing health for a number of months.

The Rev. J. W. Ball, Ph.D., was a successful missionary since 1895.
With the exception of two mission parishes in the central west, that of
Memorial, Kansas City and Grace, Lincoln, Nebr., his life was given to the
Synod of California. He served St. Mark's Church, Los Angeles, for many
years and while there manifested his self-sacrificing spirit and his desire to
see the church planted. He was a moving spirit in the organization of that
mission. At Huntington Park and Alhambra he did the same thing. In
fact at one time it was said he had given all the members of his council to
new missions. Later he organized and became pastor of Santa Monica when
he was elected as Field Missionary and organized the Beverly Hills mission. He was suddenly called home June 17, 1932.

The New Biennium

The new biennium has started with practically all the mission parishes
supplied with pastors. How different this is from a few years ago when seminaries were visited and conferences were held with theological students with
the thought of interesting them in mission parishes. With the testimony
from all sources that these are times when the hearts of men are more

easily reached by the gospel the record in ingathering during the biennium should be great. The reports for the quarter just closed seem to indicate it. With but few exceptions the missionaries after very fine reports by the Palm Sunday and Easter Season, are reporting further accessions. May we ask that all missionaries and their congregations be taken often to the throne of Grace that strength and wisdom may be given for the days and tasks that are before them.

LINGUISTIC INTERESTS
Dr. E. A. Tappert

Man's extremity is God's opportunity. This is particularly true in the field of missions. No branch of the Church has felt the stress of the times more severely than has the mission field, and none will come out with a greater blessing. When our last report was rendered, we did not realize what we would have to go through; we thought like the martyrs of old; Nebicula, transibit: It is only a cloud, it will pass away. But soon we had to learn that there would not be an immediate change, and that we would have to adjust ourselves to the conditions. This we did unflinchingly, starting at the top, doing away with overhead, which was not absolutely necessary, cutting out waste and inefficiency; closing up hopeless and unproductive work. Thus we have cut down expenses to the bone; to the very marrow of the bone. It was an arduous and at times a rather disagreeable task, but as stewards of the church's money it had to be done. And it was done without hurting a single hopeful mission, nor a single faithful missionary. The result is expansion all along the line. There has been no slackening. but great progress; since new work could be undertaken only on the savings which were made on the budgets, the support of such new work could only be small.

These are times which breed real missionaries. The Scriptures say in Lamentations: "It is good for a man that he bear the yoke in his youth." A pastor who does not learn how to sacrifice in his younger years will eventually be forced to learn it in his old age. The constituency in our linguistic field is for the most part desperately poor. By force of circumstances our missionaries must share in the universal poverty, and they do it ungrudgingly, as a true pastor should. They will be all the more highly esteemed and exercise a greater influence when things brighten up. These times are apt to bring out what is best in man. God sits and purifies (melts) the sons of Levi, and the result will be pure gold. While we groan and travail under the burden and hope for a brighter day, we should not forget God's word that he would dwell in the thick darkness, and upon the darkness shall break the morning, and what looked like a great misfortune will prove a blessing in disguise.

Our missionary efforts during the biennium have found doors wide open and hearts yearning for the ministrations of the Church. More than ever has it become evident that man does not live by bread alone, that there is a distinct need of the Church in our social order, and that where all material values have failed, the Church must not fail those who look to her for comfort and strength. While this is truly felt in the densely populated parts of our land, it is felt much more in these isolated districts, where the Church is the only agency to which the people can turn for light and guidance and help. With hundreds of thousands of our Lutheran household of faith in the most dire distress, how can the Lutheran Church permit man-made barricades to block a united effort to supply the spiritual and material needs of these suffering multitudes. If even old-age enemies, like France and Germany, can come together, driven by economic need which threatens to destroy European civilization, why should not we Lutherans be driven together by the spiritual need of our brethren? Such cooperation is particularly needed in the great Dominion of Canada. There is altogether too much overlapping and wasted effort; too little concerted action in the right direction.

There can be no question that our Lutheran Church has her greatest prospects for future growth and development in the linguistic field. As yet she has not fully grasped its importance and the urgent need of gathering this abundant harvest, before others reap where they have not sown. The Presbyterian Church, which has a limited field of her own, is expending the colossal sum of $1,105,000 for its linguistic work alone; we are expending less than $100,000, and a large part of this goes to work among non-Lutherans, Jews and Italians. Our Church must become more conscious of the fact that the growth and prosperity of our English-speaking Church in Canada depends on the conservation and proper training of our foreign-speaking Lutherans. There are only two self-supporting English Lutheran churches in Ontario today, and they are located in towns which have a large German Lutheran constituency. But the Anglicization process is going on rapidly in most of the old German churches and before long there will be a substantial English Lutheran Church on the territory of the Canada Synod.

We group our linguistic work under eight captions: 1. German; 2. Slovak; 3. Hungarian; 4. Finnish; 5. Lettish-Esthonian-Lithuanian; 6. Scandinavian; 7. Italian. 8. Jewish.

I. German Missions

The larger part of our linguistic mission work is carried on in the German language. There are no signs of abatement, but a steady increase in the number of German missions is evident. With the millions of Germans who have become expatriated through the late war, or whose stay in non-German countries of Europe has been made unbearable, it is no wonder that many thousands have flocked into the wide spaces to establish for themselves a new home. We count 151 German missions and preaching places, 90 of which are located in the Canadian Northwest. Home mission work in the Prairie Provinces is unlike any other home mission activity. In character it is very similar to Foreign Missions. These recent settlers are as destitute and unable to provide for their spiritual welfare as the savages in darkest Africa. They have absolutely no assets, only liabilities; they can produce but little and what they produce they cannot sell. They see real money only on rare occasions; how can they be expected to provide the necessary funds for salaries, or for the erection of church buildings?

Nor are we the only ones who are putting money into this work. In a recent statement the Anglican Bishop of Quippelle (center Saskatchewan) revealed that of the 500 centers only thirty are self-supporting, all others are receiving aid, and that with the most well-to-do class of people as their membership. The utmost which our people are able to do for some time to come, is to provide the pastor with food and fuel, if their crops don't fail, and to furnish labor for the building of churches. This they have been doing. In spite of drought and famine they have kept our missionaries from starvation. With much time on their hands they have willingly contributed labor for the repair and building of churches. The Church building at Emerson, Manitoba, which had been destroyed by a tornado, was rebuilt in a more substantial manner at a surprisingly low cost, and could be rededicated free of debt. At Hines Creek in the Peace River district, a neat chapel was erected at a total cost of $232.00, the people furnishing all the labor. Trees were felled and hauled over the frozen ground and then sawed into boards and rafters all by hand. One man gave forty-five days of his time, another thirty-five and others little less. Money was needed only for the purchase of shingles, nails, building paper, doors, windows, hardware and lumber for pulpit and altar, which cost $199.50, furnished by an aged couple in New York. The sum of $32.00 was expended in traveling expense for a skilled carpenter from Edmonton, who assisted in fitting doors and windows and who built altar and pulpit. The amount was contributed by the Field Missionary. Similar buildings are being erected at Flatbush, Warburg, Rosevear and Meadowview, Alta., the money having been graciously donated by Christian friends. In all we have received six such donations, three from Pennsylvania, one each from New York, Wartburg Synod and Alberta. We are exceedingly grateful to these friends for their valuable aid and encouragement which they have rendered these poor settlers, and wish them a rich measure of blessing in return. We are grateful also for the large gift of good clothing which our generous people have given in response to our appeal. They were a real Godsend to people who have no means of protecting themselves against the rigors of climate; they were a service to Him who says, "I was naked and ye clothed me."

Every faithful pastor feels the demands which the distress of so many of his parishioners make on his time and money, on the strength of body and soul. Think of the plight of these missionaries who find that almost every family in their parish presents a heart-breaking problem! Think of the plight of Pastor Wahl in Edmonton, who has rendered such valuable service in advising and settling hundreds of Lutheran families in Alberta. An endless line of guests knock at his door; men, girls and expectant mothers, in need, ask for food, shelter and care. The predicament of these expectant mothers is particularly embarrassing. The primitive one-room shacks in which they live, sometimes house two or three families, with a number of unmarried young men. His willingness to take them in is beyond question, but also his inability to carry the financial burden for these free boarders unassisted, with a salary of $1,400, out of which he must pay $500 for rent and support a family of seven. At this writing we see no way of keeping him at his blessed work; he cannot exist the way it is and we have no funds from which to supplement his salary. There will be nothing left for him but to accept a call from a congregation, at least temporarily; which is much to be regretted.

All our field men and missionaries have worked with great zeal and efficiency, and in consequence the Manitoba Synod has had an increase in membership of more than twenty per cent during the biennium. No section of our Church equals the Canadian Northwest in low cost and missionary service. None of this year's graduates, nor most of last year's, receive a salary in excess of $600 a year. The living conditions are most primitive. One of our youngest missionaries who had come from Kropp Seminary and spent a year at Saskatoon, goes into a parsonage built of sod, with walls two feet thick, warm in winter and cool in summer, yet a strange kind of parsonage. We attended his final examination. In all our experience as a member of examining committees for years we have never met a young man so well versed in all branches of theology and with such perfect command of every subject, as this young man, who willingly, even enthusiastically, goes to live in a sod house and render arduous missionary service at $50 a month. The Church should know the kind of heroic service which is being rendered by these men, and derive courage from the fact that a Church that can produce such men has the future and need not be ashamed before the world. What is being spent in this field will bring a rich harvest.

Two years ago the Manitoba Synod was mentioned as the only synod of The United Lutheran Church in America which had no work in the English language. Today, we can report fifteen major places with English services, not to mention many smaller places in which the English language is being constantly used, by missionaries A. Goos and Weidenhammer. The inevitable transition movement has started and the need of bilingual men in this formerly purely German field will become more and more pressing. The only place where we can train them is our Seminary in Saskatoon. If we want men who will fit in and who will stick, we must take them from the field and train them on the field. That is why Saskatoon Seminary is absolutely necessary for the success of the work.

So far most of our missionaries have come from European institutions, mainly from Kropp. This source of supply has definitely stopped. We must train our men on the field. Next year's graduation class will yield four native Canadians. The Church should look into this matter thoroughly, so that an adequate supply of missionaries may be assured.

The decreased income of the Board with its enforced retrenchment has made it necessary to eliminate the office of a Missionary Superintendent. Pastor Thomas Hartig, who filled this office most acceptably for many years, has received and accepted a call to Winnipeg. We cannot let this opportunity pass without paying tribute to his zeal and faithful service. He has traveled many thousands of miles in visiting the many missions of his large domain and he has saved neither effort nor sacrifice in the great task of building the Lutheran Church in the Canadian Northwest. We are grateful for his devotion and interest, and we are glad that his advice and counsel will still be available when needed.

The German work of the Canada Synod has received a new impetus through the establishment of missions at Montreal and Kitchener. The Canada Synod has undertaken some German work at Montreal under the direction of Dr. Klaehn. The Canada Synod has fourteen German missions. At present the field for German missions is rather limited, but when immigration sets in again, many new opportunities may offer.

The German work of the Wartburg Synod has made commendable progress. Two new missions were organized, one at Milwaukee, the other at Chicago. The latter was particularly interesting. A substantial group of Wolga Germans was discovered close to our Maywood Seminary, a strong congregation was organized which numbers 187 souls. It was served for a time by Professor Klotsche and students of Maywood Seminary and is now ready for its first pastor. We have no doubt that there are many similar opportunities in and around Chicago, and that this congregation of Wolga Germans is but the beginning of greater and better things.

The German Nebraska Synod will not be German much longer, if there is such a dearth of German material as the accomplishments of the last decade seem to indicate. Yet we are convinced that the centers of population on its territory harbor a large number of unchurched German Lutherans, and offer splendid opportunities for successful mission work. The office of Missionary Superintendent has been abolished.

The Texas Synod has only three German missions, with one preaching point. It is up against a strong competition on the part of the American Lutheran Church, but there should still be opportunity for German work in the fast growing larger towns.

In California, St. John's Church, Oakland, has been turned back to the Linguistic Department, and Temple Church, of San Francisco, was added. Bethel Church of San Jose was transferred to the English Department. Temple Church located in a district from which almost every other church has been removed, is badly in need of a building for its social work and growing Sunday School.

The seven German missions of the United Lutheran Synod of New York show a steady and healthy growth. It has not as yet been possible to find an approach to the many post-war Germans. Many thousands are here. We keep an eye on them, and hope that some day the Lord will give us an open door.

The four German missions and three preaching points of the Ministerium of Pennsylvania are making rather slow progress. But the territory is well churched and has many pastors who are able to serve the German element in their native tongue. Pastor Ludwig has been called by the Ministerium as its traveling missionary.

In the Pittsburgh Synod the two Siebenbuerger Saxon congregations at Cleveland, Ohio, have assumed self-support. The five remaining Saxon congregations are making a valiant effort to overcome the vicissitudes of the times.

We cannot close this report on German work without making mention of former General Superintendent Ludwig, who was intimately connected with it for so many years. While the Plan of Operation as adopted by the Board of American Missions at its organization left room for General Superintendents, the present work is not sufficient to continue Pastor Ludwig's connection with this department, but we want to give testimony to the fact that Pastor Ludwig's share in German missions will not be forgotten by those who were associated with him in the work.

We are grateful to the Women's Missionary Society, which is supporting missionaries William Wahl and Otto Goos, and hope that the greatness, importance and patricular need of the field will induce them to give it more attention and a larger measure of support. We are grateful to St. Johannes congregation, Reading, Pa., Rev. Robert Ischinger, pastor, which supports Missionary Weidenhammer to the extent of $600 per year, and ask our large German congregations to emulate its example. We are grateful to a number of congregations whose special gifts have enabled us to meet perplexing conditions and to alleviate special cases.

2. SLOVAK MISSIONS

Our Slovak constituency, though not nearly so large as the German, is of considerable proportions. Our twelve missions and some twenty-four preaching points have suffered intensely, but have held their own. Perhaps no class of people in our land has been hit so hard through the present adversity as the Slovaks. Of all our industries, steel and coal mining have been the most adversely affected, and these are the ones in which the great bulk of the Slovaks are employed. Many self-supporting congregations have scarcely been able to keep above water; some have joined forces with neighboring congregations so as to lighten their burdens; some which in normal times would have demanded the services of a pastor have decided to remain vacant indefinitely. For the first time in the history of our Slovak mission have we been able to supply all demands for pastors. Of the three young men who were to be graduated at the Philadelphia Seminary this spring, one, Stephen Medved, died shortly before his graduation. He was a good student and eager to enter the service of the Lord, but the Lord called him home at the threshold of his ministry. Through the efforts of Pastor Louis Sanjek, a very hopeful mission was organized at Guttenberg, New Jersey. Much credit is due Pastor Sanjek, who went from house to house, gathering funds with which to buy property for the congregation, and who was eminently successful in his effort. The many preaching points are being regularly visited by Pastor Dianiska in the service of Zion Synod. President Dr. Body suffered a painful accident which incapacitated him for some time. For this reason he asked the Synod to relieve him of the presidency. At the last convention, Pastor Gustav Chernansky, was elected president of Zion Synod, a young man who received his entire training in American institutions. Pastor Brndjar, one of last year's graduates, was elected secretary. One of our students, Joseph Billy, was transferred to Maywood Seminary so as to be available for mission work in Chicago. The plan to send a missionary to Canada did not materialize. Those nominated for this position declined the call, and then the stringency of funds made its execution impossible. Progress has been made in the attempt to bring the Slovak congregations into closer touch with the synods. The so-called Slovak Conference of independent pastors is still standing aloof, though a more friendly attitude toward The United Lutheran Church in America can be noted. Only with improving general conditions will come renewed activities in Slovak missions.

3. Hungarian-Wendish Missions

Our Hungarian work has expanded considerably, especially in Canada. Like the Slovak, the Hungarians are for the most part industrial workers and share in the industrial debacle. This is particularly true in the Bethlehem field. Our Akron mission has begun to branch out and has established preaching points at Lorain and Elyria, Ohio, and other places. A successful beginning has also been made with English services. Our New York mission, which has been served in connection with Caldwell, New Jersey, has become so important that a division of the parish will be sought, so that New York may have a Hungarian pastor of its own. The First Church at New Brunswick assumed self-support. The field of the Pittsburgh mission is to be enlarged, so as to include the surrounding territory, where the old people are to be served in their mother tongue and the young people to be lined up with English churches. At Caldwell preparations are in progress for the purchase of property. At Buffalo, the English work in the Hungarian congregation is assuming larger proportions. At Bridgeport, Conn., a promising work has begun by a young man, who unfortunately is here only under a student permit and must return to Hungary.

Great activity has marked our work in Canada. At Windsor, Ontario, the first Hungarian Lutheran Church in Canada was dedicated on July 31, 1932. In connection with the celebration the second Hungarian Conference was held. Great strides have been made in Ontario, where Student Ruzsa added Toronto and Hamilton to his work at Kitchener, Brantford, Galt and Welland. The future of this work seems hopeful. As a bond of union, the Hungarian Conference has begun to publish a Hungarian church paper, called "Eros Var" (A Mighty Fortress).

Of our two Wendish missions, St. John's, Newark, N. J., was temporarily taken off the funds of the Board, because the congregation refused to unite with the synod.

4. FINNISH MISSIONS

The work among the Finns is destined to command ever increasing attention. Since the Milwaukee Convention, our agreement with the Suomi Synod has been consummated and the transfer of the entire Canadian field to The United Lutheran Church in America has been effected. According to the agreement, our fifty-fifty support of Suomi Synod missions will cease within four years. Then we can concentrate our efforts on the development of the Canadian field. Unfortunately our funds are so low that we cannot avail ourselves of all the opportunities that offer. Some of the parishes had to be left vacant because there was no money to pay the missionary. At Toronto, a very promising mission was organized by Superintendent Saarinen, for which a suitable property has been acquired. At Copper Cliff, Ontario, a town of fifteen hundred inhabitants, of whom nine hundred are Finns, Pastor Hanninen has prosecuted his work with such vigor that the United Church of Canada has withdrawn its missionary from the important Sudbury district. The same happened at Sault Ste. Marie, where Pastor Pelkonen took charge. The same happened at Winnipeg, which is in charge of a student. At Montreal, St. Michael's Finnish Lutheran Church was organized with a large membership and received into the Canada Synod. It seems that in this short time we have definitely established our ascendency, and that the United Church of Canada is ready to withdraw from the field. This, of course, brings home our obligation to work this field and not to neglect our opportunities. There is no question that next to the German there is no more challenging and promising work for our Church in Canada at this time than the Finnish.

One of our problems is the training of Finnish pastors in the spirit of The United Lutheran Church in America. We can find the material, if the Church can find the money. We have an application from a student who at this time is supplying the Winnipeg mission at $50 for the season. He is extremely valuable as a linguist, since he commands the Finnish, Swedish, Norwegian, Russian, Esthonian and English languages. We hope we can engage him for our work, but we need more men and we shall have to find a way of training them, if our work is to have harmonious progress.

Like their cousins, the Magyars, the Finns also are publishing a church paper, authorized by the First Finnish Lutheran Conference, held at Copper Cliff, May 30, 1932.

5. LETTISH, LITHUANIAN, ESTHONIAN MISSIONS

Lithuanian immigration has been considerable, but it was mostly Catholic. Letts also have come in large numbers, but though nominally all Lutherans, many have been affected by communism. Of Esthonians, there are but few in this country. We have as yet no organized mission among them. We have our eye on a young man in Canada, however, who can handle three languages and hope to interest him in this work some day when he and we are ready. Meanwhile our Finnish pastors could serve them where they find them. We are in a similar predicament with the Lithuanians; their missionary has resigned and the only man we know of who could serve them acceptably, lives in Texas. We have a small group of Lithuanians in Montreal who are being served occasionally. The Lettish people could also be served in connection with some other work, though there is a sufficient number of them in Philadelphia, New York and surrounding country to occupy fully a man's time. The New York field has never been developed, yet it contains a large number of Letts, some rather prominent and interested in the Church.

The scattered groups of Lettish people in Manitoba are being regularly visited by Rev. O. Zahlis, pastor of a German congregation in Saskatchewan.

6. SCANDINAVIAN MISSIONS

Work among Scandinavians has been left to the Scandinavian bodies. Only occasionally we have taken care of Scandinavian people in connection with our German work. One of our missions in the Canada Synod at Chatham, Ontario, is largely Danish; Missionary Weidenhammer frequently officiates in Norwegian. Some Swedish work is being done in connection with our Finnish missions. Now a call has come to us from FlinFlon, Manitoba, a great mining district, where there are to be a thousand Lutherans, mostly of Scandinavian extraction. When Missionary Weidenhammer visited the field, he baptized seven Norwegian children and was urgently asked to establish a Lutheran Church. Among this year's graduates of Saskatoon Seminary, we have a Norwegian, Oigaard, who would be the man for the place. Missionary Weidenhammer has been instructed to visit the field once more to make sure that no other Lutheran body has begun work there, before we send a man into the field. There is a large work to be done among the Scandinavians in Canada. Cooperation with other Lutheran bodies would be very desirable here.

7. ITALIAN MISSIONS

Necessity demanded drastic action with regard to some of our Italian missions. The work in California, which for years has shown no progress, was discontinued upon recommendation of the Synodical Mission Committee. At Monessen, Pa., the mission is supplied every other Sunday. In Chicago little progress has been made and a change is imminent. In New York, the work has been handicapped by the lack of a church home. In Philadelphia and Erie, Pa., the work has prospered and satisfactory results have been achieved.

The conversion of the Italian is a hard and slow process. It will never be much of a success until the Spirit of God touches the Italian masses and from the midst of the Italian people will come the cry for the Light and Truth of the Gospel. To that end we must continue to pray and to testify.

With the many unchurched Lutherans in our land yet to be gathered into churches, we have neither men nor means to undertake Italian mission work on a large scale. But the millions of unchurched Italians present a challenge to the Christian Church, which our Church cannot ignore, and if we cannot do any more, we should present the testimony of the Lutheran Church to the Italian, at least in the large centers of population.

8. JEWISH MISSIONS

Last but not least, Jewish missions should always have a large place in every Christian heart. As Jesus felt that His primary call was to the lost sheep of the house of Israel, so should every Christian feel his obligation to the Jew. Jewish missions should be actuated by our spirit of gratitude to the nation which gave us Jesus, according to the flesh; by our contrition for the many wrongs which have been perpetrated against the Jew in the name of the Christian Church; but chiefly by the love of Him who wants all men to be saved and to come to the knowledge of the Truth.

The Board of American Missions has laid down a policy which emphasizes the fact that Jewish missions is the duty of every pastor and every congregation, and while Jewish missionaries are needed for the awakening and stimulation of the churches' interest by the presentation of the cause in word and script, that does not absolve Christian pastors and laymen of the duty of bringing Christ to the Jews.

Our four missionaries are acquainting the Church with this duty and are presenting Christ to the Jews: each is working in his own particular way, but all with the same purpose in mind and the same goal in view. A number of publications with a circulation of many thousands spread the knowledge of Christ to the Jew and of the Jew to the Gentile: hundreds of thousands of Christian tracts are being distributed and in services and private conversations the work is carried on. Pastor Henry Einspruch has furnished a fine translation of Martin Luther's Smaller Catechism in Yiddish, which has had a demand all over the world; a translation of the gospel according to St. Mark followed and at this writing a translation of St. John's gospel is in progress. A helpful and interesting book "When Jews Face Christ" has also come from his fertile pen. At Pittsburgh commodious quarters were secured for Christ's Mission to the Jews and dedicated as the John Legum Memorial. It contains a neat chapel and on the second floor an apartment for Pastor Bravin. Missionary Rubenstine has found the Toledo field too small and is devoting part of his time to the large Jewish population of Cleveland, Ohio. Pastor Morentz is working through the churches. A number of Jews have been baptized and led into the Christian Church and many have been influenced. We regret that scarcity of funds does not permit regular conferences of our Jewish missionaries which would prove helpful.

We are grateful to the Women's Missionary Society which has liberally supported this work. We are grateful to the Mission Committees of the different synods which have ably assisted the administration. We are grateful to the Head of the Church for His abiding presence, without whom we can do nothing, to whom be honor and glory forever and ever.

In our travels over the field, we covered more than seventy thousand miles during the biennium.

In conclusion, let me quote from an unknown author and apply to the mission obligation of the Church, "The Dead Sea."

> I gazed upon a sea, and lo! 'twas dead
> Although by Hermon's snow and Jordan fed.
> How came a fate so dire? The tale's soon told:
> All that it got it kept and fast did hold.
> All tributary streams found here their grave
> Because the sea received and never gave.
> O sea that's dead, teach me to know and feel
> That grasp and greed my doom would also seal!
> And help me, Lord, my best, my all to give
> That I may others bless, and like Thee live!

CHURCH EXTENSION AND FINANCE
Dr. Z. M. Corbe

The grouping of Church Extension and Finance may seem at first thought to be paradoxical, nevertheless at no time since the days of the Apostles has the Church ever been able to divorce the question of money from the material operations necessary for its existence on the earth.

The good name of the Church has too frequently been dragged in the mire by those whose zeal in extending the faith caused them to ignore all questions of finance, and never has this been more prevalent than in the present days of economic stress. In many instances architects, contractors, mechanics, banks and individuals have been inclined to lose all faith in a religion that allowed its followers to incur obligations without any possible resource for meeting them.

The most tragic of the Board's decisions in the past biennium has been to refuse granting aid to such congregations. The funds in Church Extension were given for the purpose of assisting missions in securing a place of worship and not to redeem illy secured loans, whether from banks or individuals, who in many cases are loyal Lutherans who had forgotten what is written in the Scriptures concerning the one who becomes a surety.

Nevertheless, had a proper Church Extension Fund been placed in the hands of this Board, it would have meant the saving this year of hundreds of thousands of dollars for congregations which have been caught in the present whirlpool of financial misfortune. The bitter lesson of adversity should prepare the way for an effective effort in 1938, the period assigned by the United Lutheran Church for securing an adequate Church Extension Fund, for its growing opportunities for expansion.

Loans to churches during the biennium were not as great as usual, due

not alone to a decreased income, but also to a definite insistence on the fulfillment of the rules which govern loans made by the Board. The total
amount loaned was $131,175, granted to 37 churches in 20 synods.

For many years an effort has been made to compensate for the inadequacy
of our funds by paying out of our current income the interest on such portions of the first mortgages of our missions as we ought to have loaned them
from Church Extension Funds had such been available. This has always
been a serious drain on our resources. The amount paid out during the
past biennium to 109 missions total $66,110, an amount which would have
made a respectable addition to the Permanent Loan Fund had this emergency
measure not been necessary.

Our chief source of income in Church Extension is from legacies, individual contributions and the amounts given by Sunday Schools at Easter.
Pastors should note that careful studies covering many years of experience
in the various denominations show that legacies to local congregations have
seldom, if ever, been a blessing. They, therefore, should urge their people
to remember the general work of the Church, especially Church Extension,
in their wills as a most suitable memorial. We would record a tribute of
appreciation for the efficient services of our attorney, George E. Neff, not
only in securing the payment of many of these legacies, but also others in
process of settlement.

To a certain degree the small return on Church Extension loans during
the past biennium, totaling $46,212, can be charged to the depression inasmuch
as during the years of prosperity the returned loans were never more than
20 per cent of what they should have been. Other reasons for this delin-
quency must be shown. Practically only one reason exists, namely, the large
debts which congregations are permitted to contract which cannot be paid
for generations to come. As long as the present epidemic continues of
building churches to accommodate festival day congregations rather than for
the religious opportunity offered by the community, just so long will be
delayed the attainment of the ideal of the Church Extension Fund, namely,
the return of loans within five to ten years so that another mission may be
aided.

FINANCES

The lengthy report required by the Treasurer makes unnecessary much
comment on the Department of Finance except to express appreciation for
the high ability of our Finance Committee and the wise counsel of our New
York banks which enabled this Board to obtain the distinction of being the
only Protestant Board of large interests to close the present year without a
deficit. Few realize the huge task of this Department with assets of and an
expense account of about a million dollars annually which necessitates the
issuance of more than 600 checks monthly. This Department, acting on the
principle that there is a stewardship of spending as well as giving, has not
always been the most popular, but it has had the supreme satisfaction of see-

ing the Divine blessing on a cause which does not forget its responsibility as a trustee.

Our invested funds are in the highest type of securities, the Committee having followed the policy of regarding safety as more important than a high rate of interest. This department during the past two years initiated movements for readjustments that were necessary in order to maintain a balanced budget and is now working on plans for further adjustments that will permit the Board to meet the decreased income on apportionment without retarding the present expansion of the Church.

We rejoice that by foregoing the advantage accruing to us in the present exchange in currency, given us by our banking facilities in Canada, we have been able to assist the Treasurer of the United Lutheran Church and the various Boards, including the Women's Missionary Society, in securing payments from the brethren in Canada by accepting Canadian checks at par, which resulted in a very appreciable gain to the Treasurers so favored.

LATIN AMERICA
Dr. F. F. Fry

Substantial progress along many lines is the record of this department. While there has been no sensational growth, consistent advance proves that the work is developing steadily.

The First All West Indies Conference in St. Thomas brought together the entire missionary force. The adventure was a pronounced success. It opened the eyes of our people to the dimensions of our opportunities. More than 600 thronged the church. The communion service, the discussion of mutual problems, the Christian fellowship were so stimulating that by unanimous vote it was decided to make it an annual affair.

The new Training School at Monteflores was dedicated July 14, 1932. Fifty-two Lutherans from all sections of the United States took the dedication cruise on the "S. S. Coamo" of the New York and Porto Rico Steamship Co. Governor James Beverley of Puerto Rico gave an address of welcome. The Chief Justice of the Supreme Court of the Island was the principal speaker. The Board was represented by Rev. C. A. Freed, D.D., the Luther League of America by its Executive Secretary, Rev. Paul M. Kinports, and the Women's Missionary Society by Miss A. Barbara Wiegand. Extensive preparations had been made by our missionaries and people in the Island. Governor and Mrs. Beverley favored the party with a special reception at the Governor's Palace. A complimentary dinner by the Steamship Company at Hotel Condado in San Juan was a feature. The party enjoyed a four hour automobile trip over the Island, visiting all of our missions. The new building provides a chapel, kindergarten, Training School for Sunday School teachers and parish workers, retreat for missionaries, library and office, as well as a commodious parsonage.

The spiritual condition is evidenced by a net gain of 16 per cent in membership. Attendance at Church and Sunday School reveals a corresponding increase. Despite their poverty which baffles description, they are turning to Christ and His Church. Their support of The United Lutheran Church in America out of dire need merits commendation.

Five missionaries were added to our force. Rev. Sergio Cobian, of Texas, is pastor of the Dorado parish consisting of Dorado, Higuillar, Maracayo and Santa Rosa. Rev. Alfredo Ortiz, graduate of the University of Puerto Rico and Hamma Divinity School, was called to San Pablo Church, Puerta de Tierra, San Juan. He ministers also to the Gandul mission in Santurce. Rev. Jamie Soler, of Buenos Aires, graduate of the Philadelphia Seminary, is developing the Spanish congregation in Harlem. Rev. Jesse W. Routte, graduate of Augustana College and Seminary in Rock Island, is assistant pastor of the Church of the Transfiguration, New York, and will open up new work in Jamaica, L. I. Rev. J. C. Pedersen has returned from California to the Virgin Islands and is house-father in the Home for Boys, Frederiksted, St. Croix.

The Church of the Good Shepherd was organized in Monteflores, San Juan, by Rev. Eduardo Roig, President of the Lutheran Missionaries' Conference. One hundred and nineteen attended Sunday School and 94 were at the first church service. The following Sunday the numbers had grown to 161 and 104. A Sunday School was started by Rev. Gustav K. Huf two miles outside of Bayamon. The average attendance exceeds 50. Rev. H. D. Whitteker introduced services in the rural district of the Island of St. Thomas with good results. A new chapel was dedicated in Higuillar. A new parsonage was added to our equipment in Toa Baja.

The missionary force in the West Indies numbers 47; a field treasurer, 12 missionary pastors, 15 missionary helpers, 13 kindergarten teachers, 3 deaconesses and 3 women workers. These serve 20 congregations and 16 mission stations, in addition to the educational work and the care of sick and neglected children. We have 13 parsonages and 5 school buildings, 3 Homes for the Aged, Ebenezer Orphanage for Girls, Queen Louise Home for Sick and Neglected Babies and a Home for Boys. The organizations include 32 Sunday Schools, 8 Daily Vacation Bible Schools, 8 daily Kindergartens, 6 Women's Missionary Societies, 8 Luther Leagues, 9 Junior Luther Leagues and 6 Light Brigades. All women workers including kindergarten teachers are supported by the Women's Missionary Society.

Two students preparing for the ministry, Francisco J. Agostini and Francisco Molina, attend the University of Puerto Rico. They are supported by the United Synod of New York.

Miss Frieda M. Hoh's unceasing activity among sick and neglected children in Puerto Rico, providing nourishing food, healing disease, comforting the sorrowful, speaking peace to the dying, everywhere bringing the consolations of the Gospel has won for her the title "The Angel of the Island." She lives in Villa Betania and administers the distribution of clothing, supplies and industrial work.

The Educational Department under the able leadership of Miss Carmen M. Villarini has gained official recognition in government and university circles. Standards have been raised, approved methods of instruction introduced together with a thorough supervision of each kindergarten.

The need of a Spanish hymnal is imperative. The hymnal in use is un-Lutheran and wholly unsatisfactory. The communion service has been translated into Spanish including the chief service, Matins, Vespers and ministerial acts. A suitable selection of hymns has been made by Dr. Alfred Ostrom and is ready for publication. The Board appeals to this convention for its good offices in promoting the publication of this Spanish hymnal.

The staff of missionaries and workers in Puerto Rico is:

Rev. and Mrs. Eduardo Roig.................Monteflores
Rev. Alfredo Ortiz ....Puerta de Tierra
Rev. and Mrs. William G. Arbaugh.... ....Santurce
Rev. and Mrs. Gustav K. Huf.............. .....Bayamon
Rev. Balbino Gonzales ....Bayamon
Rev. S. Hernandez ....Catano
Rev. G. E. Marrero ....Toa Baja
Rev. Sergio Cobian ....Dorado
Mr. Juan Zambrana ....Palo Seco
Miss Frieda M. Hoh, R.N................... .....Bayamon
Mrs. Maria Caraballo ....Bayamon
Mrs. Ramona Sotomayor ....Bayamon
Miss Carmen M. Villarini ....Monteflores
Miss Francisca Ayala ....Monteflores
Miss Marina Agostini ....Puerta de Tierra
Miss Berta Casos ....Catano
Miss Ana Luisa Dominquez.................. .....Bayamon
Miss Rosario Ojeda ....Bayamon
Miss Angilica Martinez ....Puerta de Tierra
Miss Ofelia Baldorioty ....Puerta de Tierra

VIRGIN ISLANDS

Rev. and Mrs. Herman D. Whitteker.. .....St. Thomas
Mr. Carl E. Francis................................. ....St. John's
Rev. and Mrs. Ivar O. Iverson.............. ....Christiansted
Rev. and Mrs. Eugene C. Kreider........ ....Frederiksted
Rev. J. C. Pedersen................................. ....Frederiksted
Deaconess Maren Knudsen ....Queen Louise Home, Christiansted
Deaconess Emma Francis ....Ebenezer Orphanage, Frederiksted
Deaconess Edith Prince ....Ebenezer Orphanage, Frederiksted
Mrs. Beatrice Benjamin ....Christiansted

ON FURLOUGH

Rev. Alfred Ostrom, D.D.

Rocky Boy

Our mission at Rocky Boy Indian Reservation in Montana suffered serious loss in the complete destruction by fire of the Mission House, March 6, 1932. Most of the activities of the mission were centered in this building. Any delay in replacement would have retarded the work. Thanks to the response of many friends of the mission, coupled with the payment of the fire insurance policy at its face value, we were enabled to begin construction at the most favorable season of the year. The new Mission House is ready for occupancy. It is a decided improvement on the old structure in size, arrangements and equipment.

Malcolm Mitchell, a full-blooded Cree Indian, is interpreter of the mission. Every Sunday he interprets the entire Order of the Common Service to the growing congregation of Indians. To illustrate his skill, when the well-known revivalist, Billy Sunday, unexpectedly visited the mission and spoke to the Crees, Macolm Mitchell was able to translate his wierd and graphic vocabulary into Cree without a moment's hesitation. The wholesome influence of his Christian life is invaluable. With the Board's approval he is taking a course of preparation as a lay-reader to the Indians under the Rev. William H. Gable, resident missionary.

The duties of the staff are clearly defined. Missionary Gable is in charge of the preaching, pastoral and administrative work. Mrs. Gable heads up the department of industrial products. Miss Florence Buckner directs the children of the Sunday School, religious education and supervised play.

Fifty Cree Bibles were donated to the Mission to the evident satisfaction of our Indian wards. The American Bible Society generously assumed one-half the cost of the Bibles and the total cost of transportation from London. Up to this time only one copy of the Word of God in the Cree dialect could be found in the Indian Reservation, the property of Malcolm Mitchell.

Visual instruction and promotion received an impetus through motion picture films taken by John Gable, the missionary's son and a student for the ministry. These films may be had for presentation to conventions, conferences, Sunday Schools and Societies upon application. Stereoptican slides with accompanying lecture are offered by the Board free of cost.

The new leaflet, "The Indian's Need Today," is off the press with the joint imprint of the Women's Missionary Society and the Board of American Missions. Mrs. W. F. Morehead, Literature Secretary, is the talented author.

The Caribbeans Invade New York

The sudden invasion of an alien horde insures historic notice, but overlooked are the long drawn out but no less important invasions like that of the millions of immigrants that have swarmed into New York City, in which invasion the people of the Islands of the Caribbean Sea have had their part. During the last fifty years more than a quarter of a million souls have come from the West Indies to make their home in the greatest metropolis of the world; the population of white and colored have been in about the same ratio as the population of the Islands.

For two generations these multitudes were spiritually neglected, the established churches seemingly being unable to reach them inasmuch as the white people among these West Indians spoke only Spanish; those who could speak English were of the colored race and when more than one or two applied for membership in the same congregation, they found that because their skin was black they were "creating a problem."

Within two years after the formation of the United Lutheran Church work among these people was begun by Dr. Corbe of our Board. Attention was first given to the colored people from the Virgin Islands because among them was to be found the larger number of Lutherans. The services which were started in the colored Y. M. C. A. of Harlem in 1920, grew into the present Church of the Transfiguration which now has more than one thousand colored Lutherans under its pastoral care. Paul Edward West, a native of St. Croix, but raised in Santo Domingo, had charge of this work during his student days in Wagner College and Mount Airy Seminary and after his ordination by the New York Synod was called as a pastor of this Church. The high esteem in which his faithful and zealous labors are held by his people was demonstrated by his wedding on June 1, 1932, when more than twelve hundred people overflowed St. Paul's German Lutheran Church and the congestion at the Church of the Transfiguration, where the reception was held, was so great that officers were necessary to keep the street cleared for traffic.

Every legitimate activity known to present day congregations is to be found here, but no worldly methods of raising money are tolerated. Great suffering has come to the people through the present period of unemployment and the pastor has for months secured contributions for relief and also free bread from the bakeries. This bread must be called for by him at two o'clock in the morning for distribution at the church later in the day. The attendance at the services amazes visitors and the liturgical character of the service reminds tourists of scenes witnessed in the ancient churches of Europe.

As the colored population of Metropolitan New York is over 350,000, of which 70 per cent are unchurched, one Lutheran Church is certainly not our fair share of this task. While we were wondering what steps to take next, the Lord of the harvest was preparing a man at Augustana College and Seminary at Rock Island, Illinois. Inasmuch as the Swedish Augustana Synod has as yet no work among colored people, President Brandelle and the Faculty at Rock Island offered us the services of this graduate of this institution. He was ordained by the New York Synod in 1932 and is now enthusiastically at work. Rev. J. W. Routte will be supported by the children of the Sunday Schools of the Long Island Conference.

To gather a Lutheran congregation from the tens of thousands of unchurched Spanish-speaking people in New York is a task of no small magnitude. Naturally the only Lutheran material would be the Puerto Rican converts of our Puerto Rican missions that have found their way to New York. However, these multitudes coming from all the Spanish-speaking nations of the earth, a language that in the numbers using it ranks third among civilized nations, show an increasing desire for the evangelical faith. This opens wide a door of opportunity that is being utilized by our Spanish pastor, the Rev. Jamie Soler. The attendance at services has more than trebled in the past biennium and the members are of the most substantial character. Pastor Soler graduated from Mount Airy in 1931 and was ordained by the New York Synod. The same year he visited his home in Buenos Aires, Argentina, where he was united in marriage with Miss Paula Mueller, whose culture and education abroad make her a most valuable aid in evangelization work that is filled with such peculiar difficulties.

ORGANIZATION

Officers:
  President—Rev. J. B. Markward, D.D.
  Vice-President—Rev. H. W. A. Hanson, D.D., LL.D.
  Recording Secretary—Mr. Henry F. Heuer.
  Treasurer—Rev. Zenan M. Corbe, D.D.

Staff:
  Executive Secretary—Rev. Franklin F. Fry, D.D.
  Divisional Secretary of English Missions—Rev. J. F. Seibert, D.D.
  Divisional Secretary of Linguistic Interests—Rev. E. A. Tappert, D.D.
  Attorney—George E. Neff, Esq.

Members:
  Term expiring 1932—Rev. F. O. Evers, Rev. J. M. Francis, D.D., Rev. L. H. Larimer, D.D., LL.D., Rev. L. W. Steckel, D.D., Mr. H. F. Heuer, J. A. Hoober, Esq., Mr. H. W. Bikle.

  Term expiring 1934—Rev. A. E. Bell, D.D., Rev. C. A. Freed, D.D., Rev. G. K. Rubrecht, D.D., Rev. J. C. Seegers, D.D., Mr. A. H. Durboraw, Mr. William Eck, Mr. S. F. Telleen.

  Term expiring 1936—Rev. G. A. Benze, D.D., Rev. H. W. A. Hanson, D.D., LL.D., Rev. J. B. Markward, D.D., Rev. Jacob Maurer, D.D., Mr. A. Raymond Bard, Mr. Grant Hultberg, Mr. H. L. Snyder.

Advisory Members:
  Mrs. H. C. Michael, Mrs. John M. Cook.

Divisional Committees:
  English Missions—Rev. J. C. Seegers, D.D., Rev. A. E. Bell, D.D., Rev. L. W. Steckel, D.D., J. A. Hoober, Esq.

  Linguistic Interests—Mr. William Eck, Rev. G. A. Benze, D.D., Rev. F. O. Evers, Rev. Jacob Maurer, D.D.

  Latin America—Mr. H. L. Snyder, Rev. J. M. Francis, D.D., Rev. L. H. Larimer, D.D., LL.D., Rev. G. K. Rubrecht, D.D.

  Church Extension—Mr. A. Raymond Bard, Rev. C. A. Freed, D.D., Mr. H. W. Bikle, Mr. H. F. Heuer.

Finance—Mr. Grant Hultberg, Mr. A. H. Durboraw, Mr. S. F. Telleen, Rev. H. W. A. Hanson, D.D., LL.D.

Committees :'
Conference with Foreign Board—Rev. J. B. Markward, D.D., Rev. J. C. Seegers, D.D., Rev. F. O. Evers, Mr. H. F. Heuer.

Conference with Board of Education—Rev. H. W. A. Hanson, D.D., LL.D., Rev. L. H. Larimer, D.D., LL.D., Mr. Grant Hultberg, Mr. A. H. Durboraw.

Conference with Inner Mission Board—Rev. C. A. Freed, D.D., Rev. G. K. Rubrecht, D.D., Mr. S. F. Telleen, Mr. William Eck.

Conference with Deaconess Board—Rev. G. A. Benze, D.D., Rev. A. E. Bell, D.D., J. A. Hoober, Esq., Mr. A. Raymond Bard.

Conference with Other Lutheran Bodies—Rev. J. B. Markward, D.D., Rev. G. K. Rubrecht, D.D., Rev. J. C. Seegers, D.D., Mr. Grant Hultberg, Mr. A. H. Durboraw.

Comity Conference—Rev. J. B. Markward, D.D., Rev. J. C. Seegers, D.D., Rev. F. O. Evers, Mr. Grant Hultberg, J. A. Hoober, Esq.

Ministerial Supply—Rev. H. W. A. Hanson, D.D., LL.D., Rev. J. C. Seegers, D.D., Rev. L. H. Larimer, D.D., Rev. F. O. Evers, Mr. S. F. Telleen, J. A. Hoober, Esq.

Review—Rev. A. E. Bell, D.D., Rev. G. A. Benze, D.D., Rev. C. A. Freed, D.D., Mr. A. Raymond Bard, Mr. H. L. Snyder.

Church Architecture—Rev. J. C. Seegers, D.D., Rev. F. O. Evers, Rev. Z. M. Corbe, D.D., Mr. A. Raymond Bard.

NOMINATIONS
Board of American Missions
Rev. F. O. Evers, Rev. L. H. Larimer, D.D., LL.D., Rev. H. J. Pflum, D.D., Rev. L. W. Steckel, D.D., Mr. H. W. Bikle, Mr. H. F. Heuer, J. A. Hoober, Esq.

Board of Northwestern Missions
Rev. F. O. Evers, Rev. L. H. Larimer, D.D., LL.D., Rev. H. J. Pflum, D.D., Rev. L. W. Steckel, D.D., Mr. H. W. Bikle, Mr. H. F. Heuer, J. A. Hoober, Esq.

Immigrants Mission Board
Rev. F. O. Evers, Rev. L. H. Larimer, D.D., LL.D., Mr. H. W. Bikle, Mr. H. F. Heuer.

Board of West Indies Missions
Rev. F. O. Evers, Rev. L. H. Larimer, D.D., LL.D., Rev. H. J. Pflum, D.D., Rev. L. W. Steckel, D.D., Mr. H. W. Bikle, Mr. H. F. Heuer, J. A. Hoober, Esq.

Recommendations

1. That the Board of American Missions devoutly acknowledges the guidance and blessing of the Great Head of the Church in the Home Mission achievements of another biennium and rededicates herself to her unfinished task.

2. That we record our appreciation of the loyal support and self-sacrificing labors of our home missionaries whose heroic efforts in the face of existing conditions have been an inspiration to the entire Church.

3. That we express to the synods, Women's Missionary Society, Luther League of America, Lutheran Brotherhood and the Laymen's Movement for Stewardship our gratitude for their continued assistance.

4. That in view of the imperative need of the Common Service Book and Hymnal among our Spanish speaking people and the assurance of the cordial, whole-hearted and prompt co-operation of the Common Service Book Committee, the convention be requested to authorize the publication of the Spanish Service Book and Hymnal by October 1, 1933.

5. That in view of the increasing use of benevolence for current expenses in certain local congregations to the great detriment of all mission causes, we request the Convention to appeal to synodical authorities to take urgent measures to change this condition.

6. That the United Lutheran Church go on record as disapproving the contribution of specials on the part of congregations and organizations when such congregations are not paying apportionment in full.
[Amended by the Convention, see p. 371.]

7. That in view of the evil influence upon our missions, which are forbidden the use of questionable methods of financing, the United Lutheran Church go on record as condemning the use of card parties, dancing, games of chance and all other worldly pleasures for commercial use in supporting the work of any congregation. [A substitute was adopted, see p. 339.]

8. That in view of the waste of benevolent funds in the duplication of effort in over-lapping synods, we request the United Lutheran Church to take immediate steps looking toward the consolidation of all such bodies.
[Amended by the Convention, see p. 339.]

Respectfully submitted,

J. B. MARKWARD, *President,*
HENRY F. HEUER, *Secretary,*
FRANKLIN F. FRY, *Executive Secretary.*

APPENDIX A
SELF-SUPPORTING ENGLISH MISSIONS

California Synod
San Jóse—Bethel
East Pennsylvania Synod
Downington—Messiah
Fort Washington—Oreland Parish
Upper Darby—Christ
Reading—Christ

Ohio Synod
Dayton—Westwood
Pacific Synod
Everett, Wash.—Trinity
Pittsburgh Synod
Glassport—St. John's
Rocky Mountain Synod

Illinois Synod
  Chicago—Belmont Park
  Chicago—St. Stephen's
  Riverdale—Our Saviour
  Yorkville—Bethesda
Iowa Synod
  Dubuque—St. Mark's
Kansas Synod
  Hutchinson—Zion
Maryland Synod
  Washington, D. C.—Incarnation
Nebraska Synod
  Dalton—Trinity
  York—McCool Parish
North Carolina Synod
  Burke Parish
Northwest Synod
  Woodlake, Minn.
  Beloit, Wis.—Atonement
  Phillips, Wis.—St. John's
  Salem, S. D.—Christ
Ministerium of Pennsylvania
  Burholme—Immanuel

  Denver, Col.—Messiah
South Carolina Synod
  Aiken—Graniteville Parish
Texas Synod
  Colletteville—Martin Luther
  Harlingen—Grace
United Synod of New York
  Baldwin, L. I.—St. Peter's
  Brooklyn, N. Y.—St. Philip's
  New York City—Transfiguration
  Rochester, N. Y.—Emmanuel
  Springfield Gardens, L. I.—Bethany
  Teaneck, N. J.—St. Paul's
Virginia Synod
  Manassas Parish
  Waynesboro—Grace
Wartburg Synod
  Chicago, Ill.—Mt. Clare
West Virginia Synod
  Mason Parish

SELF-SUPPORTING LINGUISTIC MISSIONS

Pittsburgh Synod
  Cleveland—St. John's,
    Siebenbuerger
  Cleveland—Teutsch (Siebenbuerger)
    Siebenbuerger

United Synod of New York
  New Brunswick, N. J.—First
    Hungarian

APPENDIX B
NEW MISSIONS

California Synod
  No. Hollywood—St. Matthew's
East Pennsylvania Synod
  Willow Grove—Holy Trinity
Georgia Synod
  Mobile, Ala.—Advent
Illinois Synod
  St. Louis, Mo.—Mizpah
Kansas Synod
  Custer City, Okla.
Michigan Synod
  Kokomo, Ind.
Ministerium of Pennsylvania
  Adamstown—Reamstown Parish
  Berlin—Wenonah Parish
  Crescentville—Lawndale Parish
  Lancaster—Rohrerstown Parish
  South Temple—Epiphany
  Wissinoming—Hope
Nebraska Synod
  Dalton—Trinity
  Sidney—Potter Parish

Northwest Synod
  Beaver Dam, Wis.
  Woodlake, Minn.
Pittsburgh Synod
  Coudersport—St. Paul's
  Slippery Rock—St. John's
  Undercliff—Bethlehem
South Carolina Synod
  Columbia—Reformation
  Swansea Parish
  Union—Augsburg
Texas Synod
  Sweetwater—Longworth Parish
United Synod of New York
  Belleville, N. J.
  Cresskill—Our Saviour
  Keyport-Matawan—Keansburg
    Parish
  Laurelton, L. I.—Epiphany
  Long Branch, N. J.—Reformation
  No. Tarrytown, N. Y.—St. John's
  Rochester, N. Y.—Transfiguration

APPENDIX C
Statistical Report—Division of English Missions

Synod	Mission Parishes June 30, 1932	New Missions since June 30, 1930	Self-Supporting since June 30, 1930	Missions Discontinued from the Budget	Accessions During the Biennium	Confirmed Membe.s June 30, 1932	Sunday School Enrollment	Brotherhood Members	Luther League Members	Women's Missionary Society Members	Value of Property	Indebtedness	Congregational Expense	Contributed Benevolences
Alleghany	1	0	0	1	14	138	167	0	28	12	$16,000		$2,299	$1,405
California	12	1	1	0	542	1,381	1,467	112	337	235	220,755	63,420	77,001	9,077
Canada	6	0	0	1	166	690	438	62	167	118	111,500	48,067	25,340	3,069
East Pennsylvania	22	1	4	0	1,040	4,581	4,436	209	486	314	930,672	462,776	207,317	16,048
Florida	6	1	0	1	151	573	502	19	69	87	149,557	68,199	21,970	3,606
Georgia	5	0	0	0	217		390	51	103	87	107,025	52,344	18,138	2,918
Illinois	5	1	4	1	1,021	2,818	2,827	345	479	222	504,345	274,587	105,621	11,305
Indiana	18	1	0	0	410	1,661	1,386	91	300	155	331,050	160,076	62,522	6,679
Iowa	12	0	1	0	190	747	651	101	112	56	98,500	22,717	20,666	2,316
Kansas	5	1	1	0	102	614	581	30	161	73	155,150	68,362	32,529	5,203
Maryland	11	1	1	0	734	2,192	2,283	186	291	210	403,600	202,059	95,791	8,545
Michigan	14	0	0	0	644	2,183	1,570	161	252	190	375,150	230,579	84,418	8,481
Ministerium of Penna.	26	1	1	0	1,222	4,948	5,356	443	594	322	749,061	420,954	183,789	15,793
Mississippi	4	0	0	0	50	426	153	0	86	49	36,100	4,848	6,306	11,143
Nebraska	20	2	2	0	200	536	547	24	87	35	48,150	20,519	11,003	3,969
North Carolina	24	2	1	0	856	4,707	2,953	428	432	707	229,850	73,620	82,251	10,082
Nova Scotia	2	0	0	0	36	405	215			30	29,925	12,300	3,606	328
Northwest	19	2	4	0	1,554	4,707	2,577	428	432	707	535,032	305,912	139,806	16,073
Ohio	21	0	1	0	635	1,955	1,777	229	290	271	508,000	237,452	102,389	9,424
Pacific	24	3	1	1	666	3,096	2,847	153	382	317	284,900	174,006	67,761	7,810
Pittsburgh	9	3	1	0	954	1,307	1,043	285	497	303	581,950	203,350	106,164	14,014
Rocky Mountain	11	0	1	0	247	1,237	1,187	94	127	174	254,350	130,722	40,962	8,481
South Carolina	6	0	1	1	295	246	190	57	204	177	92,500	11,634	22,489	2,595
Susquehanna of Cent. Pa.	7	0	0	1	169	496	437			30	22,000	575	2,806	267
Texas	45	6	2	1	2,192	7,497	6,291	44	90	66	47,600	18,873	14,268	1,432
United Synod of N. Y.	7	7	6	1	130	1,235	635	589	742	667	1,068,107	514,023	403,125	19,014
Virginia	3	1	2	1	87	700	944	89	120	74	120,218	29,195	38,230	3,615
West Pennsylvania	4	0	0	0	130	582	862	0	56	55	42,000	35,290	19,142	1,992
West Virginia	0	0	1	1	87			36	40	91	107,000	4,220	39,175	4,485
Wartburg				0										
Total	**347**	**30**	**37**	**12**	**14,657**	**54,416**	**47,375**	**4,266**	**6,984**	**5,824**	**$8,160,047**	**$3,858,579**	**$2,034,056**	**$209,367**

STATISTICAL REPORT
GERMAN MISSIONS
CALIFORNIA SYNOD

Name	Place	Organized	Bapt. Memb.	Value	Indebted
St. Johannes	Oakland, Cal.	1923	120	$12,000	$5,220
Temple	San Francisco, Cal.	1917	120	6,800	
			240	$18,800	$5,220

CANADA SYNOD

Name	Place	Organized	Bapt. Memb.	Value	Indebted
St. Johannes	Arnprior, Ont.	1891	215	$7,000	
St. Jacobus	Northcote, Ont.	1891	103	1,500	
St. Marcus	Chesley, Ont.	1894	260	5,800	
Christus	Montreal, Que.	1931	182		
Zion	Massey, Ont.	1904	187	4,000	
	Chalk River, Ont.	1904	66	1,000	
St. Paulus	Denbigh, Ont.	1868	64	2,925	
St. Stephanus	Raglan, Ont.	1887	174	4,850	$590
Christus	Maynooth, Ont.	1901	242	3,300	1,200
St. Matthaeus	East Zorra, Ont.	1853	120	7,400	
Frauenkirche	Chatham, Ont.	1931	60		
St. Peter's	Wiarton, Ont.	1888	158	15,000	1,500
Honterus, Saxon	Kitchener, Ont.	1931	50		
			1,881	$52,775	$3,290

GERMAN NEBRASKA SYNOD

Name	Place	Organized	Bapt. Memb.	Value	Indebted
Christus	Campbell, Nebr.	1900	75	$8,000	
St. Johannes	Lincoln, Nebr.	1912	90	12,900	$4,450
Christus	Pierce, Nebr.	1903	69	14,600	
St. Johannes	Norfolk, Nebr.	1902	64	19,000	5,500
Zion	Sutton, Nebr.	1896	160	6,500	
Immanuel	Lodgepole, Nebr.	1920	81	4,680	1,700
St. Paulus	Rocky Ford, Colo.	1911	100	3,000	
St. Paulus	La Junta	1915	150	3,500	
St. Paul's	Lamar, Colo.	1925	80	5,000	
St. Paul's	Linn, Kansas	1916	97	6,000	1,700
Friedens	Stillwater, Okla.	1911	91	4,000	
Zion	Perry, Okla	1907	113	1,500	
St. Petri	Creston, Nebr.	1909	195	11,000	4,000
St. Petri	Howells, Nebr.	1900	146	2,000	
Pilger	Howells, Nebr.	1891	57	2,000	
			1,568	$103,680	$17,350

WARTBURG SYNOD

Name	Place	Organized	Bapt. Memb.	Value	Indebted
Zions Wolga Ger	Bellwood, Ill.	1932	187		
Cudahy	Cudahy, Wis.	1928	310	$15,000	$12,108
Martin Luther	Chicago, Ill.	1918	210	38,000	9,200
St. John's	Chicago, Ill.,	1914	295	20,000	2,480
St. John's	West Allis, Ill.	1927	350	6,100	2,940
Tabor	Chicago, Ill.	1907	419	30,000	15,400
Unity	Milwaukee, Wis.	1931	158	10,000	7,140
Wartburg	Berwyn, Ill.	1917	168	9,000	600
			2,097	$128,100	$49,868

TEXAS SYNOD

Friedens	Vernon, Texas	1922	153	$6,200	$750
St. Michael	Ray Point, Texas	1925	88	2,000	100
Holy Cross	Pawnee, Texas	1926	67	3,000	700
St. Paul's	George West, Texas..	1924	20	1,000	800
			328	$12,200	$2,350

UNITED SYNOD OF NEW YORK

St. Luke's	Dunellen, N. J.	1930	155		
St. Paul's	Linden, N. J.	1928	250	$8,700	$1,800
Zion	Ridgefield, N. J.	1926	232	15,000	5,750
St. John's	Mamaroneck, N. Y. ..	1913	273	80,000	22,800
St. John's	No. Tarrytown, N. Y.	1895	15		
Immanuel	Madison, Conn.	1895	73	1,800	
First	Jeffersonville, N. Y. ..	1852	205	25,000	6,000
			1,203	$13,050	$36,350

MINISTERIUM OF PENNSYLVANIA

Immanuel	Lakewood, N. J.	1926	150	$3,000	$1,000
Preaching Stations	Toms River, N. J.				
	Barnegat, Beach Haven, N. J.				
	Freehold				
St. Johannes	Williamstown, N. J.	1898	63	20,000	5,750
Dreieinigkeit	Maple Shade, N. J. ..	1927	271	2,500	800
St. Timotheus	Philadelphia, Pa.	1927	100		
			584	$25,500	$7,550

PITTSBURGH SYNOD

Honterus	Gary, Ind.	1925	145	$44,000	$30,000
Christus	Canton, O.	1927	77	14,000	8,787
St. Petrus	Detroit, Mich.	1930	248		
St. Paulus	Windsor, Ont.	1930	160		
St. Johannes	Farrell, Pa.	1923	294	37,000	21,800
			924	$95,000	$60,587

MANITOBA SYNOD

St. Johannes	Dresden, N. D.	1896	194	$7,500	$60
St. Johannes	Snowflake, Man.	1927	110	250	
Preaching Sta.	Osnabruck, N. D.				
Trinitatis	Thalberg, Man.	1911	305	5,000	
St. Johannes	Gruenwald, Man.		115		
Preaching Sta.	Jackfish Lake, Man. ..		54		
St. Johannes	Froid-Culbertson, Mont.		117	1,500	150
Bethanien	Inglis, Man.		202	11,500	
Immanuel	New Cana, Man.	1901	87	400	
St. Johannes	Friedensfeld, Man.	1925	196	8,000	500
St. Johannes	Niverville, Man.	1900	57	800	
	Camper, Man.	1930	66	1,400	45

Preaching Sta. ......Graysville, Man.	1930	20		
Durban, Man.	1930	20		
Minitonas, Man.	1930	43		
Marquette, Man.	1931	19		
Portage la Prairie	1931	35		
Kenora, Ont.	1931	28		
St. Petri ....Winnipeg	1931	300	35,000	1,550
St. Johannes ....Winnipeg	1931	260	11,000	5,000
Bethlehem. ....Winnipeg	1931	87		
St. Paulus ....Elbourne, Sask.	1907	144		
St. Paulus ....Serath, Sask.	1907	92		
Dreieingkeit ....Esk, Sask.	1907	210	3,850	372
Preaching Sta. ......Kandahar, Sask.	1928	23		
St. Johannes ....Brightholme, Sask.	1916	193	6,000	300
St. Paulus ....Silver Grove, Sask. ..	1902	120	1,500	
St. Johannes ....Luseland, Sask.	1910	162	4,000	350
St. Johannes .... Stony Hill (Laird, Sask.)	1901	163	8,000	200
Immanuel ....Hubbard, Sask.	1917	100	1,000	
St. Petri ....Goodeve, Sask.	1907	115	1,060	
Preaching Sta. ......Leron, Sask.		75		
Lestock, Sask.		35		
Makwa I ....Beaver River, Sask.....	1929	43		
Makwa II ....Beaver River, Sask.....	1929	15		
Loon Forks ....Beaver River, Sask.....	1929	11		
Meadow Lake ......Beaver River, Sask.....	1929	15		
Christus ....Runciman, Sask.	1925	105		
Preaching Sta. ......Valbrand, Sask.	1928	51		
Fox Dale, Sask.	1925	35		
Boro Green	1926	24		
St. Johannes ....Shellbrook, Sask.	1924	58	100	
St. Johannes ....Sturgeon River, Sask.	1930	62	100	
Preaching Sta. ......Wood Hill, Sask.	1931	85		
Amiens	1929	36		
Dear Ridge	1928	60		
Leask, Sask.	1931	30		
Big River, Sask.	1929	40		
Stump Lake, Sask.	1932	25		
Blue Heron, Sask.	1929	46		
Shell Lake, Sask.	1928	38		
Watrous, Sask.		50		
Prince Alberta, Sask.		20		
Dreieinigkeit ....Saskatoon, Sask.		110		
St. Johannes ....Edmonton, Alta.	1903	327	20,000	6,350
St. Johannes ....New Sarepta, Alta.	1911	232	7,500	1,323
St. Johannes ....Barrhead, Alta.	1929	216	1,500	700
Preaching Sta. ......Lunford, Alta.	1929	25		
Manola, Alta.	1929	56		
Mellowdale, Alta.	1929	64		
Mosside, Alta.	1930	46		
Vega, Alta.	1931	22		
Mystery Lake	1931	26		
Immanuel ....Busby, Alta.	1929	101		
Epiphanias ....Alcomdale, Alta.	1927	41		
Dreieinigkeit ....Onoway, Alta.	1930	42		

Emaus ....Calahoo, Alta.	1930	28		
St. Johannes ....Alberta Beach		25		
Bethanien ....Thorsby-Calmar	1929	150	500	
Dreieinigkeit ....Warburg, Alta.		47		
St. Petri ....Patience-Porto Bello..		84		
St. Johannes ....Flatbush, Alta.		114		
St. Paulus ....Rosevear, Alta.		49		
Christus ....Peace Grove, Alta.		69		
Preaching Sta. ......Pamberton Hill, Alta.		40		
Fawcett, Ala.		64		
Pinedale, Alta.		40		
Edson, Alta.		24		
Westlock, Alta.		22		
Valhalla Centre, Alta.		11		
St. Paulus ....Stettler, Alta.		58		
Trinitatis ....Newbrook, Alta.		54		
Preaching Sta. ......Wolf Creek	1928	31		
Sunnybrook	1928	69		
Strawberry Creek		57		
Ellscott		34		
Hines Creek		60		
Prince George, B. C...		25		
Cherhill, Alta.		60		
St. Johannes ....Meadowview		100		
Friedens ....Ballentine, Alta.		66		
		7,211	$137,460	$30,850

SUMMARY

California Synod	240	$18,800	$5,220
Canada Synod	1,881	52,775	3,290
German Nebraska Synod	1,568	103,680	17,350
Wartburg Synod	2,097	128,100	49,868
Texas Synod	328	12,200	2,350
United Synod of New York..	1,203	130,500	36,350
Ministerium of Pennsylvania	584	25,500	7,550
Pittsburgh Synod	924	95,000	60,587
Manitoba Synod	7,211	136,460	30,850
	161,131	$704,015	$213,415

SLOVAK MISSIONS

St. Paul's ....New York, N. Y.........	1927	300	$15,000	$10,500
St. John's ....Trenton, N. J.	1907	200	20,000	3,000
Zion ....Garfield, N. J.	1919	194	16,000	3,500
Holy Trinity ....Philadelphia, Pa.	1900	125	8,000	
St. John the Bapt...Camden, N. J.	1911	45	15,000	8,575
St. John the Bapt...Pottstown, Pa.		38	1,500	
Holy Trinity ....Newark, N. J.	1893	900	85,000	35,000
Sts. Peter & Paul..Guttenberg, N. J.	1902	350	5,500	
Northampton, Pa.	1905	250	30,000	4,000
Palmerton, Pa.		40	6,000	

St. Immanuel ....Mahanoy City	1893	219	25,000	
Dr. Martin Luther Jessup, Pa.	1895	130	11,000	2,700
St. Paul's ....Port Clinton, O.	1913		11,000	200
Cairnbrook, Pa.		35	1,000	
Proctor, Vt.		25		
Bethlehem, Pa.		50		
Grassflat, Pa.				
Shepptown, Pa.		40		
Cannonsburg, Pa.		100		
Saltsburg, Pa.		30		
Buffalo, N. Y.				
Byesville, O.		100		
Cranesville, O.		50		
Dover, O.		40		
Barton, O.		100		
Philipsburg, Pa.				
Wheeling, W. Va.		50		
Muskegon Heights, Mich.		100		
Phillips, Wis.		130		
Cudahy, Wis.		100		
Tabor, Mich.		130		
Holdingsford, Minn...				
Erie, Pa.		75		
Bayonne, N. J.				
Dayton, Ohio		120		
		4,066	$250,000	$67,475

HUNGARIAN MISSIONS

Zion ....Bethlehem, Pa.		300	$45,000	$33,160
Allentown, Pa.		100	5,500	
Palmerton, Pa.				
First ....New Brunswick, N. J.	1908	387	36,000	5,700
Holy Trinity ....Caldwell, N. J.	1928	135	2,600	
Holy Trinity ....New York, N. Y.	1930	180		
Church of Our Saviour ....Buffalo, N. Y..............	1914	275		
First ....Pittsburgh, Pa.	1925	120	30,000	23,000
First ....Akron, O.	1926	137	22,000	13,000
Preaching Points....Lorain, O.				
Elyria, O.				
Windsor, Ont., Can.....	1928	162	12,000	7,500
Kitchener, Ont., Can.	1930	102		
Hamilton, Ont., Can...	1931	41		
Welland, Ont., Can.....	1930	47		
Toronto, Ont., Can.....	1931	63		
Montreal, Que., Can.	1931	66		
Preaching Points ..Brantford, Ont., Can.				
Galt, Ont., Can............				
Bridgeport, Conn.	1931	64		
		2,179	$153,100	$82,360

WENDISH MISSIONS

			Conf. Memb.	Value	In-debted
First Magyar	Perth Amboy, N. J.	1918	145	$33,000	$8,000
St. John's	Newark, N. J.		150	8,000	3,000
			295	$41,000	$11,000

LETTISH MISSIONS

St. Mark's	Philadelphia, Pa.		60
St. Mark's	New York, N. Y.		50
Preaching Stations	Sifton, Man., Can.		
	Fork River, Man., Can.		
	Morketon, Man., Can.		
	Dauphin, Man., Can.		
	Winnipeg, Man., Can.		
	West Selkirk, Man., Can.		
	Libau, Man., Can.		
	Bird River, Man., Can.		
	Le Pas., Man., Can.		
	Total for Manitoba		139
			249

LITHUANIAN MISSIONS

St. John's	Philadelphia, Pa.	70	$15,000	$5,000
	Montreal, Que., Can.	25		
		95	$15,000	$5,000

ITALIAN MISSIONS

Christ	New York, N. Y.	1924	74		
St. Peter's	Philadelphia, Pa.	1908	175	$15,000	$2,500
Neighorhood House	Philadelphia, Pa.				
Holy Trinity	Erie, Pa.	1920	285	14,000	3,500
St. Paul's	Monessen, Pa.	1918	100		
Redeemer	Chicago, Ill.	1927	39		
St. John the Divine	San Francisco, Cal.	1924	36		
Preaching Points	Fresno, Cal.	1926	31		
	Sacramento, Cal.	1927	25		
			765	$29,000	$6,000

FINNISH MISSIONS

Place	Conf. Memb.	Value	In-debted
(A) Ontario District ....Copper Cliff, Ont.	208		
Preaching Points ..Sudbury, Ont.			
Carson Mine, Ont.			
Creighton Mine, Ont.			
Naughton, Ont.			
Pyrylanmaki, Ont.			
Sault Ste. Marie, Ont.			
Newberry, Ont.			

	Windsor, Ont.	58		
	Toronto, Ont.			
St. Michaels ....Montreal, Que.				

(B) Manitoba
  District ....Winnipeg, Man. 200
  Elmo, Man. ....
  New Finnland, Sask. 3,000   1,520
  Glenside, Sask. ....
  Ivermay, Sask. ....

(C) Alberta
  District 100
Preaching Points ..Sylvan Lake, Alta. ....
  Benalto ....
  Eckville ....
  Edmonton ....
  Bright View ....
  Radway ....
  Thor Hill ....
  Fork Lake ....
  Trochu ....
  Clairesholm ....
  Barons ....
  Foremost ....
  Manyberries ....

(D) British Colum-
  bia District 100
Preaching Points Vancouver, B. C....................
  Nanaino ....
  Ladysmith ....
  Victoria ....
  Salmon Arms ....
  Webster Corner ....
  Chase River ....
  Frazer Arms ....
  Nelson ....
  New Westminster ....
  Lulu Island ....
  Yennhandon ....
  Faulkland ....
  Mara ....
  Albion ....
  Fort Henry ....

(E) Maine District 600
  South Paris, Me. 3,000
  Harrison ....
  West Barnstable 5,500
  Hyannis ....
  Sagamore ....
  North Brookline ....
  Proctor ....

(F) New York
  District   200
              North Van Etten, N. Y.............
              Spencer ....

(G) Chicago
  District .... Chicago, Ill.   195

(H) Wisconsin
  District   359
              Superior, Wis.   6,000
              Oulu-Vaino   2,200
              Marengo ....
              Brantwood   1,000
              Westborough ....

(I) Oregon
  District   193
              Portland, Ore.   8,000   3,700
              Carleton   2,000   200
              Hockinson, Wash. ....
              Vader, Wash. ....
              Toledo, Wash. ....

(J) California
  District .... Los Angeles, Cal.   51
              Reedley   35
              San Pedro ....
              San Diego ....
              Pasadena ....
              Parlier ....
              Miami, Ariz. ....
              Bisbee, Ariz. ....

(K) Washington
  District   63
              Seattle, Wash.   2,000
              Scandia ....
              Tinton ....
              East Stanwood ....

(L) Washington
  District 2.   40
              Aberdeen, Wash. ....
              Independence ....
              Kent ....
              Issaquas ....

(M) Montana
  District   100
              Butte, Mont. ....
              Milltown ....
              Hamilton ....

San Coule ....
Great Falls ....

| | 2,274 | $40,700 | $7,622 |

GENERAL SUMMARY

German Missions 152
Slovak Missions 35
Hungarian Missions 20
Wendish Missions 2
Lettish Missions 11
Lithuanian Missions 2
Finnish Missions 86
Italian Missions 9
Jewish Missions 4

321

REPORT OF TREASURER OF BOARD OF AMERICAN MISSIONS

CERTIFICATE OF AUDIT

We have audited the books of account of The Board of American Missions of The United Lutheran Church in America for the fiscal year beginning July 1, 1930, and ending June 30, 1931, and we certify that in our opinion the balance sheet as of June 30, 1931, hereto attached, correctly sets forth the fiscal position of the Board of American Missions on that date, and the consolidated statement of receipts and disbursements for the year under audit, hereto attached, contains all receipts from apportionment, contributions, and other income as recorded in the books of account, the accounting for these having been duly and properly made, and that all disbursements appearing therein were supported by proper vouchers.

TAIT, WALKER & BAKER.

BALANCE SHEET, June 30, 1931
ASSETS

Cash .... $ 46,629.37
Securities owned at Ledger Values:
  Bonds ....$ 237,628.75
  Stocks 10,285.39
  Investment Mortgage 5,000.00
  Investment Notes 1,540.00
                                                         254,454.14
Advance Payment on Monte Flores, Porto Rico.. 4,000.00
Advanced Expense Accounts 825.00
Advance Expenses a/c Estates 86.82
Loans to Churches:
  Board Loans 1,392,780.13
  Agency Loans 178,925.53
                                                       1,571,705.66

Equipment and Furnishings		9,044.76
Real Estate and Buildings:		
Owned and held by Board	394,664.00	
Held as Agent	25,670.00	
		420,334.00
Accounts Receivable (Synods)		2,507.51
		$2,309,587.26

LIABILITIES:

Loans Payable	17,200.00	
Mortgage Payable	20,000.00	
		37,200.00
		$2,272,387.26

FUNDS:

General Funds:		
Missions	78,982.43	
Church Extension	352,185.74	
		431,168.17
Endowment Funds:		
Missions	43,900.32	
Church Extension	13,819.08	
		57,719.40
Permanent Loan Fund		1,295,572.16
Memorial Loan Fund		98,739.25
McMurray Trust Fund		26,443.37
Annuity Funds		67,361.99
Designated Gifts and Sundry Special Funds:		
Missions	30,446.09	
Church Extension	60,341.30	
		90,787.39
Agency Accounts:		
Church Extension Society, New York Confer-		
ence of New York Ministerium	3,000.00	
Women's Missionary Society	175,925.53	
Sundry Churches	25,670.00	
		204,595.53
		$2,272,387.26

CONSOLIDATED STATEMENT OF RECEIPTS AND DISBURSEMENTS
Year ended June 30, 1931

Balance, July 1, 1930	$	19,674.94

RECEIPTS:

United Lutheran Church on Apportionment..........$	524,400.00
Women's Missionary Society	68,279.48
Women's Missionary Society—Designated Gifts	
and Specials	12,414.92
Synods, Churches, Societies, Individuals	12,845.11

Returned Church Extension Loans	26,922.57	
Interest and Dividends on Securities	15,779.48	
Income on Trusts (not held by the Board)	4,197.98	
Income on McMurray Trust Fund	500.00	
Contributions to Memorial Loan Fund	1,035.00	
Bequests	18,309.14	
Refunds	773.10	
Proceeds Sale of Securities	183,466.00	
Proceeds Sale of Real Estate	100.00	
Loans from Bank	185,000.00	
Designated Gifts and Specials	22,412.53	
Agency Funds: Kirch-bau Verein	3,000.00	
		1,079,435.31
Total receipts		$1,099,110.25

DISBURSEMENTS:

Loans to Churches	$ 81,800.00	
Interest Grants to Churches	31,927.71	
Salaries:		
Missionaries	431,119.06	
Secretaries and Superintendents	37,692.16	
Expenses:		
Missionaries	15,192.98	
Secretaries and Superintendents	12,110.74	
Board Meetings and Members	4,441.13	
Seminary and Student Aid	12,838.20	
Upkeep of Charitable Institutions in Virgin Islands	6,678.76	
Transmission of Designated Gifts and Specials....	24,614.93	
Payments to Annuitants	4,778.83	
Interest on Loans and Mortgages	2,604.49	
Real Estate and Buildings	3,065.00	
Equipment and Furnishings	548.17	
Maintenance: Repairs, Insurance, Taxes	2,689.08	
Expenses: McMurray Property	1,394.34	
Legal Expenses	191.25	
Refunds a/c Bequests and Estates	1,406.83	
Refund a/c Interest Income	25.00	
Repayment of Loans from Bank	185,000.00	
Securities Purchased	177,907.50	
Accrued Interest on Securities purchased	2,997.94	
Maintenance Contribution to Lutheran Church House	2,280.00	
Office Supplies and Expenses	850.48	
Telephone and Telegrams	236.12	
Sundry Expenses: Postage, etc.	876.06	
Publicity	2,976.17	
Auditing Expense	737.95	
Contribution to Home Missions Council	1,000.00	
Emergency Donation to Luther Memorial, Madi-son, Wisconsin	2,500.00	
Total disbursements		1,052,480.88

Consolidated Summary:
Balance, July 1, 1930 ....$ 19,674.94
Receipts for year ending June 30, 1931.................. 1,079,435.31

$1,099,110.25
Disbursements for year ending June 30, 1931.... 1,052,480.88

Balance, June 30, 1931 .... $ 46,629.37

Zenan M. Corbe, *Treasurer.*

REPORT OF TREASURER OF BOARD OF AMERICAN MISSIONS

Certificate of Audit

We have audited the books of account of The Board of American Missions of The United Lutheran Church in America for the fiscal year beginning July 1, 1931 and ending June 30, 1932, and we certify that in our opinion the balance sheet as of June 30, 1932, hereto attached, correctly sets forth the fiscal position of the Board of American Missions on that date, and the consolidated statement of receipts and disbursements for the year under audit, hereto attached, contains all receipts from apportionment, contributions, and other income as recorded in the books of account, the accounting for these having been duly and properly made, and that all disbursements appearing therein were supported by proper vouchers.

Tait, Walker & Baker.

BALANCE SHEET, June 30, 1932
Assets

Cash		$ 39,127.87
Securities owned at Ledger Values:		
Bonds ....$ 244,638.90		
Stocks	10,285.39	
Investment Notes	1,540.00	
		256,464.29
Advanced Expense Accounts		825.00
Advance Expenses a/c Estates...................................		174.97
Loans to Churches:		
Board Loans	1,408,139.87	
Agency Loans	193,900.53	
		1,602,040.40
Equipment and Furnishings		8,760.00
Real Estate and Buildings:		
Owned and held by Board	422,003.91	
Held as Agent	25,670.00	
		447,673.91
Accounts Receivable (Synods)		8,807.51
		$2,363,873.95

LIABILITIES:

Loans Payable	17,200.00	
Mortgage Payable	20,000.00	
		37,200.00
		$2,326,673.95

FUNDS:

General Funds:			
Missions	$	58,518.90	
Church Extension		373,903.91	
			432,422.81
Endowment Funds:			
Missions		43,700.32	
Church Extension		14,459.08	
			58,159.40
Permanent Loan Fund			1,294,849.78
Memorial Loan Fund			126,123.20
McMurray Trust Fund			25,015.45
Annuity Funds			65,188.54
Designated Gifts and Sundry Special Funds:			
Missions		37,044.10	
Church Extension		68,300.14	
			105,344.24
Agency Accounts:			
Church Extension Society, New York Conference of New York Ministerium		3,000.00	
Women's Missionary Society		190,900.53	
Sundry Churches		25,670.00	
			219,570.53
			$2,326,673.95

CONSOLIDATED STATEMENT OF RECEIPTS AND DISBURSEMENTS
Year Ended June 30, 1932

Balance, July 1, 1931	$	46,629.37

RECEIPTS:

United Lutheran Church on Apportionment	$	448,400.00	
Women's Missionary Society:			
On Budget	$76,744.04		
North Carolina Synodical	600.00		
Designated Gifts	459.70		
		77,803.74	
Contributions:			
Synods, Congregations, Individuals		11,977.73	
Final Balance, Board of Missions:			
Puerto Rico and Latin America		194.69	
Refunds		398.28	
Fund Receipts		2,037.39	
Bequests		13,693.35	
Designated Gifts and Specials (including Luther League Pledge)		36,000.81	

Interest and Dividends	14,961.95	
Proceeds from Sale of Real Estate	190.00	
New Annuities Received	3,000.00	
Loans to Churches Repaid	19,290.26	
Proceeds from Matured Securities	126,250.00	
Loan from Fifth Avenue Bank	15,000.00	
Trust Fund:		
Northern California Indian Association	1,000.00	
		770,198.20
Total receipts		$ 816,827.57

DISBURSEMENTS:

Loans to Churches	$	54,575.00
Interest Grants to Churches		34,182.33
Salaries:		
Missionaries		429,792.82
Secretaries and Superintendents		29,959.55
Expenses:		
Missionaries		11,456.36
Secretaries and Superintendents		10,856.81
Board and Committee Meetings		4,312.22
Board Members' Special Assignments		928.48
Seminary and Student Aid		6,921.80
Charitable Work: Virgin Islands		4,455.80
Transmission Designated Gifts and Specials	$ 5,051.29	
Real Estate Purchases: Out of Designated Gifts and Specials	15,731.90	
		20,783.19
Payments to Annuitants		4,596.50
Interest paid		2,084.04
Real Estate and Buildings		1,672.51
Equipment and Furnishings		405.25
Real Estate Maintenance		2,387.01
McMurray Estate Maintenance and Annuity		1,892.92
Legal Expenses		88.15
Repayment of Loan from Fifth Avenue Bank		15,000.00
Securities purchased—Gross cost		134,803.14
Contribution to Lutheran Church House		1,962.00
Office Expenses:		
Office Supplies	$ 610.05	
Telephone and telegrams	252.18	
Sundry expenses	785.08	
		1,647.31
Publicity		1,358.76
Auditing		577.75
Contribution to Home Mission Council		1,000.00
Total disbursements		$ 777,699.70

Consolidated Summary:

Balance, July 1, 1931	$	46,629.37

Receipts for year ending June 30, 1932.................   770,198.20

                                                      $ 816,827.57

Disbursements for year ending June 30, 1932......   777,699.70

Balance, June 30, 1932 ....$ 39,127.87

ZENAN M. CORBE, *Treasurer.*

MISSION BALANCE SHEET
June 30, 1931

ASSETS		LIABILITIES AND FUNDS	
Cash in General Fund......$	24,587.71	Designated Gifts ....$	3,452.90
Home Mission Endow-		Special Funds	12,548.39
ment	916.94	General Fund	58,518.90
Designated Gifts	1,453.54	Home Mission Endow-	
Harroway Fund	695.95	ment Fund	43,700.32
Kaercher Fund	1,114.36	E. M. Harroway Fund....	10,263.45
Special Funds	5,684.83	Kaercher Fund	10,779.36
Total cash ....$	34,453.33		
Bonds	99,264.11		
Stocks	3,520.88		
Advanced Expenses	825.00		
Investment Note	1,200.00		
	$139,263.32		$139,263.32

SECURITIES IN MISSION FUND ACCOUNTS

Bonds   Book Value

	Book Value
10,000 C. R. I. and P. 1st and Rfg., 4%, due 1934 ....$	9,900.00
1,500 B. and O. 1st Mtge., 4%, due 1948	1,500.00
5,000 Union El. Lt. and Pr. 1st Mtge., 5%, due 1932	5,137.50
6,000 Detroit Edison 1st Mtge., 5%, due 1933	6,175.00
1,000 Consumers' Power, 5%, due 1936	1,000.00
10,000 B. and O. Pgh. and Le. Rfg. Mtge., 4%, due 1941............	9,450.00
4,000 L. V. Gen. Cons. Mtge., 4½%, due 2003	4,000.00
4,000 Memphis Pr. and Lt. 1st and Rfg., 5%, due 1948...............	4,000.00
2,000 St. Louis Co. Gas 1st Mtge., 5%, due 1951............................	2,000.00
7,000 C. B. and Q., 4%, due 1958..	6,597.50
5,000 Pac. G. and El. 1st Mtge., 4½%, due 1957........................	4,900.00
4,000 D. and H. 1st and Mtge., 4%, due 1943.............................	3,775.00
9,000 Commonwealth Edison, 3½%, due 1932	8,997.08
5,000 4th Liberty Bonds, 4¼%, due 1933-38	5,000.00
4,000 Peoples' Gas Light and Coke Co., 4½%, due 1935............	3,976.20
4,000 Pgh. McK. and Y., 6%, due 1932	4,000.00
1,000 Metropolitan Edison, 4½%, due 1968	1,000.00
3,000 Dominion of Canada Notes, 4%, due 1932	2,855.83
15,000 New York City Notes, 6%, due 1937	15,000.00
	$ 99,264.11

Stocks
88 Shares York Trust Co. stock	3,520.88
	$102,784.99

CHURCH EXTENSION BALANCE SHEET, June 30, 1932

ASSETS:

Cash in
General Fund	
Permanent Loan Fund	
Memorial Loan Fund.$	2,166.68
Church Extension Endowment Fund	1,032.55
McMurray Trust Fund	15.78
Designated Gifts and Sundry Specials	968.13
Annuity Funds	491.40

Total cash ....$	4,674.54
Bonds	145,374.79
Stocks	6,764.51
Loans to Churches	1,408,139.87
Real Estate	422,003.91
Equipment and Furnishings	8,760.00
Due from Synods............	8,807.51
Advances a/c Estates....	174.97
Investment Note	340.00

Agency:
Loans to Churches	193,900.53
Real Estate	25,670.00

	$2,224,610.63

LIABILITIES AND FUNDS:

Mortgage Payable ....$	20,000.00
Loans Payable	17,200.00
General Fund	373,903.91
Permanent Loan Fund..	1,294,849.78
Memorial Loan Fund....	126,123.20
Church Extension Endowment Fund	14,459.08
McMurray Trust Fund	25,015.45
Annuity Funds	65,188.54
Designated Gifts and Sundry Special Funds	68,300.14

Agency Funds:
Ch. Ex. Society, N.Y., Conference	3,000.00
Women's Missionary Society	190,900.53
St. Luke's, York, Pa.	25,000.00
Harmony Grove, Pa..	500.00
Cly, Pa.	170.00

	$2,224,610.63

SECURITIES IN CHURCH EXTENSION ACCOUNTS
June 30, 1932

Bonds	Book Value
5,000 Ill. C., 4%, due 1955 ....$	4,743.75
1,000 Howard G. and C. Co., 6%, due 1937	1,000.00
3,000 El. and Peoples' Traction Co., 4%, due 1945	1,875.00
2,000 St. L. Spr. and P. 1st and Rfg., 5%, due 1939	2,000.00
1,000 Publ. Serv. Newark Terminal, 5%, due 1955	952.50
1,000 L. V. R. R. Genl. Cons. Mtge., 4%, due 2003	1,000.00
1,000 Erie El. Motor Co., 5%, due 1941	1,000.00
500 502 Park Ave. Bldg., 6%, due 1941	500.00
5,000 N. O. Tex. and Mex. 1st Mtge., 5%, due 1954	5,012.50
5,000 Penna. R. R. Genl. Mtge., 4½%, due 1965	5,043.75
5,000 West Penn. Pr. 1st Mtge. Ser. G, 5%, due 1956	5,243.75
5,000 Ala. Pr. Co. 1st Mtge. Lien and Rfg., 5%, due 1956	5,131.25
15,000 L. and N. Unified, 4%, due 1940	14,580.00
500 B. and O. 1st Mtge., 4%, due 1948	500.00
10,000 Can. Pac. Equipment, 4½%, due 1941	9,892.00
5,000 C. and N. W. 1st and Rfg. Mtge., 5%, due 2037	5,303.75
1,000 Jefferson and Placq. Dran. Dis., 5%, due 1949	1,000.00
5,000 B. and O. 1st Mtge., 5%, due 1948	5,285.00
7,000 Pub. Serv. El. and Gas of N. Y., 4½%, due 1967	6,947.50
5,000 L. and N. 1st and Rfg., 4½%, due 2003	5,100.00
6,000 So. Pac. R. R., 4%, due 1955	5,692.50

5,000 N. Y. C. R. R. Equip., 4½%, due 1932		5,000.00
4,000 Metropolitan Edison, 4½%, due 1968		4,000.00
7,000 Dominion of Canada, 4%, due 1932		6,663.61
5,000 Consumers' Power, 4½%, due 1958		5,000.00
6,000 Commonwealth Edison, 3½%, due 1932		5,998.05
6,000 Peoples' Gas Light and Coke Co., 4½%, due 1935		5,964.30
5,000 Philadelphia Electric, 4%, due 1971		4,946.39
5,000 N. Y. City, 6%, due 1937		5,000.00
15,000 U. S. Treasury Notes, due 1932		14,999.19

$145,374.79

Stocks
52 Shares Integrity Trust Co., Philadelphia		3,514.51
40 Shares Fidelity Trust Co., Pittsburgh		3,250.00

$ 6,764.51

LOANS TO CHURCHES
CALIFORNIA SYNOD

Location and Names	Dates of Loans	Maturities	Amounts
Alhambra, Grace	1925	Dec. 31, 1932	$ 4,000.00*
Berkeley, St. Michael's	1920	Sept. 16, 1932	1,650.00
Gardena, St. John's	1926	Dec. 31, 1932	3,000.00
Glendale, First	1917	June 1, 1928	500.00
Huntington Park, St. Luke's	1925	Mar. 11, 1932	1,000.00
Los Angeles:			
Hollywood	1924	May 16, 1932	5,000.00
St. Paul's	1925	Dec. 31, 1932	2,975.00
Oakland, St. Johannis	1922	Dec. 31, 1932	2,500.00
Phoenix, Ariz., Grace	1928	Aug. 28, 1933	10,000.00
Richmond, Grace	1926	Dec. 31, 1932	5,000.00
Sanger, St. Paul's	1908	Feb. 27, 1913	320.00*
San Jose, Grace	1895	Dec. 31, 1934	1,750.00
Santa Monica, St. Paul's	{1926 {1929	June 29, 1931} May 5, 1934}	15,000.00

$52,695.00

CANADA SYNOD

Brantford, Ont., St. Matthew's	1919	Dec. 31, 1932	$ 5,000.00
Galt, Ont., St. Paul's	1913	Apr. 1, 1933	550.00
Guelph, Ont., St. Paul's	1915	Jan. 20, 1931	2,000.00
Hamilton, Ont., Can., Trinity	{1915 {1923	Aug. 3, 1928} Sept. 1, 1930}	7,080.00
Kitchener, Ont., First	1913	Oct. 1, 1930	3,564.59
Montreal, Que., Redeemer	1910	July 22, 1930	4,000.00
Ottawa, Ont., St. Peter's	1913	July 1, 1930	4,000.00*

Toronto, Ont., Finnish	1931	Demand	875.00
Windsor, Ont., Hungarian	1932	Mar. 16, 1937	4,000.00
			$31,069.59

North Carolina Synod

Asheville, St. Mark's	1928 / 1932	Oct. 23, 1933 / Jan. 8, 1937	10,000.00*
Charlotte, St. Luke's	1930	Aug. 25, 1935	5,000.00
Durham, St. Paul's	1925	Dec. 31, 1932	5,000.00
Hendersonville, Grace	1922	Aug. 23, 1933	2,000.00
Highland, Good Hope	1927	June 21, 1932	2,000.00
Raleigh, Holy Trinity	1922	Aug. 8, 1930	5,000.00
Rocky Mount, Trinity	1925	Dec. 31, 1932	5,000.00
			$34,000.00

South Carolina Synod

Batesburg, Faith	1912	Nov. 1, 1932	$ 1,500.00
Clinton, St. John's	1925	Jan. 1, 1932	2,475.00
			$3,975.00

Florida Synod

Daytona, Resurrection	1925 / 1927	Dec. 7, 1933 / Mar. 20, 1932	$ 9,250.00
Hollywood, St. John's	1927	Nov. 22, 1932	7,500.00
Miami, Trinity	1929 / 1931	Apr. 15, 1934 / Sept. 28, 1936	5,000.00
St. Augustine, Memorial	1926 / 1927	Jan. 11, 1931 / Nov. 22, 1932	10,000.00
St. Petersburg, Trinity	1921	Dec. 31, 1932	15,000.00
West Palm Beach, First	1927 / 1930	Apr. 7, 1935	7,300.00
			$54,050.00

Georgia Synod

Birmingham, Ala., Christ	1921	Mar. 17, 1932	$25,800.00
Macon, Ga., Redeemer	1924	Dec. 28, 1929	5,000.00
Mobile, Ala., Advent	1932	June 30, 1937	2,500.00
			$33,300.00

Illinois Synod

Acacia Park, Chicago	1929	Dec. 28, 1934	$ 2,000.00
Aurora, Our Redeemer	1907 / 1908	May 14, 1910 / Sept. 2, 1913	2,500.00
Centralia, Redeemer	1920	Nov. 23, 1933	4,810.00
Champaign, Grace	1916	Nov. 28, 1929	2,000.00*

Chicago:

Belmont Park	1922	Dec. 15, 1930	3,500.00*
Hope-Epiphany	1916	Oct. 12, 1928	5,000.00
Oak Park	1926	1929	2,750.00
Reformation	1918	June 20, 1923	1,500.00
Riverdale, Our Saviour	1913	Oct. 15, 1918	1,000.00
St. Andrew's	1924	Nov. 10, 1929	2,500.00
St. Luke's	1907	July 17, 1931	2,500.00
Elmwood Park, Westwood	1929	Dec. 4, 1934	10,000.00*
Woodlawn Memorial	1923	Aug. 4, 1928	9,000.00*
Elmhurst, Elmhurst	1923	Sept. 24, 1928	3,000.00
Epiphany	1926	Dec. 31, 1933	3,500.00
Evanston, St. Paul's	{1925 1926 1927	Mar. 1, 1933 Mar. 1, 1934 Mar. 1, 1934	28,000.00
Macomb, Trinity	1929	Sept. 3, 1934	3,000.00
Maywood, Broadview	1926	Nov. 12, 1931	6,000.00
Murphysboro, First	1926	Oct. 21, 1931	5,000.00
St. Louis, Mo.:			
Advent	1924	Oct. 14, 1929	5,000.00*
Faith	1926	Mar. 9, 1931	6,500.00
Mizpah	1932	Mar. 18, 1937	4,000.00
Reen Memorial	1915	Oct. 30, 1918	3,300.00
St. Mark's	1881	1884	961.17
Villa Park, Grace	1930	Jan. 1, 1935	2,000.00
Waukegan, St. Paul's	1930	July 31, 1935	2,500.00
Wheaton, St. Paul's	1928	Feb. 18, 1933	4,000.00
Wilmette, English	{1921 1930	July 17, 1935 July 17, 1935	15,000.00
Illinois Synod	1930	Dec. 10, 1935	10,000.00

$150,821.17

INDIANA SYNOD

Batesville, Bethany	1912	Nov. 27, 1914	$ 1,400.00
Evansville, Christ	1923	Dec. 31, 1932	1,940.00*
Indianapolis:			
Bethany	1926	Aug. 28, 1931	4,000.00
Bethlehem	1924	Jan. 28, 1936	10,000.00
Gethsemane	1921	Sept. 21, 1929	3,000.00
Lafayette, Holy Trinity	1900	Nov. 1, 1931	9,500.00
Memphis, Tenn., First	{1926	May 8, 1931 June 1, 1932	7,500.00
Terre Haute, Unity	1924	Dec. 31, 1932	4,000.00

$41,340.00

IOWA SYNOD

Council Bluffs, St. John's	1919	Jan. 6, 1924	$ 2,000.00
Des Moines, Unity	1924	Sept. 11, 1929	3,000.00

Iowa Falls, English	1918	Apr. 11, 1931	1,000.00
Mason City, Central	1928	Dec. 14, 1935	7,500.00
Missouri Valley, St. Paul's	1926	Sept. 14, 1931	2,000.00
Muscatine, Grace	{1900 1901 1923}	Sept. 6, 1905 Sept. 11, 1928	4,000.00
Princeton, Zion	1898	Nov. 1, 1903	300.00
Valley Junction, First	1920	Jan. 14, 1931	500.00
Waterloo, Trinity	1928	Mar. 3, 1933	15,800.00
St. Luke's	{1917 1920}	{1922 1925}	1,300.00
			$37,400.00

KANSAS SYNOD

Fairmount, Mo., Fairmount	1926	Dec. 31, 1933	$ 4,900.00
Fort Smith, Ark., United	1931	Jan. 23, 1936	4,800.00*
Hutchinson, Zion	1921	Feb. 7, 1929	1,500.00
Kansas City, Kans., Trinity	1926	Dec. 31, 1934	10,000.00*
Kansas City, Mo., St. John's	{1922 1926}	May 1, 1937	10,000.00
Sedalia, Mo., Trinity	1895	Dec. 31, 1933	1,547.97
Tulsa, Okla., First	1914	June 23, 1919	1,500.00
Valley Falls, St. Paul's	{1891	Sept. 1, 1891 Dec. 9, 1896}	1,200.00
			$35,447.97

MANITOBA SYNOD

Barrhead, Alta., St. John's	1931	Mar. 1, 1933	$ 700.00
Edmonton, Alta., St. John's	1923	1926	1,500.00
So. Edmonton, Alta., St. John's	1921	1932	1,500.00
Brightholme, Sask.	{1921	Sept. 1, 1921 Sept. 1, 1929}	350.00
Esk, Sask., Gartenland	1923	Mar. 25, 1927	99.00
Golden Spike, Alta., St. John's	1927	Mar. 31, 1933	4,500.00
Friedensfeld, Alta., St. Paul's	1922	1929	50.00
Leduc, Alta., Rosenthal	1922	1927	75.00
Markinch, Sask., St. Zion's	1931	Dec. 16, 1936	1,000.00
Saskatoon, Sask.:			
Saskatoon College	{1915 1920}	1924	6,475.00
Trinity	1922	1923	1,550.00
Steinbach, Man., St. John's	1925	Sept. 7, 1934	500.00
Manitoba Synod	1931	Mar. 16, 1936	7,000.00
Winnipeg, Man., St. John's	1932	July 1, 1935	5,000.00
			$30,299.00

MARYLAND SYNOD

Baltimore:

All Saints	{1922} {1924}	June 27, 1932	$ 7,000.00
Luther Memorial	1930	Dec. 31, 1935	5,000.00
Redeemer	1928	Feb. 3, 1933	5,000.00
Brooklyn, St. John's	1928	Oct. 28, 1934	5,000.00
East Riverdale, St. John's	1923	Jan. 29, 1933	1,000.00
Maryland Synod	1928	1934	10,000.00
Lansdowne, Our Saviour	1930	Feb. 24, 1935	4,000.00

Washington, D. C.:

Incarnation	1928	Dec. 24, 1933	5,000.00
St. Stephen's	1927	July 16, 1931	5,000.00

$47,000.00

MICHIGAN SYNOD

Ann Arbor, Mich., Trinity	1893	Oct. 30, 1898	$ 2,000.00
Butler, Ind., Evangelical	{1866 {	1869} 1873}	500.00

Detroit, Mich.:

Augsburg	1926	Aug. 31, 1931	3,800.00
Hope	1926	Dec. 31, 1933	7,000.00
Luther Memorial	1926	Dec. 31, 1932	7,000.00
Michigan Synod	1929	Dec. 2, 1934	5,000.00
Nativity	{1927} {1928}	Demand	5,500.00
Reformation	1926	Dec. 31, 1932	10,000.00
St. Paul's	1920	July 22, 1925	5,000.00
Unity	1924	Dec. 31, 1932	11,450.00
Flint, Trinity	1922	Dec. 31, 1932	4,950.00
Fort Wayne, Ind., Christ	{1917} {1926} {1930}	Jan. 1, 1934	5,000.00
Gary, Ind., Grace	1924	Nov. 3, 1929	10,000.00*
Jackson, Reformation	1926	Dec. 31, 1932	3,925.00
Kalamazoo, Trinity	1928	Jan. 13, 1933	5,000.00*
Lansing, Redeemer	1923	Jan. 20, 1928	4,000.00
Pontiac, Ascension	1926	Sept. 23, 1931	6,000.00
Saginaw, Resurrection	1925	Mar. 30, 1930	2,500.00
Windsor, Ont., Can., Trinity	1924	Aug. 1, 1929	6,000.00

$104,625.00

MISSISSIPPI SYNOD

Goodman, St. Mark's	{1924 {	June 2, 1927} June 2, 1929}	$ 185.00
Laurel, Grace	1923	May 29, 1928	1,937.35

$2,122.35

NEBRASKA SYNOD

Ericson, First	1899	Feb. 27, 1904	$ 140.00
Fremont, Salem	1924	Nov. 6, 1932	13,000.00
Hooper, Grace	1916	Nov. 11, 1927	200.00
Omaha:			
First	1908	Mar. 5, 1913	1,000.00*
Grace	1896	Oct. 12, 1901	3,000.00
St. Luke's	{1909 1910}	May 1, 1933	2,625.00
Lincoln:			
Grace	1893	Dec. 1, 1898	4,000.00
St. James'	1925	Feb. 13, 1933	3,500.00
South Sioux City, First English	1925	Dec. 31, 1932	5,000.00
York, First	{1908 1922}	Nov. 14, 1913 Dec. 1, 1927}	800.00

$33,265.00

GERMAN NEBRASKA SYNOD

Havelock, Zion	1916	Aug. 15, 1921	$ 600.00
Lincoln:			
Martin Luther	{1926	Feb. 1, 1929 Feb. 1, 1937}	900.00
St. John's	1916	Oct. 31, 1919	750.00
Lodge Pole, Immanuel	{1922	July 1, 1927 July 1, 1934}	900.00
Norfolk, St. Johannis	1920	June 25, 1925	325.00

$3,475.00

UNITED LUTHERAN SYNOD OF NEW YORK

Baldwin, St. Peter's	1924	Dec. 31, 1932	$ 4,875.00
Bay Shore, L. I., St. Luke's	1930	June 28, 1935	10,000.00
Bayside West, Good Shepherd	1931	Jan. 6, 1936	3,000.00
Bellerose, Holy Trinity	1931	Apr. 6, 1936	8,000.00
Blasdell, First	1926	Dec. 31, 1932	2,000.00
Bronx, St. Paul's (Slovak)	1929	Mar. 9, 1935	5,000.00
Brooklyn:			
Calvary	1905	May 1, 1910	2,500.00
St. Andrew's	1916	July 1, 1932	5,000.00
St. Philip's	{1921 1926}	Dec. 31, 1934	4,750.00
Buffalo, Zion	1896	May 25, 1901	2,000.00
Elizabeth, N. J., St. Paul's	1931	July 1, 1936	2,000.00
East Orange, N. J., Advent	1924	Demand	200.00
Endicott, Holy Nativity	1926	Dec. 31, 1932	1,950.00
Forest Hills, Grace	1927	Dec. 31, 1933	4,000.00
Franklin Square, Ascension	1925	Dec. 31, 1932	2,975.00
Gerrittsen Beach, St. James'	1926	Dec. 31, 1932	5,000.00

Hartford, Conn., St. Paul's	1924	Dec. 31, 1933	3,600.00
Hasbrouck Heights, N. J., Trinity	1923	Dec. 31, 1932	1,000.00
Hillside, N. J., Calvary	1925	Jan. 16, 1933	5,000.00
Hoboken, N. J., Trinity	1911	Nov. 17, 1916	2,000.00
Howard Beach, St. Barnabas	1924	Dec. 31, 1932	2,900.00
Jamaica, Baisley Park, L. I.:			
Incarnation	1925	Dec. 31, 1932	3,000.00
Jamaica, Our Saviour	1924	Dec. 31, 1932	4,750.00
Jamacia, Locust Manor, L. I.:			
St. Thomas	1931	Sept. 18, 1936	5,000.00
Jersey City, N. J., Calvary	1919	July 22, 1924	1,500.00
Little Neck, L. I., Christ	1926	Dec. 31, 1932	3,000.00
Newark, N. J., Grace	1906	Jan. 20, 1933	6,000.00
New Britain, Conn., Reformation	1926	Aug. 13, 1932	4,900.00
Nutley, N. J., Trinity	1927	Dec. 31, 1933	4,000.00
Oswego, N. Y., St. Matthew's	1888	Dec. 31, 1932	1,975.00
Paterson, N. J., First	1907	Dec. 31, 1932	5,960.90
Pelham Park, Bronx, Calvary	1925	Dec. 31, 1932	9,900.00
Queens (Dunton), St. Paul's (Richmond Hill)	1925	Dec. 31, 1932	4,000.00
Richmond Hill Circle:			
Holy Comforter	1926	Dec. 31, 1931	950.00
Ridgefield, N. J., Zion	1930	Feb. 1, 1935	5,000.00
River Edge, N. J., Grace	1923	Aug. 1, 1928	3,000.00
Rochester, Emmanuel	1924	Dec. 31, 1931	4,800.00
Rutherford, N. J., St. John's	1930	June 2, 1935	5,000.00
Schenectady, First	1922	Demand	2,800.00
Second	1928	Feb. 20, 1933	5,000.00
Snyder, Ascension	1927	Sept. 1, 1932	5,000.00
Springfield Gardens, Bethany	1925	July 2, 1933	4,000.00
Syracuse, Atonement	{1918 1931}	Mar. 8, 1933	6,000.00
Teaneck, N. J., St. Paul's	1928	Dec. 31, 1935	5,000.00
Union Township, N. J., Christ	1927	Dec. 24, 1932	3,000.00
United Lutheran Synod of New York	1930	Dec. 31, 1933	8,000.00
Valley Stream, St. Paul's	1924	Feb. 21, 1933	2,250.00
Woodhaven, St. James' (Ozone Park)	1924	Dec. 31, 1931	4,000.00

$195,535.90

NORTHWEST SYNOD

Alden, Minn., Grace	1931	May 26, 1934	$ 1,500.00
Appleton, Wis., Trinity	1924	Dec. 31, 1932	4,950.00
Beloit, Wis., Atonement	{1908 1918}	Mar. 23, 1913} July 16, 1923}	8,000.00
Billings, Mont., First English	1920	Aug. 10, 1933	6,200.00
Fond du Lac, Wis., Our Saviour	1926	Dec. 31, 1932	4,970.00
'Glenburn, N. D., Trinity	1929	Apr. 26, 1934	2,000.00

Grand Forks, N. D., St. Mark's	1915	Oct.	13, 1929	900.00
Great Falls, Mont., St. John's	1927	May	14, 1932	10,000.00*
Jefferson, Wis., St. Mark's	1926	Aug.	12, 1931	700.00
Kenosha, Wis., Trinity	1931	Apr.	2, 1936	500.00
Killdeer, N. D., St. John's	1920	Oct.	27, 1925	2,000.00
Lansford, N. D., Trinity	1920	Sept.	18, 1925	900.00
Lincolnton, Minn., St. Andrew's	1925	Sept.	1, 1933	3,000.00
Livingston, Mont., Redeemer	1912	Oct.	3, 1932	5,000.00
Madison, Wis., Luther Memorial	⎰1921 ⎱1922 1924 1927	Aug.	12, 1932	39,300.00
Marinette, Wis., St. James'	1922	Jan.	6, 1927	5,000.00
Marshfield, Wis., Trinity	1924	Feb.	20, 1932	3,000.00
Milwaukee, Wis.:				
Pentecost	⎰1924⎱ ⎰1928⎱	Dec.	22, 1933	6,765.09
Resurrection	1913	Aug.	12, 1920	700.00
Washington Park	1921	Dec.	31, 1929	15,000.00
Superior, Wis., Holy Trinity	1926	June	8, 1932	5,000.00
Minneapolis, Minn.:				
Epiphany	⎰1926 ⎱1927	Jan. Mar.	4, 1931⎱ 10, 1932⎰	5,000.00
Holy Communion	⎰1910 ⎱1913	July Apr.	15, 1915⎱ 14, 1918⎰	2,000.00
Mt. Carmel	1926	Aug.	17, 1931	4,000.00
Resurrection	1923	Dec.	1, 1928	2,000.00
St. James'	1916	Oct.	12, 1921	2,000.00
Oxboro, Minn., St. Luke's	1927	Sept.	29, 1932	2,000.00
St. Paul, Minn., Ascension	1925	Mar.	2, 1933	5,500.00
Waukesha, Wis., St. Luke's	⎰1926 ⎱	July May	19, 1928⎱ 28, 1931⎰	8,000.00*
Wauwatosa, Wis., St. Matthew's........	1921	June	17, 1929	15,000.00
West Allis, Wis., First	1929	May	25, 1934	2,000.00
West Bend, Wis., Trinity	1926	Dec.	31, 1934	2,950.00
Winnipeg, Man., Can.,:				
First English	⎰1912 ⎱1921	May Oct.	7, 1915⎱ 10, 1926⎰	26,288.38
				$202,123.47

NOVA SCOTIA SYNOD

Halifax, Resurrection ,...........................	1915	Sept.	1, 1930	$ 5,000.00

OHIO SYNOD

Akron, First Hungarian	1927	July	21, 1932	$ 5,000.00
Bowling Green, First	1923	Dec.	31, 1932	3,000.00
Cleveland:				
Emmaus	1912	Mar.	4, 1916	1,150.00

Our Saviour	1930	Nov. 12, 1933	1,000.00
Parma, Redeemer	1928	Sept. 10, 1933	4,000.00
Cleveland Heights, Messiah	1924	Mar. 1, 1929	5,000.00
Columbus:			
Hilltop	1919	Dec. 31, 1932	2,000.00
Indianola		Demand	3,333.33*
Redeemer	1923	June 15, 1928	2,600.00
Continental, Christ	1897	Nov. 19, 1897	300.00
Covington, Ky., First	1920	Feb. 3, 1931	5,000.00
Dayton:			
Grace	1912	Dec. 12, 1917	1,700.00
No. Riverdale	1914	Oct. 31, 1919	1,500.00
Westwood	1916	Aug. 28, 1921	1,500.00
East Cleveland, St. James'	1919	Oct. 18, 1924	2,000.00*
Elyria, Emmanuel	1931	Nov. 25, 1936	10,000.00*
Fremont, St. Mark's	1921	Jan. 31, 1926	3,000.00
Kent, First	1908	Aug. 18, 1913	1,000.00
Lakewood, Trinity	1921	Dec. 31, 1932	10,000.00
Marion, St. Paul's	1917	Dec. 31, 1922	1,000.00
Niles, Trinity	{1924 / 1928	Dec. 31, 1933} / Oct. 22, 1933}	10,000.00
Sebring, Trinity	1915	May 1, 1918	1,000.00
Springfield, Fifth	1902	Mar. 24, 1904	2,000.00
Steubenville, Grace	1930	July 19, 1935	5,000.00
Toledo:			
Augsburg	1925	Dec. 12, 1929	5,000.00
Bethany	1927	June 7, 1932	5,000.00
Home Acres	1922	June 20, 1927	1,000.00
Messiah	1925	Dec. 31, 1932	2,000.00
Redeemer	1925	Mar. 16, 1930	5,000.00

$100,083.33

PACIFIC SYNOD

Bellingham, Wash., St. Mark's	1924	Dec. 31, 1932	$ 1,000.00*
Everett, Wash., Trinity	1920	Oct. 7, 1929	5,000.00
Longview, Wash., Trinity	{1926 / 1930 / 1931	Dec. 17, 1931} / Mar. 24, 1933} / On Demand	14,000.00*
Medford, Ore., Zion	{1926} / {1928}	Aug. 27, 1933	5,500.00
Portland, Ore., Redeemer	1925	Dec. 7, 1932	1,200.00
Salem, Ore., American	1928	Aug. 15, 1933	5,000.00
Seattle, Wash.:			
Holy Trinity	{1901 / 1903	Dec. 19, 1902} / Dec. 31, 1906}	3,500.00
St. James'	1923	Dec. 31, 1932	2,500.00
St. Mark's	1929	Nov. 3, 1934	3,500.00

University	{1926 1927 1927 1930	Dec. 10, 1931 Jan. 24, 1932 Jan. 28, 1932 Oct. 14, 1935	18,500.00*
Spokane, Wash., St. Paul's	1924	Mar. 24, 1929	3,000.00
Vancouver, B. C., Redeemer	1913	Apr. 1, 1918	5,000.00
Victoria, B. C., Grace	{1910	Oct. 29, 1913 Apr. 20, 1925	5,967.50*

$73,667.50

EAST PENNSYLVANIA SYNOD

Bristol, Zion	1920	June 4, 1933	$ 2,850.00
Collingdale, Pa., First...............................	1926	Dec. 31, 1932	5,000.00
Drexel Hill, Grace	1925	Oct. 2, 1933	5,000.00
Essington, Tinicum Memorial	1922	May 5, 1932	2,850.00
Harrisburg, St. Paul's	1924	Oct. 31, 1932	2,625.00
Merchantville, N. J., Messiah	1927	June 6, 1932	2,500.00
Narberth, Trinity	{1921 1924	Oct. 7, 1932	6,562.50
Palmyra, N. J., First	1925	Nov. 6, 1933	5,000.00
Philadelphia:			
Luther Memorial	1921	Feb. 19, 1932	5,000.00
St. Andrew's	1904	Nov. 5, 1932	1,750.00
Runnemede, N. J., Trinity	1928	May 10, 1933	2,500.00
Sea Isle City, N. J., Messiah	1918	July 1, 1919	500.00
Trenton, N. J., Bethel	1924	Mar. 22, 1932	10,000.00
West Chester, Calvary	1925	Feb. 14, 1932	1,387.50
Yeadon, Trinity	1930	Apr. 11, 1935	5,000.00
East Pennsylvania Synod	1930	June 20, 1935	10,000.00
East Pennsylvania Synod	1930	Sept. 15, 1935	4,000.00

$72,525.00

MINISTERIUM OF PENNSYLVANIA

Allentown, Redeemer	1926	Dec. 31, 1932	$ 3,000.00
Attleboro, Redeemer	1906	Dec. 31, 1932	800.00
Bethlehem, First Hungarian	1926	Feb. 28, 1934	2,500.00
Chester, Nativity	1920	Aug. 30, 1933	2,500.00
Clark's Summit, Trinity	1930	Jan. 20, 1935	4,000.00
Haddonfield, N. J., Our Saviour	1928	Dec. 31, 1932	2,500.00
Haddon Heights, N. J., Our Saviour..	1916	Nov. 1, 1932	1,700.00
Laureldale, Calvary	1930	Jan. 1, 1933	5,000.00
Mountainville, Trinity	1924	Mar. 6, 1933	4,250.00
Oaklyn, N. J., St. Mark's	1928	Dec. 31, 1931	2,500.00
Philadelphia:			
Gloria Dei	1924	June 17, 1934	12,750.00
Mediator	1923	Feb. 24, 1933	5,425.00
Reading, Nativity	1928	June 28, 1933	5,000.00

Shavertown, St. Paul's	1927	Dec. 31, 1933	2,500.00
Somers Point, Grace	1927	Dec. 10, 1932	2,500.00
West Collingswood, N. J., St. Luke's..	1917	July 23, 1930	1,775.00
West Lawn, Advent	1929	Dec. 17, 1932	5,000.00
			$63,700.00

SUSQUEHANNA SYNOD

Jersey Shore, Grace	1908	May 27, 1911	$ 500.00
Scranton, Grace	1902	July 1, 1907	1,300.00
			$1,800.00

PITTSBURGH SYNOD

Arnold, Calvary	1923	Dec. 31, 1932	$ 2,430.00
Ashtabula, First	1912	Dec. 31, 1932	1,000.00
Beaver, Holy Trinity	1931	Nov. 24, 1936	2,500.00
Butler, Trinity	1923	Dec. 31, 1932	7,975.00*
Clairton, Trinity	1929	Feb. 1, 1934	5,000.00
Cleveland, Ohio:			
St. Johannis	1924	Dec. 31, 1932	5,000.00
Teutsch	1929	Jan. 31, 1934	5,000.00
East McKeesport, St. John's	1911	Aug. 31, 1933	400.00
Farrell, St. John's	1928	May 2, 1933	4,000.00
Gary, Ind., Honterus	1927	Nov. 10, 1933	8,000.00
Monessen, St. Paul's	1910	Oct. 5, 1915	1,000.00
Pittsburgh:			
First Hungarian	1926	Dec. 31, 1932	5,000.00
Messiah	1915	Dec. 31, 1932	2,000.00
St. James'	1907	May 20, 1932	2,000.00
St. Paul's	1906	Dec. 31, 1932	700.00
Sharon, Trinity	1926	July 6, 1933	3,000.00
Swissvale, St. John's	1908	Dec. 31, 1932	2,000.00
Trafford, St. Mark's	1930	Mar. 28, 1935	3,000.00
Wesleyville, Messiah	1920	Oct. 9, 1933	3,000.00
Pittsburgh Synod	1927	June 10, 1932	4,750.00
Pittsburgh Synod	1930	Mar. 4, 1935	3,225.00
			$70,980.00

ROCKY MOUNTAIN SYNOD

Boulder, Colo., Trinity	1929	Oct. 23, 1934	$10,000.00*
Casper, Wyo., Grace	{1924} {1929}	Dec. 26, 1934	8,000.00*
Colorado Springs, Colo., First	{1894} {1929}	Sept. 20, 1934	4,912.42

Denver, Colo.:

| Messiah | 1924 | Dec. 31, 1932 | 2,000.00 |

| Trinity | {1908, 1928, 1929, 1931} | Apr. 1, 1934 | 15,000.00* |

El Paso, Texas, St. Paul's	1929	Jan. 10, 1933	1,000.00
Laramie, Wyo., First Scandinavian....	1925	July 23, 1930	4,000.00*
Pueblo, Colo., St. Mark's	1906	Aug. 3, 1932	1,500.00

$46,412.42

SLOVAK ZION SYNOD

Camden, N. J., St. John the Baptist....	1927	Aug. 6, 1932	$ 2,000.00
East Pittsburgh, Pa., Trinity	1924	Aug. 27, 1932	3,000.00
Newark, N. J., Holy Trinity	{1930, 1931, 1931}	June 30, 1935 / Jan. 24, 1936 / May 20, 1936	13,000.00

$18,000.00

TEXAS SYNOD

Dallas, First	1923	Dec. 31, 1931	$ 2,427.70
Pawnee, Holy Cross	1927	Sept. 29, 1932	600.00
San Antonio, St. Luke's	{1926, 1930}	Dec. 31, 1932 / May 6, 1935	6,100.00

$9,127.70

VIRGINIA SYNOD

Greeneville, Tenn., Reformation	1932	May 17, 1937	$ 5,000.00
Kingsport, Tenn., Trinity	1928	Nov. 10, 1933	2,500.00
Lynchburg, Va., Trinity	1922	Jan. 3, 1929	5,300.00*
Virginia Synod	1927	Jan. 15, 1928	10,000.00

$22,800.00

WEST VIRGINIA SYNOD

| Charleston, Trinity | 1925 | Nov. 2, 1932 | $ 5,000.00 |
| Clarksburg, St. Mark's | 1926 | Aug. 18, 1929 | 1,400.00* |

$6,400.00

WARTBURG SYNOD

Chicago, Ill.:

Friedens	1923	Nov. 24, 1928	$ 3,000.00
Martin Luther	1926	Dec. 10, 1931	2,000.00
Mont Clare	{1921}	Sept. 6, 1924 / Sept. 6, 1934	2,200.00
St. Johannes	1916	Dec. 19, 1921	550.00

Tabor	1927	May 17, 1932	2,000.00
Cudahy, Wis.	1930	Apr. 17, 1935	3,000.00
Guttenberg, Ia., St. Paul's	1923	Apr. 16, 1931	4,250.00
West Allis, Wis., St. John's	1929	July 28, 1933	2,000.00

$19,000.00

LOANS TO CHURCHES

Synod	Amount
California Synod	$ 52,695.00
Canada Synod	31,069.59
North Carolina Synod	34,000.00
South Carolina Synod	3,975.00
Florida Synod	54,050.00
Georgia-Alabama	33,300.00
Illinois Synod	150,821.17
Indiana Synod	41,340.00
Iowa Synod	37,400.00
Kansas Synod	35,447.97
Manitoba Synod	30,299.00
Maryland Synod	47,000.00
Michigan Synod	104,625.00
Mississippi Synod	2,122.35
Nebraska Synod	33,265.00
German Nebraska Synod	3,475.00
United Lutheran Synod of New York	195,535.90
Northwest Synod	202,123.47
Nova Scotia Synod	5,000.00
Ohio Synod	100,083.33
Pacific Synod	73,667.50
East Pennsylvania Synod	72,525.00
Ministerium of Pennylvania	63,700.00
Susquehanna Synod	1,800.00
Pittsburgh Synod	70,980.00
Rocky Mountain Synod	46,412.42
Slovak Zion Synod	18,000.00
Texas Synod	9,127.70
Virginia Synod	22,800.00
West Virginia Synod	6,400.00
Wartburg Synod	19,000.00

$1,602,040.40

Board Loans		$1,408,139.87
Agency Loans:		
*Women's Missionary Society	$190,900.53	
Church Extension Society, New York Conference	3,000.00	
		193,900.53

$1,602,040.40

xecutive Secretary of the Board, the Rev. Z. M. Corbe, Treasurer of the Board, the Rev. J. F. Seibert, Divisional Secretary of English Missions, and the Rev. E. A. Tappert, Divisional Secretary of Linguistic Interests.

Recommendations 1, 2, 3, 4 and 5 were adopted.

Recommendation 6 was amended by striking out the words "disapproving the contribution of specials on the part of" and inserting therefor the word "urging;" by striking out the words "when such congregations are not paying" and inserting therefor the words "to pay their;" by substituting for the period a comma, and by adding the words "before undertaking specials." The amended recommendation was adopted as follows:

"That the United Lutheran Church go on record as urging congregations and organizations to pay their apportionment in full before undertaking specials."

Instead of recommendation 7, Dr. Hanson presented on behalf of the Board of American Missions the following:

"That in view of the evil influence upon our missions, which are forbidden the use of questionable methods of financing, our United Lutheran Church commends Scriptural giving as the only approved method."

A motion to adopt the original recommendation of the Board of American Missions was lost. The substituted recommendation of the Board of American Missions was adopted.

It was moved and seconded to adopt recommendation 8. The Rev. J. C. Mattes raised a point of order that such a recommendation is not within the prerogative of a Board of the Church. President Knubel ruled on the point of order as follows:

"The point of order is not well taken. The recommendation of the Board is based upon 'the waste of benevolent funds in the duplication of effort in overlapping synods.' Inasmuch as the Board is compelled to live by the benevolent funds which come to it, it is a prerogative of the Board to make recommendations concerning matters affecting such benevolent funds. The Board is here merely appealing to the Church with the request that this Convention take this step because of the impelling motive that touches the life of the Board. The point of order is not well taken."

Recommendation 8 was amended by substituting for the words "to take immediate steps looking toward the consolidation of all such bodies" the words "to encourage steps looking toward the elimination of such overlapping." Recommendation 8 was adopted as amended:

"That in view of the waste of benevolent funds in the duplication of effort in overlapping synods, we request the United Lutheran Church to encourage steps looking toward the elimination of such overlapping."

On motion the following resolution was referred to the Executive Board:

"That we request the Board of American Missions to establish a department or division on rural work and life in said Board."

On motion the Secretary was instructed to dispatch a telegram to the Rev. J. B. Markward, President of the Board of American Missions, in his illness.

It was moved and carried that the report of the auditors be accepted.

The report of the Committee on Evangelism was presented by the Rev. F. C. Fry.

REPORT OF COMMITTEE ON EVANGELISM
I

Twice during the biennium your Committee on Evangelism has confronted its task, to stimulate the Church to achieve its prime, undergirding purpose, which is to conquer lives with the Gospel of eternal salvation in the abundant might of the Holy Spirit. It assembled at the Philadelphia Seminary on December 30, 1930, and at the Muhlenberg Building, Philadelphia, on January 22, 1931. The drafting of its report to this convention was committed to its chairman and secretary with the concurrence of the other members of the committee, who communicated their recommendations by correspondence, in lieu of a subsequent meeting. The motive of this procedure was prudent economy. Each of the appointees to this committee further recognized that he was commissioned to exalt Evangelism in season and out of season in the area of the Church in which he lives and, indeed, wherever his voice could be raised.

Your committee was convinced that the most effective impact would be made upon the consciousness of the Church by a unified and persistent emphasis upon a single phase of Evangelism at this time: recruiting for Christ. In that determination it did not, however, abate its insistence that retention of those already added to the Church and reclamation of the lapsed are also organically vital elements of the evangelistic ministry with which we are charged.

The most conspicuous and blameworthy dereliction of the American Lutheran Church in Evangelism has been in recruiting. Our Church in this
country began with the purpose of seeking out scattered Lutherans and
assembling them into congregations. Too frequently it is still so afflicted
with myopia as not to feel itself imperatively impelled to go out and con-
strain others, not anticipated originally as guests at the Feast of the Kingdom, to come in. Complacency in the enlistment of those who were "born
Lutherans" and anxiety only for those of this select company who have
strayed is the most blasting evidence of secularism which the Lutheran
Church in America has manifested. A sectarian church with a universal
Gospel stands self-condemned.

As *The Lutheran* declared recently in a ringing paragraph: "It is time for
us to cease making the ingathering of our scattered Lutherans the chief
objective of our work of evangelizing. We must see most clearly the foe
in front of us rather than the laggards at the sides and in the rear of the
Church Militant. It is of far less concern that we should have so many
thousands of Lutheran ancestry than that there are forty or fifty million
unbelievers in the United States and Canada as well as hundreds of millions
in the world."

II

In response to the memorial of the West Pennsylvania Synod to the Milwaukee Convention, the committee would call the attention of the petitioning
synod to the fact that not a little literature has been published and distributed
by the committee. In addition, the committee has under advisement the
preparation of additional pamphlets. Its chairman and another of its members were directed to project such supplementary publications.

III

Although the committee does not at this time feel warranted in seeking
permission to make operative the resolution of the Richmond Convention, but
deems it advisable to proceed as heretofore, it rejoices that the Executive
Board has reported adversely on the Milwaukee resolution recommending
the merger of this committee and others with the Board of Inner Missions.
It vigorously records its judgment that the interests committed to it can
most effectively be served by the maintenance of the Committee on Evangelism as a distinct entity.

IV

Because Evangelism is an integral and inalienable function of each Christian congregation and evangelistic projects must, of necessity, be prosecuted
in every locality by those who live there, rather than by a remote agency of
the Church, your committee felt that the most practical and realistic approach to its responsibility would be through a survey of the activities and
accomplishments of the synods in this enterprise. Thus it sought to obtain
a comprehensive view of what was being undertaken throughout the Church
and equipped itself to make the experiences of each synod available to the

others and to the United Lutheran Church in its entirety. Moreover, the Committee on Evangelism realized that, as it is at present constituted, with no full-time secretaries and no budgeted appropriations for extensive and sustained undertakings, such a course was mandatory if it would proceed constructively. It believed further—and the consequences would have confirmed its faith—that such an inquiry in itself would stimulate synodical Committees on Evangelism to increased exertion and vigor.

From the replies to this request for definite data, necessarily supplemented by perusal of the minutes of the conventions of all the synods during 1931 and of several in 1932, your committee has been gratified to ascertain that twenty-four synods have constituted Committees on Evangelism, one of them appointed as a direct result of this committee's investigation. In two others, the promotion and furtherance of Evangelism have been amalgamated into the responsibilities of Inner Mission Committees. In another, there is a Committee on Stewardship and Evangelism. Six apparently and, we believe, censurably, have made no organized provision for this essential interest.

Activities in Evangelism enumerated have revealed the Church's alertness to its mandate to win men's allegiance to their Saviour and the salutary emphasis which is being widely accorded to it.

(1) Institutes on Evangelism, which were commended by this committee in its reports to past conventions of the Church as effective media for the arousing and instruction of laymen and women, have been profitably conducted in many synods, conferences, cities and congregations. Synodical delegations have called attention to the United Lutheran Church's approval of such institutes at its Milwaukee Convention and presidents and secretaries of synods have likewise cited their official notification of it by the secretary of the Church.

(2) The percentage goal for annual increase in communicant membership adopted at Erie has been insistently kept before their congregations by five synods as worthy of honest endeavor.

(3) Gospel preaching missions, conducted by guest-preachers through a general exchange of pulpits or by pastors recommended by synodical committees as especially proficient or by the pastor of each congregation for himself, have been endorsed by eight synods and consistently found effective. The pre-Lenten, Lenten and Reformation seasons are favored. Theater services in the winter and preaching in parks and along city streets in the summer are projected to reach the church-shy unevangelized.

(4) Adult catechization is explicitly advanced by two synods as a markedly productive evangelistic method.

(5) Forums in which Evangelism was the sole and absorbing concern engrossed the attention of four synods, one of which has appointed an annual synodical Day of Evangelism, apart from its sessions, at which a nationally recognized exponent of this phase of the Christian life makes the presentation. Similar forums featured conference conventions in ten others. Evan-

gelism has also been urgently discussed in group assemblies of pastors and Church Councilmen with the synodical and conference presidents in another.

(6) Hortatory and instructive articles concerning Evangelism in five synodical papers have been reported. One synod devotes an entire issue of its monthly publication each year to this purpose.

(7) Six synodical committees have distributed comprehensive programs of congregational Evangelism to the churches. The assembling and vigorous functioning of congregational Committees on Evangelism were central to each. Such committees have been charged with prayer and study, canvasses of communities to locate the unchurched, definite assignments of those to be won, the conservation of church members who move from one parish to another, solicitude for the newly confirmed, the reclamation of the lapsed. At the instance of its synodical committee, an Every Member Evangelistic Visitation, apart from that in which finances are the emphasized objective, was pledged by more than one-half of the congregations of one synod.

(8) Evangelism exhibits and book-tables at synodical conventions; (9) a pronounced, evangelistic note at Church and pastoral anniversaries; and (10) evangelistic instruction in summer schools and Luther Leagues have been approved by experience.

The effectiveness of these undertakings, which has appeared dubious to many because of the intangibles inevitably involved in an exclusively spiritual ministry, has been decisively confirmed. The substantial statistical gains in membership which have made the Lutheran Church conspicuous during the biennium are convincing, as is the marked preponderance of congregations with increasing attendances at divine worship in many synods which tabulate "State of the Church" findings.

V

Men have been disillusioned. They have found no security, only a collapse, in their own presumptuous building of life. A sense of futility oppresses and blights humanity which can be dispelled only by faith. There is an imperative need of refocusing the thought of the world to discover the spiritual as the truly real. The unchanging and ever-applicable principles of the eternal Christ hold the only adequate promise of a solution of the dilemma upon which mankind is impaled. It may be that those who have been frustrated in their preoccupation in material possession will be found more approachable by Christian evangelists. The situation, at least, presents a strategy for a new attack.

"Today is the day of salvation" of the masses in greater numbers than have responded in a generation. Time presses. Humanity is fluid but, perhaps before we assemble again, it will set in new moulds. Will they be Christian? A century may not bring another such limitless opportunity for instilling the mind of Christ in the life of individuals and of society.

In this endeavor, the Church should not represent itself as a specialist in economics nor as an authority in finance. She should have no political pan-aceas to promote. Courageously and confidently let her preach the Redeemer of the Gospel and His way. By the divine alchemy of salvation, she can transform sorrow into joy.

A spiritual offensive is demanded. The times are inopportune for financial drives. They are tremendously opportune for a crusade for souls. In such mutually remote sections of the Church as Chicago, Toledo, Allentown and Charleston, concerted, evangelistic impacts upon entire communities have produced heartening effects. The depression will not bring a spiritual re-vival by itself. It has merely furrowed the ground for the seed. The seed is still the Word of God. Christian congregations must sow it lavishly. The unquenchable and constant expression of their gratitude must be Evangelism.

We should be much in prayer. We must articulate our forces. All of the organizations of our churches and their entire personnel are to be enlisted in this enterprise. Then may the Spirit of God set us aflame!

JOHN C. SEEGERS, *Chairman.*
FRANKLIN CLARK FRY, *Secretary.*

The Rev. A. Pohlman spoke on the work of the Committee on Evangelism.

The Rev. C. K. Fegley called the attention of the Convention to a medal commemorating the bicentennial of the birth of George Washington, and the tricentennial of the death of Gustavus Adolphus.

At five o'clock the Convention adjourned with prayer by the Rev. Mark O. Heller.

Monday Evening

A Memorial Service was held in St. Matthew's Church, Broad and Mt. Vernon Streets, Philadelphia, at eight o'clock Monday evening.

The Rev. F. H. Knubel conducted the service.

A memorial tribute to the Rev. M. G. G. Scherer was presented by the Rev. A. G. Voigt.

A memorial tribute to the Rev. H. E. Jacobs was presented by the Rev. N. R. Melhorn.

The Rev. J. F. Lambert read the Necrology Report.

NECROLOGY REPORT

At the beginning of this our seventh biennial report we pause a moment reverently to recall Doctor M. G. G. Scherer, our former faithful and efficient secretary. He was a Christian gentleman, a truly magnetic and dependable friend.

Our books are closed for the biennium on July first of convention years, but because of the magnificent service rendered the Church by Doctor Henry Eyster Jacobs, and since his call came before this report was completed, we include his record at this time.

Edgar L. Hildebrand had been licensed to preach, but since he still was a student in the seminary we classed him with another student, Stephen Medved, as laymen.

Lists of deceased of constituent synods of our Church were forwarded during the month of May, with the plea that necrologists revise or approve them. The majority of men we addressed favored us with replies, and so we offer the list appended.

There are records of 98 ministers, 12 laymen and 8 laywomen. Copies of each are completed and were sent to the libraries at the Gettysburg and Philadelphia seminaries, respectively.

Name	Birth Place	Birth Date	Ordination	Synod at Death	Death Place	Death Date	Place of Burial	Age Y	M	D	Years of Service
Aksim, Edward F., S. T. M.	Ahrensburg, Esthonia	Feb. 9, 1876	1900	Cn.	Waterloo, Ont., Can.	Oct. 12, 1930	Waterloo, Ont.	54	8	3	30
Amick, George W.	St. Clairsville, Pa	Apr. 16, 1861	1887	WV.	Wheeling, W. Va.	May 11, 1932	Johnstown, Pa.	71	1	25	43
Baetz, Gustav A.	Jueterbogh, Germany	Oct. 27, 1856	1881	NY.	Ozone Park, L. I., N. Y.	Feb. 25, 1931	Kew Gardens, L. I.	74	3	28	41
Baenisch, Paul, A. C. E.	Lissa, Germany	Apr. 5, 1863	1893	Cf.	Gorham, N. Y.	Aug. 20, 1931	Rochester, N. Y.	68	4	15	37
Ball, Jessie W., Ph.D.	Berlin, Pa	Dec. 29, 1870	1870	Cf.	Santa Monica, Calif.	June 17, 1932	Glendale, Calif.	61	5	18	36
Barr, William Penn.	Mauch Chunk, Pa	Feb. 16, 1867	1899	PM.	Trenton, N. J.	Dec. 14, 1930	Elizabethville, Pa.	63	9	28	31
Bartholomew, Henry J. G.	Fort Wayne, Ind.	Apr. 30, 1852	1878	Il.	Chicago, Ill.	Oct. 22, 1930	Chicago, Ill.	78	6	13	40
Baum, William M., Jr., D.D.	Winchester, Va.	June 30, 1858	1880	NY.	Canajoharie, N. Y.	Feb. 5, 1932	Reading, Pa.	73	7	5	52
Beck, Willis	Stone Church, Pa.	Feb. 12, 1876	1902	NW.	Minneapolis, Minn.	June 16, 1932	Zumbrota, Minn.	56	4	4	30
Bickle, Louis A., D.D.	Thurmont, Md.	Nov. 6, 1834	1862	NC.	Concord, N. C.	June 29, 1931	Concord, N. C.	96	7	23	46
Blint, Edward E., D.D.	Lock Haven, Pa.	Apr. 11, 1868	1893	Pg.	Pittsburgh, Pa.	Mar. 24, 1932	Lock Haven, Pa.	63	11	13	36
Bixler, Henry C.	East Berlin, Pa.	Nov. 8, 1863	1891	O.	Fort Wayne, Ind.	July 3, 1930	Fort Wayne, Ind.	66	7	25	28
Blum, Andrew	Cleveland, O.	Apr. 17, 1864	1891	NY.	Rochester, N. Y.	July 1, 1930	Adrian, Mich.	66	2	14	39
Braun, George F., D.D.	Guelscheim, Germany	Aug. 31, 1878	1900	Il.	Mendon, Ill.	July 29, 1930	Mendon, Ill.	51	10	28	30
Brezinski, Frederick, D.D.	Heydick, Germany	Nov. 2, 1872	1895	NY.	New York, N. Y.	June 14, 1932	Troy, N. Y.	59	7	12	37
Brosius, Charles H.	Ashland, Pa.	Sept. 19, 1871	1898	Sq.	Sunbury, Pa.	Aug. 14, 1931	Sunbury, Pa.	59	5	25	33
Brubeck, John J.	Staunton, Va.	Aug. 2, 1867	1895	Md.	Campgaw, N. J.	May 21, 1932	Weyer's Cave, Va.	64	9	19	35
Byers, John E., D.D.	Nr. Williamsport, Md.	May 31, 1871	1898	Md.	Baltimore, Md.	July 20, 1932	Waynesboro, Pa.	59	1	21	32
Catvert, William	Yorkshire, England	Sept. 25, 1837	1909	Ks.	La Mesa, Cal.	June 14, 1931	San Diego, Cal.	93	8	19	22
Clark, George G., D.D.	Nr. Casstown, O.	Mar. 4, 1857	1890	RM.	Rochester, Minn.	Dec. 19, 1931	Dayton, O.	74		15	41
Craun, William A., B.D.	Mt. Sidney, Va.	Nov. 28, 1880	1914	SC.	Portsmouth, Va.	Dec. 21, 1931	Mt. Sidney, Va.	51	0	23	15
Cromer, James M., D.D.	Nr. Muncie, Ind.	Oct. 3, 1850	?	RM.	Casper, Wyo.	Nov. 27, 1930	Kansas City, Mo.	80	1	24	
Curran, Joseph D., D.D.	Windsor, Pa.	Sept. 3, 1881	1911	Md.	Monrovia, Liberia.	Sept. 20, 1930	Liberia, Africa.	49	0	17	19
Dahlke, Rudolph C.	Palmyra, Mo.	Sept. 14, 1893	1918	Ia.	Nr. New Paris, Ohio.	June 2, 1932	Sheffield, Iowa.	38	8	24	14
Day, Charles H.	Nr. Annapolis, Md.	Sept. 16, 1862	1887	Cf.	Riverside, Calif.	May 11, 1932	Riverside, Calif.	69	7	27	35
Diener, George J.	Nr. Shannondale, Pa.	Nov. 1861	1891	Pg.	Butler, Pa.	Feb. 15, 1931	Prospect, Pa.	69	2	29	40
Dietterich, Elmer E.	Millville, Pa.	June 5, 1882	1890	Cn.	Montgomery, Pa.	Apr. 22, 1932	Montgomery, Pa.	49	9	24	32
Endy, George P., M.A.I.	Reading, Pa.	Mar. 14, 1849	1902	O.	Guelph, Ont., Can.	Aug. 16, 1931	Guelph, Ont.	81	5	11	29
Ernsberger, Cyrus S.	Nr. Lucas, O.	Mar. 9, 1853	1873	Ks.	Cleveland, O.	Jan. 15, 1931	Springfield, O.	77		1	58
Exline, Martin L.	Sandyville, O.	Mar. 23, 1860	1888	Ks.	Hutchinson, Kan.	July 10, 1930	Strafford, Kan.	70	4		27
Fasold, John C., Ph.D.	Sunbury, Pa.	Aug. 23, 1869	1896	Sq.	Mifflinburg, Pa.	Sept. 1, 1931	Selinsgrove, Pa.	62	0		30
Fryberger, Anthony Z.	Canton, O.	Oct. 1, 1844	1894	Mh.	Warsaw, Ind.	July 17, 1931	Warsaw, Ind.	86	8	16	26
Gaudian, Martin W.	Ratibor, Germany	Aug. 25, 1861	1886	NY.	New Britain, Conn.	Feb. 23, 1931	New Britain, Conn.	69	5	28	45
Gersib, George	Wartenburg, Germany	Dec. 19, 1881	1912	GN.	Lipscomb, Tex.	July 19, 1929	Enid, Okla.	47	5	27	17
Goll, George P.	Philadelphia, Pa.	Oct. 28, 1868	1896	FP.	Trenton, N. J.	Oct. 3, 1931	Fox Chase, Pa.	62	11	24	35
Halverstadt, Rufus A., B.D.	Nr. Leetonia, O.	Sept. 18, 1866	1894	O.	Cleveland, O.	June 8, 1931	Leetonia, O.	69	8	10	37
Hankey, Benjamin F., D.D.	Brick Church, Pa.	Apr. 27, 1854	1899	Pg.	Pittsburg, Pa.	Nov. 5, 1930	Mt. Pleasant, Pa.	64	9	17	31
Hantz, Jacob M., D.D.	Madison, Pa.	Jan. 21, 1844	1868	O.	Nr. Alliance, O.	Aug. 3, 1931	Greensburg, Pa.	87	3	12	63
Hartman, James A.	Adams Co., Pa.	Sept. 27, 1854	1881	Sq.	Sunbury, Pa.	Jan. 13, 1931	Sunbury, Pa.	76	3	16	50

Name	Birth Place	Birth Date	Ordination	Synod at Death	Death Place	Death Date	Place of Burial	Age Y	M	D	Years of Service
Heffner, William C., Ph.D.	Friedensburg, Pa.	Feb. 14, 1865	1896	Ks.	Salina, Kan.	July 29, 1931	Tremont, Pa.	66	5	15	35
Hellwege, Adolph H. F., D.D.	Krautsand, Germany	Mar. 3, 1866	1887	FM.	Wildwood, N. J.	Oct. 2, 1930	Philadelphia, Pa.	64	6	29	43
Hesse, William, D.D.	Martinsburg, W. Va.	Oct. 9, 1856	1888	WP.	Martinsburg, W. Va.	Dec. 9, 1930	Martinsburg, W. Va.	74	2	0	16
Heissler, John.	Trenton, N. J.	Feb. 15, 1863	1887	PM.	Trenton, N. J.	Sept.16, 1931	Trenton, N. J.	68	7	1	32
Heydenreich, Otto E.	Mecklenburg, Germany	July 11, 1878	1901	NY.	Hartford, Conn.	Dec. 4, 1931	Meriden, Conn.	54	4	23	30
Hilbish, William H., D.D.	Shamokin, Pa.	Oct. 28, 1867	1892	Sq.	McClure, Pa.	Jan. 19, 1932	Northumberland, Pa.	64	2	21	39
Hill, John J., D.D.	Leechburg, Pa.	Jan. 27, 1864	1891	Pg.	Gettysburg, Pa.	May 29, 1931	Gettysburg, Pa.	67	3	22	40
Hoffman, I., Chantry, D.D.	Norristown, Pa.	Apr. 13, 1864	1892	PM.	Philadelphia, Pa.	May 21, 1931	Glenside, Pa.	67	1	16	39
Hoshour, Edward E.	Glen Rock, Pa.	Sept. 18, 1863	1888	PM.	Gettysburg, Pa.	Feb. 7, 1931	Glen Rock, Pa.	67	5	5	41
Horner, Daniel M., D.D.	Lewisburg, O.	Nov. 22, 1849	1881	Id.	Cicero, Ind.	July 7, 1931	Brookville, O.	81	7	15	50
Huebner, Julius, S.T.M.	Gablonz, Bohemia	Oct. 30, 1887	1910	GN.	Lincoln, Neb.	Jan. 20, 1932	Lincoln, Nebr.	44	2	20	22
Hunton, William L., Ph.D., D.D.	Morrisburg, Can.	Feb. 16, 1864	1889	PM.	Philadelphia, Pa.	Oct. 12, 1930	Bethlehem, Pa.	66	7	26	41
Jackson, Harry A.	Nr. Organ Cave, W. Va.	Mar. 28 1897	1926	SC.	Newberry, S. C.	Jan. 31, 1931	Nr. Columbia, S. C.	33	10	3	6
Jacobs, Henry Eyster, D.D., S.T.D., LL.D.	Gettysburg, Pa.	Nov. 10, 1844	1865	PM.	Philadelphia, Pa.	July 7, 1932	Gettysburg, Pa.	87	7	27	67
Jenkins, John T.	Mahanoy City, Pa.	May 27, 1885	1913	Md.	Hanover, Pa.	May 5, 1931	Hanover, Pa.	45	11	8	18
Jones, Frank.	Choharie, N. Y.	Sept. 30, 1872	1904	NY.	Airmont, N. Y.	Nov. 14, 1929	Manorton, N. Y.	57	1	15	25
Kaehler, Frederick A., D.D.	Erie, Pa.	Sept. 21, 1850	1874	NY.	Buffalo, N. Y.	Jan. 24, 1931	Buffalo, N. Y.	80	4	3	57
Kleckner, Harry C., B. D.	Loysville, Pa.	July 11, 1878	1907	Mh.	South Whitley, Ind.	Sept.22, 1931	Constantine, Mich.	53	2	11	24
Klick, Aaron H.	Lancaster Co., Pa.	Mar. 12, 1860	1900	PM.	New Ringgold, Pa.	Dec. 3, 1930	Pine Grove, Pa.	70	8	11	30
Koehler, Theodore J.	Petrograd, Russia	Feb. 5, 1852	1874	GC.	Egg Harbor City, N. J.	Oct. 24, 1929	Egg Harbor City, N. J.	77	8	19	55
Koogle, H. A.	Nr. Myersville, Md.	June 10, 1847	1889	Ks.	Chapman, Kan.	June 8, 1932	Chapman, Kan.	84	11	28	10
Kopenhaver, William M.	Elizabethville, Pa.	Mar. 20, 1866	1900	PM.	Harrisburg, Pa.	Mar.20, 1932	Lykens Valley, Pa.	66	0	0	28
Leisenring, Philip.	Guntur, India	Dec. 8, 1881		IS.	Nadadavole, India	June 24, 1931	Guntur, India	49	6	16	..
Lentz, J. Nelson, D.L., B.D.	Glen Rock, Pa.	Dec. 23, 1861	1892	Mh.	Detroit, Mich.	Oct. 6, 1931	Detroit, Mich.	69	9	13	39
Legler, Carl.	Wolga Colony, Russia	Aug. 25, 1859	1902	Cf.	Fresno, Calif.	July 19, 1930	Fresno, Calif.	70	10	24	26
Leonard, Homer C.	Nr. Terre Haute, O.	Aug. 22, 1897	1922	O.	Roswell, N. M.	Apr. 5, 1931	St. Paris, O.	33	7	13	30
Lerch, John F.	Clarion Co., Pa.	Feb. 28, 1850	1879	O.	Warren, O.	Nov. 19, 1929	Nr. Ravenna, O.	79	8	21	44
Loch, J. W., Ph.D.	Kusel, Germany	Aug. 1, 1859	1881	L. I.	Southold L. I.	Dec. 2, 1929	Newark, N. J.	70	4	1	31
Miller, Christian.	Reading, Pa.	May 13, 1870	1900	PM.	Coplay, Pa.	Feb. 7, 1931	Allentown, Pa.	60	8	24	36
Minemeier, John J.	Nr. Warrior's Mark, Pa.	Oct. 11, 1856	1891	NY.	Philadelphia, Pa.	May 2, 1931	Dansville, N. Y.	74	6	21	40
Myers, Uriah, D.D.	Nr. Easton, Pa.	Jan. 23, 1847	1869	Sq.	Danville, Pa.	Mar. 31, 1932	Muncy, Pa.	85	2	8	51
Uchsenford, Solomon E., D.D.	New Hanover, Pa.	Nov. 8, 1855	1879	PM.	Selinsgrove, Pa.	June 19, 1932	Selinsgrove, Pa.	76	7	11	3
Plagemann, Martin.	Jabel, Germany	Apr. 10, 1900	1928	NY.	Union City, Conn.	Oct. 6, 1931	Naugatuck, Conn.	31	5	26	30
Reber, Owen.	Nr. Shoemakersville, Pa.	Oct. 3, 1858	1888	PM.	Fredericksburg, Pa.	Oct. 5, 1931	Fredericksburg, Pa.	73	0	2	31
Rice, Samuel L.	Virginia	Jan. 4, 1857	1888	Sq.	Seven Stars, Pa.	Oct. 8, 1930	Seven Stars, Pa.	73	9	4	

Name	Birth Place	Birth Date	Ordination	Synod at Death	Death Place	Death Date	Place of Burial	Age Y	Age M	Age D	Years of Service
Richardson, Harvey A.	Shanesville, O.	Nov. 27, 1855	1906	Il.	Petosky, Mich.	Sept. 17, 1930	Columbus, O.	71	10	20	24
Ringer, Calvin J.	Nr. Summit Mills, Pa.	Dec. 10, 1855	1894	Ia.	Omaha, Nebr.	Apr. 28, 1931	Wayne, Nebr.	71	4	18	36
Roof, Francis K., Jr.	Catawba Co., N. C.	Nov. 23, 1904	1930	SC.	Boyden's Arbor, S. C.	June 30, 1931	Mt. Hermon, S. C.	26	7	7	1
Roth, David A.	Albrightsville, Pa.	Mar. 16, 1866	1898	PM.	Palmerton, Pa.	June 6, 1931	Towamensing, Pa.	65	3	0	28
Samuel, Ernest W. C., O.	Hanover, Germany	Aug. 8, 1846	1878	Wg.	Trinidad, Colo.	Dec. 9, 1931	Trinidad, Colo.	85	4	1	42
Sandt, George W., D.D., LL.D.	Belfast, Pa.	Feb. 22, 1854	1883	PM.	Allentown, Pa.	Jan. 8, 1931	Easton, Pa.	76	10	16	47
Schantz, Joseph S.	Hosensack, Pa.	Jan. 23, 1875	1904	PM.	Philadelphia, Pa.	Mar. 26, 1931	Spinnerstown, Pa.	56	2	3	27
Scherer, Melanchthon G. G., D.D.	Catawba Co., N. C.	Mar. 16, 1861	1883	SC.	New York, N. Y.	Mar. 9, 1932	Charleston, S. C.	70	11	23	49
Schoch, William H.	Mifflinburg, Pa.	Feb. 16, 1839	1860	Sq.	Rochester, N. Y.	Dec. 20, 1930	Bellefont, Pa.	91	10	16	50
Scholl, Daniel, D.D.				Ks.	Seattle, Wash.						
Schwab, Arthur P.	Glenco Mills, N. Y.	Dec. 26, 1867	1918	NY.	Rochester, N. Y.	Aug. 20, 1931	Herkimer, N. Y.	63	7	24	15
Scott, William D. E.	Adams Co., Pa.	Feb. 6, 1856	1883	Md.	Manchester, Pa.	Dec. 26, 1930	Gettysburg, Pa.	74	10	20	40
Seabrook, William L., L.L.B.	Frederick, Md.	Nov. 15, 1856	1889	Md.	Westminster, Md.	Jan. 23, 1931	Gettysburg, Pa.	74	2	7	42
Shindle, Henry C.	Lancaster, Pa.	Dec. 10, 1833	1865	EP.	Narberth, Pa.	July 28, 1931	Lancaster, Pa.	92	7	18	48
Sorensen, P. A.	Schleswig Holstein, Germany	Mar. 5, 1886	1909	Il.	Metropolis, Ill.	Jan. 20, 1931	Metropolis, Ill.	44	10	15	22
Stefey, Sidney D.	Rural Retreat, Va.	Aug. 6, 1867	1890	Mh.	Nr. Camden, Ind.	Apr. 25, 1932	Mt. Pizgah, Ind.	64	8	19	42
Stetler, Isaac H., Ph.D.	Philadelphia, Pa.	Mar. 14, 1869	1895	O.	Barberton, O.	Sept. 16, 1930	Doylestown, O.	61	6	21	35
Streich, Carl I.	Heimthal, S. Russia	Jan. 16, 1873	1896	PM.	Wilkes-Barre, Pa.	Apr. 5, 1931	Philadelphia, Pa.	58	2	20	35
Trabert, George H., D.D.	Lancaster Co., Pa.	Oct. 16, 1843	1870	NW.	Minneapolis, Minn.	Sept. 16, 1931	Minneapolis, Minn.	87	11	0	50
Turner, Joseph H., D.D., LL.D.	Franklin Co., Va.	Oct. 23, 1841	1870	Md.	Baltimore, Md.	June 25, 1930	Baltimore, Md.	88	0	8	38
Ulrich, William S., D.D.	Selinsgrove, Pa.	Feb. 10, 1873	1899	Sq.	Philadelphia, Pa.	June 3, 1932	Selinsgrove, Pa.	59	8	23	33
Wenrich, Samuel	Lancaster Co., Pa.	Apr. 9, 1844	1884	PM.	Allentown, Pa.	Mar. 30, 1931	Allentown, Pa.	86	11	29	29
Wupper, Frederick, D.D.	Boehle, Germany	July 1, 1866	1891	GN.	Hot Springs, S. D.	June 26, 1932	Hooper, Nebr.	65	11	17	34
Zimbeck, Silas A.	Sharon, Wis.	Sept. 4, 1860	1893	Il.	Decatur, Ill.	Aug. 8, 1931	Sharon, Wis.	70	11	4	36
Laymen											
Albrecht, Frederick W.	Massillon, O.	Apr. 3, 1861		O.	Akron, O.	Jan. 5, 1932	Akron, O.	70	9	2	
Finley, James G.	Philadelphia, Pa.	Jan. 10, 1846		PM.	Chestnut Hill, Pa.	May 25, 1932	Philadelphia, Pa.	86	4	15	
Fritch, David D., M.D., F.M.	Berks Co., Pa.	May 4, 1848		PM.	Macungie, Pa.	Sept. 10, 1931	Macungie, Pa.	83	7	6	
*Hildebrand, Edgar L.	Baltimore, Md.	May 4, 1905	1930	Md.	Gettysburg, Pa.	Dec. 7, 1930.	Nr. Baltimore, Md.	25	7	6	
Maron, Gotthard I.	Zechlin, Germany	May 17, 1869		Mn.	Winnipeg, Can.	July 13, 1931.	Winnipeg, Can.	62	3	26	
McCreary, Harry	Leechburg, Pa.	Oct. 30, 1863		Pg.	Indiana, Pa.	Aug. 19, 1930.	Indiana, Pa.	66	9	19	
Medved, Stephen	Mahanoy City, Pa.	May 6, 1907		PM.	Philadelphia, Pa.	Apr. 23, 1932.	Mahanoy City, Pa.	24	11	17	
Moldenke, Richard, E. M., Ph.D.	Watertown, Wis.	Nov. 1, 1864		NY.	Plainfield, N. J.	Nov. 17, 1930.	White Plains, N. Y.	66	0	16	
Reinert, Henry H.	Greshville, Pa.	July 17, 1852		PM.	Boyertown, Pa.	Apr. 3, 1932.	Boyertown, Pa.	79	8	16	
Snyder, James M.	Hilltown, Pa.	Jan. 2, 1857		PM.	Philadelphia, Pa.	Apr. 17, 1932.	Philadelphia, Pa.	75	3	15	
Strohecker, Robert L.	Harrisburg, Pa.	Jan. 16, 1845		PM.	Reading, Pa.	Mar. 31, 1932.	Reading, Pa.	67	2	15	
Young, George H., Prof.	Upshur Co., W. Va.	Dec. 12, 1849		PX.	Los Angeles, Calif.	Sept. 15, 1930.	Springfield, O.	80	9	3	
*Licensed 1930											
Laywomen											
Baldwin, Maud Junkin	St. Louis, Mo.	Mar 20, 1874		PM.	Philadelphia, Pa.	Nov. 6, 1930.	St. Louis, Mo.	56	7	16	
Eisenhardt, Pauline	Nr. Tuebingen, Germany			PM.	Interlaken, Fla.	July 3, 1930.	Interlaken, Fla.	69	9	5	
Fry, Laura F.		July 21, 1863		PM.	Germantown, Pa.	Jan. 16, 1931.	Germantown, Pa.	67	5	25	
Kugler, Anna S., M.D.	Ardmore, Pa.	July 17, 1867		PM.	Philadelphia, Pa.	Oct. 22, 1930.	"Old Trappe", Church.	64	3	5	
Leamer, Ruth Richards	Geary, Kan.	Apr. 19, 1856		EP.	Guntur, India.	July 26, 1930.	Guntur, India.	74	3	7	
Seegers, Sarah Adelaide	Charleston, S. C.	July 28, 1871		WV.	Nr. Lyons, Nebr.	Aug. 17, 1931.	Sioux City, Nebr.	60	0	19	
Wattles, Mrs. William W.	Charleston, S. C.	July 24, 1867		SC.	Columbia, S. C.	Dec. 12, 1930.	Columbia, S. C.	63	4	18	
Woerner, Mrs. Lydia	Spring Station, Tx.	Sept. 28, 1860		Pg.	Pittsburgh, Pa.	June 2, 1932.	Allegheny, Pa.	82			

Humbly submitted,
JAMES F. LAMBERT, *Necrologist.*

The congregation stood in solemn attention during the reading of the report.

EIGHTH SESSION

BENJAMIN FRANKLIN HOTEL.
Philadelphia, Pennsylvania.
Tuesday, October 18, 1932, 8.45 A. M.

Matins were conducted by the Rev. L. A. Thomas.

The Convention was called to order by the President.

The Minutes of the Sixth and Seventh Sessions were read by the Secretary and declared approved.

Mr. H. F. Heuer, Chairman of Committee of Tellers No. 1, reported that Mr. Charles Steele received a majority of the votes cast for a member of the Executive Committee of the Laymen's Movement. The President declared Mr. Steele elected.

Mr. C. J. Driever, Chairman of Committee of Tellers No. 2, reported elections as follows:

For the *Board of Foreign Missions* each of the following received a majority of the votes cast:

Rev. Robert D. Clare
Rev. Chas. A. Dennig
Rev. S. W. Herman
Rev. S. T. Nicholas
John J. Bruns
Chas. H. Dahmer
Claude L. Peterman

The President declared them elected.

For the *Board of American Missions* each of the following received a majority of the votes cast:

Rev. F. O. Evers
Rev. L. H. Larimer
Rev. H. J. Pflum
Rev. L. W. Steckel
Horace W. Bikle
Henry F. Heuer
John A. Hoober

The President declared them elected.

For the *Board of Northwestern Missions* each of the following received a majority of the votes cast:

Rev. F. O. Evers
Rev. L. H. Larimer
Rev. H. J. Pflum
Rev. L. W. Steckel
Horace W. Bikle
Henry F. Heuer
John A. Hoober

The President declared them elected.

For the *Immigrants Mission Board* each of the following received a majority of the votes cast:

Rev. F. O. Evers   Horace W. Bikle
Rev. L. H. Larimer   Henry F. Heuer

The President declared them elected.

For the *West Indies Mission Board* each of the following received a majority of the votes cast:

Rev. F. O. Evers   Horace W. Bikle
Rev. L. H. Larimer   Henry F. Heuer
Rev. H. J. Pflum   John A. Hoober
Rev. L. W. Steckel

The President declared them elected.

For the *Board of Education* each of the following received a
majority of the votes cast:

Rev. G. M. Diffenderfer   C. J. Driever
Rev. P. H. Krauss   L. C. Hassinger
Rev. W. H. Traub   Ralph D. Owen
Rev. A. R. Wentz

The President declared them elected.

For the *Inner Mission Board* each of the following received
a majority of the votes cast:

Rev. S. E. Greenawalt   Robert F. Bowe
Rev. Harold S. Miller   H. C. Hoffman
Rev. J. L. Sieber

The President declared them elected.

For the *Board of Publication* each of the following received a
majority of the votes cast:

Rev. Henry Anstadt   Charles Baum
Rev. John W. Horine   M. P. Moller, Jr.
Rev. Paul E. Scherer   Claude T. Reno
Rev. Russell D. Snyder

The President declared them elected.

For the *Board of Ministerial Pensions and Relief* each of the
following received a majority of the votes cast:

Paul F. Myers   Albert F. Sittloh
F. Seiberling   Belding B. Slifer
                    D. F. Yost

The President declared them elected.

For the *Parish and Church School Board* each of the following received a majority of the votes cast:

Rev. J. D. M. Brown
Rev. M. Hadwin Fischer
Rev. F. R. Knubel

George M. Jones

The President declared them elected.

For the *Board of Deaconess Work* each of the following received a majority of the votes cast:

Rev. George N. Lauffer
Rev. William A. Wade

Harry R. Hagerty
I. Searles Runyon
Edgar W. Young

The President declared them elected.

For the *Board of the National Lutheran Home for the Aged* each of the following received a majority of the votes cast:

Rev. Henry Anstadt
Rev. Oscar F. Blackwelder
Rev. J. L. Frantz
Rev. J. E. Harms
Rev. John T. Huddle
Rev. Richard Schmidt
Rev. H. E. Snyder
Rev. F. R. Wagner
Rev. John Weidley

L. Russell Alden
W. K. Butler
F. E. Cunningham
H. T. Domer
W. H. Finckel
F. W. Kakel
Harry L. Snyder

The President declared them elected, and stated that one layman was yet to be elected to the Board of Directors of the National Lutheran Home for the Aged.

By unanimous consent it was ordered that Committee of Tellers No. 2 conduct an election by ballot for one additional layman as a member of the Board of Directors of the National Lutheran Home for the Aged immediately after the close of the morning session today.

Moved and carried that the balloting be confined to the two names which had received the highest number of votes without being elected.

The report of the Committee on Lutheran Brotherhoods was presented by the Rev. W. C. Schaeffer, Jr., a member of the Committee.

REPORT OF THE COMMITTEE ON LUTHERAN BROTHERHOOD

(For action on the recommendation in this report see p. 388.)

Through the medium of your Committee:

THE BROTHERHOOD OF THE UNITED LUTHERAN CHURCH REPORTS

The Practice of the Four Objectives

Believing that the greatest service that the Brotherhood can render to the Church is the practive of the Four Objectives, special emphasis has been laid on the importance of putting these objectives into operation.

During the biennium remarkable results have been secured in each of these lines of activity. Milwaukee, Chicago, Houston, Niagara Falls Conference, and in many other towns and districts the men have accomplished real things for the advancement of the Kingdom. In a special campaign in Chicago the Family Altar was established in four thousand homes, and in an evangelistic campaign fifteen hundred people were added to the Church. This result, in perhaps a modified form, has been secured in a number of churches where the Brotherhood has been taking the leadership in Christian work.

It is most encouraging to find that many laymen have changed their attitude toward the Church from one of indifference to active participation and definite service. It is more and more evident that the laymen want a real part in the work of the Church. The Brotherhood has come to them with a definite program, a challenging task, and they are responding to this call in ever-increasing numbers. The Brotherhood is now the center of the activity of the laymen, and regarded with great favor. It has attained the point of being a popular movement, and outlet for the pent up desire to have a real job in the Church. More and more pastors are becoming enthusiastic supporters and leaders of the men in these special lines of work.

Holding Its Own

The past biennium has been one of special difficulty, not only in missionary and educational interests, but for all the agencies of the Church as well. Many Brotherhoods in the different denominations have lost heavily. We praise God that we have held our own in numbers and advanced steadily in favor in the Church, in winning devoted advocates of the Brotherhood, in capable leaders, in the operation of our plans and projects and in general efficiency. Synodical and Conference Organizations have been formed and are functioning along true Brotherhood lines. While here and there Brotherhoods have felt compelled to fall out of line on account of the stringency of the times, others have taken the place, and the work has gone forward.

Our greatest hindrance lies in the spirit of separatism. Though the Brotherhood is the agency of the United Lutheran Church, and is charged with the task of organizing and combining the men for definite service in the Kingdom, still there are many men's organizations that do not seem to realize the importance of this combination and consider that they do not need to have a definite union with the men of the Church in general. If all of our men's organizations of every kind would come into union with the Brotherhood of the Church, we could report a great army of men, organized and being trained for definite service for the Kingdom. We could in that case secure great results in our missionary, educational and eleemosynary work.

The membership fee cannot be accused of standing in the way, since this is less than ten cents per month. No, it is still the spirit of separatism that has so many times divided and kept our Lutheran forces apart. It is the narrowness of vision in failing to see that in union there is strength and in cooperation there comes achievement. With this difficulty out of the way we can reach the goal of masculine leadership, of masculine aggressiveness, of masculine determination and power in the Church.

The Expansion of the Mulberry Lutheran Home

(For a detailed account of the history of this project we refer you to the minutes of the 1930 Convention.)

About three and a half years have elapsed since the first definite step was taken to establish the Mulberry Lutheran Home for aged Lutherans, at Mulberry, Indiana. In so short a period the buildings have been renovated and the Home opened for guests. We now have twenty-six members in the family, and additional applications coming every month, thus showing the special need of this work. The property has lent itself splendidly to this work, and we have now at Mulberry one of the finest Old People's Homes of any denomination. The total cost to us, including the first cost, furnishings and renovation, is approximately forty-five thousand dollars. If we should have undertaken to reproduce this property it would have cost us not less than a hundred thousand dollars. We rejoice, therefore, in being able to have a part in this beautiful service of love, in providing a haven of rest and peace for our beloved fathers and mothers. The Home is incorporated under the laws of the State of Indiana and is authorized by the three synods named.

The Establishment of the Iron Mountain Lutheran School for Boys and Young Men

In 1928 the Secretary of the Inner Mission Board wrote to us, requesting that we investigate the possibility of the establishment of a school for boys and young men in the mountains of Virginia, at Konnarock, adjacent to the Girl's Training School supported by the Women's Missionary Society. A full and complete report of the whole situation was submitted to the Convention in Milwaukee, October, 1930. After due consideration the Convention voted unanimously to undertake the establishment of this school.

Meetings were held by the Executive Committee of the Brotherhood and representatives of the Inner Mission Board to carry out the action of the 1930 Convention. A Board of Directors of the school was formed, consisting of members of the Inner Mission Board, of the Brotherhood and a representative from the Synod of Virginia. This Board had a meeting and proceeded to arrange to open the school. Rev. C. L. Miller, D.D., pastor of our church at Chattanooga, Tenn., was elected superintendent, and the school was opened October 1, 1931, and in due time was incorporated under the laws of the State of Virginia.

On account of the stringency of the financial condition, it was found necessary to limit the number of students to twelve. This number has since been increased by one. To our surprise we were immediately overwhelmed with applications by boys and young men from the mountains to get into this school. We now have over two hundred applications on hand.

The first school year is a matter of history now. The young men who were members of the school have shown a fine spirit, in every way co-operating to make the year a success. We rejoice especially that, under the direction of the superintendent, all the young men have been received into our congregation at Konnarock.

The property was dedicated in August, and is now a full-fledged school. The young men are being taught how to develop their mountain farms and establish normal Christian homes.

A great mountain district has fallen to our lot as a Church to redeem, not only agriculturally, but primarily to bring the people into the Kingdom of God. It is our responsibility and it is our great privilege and opportunity as well. We can thus not only strengthen the churches organized by Pastor Killinger in the mountains, but establish many new congregations and thus evangelize the whole district. We submit that this cause is one of the most appealing, necessary and important interests that has been committed to our Church, and the Brotherhood urgently asks that all men, whether in the Brotherhood or not, join hands with us in accomplishing this work to which our Lord has called us.

The past two years have been marked by a strenuous endeavor to meet the situation of reduced earnings or no earnings at all on the part of many Brotherhood men. In spite of all that could be done, our losses have been considerable. However, we thank God that we can report that others have taken their places. Indeed the month of December witnessed the largest increase of enrollment of any month in our history.

A Larger Income Necessary

However, on account of the financial conditions, and also because for the first time the Brotherhood has functioned on the income of the membership fee alone, during the year October, 1931, to October, 1932, it was necessary to limit our activities in order to avoid a debt. The expansion of the work is making a larger income necessary. We feel confident that this will come as Brotherhoods pass from the spirit of separatism to loyalty to the Church, and unite with the central organization.

This financial condition also has made it especially difficult to carry forward our special projects. Especially is this true of the School. Several times it seemed that we could not proceed, but each time answers to prayers came and we were able to meet the emergency. The superintendent has shown a heroic spirit in these times. By severe economy and self-denial on the part of all the help and by the splendid response from many men and organizations in the Church, we have been able to proceed. Through the forebearance of men to whom funds were due, and through reducing our budget to the lowest possible point, we have been able to keep the school open, but it is high time that our income must be increased, not only to meet the present needs, but also to admit young men from the mountains who are urging that they be accepted.

We should have twenty thousand dollars this coming year and a like amount for the year following, to enable us to meet the opportunity our Lord has given us at Konnarock. This sum is a small amount when it is divided among the men's organizations and other groups interested in this important work. It is not a question of our ability but of our action. If we can get responses from the organizations interested in this project, this goal will be reached. We therefore urge that every man reading this report should take the matter up in his church and arrange to make such a contribution as the Church may be able. People need but know the story of the mountain folk and of the opportunity that has come to us as a Church, and we are persuaded that the money will be forthcoming to carry this work forward.

Our Brotherhood joined with other Lutheran Bodies in a National Convention held in the city of Pittsburgh, October, 1931, under the auspices of The Federation of Lutheran Brotherhoods. The desire for a United American Lutheran Church was the predominant note. The convention did much good in that it brought to the fore our essential unity in the arousing of laymen for a larger and more effective part in the work of the Church, in giving a better appreciation of our Church and a larger vision of the place of the Lutheran Church in America. Since this organization has no legislative power nothing occurred requiring the consideration of this body.

We thank God for the privilege of serving our Lord in this work, and assure the Church that it is our earnest and sincere purpose to develop the Brotherhood that it may continue to serve the Church in ever increasing effectiveness and power.

H. E. ISENHOUR, *President.*
J. W. KAPP, *Executive Secretary.*

RECOMMENDATION

It is recommended that this inspiring report of the Brotherhood be received with a vote of hearty appreciation for Brotherhood leaders and executives and with enthusiastic approval of the Brotherhood's program and policies.

Respectfully submitted,

DAVID A. DAVY, *Chairman.*

Dr. Schaeffer introduced the Rev. C. L. Miller, who is in charge of the Iron Mountain Lutheran School, and Mr. J. Milton Deck, who addressed the Convention.

The recommendation of the Committee was adopted.

The following resolution was presented, and on motion was referred to the Executive Board with commendation and power to act:

"That the Brotherhoods of Constituent Synods and Conferences of the United Lutheran Church collaborate with the Board of Education and the Committee on Publicity in a publicity program on benevolence, by the use of motion pictures and a central exchange of the same for visual education."

At this time the special order, the report of the Commission on Investments, as to its investigation of the Treasurer's Report and the Auditor's Certificate of the Board of Ministerial Pensions and Relief, was presented by Dr. E. Clarence Miller, Chairman of the Commission.

REPORT OF THE COMMISSION ON INVESTMENTS ON THE FINANCIAL REPORT OF THE BOARD OF MINISTERIAL PENSIONS AND RELIEF

(For action on the recommendation in this report see p. 390.)

Your Commission has held two prolonged meetings, one with officers and members of the Board of Ministerial Pensions and Relief who have accorded their full co-operation.

Because of the scope of the resolution adopted by the Church, much more time will be needed to complete our work. However, we present the following findings and conclusions at this point as required by the resolution as finally adopted.

I

We have in our minutes a statement made by the mover of the resolution to investigate the Board's financial report, as follows: "There is not any question and there has not been any question with respect to the personal or official integrity of any member of the Board." We desire at the outset to emphasize this point because of erroneous conclusions which may be drawn from discussions on the floor of the Convention.

Your Commission recognizes that the officers, and particularly the treasurer of the Board, have put forth a great amount of conscientious effort in connection with the endowment funds in their charge.

II

At the Erie Convention of the Church in 1928, the Treasurer of the Board made a statement to the Convention as to the manner in which it proposed to invest up to $1,000,000 of the Board's funds in guaranteed first mortgages.

At the Milwaukee Convention of the Church in 1930, the report of the Board, including full details of mortgages and other investments held, was placed before the Church.

III

The reports of the treasurer authenticated by competent auditors, as found in the Minutes of the Conventions of the Church, must be accepted as prima facie evidence of the financial transactions of the Board and of the situation as pertaining to its investments.

In the absence of competent proof to the contrary, we accept them as faithful and accurate records.

IV

Your Commission concludes from its preliminary investigation that the methods pursued by the Board in the investment of the funds committed to its charge may be open to question in the following specific particulars:

1. Its mortgage investments do not appear to be well diversified. A large proportion of its funds were placed in mortgages on properties located in one section of Philadelphia, all guaranteed by the Bank of Philadelphia and Trust Company, later merged with the Bankers Trust Company, which has since closed its doors.

2. The investment of $500,000 in any one mortgage appears too large, considering the size of the fund at the Board's disposal. (It should be noted in passing that the one mortgage of this amount held by the Board is not in default and appears to be substantially secured.)

3. It appears that the Board did not have an adequate organization for an independent appraisal of properties and relied wholly on the bank which guaranteed and sold the mortgages to the Board.

V

All institutional holders of large endowments may be expected to suffer some losses in this period of unusual stress. This Board will, in all probability, be no exception to the rule. The degree of loss only time can determine.

Let it be said at this point, that in selecting as investments mortgages secured by improved real estate, on which properties such mortgages are first liens, the Board chose a basic type of security, the intrinsic value of which, even in the event of foreclosure, is not destroyed and which may, in many cases, return in actual proceeds more than the amount invested.

VI

Early in 1929 the Board determined to limit the amount of funds to be invested in first mortgages, and carried this policy into effect in July of that year, after which time no additional funds have been invested in this type of security.

VII

With respect to the bonds' investments, we note that while there has been depreciation in market value, none have defaulted in interest. The Commission believes that these bonds were generally of high character at the time of purchase, showing that security of the principal rather than rate of income was given first consideration.

VIII

The Commission proposes to continue its investigation and make full report to the Executive Board for such action as it may determine.

We further propose, in the exercise of the powers conferred on us by this Convention, to advise and assist the Board of Ministerial Pensions and Relief in arranging an approved procedure for administering its permanent funds.

With this in view, we recommend the following resolution for adoption:

Resolved: That the Board of Ministerial Pensions and Relief be instructed to co-operate with the Commission on Investments in continuing the Commission's investigation as directed by the Church and in setting up such organization and procedure as shall assure the maximum protection to the invested and investible funds of the Board.

After extended discussion, the resolution attached to the report was unanimously adopted.

On motion the auditors' report of the Board of Ministerial Pensions and Relief was accepted.

The report of the Committee on Women's Work was presented by the Rev. F. M. Urich, Chairman of the Committee.

REPORT OF THE COMMITTEE ON WOMEN'S WORK

With characteristic zeal and true Christian optimism the women of the Church have met the difficult problems and the additional burdens imposed upon their work by the untoward conditions that have prevailed during the last two years.

We can not commend too highly the devotion, the wisdom and the resourcefulness displayed by our women in the effort to achieve a more effective missionary program in our congregations and to provide plans and methods by which missions, both in theory and practice, may be more urgently laid upon the heart of the Church.

The Chairman of the Committee on Women's Work has been privileged to attend all the meetings of the Executive Board of the Women's Missionary Society during the biennium, and begs leave to express herewith his appreciation of the generous and courteous treatment accorded to him at all times.

Close observation of the spirit underlying the work of the Women's Missionary Society has confirmed the impression that the tremendous success which has attended the efforts of this consecrated group of women to arouse interest in missions and to develop a sound policy of mission administration, is not due to superficial causes but to a deep and vital understanding of the claims of the Gospel.

In building the structure of their mission enterprise our women have steadfastly kept in view the work of the Church as a whole. They have consciously elected to broaden the scope of their activities, with the result that every department of the Church's work has felt the impact of their influence.

An examination of the literature and a survey of the budget of the Women's Missionary Society will disclose the effort made to coordinate the activities of the Society with the work of the various Boards of the Church.

This wider approach to the whole problem of missions has not only benefited the activities of the Society, but it has also helped to stimulate greater interest in the benevolences of the local congregation.

The Report of the Executive Board of the Women's Missionary Society herewith appended is worthy of careful perusal by pastors and church workers in general. It is manifestly more than a mere tabulation of statistics. In outward form it is impressive, indeed, but its inner significance lies in the fact that it is a first-class exhibit in applied Christianity.

No interpretation of the figures presented would be complete without due appreciation of the earnest prayers and the unselfish labors that have undergirded the noble and inspiring task to which the women of the United Lutheran Church in America have committed themselves.

Respectfully submitted,

The Committee on Women's Work,

FRANK M. URICH, *Chairman.*

REPORT OF THE EXECUTIVE BOARD OF THE WOMEN'S MISSIONARY SOCIETY

July 1, 1930— *July* 1, 1932

The seventh biennial report is presented for permanent record and for guidance in our work for the coming biennium. The most striking fact in all the report is the evident, yet unrecorded loyalty and faithfulness of the

Women's Missionary Society in holding up the hands of the missionaries. There is no mention of the volume of prayer which has been flowing steadily. There has been no special campaign for funds. The blessing which has come, however, we feel confident could have come only through prayer. Our finances show decreases not nearly so large as we might have expected. There has been an increase in membership in some places where an awakened interest has laid claim to the hearts of the women. There has been closer observance of the injunction "Be not slothful in business," as shown in the report of every department secretary. Our young women have made notable progress in their organizations and service. The Fourth Young Women's Congress, with its large advance enrollment of young women, who at their own expense, will meet for a day of missionary education and inspiration, is proof that they do care for the things of the spirit. Our Light Brigades have kept pace in gifts and numbers and in use of every means to educate the children in missions.

In grateful acknowledgement to God for the task committed to our hands we look forward to another biennium in which to serve in the missionary enterprise.

SYNODICAL SOCIETIES

In thirty-one of the synods there are Women's Missionary Societies: Alleghany, California, Canada, East Pennsylvania, Florida, Georgia, Illinois, Indiana, Iowa, Kansas, Maryland, Michigan, Mississippi, Nebraska, (English), Nebraska (German), New York, North Carolina, Northwest, Nova Scotia, Ohio, Pacific, Ministerium of Pennsylvania, Pittsburgh, Rocky Mountain, South Carolina, Susquehanna, Texas, Virginia, Wartburg, West Pennsylvania, West Virginia.

EXECUTIVE BOARD, BOARD OF TRUSTEES, OFFICERS

The members of the Executive Board are also members of the Board of Trustees.

EXECUTIVE BOARD

	Elected	Re-elected
President, Miss Flora Prince	1930	....
Vice-President, Mrs. C. E. Gardner	1930	....
Recording Secretary, Mrs. H. C. Michael	1930	....
Treasurer, Mrs. J. M. Cook	1928	1930
Statistical Secretary, Mrs. J. M. Bramkamp	1928	1930

	Elected	Terms Expire
Mrs. S. R. Kepner	1926	1932
Mrs. A. V. Pohlman	1926	1932
*Mrs. A. B. Leamer	1926	1932
Mrs. A. O. Mullen	1926	1932
Mrs. Thomas Frack	1928	1934
Mrs. Theodor Kemnitz	1928	1934
Mrs. R. N. McMichael	1928	1934
Mrs. A. M. Obenauf	1928	1934
Mrs. W. M. Snyder	1928	1934
Mrs. Eldridge Copenhaver	1930	1936
Mrs. N. K. Feddersen	1930	1936
**Miss A. C. Bornholdt	1930	1936
Mrs. J. A. Linn	1930	1936

Mrs. Philip M. Rossman 1930   1936
***Mrs. G. H. Haase 1930   1932

*Mrs. A. B. Leamer died August 17, 1931.
**Miss Bornholdt resigned October, 1931.
***Mrs. Haase was elected to fill the unexpired term of Mrs. O. D. Baltzly.

BOARD OF TRUSTEES

President, Vice-President and Recording Secretary are the same as for the Executive Board. Treasurer, Miss Flora Prince. The members are the same as for the Executive Board. The 1932 convention is charged with the responsibility of electing a President, Vice-President, Recording Secretary, Treasurer and Statistical Secretary. The present officers are all eligible for re-election.

BOARD MEETINGS

The Executive Board has held six meetings during the biennium. The first meeting was held in the Church of the Holy Communion, Racine, Wisconsin, the day following the close of the biennial convention in 1930, and the other meetings were held in the Muhlenberg Building, Philadelphia. The dates of the meetings were: October, 1930; February, June and October, 1931; and April, 1932.

ADMINISTRATIVE COMMITTEE

The administrative Committee consists of the five officers of the Executive Board. There have been nine meetings of the Committee in the Muhlenberg Building, Philadelphia: October and December, 1930; February, June, October and December, 1931; February, April and July, 1932.

STAFF

The staff appointed is as follows: Executive Secretary, Amelia D. Kemp; *Executive Secretary of Literature, Mrs. Charles L. Fry; Field Secretary, Mrs. H. C. Bell; Secretary for Young Women, Nona M. Diehl; Light Brigade Superintendent, Mrs. C. K. Lippard; Secretaries for Women Students, Mary E. Markley and Mildred E. Winston.

DEPARTMENTS

The following department secretaries were appointed: Annuity, Mrs. D. A. Davy; Box Work, Mrs. F. F. Fry; Deaconess, Mrs. W. P. M. Braun; **Extension, Mrs. A. C. Schenck; India Lace, Mrs. A. S. Woll; Life Membership and In Memoriam, Mrs. L. K. Sandford; Mission Study, Mrs. C. P. Wiles; Patron and Protege, Eleanor M. Robinson; Thank Offering, Mrs. John I. Meck; West Indies, Beulah Weiser.

LITERATURE COMMITTEE

Appointed by Executive Board: Mrs. B. E. Copenhaver, Chairman; *Mrs. Charles L. Fry, Executive Secretary of Literature; Mrs. H. S. Bechtolt, Mrs. C. T. Benze, Mrs. C. F. Kuder, Mrs. E. S. Lewars, Mrs. Virgil B. Sease, Mrs. D. Burt Smith. Ex-officio by virtue of office: Mrs. E. W. Althof, Mrs. W. P. M. Braun, Miss Nona M. Diehl, Mrs. C. K. Lippard,

Doctor Mary E. Markley, Mrs. J. F. Seebach, Mrs. C. P. Wiles, Mrs. A. C. Schenck.

---

*Mrs. Fry resigned June, 1931, and died October 22, 1931.
**In October, 1931, this was changed to "Visitation."

CANDIDATE COMMITTEE

Doctor Mary E. Markley was appointed chairman with Mrs. Philip M. Rossman and Amelia D. Kemp as members.

COMMITTEE ON INTERDENOMINATIONAL RELATIONSHIPS

The Committee is: Mrs. Philip M. Rossman, Chairman; Mrs. F. F. Fry, Mrs. A. V. Pohlman and Amelia D. Kemp.

ADVISORS TO CHURCH BOARDS

By appointment the following served as advisors to the Boards of the Church: Board of American Missions: Mrs. H. C. Michael, Mrs. A. B. Leamer; Board of Foreign Missions: Miss Flora Prince and Mrs. S. R. Kepner; Board of Education: Mrs. A. V. Pohlman, Mrs. C. E. Gardner, Miss Dorothea Hess; Deaconess Board: Mrs. A. M. Obenauf, Mrs. W. P. M. Braun; Board of Ministerial Pensions and Relief: Mrs. A. O. Mullen and Mrs. Oscar C. Schmidt; Inner Mission Board: Mrs. W. A. Snyder, Mrs. M. J. Bieber.

MISSIONS AND THE MISSIONARIES

Our missionaries serve under the Board of the Church in the regular fields of the Church. The distribution of support is as follows:

UNDER THE BOARD OF AMERICAN MISSIONS

In the United States	*Supported by Special Funds*
California, Alhambra, Grace	California Women's Missionary Society
Illinois, Westwood, Elmwood Park	Christ Church, Chicago
Michigan, Kalamazoo. Trinity	Michigan Women's Missionary Society
Montana, Great Falls, St. John's	Alleghany Women's Missionary Society
New Jersey, Vineland, Redeemer	Ministerium of Pennsylvania Women's Missionary Society
North Carolina, Asheville, St. Mark's	North Carolina Women's Missionary Society
Ohio, Elyria, Emmanuel	Ohio Women's Missionary Society
Pennsylvania, Butler, Trinity	Pittsburgh Women's Missionary Society
Tennessee, Nashville, St. Paul's	Indiana Women's Missionary Society
Wisconsin, Waukesha, St. Luke's	Northwest Women's Missionary Society
Alaska, Juneau, Resurrection	Supported by General Funds
Arkansas, Fort Smith	Supported by General Funds
California, Santa Barbara, Grace	Supported by General Funds
Colorado, Boulder, Trinity	Supported by General Funds
Denver, Barnitz Memorial	Supported by General Funds
Pueblo, St. Mark's	Supported by General Funds

Florida, West Palm Beach................Supported by General Funds
Illinois, Chicago, Belmont Park........Supported by General Funds
   Tabor ....Supported by General Funds
Indiana, Gary, Grace ....Supported by General Funds
Kansas, Kansas City, Trinity............Supported by General Funds
Montana, Rocky Boy Indian
 Reservation ....Supported by General Funds
North Carolina, Watauga Parish......Supported by General Funds
New York, Endicott, Holy
 Nativity ....Supported by General Funds
Pennsylvania, Pittsburgh, Messiah....Supported by General Funds
South Carolina, Rock Hill, Grace....Supported by General Funds
Virginia, Lynchburg............................Supported by General Funds
Washington, Bellingham, St.
    Mark's ....Supported by General Funds
   Longview, Trinity......Supported by General Funds
   Seattle, University......Supported by General Funds
Wyoming, Casper, Grace....................Supported by General Funds
   Laramie, Wyoming..........Supported by General Funds

In Canada
 Quebec, Montreal, Redeemer..............Supported by General Funds
 British Columbia, Victoria, Grace....Supported by General Funds

Women Missionaries   *Supported by Special Funds*
 Miss Florence Buckner
  Rocky Boy Indian Reservation......Northwest Women's Missionary
            Society
 Miss Cora Pearl Jeffcoat
  Watauga Parish, North Carolina..Light Brigades
 Miss Amy Louis Fisher
  Watauga Parish, North Carolina..Supported by General Funds
 *Miss Marie Gerlach
  Jewish Mission, Baltimore, Md.....Supported by General Funds
 Miss Frieda Hoh
  Porto Rico ....Supported by General Funds
 Sister Maren Knudsen
  Frederiksted, Virgin Islands ....Supported by General Funds
 Sister Emma Frances
  Frederiksted, Virgin Islands ....Supported by General Funds
 Sister Edith Prince
  Frederiksted, Virgin Islands ....Supported by General Funds

UNDER THE INNER MISSION BOARD
The faculty of the Konnarock Training School, Konnarock, Va.
Supported by Special Funds

Miss Helen Dyer, Principal................Maryland Women's Missionary
            Society
Miss Margaret Howard......................Washington, D. C., Missionary Union

Miss Olive Salem..............................

Miss Katrina Umberger.....................

Miss Sadie Ponwith...........................

Miss Ida Twedten...............................

Two of these four are supported by General Funds
The Northwest Women's Missionary Society contributes part support for one teacher
The New York Conference of New York Women's Missionary Society contributes full support for one teacher

*Appointed January, 1931.

UNDER THE BOARD OF FOREIGN MISSIONS

Africa   *Supported by Special Funds*
Sister Laura Gilliland...........................Alleghany Women's Missionary
    Society
Mrs. C. E. Buschman...........................Temple Church, Philadelphia, Pa.
Miss Marie Jensen...............................Messiah Church, Williamsport, Pa.
Miss Mabel Dysinger.........................Pittsburgh Women's Missionary
    Society
Miss Elsie Otto.....................................West Virginia Women's Missionary
    Society

China
Miss Erva Moody.................................Illinois Women's Missionary Society
Miss Lydia Reich.................................Epiphany Church, Milwaukee, Wis-
    consin
Miss Clara Sullivan.............................North Carolina Women's Missionary
    Society

India
Miss Selma Anderson.........................Emmanuel Church, Souderton, Pa.
Doctor Mary Baer...............................Maryland Women's Missionary
    Society
Miss Mette K. Blair............................Kountze Memorial Church, Omaha,
    Nebraska
Miss Mary S. Borthwick....................Church of the Holy Communion,
    Philadelphia, Pa.
Doctor Nellie Cassell.........................Christ Church, Baltimore, Maryland
Miss Agnes Christenson......................Kansas Conference, Augustana
Miss Edith Eykamp............................Unity Church, Chicago, Illinois
Miss Susan Glatz.................................Kodaikanal School Board
Miss Emma Johnson...........................Young Women's Missionary Society,
    Trinity Church, Rockford, Illinois
Miss Ada Kron.....................................Augustana Women's Missionary
    Society
Miss Clara J. Leaman..........................St. Paul's Church, Carlisle, Pa.
Miss Hilma Levine..............................Augustana Women's Missionary
    Society
Miss Verna Lofgren............................Augustana Women's Missionary
    Society
Miss Mabel H. Meyer........................New York Women's Missionary
    Society
*Miss Louisa Miller..............................Two Friends
Doctor Grace L. Moyer......................Light Brigades
Miss Alice J. Nickel............................Church of the Good Shepherd,
    Brooklyn, N. Y.
Dr. Betty Nilsson................................Augustana Women's Missionary
    Society
Miss Annie E. Sanford.......................West Pennsylvania Women's Mission-
    ary Society
Miss Lilith Schwab.............................Kansas Women's Missionary Society
Miss Frances Segner...........................West Pennsylvania Women's Mis-
    sionary Society

---

*This to be transferred to Dr. Beal when Dr. Beal returns to India.

Miss Agatha Tatge..............................Advent Church, New York City
Miss Jessie Thomas...........................Ohio Women's Missionary Society
Miss Emilie S. Weiskotten...............Ministerium of Pennsylvania Women's
                                     Missionary Society
Miss Florence M. Welty....................Indiana Women's Missionary Society
Miss Pauline Whitteker......... ....Trinity Church, Lancaster, Pa.
Miss Christie Zimmerman.................Susquehanna Women's Missionary
                                     Society

Japan

Miss Grace M. Beers...........................Pittsburgh Women's Missionary
                                     Society
Miss Helene H. Harder......................German Nebraska Women's Mission-
                                     ary Society
Miss Martha M. Harder....................East Pennsylvania Women's Mission-
                                     ary Society
Miss Mary E. Heltibridle....................Maryland Young Women
Miss Faith G. Lippard........................Northwest Women's Missionary
                                     Society
Miss Annie Powlas.............................Light Brigades
Miss Helen M. Shirk..........................Ministerium of Pennsylvania Women's
                                     Missionary Society
Miss Maya Winther............................Danish United Lutheran Church

Africa

*Miss Irene Block................................Supported by General Fund
Miss Bertha Koenig...........................Supported by General Fund

China

Miss Frieda Strecker.........................Supported by General Fund
Miss Elvira Strunk.............................Supported by General Fund
Miss Kathe Voget...............................Supported by General Fund

India

Miss Emma Baer................................Supported by General Fund
Miss Jessie Cronk..............................Supported by General Fund
Miss Edna Engle.................................Supported by General Fund
Miss Charlotte Hollerbach.................Supported by General Fund
Miss Hilda Kaercher..........................Supported by General Fund
Miss Lottie Martin............................Supported by General Fund
Miss Maida Meissner...................... ...Supported by General Fund
Miss Hildegarde Swanson..................Supported by General Fund

Japan

Miss Martha B. Akard........................Supported by General Fund
Miss Marion E. Potts..........................Supported by General Fund
Miss Maude Powlas............................Supported by General Fund

South America

Miss Corinne Menges..........................Supported by General Fund
Miss Myrtle Wilke...............................Supported by General Fund

---

*Resigned June, 1931.

India
> Miss Agnes I. Schade...........................Retired
> Miss Katharine Fahs............................Retired
> Miss Ellen Schuff...............................Died December, 1931
> Doctor Arline Beal.............................Reappointed February, 1932, and sails
> October, 1932

STAFF

Three changes in the staff are to be noted. The Executive Secretary of Literature, Mrs. Charles L. Fry, resigned February 1, 1931. Mrs. W. F. Morehead of Salem, Virginia, was appointed to succeed Mrs. Fry in that important work, and came to the Philadelphia office July 1, 1931.

Mrs. H. C. Bell, Field Secretary, presented her resignation April 13, 1932, to become effective January 1, 1933. No appointment for her successor will be made this biennium.

The Superintendent of Light Brigades, Mrs. C. K. Lippard, resigned June 30, 1932, to return to the mission field in Japan. Mrs. Mabel Fenner, of Elyria, Ohio, has been appointed Secretary for Light Brigades and will assume office October 1, 1932.

DEPARTMENTS

One change in the departments was made, when in October, 1931, the Executive Board voted that the name of the department known as "Extension" should be changed to "Visitation."

Mrs. David A. Davy, Annuity Secretary, presented her resignation June 30, 1932, and no successor has been appointed.

NEW MISSIONARIES, 1932

We will send to China in September, 1932, in order that she may enter the North China Language School in October, Miss Mae Leone Rohlfs of Davenport, Iowa. Miss Rohlfs was commissioned in her home church July 10, 1932, St. Paul's, Davenport. The pastor is Rev. J. A. Miller, D.D., Rev. Stewart W. Herman, D.D., President of the Board of Foreign Missions, commissioned Miss Rohlfs.

We will send to India in October two missionaries: Miss Amelia Lusetta Brosius of Rebuck, Pennsylvania, and Doctor Barbara E. DeRemer of Williamsport, Pennsylvania. These missionaries will be commissioned by the President of the Board of Foreign Missions at the Biennial Convention in Baltimore, October 2, 1932.

KONNAROCK SCHOOL BOARD

The members of the Women's Missionary Society on the Konnarock School Board and the terms they serve are:

Terms Expire
Mrs. W. F. Morehead...December, 1936
Mrs. S. R. Kepner... 1934
Miss Flora Prince... 1934
Mrs. G. W. McClanahan........,..................................... 1932

The Administrative Committee at its meeting July 6 and 7, 1932, nominated Mrs. Theodor Kemnitz of Louisville, Ky., to succeed Mrs. G. W. McClanahan.

KUGLER-WOERNER MEMORIAL FUND

At the meeting of the Executive Board, October, 1931, the plan for a memorial for Doctor Anna S. Kugler was enlarged to include Doctor Lydia Woerner, and the fund to be established will be known as the Kugler-Woerner Memorial Fund. The committee appointed was Amelia D. Kemp, chairman, Mrs. Charles L. Fry and Mrs. A. M. Obenauf. After the death of Mrs. Charles L. Fry, the Board appointed Mrs. C. F. Kuder of Philadelphia to the committee. There is no stated amount for the total of this fund. The goal is that both the Kugler Hospital and the Rajahmundry Hospital in India shall be reconditioned. The India Council has been on the alert to co-operate in every way, and an important and thorough survey of the medical work in India has been made by a committee composed of the physicians of our India mission and two from outside. Both hospitals are in need of standard up-to-date equipment, including X-ray machines and other apparatus. On recommendation adopted by the 1930 biennial convention, plans were made to launch the memorial for Doctor Kugler. At the 1932 biennial convention, therefore, with the inclusion of a memorial for Doctor Lydia Woerner, the plans are now under way.

CRONK MEMORIAL FUND

At the meeting of the Executive Board, April, 1932, the committee for the Cronk Memorial Fund presented the following recommendations which were adopted:

That if Grace College is not a reality by the beginning of the college year in 1934, the Cronk Memorial Fund shall be allocated to some object to be recommended by the Executive Board.
That official notice of this action be given to the President of the Grace College Board, the Rev. J. Henry Harms, D.D.
That the Executive Board grant permission to the Cronk Memorial Committee to release immediately these recommendations to Synodical Presidents and Chairmen for the Cronk Memorial Fund.

MRS. A. B. LEAMER

Mrs. Leamer was elected to membership on the Executive Board at the Biennial Convention in 1926 for six years, to retire in 1932. At her first attendance at a meeting of the Executive Board we recognized what resources were at command. Mrs. Leamer had been devoted to the work of the Church and the Women's Missionary Society from the time of her young womanhood. She was most careful wherever she served. For over twenty years her work in the Iowa Women's Missionary Society was an influential factor in that Society. Four and a half years ago she went to Charleston, West Virginia, to live. So well did she adapt herself to that community and Society that friends there report it seemed to them that she had always lived there. The congregations which her husband has served were blessed in having such a pastor's wife. The Women's Missionary Societies into which she put great devotion are richer for her happy spirit having been among them. The Executive Board gained a friend whose going was an irreparable loss. Mrs. Leamer was wise, just, careful and entered into the problems of the Executive Board with a characteristic sense of responsibility for the decisions made by the Board.

Mrs. Charles L. Fry

At the meeting of the Executive Board, February, 1931, Mrs. Fry resigned as Executive Secretary of Literature, the resignation to become effective June 30, 1931. The Board accepted the resignation very reluctantly and only because Mrs. Fry's statement concerning her health was so convincing that no other course could be followed. The deepest appreciation was felt for Mrs. Fry's twenty-two years of service as Secretary of Literature, first with the General Council Federation and continuing after the merger. Acknowledgment was made of her influential capacity in many activities of the Church and the Missionary Society. There was genuine regret in anticipating severing the close relation with Mrs. Fry in the daily work at the headquarters offices. It was difficult to see the way clearly without her friendly counsel, wise judgments and far seeing plans. On October 12 she attended the meetings of the Executive Board. A few days later she was present at the Philadelphia meeting addressed by Doctor Kagawa of Japan. In another week, suddenly and quietly, she went back to her Heavenly Father.

Mrs. C. K. Lippard

Mrs. Lippard returned July 16, 1926, from Japan, where she and Doctor Lippard were missionaries. On account of the illness of their daughter, Lois, it was necessary for them to remain in America. On May 25, 1927, we called Mrs. Lippard to serve as Light Brigade Superintendent to succeed Mrs. E. C. Cronk. Mrs. Lippard has made a helpful contribution to the children's work, and we are grateful to her. In the summer of 1931 the daughter, Lois, was called home after ten years of invalidism. Mrs. Lippard resigned the Light Brigade work June 30, 1932, and sailed July 16, 1932, for Japan, to which field Doctor Lippard has been reappointed. May God's blessing follow.

Mrs. H. C. Bell

Mrs. Bell has been serving as Field Secretary since 1923. Her travels have brought stimulation to the work—North, South, East, West. At the meeting of the Executive Board, April, 1932, Mrs. Bell presented her resignation to become effective January 1, 1933. We can scarcely measure the gap in the staff which this resignation causes, and were it not for the circumstances which demand Mrs. Bell's presence at home we should be loath to give her up just now. The full record of Mrs. Bell's accomplishments is a succession of good works—leader of children, Bible teacher, Y. W. C. A. Secretary, Mission Study Teacher, Executive Board Member and Field Secretary. For many years the monthly prayer calendar and the programs for the week of Prayer and Lenten Self-Denial were her care and joy. Her interest and influence in home missions gave many new courage and hope.

The Budget

The budget to be presented for adoption at the Biennial Convention has been prepared with emphasis on "No reduction anywhere except at home base." It will be noted that in the general total the Kugler-Woerner Memorial which would ordinarily appear as a "Special" and therefore added to the total, is omitted. We have no "Repayment balance on loan" for *we have paid the debt in full.* Also there is no item for "Interest on loan" since there is no debt. These items make a difference in comparison with the total budget of 1930-32. In the headquarters offices those who have left our employ within the past two years have not been replaced. Others have carried their work in the clerical staff. In the new budget all salaries have been reduced for both executive and clerical staff by ten per cent.

PROPOSED BUDGET
January 1, 1933 to January 1, 1935

Board of American Missions		$147,944.00
Salaries English Pastors	$66,444.00	
Salaries Women Missionaries	17,800.00	
Expense and Equipment, Watauga, N. C.	2,000.00	
Parish Worker	$1,000.00	
Nurse	1,000.00	
	$2,000.00	
Linguistic Interests		10,000.00
Salaries	$7,190.00	
Students for the Ministry	2,810.00	
	$10,000.00	
Loans to Churches		20,000.00
Interest Requirements		15,000.00

Rocky Boy Indian Reservation... 4,600.00
    Travel of Missionaries $800.00
    Maintenance of Mission 3,800.00

                                       $4,600.00

West Indies 12,100.00
    Travel of Missionaries $1,500.00
    Queen Louise Home 5,200.00
    Milk Fund for Porto Rico 1,000.00
    Salaries Kindergarten Teachers................ 4,400.00

                                       $12,100.00

                                                $147,944.00

Board of Education 5,400.00
Board of Ministerial Pensions and Relief.. 9,000.00
Inner Mission Board 20,000.00
    (Konnarock Training School—Salaries, Maintenance, Health Work)

Board of Foreign Missions $409,956.00
 Africa $35,300.00
    Salaries $13,600.00
    Travel 4,500.00
    Maintenance 13,200.00
    Medical Work 4,000.00

                                       $35,300.00

China 37,890.00
    Salaries $11,840.00
    Travel 1,650.00
    Maintenance 17,400.00
    Share in purchase price (final payments) 7,000.00

                                       $37,890.00

India 223,456.00
    Salaries $64,600.00
    Travel 6,600.00
    Maintenance 152,256.00

                                       $223,456.00

Japan 85,710.00
    Salaries $26,350.00
    Travel 1,500.00
    Maintenance 57,860.00

                                       $85,710.00

South America 27,600.00
    Salaries $7,200.00
    Travel 400.00

Maintenance 20,000.00

$27,600.00

$409,956.00

Total to Boards of the Church $592,300.00

Boards of the United Lutheran Church...$592,300.00
Interdenominational Boards and Committees.. 8,370.00

Council of Women for Home Missions........................ $920.00
    Migrant Work $200.00
    Committee Work 500.00
    Dues 220.00

$920.00

Federation of Women's Boards of Foreign Missions....   250.00
    Christian Literature Committee $100.00
    Dues 150.00

$250.00

Foreign Missions Conference of North America........   1,000.00
Missionary Education Movement 400.00
Missionary Review of the World 100.00
Summer Schools 700.00
Christian Colleges in the Orient 5,000.00
    Madras $2,000.00
    Vellore 2,000.00
    St. Christopher's 1,000.00

$5,000.00

$8,370.00

Specific Appropriations 72,900.00
    Literature Committee $18,000.00
    Lutheran Woman's Work—Life Membership Supple-
        ment 7,000.00
    Interest to Annuitants 28,000.00
    Biennial Convention, 1934 ....   18,000.00
    Pension—Retired Missionary 400.00
    Emergencies 1,500.00

$72,900.00

Administration 69,569.00
    Rent of rooms, 7th floor, Muhlenberg Building............ $8,634.00
    Telephone 650.00
    Expense account—headquarters, officers, department
        secretaries 5,000.00
    Stationery and report blanks 600.00
    Board and Administrative Committee meetings............   8,000.00

Travel representatives to meetings	750.00
Bonds for Treasurers	125.00
Field Travel (divided between Young Women and Light Brigade)	1,000.00
Salaries (executive and clerical staff, 17 people)........	44,810.00
Accountant	800.00
Auditors	1,200.00

$69,569.00

Total Proposed Budget $743,139.00

Other Items:

Board of American Missions: Possible new work $5,000.00
(If Chicago Italian woman worker is approved by Board of American Missions, her support will have first claim on new work)

Board of Foreign Missions: Possible exchange on salaries........ 7,180.00
(South America, $720.00; India, $6,460.00).

Total $12,180.00

RECOMMENDATIONS

During the past biennium unusual blessings have been ours, therefore in deep humility and gratitude to God we offer these recommendations:

1. That in view of the splendid record herein contained, in the face of unusual economic conditions, we express gratitude to God for the divine guidance that has marked our way, and declare and emphasize an unshaken faith in the future progress of this organization.

2. That in this time of world-wide social unrest we urge the women of the United Lutheran Church to stand firm for law, order and peace, and to exercise their right to help keep the country safe for the youth of the land.

3. (a) That a committee be appointed to review the findings of the committee on the status and work of women in the Church, and to bring in definite recommendations for the future development of the organized work of women in the Church.

(b) That we enlist the interest of a larger number of women in our Church by presenting to them the possibilities for Christian service through the missionary activities of the Church at home and abroad.

(c) That we urge definite study of missions, more frequent inspirational public meetings and the use of every possible means for wider contacts with the women of our Church.

4. That a member of the Women's Missionary Society be appointed to present definite plans for the development of a sense of stewardship among the women of the Church.

5. That we express gratitude to the officers of the Women's Missionary Societies of our synods, and to the general and synodical secretaries for their untiring efforts in promoting the work in synods and in the departments.

6. That we commend the high type of literature produced by our Literature Committee, and recognize its helpfulness in the missionary education program of the Church.

7. That since *Lutheran Woman's Work* is the official organ of the Women's Missionary Society and vital to its work, that we make special

effort during this biennium to increase the subscription list and the reading of the magazine.

8. That we repeat the request of 1930 that invitations for the entertainment of Biennial Conventions be in the hands of the Executive Board at least four months prior to the convention at which the invitation is presented.

9. That the Christmas offering for 1932 and the undesignated Lenten Self-Denial Offering for 1933 be given to the Linguistic work on the budget of the Board of American Missions.

10. That the Christmas offering for 1933 and the undesignated Lenten Self-Denial Offering for 1934 be given to our budgeted work in Africa.

11. That tributes to departed friends be made in May each year through the Life and In Memoriam department instead of promoting special memorial funds.

12. That the budget adopted at this convention become operative January 1, 1933, and continue in force without change until December 31, 1934, unless in the judgment of the Executive Board funds will allow restoration either wholly or in part of the decreases made.

Respectfully submitted,
The Executive Board,
By Amelia D. Kemp, <i>Executive Secretary.</i></div>

July 9, 1932.

Dr. Urich presented Miss Flora Prince, President of the Women's Missionary Society, who addressed the Convention. The Rev. C. A. Freed, President of the South Carolina Synod, responded. Dr. Urich presented Miss Amelia D. Kemp, Executive Secretary of the Women's Missionary Society, and Mrs. W. F. Morehead, Chairman of the Literature Committee, who addressed the Convention. The other officers of the Women's Missionary Society, Mrs. J. M. Cook, Mrs. O. C. Schmidt and Mrs. H. C. Michael were also introduced to the Convention.

At twelve o'clock the Convention adjourned with prayer by the Rev. L. A. Thomas.

NINTH SESSION

Benjamin Franklin Hotel.
Philadelphia, Pennsylvania.
Tuesday, October 18, 1932, 2.00 P. M.

Devotions were conducted by the Rev. J. Reble, and the President called the Convention to order.

The report of the Committee of Reference and Counsel was presented by the Rev. H. Brezing, Chairman of the Committee.

Report of the Committee of Reference and Counsel

1. Today the Rev. G. U. Wenner, New York City, and his congregation (Christ Lutheran Church) celebrate the sixty-fifth anniversary both of the pastorate of Dr. Wenner and of the founding of the congregation. Your Committee believes that this unusual event deserves recognition and recommends that the Secretary be instructed to telegraph congratulations.

2. In acknowledgment of the many courtesies shown to the Convention, we recommend the adoption of the following resolution:

Resolved, That this Convention express its gratitude and appreciation for the fine hospitality extended to us by the City of Philadelphia and its Lutheran churches; the generous and considerate co-operation of the press; the speakers at the Convention services and public meetings for their compelling messages; the choirs who assisted in these events; the Lutheran Social Union and the Women's League for their splendid and most interesting program of entertainment; the students of the Mt. Airy Seminary for their leadership at our devotions; the police department for its escort on the excursion to The Trappe and Valley Forge; the management of the Benjamin Franklin Hotel for its many favors; and, most particularly, to the alert and courteous chairman of the Committee for Entertainment and the members of his committee who ministered so graciously to all our needs, and to all others co-operating for kindnesses too many to mention.

3. Your Committee is happy to bring to the attention of the Convention the fact that a telegram from the American Lutheran Church in response to our message of greeting has been received. It announces that the Rev. G. E. Lenski, Washington, D. C., has been appointed their representative to our body. He will be here on Wednesday morning and we recommend that he be heard when he appears.

4. Inasmuch as this is the last opportunity provided for the Committee of Reference and Counsel to report, I am taking the liberty as chairman to present a resolution which has just come to me:

Resolved, That in presenting their financial statements, all boards and agencies holding capital assets invested in securities be instructed to include in each instance a statement of the current market value of such securities.

Recommendations 1, 2, 3, and 4 were adopted.

The President announced that the Executive Board will give earnest study to the program for the next convention so that the regular agencies will not be crowded out of favorable places.

The report of the Committee on Moral and Social Welfare was presented by the Rev. W. H. Greever, Chairman of the Committee.

REPORT OF THE COMMITTEE ON MORAL AND SOCIAL WELFARE

(For action on the resolutions in this report see p. 419.)

The Committee was organized with Dr. W. H. Greever as chairman and Dr. J. Henry Harms as secretary. As the Milwaukee Convention referred no specific subjects to this Committee for consideration during the past biennium, the Committee presents, in outline, some results of a study of moral and social welfare in general, with special reference to existing conditions, recent events, notable trends and representative pronouncements.

The whole Church is called upon, by the acute distress of present conditions, to make as deep, thorough and definite study of this subject as is possible. Even more, *the Church is challenged.* In the face of its claim to find the solution of all human problems in the Christian religion, the Church is boldly charged with failure in practical results, and the enemies of the Christian religion make this charge of failure an argument against the Christian religion itself. The answer that the Church, through applied Christianity, as a leaven and otherwise, has done more for society than its enemies will admit is valid, but it is not an adequate answer, and will not be adequate until the Church has done all it can do for social welfare. That is the point of the present challenge.

Undoubtedly the chief cause for whatever failure the Church shows in its service to society is a lack of a *will to do,* but it is certain that another great cause, perhaps, in no small degree responsible for the lack of will, is lack of understanding of the "what," "why" and "how" involved. This is manifest in the vagueness of views, the casuistry of programs, the inadequacy of means and impulsiveness of procedure proposed by many recognized as leaders in what they call social service. The almost fanatical concern for incidental ills, far from the heart of society, the inauguration of movements on this, or that, or the other account, or the almost inevitable resort to effort for special legislation to regulate life in particular points, are characteristic of many misguided enthusiasts for social welfare. But in the absence of other voices and for the lack of better leadership, it is not uncommon for some of the best people in the Church to follow these enthusiasts—where they can see tangible results that may be beneficial to society, but not always for fundamental good. The zeal and intent may be most commendable, but the view is often superficial and the results more apparent than real.

PRELIMINARY INQUIRIES

In the effort to get to clearer and deeper conceptions of that which is most basic to most effective service for moral and social welfare, and to get to the foundation for an adequate and definite program, we propose certain inquiries, which if answered according to facts and principles, correctly interpreted, will contribute much to that end.

1. Is there general agreement on the meaning of "welfare"? Literally, it

means "going well." But what do we mean by "well"? To the Christian it means the realization of the power, blessings and joys of true religion, but to the worldling it means the possession of material wealth, power over other men, and the gratification of carnal desires, passions, and appetites. So it is necessary to use the qualifying word "Christian" and "welfare," "social" and "moral" to make our meaning clear. Even then we will still find wide difference in definitions, for not all who call themselves "Christian" agree as to what the "Christian view" of a particular subject is. There are Lutheran Christian views, even, which are distinctive in their differences from all others.

2. What do we mean by "social"? Those who hold that society is an entity, in itself, and that it possesses the attributes of personality, propose that society be dealt with directly as a person—that it be educated, or reformed, or restrained, or punished. Those who hold, to the contrary, that society possesses no such personal entity, but that it is the *relationship* between individuals that constitutes society, propose that society is to be made better through changes in its individual members. That distinction is not academic, but is of fundamental practical importance in any proposed course of dealing with the so-called social ills or problems. It involves the practical question immediately as to whether betterment is to be sought by dealing with men *en masse,* or as individuals, or both. Our claim is that *en masse* effort is effective only in what it contributes to the reaching of the individual.

3. What do we mean by "moral"? Morality is primarily a personal matter. Further, morality is a matter concerned with personal responsibility. It is on that account an individual matter. It is primarily a matter of the *will,* and being involved in action as the expression of the free exercise of the will, it is, therefore, a matter of inner attitude. A man's inner attitudes determine his character. The inner attitudes are the products of motives as they influence the will. Motives are products of accepted dynamic principles, modified by desires and judgments—desires as they express feeling, and judgments as they express appraisal of values. Such judgments constitute ideals. By ideals a man is guided, and by feelings he is motivated. *But his morality is determined by the free exercise of his will.* Since the dynamic principles of the true life, and the revelation of the true values of life, and the desires of the holy life come from God alone, it follows that sound and vital morality depends upon true religion, as social welfare depends upon sound morality.

4. What do we mean by "religion"? Some make religion consist chiefly in a body of beliefs, some in a particular course of life, some in forms, and acts of worship and some in specific inner experiences. No one of these, nor all combined, includes the *essence* of the Christian religion, which can be conceived of only as a *relationship* between a man and God,—a relationship which is religion in essence because it is (a) a *personal* relationship, between man as person and God as person; (b) a *vital* relationship, union of *souls* of

man with God, pure *spirit;* (c) a *reciprocal* relationship, where there is communion and fellowship through union; (d) a *conscious* relationship, where communion and fellowship are *experienced realities.* Such a relationship is effected alone through personal faith in the Lord and Saviour, Jesus Christ.

Where such a relationship exists between man and God, the *elements* of religion become manifest in experience, which are, on the human side, (a) reverence, (b) trust, (c) love, (d) readiness of will to obey God. Likewise the blessedness of religion is experienced in (a) assurance, (b) peace, (c) satisfaction, (d) joy and (e) eternal life. Doubt and fear and all distress arising out of sin and separation from God are banished. In this relationship, established through the Gospel of grace, a man's whole being is brought into harmony with God's Spirit and Will, and God dwells in him, the light and power of his life. Thus his motives are made pure and holy because they are in harmony with God's motives. His ideals are made true, his judgments of values are rectified, his attitudes are determined in righteousness, and, in the power of God, he goes out to the highest possible service to his fellowman, effectively equipped to deal with every social problem.

Accepting it as our task to work for the best possible moral and social order, we identify defects in the existing order, and propose ideals and aims, and specify means and measures, for betterment, according to the foregoing definitions.

The Task as Related to Social Ills

In any general contemplation of the social order in which we are living the attention is challenged immediately by what we recognize as *social ills.* They are many, varied and universal. They all are but symptoms indicating the more grave *moral diseases* of poisoned human nature, yet they affect the social life so vitally and in such great degree that they require more attention than that incident to their use in the deeper diagnosis. The task of social betterment receives much light on its nature and magnitude through a clear and comprehensive view of the social ills. As a help in this study we present an enumeration of such major ills as are most notorious in current life. Without attempt to be technical, and merely for the sake of practical convenience, we classify these ills under four groups.

1. *Those which involve money:*—social-economic ills.

(1) *Gambling.* If gambling is rightly judged to be a social ill, an analysis will show wherein the judgment is justified. The distinctive *intent* in gambling is *to get something for nothing*—gain without production. The frequent attendants upon gambling are deception and trickery. In some forms of "trade," as well as in some games, the end is accomplished by "manipulations." Sometimes advantage is taken by the secret use of knowledge which rightly belongs to another who does not have it. Gambling is a social ill, because it is a deliberate and *overt disregard for personal rights.* Gambling,

itself a social ill, is directly and indirectly responsible for more social ills, not commonly associated with it, than most men even dream.

(2) *Racketeering*. Racketeering is a new name for an old crime (robbing by force) used to designate that crime in its modern organized, systematized, wholesale form. It does boldly what has always been done in some measure, more subtly,—it collects by force, without regard for rights or laws, through the intimidation and peril of life, what the racketeer wants, and compels men to work for him under compulsion worse than the most abject slavery. It is an old evil, gone violent and unmasked. But it is akin to injustice and oppression long practiced under tolerance of an indifferent social order by many individuals and corporations,—through competitions, combinations and monopolies,—by force not as terrorizing as guns but no less destructive.

(3) *Exploitations*. An authoritative definition of "exploitation" is: "Selfish or unfair utilization." In that sense it is used here to designate a particular social-economic ill. The purpose of exploitation is always immediate *selfish gain*, though the ill to society may not be immediately apparent, as in the wanton waste of great natural resources—timber, soil, minerals, etc., to the privation of unborn generations. Or the ill may be very immediate where some great calamity or need is exploited by those who control supplies. Or the ill may be continuous where mercenary motives prevail in an economic system, as when capital and labor wage warfare, each often from the same motive.

(4) *Bribery*. Bribery involves the betrayal of trust and the surrender of honor on the part of all concerned. It is destructive of the very foundations of the social, economic, civil order. It does not always involve the passing of money, for men are bribed in more ways than one, but it always means the sacrifice of honor which has no money evaluation. The wrong is all the greater when one sells that which is not his to be bartered, without the knowledge of those who are made to suffer, as is done so often by those in positions of public trust, whether it be a "tip" or a conviction, a vote or a veto. The prevalence of this is a menace to every man's security, but the complacency with which it is "taken for granted" and tolerated is a corrupting poison in the whole body of society.

With just a little elaboration many common and sharp, shrewd practices in manufacturing, marketing, advertising, financing, etc., could be listed under these headings with undeniable propriety, and the fact should be noted that by common commendation of many of these practices as evidences of business ability, society but confesses its own sad state of debility.

2. *Those which involve social contagions.*

The ills we specify here are ills which primarily are injurious to the individual afflicted by them, but because they are contagious they are of tremendous social import.

(5) *Profanity*. Profanity is disregard for the sacred. The sacred is that which by common sanction is set apart as worthy of universal reverence,

and is held as inviolate. The common sanction may not include all that is worthy of reverence, and it may include some things that are not worthy, but nevertheless such sanction is the *strongest bond in the social unity*. He who despises and violates that sanction breaks the social bond, and profanity is not only a sin against God, but it also works organic injury to society.

(6) *Dissipation.* All waste is dissipation. All dissipation is loss both to individual and social welfare. Individual loss always involves social loss. Dissipation appears in waste of time, talents, money and spiritual vigor; and in forms of drunkenness, gluttony, idleness, play, prodigality and many indulgences of passions and appetites.

(7) *Diseases.* The avoidable prevalence of many destructive and fatal diseases, mental as well as physical, due to voluntary sin, carelessness, poverty, blameworthy ignorance, and programs of living, works havoc to social welfare.

(8) *Suicide.* The increase of suicide in recent times challenges particular attention, as it rends the hearts and depresses the spirits of multitudes and affects them in their social relationships. It does not lessen the moral and spiritual disaster of suicide to ascribe it to a state of irresponsibility, including insanity, as long as the social order condones and perpetuates the conditions which cause such a state. Many suicides in these times are not so much due to a collapse of nerves as to the acceptance of that false philosophy of life which denies the hope of immortality and repudiates religious sanctions for the present life. The prevalence of suicide shows a *low appraisal of life itself*, the most dangerous of all menaces to social welfare.

3. *Those which more distinctly involve the inner life in social relationships.*

(9) *Sex-laxity.* Perhaps, for social welfare, in a fundamental practical way, more depends upon the purity of sex-feeling and the sanctity of sex-function than upon any other single thing, for it is here that the character of the primary unit of society, the family, is determined. And the family is not only the primary unit of society but it is the fountain from which all social life continuously issues,—new with each succeeding generation. Nothing in the whole moral experience of man is more difficult than the maintenance of that purity and sanctity against the urges of the strong animal passions, inseparable from sex consciousness. When the animal, sex passions are allied with other evil motives, like the money-motive, the worldly social-ambition motive, etc., it is no wonder that they manifest their corrupting power in obscenity, gross sex immorality, easy divorce and the practical repudiation of marriage as a sacred institution. Let it be noted that in the New Testament lists of social evils, sex-immorality is always put in the first place.

(10) *Lawlessness.* Human laws, whether written or unwritten, are *expressed terms of social contract*, unless imposed by a dictator, and are sanctioned for the protection and promotion of social welfare. The unity, peace, freedom, and prosperity of society depends upon respect for and observance of those terms of social contract. Disrespect for law always

precedes the violation of law, is always more widespread than overt violation, and is always more detrimental to society.

(11) *Organized agencies.* Most of the ills already enumerated are abetted and promoted, in greater or less degree, through certain organized agencies, from which society receives much good service, to be greatly appreciated, but society dares not on account of great, good service to close its eyes to the malservice of which we now speak.

(a) *The Press.* The press is one of the greatest of modern agencies for good, a fact appreciated by the Church in peculiar degree. Yet it is to be most deeply regretted that only too often great sections of it are perverted to the service of evil. This applies to the news-press, the periodical-press, and the book-press—where abuses and misuses of public contact and power are too apparent to need designation.

(b) *The Theater.* The theater, whether stage or screen, is likewise potentially an agency for good, but, in many instances, it has been perverted, especially the screen, to the service of evil to such a degree, and has been so calloused to reasonable censorship as to raise a veritable storm of protest from those most concerned for social and moral welfare. "Movie" and "Menace" have sometimes so nearly become synonyms in relation to morals that many seem to be justified in seeking drastic action for the protection of the millions of boys and girls to whom the screen makes its strongest appeal.

(c) *Societies and "Movements."* To specify fully and fairly under this heading would require reference to organized atheism, to schools of materialism, to paganistic sects, to organized selfishness in many forms, to bands of fanatics and radicals—everyone loaded with dynamite and digging at the foundations of our social order.

4. *Those which are divisive and militate against unity and harmony in society.*

(12) *In the family.* Infidelity between husbands and wives, disloyalty between parents and children, clashing views on standards of living, undisciplined temperaments, etc.

(13) *Between races.* Distinct races are a fact, and not necessarily to the hurt of social welfare, but racial prejudices, superiority and inferiority complexes, traditions and attendant anti-social attitudes militate against social welfare in racial relationships.

(14) *Between nationalities.* Much of the same anti-social feeling and attitudes which separate races are responsible for antagonisms between nations, to which may be added competitions, jealousies, greed, grudges—from which come wars and rumors of wars.

(15) *Between groups.* There are divisive social ills *within* nations and races. In some places society is divided into castes, in others into classes, though in the social significance the differences are in terms only. The existence of classes in society is natural and inevitable on certain grounds—differences in ability, in tastes, temperament, etc., but it is when classifica-

tion is *arbitrary and forced*, unjustly, with abridged privilege and liberty that it becomes a social ill and moral evil. No society enjoys welfare where there are suppressed and underprivileged classes upon whom privileged classes prey. On the other hand, society must always find a problem in the great class for whom no degree of privilege, beyond that of simply living, will better its members—the *morons*. It is not the *existence* of classes, but the *attitude* of class toward class which constitutes the class-social ill.

(16) *In conditions.* When conditions affect the lives of many people to their hurt, and they are powerless to change such conditions maintained by the will of others, there are social ills in those conditions. The economic system under which we have been living illustrates great wealth and luxury and abject poverty in sight of each other, but separated by an impossible gulf; leisure because of no need to work and enforced idleness because of no opportunity to work; the palace towering over the hovel; privilege and underprivilege.

THE TASK AS RELATED TO MORAL EVILS

We observe that the social ills enumerated are universal, varying only in degree and form in different sections of society, but found in every age and in every country. We have called them *"social ills"* in order to emphasize a fundamental distinction between them and *moral evils*. These social ills are the effects from moral evils as *causes*. Social ills may be regarded as symptoms of chronic diseases, but if some of them appear to be diseases rather than symptoms, it yet remains true that the diseases or roots and germs are to be found in moral evils. *The moral evils are inherent in unregenerated human nature.* All moral evils are comprehended in one word,—sin, and sin, like religion, consists in a definite relationship to God,—rebellion. The form of sin from which nearly all social ills arise may be comprehended in one word,—selfishness.

Specific forms of moral evils are pointed out in certain lists found in the New Testament, and are more vividly portrayed in Luther's explanation of the Ten Commandments.

When the social ills are traced to their origins, the course leads inevitably and invariably to moral evils. But moral evils are aways individual matters. They characterize social relationships and determine social conditions, but they belong to the individual person. This throws clear light upon our task. If we are to secure social welfare we must effect the spiritual regeneration and the moral renovation and sanctification of the individuals who, in their personal relationships, constitute society. Anything else is an external treatment of symptoms for the cure of an internal disease. The task before us only overwhelms us with the impossibility of performing it by human wisdom and power alone.

THE TASK AS RELATED TO DIVINE PROVISION

God has immeasurable concern for human welfare, according to His perfect conception of what welfare is. He has presented His plan and provided the means for its realization. He gives assurance of its adequacy and of its effectiveness. Where His plan has been followed and His means used, there the highest welfare has been experienced. How presumptuous it is in any man to seek any modification of plan or means, by either subtraction or addition, or to question either His wisdom or His honor!

This is what God says is necessary and what He does for moral and social welfare.

1. He says that man *must be delivered from sin,*—guilt, power, and consequences,—before he even can know what welfare is. Such deliverance He offers through Jesus Christ, His Son, our Saviour.

2. He says that the natural man *must be born again.* Such regeneration He effects by the Holy Spirit through His Word of Grace, especially in baptism.

3. He says that man must be nurtured, confirmed, and strengthened in the new life so that he is spiritually renovated, transformed, and sanctified, and his whole being brought into harmony with His will. All of this He does for everyone who accepts it, by the Holy Spirit, through His Gospel, especially in the Sacrament of the Lord's Supper.

4. He says that all who accept these gifts of grace *become His children* to live together in one great *brotherhood,* each seeking the welfare of every other in loving unselfishness, and all working together with Him to bring His salvation to all mankind. Accordingly He has established His *Church* for the edification of His children and for the execution of His purposes toward unsaved men. To the Church He has committed His means of grace, and through the Church He has placed upon the individual Christian the responsibility of human agency in the application of His effective means for the realization of the only true moral and social welfare.

The Task as Related to the Church

The Church does not have an open and uncontested field for its endeavor in behalf of moral and social welfare. The Church is only a part of society and the greater part of society is not only unchristianized, fostering the forces of evil, but the various portions of unchristianized society also have their codes and moral standards and programs for betterment. These conflict with those of the Church in regard to needs, aims, means and measures. Then, too, the true Church, composed of those who are truly in harmony with God's will, is not identical with the organized Church in which are many who are no more Christianized than many of those outside the Church. It is no uncommon thing for social workers outside of the Church to enlist the support of our people in programs of but superficial and temporal benefit. This is *a challenge for stronger leadership in the Church,* for a more positive and clear-cut statement of principles and a more aggressive and effective program.

No matter what the conflicts, or the compromises, or calls for cooperation from outside of the Church may be, the *full responsibility* for the promotion of moral and social welfare in any real sense, *remains upon the Church.*

We proceed to specify the chief things essential to the Church in any effective endeavor for moral and social welfare.

1. The Church must realize clearly what the defects and evils in the present social order are, and from what they come. This we have sought to indicate in the above.

2. The Church must realize clearly what the social order is to be when its task is accomplished. This we attempt to show by pointing out certain essentials that must characterize the ideal order.

(1) An order in which the *meaning of life* is construed according to the purpose of its divine author: The realization, in the development of perfect personality, of the eternal spiritual values, comprehensively specified as follows:

a. *The Good,*—whatever *pertains to* or *contributes to* the perfection of personality.

b. *The True,*—the essential, eternal *realities* in which all values inhere, for the enduement and enrichment of personality.

c. *The Beautiful,*—perfection itself, to be realized and experienced by personality in purity, unity, harmony and glory, in all relationships.

(2) An order in which the value and potentialities of personality are correctly appraised, duly appreciated and consistently sought.

(3) An order in which *justice* secures to everyone full measure of opportunity for the realization of the possibilities of his personality.

Justice, *in its purpose,* is to *maintain* the rights inherent in the nature, value and potentialities of personality, to the realization of "welfare" in the attainment, acquirement and enjoyment of the substance of those rights within the sphere of liberty; and, *in its spirit,* justice is *to have and manifest the will to promote* the welfare of every personality without partiality.

(4) An order in which true religion unifies and harmonizes the life of individuals in a practical *brotherhood,* through the experience of individual fellowship with the common Father,—God.

(5) An order in which the practical brotherhood expresses itself through loving, unselfish service, by the administration of true Christian *stewardship.*

The Gospel in the hearts of men regenerates and sanctifies so that such an ideal social order is effected and moral and social welfare is achieved. If it be said that such an order is ideal and is beyond human achievement in this world, the answer is that the Christian can aim at nothing less, cannot even make compromises or excuses, and that all betterment must come from the effort to attain to this ideal. This is the only practically effective way to welfare, no matter how far the ideal is above the real.

These specific aims may be placed alongside the catalogued moral evils and social ills and it will be seen that they furnish the specific correction and cure for every evil and ill. When the Gospel is brought effectively to a man's heart, in its purity, power and principles, it brings God into that heart to give it purpose, motive and will in harmony with God's purpose, motive and will.

3. The Church must think and act in consistency with the facts and principles involved in this task.

(1) With reference to human nature.

a. Facts: That human nature, per se, *possesses the essential attributes* of personality,—intelligence, emotion and will; and, That human nature, since sin entered the world, is in a *state of depravity* until regenerated.

b. Principle: A power is to be applied to corrupt human nature which will change its state by regeneration and renovation, but *without violence* to the essential attributes of personality:

(a) Convincing the mind.

(b) Convincing the conscience.

(c) Converting the will.

(d) Consecrating the heart.

(2) With reference to the Gospel.

a. Fact: The Triune God deals directly with the individual man,—redeeming, regenerating, renovating and sanctifying him.

b. Principle: The mystical nature of the divine operation must be recognized, because the inner spiritual transformation is so effected as to *institute the Kingdom of God,* "which cometh not with observation."

Thus any idea of the real or permanent solution of moral and social problems by law alone, or any other merely human means, is dissipated, and any seeming benefits from such are recognized as no more than temporary alleviations.

4. The Church must strictly and faithfully use the divinely appointed means for the christianization of men, without subtraction or addition, in both content and implication, which means are: The Word and Sacraments.

5. The Church must employ those measures in this work which are divinely commanded and approved, and are consistent with means and needs. These measures are:

(1) *Preaching,*—the public proclamation of the Gospel and the conduct of *Worship.*

(2) *Administration of the Sacraments,*—the individualizing of the means of grace for personal appropriation.

(3) *Teaching,*—the exposition and interpretation of the Gospel for personal acceptance and application.

(4) *Witnessing,*—testimony to the *experience* of the power and blessedness of the Gospel and to assurance of the truth of its factual claims, in confirmation of the faith by which its blessings are received.

(5) *Demonstration, or ministration,*—the exemplification of the power of the Gospel in such a life of spiritual purity and beauty, and of Christ-like attitudes and loving service as will "adorn the Gospel," and recommend it by its fruits. Verbal testimony requires the life testimony for its confirmation to effectiveness. This is done through *ministration,* especially the ministration of mercy.

Through these measures of transmission the Gospel enters the hearts of the individual man and permeates society like the leaven in the lump. Thus it effects the only transformations possible for real moral and social welfare.

6. The Church must not be afraid and must not fail to condemn evil. It must follow the example of the Prophets in the Old Testament and of Christ and the Apostles in the New. Sometimes it must censure severely, and sometimes it must denounce acts and courses of conduct. It is here that the Church makes a right use and application of the law. But it cannot censure except it act in a sense as a censor. If such a thing were possible the Church should serve as a "conscience for the world." Every physician who makes his treatment effective recognizes and points out the nature and power of the disease, for which the treatment is given.

At the Lutheran World Convention in Copenhagen Dr. Knubel said that the Church is called to "a ministry of condemnation" in its relation to society. He said: "In a world of wrong silence in itself would often be sin. Christ and His Church do not, however, condemn as the world condemns. Judgment is not the purpose. The great difference is that they so condemn as to lead to repentance. Such condemnation is born of and guided by love."

7. The Church must recognize its *responsibility* for the realization of God's will for the temporal and eternal welfare of all mankind, and must work according to His plan.

The execution of His plan, by the use of His means, through His approved measures would so exalt piety, and so invigorate and promote Christian brotherhood, and to develop Christian stewardship that an incorruptible citizenship would control the destinies of the state, wealth would become the servant of all, the conflict between labor and capital would cease, sex immorality with its diseases would disappear, divorce courts would be closed, leisure would be used for the enrichment of personality instead of indulgences in dissipations, the under-privileged would find open doors of opportunity, and this would be like another world. *This all depends upon the faithfulness of the Church,* which needs only actually to enlist, in active endeavor, everyone it has enrolled into nominal membership. No new program needs to be set up. No new machinery needs to be added. *The great need is spiritual impulse.* The responsibility rests ultimately, as primarily, upon the individual man in the church, but for all cooperative endeavor the organization is already complete and sufficient. When we come down to the purely practical aspect of this matter, with our general observations before us, we find the key to *solution,* if we think of our subject as a problem, or to *success* if we think of it as an enterprise, in the *will to do.* If we look at the Church, with the charge of blameworthy degree of failure against it, we know that it is a human failure, and we center our attention upon the *leadership of the Church,* particularly upon the pastor. If we are not willing to charge him with responsibility for failure in his community, we are ready to credit him with being the key-man to success. If the pastor has clear views upon applied Christianity, *through brotherhood and stewardship,* if he has full faith in the power of the Gospel to produce brotherhood and induce stewardship, if he has a deep experience of the blessedness of vital religion and *practices* both brotherhood and stewardship, if he has the zeal of a true disciple of Jesus Christ,—is filled with His love, and preaches, teaches, testifies and lives accordingly,—he will be a social servant who can show definite results, and he will be a missionary who will win and enlist others,—within his church council, in his Sunday school, in his missionary societies, among the men and children groups and in his congregation as a whole, and thus will the community be reached. When a man is identified with God through communion, God communicates love for fellowman to his heart and spiritual impulse is begotten, which is first compassion, then passion and then personal concern and Christ-like service.

This joint enterprise, between God and man, for the realization of man's supreme interests and for the glory of Almighty God, claims the full measure of human loyalty and endeavor, as it is assured of divine faithfulness and power.

We recommend the following resolutions:

1. *Resolved,* That the outline presented above be referred to the congregations and educational agencies of the United Lutheran Church for study and discussion, preferably in groups, dividing and adapting matter according to circumstances, and arranging for a sufficient number of periods, with efficient leaders, to cover the subject with due deliberation. [Supplemented by the Convention, see p. 419.]

2. *Resolved,* That the United Lutheran Church records its feeling of horror and shame on account of the outrageous crimes committed in recent times, of which the kidnapping and murder of the Lindbergh baby is cited as one of the most appalling; that it recognizes a general spirit of lawlessness as the background of such crimes; and that it charges its people conscientiously and actively to uphold the sacredness and the majesty of the law of the land, and to recognize and practice Christian stewardship in the strict observance of all duties involved in Christian citizenship, including proper preparation for right action at the ballot box.

3. *Resolved,* That the United Lutheran Church hereby expresses its deepest concern on account of the distress arising from present economic conditions, especially on account of the sufferings of millions of unemployed people and those dependent upon them; and that it implores its members everywhere to use this opportunity to demonstrate the spirit of Christ through kind, sympathetic assistance wherever it can be given; and, since such conditions as now prevail may characterize any particular economic system, it declares it to be its conviction that the practice of true Christian Brotherhood and Stewardship is the only universally effective security for economic and social justice, and points to the promotion of the same as a basic duty of the Church in seeking to remedy causes, while it gives special aid for the immediate relief of present suffering.

4. *Resolved,* That the United Lutheran Church adopt the following submitted by a special committee after investigation and careful study of the particular subject:

Whereas, Throughout our land and nearly the whole civilized world, the moving picture has become a great center of attraction for the vast multitude of people, and especially for the young, and

Whereas, Notwithstanding the wonderful possibilities for both instruction and entertainment in pictures of good moral standard, the great commercial producing companies so often persist in forcing, through the block booking system, upon the communities of our land, a dangerously high percentage of pictures that are salacious and inciting to crime, and in pushing the sale of these in Europe and in Mohammedan and "heathen" lands, to the shame and injury of our American civilization, and to the great hindrance of our missionary work.

Therefore, Be It Resolved, That our United Lutheran Church in America hereby registers its strongest protest against the making, showing and sale of such pictures, as many prove to be most insidious forms of moral poison, and urges its pastors, teachers, parents and others to take a stand against this evil as it is brought into their communities.

Further, Be It Resolved, That as representatives of the great Lutheran Church we hereby petition the Senate and the House of Representatives of the United States of America to enact a law for the Federal supervision of moving pictures, the present system of censorship having shown itself to be ineffective. This supervision, to be of real worth, should be applied by Federal inspectors *before* the proposed pictures are filmed, and should extend to interstate and foreign commerce.

[This paragraph was stricken out by the Convention, see p. 419.]

WILLIAM H. HAGER, *Chairman.*
W. A. SADTLER
C. E. BRANDORFF.

5. *Resolved,* That this Convention hereby instructs the Committee on Moral and Social Welfare to make Facts and Influences in Modern Education in Relation to Morals the subject of special investigation and study during the next biennium, and to report results to the next Convention.

For the Committee,
W. H. GREEVER, *Chairman.*

Dr. Greever introduced the Rev. J. H. Harms who addressed the Convention.

Resolution 1 was amended by adding the words "and that we ask the Executive Board to consider the possibilities of more widespread publication of this report."

The resolution as amended was adopted.

Resolutions 2 and 3 were adopted.

It was moved and seconded to adopt resolution 4.

Dr. Greever asked that Mr. W. H. Hager and the Rev. W. A. Sadtler be given the privilege of addressing the Convention at this time.

It was moved and carried that resolution 4 be amended by striking out the last paragraph beginning with the words "Further, Be it resolved, That as representatives," etc.

The resolution as amended was adopted.

Resolution 5 was adopted.

The report of the Commissioners to the National Lutheran Council was presented by the Rev. P. W. Koller, Chairman of the Commissioners.

REPORT OF THE COMMISSIONERS TO THE NATIONAL LUTHERAN COUNCIL

(For action on the recommendations in this report see p. 426.)

Your Commissioners have the honor to submit their report of the work of the National Lutheran Council for the past biennium of The United Lutheran Church in America.

The full extent and importance of the work of the National Lutheran Council is not known as it should be throughout the Lutheran Church in America. It is in the providence of God the best known Lutheran agency in the world. It has been able to make contacts the world around that are most valuable and at the same time to serve all of our Lutheran bodies in America. Matters which seem to be the business of no particular Lutheran body are quietly done by the National Lutheran Council.

The Commissioners report on the National Council's work for the period beginning July 1, 1930, up to and including June 30, 1932. The report covers the following activities of the Council.

The functions of the National Lutheran Council, as outlined and defined in its governing regulations, are broadly classified into two spheres of activity:

A. Regular work, which is the home program, and

B. Emergency work, until this time largely confined to relief work among Lutherans in other lands.

When the National Lutheran Council decided in January, 1930, that, in addition to the regular administration of all affairs of the Lutheran World Convention, its Executive Committee should also assume the responsibility of administering all World Service funds and the giving of relief to suffering and endangered Lutheran churches throughout the world, it did so in order that the home program of the Council might be developed and carried out more fully. Conditions which have existed since that time have made it practically impossible to enlarge the home program as it was intended.

The regular work of the National Lutheran Council, as prescribed and defined in its regulations, is classified under three departments: Representation, Statistical and Reference Library Service, and Publicity. Under Representation may also be included the executive administration of the affairs of the Council. The following are listed and briefly described as cases coming under this department in the last two years.

1. The White House Committee on Child Health and Protection. Infor-

mation was supplied to the committee concerning the care and nurture of the Lutheran Church and all its agencies for children. In this connection it was necessary to give a comprehensive survey of all effort made to safeguard and preserve and develop the physical and spiritual welfare of children. Included in the survey were the activities of Sunday Schools, Luther Leagues, Young People's Societies, Boys' Clubs, Girls' Clubs, Summer Vacation Bible Schools, Camps, etc.

2. The President's Organization for Unemployment Relief. As a common agency of its participating Lutheran bodies the National Lutheran Council was called upon to cooperate with the President's Organization for Unemployment Relief in enlisting the sympathy, and favorable action of the bodies and of the pastors within the bodies in the effort to relieve unemployment and its consequent distress by urging from the pulpit and other channels, the return of boys and girls to school, rather than seeking employment, and urging each congregation to take care of the needy within its own membership, and to participate in the efforts of the community in which it is located to relieve the distress of those who were unfortunate and unemployed.

3. In the interest of securing the prompt release of captured Lutheran missionaries in China, it was necessary to communicate with the Department of State on several occasions.

4. Several cases of foreign students who wished to enter the United States for the purpose of further studies to become missionaries were referred to the National Lutheran Council in order to facilitate the securing of student visas for this purpose.

5. Contact was made with the General Committee on Army and Navy Chaplains and Chief of Chaplains of both the Army and the Navy in order to represent the interests of the Lutheran Church and her chaplains. In view of our activity in this direction, the Executive Director of the National Lutheran Council was made a Member-at-Large of the Executive Committee of the General Committee on Army and Navy Chaplains.

6. The National Lutheran Council was requested by the heirs in Poland of a deceased Polish man in the United States, through their pastor in Poland, to execute the final settlement of his estate. Power of Attorney was granted to the Executive Director and the estate finally settled to the satisfaction of the heirs.

7. Representation of the interests of the Lutheran Church in the "Church of the Air" of the Columbia Broadcasting System, through whose courtesy seven broadcasts were assigned to the Lutheran Church, made it possible to have the services conducted by pastors from five different Lutheran bodies. The "Church of the Air" will again be resumed in the early fall, the first Lutheran broadcast coming on the convention Sunday of the United Lutheran Church. Arrangements have already been made to broadcast from Philadelphia. A leading churchman of the United Lutheran Church in Philadelphia is being requested to be in charge of the service. Upon our suggestion the

Columbia Broadcasting System has assured us that the service will be extended to forty-five minutes. The uniform courtesy of the Columbia Broadcasting System in providing a full hour for the Lutheran broadcast on Easter Sunday by Dr. Tulloss and bringing the Wittenberg Choir from Springfield to Columbus, as well as the special scheduling of the St. Olaf Choir on Sunday afternoon, May 7, is deserving of recognition and grateful appreciation.

8. By authorization of the Commissioners of the National Lutheran Council in the annual meeting of 1931, the Executive Director began the publication of "The National Lutheran," which is being published bi-monthly and sent to all the pastors in the participating Lutheran bodies. The publication and mailing of this bulletin without cost to the pastor is made possible through the courtesy of the Lutheran Brotherhood.

STATISTICAL AND REFERENCE LIBRARY SERVICE

This department of the work of the National Lutheran Council is under the able and efficient direction of Dr. G. L. Kieffer, as Reference Librarian and Statistician, with whom Dr. O. M. Norlie cooperates as Consultant Librarian. The department is called upon frequently to furnish information concerning a great variety of subjects pertaining to the Lutheran Church. Considerable research is required to furnish all the material that is desired from time to time.

1. The articles furnished within the last two years include historical data, organization and development of Lutheran synods and church bodies, information concerning pioneer pastors and congregations, bibliography, United States Census of Religious Bodies, 1926, the percentage of different languages in the Lutheran Church in the United States and Canada, the percentage of illiteracy of the various countries of the world, the Lutheran churches of America, the Lutheran churches of Greater New York, and similar articles.

2. Dr. Kieffer has also contributed articles to a number of reference works on the Lutheran Church, as for instance: "The Present Organization of the Lutheran Church in America" for Schaff's Creeds of Christendom; an article for the "American Year Book"; an article for the Encyclopedia Brittannica, and extended correspondence with G. and C. Merriam Company, publishers of Webster's International Dictionary. These and other articles have all been prepared and authenticated by historical research in order that the true facts of the Lutheran Church shall be known.

3. Statistical and Reference Library service is also responsible for the assembling, compiling and preparation of the statistical and historical information contained in the Lutheran World Almanac. The recent edition of the Lutheran World Almanac, which appeared a few months ago, has been so well received that all but a few hundred copies of the entire edition have been sold. More and more, this reference book of Lutheran facts and figures is finding its way into the public libraries and to the best of editors and writers.

4. The statistical department continues to gather and compile the reports of all Lutherans in America from year to year. Annually these summary figures are released to all our Lutheran editors and to a great number of the daily press.

5. The efficient service of Dr. Kieffer as the statistician of the United Lutheran Church and of the National Lutheran Council, earned for him the well deserved recognition which the "Christian Herald" gave him in asking that he complete the figures of the reports of the churches upon the death of Dr. H. K. Carroll. Since then he has been asked to continue in this work and has organized the statisticians of the various religious bodies in the United States as an association of which he is the president.

Publicity

6. During the past biennium the Publicity Bureau of the National Lutheran Council has maintained active contact with the press and wire agencies throughout the United States and Canada, and has issued many releases direct to the newspapers of the country. The Bureau has come to be recognized as an authentic official source of church news. By enlisting the cooperation of publicity agencies, correspondents and press bureaus throughout the Lutheran Church, it has been possible to gather a great deal of news, which in turn has been given wider publicity by being released to a large circle of newspapers.

2. The Bureau also acts as a clearing house of Lutheran news all over the world, which is released to the Lutheran editors and executive officers within the Church, as well as to a number of religious editors of the daily press through a weekly News Bulletin.

3. At the request of the Lutheran Editors' Association, a series of syndicated articles were released to the editors. At the present time the Bureau is furnishing a series of five articles on Gustavus Adolphus in commemoration of the tercentenary of his death.

4. Mr. W. P. Elson, who for a number of years was in charge of the Publicity Bureau, is since January 1, 1932, devoting only one day a week to this work. He is in charge of the releases that are made to the press and wire agencies and to the newspapers. The other work of the Bureau has been assumed by the remaining members of the staff. It was necessary to make this adjustment in order to balance the budget, the income of the Council having decreased materially in the last few years.

5. It should also not be overlooked that a great deal of the time and energy of the staff of the Publicity Bureau is used to prepare and mail the literature that is sent out in the interest of Lutheran World Service. All the mimeographing, multigraphing, addressing and mailing incident to the appeal for funds for Lutheran World Service is borne by the Publicity Bureau.

Emergency Work

1. Since 1930 the administration and distribution of all releases for the World Service program has been definitely committed to the Executive

Committee of the Lutheran World Convention. This action was taken in the annual meeting of the Council in January, 1930, in order to enable the Council to develop and enlarge its home program. Circumstances and conditions which have prevailed since then have made it practically impossible to carry out this purpose to any great degree. A number of projects which properly come within the range of the function of the National Lutheran Council have had to be temporarily postponed because of the lack of funds.

It is the consensus of opinion of a number of leaders of the Lutheran Church that the shifting of the emphasis from the World to the American program was a very wise provision.

2. World Service. As the common agency of the participating Lutheran bodies, the National Lutheran Council continues to be the organization through which funds contributed by American Lutherans are to be raised for the Lutheran World Service program. The economic situation of the last two years has made it increasingly more difficult to raise sufficient amounts to care for the whole program in an adequate manner. The total amount raised from American sources in 1930 amounted to $41,551.94, whereas in 1931 the amount was $25,377.59. The request for 1932 by the Executive Committee of the Lutheran World Convention is $70,000, including $10,000 for the Harbin refugees.

3. With reference to the German-Russian Lutheran refugees concerning whom Dr. Morehead reported there were about 400 in Harbin, Manchuria, and that an ultimatum had been delivered that they must leave or they would be deported to Russia, it was decided to add the sum of $10,000 to the regular budget of World Service for the relief of the refugees. Developments after the meeting of the Council proved that it was necessary to remove them as soon as possible. Accordingly, plans were made and negotiations were entered into for their transportation and settlement to another country. To accomplish this at least $56,805 was necessary, according to the lowest estimate of expenses. Dr. Morehead then requested the National Lutheran Council to raise $20,000 instead of the $10,000 which had been voted, and requested the Lutherans of Europe to share in the responsibility. When sufficient funds were on hand to pay for their transportation it was arranged to forward them from Shanghai to Brazil where they are to be settled, hoping to secure the balance necessary for their settlement later. Dr. Morehead became ill in May and was compelled, upon the advice of his physician, to relinquish his duties temporarily in order to recover his health. Dr. L. W. Boe, the second American member of the Executive Committee of the Lutheran World Convention, then assumed the responsibility, which he in turn delegated to Dr. Knubel and the Executive Director, since it was impossible for him to devote his entire time to it.

Note: The time of the arrival of the refugees in Brazil and the exact place of their settlement has not been definitely learned.

4. The active participation and cooperation of the Lutheran Student's Association of America in support of the Lutheran Seminary in Leningrad, is deserving of mention.

PERSONNEL AND BUDGET

The membership of the Council is as follows: Church Bodies officially participating and their commissioners: United Lutheran Church in America, Rev. J. A. W. Haas, D.D., LL.D., Rev. C. E. Krumbholz, Rev. L. W. Steckel, D.D., Rev. C. A. Freed, D.D., Rev. P. W. Koller, D.D., Hon. E. F. Eilert, C.S.D., Mr. G. F. Greiner, Rev. E. B. Burgess, D.D., LL.D., Rev. E. P. Pfatteicher, Ph.D., D.D., Norwegian Lutheran Church of America, Rev. J. A. Aasgaard, D.D., Rev. L. W. Boe, D.D., LL.D., Rev. J. A. O. Stub, D.D.; The Evangelical Lutheran Augustana Synod in North America, Rev. G. A. Brandelle, D.D., LL.D., Rev. Peter Peterson, D.D.; American Lutheran Church, Rev. C. C. Hein, D.D., Rev. E. Poppen, D.D., Rev. E. H. Rausch, D.D., LL.D., Rev. F. H. Meyer, D,D.; The United Danish Evangelical Lutheran Church in America, Rev. N. C. Carlsen, D.D.; Lutheran Free Church, Rev. T. O. Burntvedt; Icelandic Evangelical Lutheran Synod in North America, Rev. K. K. Olafson. Other Church Bodies unofficially participating in Lutheran World Service programs: Danish Lutheran Church, Eielsen Synod, Lutheran Brethren, Suomi Synod, and the Finnish Apostolic Church.

Note: During the Biennium we lost Commissioner Dr. M. G. G. Scherer, who has been a member from the very organization of the Council and who will be greatly missed, as his participation in the work of the Council has always been wise and worthy.

Officers are as follows: President, Rev. G. A. Brandelle, D.D., LL.D.; vice-president, Rev. C. C. Hein, D.D.; secretary, Rev. N. C. Carlsen, D.D.; treasurer, Hon. E. F. Eilert, C.S.D.

Executive Committee: Rev. G. A. Brandelle, D.D., LL.D.; Rev. C. C. Hein, D.D.; Rev. N. C. Carlsen, D.D.; Hon. E. F. Eilert, C.S.D.; Rev. E. B. Burgess, D.D., LL.D.; Rev. E. H. Rausch, D,D., LL.D.; Rev. T. O. Burntvedt; Rev. J. A. Aasgaard, D.D.

Since September 1, 1930, the work of the National Lutheran Council has been under the direction of Rev. Ralph H. Long, D.D., Executive Director. Rev. F. H. Meyer, D.D., pastor of Fordham Lutheran Church, New York City, served as acting Director from February 1, 1930, until September 1, 1930. On February 1, 1930, Rev. John A. Morehead, D.D., LL.D., Th.D., S.T.D., then Executive Director, relinquished this position to become the full-time president of the Lutheran World Convention.

The total budget of the Council as pro rated through its participating bodies now amounts to $37,029.35. The proportionate share of this allocated to the United Lutheran Church is $18,488.87; of this amount the United Lutheran Church paid in 1930, $16,215; in 1931, $15,065, and based on the receipts for the first half of this year the total amount in 1932 will hardly exceed $13,000. The allocation of the entire budget is as follows: United Lutheran Church, $18,488.87; Norwegian Lutheran Church, $6,066.89; Augustana Synod $4,678.36; American Lutheran Church, $6,800; United Danish Church, $374.82; Lutheran Free Church, $500; Icelandic Synod, $120.41.

This rather extended and detailed outline gives a fairly complete picture of the work of the National Lutheran Council during the past biennium. It should, however, be remembered that much of the influence is intangible and cannot be tabulated. This fact is embodied in one of the resolutions of the last meeting of the Council, in which it is stated:

"The united efforts of the co-operative bodies through this agency has created a bond of sympathy and understanding that can hardly be estimated or understood. These are contributions to the Lutheran Church which may well justify all that the Council has cost in time, money and sacrifice."

RECOMMENDATIONS

Your Commissioners offer the following recommendations:

1. That the United Lutheran Church pay its share of the budget, $18,488.87, for the maintenance of the National Lutheran Council.
[Withdrawn by the Commissioners.]

2. That the 1932 world service program for $70,000 be approved and that pastors and parishes of all constituent synods be encouraged and urged to contribute their proportionate part of this world service program. In the $70,000 is included $10,000 for the transportation of the Harbin refugees to Brazil, South America.

3. That if a successor for Dr. M. G. G. Scherer on the National Lutheran Council has not been selected we authorize the president of the United Lutheran Church to make such an appointment.
[Withdrawn by the Commissioners.]

Material for the Lutheran World Almanac and articles from the Council have been quoted in this report.

Respectfully submitted,

PAUL W. KOLLER,
For the Commissioners.

Recommendation 1 was withdrawn because it was already covered by the action of the Convention on the budget.

Recommendation 2 was adopted.

Recommendation 3 was withdrawn.

The report of the Committee on Women as Congregational Representatives was presented by the Rev. S. Billheimer, Chairman of the Committee.

REPORT OF THE COMMITTEE ON WOMEN AS CONGREGATIONAL REPRESENTATIVES

(For action on this report see p. 430.)

The committee was appointed to study and summarize (1) the biblical teachings and interpretation, and (2) the questions of church polity bearing upon the two Memorials from the Texas Synod, (Minutes of the Seventh

Biennial Convention of The United Lutheran Church in America, 1930, pp. 142-3) :

"8. From the Texas Synod:
    1930
'(1)   That we memorialize The United Lutheran Church in America in the matter of women delegates to meetings of synod to determine whether or not such procedure is unscriptural.'
    1929
'Beschlossen, dass wir, die Texas Synode, die Vereinigte Lutherische Kirche von Amerika ersuchen, ein Gutachten ueber diese Frage zu geben: Ist die Gemeindevertretung seitens der Frauen der Gemeinde schriftwidrig?'"

The undersigned are of the opinion that the election of women as congregational representatives is not unscriptural. This view is based on the following considerations:

1. BIBLICAL TEACHINGS AND INTERPRETATION

a. No Scripture passage expressly forbids such election or representation. The two passages, I Cor. 14: 34-35 and I Tim. 2: 11-12, which have been held to forbid this procedure, have no direct and immediate application to the question raised in these Memorials. Their immediate application was to the question whether women were to be permitted to "speak" or to "teach" in the churches. This was in a social order in which such public speaking, not only in the churches but in any public meeting, would have been considered exceedingly improper. Literally applied, these passages would prohibit women from teaching in our Sunday schools; and, to be consistent, would involve radical changes in the present development of our church life and organization.

b. The attitude and the general principle which should govern the Church in answering these Memorials are revealed by St. Paul in Gal. 3: 28, where he sets forth the ideal of spiritual equality in Christ. This could not be reached at once, but its gradual application should not be hindered simply because conditions in some of the New Testament churches made it necessary for women to "keep silence." Under the guidance of the Holy Spirit, as promised by the Saviour, the Church has been brought nearer to the realization of this spiritual ideal; and actual retrogression would result if our modern churches were to limit themselves to a literal application of the specific practice recommended to these ancient churches.

c. The mind of Christ, as revealed by Scripture, must be our final authority for the solution of these problems. While maintaining the divine order of creation (Matt. 19: 4), Jesus manifested unusual sympathy for women and accepted their ministries. His admission of them into the circle of his fellowship secured for them their place in the infant church (Acts 1: 14).

2. CONSIDERATIONS BEARING ON CHURCH POLITY

With reference to the second question, it is our opinion that there is nothing in our Lutheran polity to prevent the election of women as congregational representatives. Our Confessions are very clear on the liberty of the Church, under the guidance of the Holy Spirit and in harmony with the explicit limitations of Scripture. When the interests of a congregation can be served better by the election of a woman as delegate to synod, such congregation should feel free to do so. It is in the exercise of this liberty that several of our older and larger district synods have occasionally seated women delegates, and the same is true of two other Lutheran groups in this country. But in all such procedure the following considerations ought to be kept in mind:

a. The conception of spiritual equality in Christ does not alter the fact that, by divine appointment, certain spheres of Christian service are more natural or normal to men, while other types of service can be best performed by women. Since the Church deeply deplores those social, industrial, and economic conditions which oppose the Christian home, the glory of motherhood and the rearing of children in the nurture and admonition of the Lord, it should encourage the fulfillment of those duties by the exercise of care in the organization and assignment of its work.

b. After securing the views of a number of representative women of our Church, we find no marked desire on their part to assume a larger share in the administrative work of the Church. Where service can be rendered equally well by the men, they should not be permitted to shift upon the women their responsibility for the welfare of the congregation and the spread of the gospel. Disregard of this principle would result in lack of good order, evasion of duty and the diversion of women from those tasks which are peculiarly their own, such as are found in the educational work of the Church, the various phases of Inner Mission work and the female Diaconate.

c. These same principles should be applied to all questions concerning the election of women to membership in the Church Council, as delegates to the Biennial Convention, or as members of the General Boards. But wherever the question of the conducting of formal public services by women has been raised in Lutheran circles, it has always been answered by refusing to women the regular administration of the Means of Grace.

d. Where difference of opinion on these questions exists, congregations and synods alike should deal with it in the spirit of mutual tolerance, in order that the law of Christian love may have free course in maintaining the peace and unity of our Church.

3. Recommendation

With these considerations in mind, the undersigned recommend that the reply of The United Lutheran Church in America to the Memorials from the Texas Synod be as follows:

"The election of women delegates to meetings of synod is not unscriptural."

> Stanley Billheimer.
> Raymond T. Stamm.
> Claude T. Reno.
> Flora Prince.

Dr. Billheimer introduced the Rev. J. C. Mattes, a member of the Committee, who presented a minority report as follows:

MINORITY REPORT

The undersigned, to his great regret, is compelled to submit the following report dissenting from the report of the other members of the Committee on Women as Congregational Representatives for the reasons herein stated.

Under all normal conditions the election of women delegates to synodical meetings and to membership in Church Councils is unscriptural because the placing of women in positions of authority over men in the official direction and ruling of the Church, or in the conduct of its public worship, is expressly forbidden by St. Paul in I Tim. 2:11-12. That this passage of Holy Writ is to be so understood is the opinion of practically all learned commentators and has been the unanimous understanding of the universal Church for almost nineteen hundred years. Even those who have differed most widely on other points of doctrine or discipline have been agreed on this point till very recent days. The context of the passage furthermore makes it clear that St. Paul has in mind the natural distinctions between the sexes, as they were established by the immutable and eternal order of creation, and that this prohibition has nothing whatsoever to do with certain customs of the times. To attempt to remove the binding character of this statement on the plea that it is only applicable to certain ages, and is conditioned by ancient customs, is to introduce a principle of exegetical evasion that is most dangerous and one by which the authority of very many passages of Scripture can be deleted when desired.

That the election of women delegates to synods would place them in a position of ruling over man and even of teaching doctrine, on occasion, becomes clear if we consider but one possible case. Should a doctrinal question arise, it would be the right of such a woman delegate to debate it and thus teach and preach in a public assembly of the Church.

The restriction here imposed by St. Paul in no wise impairs the honor shown to womankind nor does it conflict with the spiritual equality of men and women, any more than do the restrictions imposed by differences of age or natural endowments. Nor does it in any way conflict with Galatians 3:28. To cite the latter passage as contradicting this one in First Timothy is to violate the sound rule of exegesis that a more general passage is to be interpreted in the light of the one that is more specific and particular.

Neither can it disagree with the mind of Christ, which St. Paul knew better than we, for the Lord who gladly accepted the ministrations of women and welcomed them, together with the children, to His circle, nowhere commissioned them to direct or rule His Church, any more than He commissioned children for that purpose, but confined all such activities to grown men.

In Lutheran polity this has been the accepted and undisputed position up to our own times. While the Lutheran Church has welcomed women to all phases of the ministry of serving love, in which they not only excel men but in which, due to the different qualifications conferred on the sexes by the order of creation, they are able to render services for which men are not normally qualified. It is in such ministrations and in the divinely given task of motherhood and the care of the young that the New Testament finds the highest crown of womanly glory. Here is a mission just as vital, honorable and glorious as the government of the Church and one for which women are pre-eminently fitted by their God-given endowments.

Therefore, the undersigned respectfully submits in conformity with the unanimous interpretation of the universal Church of all ages (excepting a minority of Christendom in the most recent times and some fanatical sects of various ages) that, under normal conditions the electing of women to ruling places in the administration of the general work of the Church or congregation is unscriptural. To avoid confusion it must also be understood that this universal application of the words of St. Paul has always been clearly interpreted as not applying to the teaching of the young (Sunday school, for example) nor to the work of women among women, of which the Deaconess Board might serve as an example in our own day.

JOHN C. MATTES.

On motion both the report of the Committee and the minority report were referred to a new committee, to be appointed by the President, to study this matter further and report to the next Convention of The United Lutheran Church in America.

The Convention then proceeded to items of unfinished business.

The report of the Parish and Church School Board was presented by the Rev. F. M. Urich, President of the Board.

REPORT OF THE PARISH AND CHURCH SCHOOL BOARD

The Parish and Church School Board herewith submits its regular biennial report to The United Lutheran Church in America.

In this report the Board repeats, for the information of the Church and for the inspiration of its workers, the objectives for which it was created; it describes the efforts and the progress it has made toward a fuller realization of these objectives; and it pledges to the Church a courageous and a careful continuance of the work committed to it. The report is presented under the following headings:

I.   The Objectives of the Board.
II. The Activities of the Board.
III. The Pledge of the Board.

I. The Objectives of the Board.

The Board continuously keeps before it the following five specific objectives:

A. The efficient administration of the operations of the Board.

B. The formulation of a comprehensive plan of parish education for the Church.

C. The preparation of a comprehensive and effective curriculum for parish education.

D. The development of a consecrated and effective leadership for parish education.

E. The promotion of parish education in the Church.

These objectives are a simple summary and outline of the task which the Church has committed to the Parish and Church School Board. They are stated in the constitution of the Board in detail as follows:

"The object of this Board shall be to develop and execute a system or systems of literature for use in the home, the parish and the Church schools; to organize schools for weekday Christian training; to plan methods of school administration; to recommend books for the library; to outline programs for Summer Assemblies, Sunday School Conventions and Normals and all festival occasions of the Church; to prepare hymnals; to have oversight over and control of whatever pertains to the best interests of the parish and the Church school. It shall carry on its work in the name of The United Lutheran Church in America, and in accordance with the Doctrinal Basis, Constitution, Acts and Rulings of said United Lutheran Church in America."

"Section 1. The Board shall have power to prosecute the work entrusted to it. It shall prepare a system or systems of lessons for the religious training of the young in the Sunday Bible School, Weekday Bible Training School, Catechetical Class, Christian Kindergartens, Daily Vacation Bible School, Teacher Training, Young People's Societies, Boys' and Girls' Organizations, Home Studies in the Christian Religion for parents and children, and such other efforts by which the members of the Church will be confirmed in their holy faith. The system or systems shall be known as the Christian Training Series of The United Lutheran Church in America, and shall be under its control. It shall supply all the material necessary for the thorough development of all these agencies.

"Section 2. The Board shall keep itself informed concerning the best methods in parish and Church school work and administration and shall publish literature, tracts, magazines and books for the information and assistance of parents, pastors and teachers. It shall recommend suitable books for libraries and the home, and encourage and stimulate Lutheran writers in the preparation of such literature. After consultation with the Common Service Book Committee it shall prepare hymnals for Church school use.

"Section 3. It shall have oversight and control of the Church school. It shall prepare plans, methods of operation, and programs for Summer Assemblies, Sunday School Conventions and Normals, and other festival occasions of the Church."

II. The Activities of the Board.

The activities of the Board are here arranged under the five specific objectives of the Board as outlined above. This outline is followed in order that the Church may be able to see how far the Board has progressed toward a complete realization of its work.

A. The Efficient Administration of the Operations of the Board.

1. Reorganization of the Board.

    a. The Officers of the Board are as follows:

        (I) President: Rev. Frank M. Urich, D.D.
                                      Philadelphia, Pa.
        (II) Vice-President: Rev. F. R. Knubel,
                                        Rochester, N. Y.
        (III) Secretary: Rev. D. Burt Smith, D.D.,
                                      Philadelphia, Pa.
        (IV) Treasurer: Mr. George M. Jones,
                                        Reading, Pa.

    b. The Standing Committees of the Board:

During the biennium, the Board changed its By-Laws, reorganizing its operations under four standing committees in place of the former six and a number of special committees. The four new standing committees, and the work referred to each, are as follows:

(I) Committee on Field Work:

    (A) The promotion of parish education through:
        (1) Field Secretaries
        (2) The Parish School Magazine
        (3) Visitation by Editors
        (4) Leadership Training Program
        (5) Church School Plans and Equipment
    (B) The promotion of leadership training through:
        (1) Congregational Classes
        (2) Community Classes
        (3) Correspondence Courses
        (4) Summer Schools
        (5) Leadership Training Camps (Nawakwa)
        (6) Colleges and Seminaries
        (7) The Parish School Magazine
        (8) Workers' Libraries
        (9) Special Literature, Tracts and Folders
       (10) Visitation by Secretaries and Editors
       (11) Issuing of certificates, diplomas and teacher accreditations, etc.
       (12) Recording of credits

(II) Committee on Literature:

    (A) The Preparation of Materials for:
        (1) The Augsburg International Uniform Lessons
        (2) The Lutheran Graded Series
        (3) The Christian Life Course
        (4) The Vacation Church School Texts
        (5) The Weekday Church School Texts
        (6) The Parish School Magazine
        (7) Lutheran Boys and Girls
        (8) Lutheran Young Folks
        (9) The Parish School Hymnal
       (10) The Children's Hymnal and Service Book
       (11) Services for Special Days

(12) Leadership Training Textbooks
(13) A Home Course
(14) Workers' Libraries
(15) Special Literature, Tracts and Folders
(B) Stimulation of Lutheran Authorship
(III) Committee on Organization and Administration of Parish Education:
  (A) The Formulation of a Comprehensive Plan of Parish Education for:
    (1) The Congregation
    (2) The Synod
    (3) The United Lutheran Church in America
  (B) Church School Plans and Equipment
  (C) Defining Relationships With:
    (1) Other Boards and Agencies of the Church
    (2) Outside Agencies
  (D) Surveys and Research
(IV) Committee on Finance:
  (A) Arrange the Budget
  (B) Present the Budget to the Executive Board of The United Lutheran Church in America
  (C) Have General Supervision of Disbursements

c. The employed personnel of the Board:

The Board called the Rev. S. White Rhyne, one of its former field secretaries, to become its first Executive Secretary. Headquarters for the Board were established in the Muhlenberg Building, Philadelphia, Pa., and the Executive Secretary took up his duties June 1, 1931.

The present employed personnel of the Board is:

Executive Secretary:	Rev. S. White Rhyne
Editors:	Rev. Chas. P. Wiles, D.D.
	Rev. D. Burt Smith, D.D.
	Rev. Paul J. Hoh
Assistant Editor:	Miss Mabel Elsie Locker
Field Secretaries:	Rev. C. H. B. Lewis, D.D.
	Rev. Paul E. Keyser

d. Deaths:

Since the Board made its last report to the Church, two faithful members of its staff have passed away, Rev. William Lee Hunton, Ph.D., D.D., and Miss Maud Junkin Baldwin, B.R.E. Dr. Hunton was also a former member and secretary of the Board. The following is a quotation from "the Minute placed upon the records of The Parish and Church School Board as a permanent memorial to the lives and labors of these devoted servants of God":

"That we herewith record our deep appreciation of the earnest, faithful and consecrated service rendered by Dr. Hunton and Mrs. Baldwin in the field of our Sunday School literature and in many other departments of the Church's work.

"That we recall with affectionate esteem the many evidences of their unselfish zeal and fidelity in addressing themselves to the multiform tasks that claimed their time, talent and physical strength.

"That we are deeply conscious of the loss we have sustained by their removal from our ranks and pray that new leaders may spring up to take the place of those whose earthly labors have ended and who have so greatly enriched our lives as we worked side by side with them in the furtherance of Christ's Kingdom."

2. Nominations.

The four members of the Board whose terms expire at this convention are nominated for re-election:

Rev. J. D. M. Brown, Litt.D., 1620 Walnut St., Allentown, Pa.
Rev. M. Hadwin Fischer, Ph.D., Gettysburg, Pa.
Rev. F. R. Knubel, 330 Barrington St,, Rochester, N. Y.
Mr. George M. Jones, 5 N. 4th St., Reading, Pa.

3. Conferences.

a. Conference of the Board of Education:

The Rev. Chas. P. Wiles, D.D., attended the Conference called by the Board of Education in Washington, D. C., December 19-20, 1930.

b. Intersynodical Conference on Elementary Education:

The Rev. Chas. P. Wiles, D.D., and the Rev. D. Burt Smith, D.D., attended and participated in the two meetings of Intersynodical Conference on Elementary Education held in Chicago during the biennium.

"At these conferences, principles and methods were discussed, looking toward a better understanding of the conceptions held by the different Lutheran bodies of the conferences in the matter of elementary Christian education. Well prepared papers were presented and thoroughly discussed. While there is no tangible outcome from these conferences to be expected in the near future, yet it seems advisable to continue them. The Board is glad to have its representatives take part in the conferences and will continue their appointment."

B. The Formulation of a Comprehensive Plan of Parish Education.

In compliance with the resolutions of the Milwaukee Convention of The United Lutheran Church in America, instructing the Board to prepare a comprehensive plan of parish education, the Board directed its secretarial staff to make a study of the problem and to formulate the plan. Work was begun as soon after the last convention of the Church as it was possible to make adjustments in the work of the Board. For the past ten months the Executive Secretary and the two Field Secretaries of the Board have addressed themselves to the task exclusively. The President of the Board and the Committee of the Board, to which this work is referred, have closely supervised the procedure of the secretaries and have instructed the secretaries to continue their work without ceasing until it is completed. A full report of the work to date has been made to the Executive Board of The United Lutheran Church in America.

C.   The Preparation of a Comprehensive and Effective Curriculum for Parish Education.

The following curriculum materials have been prepared, or are in the process of being prepared, under the auspices of the Parish and Church School Board.

Curriculum Material	*Prepared or Being Prepared*	*Editor or Author*
1. The Augsburg International Uniform Lessons:	Prepared Quarterly	Drs. Wiles and Smith (Editors)
a. Little Ones: Papers Cards Charts	Prepared Quarterly	Dr. Wiles (Editor)
b. The Junior Lesson Book	Prepared Quarterly	Miss Mabel Elsie Locker (Author)
c. The Intermediate-Senior Lesson Book	Prepared Annually	Rev. D. Burt Smith, D.D. (Author)
d. The Young People's Lesson Book	Prepared Annually	Rev. D. Burt Smith, D.D. (Author)
e. The Adult Lesson Book	Prepared Annually	Rev. D. Burt Smith, D.D. (Author)
f. The Home Department Lesson Book	Prepared Annually	Drs. Smith and Wiles (Authors)
g. The Augsburg Teacher	Prepared Monthly	Dr. Wiles (Editor and Author)
h. The Lesson Commentary	Prepared Annually	Drs. Wiles and Smith (Authors)
i. The Lutheran Page	Prepared Weekly	Rev. D. Burt Smith, D.D. (Author)
2. The Lutheran Graded Course: In bound book form only.	Completed	
a. Bible Stories (Teacher and Pupil)		
b. Bible Readings		
c. Bible History (Teacher and Pupil)		
d. Bible Facts and Scenes (Teacher and Pupil)		
e. Bible Biography		
f. Bible Teachings		
g. Bible Outlines		
h. In Mother's Arms (Teacher and Pupil)		

Curriculum Material	Prepared or Being Prepared	Editor or Author
3. The Christian Life Course		Rev. Paul J. Hoh (Editor)
Nursery Department:		
a. A Nursery Course: Teacher's Book— Pupil's Leaflet	Ready Oct. 1933	Mrs. Marion Poppen Athy (Author)
Beginners Department:		
b. The Heavenly Father's Little Ones Teacher's Book— Pupil's Leaflet	Completed	Mrs. Marion Poppen Athy (Author)
c. The Heavenly Father's Children— Teacher's Book— Pupil's Leaflet	Ready Oct. 1932	Mrs. Marion Poppen Athy (Author)
Primary Department:		
d. Our Homes Teacher's Book— Pupil's Leaflet	Completed	Mrs. Mabel B. Fenner (Author)
e. Our World Teacher's Book— Pupil's Leaflet	Ready Oct., 1932	Mrs. Mabel B. Fenner (Author)
f. Our Friends Teacher's Book— Pupil's Leaflet	Ready Oct., 1933	Mrs. Mabel B. Fenner (Author)
Junior Department:		
g. God's Heroes Teacher's Book— Pupil's Book	Completed	Miss Mabel Elsie Locker (Author)
h. God's Workers Teacher's Book— Pupil's Book	Ready Oct., 1932	Miss Mabel Elsie Locker (Author)
i. God's Book Teacher's Book— Pupil's Book	Ready Oct., 1933	Miss Mabel Elsie Locker (Author)
Intermediate Department:		
j. Christian Boys and Girls Teacher's Book— Pupil's Book	Completed	Rev. Ernest J. Hoh (Author)
k. Men and Women of God Teacher's Book— Pupil's Book	Ready Oct., 1932	J. Conrad Seegers, Ph.D. (Author)
1. The Story of God's People Teacher's Book— Pupil's Book	Ready Oct., 1933	Rev. Paul I. Morentz and Rev. Paul J. Hoh (Authors)
Senior Department:		
m. The Christian Church Teacher's Book— Pupil's Book	Completed	Revs. O. F. Nolde, Ph.D., George R. Seltzer, Paul J. Hoh (Authors)

Curriculum Material	Prepared or Being Prepared	Editor or Author
n. The Christian Life Teacher's Book— Pupil's Book	Ready Oct., 1932	Revs. O. Fred Nolde, Ph.D., Paul J. Hoh
o. Life Problems	Ready Oct., 1933	Rev. Paul J. Hoh (Author)
4. Religious Education Texts for Vacation Schools:•	Completed	Mrs. Maud Junkin Baldwin (Editor and Author)
Primary Department: a. The Heavenly Father and His Children Teacher's Book Pupil's Memory Book Large Pictures	Completed	Mrs. Maud Junkin Baldwin (Editor and Author)
b. Serving the Heavenly Father Teacher's Book Large Pictures Pupil's Memory Book	Completed	Mrs. Maud Junkin Baldwin (Editor and Author)
c. Jesus and His Followers Teacher's Book Large Pictures Pupil's Memory Book	Completed	Mrs. Maud Junkin Baldwin (Editor and Author)
Junior Department: d. Stories of the Early Hebrew Heroes Teacher's Book Large Pictures Pupil's Memory Book	Completed	Mrs. Maud Junkin Baldwin (Editor and Author)
e. Stories of Jesus Teacher's Book Picture Folder Pupil's Memory Book	Completed	Mrs. Maud Junkin Baldwin (Editor and Author)
f. Stories of Early Church Heroes Teacher's Book Picture Folder Pupil's Memory Book	Completed	Mrs. Maud Junkin Baldwin (Editor and Author)
5. Religious Education Texts for Weekday Schools:	Completed	
Primary Department: a. God and His Helpers Teacher's Manual Pupil's Book	Completed	Mrs. Mabel B. Fenner (Author)

Curriculum Material	Prepared or Being Prepared	Editor or Author
b. Jesus and His Friends Teacher's Manual— Pupil's Book	Completed	Mrs. Mabel B. Fenner (Author)
c. God's Good Gifts Teacher's Manual— Pupil's Book	Completed	Mrs. Mabel B. Fenner (Author)
Junior Department: d. God's Great Plan for Mankind Teacher's Manual— Pupil's Book	Completed	Miss Eva M. Stilz (Author)
e. God's Care for Mankind Teacher's Manual— Pupil's Book	Completed	Miss Eva M. Stilz (Author)
f. God Working Through Mankind Teacher's Manual— Pupil's Book	Completed	Miss Eva M. Stilz (Author)
6. The Parish School Magazine	Prepared Monthly	Drs. Wiles and Smith (Editors) Miss Mabel Elsie Locker (Asst. Editor)
7. Lutheran Boys and Girls	Prepared Weekly	Dr. Wiles (Editor) Miss Gilbert and Miss Albert (Asst. Editors)
8. Lutheran Young Folks	Prepared Weekly	Drs. Wiles and Smith (Editors) Miss Albert (Assistant Editor)
9. The Parish School Hymnal	Completed	
10. The Children's Hymnal and Service Book	Completed	
11. Special Services: Christmas Easter Children's Day Rally Day	Prepared Annually	
12. Dedication of a Church House	Completed	
13. Office for The Induction of Officers and Teachers	Being Prepared	
14. Pamphlet on Church School Plans and Equipment	Being Prepared	

All materials prepared under the auspices of the Parish and Church School Board have always been published, distributed, and sold by the Board of Publication. In turn, the Board of Publication pays the salaries, provides the offices and the equipment, and furnishes the stenographic assistance for the editors and the assistant editor of the Parish and Church School Board.

The Augsburg International Uniform Lesson Course

This course has been continued as in the previous bienniums except for the change in the names of two lesson books. The Intermediate Lesson Book was changed to The Intermediate-Senior Lesson Book and The Senior Lesson Book was changed to The Young People's Lesson Book. This change was made to clear up confusion in orders placed for materials and to assist the schools in better grading of pupils.

The Lutheran Graded Course

This course is still made available in bound book form from Bible Stories through Bible Outlines.

The Christian Life Course

The Board has been able to prepare this course according to the schedule announced in the last report to the Church. The first five courses of the fifteen planned appeared in time for introduction into our Church Schools October 1, 1931. The courses have met with almost universal satisfaction, and, though there have been minor criticisms, the general approval of the Church is evidenced by the fact that more than 300,000 copies are now in use each quarter. More than three hundred thousand pupils and teachers in our Church Schools are using this course each Sunday. Five additional courses are now ready for introduction into the Church Schools October 1, 1932, and the five remaining courses will be ready for introduction October 1, 1933. A Course for the Nursery Department is included in the Courses promised for the fall of 1933. This course will consist of a teacher's book with fifty-two lessons and a weekly illustrated leaflet for the nursery pupils.

Considerable space in our official magazine, The Parish School, has been devoted to a consideration of The Christian Life Course and teachers who have followed these articles have been greatly benefitted by them. The new course and the magazine are commended to your consideration.

The Parish School Magazine

The Parish School Magazine is being made more practical each year. The department on Children's Work has been found very helpful by workers with children. The coming year a department for young people, a department for adults, and a monthly workers' conference program for the meeting of the teachers and officers of the Church Schools will be introduced.

New Pamphlets

Two new pamphlets of much value to Church School workers will be completed within the next year. These pamphlets are:

"An Office for The Induction of Officers and Teachers in a Church
School."

"Church School Plans and Equipment."

D. The Development of a Consecrated and Effective Leadership for Parish Education

The Board considers this one of the most important objectives of its work. It is not sufficient merely to prepare materials for parish education. There must be developed an intelligent, effective, and consecrated leadership for parish education. The preparation of materials for parish education and the development of leadership for parish education must go hand in hand.

The Board is prepared to suggest leadership training courses to congregations, community schools, and synodical summer schools. Teachers are accredited, certificates of credit and diplomas are issued, and assistance is given to the organization of all types of training schools. At the present time two types of courses are suggested: an elementary Course and a standard Course. During the past biennium, the Board accredited 244 teachers, and issued 600 final certificates of credit for the elementary course. In the same period, Lutheran workers have earned 10,092 standard certificates. This number includes those issued directly by our Board and those issued by the International Council of Religious Education. The Board has issued 97 standard diplomas directly from its offices during the biennium. No record of the number of diplomas issued to Lutheran students by the International Council of Religious Education is now available.

Nawakwa Leadership Training Camp

Nawakwa Leadership Training Camp completed two splendid seasons of work during the biennium. The Rev. M. Hadwin Fischer, Ph. D., has been continued as director and Miss LaVene Grove as associate director. Substantial material equipment has been added to the camp during this period.

The following statistics give an idea of the scope of the work:

Year	Faculty Members	Students	Standard Leadership Training Credits
1930	26	439	390
1931	28	485	464

E. The Promotion of Parish Education in the Church

1. Field Secretaries:

a. A New Policy in Field Work—

The Board depends primarily upon its Field Secretaries for the promotion of parish education in the Church. In order to extend this work and to give an even development to it throughout the entire church, a new policy in field work has been adopted. It will now be the duty of the Field Secretaries to assist synods, or groups of synods, to develop their own programs of parish education. Strong synodical committees on parish education will be urged and the Field Secretaries will cooperate with them in building a synodical program and in promoting it in the parish. The two Secretaries will now be known simply as Field Secretaries of the Parish and Church School Board and will serve the territory of The United Lutheran Church in America in place of certain districts. The change of policy means that the Board will now offer its Secretaries to the synods in an advisory and supervisory capacity in building a parish program, but will leave the active development of the program to the synods themselves. Only when great need demands, and only when time will permit, will the Field Secretaries do specific work in parishes.

b. The Field Secretaries Taken From the Field—

In order that the Board might carry out the instructions of The United Lutheran Church in America to formulate a comprehensive plan of parish education, it was necessary to call the Field Secretaries from the field temporarily. During the last year of the biennium the Field Secretaries, together with the Executive Secretary, have given themselves exclusively to this work. It has meant that the Church has had to suffer the loss of these men in the field, but the Board felt that their services were essential in the formulation of the plan. A few of our church leaders have not been able to understand this procedure, but in most cases the Church has given a sympathetic hearing to our explanation.

During the first year of the biennium the Field Secretaries did specific work in the promotion of parish education. The field secretaries and the editors assisted in preparing the schedules of 27 Synodical Summer Schools and participated in their programs. Sixteen synodical meetings were attended and the cause of parish education presented and personal conferences conducted. Twenty-four community leadership training schools were set up and conducted. Sunday School Associations and Church School Conferences were promoted throughout the Church. Addresses were made and sermons preached on the theme of religious education. Three series of lectures were delivered in as many seminaries and various meetings were held with synodical officials and synodical committees on parish education. A conference of synodical workers was promoted to which the Alleghany, Indiana, Michigan, Ohio, Pittsburgh, and West Virginia Synods sent representatives. Definite action by several synods toward the improvement of their educational programs resulted from this conference. The work of the field secretaries is indispensable to the work of the Board and to the cause of parish education.

2. Synodical Secretaries of Religious Education.

The following recommendation was approved by the Board and is being carried out:

That the "Executive Secretary and the Field Secretaries encourage through the proper synodical officials the appointment of directors of religious education and committees on religious education in the synods, conferences, and congregations."

3. A Prospectus of the Christian Life Course.

To assist the congregations in introducing the Christian Life Course, the Board has prepared a prospectus of the course which was published and widely distributed, without cost, by the United Lutheran Publication House.

4. The Parish School Magazine.

"The Parish School" is a magazine of religious education. It is used primarily for the promotion of parish education in the Church. Teachers, officers, parents, and workers in all phases of religious education find in it solutions for many of their teaching problems.

III. The Pledge of the Board

The Parish and Church School Board and its staff realize the extent of their task and feel very keenly their responsibility. They see the 3,942 congregations of our Church in the United States and Canada; they see the 1,424,386 baptized members of our congregations; they see the great host outside the Church; they see all those who need to be taught and trained to teach; and they pledge themselves to continue their work in an ever-increasing fulfillment of their objectives. Carefully but courageously the Board will administer the trust which the Church has committed to it.

FRANK M. URICH, *President.*

D. BURT SMITH, *Secretary.*

S. WHITE RHYNE, *Executive Secretary.*

REPORT OF THE TREASURER OF THE PARISH AND CHURCH SCHOOL BOARD

CASH RECEIPTS AND DISBURSEMENTS

July 1, 1930, *to June* 30, 1931

Balance in Bank, July 1, 1930 ....$15,429.48

RECEIPTS:
Received from the United Lutheran Church on account
of Apportionment $11,340.00
Interest on Bank Deposits 245.92

Total Receipts 11,585.92

$27,015.40

DISBURSEMENTS:
Salaries, Field Secretaries, Current Period...................$10,275.00
Salaries, Field Secretaries, in advance............................   650.00
Expenses, Field Secretaries 2,204.81
Expense Advance 100.00
Expenses, Travel, etc., Board Meetings, etc...................   989.37
Expenses Editors' Travel, etc. 382.65
Literature 12.00

Leadership Training Camp:

Director's Salary	375.00
Expenses	347.92
Auditing	25.00
Premium on Treasurer's Bond	25.00
Office Furniture and Fixtures	490.24
Moving Expenses	200.00
Office and General Expenses	75.69

Total Disbursements 16,152.68

Balance in Bank, June 30, 1931..$10,862.72

CASH RECEIPTS AND DISBURSEMENTS
July 1, 1931, to June 30, 1932

Balance in Bank, July 1, 1931..$10,862.72

RECEIPTS:

Received from The United Lutheran Church on account of Apportionment $10,980.00

Interest on Bank Deposits 153.63

Total Receipts 11,133.63

                   $21,996.35

DISBURSEMENTS:

Salaries, Executive and Field Secretaries—Current Period	$10,450.00
Expenses, Executive and Field Secretaries	2,868.42
Advanced for Expenses	100.00
Travel and Expenses——Board Meetings, etc	423.52
Travel and Expenses—Editors	524.89
Literature	150.86
Leadership Training Camp:	
Director's Salary	375.00
Expenses	374.47
Auditing	25.00
Premium on Treasurer's Bond	25.00
Office Furniture and Equipment	578.20
Rent	540.00
Printing, Postage and General Office Expenses	227.51

Total Disbursements 16,662.87

Balance in Bank, June 30, 1932.. $5,333.48

Respectfully submitted,

GEORGE M. JONES, *Treasurer.*

Philadelphia, Pa., July 26, 1932.

We have audited the books of account of the Parish and Church School Board of the United Lutheran Church in America, for the biennium beginning July 1, 1930, and ending June 30, 1932, and we hereby certify that, in our opinion, the foregoing statements of Cash Receipts and Disbursements are in accordance with the books of account, and are true and correct.

TAIT, WALKER & BAKER,

Accountants and Auditors.

It was moved and carried that the report of the auditors be accepted.

By common consent the report of the Committee on Memorials from Constituent Synods was presented at this time by the Rev. G. A. Greiss, Chairman of the Committee.

REPORT OF COMMITTEE ON MEMORIALS FROM CONSTITUENT SYNODS

(For action on the recommendations in this report see pp. 447, 449.)

Memorials From Constituent Synods

1. *From the Florida Synod*:

"That since the year 1934 will be the two hundredth anniversary of the landing of the Salzburgers in Georgia, and since the Georgia-Alabama Synod proposes to invite the 1934 Convention of the United Lutheran Church to meet in Savannah, we, the Florida Synod, do hereby urge said body to accept this invitation when presented, and instruct our secretary to convey this action to the secretary of the United Lutheran Church and to the president of the Georgia-Alabama Synod."

PAUL G. McCULLOUGH, *Secretary.*

2. *From the Illinois Synod*:

"*Resolved,* That we, the Illinois Synod, memorialize The United Lutheran Church in America to sponsor a concerted and church-wide program of evangelism, stressing the winning of souls, the establishment of the Family Altar in the homes of our people, and the organization of adult catechetical classes."

ROY CATLIN, *President.*

3. *From the Maryland Synod*:

"*Whereas,* budget making and budget payments in the Constituent Synods are not upon a uniform basis; be it

"*Resolved,* That the Evangelical Lutheran Synod of Maryland memorialize The United Lutheran Church in America to consider the advisability of recommending some principles of budgeting for The United Lutheran Church in America and the Constituent Synods."

JOHN B. RUPLEY, *Secretary.*

4. *From the Nebraska Synod*:

(A.) "The United Lutheran Church in America, assembled in general convention at Philadelphia, October, 1932, is hereby respectfully and urgently petitioned to consider ways and means by which the various official periodicals of the Church, its auxiliary organizations, and its boards and committees, may be published in one-volume-monthly form; and, if feasible, to take immediate steps looking to the accomplishment of the same."

(B.) "The United Lutheran Church in America, assembled in general convention at Philadelphia, October, 1932, is hereby respectfully and urgently petitioned by the Evangelical Lutheran Synod of Nebraska:

"First: To declare and define the aim and function of the Board of Education as they pertain to the colleges and seminaries of The United Lutheran Church in America;

"Second. To consider the advisability of devoting a larger percentage of the budget of the Board of Education to the purposes of Christian education."

WILLIAM IRA GUSS, President.
FRED C. WIEGMAN, Secretary.

5. *From the New York Synod:*

(A.) "That The United Lutheran Church in America at its convention in Philadelphia, in 1932, be memorialized 'to institute a National Radio Broadcast, if possible, in connection with the National Lutheran Council.'"

(B.) "*Resolved*, That the United Lutheran Synod of New York memorialize The United Lutheran Church in America, to request the Federal Council of the Churches of Christ in America that before making public pronouncements and representations with regard to issues of public concern, for which pronouncements and representations certain official Church bodies may not wish to be held responsible, to ascertain first when possible the position of all such bodies involved, consultative or otherwise; and to list such as may not be in agreement."

PAUL ANDREW KIRSCH, Secretary.

6. *From the Pacific Synod:*

"*Whereas*, the Reverend J. C. Kunzmann, D.D., has been looking forward to his eightieth birthday, December 31, 1932, and his retirement from the presidency of the Pacific Theological Seminary, and in the expectation of the completion of the $250,000 Equipment and Endowment Fund, which was hindered and made impossible during the present depression; and

"*Whereas*, by that date he and his devoted wife will have served the Church most efficiently for over fifty-four years, more than twenty years spent in three parishes,—Kittanning, Greensburg, and Pittsburgh, Pennsylvania—twenty years and one month in the home mission work of the General Council and The United Lutheran Church in America, and now over thirteen years as president of the Pacific Theological Seminary, in all of which positions he has rendered most valuable service to the entire Church; and

"*Whereas*, the Board of the Pacific Theological Seminary in grateful recognition of his services to the Church has made itself responsible for $1,000 per year during his life as an honorarium; therefore be it

"*Resolved,* That the Pacific Synod in convention assembled memorialize The United Lutheran Church in America for an additional $1,000 per annum during the remaining years of the life of the Reverend J. C. Kunzmann, D.D., toward such an honorarium."

W. I. Eck, Secretary.

7. *From the Ministerium of Pennsylvania:*

(A.) "*Resolved,* That the Ministerium (of Pennsylvania) petition the United Lutheran Church to sever its consultative relation with the Federal Council of Churches." (Minutes of 1931, page 163.)

(B.) "We (the Ministerium of Pennsylvania) express our pleasure to The United Lutheran Church in America for the acceptance of the invitation to hold its Eighth Biennial Convention in Philadelphia this coming October, and pray that through the outpouring of God's Holy Spirit upon this Convention much good may be accomplished for the Church." (Minutes of 1932, page 38.)

(C.) "We (the Ministerium of Pennsylvania) memorialize the United Lutheran Church to make a (phonographic) record of the ideal rendition of the music of The Service." (Minutes of 1932, page 43.)

W. L. Stough, Secretary.

8. *From the Pittsburgh Synod:*

"That the United Lutheran Church undertake a systematic study of Army Chaplains' Work relative to placing our chaplains' work in the hands of the National Lutheran Council. Under the term, 'chaplains' work,' we would include the following for consideration:

"a.   A more effective method for the recruiting of the best men possible for this service over against the haphazard way at present.

"b.   The establishing of a system of reports from our chaplains in the field.

"c.   The maintenance of a fund for our chaplains' assistance.

"d.   The establishing of a method for the sending of information and publicity articles from the respective synod of the chaplain.

"e.   Making of arrangements for our chaplains to be present at their respective synod meetings, with expenses paid. (The government will grant leave of absence but does not pay expenses.)"

Henry H. Bagger, President.
Frank W. Ash, Secretary.

9. *From the Virginia Synod:*

"That the Lutheran Synod of Virginia overture The United Lutheran Church in America to officially proclaim Rogata Sunday, the fifth Sunday after Easter, Rural Life Sunday."

C. W. Cassell, Secretary.

10. *From the West Virginia Synod*:
"I move that this synod memorialize The United Lutheran Church in America to consider the advisability of effecting economy in administration by holding the next convention of the Church three years hence instead of two years hence."

C. A. PORTZ, *Secretary.*

11. *From the Synod of East Pennsylvania*:
"That the United Lutheran Church hold the General Convention of the Church triennially instead of biennially."

WILLIAM C. NEY, *President.*
E. ALLAN CHAMBERLIN, *Secretary.*

The COMMITTEE ON MEMORIALS FROM THE CONSTITUENT SYNODS, with respect to the foregoing memorials, recommends as follows:

1. That the memorial from the Florida Synod be referred to the Committee of Synodical Presidents to whom have been referred the invitations to the United Lutheran Church for the place of its next convention.

2. That the memorial from the Illinois Synod be referred to the Committee on Evangelism for favorable consideration.

3. That the memorial from the Maryland Synod be referred to the Executive Board.

4. (A) That the first memorial from the Nebraska Synod be referred to the Committee on Church Papers.
(B) With respect to paragraph "First" of the second memorial from the Nebraska Synod, the Committee believes that the object sought has been accomplished by the adoption of the Constitution of the Board of Education. With respect to paragraph "Second" of said memorial, the Committee recommends that this matter be referred to the Board of Education.

5. (A) Concerning the first memorial from the New York Synod, the Committee has obtained the following facts:
In the present arrangements for broadcasting over national hook-ups the Columbia Broadcasting Company has contributed to the cause of Protestant Radio Services a one-half hour period each Sunday morning at 10.00 o'clock (E. S. T.), which is known as the Church of the Air. The National Lutheran Council has procured the assignment of about seven Sundays each year to the Lutherans.
The National Broadcasting Company conducts a National Forum Period each Sunday afternoon at 3.30 o'clock. It will not permit any denomination as such to occupy this time, but it does invite individual ministers to speak. In 1931 Dr. Knubel was invited to use nine hours and in 1932 he was invited to use thirteen half hours, covering a period from August 1st to November 1st. In the 1932 broadcasts Dr. Knubel has been assisted by Dr. Paul Scherer. The National Broadcasting Company donates the station time, but requires that its staff of musicians and vocalists be used and paid for. Dr. Knubel's broadcasting has been sponsored by the Lutheran Lay-

men's Radio Committee, a voluntary group, who have provided the funds to defer the cost of the music.

The Church of the Air period of the Columbia Broadcasting Company is sponsored by a joint Protestant Committee.

Both broadcasting companies refuse to sell any time to any single Protestant denomination.

In view of the foregoing facts, the Committee recommends:

(a) That this convention of the United Lutheran Church express its appreciation of the invitation of the National Broadcasting Company to our president to give radio messages at stated periods during the last two years, and that the secretary of the Church be instructed to convey this expression to the National Broadcasting Company.

(b) That this convention likewise express to the Lutheran Laymen's Radio Committee its appreciation of their service and efforts to collect the funds necessary to meet the expense of the music used in the broadcasts of Dr. Knubel and Dr. Scherer, and that this committee be urged to effect a permanent organization.

(c) That the Executive Board be requested to arrange with the Lutheran Laymen's Radio Committee for regular reports to the conventions of the United Lutheran Church, similar to the privilege now extended to the Lutheran Historical Society and the Lutheran Church Book and Literature Society.

(B.) Concerning the second memorial from the New York Synod and the first memorial (7. (A.)) from the Ministerium of Pennsylvania, both of which treat of the same matters, the committee has obtained the following facts:

The Federal Council of the Churches of Christ in America, at the present time, is engaged in a re-examination of its functions and structure through a committee of which the Rev. Dr. G. W. Richards, of Lancaster, Pa., is chairman. This committee has taken into consideration the criticisms which have come from our own and other quarters and will report to the meeting of the Federal Council in Indianapolis, in December of this year.

Since our relationship to the Federal Council is not one of full organic connection, Christian courtesy might best be shown by taking no action on either of these memorials at this time and your committee so recommends.

It is further recommended that the Executive Board be requested to appoint visitors, in such number as it may judge best, to the Indianapolis meeting of the Federal Council.

It is further recommended that these visitors be requested to make prompt report to the Executive Board, and that the Executive Board thereupon re-examine our relationship to the Federal Council and make recommendations to the next convention of the United Lutheran Church.

6. Concerning the memorial from the Pacific Synod it is recommended that this convention express its appreciation and gratitude to the Rev. J. C. Kunzmann, D.D., for his devoted service to the Church rendered during his long ministry of more than fifty-four years and that the request for an honorarium be referred to the Board of Ministerial Pensions and Relief.

7. (A.) See 5 (B.)

(B.) Concerning the second memorial from the Ministerium of Pennsylvania and in reply to the Ministerium's expressions of pleasure in the selection of Philadelphia as the place for the Eighth Biennial Convention, the committee recommends the adoption of the following resolution:

Resolved: That the United Lutheran Church in convention assembled does hereby express its deep appreciation of the opportunity to hold its Eighth Biennial Convention in the City of Brotherly Love amid scenes so rich in historical significance both to our Government and to our particular Church.

(C.) Concerning the third memorial from the Ministerium of Pennsylvania, the committee recommends its adoption and that the project be referred to the Common Service Book Committee and the Committee on Church Music, jointly, with power to act.

8. Concerning the memorial from the Pittsburgh Synod the committee recommends that the United Lutheran Church take cognizance of the work of its chaplains in the armed forces of our country and give favorable consideration to the suggestions contained in the memorial and that the matter be referred to the Executive Board.

9. Concerning the memorial from the Virginia Synod, the committee recommends that no action be taken.

10 and 11. Concerning the memorials from the West Virginia Synod and the East Pennsylvania Synod, the committee recommends that no change be made in the present arrangements of the United Lutheran Church of meeting biennially.

Respectfully submitted,

GEORGE A. GREISS, *Chairman.*

Recommendation 1 adopted.

Recommendation 2 adopted.

Recommendation 3 adopted.

Recommendation 4, (A) and (B), adopted.

Recommendation 5, (A), (a), (b), (c) and (B), adopted.

Recommendation 6 adopted.

Recommendation 7, (B) and (C), adopted.

Recommendation 8 adopted.

It was moved and carried that recommendation 9 be referred to the Executive Board for further study.

Recommendations 10 and 11 adopted.

The report of the Committee on President's Report was presented by the Rev. W. G. Boomhower, Chairman of the Committee.

REPORT OF THE COMMITTEE ON PRESIDENT'S REPORT

(For action on the recommendations in this report see p. 451.)

The seventh report of our President to The United Lutheran Church in America in Convention has impressed the committee appointed to consider it profoundly and as a result the members of that committee join in urging the delegates to this convention to pay earnest attention to all he has said in this official document. He has spoken out of an experience of fourteen years and this remarkable term of service, we declare, has been filled with a labor of investigation, planning and supervision, which makes him competent to speak with the best judgment possible. We would put before you again these words of President Knubel:

"First of all, evangelism is the prime necessity of the Christian heart, for that heart must win others to the same faith. It represents the fundamental attitude of the Church towards the world, and is the one means whereby the Church maintains her necessary independence of the world. She can never be a mimic of the world while she knows that the world needs evangelism, that the world is wrong and must be converted."

This carries the burden of his message and points the way to progress. Inspired by these words we express:

1. Our appreciation of the nature of this report, interpreting it as a spiritual communication and admonishing the convention that it is to be spiritually discerned. We regard this report as having special value because of its sequence, following as it does other vital subjects treated in earlier years and standing in very proper relation to all the major concerns of the administration.

2. We recognize that in his emphasis on evangelism and in his interpretation of the prime responsibility of the Church, our president conjoins and strengthens many expressions of grave concern heard here such as memorials from synods, reports of committees and deliberations on the floor, all converging on the subject of evangelism.

3. We have recognized as a committee the keenness and accuracy with which the report describes conditions in the world and discloses the causes of present confusion and distress and we accept the faults and failures of the Church noted herein as our own and we call upon this gathering to humble itself before God and beseech of Him a guiding Spirit Who shall direct us in the way of amendment and recovery.

4. We call upon our delegates to resolve, upon returning to their parishes, to show our people the connection between a shortage of benevolent funds and offerings and spiritual shortcomings in the Church and to point out that an absence of evangelistic fervor which, in some instances, is first lacking in our pastors, is generally accompanied by the material embarrassment of the Church.

Before proceeding to some recommendations we would offer a testimony of deep concern felt by our committee and by many who have spoken to us at this convention, over the absence of a spiritual awakening in our times, the meager use and support of our Church papers and the decline in our benevolent giving. We say this in order to assure our President and do justice to the hearts of some delegates as we know them.

5. And now we recommend that our United Lutheran Church by means of such programs and agencies as are ready for the work or are contemplated shall ardently promote:

(a.) More spiritual efforts in our catechetical classes so that the adolescents in our Church may truly experience a work of saving and persisting grace in their lives.

(b.)   Much more than formal catechetical work with adults entering the Church in order that all such may indeed be converted to the way of God and truly live under Him in His Kingdom here as hereafter.

(c.)   More skillful and hearty effort on the part of our members in good standing to win unsaved members of their families, thereby making their families genuinely Christian and also by example, testimony and personal service to bring in people from the world to hear the transforming Gospel and learn of Christ's redeeming love.

(d.)   The gathering of pastors throughout our synods, especially in communities where a deep concern over these matters is felt, to give them encouragement and training for working together in preaching missions and special services and in directing the lay activities possible so that the apostolic labors of evangelism may be carried on triumphantly in our day.

6.   Finally, and in view of the great need of evangelism as articulated this year by our President, particularly since memorials on this most vital subject have been presented by one or more synods, we would declare as a convention that we look most favorably on the proposal that a Director of Evangelism be appointed for the Church as a whole and trust that this will be done at some good time to be agreed upon by the Executive Board and the Committee on Evangelism.

In the meantime we commend to all synods the good work being done in this field of evangelism by several synods and urge bodies that are not functioning in the promotion of evangelism to undertake synod-wide programs in these days of opportunity.

Respectfully submitted,
W. G. Boomhower, Chairman.

On motion the two recommendations were adopted.

Committee of Tellers No. 2 reported that Mr. D. P. Deatrick, having received the highest number of votes, was elected to the Board of the National Lutheran Home for the Aged.   The President declared him elected.

At five o'clock the Convention adjourned with prayer by the Rev. J. Reble.

TENTH SESSION

Benjamin Franklin Hotel.
Philadelphia, Pennsylvania.
Tuesday, October 18, 1932, 8.00 P. M.

Vespers were conducted by the Rev. H. C. Michael.

The President called the Convention to order and stated that the special order of business for this time was Item II, 9 of the report of the Executive Board on the Training of Ministers and Teachers, as contained in the Supplemental Report of the Executive Board, Item "A."

By unanimous consent the motion to adopt item I, under "VI. Recommendations" (see p. 175), postponed to this session, was withdrawn; and, at the suggestion of the Chair, it was decided to take up the consideration of the recommendations and preamble seriatim.

Before taking action on the recommendations, the Convention proceeded to consider the form of the recommendations. The Rev. P. W. Roth gave notice of a proposed change to the preamble.

I, Items 1 to 6. No change proposed.

I, Item 7, was on motion changed to read as follows:

"That in view of the recommendation (7) of the Commission on Survey of Canadian Synods, which was adopted, the Seminaries at Waterloo and Saskatoon be continued."

II, Item 8, a, b, c. No change proposed.

III. *As to a New Institution,* was on motion changed to read:

"That the Church ask the Commission of Adjudication to inform and instruct it as to whether or not the action of the Washington Convention (Minutes 1920, p. 60) rightly interpreted the Constitution with regard to the establishment and control of a theological seminary."

IV, *As to the Effecting Agency,* was on motion changed to read:

"That the Church request the Board of Education to approach the constituent synods and the theological seminaries with reference to the question of approving the program indicated in the above recommendations."

The preamble to the recommendations was changed by inserting after the parenthesis and before the word "we," the words "and in full and clear recognition of the fact that according to the Constitution of the United Lutheran Church as interpreted by the Joint Committee on Ways and Means in advance of the merger of the three General Bodies, the control of theological seminaries is the function of the synods."

No other changes to the form of the recommendations were proposed.

It was moved and seconded to adopt the whole of "VI. Recommendations." After extended debate the previous question was moved and carried. The President put the question on the adoption of "VI. Recommendations" and it was carried. The final action on this item, therefore, reads as follows:

VI. Recommendations

In view of the foregoing findings and for the best interests of The United Lutheran Church in America in the exercise of the power of advice and counsel which belongs to the United Lutheran Church in accordance with the decision of the Commission of Adjudication (Second Supplementary Report, Milwaukee Convention Minutes, pp. 409-412), and in full and clear recognition of the fact that according to the Constitution of the United Lutheran Church as interpreted by the Joint Committee on Ways and Means in advance of the merger of the three General Bodies, the control of theological seminaries is the function of the synods; we express it as our judgment and do hereby advise:

I. *As to the Number and Location of Seminaries, with Supporting Synods*:

1. That Southern Seminary be continued, developed, and supported by the following synods:
Virginia, North Carolina, South Carolina, Georgia-Alabama, Florida, Mississippi.

2. That Hartwick, Gettysburg, Susquehanna and Philadelphia seminaries be merged, and be supported by the following synods:
Ministerium of Pennsylvania. United New York, East Pennsylvania, Slovak-Zion, West Pennsylvania, Susquehanna, Alleghany, Pittsburgh, Maryland and West Virginia.

3. That Hamma and Chicago seminaries be merged, and be supported by the following synods:
Ohio, Indiana, Michigan, Illinois, Wartburg.

4. That Western, Martin Luther and Northwestern seminaries be merged and be supported by the following synods:
Northwest, Nebraska, German Nebraska, Rocky Mountain, Kansas, Texas and Iowa.

5. That a seminary on the Pacific Coast be supported by the Pacific and California Synods.

6. That, at least until the future of the Pacific Seminary has been determined, the Board of Education be asked to pay for the transportation of

students for the ministry from the Pacific Synod to the proposed Western Seminary.

7.   That in view of the recommendation (7) of the Commission on Survey of Canadian Synods, which was adopted, the Seminaries at Waterloo and Saskatoon be continued.

II.   *As to Specific Responsibilities:*

8.   That the Church ask the proposed seminaries to undertake the following specific responsibilities:

a.   The proposed Eastern Seminary—A special department for the training of teachers, scholars, editors, foreign missionaries, etc.

b.   The proposed Central Seminary—A special department for the training of layworkers and workers in the field of inner missions.

c.   The proposed Western Seminary—The training of men to serve in churches requiring the use of other languages than English, and also the development of special training in the problems of the rural parish.

III.   *As to a New Institution:*

9.   That the Church ask the Commission of Adjudication to inform and instruct it as to whether or not the action of the Washington Convention (Minutes, 1920, p. 60) rightly interpreted the Constitution with regard to the establishment and control of a theological seminary.

IV.   *As to the Effecting Agency:*

10.   That the Church request the Board of Education to approach the constituent synods and the theological seminaries with reference to the question of approving the program indicated in the above recommendations.

The report of the Executive Board was adopted as a whole.

The report of the Board of Publication was presented by the Rev. S. W. Herman, Secretary of the Board.

REPORT OF THE BOARD OF PUBLICATION

The new manufacturing plant mentioned in our Report to the 1930 Convention was completed and occupied in the fall of 1930. A new two-color press, a linotype, and a new vertical job press have been added to our equipment. This additional equipment was made necessary by the increased demands made on our printing plant by the new Christian Life Course of Sunday School lessons.

OUTSTANDING ACHIEVEMENTS

The two outstanding achievements of the biennium have been the completion of the six volume edition of Luther's Works, and the production of the first year's course in the Christian Life series. Most of the quarterlies for the first quarter of the second year's course in this series were ready by the close of June, this year, and it is planned to continue the publications of additional quarterlies in ample time before the beginning of each quarter. It is hoped to have the full three years' course completed by May 1, 1934.

The demand for this new lesson material far exceeded our expectations at the beginning of the introduction of the Course last fall. This has materially helped to keep our entire force of employees busy during the past year, and has enabled us to present an encouraging report of the business done, despite the trying times we have been passing through during the biennium.

New Books

Several new books have been published during the biennium, though the number is not as great as in some previous periods. Attention is called to the following:

"The Christian Way of Liberty," by Rev. J. A. W. Haas, D.D.; "Consecrated Leadership," by Rev. A. J. Traver, D.D.; "In the Presence," by Rev. Paul Z. Strodach, D.D.; "A Plea for Lay Evangelism," by Rev. Carroll J. Rockey, D.D.; "Lenten Calendar for 1932," compiled by Rev. C. B. Foelsch, Ph.D.; and "His Glorious Hour," a booklet of Lenten meditations by Rev. Paul Z. Strodach, D.D. Volumes III, IV, V, and VI of the Works of Martin Luther were also issued during the biennium.

The Lesson Commentary on the Uniform Sunday School lessons and the Year Book of the United Lutheran Church have been continued each year during the biennium.

A Christmas Pageant entitled "Immanuel" by the Rev. Wilfried Tappert was published in the fall of 1931.

"The Order for Confirmation," an attractive confirmation booklet, was issued early in 1931, followed by a similar booklet, "The Order for the Baptism of Infants," in the fall of the same year.

A total of 133,500 new books and booklets were published during the biennium.

Books Reprinted

Among the books under this classification may be mentioned The Parish School Hymnal, The Junior Class Manual, Other People's Children, The Common Service Book,—regular music and Mission editions, the various Catechisms, The Story of Jesus, Doctrinal Theology of the Evangelical Lutheran Church, The Augsburg Confession, Preparation for Teaching, The Children's Hymnal and Service Book, The Story of the Church, A Catechism in Christian Worship, How to Teach in Sunday School, and The Book of Worship with tunes.

The total of reprinted books is 296,250.

Pamphlets and Tracts

New pamphlets and tracts have been issued in a total of 500,500 copies and previously issued similar publications have been reprinted in a quantity of 166,000 copies.

Children's Services for Christmas, Easter, Children's Day and Rally Day have been published each year; and the Church Year Calendar has been continued as heretofore. An "Order of Services for Lay Conventions," prepared by the Common Service Book Committee, was published in May this year.

PERIODICALS

The various periodicals in the Lutheran Graded Series were discontinued at the close of 1931. The Church and Sunday School papers and the various monthlies and quarterlies in the Augsburg Uniform Lesson Series have been continued throughout the biennium. The total circulation of these periodicals, including the Lutheran Graded Series, was 855,650 at the close of the first fiscal year of the biennium, and 641,900 at the close of the last year. To the total of periodical circulation for the second year of the biennium should be added the distribution of the Christian Life Course Series which amounts to 310,000 for each quarter. This will bring the total circulation of weeklies, monthlies and quarterlies up to 951,900.

CHURCH PAPERS

The official papers of the Church, "The Lutheran" and "Lutherischer Herold," have been issued regularly each week during the biennium. Both of these papers have suffered a diminished circulation and decreased advertising revenue during this period of depression. "The Lutheran," having the larger circulation of the two, has experienced the greater reduction in its subscription and advertising income. As these papers carry the message of the Church to its membership each week, they deserve the whole-hearted support of the Church if they are to be effective messengers.

GENERAL BUSINESS

The Accounting and Financial reports give figures in detail of the business done during the biennium, and the financial standing of the Board at the present time.

ORGANIZATION

The Board has continued to meet regularly four times each year and the Executive Committee has met monthly. These meetings have been well attended and the Board has conducted your publication business with unanimity and close attention to all its details.

The organization meeting for the biennium was held on October 21, 1930, when the following officers were elected:

Mr. D. F. Yost, President.
Mr. E. G. Hoover, Vice-President.
Rev. S. W. Herman, D.D., Secretary.
Mr. John M. Snyder, Treasurer.

One of the valued members of the Board—Mr. Croll Keller, died on May 11, 1931. He was a member of the Board of the Lutheran Publication Society at the time of the merger and was elected to membership on this Board at the first convention in 1918. With the exception of a two-year interval, he served on your Publication Board continuously until his death. He was a regular attendant at the meetings, and his counsel and advice were highly regarded by his fellow members of the Board, who desire to register their appreciation of his devoted services.

Mr. John M. Snyder resigned in April, 1931, after rendering years of faithful service as vice-president and treasurer of the Board. This resignation was presented on account of health conditions, which prevented full participation in the Board Meetings, and was accepted with the regrets of the Board.

On nomination of the Board, the Executive Board of the Church elected Mr. Wm. G. Semisch to fill the vacancy caused by the death of Mr. Croll Keller, and the Hon. Claude T. Reno to fill that caused by the resignation of Mr. John M. Snyder.

TERMS EXPIRING WITH THIS CONVENTION

Those whose terms expire at this time are:

Rev. Henry Anstadt, D.D.
Rev. Stanley Billheimer, D.D.
Rev. John W. Horine, D.D.
Rev. C. M. Jacobs, D.D., LL.D., L.H.D.
Charles Baum, M.D.
Mr. M. P. Moller, Jr.
Hon. Claude T. Reno.

The Board has placed in nomination the following:

Rev. Henry Anstadt, D.D.
Rev. John W. Horine, D.D.
Rev. H. F. Baughman.
Rev. Prof. Russell D. Snyder.
Charles Baum, M.D.
Mr. M. P. Moller, Jr.
Hon. Claude T. Reno.

Concerning the proposal of the Ministerium of Pennsylvania, referred to the Board by the last convention (Minutes 1930, p. 143), the following action has been taken:

1. The Board is in hearty sympathy with the purpose of the proposal, which is to provide the Church with English translations of important Lutheran literature, classical and current, now available only in other languages. As an evidence of this, the Board calls attention to the publication, since the last convention, of four additional volumes of Luther's Works in English and the recent publication of Elert's *Outline* and Boehmer's *Jesuits*. The Board has also secured the manuscript of a translation of a recent work on the life of Luther. As a publication policy, the Board is ready to publish any needed works of this kind and is ready, if necessary, to publish such works at a financial loss.

2. The Board does not approve the setting aside of an endowment for this purpose, believing that this action would be both unnecessary and unwise. It would be unnecessary because the Board will normally be in a position to publish such works without the aid of endowment funds. It would be unwise, because it would require the sequestration of funds which might be needed for other purposes of the Church.

The Board is deeply conscious of the trust placed in it by the Church and recognizes with gratitude the splendid support given by the Pastors, Churches, Sunday Schools and other organizations, and the members in general of our beloved United Lutheran Church. This has been an encouragement and help to us and the members of the Board in our work.

Respectfully submitted,

DANIEL F. YOST, *President.*

S. W. HERMAN, *Secretary.*

CONSOLIDATED PROFIT AND LOSS ACCOUNT

For the Year Ended June 30, 1931

Gross Sales of Books, Periodicals, etc.		$683,308.95	
Less Returns and Allowances		7,735.45	
Net Sales			$675,573.50
Cost of Sales:			
Inventory, July 1, 1930		$267,055.55	
Purchases of Material, Printing and Binding	$122,843.67		
Purchases of Publications for resale	202,018.09		
Printing Department Wages and Editorial Salaries	115,979.07		
Manuscripts and Contributors	11,630.52		
Royalties	1,183.08		
Shipping and Delivery Expense, including Postage	10,127.38		
Insurance	2,858.41		
Rent	18,000.00		
Taxes	1,992.61		
General Manufacturing Expenses	4,389.96		
Depreciation on Machinery, etc.	13,155.84		
		504,178.63	
		$771,234.18	
Less Inventory, June 30, 1931		270,896.30	
		$500,337.88	
Less:			
Sales of Waste, etc.	$1,899.96		
Discount on Sales	1,880.89		
Returned Merchandise	379.05		
		4,159.90	
Cost of Sales			496,177.98
Gross Profit on Sales			$179,395.52

Selling, Administrative and General Expenses, including Appropriation to United Lutheran Church
House:

Executive and Office Salaries	$72,036.03	
Expenses of Board Meetings	1,103.15	
Telephone and Telegraph	1,240.42	
Advertising	5,202.92	
Legal and Auditing	1,763.40	
Subscriptions and Dues	1,102.85	
Christian Life Course	9,920.79	
*Pensions	1,816.69	
Bad Debts	1,219.37	
General Expense	8,475.04	
Depreciation Furniture and Fixtures	1,235.26	
Appropriation United Lutheran Church House, 39 E. 35th St., New York, N. Y.	25,000.00	
Branch Offices:		
Light and Heat	475.52	
Insurance	372.33	
Parcel Post and Delivery	3,180.35	
Taxes	127.71	
Bank Charges	105.40	
Rent	5,050.00	
		139,427.23
Total Profit from Operations		39,968.29
Other Income:		
Interest and Dividends on Securities	$6,516.28	
Interest on Bank Deposits	2,020.37	
Profit on Sale of Fixed Assets	2,801.39	
		11,338.04
		$51,306.33
Other Deductions:		
Moving Expense (Printing Plant)	$5,971.80	
Loss on Operations of Buildings	10,199.01	
		16,170.81
Net Profit for Period		$35,135.52

CONSOLIDATED PROFIT AND LOSS ACCOUNT
For the Year Ended June 30, 1932

Gross Sales of Books, Periodicals, etc.		$711,540.01
Less Returns and Allowances		14,211.10
Net Sales		$697,328.91
Cost of Sales:		
Inventory, July 1, 1931		$270,896.30
Purchases of Material, Printing and Binding	$134,305.47	
Purchases of Publications for resale	157,933.40	
Printing Department Wages and Editorial Salaries	122,981.37	
Manuscripts and Contributions	9,772.67	

Royalties	975.51	
Shipping and Delivery Expense, including Postage	20,188.29	
Insurance	1,858.98	
Rent	18,000.00	
Taxes	4,067.01	
General Manufacturing Expenses................	7,409.52	
Depreciation on Machinery, etc....................	14,644.69	
Christian Life Course	18,356.41	
		510,493.32
		$781,389.62
Less Inventory, June 30, 1932........................		262,925.38
		$518,464.24
Less:		
Sales of Waste, etc.....................................	$1,461.60	
Advertising and Stationery Printed........	7,032.21	
		8,493.81
Cost of Sales		509,970.43
Gross Profit on Sales....................................		$187,358.48
Selling, Administrative and General Expenses, including Appropriations:		
Executive and Office Salaries..........................	$74,870.77	
Expenses of Board Meetings...........................	931.10	
Telephone and Telegraph	1,255.44	
Advertising	5,790.38	
Legal and Auditing	1,642.55	
Subscriptions and Dues	963.88	
Bad Debts	7,303.53	
General Expense	7,358.79	
Depreciation Furniture and Fixtures	1,446.64	
Commissions Paid	134.44	
Stationery and Supplies	2,488.72	
Appropriations:		
United Lutheran Church	35,000.00	
Lutheran Historical Society	500.00	
World Sunday School Convention............................	75.00	
Branch Offices:		
Insurance	240.30	
Taxes and Water Rent.................................	27.10	
Shipping, Delivery and Postage....................	2,073.60	
Bank Charges	147.15	
Rent	5,020.00	
Balance in Closed Bank Written Off......................	953.57	
		148,222.96
Total Profit from Operations........................		$39,135.52
Other Income:		
Interest and Dividends on Securities............................	$7,086.35	

Interest on Bank Deposits.. 1,055.46
Discount Earned on Purchases.. 1,373.98
Bad Debts Recovered 167.23

                                                                                    9,683.02

                                                                                  $48,818.54

Other Deductions:
  Loss on Sale of Assets... $394.30
  Loss on Operations of Buildings 5,050.57
  Interest Paid 80.66

                                                                                    5,525.53

     Net Profit for Period... $43,293.01

REPORT OF ASSETS AND LIABILITIES
As of June 30, 1932
ASSETS

Cash in Banks and on Hand..$137,696.38
Notes Receivable 62.00
Accounts **Receivable:**
  Merchandise $172,473.67
  Advertising 1,537.85
  Unpaid Subscriptions 428.89

                                                         $174,440.41
     Less Reserve for Bad and Doubtful Accounts............ 15,000.00

                                                                                    159,440.41
Rentals Receivable 980.00
Accrued Interest on Investments... 1,917.47
Merchandise and Stock on Hand in Philadelphia and Branch
  Offices 262,925.38
Securities at Market Value June 30, 1932.. 91,367.50

                                                                                  $654,389.14
Legacies and Bequests, with Accumulations... 5,017.57
Prepaid Insurance 3,110.96
Prepaid Taxes 2,986.97
Cash in Closed Banks... 875.86
Plant and Equipment:
  Land $261,859.50
  Buildings $728,279.81
  Machinery and Equipment............................ 144,199.28

                                                         $872,479.09
     Less Reserve for Depreciation...................... 168,398.54

                                                                                    704,080.55

                                                                                    965,940.05

                                                                                  $1,632,320.55

LIABILITIES

Accounts Payable	$16,070.56
Accounts Receivable, Credit Balances	965.82
Accrued Salaries, Royalties and Taxes	5,657.23
Amount due Subscribers on Subscriptions for Periodicals $76,222.90	
Prepaid Advertising 23.52	
	76,246.42
Legacies and Bequests, with Accumulations	5,017.57
Net Assets	1,528,362.95
	$1,632,320.55

SECURITIES IN THE DEPRECIATION RESERVE FUND
AT MARKET VALUE AS OF JUNE 30, 1932

$5,000	Baltimore & Ohio 1st Mtg. 4s, 1948	$3,537.50
4,600	E. & P. Traction Certfs. 4s, 1945	920.00
6,000	Lehigh Coal & Navigation 4½s, 1954	4,920.00
5,000	Lehigh Valley Railroad 4s, 2003	1,506.25
3,000	United Traction of Pittsburgh 5s, 1997	615.00
5,000	Reading Company Gen'l 4s, 1997	3,350.00
10,000	Baltimore & Ohio Southwestern 1st 5s, 1950	5,350.00
5,000	Reading Jersey Central 4s, 1951	2,750.00
5,000	Pennsylvania Railroad 5s, 1964	3,150.00
10,000	Philadelphia Company 5s, 1967	7,512.50
5,000	Metropolitan Edison 4½s, 1968	3,525.00
10,000	Penn Central Light & Power 1st 4½s, 1977	6,300.00
5,000	Missouri Pacific 1st Series F 5s, 1977	1,250.00
5,000	Illinois Central 4¾'s, 1966	1,075.00
8,000	Phila. Electric Gold Tr. Certfs. 5s, 1948	7,600.00
5,000	New Orleans, Texas & Mexico 1st 5s 1954	1,000.00
8,000	American Gas Electric Gold Deb. 5s, 2028	5,900.00
5,000	Central Illinois Public Service 5s, 1968	2,900.00
5,000	Public Service Co. of Northern Illinois 4½s, 1978	3,050.00
5,000	Pennsylvania Company 4¾s, 1963	3,268.75
5,000	Chesapeake & Ohio 4½s, 1993	3,550.00
5,000	Railway Express Agency 5s, 1938	4,850.00
5,000	Texas & Pacific "C" 5s, 1979	1,725.00
10,000	Pennsylvania Power & Light 1st 4½s, 1981	8,100.00
5,000	Commonwealth Edison 4s Series F, 1981	3,662.50

PERMANENT FUNDS
Summary of Cash Account July 1, 1931 to June 30, 1932

Balance, July 1, 1930		$740.45
Receipts:		

	Year Ended June 30, 1931	Year Ended June 30, 1932
Income from Investments	$375.00	$375.00
Interest on Bank Balances	30.98	31.14
	$405.98	$406.14

	812.12
	$1,552.57

Disbursements :
  None ....

Balance, June 30, 1932...$1,552.57

PERMANENT FUNDS
Balance Sheet as of June 30, 1932
ASSETS

Cash in Bank $1,552.57
Investments at Market Value, June 30, 1932:
  $1,000 Illinois Central Equipment Trust 5s, 1933.............. $900.00
  1,000 Chicago, Rock Island and Pacific Equipment Trust
        5½s, 1933 .... 825.00
  4,000 Altoona and Logan Valley Electric Rwy. Co. 4½s,
        1933 .... 480.00
  1,000 Lehigh Valley Railroad 4½s, 2003.......................... 360.00
  1,000 Western New York and Pennsylvania Railroad
        5s, 1937 .... 900.00

                                                              3,465.00

                                                              $5,017.57

LIABILITIES

Funds :
  John Rung Legacy $3,000.00
  David W. Beidle Bequest.. 200.00

                                                              $3,200.00
Accumulated Interest and Adjustment of Securities to Market
  Values 1,817.57

                                                              $5,017.57

Respectfully submitted,
GRANT HULTBERG, *Business Manager.*

Philadelphia, Pa., July 27, 1932.
  We have examined the books of account of the Board of Publication of The
United Lutheran Church in America, for the biennium beginning July 1,
1930, and ending June 30, 1932, and we hereby certify that the foregoing
Profit and Loss Statements, setting forth the result of the operations for
the biennium under audit, together with the Balance Sheet as of June 30,
1932, setting forth the financial condition at that date, are in our opinion, true
and correct.

TAIT, WALKER & BAKER,
Accountants and Auditors.

  Dr. Herman introduced Dr. Grant Hultberg, Business Manager
of the Publication House, and the Rev. Paul J. Hoh, Editor
of the Christian Life Course of Sunday school literature.

It was moved and carried that the report of the auditors be accepted.

At 10.15 P. M. the Convention adjourned with prayer by the Rev. H. C. Michael.

ELEVENTH SESSION

BENJAMIN FRANKLIN HOTEL.

Philadelphia, Pennsylvania.

Wednesday, October 19, 1932, 8.45 A. M.

Matins were conducted by the Rev. P. R. Siebert.

The President called the Convention to order.

On motion the Minutes of the Eighth, Ninth, Tenth and Eleventh Sessions were referred to the Executive Board for approval.

The report of the Committee on Church Music was presented by the Rev. G. C. Rees, Chairman of the Committee.

REPORT OF THE COMMITTEE ON CHURCH MUSIC

The Committee on Church Music met in Philadelphia, Pa., at the Publication House, on April 30, 1931. At this time the Rev. Gomer C. Rees, D.D., was elected chairman and the Rev. George R. Seltzer, secretary. The discussions at this meeting evidenced much interest in the activities of the committee. The earnest desire throughout was to assist the Church as far as possible in maintaining the high ideals of Christian worship. For the sake of brevity we refrain from giving all the details of this conference, although the main elements will appear in this report.

CONVOCATIONS

During the biennium four convocations were held. At three of these the complete program of the committee was presented and at the fourth the major parts were given consideration.

The first convocation was held on October 24, 1930, under the auspices of the Lutheran Ministers' Association of Washington, D. C., in Keller Memorial Church, the Rev. S. F. Nicholas, D.D., pastor. Dr. Reed, Dr. Rees, the Rev. Seltzer and Mr. Sykes, Mus.D., were on the program and were ably assisted by the combined choirs of the Washington churches.

On November 11, 1930, two sessions were held in connection with the Middle Conference of the Maryland Synod in St. Mary's Church, Silver Run, Md., the Rev. W. E. Saltzgiver, pastor. Dr. Reed spoke in the afternoon on "The Church Services and Their Music" and the chairman of the committee addressed the convention in the evening on the subject, "The

Music of Our Hymns." On each occasion practical demonstrations were given.

The complete program of the committee was presented in Temple Lutheran Church, Altoona, Pa., the Rev. F. R. Greninger, pastor, on January 29, 1931, under the auspices of the Lutheran Ministers' Association of that city. Dr. Reed and Dr. Rees were in charge of the program. They received very effective assistance from the combined choirs of the Altoona churches.

The chairman of the committee conducted a convocation at Fairmont, W. Va., on November 5, 1931, in Grace Church, the Rev. W. P. Cline, D.D., pastor. The complete program of the committee was presented under the auspices of the Synod of West Virginia. This convocation was marked by the excellent assistance of the choir of Grace Church. The attendance at the three sessions was very good and a more than ordinary degree of interest was manifested.

In addition to the above activities, individual members of the committee have been called upon from time to time to present certain features of our work and have gladly responded.

Prospective Publications

We are pleased to report that one of the members of this committee, namely, Dr. Harry A. Sykes, of Lancaster, Pa., has prepared an excellent musical interpretation of the principal services. We believe that this material will be of great benefit to organists and choir directors. The manuscript was examined by certain former and present members of the committee and has now been submitted to our Publication House with the hope that it will be approved and published at an early date.

We also note with pleasure that the Ministerium of Pennsylvania is memorializing this convention of the United Lutheran Church to make a phonographic record of the ideal rendition of the music of The Service. This is another evidence of the interest of the Church, for this action was not suggested in any way by the committee, although the committee did discuss the matter several years ago. We heartily endorse the request.

Requests for More Musical Material

The chairman of the committee has received a number of requests for musical material not now furnished in the Common Service Book because of the lack of space. The best we could do was to refer such inquirers to certain former publications of the "Church Book" and the "Book of Worship" or parts of those books. These publications, of course, do not adequately meet the present need on account of the different material found in portions of the Common Service Book. Naturally, our answers to such requests could not prove very satisfactory. In addition, there would be practical difficulties which are quite apparent.

We believe, therefore, that this need of the Church should be met, for we feel that there will be an increasing demand for such musical material. We should, for example, provide chants for the Psalms and Canticles; also proper settings for the Invitatories, Versicles and such other parts of any service that would require musical treatment.

We direct special attention to the antiphons which seem to be used so seldom. For these we know principally the Gregorian settings. We should like to have settings for use with Anglican chants. We realize that there is practically no precedent for this use, yet it seems a pity that this beautiful enrichment of our services should be neglected. We know the difficulties surrounding this suggestion. To produce worthy churchly music for these antiphons would require fine musicianship, deep liturgical appreciation and a real spirit of devotion. Such a result might not be available for quite a while, since it would likely be a matter of gradual growth; yet we believe it a worthy attainment for which to strive.

In this connection, permit us to remind you that the chairman and the secretary of the Committee on Church Music are at present also members of the Common Service Book Committee, which presents the opportunity for real co-operation between the two committees in all that pertains to the worship of the Church.

Music for Organists and Choirs

For our organists and choirs we recommend that great care be exercised in choosing the best music available. This does not mean necessarily the most difficult, but that which can be presented in such a manner as to enhance the true spirit of worship in the congregation. Much material of this kind can be secured if we patiently look for it.

Although it may entail considerable effort, we hope that we shall be able to bring into practical use more of the musical treasures of our church. A church which numbers J. S. Bach and other great musicians among her members ought not to forget the rich heritage of the past. Other groups are showing their appreciation by the use of such material. We desire that our church also may be inspired by these compositions.

Churchly Music in the Sunday School

We again emphasize the necessity of training the children of the Church in the way of true worship. The reason for this is so clear that we scarcely need to enlarge upon it. However, we do urge upon all who deal with the young people that they use their utmost endeavor to teach them to love the liturgy and hymns of the Church. Eliminate all trivial musical nonsense from the Sunday school and give to the children the high privilege of worshiping God in spirit and in truth.

Concerning Advancement

Looking back over a considerable period of time spent in the musical activities of the Church, we feel gratified at the evident progress that has been made. In the past, under the splendid leadership of Dr. J. F. Ohl and other men of like mind, we have noted this advancement. We desire also to do our full part in continuing to magnify the finest principles and practices in the musical expression of Christian worship.

We hold ourselves ever in readiness to serve the Church.

GOMER C. REES, Chairman.
GEORGE R. SELTZER, Secretary.

On motion of the Rev. G. C. Rees it was

Resolved, That this body send its cordial greetings and best wishes to the Rev. J. F. Ohl with the assurance that we hold in grateful remembrance his splendid services to the Church.

On motion of the Rev. G. C. Rees it was

Resolved, That the Committee on Church Music be authorized to prepare a setting of the Psalter to Anglican Chants and also provide music for the Antiphons, Invitatories, Versicles, Graduals, Canticles and such other parts of the Common Service Book as may require musical material.

The report of the Committee on Church Architecture was presented by the Rev. L. D. Reed, Chairman of the Committee.

REPORT OF THE COMMITEE ON CHURCH ARCHITECTURE

(For action on the recommendation in this report see p. 474.)

Nine regular meetings of the committee, attended chiefly by the members in or near Philadelphia, were held during the biennium. Fewer meetings were required than in previous periods because of the general falling off in church building as a result of the general business depression.

Due to ill-health, Dr. J. F. Ohl, chairman of this committee for many years, resigned at the beginning of the biennium. Dr. Ohl had been a member of this committee and its chairman since its organization, having also served on a similar committee of the General Council. The committee wishes to take this opportunity to express its appreciation of the faithful and helpful services rendered by Dr. Ohl over a period of many years. We regret that he is no longer able to be actively engaged in this work in which he took such a keen interest and to the development of which he so greatly contributed.

At the organization meeting held December 1, 1930, the Rev. Luther D. Reed, D.D., formerly secretary to the committee for sixteen years, was elected chairman, and Charles A. Scheuringer, secretary.

The committee also notes the loss by death of Mr. Albert F. Schenck, architect, of Philadelphia, in December, 1931. Mr. Schenck had been a member for many years. He was extremely interested in the work, faithful in attendance, and ever ready to offer helpful and constructive suggestions. The committee regrets the loss of a valuable member.

COMMITTEE ACTIVITIES

In the performance of its work during the past biennium, **thirty-four sets** of plans have been reviewed by the committee. These came from sixteen states and Canada.

Reports and suggestions were rendered, a summary of which is given later. Where necessary, suggestions have been accompanied by simple pencil sketches.

The unusually small number of plans—about one-third as many as four years ago—is undoubtedly due to economic conditions. Not a single plan has been received during the four months prior to the preparation of this report. The extensive correspondence and the many conferences held, show that interest in church building is unabated, although there has been a very general suspension of new construction. Congregations should be advised, however, that the present relatively low cost of building offers a favorable opportunity to secure new constructions if these can be financed.

The secretary, at his own expense, prepared two sets of plans with working drawings for mission churches, and presented them to the committee. The committee thankfully accepted and approved them, and published them as the first numbers in a series of "Standard Plans."

CONFERENCES AND CORRESPONDENCE

While a comparatively small number of plans were reviewed by the committee itself, many conferences were held and an extensive correspondence was carried on with pastors, building committees, and architects by the chairman and the secretary. The chairman received letters from 149 different persons in twenty-nine states and Canada, and the secretary sixty-five letters from thirteen states and Canada, a slight increase over the number of two years ago. Twenty personal conferences were held with pastors and architects in addition to several conferences with the Church Councils of St. John's Church and of Christ Church, Allentown, Pa. Illustrated lectures on church building were also given.

The chairman actively collaborated with the architects, Messrs. Frank H. Watson, Edkins and Thompson, and the college authorities, in the development of the plans for the Egner-Hartzell Memorial Chapel at Muhlenberg College, and prepared the entire scheme of symbolism for the stained glass windows, interior and exterior carvings and other decoration.

The Rev. E. A. Trabert conferred with pastors and building committees on the Pacific Coast and the Rev. George H. Schnur, D.D., was active in a similar way in the Pittsburgh Synod.

The committee was represented by the chairman at the conference of the Associated Bureaus of Church Architecture held in Cleveland, Ohio, November, 1930. Dr. Reed, the chairman, and C. A. Scheuringer, the secretary, represented the committee at the conference of the Associated Bureaus in New York City, December 17 to 19, 1931. Following an interesting discussion of "The Contemporary Renaissance of Christian Art," by Professor Joseph Hudnut, of Columbia University, and "Certain Aspects of Modern Church Building," by Dr. Ralph Adams Cram, noted church architect, "The Viewpoint of the Church" was presented by Dr. Reed. At the close of the conference, Dr. Reed was elected chairman of the Associated Bureaus. The next meeting will be held in Chicago, in December, 1932.

PUBLICATIONS

Attention is called to the following publications of the committee which are available without cost, upon request:

"Church Principles in Church Architecture"—a 20-page pamphlet prepared by the chairman, Dr. Reed, now in its third printing.

"Practical Suggestions for Building Committees"—a pamphlet which has been freely distributed and recently reprinted.

"Architectural Leaflets"—a series of attractive four-page folders containing cuts of successful Lutheran church buildings with descriptive writeup. Additional leaflets of new designs are being printed and will be available next fall.

"Space Requirements for Church Organs"—a valuable statement prepared by Dr. Ohl, in collaboration with representatives of one of the large organ building companies.

PLANS APPROVED AND COMMENDED

The following plans were approved for general excellence, minor suggestions being made by the committee in almost every case:

Bethlehem Church, Indianapolis, Ind., Rev. A. K. Trout, pastor; R. G. Foltz, Architect, Indianapolis. A very attractive exterior design and at a very moderate cost.

First English Church, Schenectady, N. Y., the Rev. Herbert D. Shimer, Pastor; Messrs. Cherry & Matz, Architects, New York. Preliminary plans first submitted showed good planning, fine proportions, and an excellent design. Suggestions included the possible omission of the tower, widening of the aisles, relocating the organ and the use of a level floor in place of a sloping floor in the nave.

Chapel St. James' Community Church, Stewart Manor, Garden City, L. I., the Rev. Edward T. Morecroft, Pastor; Messrs. Steffins & Gustafson, Architects, New York. These plans were commended for excellence in design.

St. John's Church, Richlandstown, Pa., the Rev. E. E. Landis, Pastor; Charles Talley, Architect. Revised plans submitted in accordance with the committee's suggestion were approved and commended.

First English Lutheran Church, Sacramento, California, the Rev. C. F. Crouser, Pastor; W. E. Coffman, Architect. A pleasing design in Spanish style approved with minor suggestions.

Chapel Church of the Redeemer, Lansing, Michigan, the Rev. F. F. Madsen, Pastor; W. S. Holmes, Architect. Preliminary plans were returned with minor changes suggested in the chancel, altar rail, etc. Revised plans were commended.

Church and Parish Building of the Epiphany, Hemstead, L. I., the Rev. Walter C. Ruccius, Pastor; Messrs. Cherry & Matz, Architects, N. Y. Suggestions were made as to relocation of console, widening of aisles, communion rail, etc. Revised plans approved and commended as assuring a churchly building.

PLANS APPROVED

Good Shepherd Church, Bayside, L. I., the Rev. J. D. Wein, Pastor; Lewis Grandgent, Architect, N. Y. Approved after suggestions covering rearrangement of chancel were accepted.

Sunday School Addition, Dallas, Texas, through Dr. Hancher's office. A temporary building, approved subject to rearrangement of objectionable features.

Reformation Church, Columbia, S. C., the Rev. Wynne C. Boliek, Pastor; J. B. Urquhart, Architect, Columbia, S. C. Approved with a suggestion for a better location for the font.

St. Mark's Church, Asheville, N. C., a mission congregation; Rev. E. R. Lineberger, Pastor; Messrs. Lord & Lord, Architects, Asheville, N. C. Approved with a suggested change of main entrance feature.

St. Luke's Church, Bear Poplar, N. C. Alternate plans considered for chancel arrangements, the plan of the American Seating Co. being approved with minor changes.

Grace Church, Alden, Minn., Rev. C. H. Eckhoff, Pastor. Plans were approved after suggested changes had been accepted by the local church committee.

Holy Trinity Church, Bellerose, L. I., the Rev. W. John Derr, Pastor; Cherry & Matz, Architects, N. Y. Approved with suggestions concerning chancel arrangements.

St. Paul's Church, Linden, N. J., the Rev. J. F. Bauchmann, Pastor. Revised drawings incorporating suggestions for re-designing the exterior were approved.

St. Paul's Church, Leetonia, Ohio, the Rev. H. C. Brillhart, Pastor. A number of suggestions accompanied by sketches were forwarded.

Plans for church at North Kannapolis, N. C., received from Mr. E. W. Wagoner, Salisbury, N. C. Plans revised in accordance with suggestions and approved.

Trinity Church, Long View, Washington, the Rev. Arthur M. Knudsen, Pastor. Suggestions for improvement of acoustic conditions forwarded.

Temple Evangelical Church, San Francisco, California, the Rev. H. F. Schmidt, Pastor. Due to the limited funds available, these plans while not entirely satisfactory were approved as being the best that could be obtained under the circumstances.

Hope Evangelical Church, Toledo, Ohio, the Rev. Franklin E. Stroebel, Pastor; Paul T. Cahill, Architect, Toledo, Ohio. Revised drawings incorporating suggestions for the re-designing of main entrance, windows and reconstruction of roof trusses were approved.

Lutheran Church of Lawrence, Mass. Plans received through Rev. H. Mackensen, Superintendent of Home Missions, New York, for alterations to a residential building to serve as a temporary chapel and parsonage were approved as a temporary procedure.

Lutheran Church of Haddon Heights, N. J., the Rev. Bernard W. Krapf, Pastor; Roscoe Cook Tindall, Architect, Wilmington, Del. Tentative plans for the future development of a church and parish house were submitted and constructive suggestions were given by the committee.

St. Thomas' Church, Jamaica, L. I., the Rev. Walter F. Frey, Pastor. The original plans were not approved because of impractical arrangement of building on the lot, and poorly designed plan and elevation. Due to lack of funds for architectural fees, the committee offered to provide a new set of plans without cost. This offer was accepted and plans prepared and forwarded.

Reformation Church, Greenville, Tenn., the Rev. L. A. Wertz, Pastor; D. R. Beeson, Architect. The original plans were not approved. After considerable correspondence, the committee finally instructed the secretary to prepare other designs, one of which was accepted by the Building Committee.

South Temple, Penna., Mission Church. Plans submitted through Rev. U. S. G. Bertolet, Missionary Superintendent. The plans were prepared by a local construction company, were submitted and approved after incorporating changes suggested by the secretary.

Church of the Good Shepherd, Philadelphia, the Rev. C. K. Lippard, Pastor. The original plans for this mission church were prepared by a local contractor and were not approved. A new design was later prepared by the secretary, at no cost to the mission, and approved by the committee.

Church of the Redeemer, Milwaukee, Wisconsin; Judell & Bogner, Architects. Four different tentative designs in plan were sent to the committee, requesting its opinion as to the various plans submitted. The plans contemplate the erection of a new church building and the remodeling of the existing building for Sunday school purposes with additions to accommodate this rapidly growing congregation. After consideration, a number of recommendations were submitted to Mr. A. T. Martsolf of the church committee.

Concordia Church, Chestnut Hill, Pa., E. A. Early, Architect, Philadelphia. Suggestions were made concerning the choir arrangement, pulpit and lecturn, etc., and the plans approved.

Hungarian Evangelical Lutheran Church (Mission), Windsor, Ontario, Canada, the Rev. J. L. DePapp, Pastor. Plans submitted through Dr. F. F. Fry, Executive Secretary of the Board of American Missions, were deficient in practical arrangement and churchly character. They were not approved but returned with the request that they be re-designed. The congregation having no funds available for this purpose was unable to meet the committee's request that they be re-designed. A new design with a complete set of working drawings was prepared by the secretary, approved by the committee and presented to the Mission without cost.

Ascension Church, Shelby, N. C., the Rev. E. C. Cooper, D.D., Pastor. Preliminary plans submitted through Mr. E. W. Wagoner with minor suggestions were returned. Final drawings later submitted and approved.

Church of the Epiphany, Pleasantville, N. J., the Rev. E. A. Lebo, Pastor. Plans for church and Sunday school building received through Rev. A. C. Schenck, Missionary Superintendent. A sketch suggesting rearrangement of Sunday school wing was made by the secretary, accepted by the pastor and the plans finally approved.

PLANS NOT APPROVED

Church of the Redeemer, Houston, Texas, the Rev. Fred W. Kern, Pastor; C. N. Nelson, Architect, Houston, Texas. Plans submitted through Dr. Seibert, were generally satisfactory, the exterior was considered so poor that a re-designing was requested.

St. Paul's English Church, the Rev. George C. Ackerly, Pastor, Rensselaer, N. Y. Plans for additions to the existing church, except for minor changes, were considered satisfactory, but the exterior was inadequate. Three suggested sketches for exterior design were forwarded by the secretary. No reply having been received, the plans have not been approved to date.

Holy Trinity Church, New Castle, Indiana, the Rev. H. G. Beeman, Pastor; R. C. Gotwald, Architect, Springfield, Ohio. Plans which had not been submitted to this committee were prepared five years ago under a previous pastorate, the foundation being built at that time of used materials and construction stopped. The building program revived and the original plans were submitted. While the plans could have been made satisfactory with minor changes, the exterior was considered impossible. The architect refused to make revisions, he having retired from practice. The committee offered to re-design the building for a nominal fee. No reply having been received, the plans at this writing are not approved.

PLAN OF SERVICE

The unsatisfactory economic conditions prevailing during the past two years made it impracticable to establish a Bureau of Architecture as outlined and recommended in the committee's report of 1930. Realizing the necessity for some definite service, primarily for mission congregations, a plan has been formulated which comprises the usual reviewing of plans, specifications, conferences for discussion and arrangement of preliminary floor plans at no charge, except where such conferences are held at distant places, in which case a charge for expenses would be made. In addition, the secretary is to make sketches as authorized by the committee for the improvement of unsatisfactory plans. In several instances where an architect has not been available or where funds have been extremely limited, the committee has furnished complete designs and working drawings without cost.

As partial remuneration for the time and labor involved, the committee, acting under an agreement with the Executive Board, authorized an annual allowance to the secretary of $300 for architectural service and $100 a year for secretarial service.

STANDARD PLANS FOR MISSIONS

In response to many requests from mission superintendents, and from recently established mission congregations themselves the committee has given earnest consideration to the subject of providing standard building plans which might be used, with necessary modifications, by missions so situated that the services of an architect are not available, or where financial conditions make it impossible for the mission to pay the standard fee of a competent architect. In such cases recourse is often had to a local carpenter or builder, or possibly a partially trained draughtsman, who is not fully qualified either to design the building or to properly supervise its construction. The congregation eventually secures a poorly planned building, uneconomical in cost and unchurchly in character.

The committee believes that it should not compete with the architectural profession by cutting standard fees for regular services, and that it should not attempt to do the work of competent architects when these can be engaged. Since it is clearly its duty, however, to endeavor to raise the architectural standard of our church buildings, the committee has undertaken to offer a definite service to mission congregations who may desire it for buildings which will not exceed $20,000 in cost of construction. It has approved two standard plans prepared by the secretary, the original designs of which are on exhibition at this convention. These include floor plans, alternate exterior designs and complete working drawings and specifications for buildings to cost from approximately $6,000 to $15,000. Sufficient sets of the working drawings for actual construction may be purchased from the committee at a nominal charge not exceeding one per cent of the estimated cost of the building. The committee hopes to prepare additional plans of this same character from time to time, providing for inexpensive but churchly types of buildings with as much variety in cost and design as may be possible.

Where these plans are purchased from the committee, congregations should bear in mind that it will be necessary to secure competent technical supervision of construction if the quality of the building is to be maintained and the cost held to the lowest level.

RECOMMENDATION

Due to the uncertainty of conditions and the inadvisability of planning for any extensive development of the work of the committee at this time:

The committee requests approval of the continuance of the plan of service for mission congregations as outlined in this report, with the understanding that financial arrangements will be subject to the approval of the Executive Board.

Respectfully submitted,
LUTHER D. REED, *Chairman.*
CHARLES A. SCHEURINGER, *Secretary.*

The recommendation was adopted.

The report of the Statistical and Church Year Book Committee was presented by the Rev. G. H. Schnur, Chairman of the Committee.

THE REPORT OF THE STATISTICAL AND CHURCH YEAR BOOK COMMITTEE

(For action on the recommendations in this report see p. 523.)

The Statistical and Church Year Book Committee of The United Lutheran Church in America, during the years 1930-32, had the co-operation of the statistical secretaries of the Constituent Synods of The United Lutheran Church in America. At the

CONFERENCE OF THE STATISTICAL SECRETARIES

of The United Lutheran Church in America held at the time of The United Lutheran Church Convention in Milwaukee, Wisconsin, on Tuesday, October 7, 1930, representatives from twenty-two constituent synods were present. At that conference the following subjects were discussed:

Standard Parochial Statistics and Blank; Ten-Year Comparison of the Parochial Statistics; Standard Assembly Sheet; Standard State of the Church Blank; Standard System of Parish Records and Congregational Auxiliary Blanks.

The statistical secretary, the Reverend George Linn Kieffer, D.D., Litt.D., resolved the conference into a school and instructed the statistical secretaries as to how to introduce a balance sheet for the constituent synod from the parochial reports.

The minutes of the constituent synods, as to uniformity, content, method of arrangement of content, etc., were also studied and recommendations made looking forward to action which would bring about greater uniformity.

The Reverend S. Gunderman, the Reverend C. E. Butler and Mr. Harry E. Pugh were appointed a committee on uniform practice in relationship and standing of the statistical secretaries. This committee's report was later adopted by the conference as follows:

(a.)   That this conference of statistical secretaries of constituent synods requests the synods to consider the advisability of making their statistical secretaries members of the executive committee of the synod where such is not now the case; or, at least making provision for having the statistical secretary sit in at the meeting of the Executive Committee of the Synod, especially when matters concerning the statistical work of the synod is to be taken up. A similar arrangement concerning other boards and committees might prove profitable to the constituent synods.

(b)   Resolved that the conference of the statistical secretaries request the Statistical and Church Year Book Committee of the United Lutheran Church to petition the Executive Board of the United Lutheran Church to consider the advisability of inviting the statistical secretary of the United Lutheran Church to sit in the meeting of the Executive Board when matters concerning the statistical work of the United Lutheran Church are under consideration.

The conference went on record petitioning the constituent synods of The United Lutheran Church in America to use the Standard State of the Church Blank in 1932 and every three years thereafter, pointing out that the Standard Parochial Blanks are entirely different from the Standard State of the Church Blank, the former being the pastor's report on the condition of the congregation, the latter being the church council's report on the condition of the congregation, only being attested by the pastor.

It was found that the following constituent synods used the Standard State of the Church Blank: United North Carolina, United New York, Maryland, South Carolina, Virginia, Alleghany, Indiana, Illinois, Mississippi, Michigan, Georgia-Alabama, Nebraska, California, Rocky Mountain, Northwest and West Virginia.

The other constituent synods had as yet not introduced the Blank.

The Reverend George H. Schnur, D.D., presented and explained the use of the Parish Register as well as the Auxiliary Cards and Blanks available for the use of the pastor.

The conference recommended the procedure with the publication of the Statistical Handbook. The Reverend George L. Kieffer, D.D., Litt.D., explained the value of graphically presenting statistics and gave a bibliography of books available to aid in the preparation of graphs.

The conference also discussed the statistical historical job confronting every statistical secretary and recommended that the statistical secretaries go to work in preparing statistical and historical studies in their respective constituent synods of The United Lutheran Church in America similar to the excellent study made by former Statistical Secretary C. L. Ramme for the Rocky Mountain Synod as published in the minutes of that synod in 1928.

The conference also extended to the constituent synods who have continued their statistical secretaries in office over a long period of time its appreciation that the constituent synods have manifested wisdom in permitting this extremely technical work to remain in experienced hands.

The statistical secretaries of the constituent synods in most cases have made conscientious preparation and training in technique and earnestly endeavored to arrive at statistical accuracy, all of which accrues to the benefit and standing of The United Lutheran Church in America.

The following statistical secretaries of the following constituent synods were present:

Ministerium of Pennsylvania—Reverend Ira F. Frankenfield.
United Lutheran Synod of New York—Reverend A. L. Dillenbeck, D.D.
Synod of Maryland—Reverend W. G. Minnick.
Virginia Synod—Mr. Harry E. Pugh.
Ohio Synod—Mr. Amor W. Ulrici.
East Pennsylvania Synod—Reverend J. D. Krout, D.D.
Alleghany Synod—Reverend C. P. Bastian.
Pittsburgh Synod—Reverend George H. Schnur, D.D.
Iowa Synod—Reverend L. H. Lesher.
Michigan Synod—Reverend L. F. Gunderman.
Georgia-Alabama Synod—Mr. D. E. Wilson.
Synod of California—Reverend John E. Hoick.
Northwest Synod—Mr. Chas. A. Gottschalk.
Pacific Synod—Reverend Theo. A. Jansen.
West Virginia Synod—Reverend C. E. Butler.

Those present, not statistical secretaries, were:

United Synod of North Carolina—Reverend J. L. Morgan, D.D., president.
Synod of South Carolina—Reverend C. J. Shealy, president.

And the official representatives:

United North Carolina Synod—Reverend G. H. Rhodes.
Kansas Synod—Reverend H. J. McGuire.
South Carolina Synod—Mr. E. H. Schirmer.
Nebraska Synod—Reverend W. A. Klink.
Wartburg Synod—Reverend G. Kempf.
German Nebraska Synod—Reverend William Harder.
Manitoba Synod—Reverend Professor H. W. Harms.

The secretary of the Virginia Synod, the Reverend C. W. Cassell, was also present.

The conference expressed by a motion its appreciation of the value of the conference. The statistical secretaries requested that a similar conference be held at the time of the Convention of the United Lutheran Church in Philadelphia. This conference will be held on Wednesday, October 12, 1932, at 10.00 A. M., in Room 825, in the Muhlenberg Building, 1228 Spruce Street,

Philadelphia, Pa. These conferences, which have been held at Buffalo, Chicago, Richmond, Erie and Milwaukee, have indeed proven most valuable.

LIST OF STATISTICAL SECRETARIES

The following served as statistical secretaries of the constituent synods of The United Lutheran Church in America during the biennium, 1930-32:

		1931	1932
1	Ministerium of Pennsylvania	Rev. I. F. Frankenfield	Rev. I. F. Frankenfield
2	United Synod of New York	Rev. A. L. Dillenbeck, D.D.	Rev. A. L. Dillenbeck, D.D.
3	United Synod of North Carolina	Rev. E. H. Kohn, D.D., Ph.D.	Rev. E. H. Kohn, D.D., Ph.D.
4	Synod of Maryland	Rev. W. G. Minnick	Rev. W. G. Minnick
5	Synod of South Carolina	Rev. H. S. Petrea	Rev. H. S. Petrea
6	Synod of West Pennsylvania	Rev. D. S. Martin, D.D.	Rev. D. S. Martin, D.D.
7	Synod of Virginia	Mr. H. E. Pugh	Mr. H. E. Pugh
8	Synod of Ohio	Mr. A. W. Ulrici	Mr. A. W. Ulrici
9	East Penna. Synod	Rev. J. D. Krout, D.D.	Rev. J. D. Krout, D.D.
10	Alleghany Synod	Rev. B. F. Rudisill	Rev. B. F. Rudisill
11	Pittsburgh Synod	Rev. G. H. Schnur, D.D.	Rev. G. H. Schnur, D.D.
12	Indiana Synod	Mr. H. D. C. Loemker	Mr. H. D. C. Loemker
13	Illinois Synod	Mr. Frederick Sachse	Mr. Frederick Sachse
14	Texas Synod	Rev. F. W. Henkel	Rev. F. W. Henkel
15	Susquehanna Synod of U. L. C. A.	Rev. C. S. Bottiger	Rev. C. S. Bottiger
16	Mississippi Synod	Rev. E. K. Counts*	Rev. J.L. Drafts
17	Synod of Iowa	Rev. L. H. Lesher	Rev. L. H. Lesher
18	Michigan Synod	Rev. L. F. Gunderman	Rev. L. F. Gunderman
19	Synod of Georgia-Alabama	Mr. D. E. Wilson	Mr. D. E. Wilson
20	Synod of Canada	Rev. O. Stockman	Rev. O. Stockman
21	Synod of Kansas	Rev. A. L. Groseclose	Rev. A. L. Groseclose
22	Synod of Nebraska	Rev. H. Dumler	Rev H. Dumler
23	Wartburg Synod	Rev. H. R. Pontow	Rev. H. R. Pontow
24	German Synod of Nebraska	Rev. P. Waldschmidt	Rev. P. Waldschmidt
25	Synod of California	Rev. J. E. Hoick*	Rev. J. L. Sawyer
26	Rocky Mountain Synod	Rev. A. H. Schnake	Rev. A. H. Schnake
27	Synod of the Northwest	Mr. C. A. Gottschalk	Mr. C. A. Gottschalk
28	Manitoba Synod	Rev. W. Magnus	Rev. W. Magnus
29	Pacific Synod	Rev. T. A. Jansen	Rev. T. A. Jansen
30	Nova Scotia Synod	Rev. E. V. Nonamaker	Rev. E. V. Nonamaker
31	Synod of West Virginia	Rev. C. E. Butler	Rev. C. E. Butler
32	Slovak Zion Synod	Rev. A. B. Svasko	Rev. A. B. Svasko
33	Florida Synod	Mr. P. Fischer	Mr. P. Fischer

* Resigned.

Addresses of laymen listed above:

Mr. H. E. Pugh, Statistical Secretary of Virginia Synod, 105 Lancaster Road, Richmond, Virginia.

Mr. A. W. Ulrici, Statistical Secretary of Ohio Synod, 3747 Elsmere Ave., Cincinnati, Ohio.

Mr. H. D. C. Loemker, Statistical Secretary of Indiana Synod, 2151 Emerson Ave., Louisville, Kentucky.

Mr. Frederick Sachse, Statistical Secretary of Illinois Synod, 562 Earlston Road, Kenilworth, Illinois.

Mr. D. E. Wilson, Statistical Secretary of Georgia-Alabama Synod, 3242 W. Shadowlawn Ave., S. W., Atlanta, Georgia.

Mr. C. A. Gottschalk, Statistical Secretary of Northwest Synod, 5543 N. Holton Street, Milwaukee, Wisconsin.

Mr. P. Fischer, Statistical Secretary of Florida Synod, P. O. Box 15, Lakeland, Florida.

While time does bring changes in personnel, the specialized field of statistics requires trained and experienced men. It is interesting to note in looking over the rolls of the statistical secretaries since 1919 how many of these men now at their post of duty have continued at their task, striving for greater accuracy. Recognition of the statistical field as a specialized field requiring a mind with an aptitude for mathematics and minutest details should be emphasized and kept in mind by all.

PRINTED MINUTES: PROGRESS IN UNIFORMITY AND STANDARDIZATION

The latest complete set of available Minutes (1931) of the thirty-three constituent synods of The United Lutheran Church in America does show progress in uniformity in meeting the requirements of standardization.

Now, all of the constituent synods excepting two—the Slovak Zion Synod and the Manitoba Synod—use the Standard Parochial Assembly Sheet in their Minutes. These two synods should do so in their next printed Minutes not later than 1933.

All of the constituent synods, excepting the Mississippi Synod, printed totals for their entire synod. The Mississippi Synod should do so in its next printed Minutes not later than 1933.

Twenty-one of the constituent synods printed comparisons, either by totals showing the previous year's figures, or by increase or decrease over the previous year's report. The rest of the constituent synods should do so in their next printed Minutes not later than 1933. They are—Slovak Zion, United New York, United North Carolina, Indiana, Pacific, Wartburg, German Nebraska, Northwest, Manitoba, and Nova Scotia.

The Alleghany Synod prints totals and comparisons, but does not print grand totals for the entire synod and comparisons.

The Indiana Synod and the Pacific Synod print only totals but no grand totals for the entire synod and no comparisons.

The three last-mentioned synods, namely—Alleghany, Indiana and Pacific —should do so in their next printed Minutes not later than 1933.

Two of the Constituent Synods—German Nebraska and Texas—exceeded two pages in printing the rubrics of the Standard Parochial Blank. These synods, by 1933, should conform to the standard which is two pages.

Two of the Constituent Synods—Wartburg and Manitoba—printed rubrics across the narrow width of the page. These synods, by 1933, should conform in their next printed Minutes to the standard method of placing the parochial blanks in their Minutes, namely, lengthwise on two pages.

Inserts seem to have disappeared, we hope forever. The size of the printed Minutes is practically uniform—6 x 9—making bound volumes of Minutes possible. The secretaries of the constituent synods should see to it that the printer does not waste space by using less than forty-one lines to a page in printing the Standard Parochial Blank on two pages lengthwise in the Minutes.

The Statistical and Church Year Book Committee

The Statistical and Church Year Book Committee held one meeting during the biennium in the Lutheran Church House, 39 East 35th Street, New York, N. Y., on Wednesday, February 11, 1931, at 10.30 A. M. All of the members of the committee were present with the exception of the Reverend C. J. Rockey, D.D., who was excused.

The Reverend George H. Schnur, D.D., was elected chairman of the committee and the Reverend George L. Kieffer, D.D., Litt.D., was elected secretary-treasurer of the committee.

Tools for Pastors

1. *The Standard Parochial Blank.* The Standard Parochial Blank was revised and put in final form and plated during the past biennium.

2. *The Parish Register.* The Parish Register, which appeared some years ago under the editorship of the Reverend George H. Schnur, D.D., by the authority of the Statistical and Church Year Book Committee, is being rapidly introduced into the congregations of The United Lutheran Church in America.

3. *The Synodical Statistical Cards, or, The Auxiliary Parochial Cards.* These are a set of seven cards. This set of seven cards is being found to be a necessity for both pastors and synod officials in having a ten-year parochial record available.

4. *Auxiliary Blanks.* Your committee after a study of about ten years finally completed and released, under the editorship of the Reverend George L. Kieffer, D.D., Litt.D., a fairly complete set of Standard Auxiliary Blanks for congregations, to be used by officers of the church, church schools, organizations, church councils, etc., in preparing monthly, quarterly, semi-annual and annual reports. A blank for the Every Member Evangelistic Visitation and the Standard Canvass Card for canvassing of communities have also been provided. These blanks are described in a very attractive folder published by the United Lutheran Publication House, entitled, "A Complete and Uniform System for Keeping Church Records, Auxiliary Blanks and Additional Standard Forms for Congregations and The Parish Register, etc." Close examination of these blanks will reveal their simplicity and the fact that it will be easier to keep church records by the use of these blanks than by any other known method. The use of these blanks in every one of the

United Lutheran Church congregations is urged. Quite a number of the constituent synods have already introduced them, presenting a sample set to every congregation.

5. *The State of the Church Blank.* The State of the Church Blank has been rapidly revised. An effort will be made to secure a report on the use of this blank in many of the constituent synods of The United Lutheran Church in America. This data will be presented at the conference of the statistical secretaries in Philadelphia and recommendations will be made from this conference to the Statistical and Church Year Book Committee looking to the revision and the possible plating of this blank. This blank can be greatly improved. It is a vital blank and is the only blank providing for a regular report from the congregation to the constituent synod in that the report is to be filled out by the secretary of the congregation.

SERVICE RENDERED

Your committee through the statistical secretary of The United Lutheran Church in America has supplied The United Lutheran Church in America statistics to the National Lutheran Council for the Lutheran World Almanac for 1931-33; the annual releases of the Lutheran statistics to the *Christian Herald* as published in the annual religious statistics in the *Christian Herald* for 1931-32 (the Reverend George L. Kieffer, D.D., Litt.D., succeeding the Reverend Doctor Henry King Carroll as General Church Statistician) ; to the Reverend Doctor H. S. Myers, of the United Stewardship Council, for the Benevolence Statistics for 1931-32; to the editors of the Encyclopedia Americana, the International Year Book, for their articles on the Lutherans and to various other editors and authors.

SALARY SURVEY

Your committee through the statistical secretary of The United Lutheran Church in America in the Fall of 1931 made a preliminary salary survey for The United Lutheran Church in America by securing from each of the presidents of the thirty-three constituent synods the answer to a questionnaire of seven rubrics. The survey reveals that in the Fall of 1931 there were 3,323 ordained ministers on the rolls of The United Lutheran Church in America; 2,632 of these had congregational pastorates; 691 were without congregational pastorates. Of this number 265 were retired or pensioned, leaving 426 who were theological seminary. college and academy officers, professors and teachers, foreign missionaries, synodical and United Lutheran Church in America executives, chaplains, superintendents of institutions and Inner Mission workers on full time and those without any field of service. The highest salary paid as reported was $9,000 and parsonage; the lowest salary paid was $500; the average salary paid for the entire United Lutheran Church is between $1,900 and $2,000. For comparison's sake and in order to analyze that number of 526 more closely, another questionnaire in a more extended form is being released in the Fall of 1932.   It is to be hoped that the returns from this can be tabulated in time to be published in *The Lutheran* prior to the Convention of The United Lutheran Church in America.   The study of the number of deaths that occur from year to year reveals an average of fifty with a tendency to increase each year.   There are also about fifty ordained men each year who retire or enter the pension rolls and an average yearly seminary output of about one hundred.   It becomes quite evident that even though there may be now an apparent over-supply of ministers, the number that should enter the colleges with the ministry in view each year should be between one hundred and one hundred and fifty, in order to maintain the supply seven years hence.   The East Pennsylvania Synod publishes a Salary Survey yearly in connection with the Minutes of the Synod.   This has been done since 1920 with gratifying results.

The Statistical Handbook
The Statistical Handbook remains an unfinished task.   While an effort was made to gather the parochial statistics of the various constituent synods incomplete co-operation made the completion of the handbook too expensive.   Consultation with the business manager of the United Lutheran Publication House, Mr. Grant Hultberg, resulted in the postponement of the publication of this work, which should be produced as soon as possible.   A way should be found to produce this work, the cost of which would not be prohibitive as it appears to be now.

Incomplete and Inaccurate Parochial Statistical Reports
Not every man can add even the smallest sum.   Fewer can maintain mathematical tables looking toward the production of a balance sheet report.   Accurate and complete reports are, therefore, only possible where the statistical secretaries of the constituent synods actually complete and balance the parochial reports as received from the pastors.   That this is not done by quite a number of the statistical secretaries is evident when the printed parochial reports of the constituent synods are placed upon the adding machine.   If the congregational lines are not balanced the total for the constituent synod naturally will not be balanced, and just as true if the lines representing the reports of the constituent synods are not balanced the report for The United Lutheran Church in America will not be balanced.   Your committee through the statistical secretary has maintained a balanced report for The United Lutheran Church in America since the first report in 1919.

Reckoning of Membership
The "Confirmed Membership" and the "Communing Membership" of the congregations of the constituent synods of The United Lutheran Church in America still show the effect and influence of financial responsibility.   It is unfortunate when one report is made to the statistical secretary of the con-

stituent synod, a dissimilar report is made to the United States Census Bureau and an altogether different report published in a local church directory, all covering the same period of time. Facts should be adhered to in all instances. In the future the statistics of the churches as published in the *Christian Herald* will be compiled upon the basis of the "Baptized Membership" according to the percentages of those over thirteen years of age as revealed by the most recent United States Religious Census. The variance in the reports on "Confirmed" and "Communing Membership" will, therefore, no longer influence the standing of the Lutheran Church among the various Religious Bodies in the United States, and since practically all of the General Lutheran Church Bodies are given to involving either "Confirmed" or "Communing Membership" in their financial system, the standing of either of the General Lutheran Church Bodies will hardly be impaired when the various General Lutheran Church Bodies are compared. It is to be hoped that all finances in the entire Lutheran Church some day will be based upon the record of the past according to the degree of expectancy. There is no necessity for mixing finances and church membership. Wherever there is a period of time and individual units of achievements can be tabulated the lines of expectancy are easily determined to guide in the future.

END OF THE FISCAL YEAR

All of the constituent synods of The United Lutheran Church in America now conform to the standard—ending their fiscal year December 31st, the end of the calendar year. The Statistical and Church Year Book Committee has pioneered in this and is being copied by other religious bodies in America.

THE UNITED STATES CENSUS OF RELIGIOUS BODIES, 1936

It is not too early to begin to think of the taking of the next Census of Religious Bodies. This will require the preparation of a complete directory of the congregations of The United Lutheran Church in America as of 1936. It cannot be done in a single year or in a few months, but will require the checking of all of the Minutes of the constituent synods from 1926 to 1936, because every congregation which in the eyes of the law of the United States is an incorporated legal entity has to be accounted for whether still existing, disbanded or merged. The National Lutheran Council has already begun the checking of the card file of the Lutheran congregations in the United States which includes the directory of the United Lutheran Church congregations.

VISITATION OF SEMINARIES

The statistical secretary, the Reverend George L. Kieffer, D.D., Litt.D., visited in April, 1932, the following theological seminaries of The United Lutheran Church in America during that month: Lutheran Theological Seminary of Gettysburg, Pa.; Hamma Divinity School and Wittenberg College of Springfield, O.; and Lutheran Theological Seminary of Maywood, Chicago, Ill., and explained the statistical work in The United Lutheran Church in America to the students and members of the faculties present. The expenses of the trip for the visitation were taken care of by the National Lutheran Council.

The Reverend Ira F. Frankenfield, a member of the Statistical and Church Year Book Committee, made a similar visit to the Philadelphia Lutheran Theological Seminary, Mt. Airy, Philadelphia, Pa.

Expenses

The expenses of the Statistical and Church Year Book Committee in the form of postage and traveling have been taken care of by the treasurer of The United Lutheran Church in America, the amount being recorded in the treasurer's report.

Charts and Graphs

The chairman of the Statistical and Church Year Book Committee and the statistical secretary of The United Lutheran Church in America beg permission to present such charts and graphs as they may deem advisable at the time of the convention which will be based upon the very latest parochial statistics and which may or may not be desired as part of the minutes of the convention.

Parochial Statistics of The United Lutheran Church in America for 1930-31

The tables showing the totals for the parochial statistics of the constituent synods as well as of The United Lutheran Church in America for the year 1930 are hereby appended. (Note.—Committee: They are the same as in the 1932 United Lutheran Church in America Year Book.) Tables showing the totals for the parochial statistics of the constituent synods, as well as for The United Lutheran Church in America for the year 1931 will be available for the minutes of the convention. (Note.—Committee: They will be the same as for the 1933 United Lutheran Church in America Year Book.)

The Year Book of The United Lutheran Church in America

At the meeting of the committee in February, 1931, the Reverend George H. Schnur, D.D., was re-elected editor of the Year Book for the years 1932 and 1933.

At that same meeting your committee passed upon and approved the contents of the Year Book for 1932, the statistical material and the alphabetical directory of ministers being provided by the statistical secretary of The United Lutheran Church in America while the rest of the material of the Year Book remained in the hands of the editor. When, for the sake of economy, the usual annual meeting of the committee for 1932 was omitted, the preparation of the Year Book for 1933 was left entirely in the hands of the editor and the statistical secretary. Ordinarily the Statistical and Church Year Book Committee assumes the responsibility for the contents of our Year Book.

OUR DEPARTED WORKERS

Three times during this year the angel of death has taken away a man whose work has meant much to the Lutheran Church Year Book.

1. The Reverend Solomon E. Ochsenford, D.D., was the editor of the Lutheran Church Almanac (G. C.) 1883-1905, a term of twenty-three years, besides writing a great deal for other periodical literature of the Church. His monumental work was the "Documentary History of the General Council," a book of lasting value. He was born near New Hanover, Pa., on November 8, 1855, and was baptized in the old Falkner Swamp Church, one of our oldest congregations in Pennsylvania. He entered into rest June 19, 1932, after a life of almost four-score years filled with good works.

2. The Reverend William M. Kopenhaver was the last editor of the Lutheran Church Almanac of the General Council, 1906-1916; a co-editor of the Lutheran Church Year Book, 1917-1919; and, again, editor of the Year Book of the United Lutheran Church, 1921-1926. Thus he served in all for twenty years. At the time of the merger he was appointed a member of the Statistical and Church Year Book Committee, of which he was a valuable member until failing health brought on his resignation. He died at his sister's home in Harrisburg on his sixty-sixth birthday, on March 20, 1932, and was buried in the cemetery in the beautiful Lykens Valley, near Elizabethville, Pennsylvania, his birthplace. As a pastor at Macungie, Pa., for many years, as statistician of the Allentown Conference of his synod, as well as editor of the Year Book for two decades, he will be long remembered. He was a conscientious and faithful servant of the Lutheran Church.

3. The Reverend Melanchthon G. G. Scherer, D.D., born in Catawba Co., N. C., on March 16, 1861, entered into life March 9, 1932. Elsewhere we read of his many-sided life and labors. In this report we think of him as the leading spirit of our committee. What a wonderful family he sprang from! The writer of this memorial attended Sunday school in early childhood in a congregation founded in the Wabash Valley by his grandfather, the Reverend Jacob Scherer and heard many interesting stories of that pious pioneer. And how glad we have been in these later years to count his grandson, our beloved secretary of the Church, as a friend. His scholarship, his good judgment, his common sense, his kindly consideration, altogether guided us so continually that our statistical committee will sorely miss him.

RECOMMENDATIONS

1. That the constituent synods be requested in the printing of their minutes to make the pages after the title page a calendar page, indicating the special days and dates of The United Lutheran Church in America and the special days and dates of the constituent synod, and also a table showing

the use of the Budget Benevolence Dollar of The United Lutheran Church in America and one showing the use of the Budget Benevolence Dollar of the constituent synod, or a table showing a combination of both.

2. That we request the constituent synods to urge their congregations to use "The Parish Register," prepared by your committee for use in congregations of The United Lutheran Church in America.

3. That we request the constituent synods to provide Standard Parish Record Cards for the statistical secretaries and that the constituent synods urge the pastors to use these Parish Record Cards to provide ready comparative parochial tables.

4. That we request the constituent synods to make use of the Standard State of the Church Blank as provided by the Statistical and Church Year Book Committee of The United Lutheran Church in America.

5. That we request the constituent synods to introduce in the congregations of The United Lutheran Church in America the Standard Auxiliary Congregational Blanks.

6. That we request all the constituent synods of The United Lutheran Church in America in the preparation of their minutes to conform to the standard as to size and to style and to the arrangement of content.

7. That we request all the constituent synods to use the Standard Parochial Blanks and the Standard Assembly Sheets in complete form.

8. That the constituent synods be requested to co-operate with the Statistical and Church Year Book Committee of The United Lutheran Church in America in the publication of a Statistical Handbook of The United Lutheran Church in America, the first to appear in 1935 to contain the 1934 parochial statistics of the constituent synods and to be published every ten years thereafter.

9. That the constituent synods be again requested to make provision for their statistical secretaries at future conventions of The United Lutheran Church in America in order that they may attend the conference as statistical secretaries which will meet at the time of the convention.

10. That we request that the fiscal years of all of the congregations and synod organizations be made concurrent with the calendar year ending December 31st each year and that all published reports and statistics be of the date of December 31st of the previous year.

11. That we request the constituent synods to prepare statistical and graphic histories of their synod and of their congregations.

Respectfully submitted,

The Statistical and Church Year Book Committee,

GEORGE H. SCHNUR, *Chairman.*

GEORGE L. KIEFFER, *Secretary-Treasurer.*

CHARLES W. LEITZELL.

JOSEPH D. KROUT.

IRA F. FRANKENFIELD.

C. J. ROCKEY.

HARRY E. PUGH.

The Report of the Statistical Secretary of the United Lutheran Church in America

The report of the statistical secretary of The United Lutheran Church in America is in part embodied in the report of the Statistical and Church Year Book Committee. Attention is especially called to the part of the committee's report referring to charts and graphs.

The statistical secretary desires to express appreciation, especially to the statistical secretaries of the various constituent synods, to the officers of the various constituent synods and heads of various institutions, organizations and societies for their loyal co-operation in the answering of many questionnaires.

In completing the work of the present biennium the statistical secretary is conscious of the fact that the Lutheran Church, especially The United Lutheran Church in America, has been a leader in the field of religious statistics since 1919. A review of the various reports of the Statistical and Church Year Book Committee, as printed in the Minutes of the United Lutheran Church since 1920, reveals a story of laying foundations and the establishment of principles, all of which have accrued to the benefit of The United Lutheran Church in America and the Lutheran Church's position in religious statistics.

Your statistical secretary, in the summer of 1919, was the compiler of the 1920 Year Book of The United Lutheran Church in America. In the summer of 1920 your statistical secretary compiled the parochial tables which appeared in the 1921 Year Book. The parochial statistics which have appeared in the Year Books and the Minutes of The United Lutheran Church in America since 1920 have been prepared by your statistical secretary who was elected the statistical secretary of The United Lutheran Church in America, on February 10, 1921, at a salary of $500 per annum (increased to $600 in December, 1924, and to $800 in 1928).

The expenses of the statistical secretary in the form of postage and traveling expenses have been taken care of by the treasurer of The United Lutheran Church in America as a part of the expenses of the Statistical and Church Year Book Committee, but since 1919 the clerical help, office space, etc., incident to the statistical work of The United Lutheran Church in America, has been provided by the National Lutheran Council.

Your statistical secretary is conscious of the fact that there is yet much to be done in the statistical field of The United Lutheran Church in America. First, in the form of the completion of statistical histories covering the various constituent synods of The United Lutheran Church in America and the various General Lutheran Church Bodies merged in The United Lutheran Church in America; the revision of the Standard State of the Church Blank and other blanks, so that they can be put in plated form, and, the publication of the Statistical Handbook, as of 1935 and every ten years thereafter, always preceding the United States Census of Religious Bodies, thus providing a congregational roll of The United Lutheran Church in America for the United States Bureau of Census, Department of Commerce, Washington, D. C.

Respectfully submitted,

GEORGE LINN KIEFFER, *Statistical Secretary.*

Report of the Editor of the Year Book of the United Lutheran Church in America

To the regular biennial report, which will be found included in the report of the standing committee, we wish to add a few words. It is now eighty-three years since T. Newton Kurtz founded the Lutheran Almanac at Baltimore, Maryland.

Volume LXXXIII, the Year Book of The United Lutheran Church in America for 1933, which is now almost ready for the press, completes my seven years' service as editor. I have enjoyed the work very much and am grateful to the Church for the privilege of this opportunity during these years of adaptation and development of our United Church. The annual bird's-eye view of our Church's work found in our editorial pages and the continued accurate presentation of historical anniversaries that are both interesting and valuable to Lutheranism in the calendar pages and, in special cases, with editorial mention, alongside of the statistical department has involved many hours of careful attention to detail. But it has been a labor of love.

That our Year Book may continue as an increasingly valuable storehouse of fact and progress for The United Lutheran Church in America is our hope.

Respectfully submitted,

GEORGE H. SCHNUR, *Editor.*

STATISTICAL REPORT OF THE UNITED LUTHERAN CHURCH IN AMERICA FOR THE YEAR 1930

PAROCHIAL

Index No.	Synod	When Organized	Pastors	Parishes	Congregations	Membership: Baptized	Membership: Confirmed	Membership: Communing	Accessions Children: Baptism	Accessions Children: Otherwise	Accessions Adult: Confirmation	Accessions Adult: Baptism	Accessions Adult: Certificate	Accessions Adult: Otherwise	Losses Children: Death	Losses Children: Otherwise	Losses Adult: Death	Losses Adult: Certificate	Losses Adult: Otherwise	Church Papers: No. Sub. to Official Papers	Church Papers: No. S. S. Papers Distributed	Church Papers: No. Sub. to Other Ch. Papers
1	Ministerium of Penna.	Aug. 15, 1748	460	374	594	291417	198292	140873	6855	2913	6549	442	2765	2262	456	2987	2971	1997	4823	6606	15916	5935
2	United Synod of N. Y.	Oct. 23, 1786	454	413	424	224978	152649	188910	4689	3974	5081	326	1837	3500	282	3736	2048	1030	3838	4301	15411	3357
3	United Synod of N. C.	May 2, 1803	106	90	162	35519	24782	18887	850	205	667	148	550	66	56	111	186	311	1355	1223	2570	2463
4	Synod of Maryland	Oct. 11, 1820	120	101	139	66042	48592	30983	1482	546	1503	204	879	587	56	808	712	550	1355	1755	4727	1977
5	Synod of S. Carolina	Jan. 14, 1824	110	94	160	27654	20158	13222	463	117	567	69	361	78	20	78	201	321	433	1555	1812	1976
6	Synod of West Penna.	Sept. 5, 1825	94	76	160	60699	45183	33905	1175	266	1267	273	665	276	62	201	735	513	243	1069	2471	936
7	Synod of Virginia	Aug. 10, 1829	94	76	168	24995	19785	12203	409	245	402	251	361	139	19	139	264	258	3374	3225	3739	2730
8	Synod of Ohio	Nov. 7, 1836	251	206	281	82812	56567	34304	1867	993	1950	552	1625	1076	94	781	939	1117	991	2023	22689	2433
9	East Penna. Synod	May 2, 1842	168	124	168	72440	52259	34163	1517	718	1415	305	1126	211	61	617	693	696	407	867	6915	1722
10	Alleghany Synod	Sept. 9, 1842	74	67	146	40120	30029	19984	645	134	669	147	367	265	60	265	393	392	2135	3054	5961	2077
11	Pittsburgh Synod	Jan. 15, 1845	268	223	319	121416	83774	52589	2819	1203	2714	369	1332	1449	181	1556	1002	1099	1260	3054	24329	23874
12	Indiana Synod	Oct. 28, 1848	67	59	79	16441	12636	8515	363	191	441	122	232	239	19	366	190	190	552	476	3638	502
13	Illinois Synod	Sept. 18, 1851	141	120	138	55543	37167	26531	1569	1337	1811	357	774	1462	63	1020	413	439	476	996	12357	2105
14	Texas Synod	Nov. 10, 1851	28	29	28	6031	4083	3130	145	81	262	183	36	88	19	97	44	38	256	256	476	540
15	Susq. Synod of Cen. Pa.	Sept. 25, 1855	105	81	162	51761	39075	25662	1038	256	1890		602	275	63	789	489	408	858	925	5723	948
16	Mississippi Synod	Feb. 21, 1855	6	5	12	779	636	313	18	12	9	5	18	3	57	3	5		31	31	105	45
17	Synod of Iowa	July 3, 1855	31	32	32	15922	10200	6574	381	232	473	128	296	246	18	161	94	118	224	288	3947	463
18	Michigan Synod	Sept. 27, 1855	68	63	89	22787	16067	9755	533	882	462	156	405	534	29	179	162	177	775	502	5501	1003
19	Synod of Georgia-Ala.	Oct. 20, 1860	81	17	29	6367	4029	2721	151	79	119	31	79	89	2	2	43	69	206	368	697	380
20	Synod of Canada	July 21, 1861	81	60	87	26857	17879	13866	660	197	667	8	123	384	41	148	225	116	251	1524	2014	520
21	Synod of Kansas	July 21, 1868	48	36	48	10493	7534	5046	212	191	230	68	198	247	24	116	99	132	251	321	2775	649
22	Synod of Nebraska	Nov. 5, 1871	48	44	56	20123	13870	9068	621	167	578	191	280	305	38	468	125	203	218	615	3675	701
23	Wartburg Synod	Sept. 1, 1875	57	47	57	19876	12395	9421	480	221	468	41	305	366	36	86	86	28	52	529	1450	318
24	Ger. Nebraska Synod	July 24, 1890	86	44	86	17038	11689	8159	434	113	404	47	64	30	36	52	121	40	88	300	848	343
25	Synod of California	Apr. 2, 1891	24	82	37	9760	7697	4296	282	321	233	32	219	373	13	205	82	128	237	529	1749	132
26	Rocky Mt. Synod	May 6, 1891	24	24	16	3722	2620	1725	112	153	105	30	93	133		60	28	51	124	162	1135	1243
27	Synod of the N. W.	Sept. 22, 1891	101	16	89	47272	30089	22931	1478	1155	1590	168	390	1419	51	1461	243	327	2102	1024	6961	380
28	Manitoba Synod	Sept. 16, 1897	48	83	89	13471	7697	5563	588	182	405	16	113	169	132	171	132	42	344	3300	125	291
29	Pacific Synod	Sept. 26, 1901	35	38	29	5318	3315	2008	167	7	186	15	25	101	36	19	36	42	125	139	1510	63
30	Nova Scotia Synod	July 10, 1903	8	23	8	5419	3142	1739	131	46	147	30	103	45	10	24	48	12	69	251	263	1616
31	Synod of W. Va.	Apr. 17, 1912	22	8	35	6716	4387	3129	161		130				6		38	55		327	1829	156
32	Slovak Zion Synod	June 10, 1919	22	20	31	12606	8001	6943	403		299			73	1	26	176		40		156	86
33	Florida Synod	Jan. 15, 1929	13	13	12	1992	1475	1049	32	99	32	1	53				20	55		96	370	
34	Totals for U. S. and Canada		3284	2752	3942	1424386	987231	682167	32730	17236	32650	4722	16087	17177	1764	16750	13041	10893	26336	39431	163710	61808
35	Totals Outside U. S. and Canada		144		1704	160181	69921	69430	141	16	4631	7586	16	2784	41	16	2360	28	8103	27		
36	U. L. C. World Total		3428	2752	5646	1584567	1057152	751597	32871	17252	37281	12308	16103	19961	1805	16766	15401	10921	34439	39458	163710	61808

STATISTICAL REPORT OF THE UNITED LUTHERAN CHURCH IN AMERICA FOR THE YEAR 1930—Continued

	PAROCHIAL																			FINANCIAL		
	CHURCH SCHOOLS									STUDENTS				CHURCH SOCIETIES						Valuation of Church Property		
	SUNDAY					WEEKDAY								MEN'S		WOMEN'S		YOUNG P.				
Index Number	Number	Officers and Teachers	Scholars	Home Dep't	Cradle Roll	Number	Teachers	Scholars	Catechumens	Ministry	Deaconess	In Lutheran Institutions	In Non-Luth. Institutions	Number	Members	Number	Members	Number	Members	Church Edifices	Parsonages	School and Parish Houses
1	596	12300	121128	5195	11773	134	1011	13144	8479	94	15	349	1661	237	11337	816	37341	662	24170	22963448	2411775	2078800
2	411	7814	65976	1790	8345	102	416	4664	5903	109	23	170	1414	290	13632	711	33415	770	21867	22218727	2935200	3120500
3	157	2309	24403	199	1001	95	436	7889	2761	6	3	171	283	55	1208	146	4321	198	5679	2862516	395111	176040
4	140	3699	36064	1806	3926	21	169	1726	1868	40	3	86	488	52	2701	234	4616	219	7270	6777318	738800	416600
5	107	1390	14071	130	743	59	381	6352	1566	19	4	166	247	27	897	146	4067	162	4487	1463950	258150	131300
6	159	3965	45074	1360	3672	27	174	2705	3928	24	1	146	469	38	2018	233	18541	179	7122	5005900	591130	315775
7	154	5181	51051	1510	1292	54	277	3243	4095	6		86	214	21	658	151	9469	130	4153	1941670	386065	93600
8	273	4002	39190	1303	3324	31	133	2157	2772	24	3	120	716	155	5483	492	18541	291	6755	9087600	966950	529500
9	158	2417	22792	997	3537	45	297	3630	2667	51		75	600	95	4744	312	13499	269	8305	7719477	1025382	752975
10	113	5808	25570	2420	2079	50	330	4403	1471	17	1	196	405	24	1216	157	18147	116	3915	3154100	452629	174189
11	306	1043	9076	396	6517	77	395	5177	5162	63	5	116	815	160	5804	540	14836	405	11530	10445505	1446300	510100
12	68	2403	27435	302	750	14	61	770	568	10	1	12	378	26	701	126	4137	74	1544	1719950	222950	67400
13	137	248	2048	28	2667	27	177	2165	1765	27	2	107	153	86	3537	289	7414	253	7248	5181061	642463	279650
14	28	3232	33631	1461	125	5	13	185	203	4			28	86	126	33	1028	33	791	140400	46500	36650
15	167	269	2048		2425	29	206	2223	2112	27	1	107	420	47	2172	204	7380	149	4602	4269400	504554	166000
16	10	662	6025	47	12	8	8	46	40	1			9			10	117	6	110	34150	6100	
17	31	1409	11311	272	702	11	65	546	989	9		29	152	17	540	64	2396	54	1772	1008236	156500	3000
18	86	357	2708		998	7	46	583	814	11		32	183	23	847	127	4325	80	1779	2833089	234900	108000
19	23	877	6600	9	207	7	60	628	216	7		15	65	10	310	46	1251	39	946	639900	49420	107000
20	78	699	5662	80	966	23	24	572	789	8	1	25	43	8	291	68	2814	69	2146	1077030	215725	77500
21	43	975	5801	203	414	4	22	421	286	12		13	152	17	509	95	2773	54	1203	1380840	199600	43500
22	52	558	2353		1071	13	61	560	1030	23		89	245	13	382	89	2664	66	1947	1224150	162972	18000
23	41	351	3932	12		20	28	518	509	9	3			22	794	64	2907	48	1372			
24	55	476	1772	47	102	4	5	578	439	9		8	28	9	24	61	1623	32	2064	696500	132300	14050
25	37	246	2017	363	363	4	23	103	525	10		8	134	19	697	70	2236	58	1240	1553300	72000	3000
26	15	1824	2138	329	329	23	92	275	173	2	3		41	8	184	30	773	24	490	486100	35700	5000
27	86	130	14648		2115	61	50	1295	2612	24		54	436	62	2250	155	5749	184	4758	4105484	337900	189100
28	67	279	1181	44		3	11	1875	288	16	2	24	20			19	399	31	648			
29	29	169	3442		273			111	58	3	1	5	34	14	230	48	1097	41	727	428800	59800	2000
30	19	471	1112	102	31	11	55	730	347	2		4	12			21	675	5	128	195400	29400	1000
31	30	66	880		244	84	149	3044		5		9	84	15	364	50	1345	38		711200	126801	2000
32	22	125			36	2	8	109	50										890	530000	129000	23500
33	13											3	23	3	35	20	499	18	275	384923	64500	3200
34	3711	67329	641053	23615	60029	1127	5216	72427	54485	672	64	2430	9952	1559	63691	5627	212558	4757	141933	122139124	15036577	9448929
35	1077	2195	56157			1135	1823	42062	145	191		3	18			6	91	8	273	2553000	55000	11363
36	4788	69524	697210	23615	60029	2262	7039	114489	54630	863	64	2433	9970	1559	63691	5633	212649	4765	142206	124692124	15091577	9460292

STATISTICAL REPORT OF THE UNITED LUTHERAN CHURCH IN AMERICA FOR THE YEAR 1930—Concluded

FINANCIAL

Index Number	Valuation of Church Property				Congregational Expenses			Apportioned			Congregational Benevolence — Unapportioned					Total Unapportioned Benevolence	Summary	
	Endowment	Other Property	Total Valuation	Indebtedness	Current	Unusual	Total	Paid	Excess	Deficit	Education	Foreign Missions	Home Missions	Inner Missions	Other Benevolence		Total Benevolence	Total Expenditures
1	1162191	1143880	29760094	4049907	1721155	1146635	2867790	395885	2749	247029	9408	52494	15106	137385	42024	256417	652302	3520092
2	834034	1949861	30958322	5082045	2016207	740054	2756261	249134			74196	28991	15411	132912	32798	284308	533442	3289703
3	20900	181678	3636245	415471	212330	122862	335192	43565	200	33837	8823	9508	7186	13721	8929	48167	91732	426924
4	119607	215601	8267926	1194413	556954	441474	998428	120626	1343	22301	5105	23043	9830	67676	20104	125758	246384	1244812
5	14000	146658	2014058	233172	144865	109856	254721	27829	101	32885	52247	4519	3030	12511	6731	79038	106867	361588
6	294073	339775	6546653	408579	455121	291390	746511	124462	4206	31266	3414	21255	5111	30921	12413	73114	197576	944087
7	84150	109332	2614817	187192	172781	116526	289307	36689	338	23884	1417	6563	3134	19190	8637	38941	75630	364937
8	128809	509244	11222103	1197113	877064	269901	1146965	209225	2344	58123	4417	32925	8411	62793	34242	142788	352013	1498978
9	189747	401885	10089466	1619700	742273	290003	1032276	136443	328	17223	9084	33936	12651	71448	17903	145022	281465	1313741
10	49089	104647	3934654	315077	305631	92807	398438	87469	5035		3504	5109	2061	26735	22617	60026	147495	545933
11	168301	973204	13543410	2299250	1014854	373952	1388806	202073		64687	8290	29818	15578	105143	33481	192310	394383	1783189
12	102600	154111	2267014	352670	220687	98554	319241	49417	65	13216	1758	4070	678	17934	5366	29806	79223	398464
13	62939	116530	6282643	1518587	571365	286863	858228	107322	69	27474	4105	17793	9430	37040	15565	83933	191255	1049483
14	150	10793	234493	36506	31691	14017	45708	4310	35	8783	187	319	419	1717	822	3464	7774	53482
15	116724	185092	5241770	490488	366684	135470	502154	95547	882	28521	3419	10693	1379	24365	9713	49569	145016	647170
16		40250	40250	6100	4408	1085	5493	581		599	55	74	50	143	157	479	1060	6553
17	5500	48085	1221321	298224	145865	23462	169327	14979		12388	452	1814	448	4560	1728	9002	23981	193308
18	10775	31748	1318512	807422	106643	207848	314491	34991	63	13899	569	5212	930	7934	3128	17773	52764	367255
19	20095	30700	841115	142417	54582	31669	86251	11588	6	3649	969	2489	2226	5651	1665	13000	24588	110839
20	27800	61180	1459235	107381	162509	19610	182119	33133	1228	3426	1748	2832	472	6230	3869	15151	48284	230403
21	7310	37015	1668265	202854	127976	32074	160050	22490	36	5846	283	2296	1195	8303	3131	15208	37698	197748
22	19497	141430	1566049	97703	152168	34814	186982	38567	70	14602	772	4839	1815	11837	5325	24588	63155	250137
23		191480	1191480	123524	115769	40330	156099	11696							4001	4001	15697	171796
24	6800	21900	870550	27644	62395	11218	73613	7467	8	7289	2818	1641	746	1914	8638	15757	23224	96837
25	1152	59887	1694339	272984	125922	28645	154567	13690		1557	345	1925	1682	6403	4682	15037	28727	183294
26	51	14011	540862	239956	44672	22682	67354	6518	344						4237	4237	10755	78109
27	5900	89570	4727954	1761302	419266	162139	581405	78678			2701	6817	2892	20079	13323	45812	124490	705895
28		341078	341078		41644		41644	6637		1126	100	99	99	99	1142	1539	8176	49820
29	500	18375	509475	197253	53797	15976	69773	8087			973	560	252	2327	1097	5209	13296	83069
30		6300	232100	19777	20752	7167	27919	2374		4554	75	134	54	1625	762	2650	5024	32943
31	1050	76500	917551	162355	72188	23436	95624	13139	16		10	1640	370	2881	3736	8637	21776	117400
32	6000	6000	688500	91858	75120	200	75320	1191		1088					1968	1968	3159	78479
33	1250	5500	459373	172930	28937	18154	47091	3494			157	186	459	841	768	2411	5905	52996
34	3454994	8723053	158801677	24133654	11325480	5109667	16435148	2199196	19466	707345	200476	319841	124243	838587	331973	1815120	4014316	20449464
35		58000	2677363		204753		204753								27092	27092	27092	231845
36	3454994	8781053	161479040	24133654	11530233	5109667	16639901	2199196	19466	707345	200476	319841	124243	838587	359065	1842212	4041408	20681309

COMPARATIVE STATISTICAL REPORT OF THE UNITED LUTHERAN CHURCH IN AMERICA
FOR THE YEARS 1920, 1921, 1922, 1923, 1924, 1925, 1926, 1927, 1928, 1929, 1930

PAROCHIAL

Index Number	Year	Pastors	Parishes	Congregations	Membership Baptized	Membership Confirmed	Membership Communing	Accessions Children Baptism	Accessions Children Otherwise	Accessions Adult Baptism	Accessions Adult Confirmation	Accessions Adult Certificate	Accessions Adult Otherwise	Losses Children Death	Losses Children Otherwise	Losses Adult Death	Losses Adult Certificate	Losses Adult Otherwise	Church Papers No. Sub. to Official Papers	Church Papers No. S.S. Papers Distributed	Church Papers No. Sub. to Other Ch. Prs.
1	1930	3284	2752	3942	1424386	987231	682167	32730	17236	4722	32650	16087	17177	1764	16750	13041	10893	26336	39431	163710	61808
2	1929	3274	2750	3925	1399408	971187	680836	33195	18412	5235	34247	17181	17889	1913	16855	13561	11678	27406	40329	165940	58505
3	1 Year's Gain	10	2	17	24978	16044	1331														3303
4	1 Year's Decrease							465	1176	513	1597	1094	712	149	105	520	785	1070	898	2230	
5	1930	3284	2752	3942	1424386	987231	682167	32730	17236	4722	32650	16087	17177	1764	16750	13041	10893	26336	39431	163710	61808
6	1928	3272	2790	3906	1370183	949188	676839	34530	17594	4896	33044	16725	17506	2010	16413	13184	11241	25976	41809	163027	57123
7	2 Years' Gain	12		36	54203	38043	5328								337			360		683	4685
8	2 Years' Decrease		38					1800	358	174	394	638	329	246		143	348		2378		
9	1930	3284	2752	3942	1424386	987231	682167	32730	17236	4722	32650	16087	17177	1764	16750	13041	10893	26336	39431	163710	61808
10	1927	3184	2689	3881	1321780	933650	676496	33668	18264	5397	33871	18704	20012	2023	14772	12677	12117	24464	43917	162246	49825
11	3 Years' Gain	100	63	61	102606	53581	5671								1978	364		1872		1464	11983
12	3 Years' Decrease							938	1028	675	1221	2617	2835	259			1224		4486		
13	1930	3284	2752	3942	1424386	987231	682167	32730	17236	4722	32650	16087	17177	1764	16750	13041	10893	26336	39431	163710	61808
14	1926	3127	2706	3876	1315620	916858	677287	34562	17573	5178	25451	16866	19781	1983	12789	11758	11467	22831	50684	167418	38573
15	4 Years' Gain	157	46	66	108766	70373	4880				7199				3961	1283		3505			23235
16	4 Years' Decrease							1832	337	456		779	2604	219			574		11253	3708	
17	1930	3284	2752	3942	1424386	987231	682167	32730	17236	4722	32650	16087	17177	1764	16750	13041	10893	26336	39431	163710	61808
18	1925	3011	2649	3875	1276176	886840	669695	35307	16658	5536	31071	17366	18504	2004	12335	11454	12111	23935	50735	174447	36101
19	5 Years' Gain	273	103	67	148210	100391	12472		578		1579				4415	1587		2401			25707
20	5 Years' Decrease							2577		814		1279	1327	240			1218		11304	10697	
21	1930	3284	2752	3942	1424386	987231	682167	32730	17236	4722	32650	16087	17177	1764	16750	13041	10893	26336	39431	163710	61808
22	1924	2983	2643	3829	1238009	856180	645836	35138	14029	5746	31020	17314	18090	1982	9918	11250	11887	23356	50224	162037	39471
23	6 Years' Gain	301	109	113	186337	131051	36331		3207		1630				6832	1791		2980		1673	22337
24	6 Years' Decrease							2408		1024		1227	913	218			994		10793		
25	1930	3284	2752	3942	1424386	987231	682167	32730	17236	4722	32650	16087	17177	1764	16750	13041	10893	26336	39431	163710	61808
26	1923	2924	2566	3812	1201401	839279	633184	33837	12419	4472	28188	15600	16125	2244	9788	11518	11016	25436	47618	152731	34708
27	7 Years' Gain	360	186	130	222985	147952	48983		4817	250	4462	487	1052		6962	1523		900		10979	27100
28	7 Years' Decrease							1107						480			123		8187		
29	1930	3284	2752	3942	1424386	987231	682167	32730	17236	4722	32650	16087	17177	1764	16750	13041	10893	26336	39431	163710	61808
30	1922	2900	2501	3732	1164550	819063	621123	36016	12704	5599	30954	15829	16445	2334	9370	11741	10934	25650	49267	144631	33867
31	8 Years' Gain	384	251	210	259836	168168	61044		4532		1696	258	732		7380	1300		686		19079	27941
32	8 Years' Decrease							3286		877				570			41		9836		
33	1930	3284	2752	3942	1424386	987231	682167	32730	17236	4722	32650	16087	17177	1764	16750	13041	10893	26336	39431	163710	61808
34	1921	2887	2492	3803	1147007	801250	597768	37403	11773	5302	30467	16456	16500	2392	8921	11051	11475	25485	36969	118139	21454
35	9 Years' Gain	397	260	139	277379	185981	84399		5463		2183		677		7829	1990		851	2462	45571	40354
36	9 Years' Decrease							4673		580		369		628			582				
37	1930	3284	2752	3942	1424386	987231	682167	32730	17236	4722	32650	16087	17177	1764	16750	13041	10893	26336	39431	163710	61808
38	1920	2812		3775	1117938	791400	580018	36438		4834	29380	15214	14571			11554	11610	26550			
39	10 Years' Gain	472		167	306448	195831	102149				3270	873	2606			1487					
40	10 Years' Decrease							3708		112							717	214			

COMPARATIVE STATISTICAL REPORT OF THE UNITED LUTHERAN CHURCH IN AMERICA FOR THE YEARS 1920, 1921, 1922, 1923, 1924, 1925, 1926, 1927, 1928, 1929, 1930—Continued

PAROCHIAL

In ex number	SUNDAY Number	SUNDAY Officers and Teachers	SUNDAY Scholars	SUNDAY Home Dep't	SUNDAY Cradle Roll	WEEKDAY Number	WEEKDAY Teachers	WEEKDAY Scholars	Catechu-mens	STUDENTS Ministry	STUDENTS Deaconess	STUDENTS In Lutheran Institutions	STUDENTS In Non-Luth. Institutions	MEN'S Number	MEN'S Members	WOMEN'S Number	WOMEN'S Members	YOUNG P. Number	YOUNG P. Members	Church Edifices	Parsonages	School and Parish Houses
1	3711	67329	641053	23615	60029	1127	5216	72427	54485	672	64	2430	9952	1559	63691	5627	212558	4757	141933	122139124	15036577	9448929
2	4215	66800	636121	24564	63218	1056	4870	68082	50009	661	33	2635	9034	1471	63799	5488	210328	4698	137624	120574104	15170989	8966309
3	504	529	4932	949	3189	71	346	4345	4476	11	31	205	918	88	108	139	2230	59	4309	1565020	134412	482620
4																						
5	3711	67329	641053	23615	60029	1127	5216	72427	54485	672	64	2430	9952	1559	63691	5627	212558	4757	141933	122139124	15036577	9448929
6	3671	65465	624908	26046	65787	1033	4513	65123	51212	709	44	2678	8967	1436	63646	5322	209318	4385	133105	114446734	14764569	7486380
7	40	1864	16145	2431	5758	94	703	7304	3273	37	20	248	985	123	45	305	3240	372	8828	7692390	272008	1962549
8																						
9	3711	67329	641053	23615	60029	1127	5216	72427	54485	672	64	2430	9952	1559	63691	5627	212558	4757	141933	122139124	15036577	9448929
10	3651	64212	613863	25826	65544	928	4183	58491	48823	261	52	2626	8338	1383	63146	5181	208003	3986	133682	108956533	14598321	6830516
11	60	3117	27190	2211	5515	199	1033	13936	5662	411	12	196	1614	176	545	446	4555	771	8251	13182591	438256	2618413
12																						
13	3711	67329	641053	23615	60029	1127	5216	72427	54485	672	64	2430	9952	1559	63691	5627	212558	4757	141933	122139124	15036577	9448929
14	3524	62609	608261	27309	65938	647	3157	45366	48272	851	79	2632	7555	1294	59190	4830	199855	3835	130552	99894373	13881748	5198535
15	187	4720	32792	3694	5909	480	2059	27061	6213	179	15	202	2397	265	4501	797	12703	922	11381	22244751	1154829	4250394
16																						
17	3711	67329	641053	23615	60029	1127	5216	72427	54435	672	64	2430	9952	1559	63691	5627	212558	4757	141933	122139124	15036577	9448929
18	3531	59940	590169	28187	65706	651	2704	42372	49216	826	90	2551	6753	1211	56892	4515	184475	3547	122380	86288340	12532190	3919089
19	180	7389	50884	4572	5677	476	2512	30055	5269	154	26	121	3199	348	6799	1112	28083	1210	19553	35850784	2504387	5529840
20																						
21	3711	67329	641053	23615	60029	1127	5216	72427	54485	672	64	2430	9952	1559	63691	5627	212558	4757	141933	122139124	15036577	9448929
22	3515	59205	571737	28028	63853	557	2051	38824	49310	828	68	2530	5841	1213	56605	4307	181449	3400	120277	78525563	11169150	3136620
23	196	8124	69316	4413	3824	570	3165	33603	5175	156	4	100	4111	346	7086	1320	31109	1357	21656	43613561	3867427	6312309
24																						
25	3711	67329	641053	23615	60029	1127	5216	72427	54485	672	64	2430	9952	1559	63691	5627	212558	4757	141933	122139124	15036577	9448929
26	3440	56863	552872	22164	61995	523	1638	28438	45238	746	67	2381	5402	1137	53706	4151	174535	3200	115726	70971368	10415614	2463970
27	271	10466	88181	1451	1966	604	3578	43989	9247	74	3	49	4550	422	9985	1476	38023	1557	26207	51167756	4620963	6984959
28																						
29	3711	67329	641053	23615	60029	1127	5216	72427	54485	672	64	2430	9952	1559	63691	5627	212558	4757	141933	122139124	15036577	9448929
30	3465	55330	555510	28446	59264	490	1453	25149	35311	717	59	2015	4520	1102	52525	4013	173270	3132	115234	65598841	9237584	1584150
31	246	11999	85543	4831	765	637	3763	47278	19174	45	5	415	5432	457	11166	1614	39288	1625	26699	56540283	5798993	7864779
32																						
33	3711	67329	641053	23615	60029	1127	5216	72427	54485	672	64	2430	9952	1559	63691	5627	212558	4757	141933	122139124	15036577	9448929
34	3682	54268	522691	26142	52148	375	954	17534	34034	582	85	1712	4292	967	47052	3618	154089	3694	106842	62193694	8138433	878400
35	29	13061	118362	2527	7881	752	4262	54893	20451	90	21	718	5660	592	16639	2009	58469	1063	35091	59845430	6898144	8570529
36																						
37	3711	67329	641053	23615	60029	1127	5216	72427	54485	672	64	2430	9952	1559	63691	5627	212558	4757	141933	122139124	15036577	9448929
38	3399	52939	515815	23506	46300	190	326	7070	44334	577	46	1838	4316	892	39426	3547	139205	2367	92822		6928456	
39	312	14390	125238	109	13729	937	4890	65357	10151	95	18	592	5636	667	24265	2080	73353	2390	49111		8108121	
40																						

COMPARATIVE STATISTICAL REPORT OF THE UNITED LUTHERAN CHURCH IN AMERICA
FOR THE YEARS 1920, 1921, 1922, 1923, 1924, 1925, 1926, 1927, 1928, 1929, 1930—Concluded

FINANCIAL

Index Number	VALUATION OF CHURCH PROPERTY				CONGREGATIONAL EXPENSES			CONGREGATIONAL BENEVOLENCE									SUMMARY	
								APPORTIONED				UNAPPORTIONED						
	Endowment	Other Property	Total Valuation	Indebtedness	Current	Unusual	Total	Paid	Excess	Deficit	Education	Foreign Missions	Home Missions	Inner Missions	Other Bene.	Total Un-apportioned Bene.	Total Benevolence	Total Expenditures
1	3454994	8723053	158801677	24133654	113253480	5109667	16435148	2199196	19466	707345	200476	319841	124243	838587	69748	1815120	4014316	20449464
2	3133547	8525702	156370657	23432357	11197569	6507199	17704768	2295612	26748	590494	182290	310166	135858	1173850	401721	2203885	4499497	22204265
3	321447	197351	2431026	701297	127911	1397532	1269620	96416		116851	18186	9675	11615	335263	69748	388765	485181	1754801
4																		
5	3454994	8723053	158801677	24133654	113253480	5109667	16435148	2199196	7282	707345	200476	319841	124243	838587	331973	1815120	4014316	20449464
6	2932175	7585846	148701861	19416910	10761252	7261869	18051503	2109023	28470	794562	270776	247455	132640	1673710	331973	2823242	4932265	22983768
7	522819	1137207	10099816	4716744	564228		90173		9004	87217		72386	8397	482380			917949	2534304
8																		
9	3454994	8723702	158801677	24133654	113253480	2152202	1616355	2199196		707345	200476	319841	124243	835123	150407	1008122	4014316	20449464
10	2757866	7523560	140609870	17883930	11487001	5109667	18521226	2156391	19466	623483	434917	320647	129359	838587	515817	1881271	4037662	22558888
11	697128	1200142	18191807	6249724	161521	8034224	42805		31925	83862	234441	806	5116	480531	183844	66151	23346	2109424
12																		
13	3454994	8723702	158801677	24133654	113253480	2924557	2086078	2199196	12459	707345	200476	319841	124243	838587	331973	1815120	4014316	20449464
14	2547063	7441745	128964264	15300109	9443178	5109667	18094191	1853225	19466	460334	300820	268875	100063	314697	441606	1260061	3279286	21373277
15	907931	1281957	29337413	8833545	1882302	8651013	345971		30138	247011	100354	509966	24180	523890	109633	389059	735030	923813
16																		
17	3454994	8723702	158801677	24133654	113253480	3541346	1659043	2199196	10672	707345	200476	319841	124243	838587	331973	1815120	4014316	20449464
18	2383469	6733780	118856868	11457989	8676760	5109667	15691423	1828761	19466	458335	623116	218881	110766	403638	672022	188323	3711884	19403307
19	1071525	1989922	46944809	12675665	2648720	7014663	743725	370435	41395	249010	422640	100960	13477	434949	194749	1626797	302432	1046157
20																		
21	3454994	8723702	158801677	24133654	113253480	1904996	16435148	2199196	21929	707345	200476	319841	124243	838587	331973	1815120	4014316	20449464
22	2281248	5806395	101368976	9265083	8041334	5109667	14859760	1748347	19466	390112	320448	256387	160597	354336	341049	1763990	3512337	18372097
23	1173746	2917307	57432701	14868571	3284146	6818421	1575388	450849	44595	317233	119972	63254	36354	484251	264915	51130	501979	2077367
24																		
25	3454994	8723702	158801677	24133654	113253480	1708754	16435148	2199196	25129	707345	200476	319841	124243	838587	340049	1815120	4014316	20449464
26	2007027	4973232	90831211	7441246	7387593	4635721	12023314	1605290	19466	378486	318056	227718	86762	261050	596888	1488474	3093764	15117078
27	1447967	3750470	67970466	16692408	3937887	473946	4411834	593906	48060	328859	117580	92123	37481	577537		326646	920552	5332386
28																		
29	3454994	8723702	158801677	24133654	113253480	5109667	16435148	2199196	28554	707345	200476	319841	124243	838587	331973	1815120	4014316	20449464
30	1851134	3701544	81973253	7047140	6816399	8009146	10825545	1513077	45338	368687	292682	155599	72287	233324	777002	1530894	3043971	13869516
31	1603860	5022158	76828424	17086514	4509081		5609603	686119		338658	92206	164242	51956	605263	284226	284226	970345	6579948
32																		
33	3454994	8723702	158801677	24133654	113253480	2899479	16435148	2199196	25862	707345	200476	319841	124243	838587	445029	1815120	4014316	20449464
34	1895798	2400790	76507115	6011472	6621268	5109667	10456403	1449132	19466	342307	569521	140190	66369	240927	884653	1901660	3341792	13798195
35	1559196	6322912	82294562	18122182	4704212	5978745	5978745	750064	62601	365038	569060	179651	57874	597660	552680	86540	672524	6651269
36																		
37	3454994	8723702	158801677	24133654	113253480	5109667	16435148	2199196	43135	707345	369045	319841	124243	838587	331973	1815120	4014316	20449464
38	2065974		70142813	55818845	5630943	2968750	8599693	1206115	19466		200476	233909	36017	233909	983743	1865798	3071913	11671606
39	1389020		88658864	18551809	5694537	2140917	7835455	993081			612129		88226	604678	651770	50678	942403	8777858
40											411653							

STATISTICAL REPORT OF THE UNITED LUTHERAN CHURCH IN AMERICA—1930
1930 and 1929 Gains Compared

PAROCHIAL

Index Number		Pastors	Parishes	Congregations	Membership			Accessions						Losses						Church Papers		
					Baptized	Confirmed	Communing	Children		Adult				Children		Adult			No. Sub. to Official Papers	No. S.S. Papers Distributed	No. Sub. to Other Ch. Papers
								Baptism	Otherwise	Baptism	Confirmation	Certificate	Otherwise	Death	Otherwise	Death	Certificate	Otherwise			
1	1930 Gain	10	2	17	24978	16044	1331	465	1176	513	1597	1094	712	149	105	520	785	1070	898	2230	3303
2	1930 Decrease								818	339	1991	456	383	97	442	377	437	1430		2913	1382
3	1929 Gain	2		19	29225	21999	3997	1335											1480		
4	1929 Decrease		40					870											582		
5	1930 Net Gain	8	42	2	4247	5955	2666		1994	852	3588	1550	1095	52	547	897	1222	2500		5143	1921
6	1930 Net Decrease																				

STATISTICAL REPORT OF THE UNITED LUTHERAN CHURCH IN AMERICA—1930
Including Statistics Outside Continental United States and Canada

PAROCHIAL

Index Number	Country	Province	When Organized	Pastors	Congregations	Membership			Accessions						Losses						Church Papers		
						Baptized	Confirmed	Communing	Children		Adult				Children		Adult			No. Sub. to Official Papers	No. S.S. Papers Distributed	No. Sub. to Other Ch. Papers
									Baptism	Otherwise	Baptism	Confirmation	Certificate	Otherwise	Death	Otherwise	Death	Certificate	Otherwise			
1	India	Madras	1842	For. 28, Nat. 50	1566	149743	64238	64238			7582	3662		2780			2314					
2	Africa	Liberia	1860	For. 6, Nat. 0	5	350	211	211				72							8089			
3	Japan	Kyushu-Hondo	1892	For. 13, Nat. 20	25	2259	1261	1261				406					32	12				
4	China	Shantung	1898	For. 6, Nat. 0	71	1613	1298	1298				190										
5	Virgin Islands	U. L. C.	1666	U. L. C. 4	5	2137	1012	905				78	5									
6	British Guiana	N. Amsterdam	1889	For. 2, Nat. 0	6	500	400	400				44										
7	Porto Rico	U. L. C. & O.	1898	U. L. C. 8, O. 1	18	1771	1061	677	63			145	11		21	5	14	16		12		
8	Argentina	Buenos Aires	1908	For. 3, Nat. 3	8	708	440	440	78	16	4	34		4	20	11	14			15		
9	Total Outside U. S. & Can.			144	1704	160181	69921	69430	141	16	7586	4631	16	2784	41	16	2360	28	8103	27		
10	Total U. S. and Canada			3284	3942	1424386	987231	682167	32730	17236	4722	32650	16087	17177	1764	16750	13041	10893	26336	39431	163710	61808
11	World Total U.L.C. in A.			3428	5646	1584567	1057152	751597	32871	17252	12308	37281	16103	19961	1805	16766	15401	10921	34439	39458	163710	61808

STATISTICAL REPORT OF THE UNITED LUTHERAN CHURCH IN AMERICA—1930
1930 and 1929 Gains Compared—Continued

PAROCHIAL · FINANCIAL

Index Number	Church Schools — Sunday: Number	Officers and Teachers	Scholars	Home Dep't.	Cradle Roll	Weekday: Number	Teachers	Scholars	Catechumens	Students: Ministry	Deaconess	In Lutheran Institutions	In Non-Lutheran Institutions	Church Societies — Men's: Number	Members	Women's: Number	Members	Young P.: Number	Members	Valuation Church Property: Church Edifices	Parsonages	School and Parish Houses
1	504	529	4932		3189	71	346	4345	4476	11		31	918	88	108	139	2230	59	4309	1565020	134412	482620
2	544	1335	11213	949	2569	23	357	2059	1203	48	11	205	67	35	153	166	1010	313	4519	6127370	406420	1479927
3				1482								43										
4		806		533	620	48	11	1386	5679	59	42	162	851	53	261	27	1220	254	210	4562350	540832	997307
5																						
6	1048		6281																			

STATISTICAL REPORT OF THE UNITED LUTHERAN CHURCH IN AMERICA—1932
Including Statistics Outside Continental United States and Canada—Continued

PAROCHIAL · FINANCIAL

Index Number	Church Schools — Sunday: Number	Officers and Teachers	Scholars	Home Dep't.	Cradle Roll	Weekday: Number	Teachers	Scholars	Catechumens	Students: Ministry	Deaconess	In Lutheran Institutions	In Non-Lutheran Institutions	Church Societies — Men's: Number	Members	Women's: Number	Members	Young P.: Number	Members	Valuation Church Property: Church Edifices	Parsonages	School and Parish Houses
1	1054	1836	48375			1049	1627	37487		172										1200000		
2		23	336			12	23	404												75000		
3		30	2073			9	30	1273												650000		
4		52	854			41	62	1539		8		1	8							185000		
5	5	86	1095			2	11	146	78	4						3	55	2	67	113000	15000	
6		10	470			5	10	259		1										20000		
7		112	2438			6	14	220		4										102000		
8	18	46	516			11	46	734	67	2		2	10			3	36	6	206	208000	40000	11363
9	1077	2195	56157			1135	1823	42062	145	191		3	18	1559	63691	6	91	8	273	2533000	55000	11363
10	3711	67329	641053	23615	60029	1127	5216	72427	54485	672	64	2430	9952			5627	212558	4757	141933	122139124	15036577	9448929
11	4788	69524	697210	23615	60029	2262	7039	114489	54630	863	64	2433	9970	1559	63691	5633	212649	4765	142206	124692124	15091577	9460292

STATISTICAL REPORT OF THE UNITED LUTHERAN CHURCH IN AMERICA—1930
1930 and 1929 Gains Compared—Concluded

FINANCIAL

INDEX NUMBER	VALUATION OF CHURCH PROPERTY				CONGREGATIONAL EXPENSES			CONGREGATIONAL BENEVOLENCE									SUMMARY	
								APPORTIONED				UNAPPORTIONED						
	Endowment	Other Property	Total Valuation	Indebtedness	Current	Unusual	Total	Paid	Excess	Deficit	Education	Foreign Missions	Home Missions	Inner Missions	Other Benevolence	Total Un-apportioned Benevolence	Total Benevolence	Total Expenditures
1	321447	197351	2431026	701297	127911	1397532	1269620	96416	7282	116851	18186	9675	11615	335263	69748	388765	485181	1754801
2	201372	939856	7668790	4015447	436317	754670	346735	186589	1722	204068	88486	62711	3218	499860	80659	619357	432768	779503
3																		
4	120075	742505	5237764	3314150	308406	642862	925885	283005	5560	320919	106672	53036	14433	164597	10911	230592	52413	975298
5																		
6																		

STATISTICAL REPORT OF THE UNITED LUTHERAN CHURCH IN AMERICA—1930
Including Statistics Outside Continental United States and Canada—Concluded

FINANCIAL

INDEX NUMBER	VALUATION OF CHURCH PROPERTY				CONGREGATIONAL EXPENSES			CONGREGATIONAL BENEVOLENCE									SUMMARY	
								APPORTIONED				UNAPPORTIONED						
	Endowment	Other Property	Total Valuation	Indebtedness	Current	Unusual	Total	Paid	Excess	Deficit	Education	Foreign Missions	Home Missions	Inner Missions	Other Benevolence	Total Un-apportioned Benevolence	Total Benevolence	Total Expenditures
1			1200000		175866		175866								25325	25325	25325	201191
2			75000		427		427											427
3			650000		13372		13372											13372
4			185000		3130		3130											3130
5		30000	158000		3500		3500								962	962	962	4462
6			20000		1913		1913											1913
7			181363		3077		3077								805	805	805	3882
8		28000	208000		3468		3468											3468
9		58000	2677363		204753		204753								27092	27092	27092	231845
10	3454994	8723053	158801677	24133654	11325480	5109667	16435148	2199196	19466	707345	200476	319841	124243	833587	331973	1815120	4014316	20449464
11	3454994	8781053	161479040	24133654	11530233	5109667	16639901	2199196	19466	707345	200476	319841	124243	833587	359065	1842212	4041408	20681309

UNITED LUTHERAN CHURCH IN THE UNITED STATES AND CANADA
COMPARISON OF TOTALS OF ACCESSIONS AND LOSSES, NET VALUATION AND PER CAPITA

COMPARISON OF TOTALS OF ACCESSIONS AND LOSSES

1930 Total Accessions	120,602	1930 Total Losses	68,784
1929 Total Accessions	126,159	1929 Total Losses	71,413
1930 Decrease in Accessions	5,557	1930 Decrease in Losses	2,629
1929 Increase in Accessions	2,652	1929 Increase in Losses	2,589
1930 Net Decrease in Accessions....	8,209	1930 Net Decrease in Losses	5,218

1930 Accessions Gain Over Losses	51,818
.1929 Accessions Gain Over Losses	54,746
1930 Loss in Accessions Gain Over Losses	2,928
1929 Gain in Accessions Gain Over Losses	63
1930 Net Loss	2,991

NET VALUATION

1930 Total Valuation	$158,801.677	1926 Net Valuation	$113,664.155
1930 Total Indebtedness	24,133,654	1925 Net Valuation	100,398,878
		1924 Net Valuation	92,103,946
1930 Net Valuation	134,668,023	1923 Net Valuation	83,389,965
1929 Net Valuation	132,938,294	1922 Net Valuation	74,926,113
		1921 Net Valuation	70,495,643
1930 Gain Net Valuation	1,729,729	1920 Net Valuation	64,560,968
1928 Net Valuation	129,284,951		
1927 Net Valuation	122,725,940		

PER CAPITAS

	Current Expenses	Unusual Expenses	Total Congregational	Apportionment Benevolence Paid	Total Benevolence	Total Expenditures
1930 Per Capita..........(987,231 cf.m.)	$11.06	$5.17	$16.64	$2.22	$4.06	$20.71
1929 Per Capita..........(971,187 cf.m.)	11.42	6.70	18.23	2.36	4.63	22.86
1930 Gain Per Capita..........	....	....	....	....	....	....
1930 Loss Per Capita..........		.36	1.53	1.59	.14	.57	2.15
1928 Per Capita..........(949,188 cf.m.)	11.33	7.65	19.01	2.22	5.11	24.21
1929 Gain Per Capita..........	.09			.14		
1929 Loss Per Capita..........		.95	.78		.48	1.35
1927 Per Capita..........(933,650 cf.m.)	11.23	8.59	19.84	2.31	4.32	24.16
1926 Per Capita..........(916,858 cf.m.)	10.30	9.44	19.73	2.02	3.58	23.31
1925 Per Capita..........(886,840 cf.m.)	9.78	7.91	17.69	2.06	4.19	21.88
1924 Per Capita..........(856,180 cf.m.)	9.39	7.96	17.36	2.04	4.10	21.46
1923 Per Capita..........(839,279 cf.m.)	8.80	5.52	14.33	1.91	3.52	18.00
1922 Per Capita..........(819,063 cf.m.)	8.32	4.89	13.21	1.84	3.71	16.93
1921 Per Capita..........(801,250 cf.m.)	8.26	4.79	13.05	1.79	4.17	17.22
1920 Per Capita..........(791,400 cf.m.)	7.15	3.75	10.90	1.52	3.88	14.78

STATISTICAL REPORT OF THE UNITED LUTHERAN CHURCH IN AMERICA FOR THE YEAR 1931

Index No.	Synod	When Organized	Pastors	Parishes	Congregations	Membership Baptized	Membership Confirmed	Membership Communing	Acc. Children Baptism	Acc. Children Otherwise	Acc. Adult Confirmation	Acc. Adult Baptism	Acc. Adult Certificate	Acc. Adult Otherwise	Loss Children Death	Loss Children Otherwise	Loss Adult Death	Loss Adult Certificate	Loss Adult Otherwise	Ch. Papers Official	Ch. Papers S.S. Distributed	Ch. Papers Other Ch.
1	Ministerium of Penna.	Aug. 15, 1748	455	381	597	293436	198772	141565	6882	3363	6735	563	2823	2303	443	3742	3098	1863	6488	6286	15543	6968
2	United Synod of N.Y.	Oct. 23, 1786	467	398	429	229655	155563	100839	4405	4213	4560	354	1730	3046	247	3190	1969	758	4136	3321	11157	3623
3	United Synod of N.C.	May 2, 1803	113	90	161	33565	25235	18939	630	165	514	138	338	31	101	155	149	361	167	447	1419	1873
4	Synod of Maryland	Oct. 11, 1820	140	101	139	68659	49578	31133	1504	530	1564	71	728	552	15	130	603	490	575	1593	4218	1636
5	Synod of So. Carolina	Jan. 14, 1824	70	57	109	28170	20637	13424	493	210	524	279	456	43	65	130	201	373	101	789	1771	1422
6	Synod of West Penna.	Sept. 4, 1825	121	76	160	61660	45843	33977	1207	314	1107	268	678	318	81	182	676	399	644	1540	3706	1257
7	Synod of Virginia	Aug. 5, 1829	94	197	167	25649	20391	12532	427	138	447	341	360	164	81	683	216	205	207	2783	5531	2324
8	Synod of Ohio	Nov. 7, 1836	252	136	280	81220	55332	34072	1941	771	1864	202	1216	940	51	958	945	887	3505	2054	20851	2266
9	East Penna. Synod	May 2, 1842	188	69	160	74452	48893	19582	1560	1260	1372	326	727	893	42	146	665	904	1228	789	6738	1740
10	Allegheny Synod	Sept. 9, 1842	82	219	146	40682	31098	19582	726	157	814	141	382	199	153	263	394	287	442	2804	5507	1164
11	Pittsburgh Synod	Jan. 15, 1845	270	59	319	124364	86069	52950	2662	1632	2737	366	1209	2123	13	1609	951	910	2239	922	24858	22017
12	Indiana Synod	Oct. 28, 1848	59	123	78	17250	13372	8610	294	260	411	244	286	252	13	858	147	246	264	468	3994	300
13	Illinois Synod	Sept. 18, 1851	151	27	136	39066	30066	26927	1476		1892		688	1236	61	86	399	462	1201	135	10724	1986
14	Texas Synod	Nov. 1851	24	81	29	6054	4165	3085	133	60	212	6	41	67	8	838	64	28	191	921	333	701
*15	Susq. Synod of U.L.C.A.	Feb. 21, 1855	108	6	161	52446	39510	25539	1123	288	966	153	604	380	61	2	465	420	525	28	5751	678
16	Mississippi Synod	July 25, 1855	6	6	11	813	666	315	25		20	173	14	5		20	7	7	20	255	60	41
17	Synod of Iowa	Sept. 3, 1855	36	33	33	17189	11103	7273	510	235	537	11	319	295	25	109	115	157	204	390	3170	676
18	Michigan Synod	Oct. 27, 1855	67	63	87	22994	16399	9661	576	324	579	77	336	335	16	700	165	158	715	341	5015	862
19	Synod of Georgia-Ala.	July 21, 1860	19	18	30	6445	4061	2985	112	99	106	218	125	70	56	24	61	50	198	1079	663	495
20	Synod of Canada	July 21, 1861	81	64	92	28041	18740	14718	706	307	667	54	330	431	161	161	229	143	249	329	2020	571
21	Synod of Kansas	Nov. 5, 1868	52	36	44	10703	7797	4970	212	130	219	38	189	140	14	127	88	72	168	271	2821	555
22	Synod of Nebraska	Sept. 1, 1871	61	49	54	19728	13590	9457	791	258	757	35	254	339	23	600	113	247	1460	607	4006	602
23	Wartburg Synod	1875	80	74	46	19750	13315	9527	467	349	446	189	51	376	29	392	155	26	528	395	1436	
24	Ger. Nebraska Synod	July 24, 1890	66	38	85	17642	11835	9368	434	436	440		43	115	47	268	128	59	23	862	306	
25	Synod of California	Apr. 6, 1891	25	16	38	9841	6410	3949	185	124	312		252	292	2	42	92	205	647	395	1836	391
26	Rocky Mt. Synod	May 1891	102	81	16	3673	2597	1756	91		88		84	67		99	33	38	187	330	1159	118
27	Synod of the Northwest	Sept. 22, 1891	50	42	89	49125	31292	24417	1428	1678	1765	189	469	1407	74	1093	237	344	1918	149	6160	1223
28	Manitoba Synod	Sept. 16, 1897	38	30	127	15185	8844	6412	626		459	27	53	229	5	250	136			987	125	380
29	Pacific Synod	Sept. 26, 1901	28	28	30	5381	3325	1894	190	280	191		17	13		24	27	61	273	3300	1526	391
30	Nova Scotia Synod	July 1903	10	8	31	5498	3178	1767	156	18	110	18	28	28	13	24	50	5	58	140	263	51
31	Synod of West Virginia	Apr. 17, 1912	21	21	37	6863	4551	3207	134	42	175	42	86	38	13	44	55	33	52	198	1864	1472
32	Slovak Zion Synod	June 10, 1919	22	18	31	12527	8630	7217	316	5	322			54	1		114	7	11	288		
33	Florida Synod	Jan. 15, 1929	14	17	13	2051	1563	998	61	26	53	9	58			41	19	36	23	629	359	122
34	Totals for U. S. and Canada		3401	2764	3965	1450754	1001520	691627	32594	18974	32965	5000	14946	16781	1708	17594	12766	10241	28647	35563	155446	58811
35	Totals Outside U. S. and Canada		148		1708	166004	73820	73321	153	21	5978	9943	19	3649	63	24	3210	50	10306	45		
36	U. L. C. A. World Total		3549	2764	5673	1616758	1075340	764948	32747	18995	38943	14943	14965	20430	1771	17618	15976	10291	38953	35608	155446	58811

*Formerly Susq. Synod of Central Pa.

STATISTICAL REPORT OF THE UNITED LUTHERAN CHURCH IN AMERICA FOR THE YEAR 1931—Continued

		PAROCHIAL												CHURCH SOCIETIES						FINANCIAL		
		CHURCH SCHOOLS								STUDENTS				MEN'S		WOMEN'S		YOUNG P.		Valuation of Church Property		
		SUNDAY				WEEKDAY																
Index Number	Number	Officers and Teachers	Scholars	Home Dept.	Cradle Roll	Number	Teachers	Scholars	Catechumens	Ministry	Deaconess	In Lutheran Institutions	In Non-Luth. Institutions	Number	Members	Number	Members	Number	Members	Church Edifices	Parsonages	School and Parish Houses
1	609	12835	124992	4763	12035	154	1227	14629	8967	108	16	312	1772	261	12620	829	36543	745	25639	23147804	2362690	212359
2	419	8000	66592	1937	8849	96	428	4841	5823	99	7	151	1409	300	13552	742	33048	795	22287	23283746	2891088	3311556
3	310	1517	17178	1917	1014	50	287	4910	868	7	7	87	198	44	2522	109	2260	155	7547	2947566	393561	176800
4	139	3669	35637	3596	3596	22	204	2032	2334	41	8	85	458	57	944	229	10551	239	7549	6604073	737066	386276
5	109	1356	14493	218	673	60	436	7340	1629	23	4	142	200	29	723	152	4497	183	5321	1511550	252399	167900
6	159	4001	45551	1290	3376	24	158	2545	3542	36	1	140	490	36	4944	244	9686	198	7287	5227300	568500	370900
7	154	1763	16891	1251	1248	76	406	4018	2355				204	20	5100	160	4135	302	4386	1963695	397065	89300
8	275	5229	51774	1140	2502	25	116	2006	3005	40		242	647	143	2063	511	18324	271	7224	9046400	933130	531500
9	158	4267	39859	3529	3651	43	292	3415	1709	41	5	104	611	100	5474	312	12887	127	8174	7822060	1014582	686300
10	114	2419	22146	976	1974	48	354	4357	1347	27		64	395	38	855	175	5252	424	3801	3183670	448929	124800
11	300	5803	53340	2483	6534	71	366	4815	4898	57		179	855	159	2777	561	18406	251	11870	10548495	1431032	454800
12	71	1114	9639	334	2966	15	56	720	955			64	140	29	129	142	4339	29	1741	1385500	239950	56750
13	136	3089	28118	48	160	32	260	2494	2432	34	4	113	432	82	2509	288	9790	142	7630	5114800	654706	264950
14	28	239	1978	1495	2617	3	8	71	236	4	0	6	26			33	1044	8	668	1385000	47500	47500
15	166	3264	33646			27	218	2456	1863	29	6	104	388	49	599	201	7304		4964	4380400	505533	38500
16	9	56	327	83	12	3	13	131	41		2			1		7	87		131	32050	6100	180700
17	32	694	6361	312	764	9	95	850	1344	10		39	185	19	829	73	2595	80	1920	1032236	154000	3000
18	85	1411	11706		976	8	39	418	989	11		30	146	27	263	132	4301	48	1902	2806235	215050	104500
19	24	368	2884	8	156	8	64	715	283	11		13	52	13	345	45	1208	75	1078	646416	47920	107000
20	81	890	6951	75	1107	27	29	668	783	5		22	40	13	471	71	3048	60	2274	1098030	215425	78000
21	42	699	4546	67	522	9	29	501	351			12	147	16	417	97	2816	82	401	1363090	209600	34000
22	55	1007	8713		980	17	101	1010	972	18		69	189	21	788	104	2867	48	2368	1309050	181672	4100
23	41	557	5907	34	139	18	27	538	801		7					63	2966		973			
24	62	437	4351	38	411	29	35	605	309	11	1	35	50	20	667	67	1713	34	1306	717800	217700	10000
25	38	519	4013	119	289	6	12	127	440	8	3	10	207	9	202	74	2246	68	462	1566850	74000	3000
26	13	239	1715	28	2146	2	11	115	95	1			63			30	771	21	5089	479100	35500	5700
27	88	1878	15086			31	110	1668	2330	20		46	481	65	2350	169	6006	200	861	4096410	336410	150600
28	82	168	2321	41	347	70	49	1971	299	23		24	20		241	21	487	36	864	379654	48109	2000
29	29	315	2309		35	3	11	86	98	4		7	53	13		48	1065	37	164	198400	31400	3000
30	18	160	1104	89	257				367	6		6	13		341	21	587	6	864	712000	126801	2000
31	30	467	3288			9	56	696	32	6		26	67	15		49	1273	34	547	389000	84000	25000
32	25	78	1129			26	34	1351	83	1		3	18			8	404	12	250	351000	66000	3200
33	12	137	1091	31	31	2	8	108				1	36		24	17	422	15				
34	3913	68645	645636	22721	59961	1021	5544	72207	51580	722	60	2158	10000	1597	64866	5784	212918	5015	145305	123921030	14928118	9504622
35	1191	210	59401			1136	29	41006	16455	64		3	18	515	11368	424	8453	31	830	225000	55000	11750
36	5104	68855	705037	22721	59961	2157	5573	113213	68035	786	60	2161	10018	2112	76234	6208	221371	5046	146135	124146030	14983118	9516372

STATISTICAL REPORT OF THE UNITED LUTHERAN CHURCH IN AMERICA FOR THE YEAR 1931—Concluded

FINANCIAL

Index Number	Valuation of Church Property				Congregational Expenses			Congregational Benevolence									Summary	
								Apportioned				Unapportioned						
	Endowment	Other Property	Total Valuation	Indebtedness	Current	Unusual	Total	Paid	Excess	Deficit	Education	Foreign Missions	Home Missions	Inner Missions	Other Benevolences	Total Un-apportioned Benevolence	Total Benevolence	Total Expenditures
1	1204649	1383269	30222002	3987322	1752291	817810	2570101	360806	792	280473	15144	37833	11433	75411	47485	187306	548112	3118213
2	877933	1585844	31954167	4994735	1850334	601482	2451836	250995	3531	254618	26879	20583	14189	70713	34404	166768	417763	2869599
3	71100	79675	3668702	419288	210241	92617	302858	40294	435	51794	4659	6914	5753	11358	7049	35733	76027	378885
4	99560	558953	8385928	1305172	546495	283185	829680	110519	1186	28623	3916	21413	8663	35317	16630	85939	196458	1026138
5	14150	147642	2093641	276222	138045	169975	308020	22303	107	33236	32896	4291	2070	9799	7279	56335	78638	386658
6	303683	306765	6777148	473196	441997	186366	628363	118704	4541	35973	4358	18109	4367	17841	14377	59052	177756	806119
7	87127	108128	2645315	188716	163751	48828	212579	34412	64	27918	761	6329	3222	13271	7791	31374	65786	278365
8	140954	508191	10116398	1208810	817372	234624	1051996	186664	446	85260	4511	23824	1094	28438	29545	97412	284076	1336072
9	190651	402805	3944664	1595618	726574	207305	933879	128193	209	35919	6338	31966	10434	54110	117665	245884	1179737
10	46930	40335	13442094	285484	280939	70328	351257	77387	3843	23685	4003	7118	2107	14311	46437	123834	475091
11	165466	842301	2351560	2275154	979895	278681	1258576	170944	160	98104	45306	2023	13948	61361	18898	170416	341360	1599936
12	73550	157760	6205401	401274	189356	145795	335151	360329	72	13750	889	3741	873	9689	27778	18961	55290	390441
13	55505	115440	237870	1476439	530212	146432	676644	93729	11	46546	1909	13856	6709	21644	3769	57635	151364	40489
14	650	12720	5330074	34807	28581	6504	35085	3216	574	10252	100	7680	90	1088	13517	2188	5404	577295
15	168206	94235	38150	538107	351846	113024	464870	82439		34905	3196		1815	10198	7097	29986	112425	4992
16				5723	3340	844	4184	616		170	11	18	18	46	192	192	808	
17	5700	38024	1232960	295656	147239	12130	159369	13963	47	16625	2536	1307	761	2179	99	8907	22870	182239
18	14175	28027	3167987	807593	197226	48173	245399	31986		17512	217	3190	777	3529	2124	10527	42513	287912
19	20595	38700	860631	155885	54364	22340	76704	10103	619	5874	1132	763	789	2956	2814	7227	17380	94084
20	30300	70129	1491884	103474	157170	26860	184030	29707	13	2613	3462	2846	835	2935	1637	15134	44841	228871
21	8509	29595	1644794	207454	135529	25511	161040	20198		7850	6580	1656	632	4608	5056	16334	36532	197572
22	6902	130990	1632714	135562	143702	33723	177425	35830		18835	16344	3569	1522	4777	2858	29325	65155	242580
23		1153539	1153539	140067	112985	34101	147086	10483							3113		14764	161850
24	7000	33405	975350	30832	82019	16272	98291	6945		7795	7206	977	1539	2320	4281	4281	20804	119095
25	4250	13400	1681505	271497	125362	52239	177601	13084	174	3037	232	1699	787	4911	1817	13859	23619	201220
26	55	83950	533455	227020	46968	21417	68385	5754			1154	221	109	920	2906	10535	9362	77747
27	3377	351979	467047	417363	106621		523984	74930			1689	6454	4307	11667	1204	3608	112404	636388
28		23016	452779	206199	45928	8351	45923	5458	466	3767	100	100	100	193	13347	37474	6525	52453
29		7000	239800	18950	49921	1601	58272	6572		3907	829	330	354	842	574	1067	10228	68500
30		77114	917965	159504	21505	15416	23105	2670	3	5071	56	44	19	68	1301	3656	3571	26677
31	50	3000	501955	106806	70913	15295	86329	11830	1749		104	1502	339	900	714	4714	16544	102873
32	955	2900	423200	161406	14385	17667	15295	913		5071		25	43	15	1869	316	1229	16524
33					21601		39268	3020		1517	43	228	192	521	233	1735	4755	44023
34	3601982	8550781	160506533	24197701	10855469	3847132	14702601	2000996	19051	1156477	196560	250896	109890	478246	297457	1333049	3334045	18036646
35		2454200	2745950		185915		185915								35299	35299	35299	221214
36	3601982	11004981	163252483	24197701	11041384	3847132	14888516	2000996	19051	1156477	196560	250896	109890	478246	332756	1368348	3369344	18257860

COMPARATIVE STATISTICAL REPORT OF THE UNITED LUTHERAN CHURCH IN AMERICA FOR THE YEARS 1921, 1922, 1923, 1924, 1925, 1926, 1927, 1928, 1929, 1930, 1931

Index	Year	Pastors	Parishes	Congregations	Memb. Baptized	Memb. Confirmed	Memb. Communing	Acc. Children Baptism	Acc. Children Otherwise	Acc. Adult Baptism	Acc. Adult Confirmation	Acc. Adult Certificate	Acc. Adult Otherwise	Loss Children Death	Loss Children Otherwise	Loss Adult Death	Loss Adult Certificate	Loss Adult Otherwise	Church Papers Official	Church Papers S.S. Distributed	Church Papers Other Ch. P'rs
1	1931	3401	2764	3965	1450754	1001520	691627	32594	18974	5000	32965	14946	16781	1708	17594	12766	10241	28647	35563	155446	58811
2	1930	3284	2752	3942	1424386	987231	682167	32730	17236	4722	32650	16087	17177	1764	16750	13041	10893	26336	39431	163710	61808
3	1 Year's Gain	117	12	23	26368	14289	9460		1738	278	315				844			2311			
4	1 Year's Decrease							136				1141	396	56		275	652		3868	8264	2997
5	1931	3401	2764	3965	1450754	1001520	691627	32594	18974	5000	32965	14946	16781	1708	17594	12766	10241	28647	35563	155446	58811
6	1929	3274	2750	3925	1399408	971187	680836	33195	18412	5235	34247	17181	17889	1913	16855	13561	11678	27406	40329	165940	58505
7	2 Years' Gain	127	14	40	51346	30333	10791		562						739			1241			306
8	2 Years' Decrease							601		235	1282	2235	1108	205		795	1437		4766	10494	
9	1931	3401	2764	3965	1450754	1001520	691627	32594	18974	5000	32965	14946	16781	1708	17594	12766	10241	28647	35563	155446	58811
10	1928	3272	2790	3906	1370183	949188	676839	34530	17594	4896	32256	16725	17506	2010	16413	13184	11241	25976	41809	163027	57123
11	3 Years' Gain	129		59	80571	52332	14788		1380	104	709				1181			2671			1688
12	3 Years' Decrease		26					1936				1779	725	302		418	1000		6246	7581	
13	1931	3401	2764	3965	1450754	1001520	691627	32594	18974	5000	32965	14946	16781	1708	17594	12766	10241	28647	35563	155446	58811
14	1927	3184	2689	3881	1321780	933650	676496	36668	18264	5397	33871	18704	20012	2023	14772	12677	12117	24464	43917	162246	49825
15	4 Years' Gain	217	75	84	128974	67870	15131		710						2822	89		4183			8986
16	4 Years' Decrease							4074		397	906	3758	3231	315			1876		8354	6800	
17	1931	3401	2764	3965	1450754	1001520	691627	32594	18974	5000	32965	14946	16781	1708	17594	12766	10241	28647	35563	155446	58811
18	1926	3127	2706	3876	1315620	916858	677287	34562	17573	5178	25451	16866	19781	1983	12789	11758	11467	23935	50684	167418	38573
19	5 Years' Gain	274	58	89	135134	84662	14340		1401		7514				4805	1008		5816			20238
20	5 Years' Decrease							1968		178		1920	3000	275			1226		15121	11972	
21	1931	3401	2764	3965	1450754	1001520	691627	32594	18974	5000	32965	14946	16781	1708	17594	12766	10241	28647	35563	155446	58811
22	1925	3011	2649	3875	1276176	886840	669695	35307	16658	5536	31071	17366	18504	2004	12335	11454	12335	23356	50735	174407	36101
23	6 Years' Gain	390	115	90	174578	114680	21932		2316		1894				5259	1312		5291			22710
24	6 Years' Decrease							2713		536		2420	1723	296			1870		15172	18961	
25	1931	3401	2764	3965	1450754	1001520	691627	32594	18974	5000	32965	14946	16781	1708	17594	12766	10241	28647	35563	155446	58811
26	1924	2983	2643	3829	1238000	856180	645836	35138	14029	5746	31020	17314	18090	1982	9918	11250	11887	25436	50224	162037	39471
27	7 Years' Gain	418	121	136	212745	145340	45791		4945		1945				7676	1516		3211			19340
28	7 Years' Decrease							2544		746		2368	1309	274			1646		14661	6591	
29	1931	3401	2764	3965	1450754	1001520	691627	32594	18974	5000	32965	14946	16781	1708	17594	12766	10241	28647	35563	155446	58811
30	1923	2924	2566	3812	1201401	839279	633184	33837	12419	4472	28188	15600	16125	2244	9788	11518	11016	25650	47618	152731	34708
31	8 Years' Gain	477	198	153	249353	162241	58443		6555	528	4777				7806	1248		2997		2715	24103
32	8 Years' Decrease							1243				654	656	536			775		12055		
33	1931	3401	2764	3965	1450754	1001520	691627	32594	18974	5000	32965	14946	16781	1708	17594	12766	10241	28647	35563	155446	58811
34	1922	2900	2501	3732	1164550	819063	621123	36016	12704	5599	30954	16345	16445	2334	9370	11741	10934	25485	49267	144631	33867
35	9 Years' Gain	501	263	233	286204	182457	70504		6270		2011		336		8224	1025		3162		10815	24944
36	9 Years' Decrease							3422		599		1399		626			693		13704		
37	1931	3401	2764	3965	1450754	1001520	691627	32594	18974	5000	32965	14946	16781	1708	17594	12766	10241	28647	35563	155446	58811
38	1921	2887	2492	3803	1147007	801250	597768	37403	11773	5302	30467	16456	16500	2392	8921	11051	11475		36969	118139	21454
39	10 Years' Gain	514	272	162	303747	200270	93859		7201		2498		281		8673	1715				37303	37357
40	10 Years' Decrease							4809		302		1510		684			1234		1406		

COMPARATIVE STATISTICAL REPORT OF THE UNITED LUTHERAN CHURCH IN AMERICA FOR THE YEARS 1921, 1922, 1923, 1924, 1925, 1926, 1927, 1928, 1929, 1930, 1931—Continued

Index Number	CHURCH SCHOOLS — SUNDAY Number	Officers and Teachers	Scholars	Home Dept.	Cradle Roll	WEEKDAY Number	Teachers	Scholars	Catechumens	STUDENTS Ministry	Deaconess	In Lutheran Institutions	In Non-Luth. Institutions	CHURCH SOCIETIES — MEN'S Number	Members	WOMEN'S Number	Members	YOUNG P. Number	Members	FINANCIAL — Church Edifices	Parsonages	School and Parish Houses
1	3913	68645	645636	22721	59961	1021	5544	72207	51580	722	60	2158	10000	1597	64866	5784	212918	5015	145305	123921030	14928118	9504622
2	3711	67329	641053	23615	60029	1127	5216	72427	54485	672	64	2430	9952	1559	63691	5627	212558	4757	141933	122139124	15036557	9448929
3	202	1316	4583	894	68	106	328	220	2905	50	4	272	48	38	1175	157	360	258	3372	1781906	108459	55693
4																						
5	3913	68645	645636	22721	59961	1021	5544	72207	51580	722	60	2158	10000	1597	64866	5784	212918	5015	145305	123921030	14928118	9504622
6	4215	66800	636121	24564	63218	1056	4870	68082	50009	661	33	2635	9034	1471	63799	5488	210328	4698	137624	120574104	15170989	8966309
7	302	1845	9515	1843	3257	35	674	4125	1571	61	27	477	966	126	1067	296	2590	317	7681	3346926	242871	538813
8																						
9	3913	68645	645636	22721	59961	1021	5544	72207	51580	722	60	2158	10000	1597	64866	5784	212918	5015	145305	123921030	14928118	9504622
10	3671	65465	624908	26046	65787	1033	4513	65123	51212	709	44	2678	8967	1436	63646	5322	209318	4385	133105	111444673	14764569	7486380
11	242	3180	20728	3325	5826	12	1031	7084	368	13	16	520	1033	161	1220	462	3600	630	12200	9474296	163549	2018242
12																						
13	3913	68645	645636	22721	59961	1021	5544	72207	51580	722	60	2158	10000	1597	64866	5784	212918	5015	145305	123921030	14928118	9504622
14	3651	64212	613863	25826	65544	928	4183	58491	48823	851	52	2626	8338	1383	63146	5181	208003	3986	133682	108956533	14599321	6830516
15	262	4433	31773	3105	5583	93	1361	13716	2757	129	8	468	1662	214	1720	603	4915	1029	11623	14964497	329797	2674106
16																						
17	3913	68645	645636	22721	59961	1021	5544	72207	51580	722	60	2158	10000	1597	64866	5784	212918	5015	145305	123921030	14928118	9504622
18	3524	62609	608261	27309	65938	647	3157	45366	48272	826	79	2632	7555	1294	59190	4830	199855	3835	130552	99894373	13881748	5198535
19	389	6036	37375	4588	5977	374	2387	26841	3308	104	19	474	2445	303	5676	954	13063	1180	14753	24026657	1046370	4306087
20																						
21	3913	68645	645636	22721	59961	1021	5544	72207	51580	722	60	2158	10000	1597	64866	5784	212918	5015	145305	123921030	14928118	9504622
22	3531	59940	590169	28187	65706	651	2704	42372	49216	828	90	2551	6753	1211	56892	4515	184475	3547	122380	86288340	12532190	3919089
23	382	8705	55467	5466	5745	370	2840	29835	2364	106	30	393	3247	386	7974	1269	28443	1468	22925	37632690	2395518	5585533
24																						
25	3913	68645	645636	22721	59961	1021	5544	72207	51580	722	60	2158	10000	1597	64866	5784	212918	5015	145305	123921030	14928118	9504622
26	3515	59205	571737	28028	63853	557	2051	38824	49310	746	68	2530	5841	1213	56605	4307	181449	3400	120277	78525563	11169150	3136620
27	398	9440	73899	5307	3892	464	3493	33383	2270	24	8	372	4159	384	8261	1477	31469	1615	25028	45395467	3758968	6368002
28																						
29	3913	68645	645636	22721	59961	1021	5544	72207	51580	722	60	2158	10000	1597	64866	5784	212918	5015	145305	123921030	14928118	9504622
30	3440	56863	552872	28446	61995	523	1538	28438	45238	717	67	2381	5402	1137	53706	4151	174535	3200	115726	70971368	10415614	2463970
31	473	11782	92764	5725	2034	498	3906	43769	6342	24	7	223	4598	460	11160	1633	38383	1815	29579	52949662	4512504	7040652
32																						
33	3913	68645	645636	22721	59961	1021	5544	72207	51580	722	60	2158	10000	1597	64866	5784	212918	5015	145305	123921030	14928118	9504622
34	3465	55330	555510		59264	490	1453	25149	35311	582	59	2015	4520	1102	52525	4013	173270	3132	115234	65598841	9237584	1584150
35	448	13315	90126		697	531	4091	47058	16269	140	1	143	5480	495	12341	1771	39648	1883	30071	58322189	5690534	7920472
36																						
37	3913	68645	645636	22721	59961	1021	5544	72207	51580	722	60	2158	10000	1597	64866	5784	212918	5015	145305	123921030	14928118	9504622
38	3682	54268	522691	26142	52148	375	954	17534	34034	582	85	1712	4292	967	47052	3618	154089	3694	106842	63193694	8138433	878400
39	231	14377	122945	3421	7813	646	4590	54673	17546	140	25	446	5708	630	17814	2166	58829	1321	38463	60727336	6789685	8626222
40									3421													

COMPARATIVE STATISTICAL REPORT OF THE UNITED LUTHERAN CHURCH IN AMERICA
FOR THE YEARS 1921, 1922, 1923, 1924, 1925, 1926, 1927, 1928, 1929, 1930, 1931—Concluded

FINANCIAL

Index Number	Valuation of Church Property — Endowment	Other Property	Total Valuation	Indebtedness	Cong. Expenses — Current	Unusual	Total	Apportioned — Paid	Excess	Deficit	Education	Unapportioned — Foreign Missions	Home Missions	Inner Missions	Other Benevolence	Total Unapportioned Benevolence	Summary — Total Benevolence	Total Expenditures
1	3601982	8550781	160506533	24197701	10855469	3847132	14702601	2000996	19051	1156477	196560	250896	109890	478246	297457	1333049	3334045	18036646
2	3454994	8723053	158802677	24133654	11325480	5109667	16435148	2199196	19466	707345	200476	319841	124243	838587	331973	1815120	4014316	20449464
3	146988	172272	1703856	64047	470011	1262535	1732547	198200	415	449132	3916	68945	14353	360341	34516	482071	680271	2412818
4	.....	.....	.....	.....	.....	.....	.....	.....	.....	.....	.....	.....	.....	.....	.....	.....	.....	.....
5	3601982	8550781	160506533	24197701	10855469	3847132	14702601	2000996	19051	1156477	196560	250896	109890	478246	297457	1333049	3334045	18036646
6	3133547	8525702	156370651	24332357	11197569	6507199	17704768	2295612	26748	590494	182290	310166	135858	1173850	401721	2203885	4499497	22204265
7	468435	25079	4135882	765344	342100	2660067	3002167	294616	7697	565983	14270	59270	25968	695604	104264	870836	1165452	4167619
8	.....	.....	.....	.....	.....	.....	.....	.....	.....	.....	.....	.....	.....	.....	.....	.....	.....	.....
9	3601982	8550781	160506533	24197701	10855469	3847132	14702601	2000996	19051	1156477	196560	250896	109890	478246	297457	1333049	3334045	18036646
10	2932175	7588546	147018061	24416910	10761252	7261869	18051503	2109023	28470	794562	270776	247455	132640	1673710	482380	2823242	4932265	22983768
11	669807	964935	11804672	4780791	94217	3414737	3348902	108027	9419	361915	74216	3441	22750	1195464	184923	1490193	1598220	4947122
12	.....	.....	.....	.....	.....	.....	.....	.....	.....	.....	.....	.....	.....	.....	.....	.....	.....	.....
13	3601982	8550781	160506533	24197701	10855469	3847132	14702601	2000996	19051	1156477	196560	250896	109890	478246	297457	1333049	3334045	18036646
14	2757866	7523560	140009870	17883930	11487001	8034224	18521226	2156391	31925	623483	434917	320647	129359	480531	515817	1881271	4037662	22558888
15	844116	1027221	19896663	6313771	631532	4187092	3818625	155395	12874	532994	238357	69751	19469	2285	218360	548222	703617	4522242
16	.....	.....	.....	.....	.....	.....	.....	.....	.....	.....	.....	.....	.....	.....	.....	.....	.....	.....
17	3601982	8550781	160506533	24197701	10855469	3847132	14702601	2000996	19051	1156477	196560	250896	109890	478246	297457	1333049	3334045	18036646
18	2547063	7441745	128964264	15300109	9443178	8651013	18094191	1853225	30138	460334	300820	268875	100063	314697	441606	1426061	3279286	21373277
19	1054919	1109036	31542269	8897592	1412291	4803881	3391590	147771	11087	663143	104260	17979	9827	163549	144149	93012	54759	3336631
20	.....	.....	.....	.....	.....	.....	.....	.....	.....	.....	.....	.....	.....	.....	.....	.....	.....	.....
21	3601982	8550781	160506533	24197701	10855469	3847132	14702601	2000996	19051	1156477	196560	250896	109890	478246	297457	1333049	3334045	18036646
22	2383469	6733780	111856868	11457989	8676760	7014663	15691423	1828761	41395	458335	623116	218881	110766	403638	526722	1883123	3711884	19403307
23	1218513	1817001	48649665	12739712	2178709	3167531	988822	172235	22344	693142	426556	32015	876	74608	229265	550074	377839	1366661
24	.....	.....	.....	.....	.....	.....	.....	.....	.....	.....	.....	.....	.....	.....	.....	.....	.....	.....
25	3601982	8550781	160506533	24197701	10855469	3847132	14702601	2000996	19051	1156477	196560	250896	109890	478246	297457	1333049	3334045	18036646
26	2281248	5806395	101368976	9265083	8041334	6818421	14859760	1748347	44595	390211	320448	256587	160597	354336	672022	1763990	3512337	18372097
27	1320734	2744386	59137557	14932618	2814135	2971289	157159	252649	25544	766365	123888	5691	50707	123910	374565	430941	178292	335451
28	.....	.....	.....	.....	.....	.....	.....	.....	.....	.....	.....	.....	.....	.....	.....	.....	.....	.....
29	3601982	8550781	160506533	24197701	10855469	3847132	14702601	2000996	19051	1156477	196560	250896	109890	478246	297457	1333049	3334045	18036646
30	2007027	4973232	90831211	7441246	7387593	4635721	12023314	1605290	48060	378486	318056	227718	86762	261050	596888	1488474	3093764	15117078
31	1594955	3577549	69675332	16756455	3467876	788589	2679287	395706	29009	777991	121496	23128	5691	217196	299431	155425	551131	2919568
32	.....	.....	.....	.....	.....	.....	.....	.....	.....	.....	.....	.....	.....	.....	.....	.....	.....	.....
33	3601982	8550781	160506533	24197701	10855469	3847132	14702601	2000996	19051	1156477	196560	250896	109890	478246	297457	1333049	3334045	18036646
34	1851134	3701544	81973255	7047140	6816399	8009146	13825545	1513077	45328	368687	292682	155599	72287	233324	777002	1530894	3043971	13869516
35	1750848	4849237	78533280	17150561	4039070	4162014	3877056	487519	26277	787790	96122	95297	37603	244922	479545	197845	290074	4167130
36	.....	.....	.....	.....	.....	.....	.....	.....	.....	.....	.....	.....	.....	.....	.....	.....	.....	.....
37	3601982	8550781	160506533	24197701	10855469	3847132	14702601	2000996	19051	1156477	196560	250896	109890	478246	297457	1333049	3334045	18036646
38	1895798	2400790	76507115	6011472	6621268	3835135	10456403	1449132	62601	342307	569521	140190	66369	240927	884453	1901660	3341792	13798195
39	1706184	6149991	83999418	18186229	4234201	11997	4246198	551864	43350	814170	372961	110706	43521	237319	587196	568611	7747	4238451
40	.....	.....	.....	.....	.....	.....	.....	.....	.....	.....	.....	.....	.....	.....	.....	.....	.....	.....

STATISTICAL REPORT OF THE UNITED LUTHERAN CHURCH IN AMERICA—1931
1931 and 1930 Gains Compared
Also 11 and 12 Years Comparisons, Percentages and Averages

PAROCHIAL

Index Number		Pastors	Parishes	Congregations	MEMBERSHIP			ACCESSIONS								LOSSES					CHURCH PAPERS		
					Baptized	Confirmed	Communing	CHILDREN Baptism	CHILDREN Otherwise	ADULT Baptism	ADULT Con-firmation	ADULT Certificate	ADULT Otherwise	CHILDREN Death	CHILDREN Otherwise	ADULT Death	ADULT Certificate	ADULT Otherwise	No. Sub. to Official Papers	No. S.S. Papers Distributed	No. Sub. to Other Ch. Papers
1	1931 Gain	117	12	23	26368	14289	9460	136	1738	278	315	1141	396	56	844	275	652	2311	3868	8264	2997
2	1931 Decrease																				
3	1930 Gain	10	2	17	24978	16044	1331	465	1176	513	1597	1094	712	149	105	520	785	1070	898	2230	3303
4	1930 Decrease																				
5	1931 Net Gain	107	10	6	1390		8129		2914	791	1912				909			3381	2970	6034	
6	1931 Net Decrease					1755		329				47	316	93		245	133				
7	1919 Total	2843		3473	1094153	776582	474553	24785	7945	4400	27645	13915	9235			14073	10664	23467			
8	11 Years' Gain from 1919 to 1930	441		469	330233	210649	207614	7945		322	5005	2172	7942			1032	229	2869			
9	11 Years' Decrease from 1919 to 1930																				
10	11 Years' Percentage Gain from 1919 to 1930	15.51		13.50	30.18	27.12	43.75	32.05		7.31	18.10	15.60	85.99			7.33	2.14	12.22			
11	11 Years' Percentage Decrease from 1919 to 1930																				
12	11 Years' Average Percentage Gain from 1919 to 1930	1.41		1.23	2.74	2.47	3.98	2.91		0.66	1.65	1.42	7.82			0.67	0.19	1.11			
13	11 Years' Average Percentage Decrease from 1919 to 1930																				
14	12 Years' Gain from 1919 to 1931	558		492	356601	224938	217074	7809		600	5320	1031	5336			1307	423	5180			
15	12 Years' Decrease from 1919 to 1931																				
16	12 Years' Percentage Gain from 1919 to 1931	19.66		14.17	32.59	28.96	45.74	31.50		13.63	19.27	7.40	57.78			9.28	3.96	22.07			
17	12 Years' Percentage Decrease from 1919 to 1931																				
18	12 Years' Average Percentage Gain from 1919 to 1931	1.64		1.18	2.72	2.41	3.81	2.62		1.14	1.60	0.62	4.81			0.77	0.33	1.84			
19	12 Years' Average Percentage Decrease from 1919 to 1931																				
20	1920 Total	2812		3775	1117938	791400	580018	36438		4834	29380	15214	14571			11554	11610	26550			
21	11 Years' Gain from 1920 to 1931	589		190	332816	210120	111609	3844		166	3585	268	2210			1212	1369	2097			
22	11 Years' Decrease from 1920 to 1931																				
23	11 Years' Percentage Gain from 1920 to 1931	20.94		5.03	29.77	26.55	19.24	10.55		3.43	12.20	1.76	15.16			10.48	11.79	7.89			
24	11 Years' Percentage Decrease from 1920 to 1931																				
25	11 Years' Average Percentage Gain from 1920 to 1931	1.90		0.46	2.71	2.41	1.75	0.96		0.33	1.11	0.16	1.38			0.95	1.07	0.72			
26	11 Years' Average Percentage Decrease from 1920 to 1931																				

STATISTICAL REPORT OF THE UNITED LUTHERAN CHURCH IN AMERICA—1931
1931 and 1930 Gains Compared
Also 11 and 12 Years Comparisons, Percentages and Averages—Continued

Index Number	CHURCH SCHOOLS — SUNDAY: Number	Teachers and Officers	Scholars	Home Dep't	Cradle Roll	WEEKDAY: Number	Teachers	Scholars	Catechumens	Ministry	STUDENTS: Deaconess	In Lutheran Institutions	In Non-Luth. Institutions	CHURCH SOCIETIES — MEN'S: Number	Members	WOMEN'S: Number	Members	YOUNG P.: Number	Members	FINANCIAL — VALUATION CHURCH PROPERTY: Church Edifices	Parsonages	School and Parish Houses
1	202	1316	4583			106	328	220	2905	50			48	38	1175	157	360	258	3372	1781906	108459	55693
2		529	4932	894	68						4	272	918	88		139	2230	59	4309	1565020		482620
3	504	787		949	3189	106	346	4345	4476	11	31	205			108						134412	
4	706		349	55	3121	71									1283	18	1870	199	937	216886	25953	
5						177	18	4565	7381	39	35	67	870	50								426927
6																						
7	3412	53524	514924	19019	32228	109	130	4779	36689	526	14	223	611	708	32550	2811	104760	2114	81746		2071193	
8	299	13805	121129	4596	27801	1018	5086	67648	17796	146	50	2207	9341	851	31141	2816	107798	2643	60187		12965384	
9	8.76	25.79	23.52	24.16	86.26	933.94	3912.30	1401.55	48.50	27.75	357.19	989.68	1528.80	120.19	95.66	100.17	102.89	125.02	73.62		625.98	
10	0.80	2.35	2.14	2.20	7.84	84.90	355.66	127.41	4.41	2.52	32.47	89.97	138.98	10.92	8.70	9.10	9.35	11.37	6.69		56.90	
11																						
12																						
13																						
14	501	15121	130712	3702	27733	912	5414	67428	14981	196	46	1935	9389	889	32316	2973	108158	2901	63559		12856925	
15	14.68	28.25	25.37	19.46	86.05	836.69	4164.61	1413.01	40.58	37.26	328.57	867.71	1536.66	125.56	99.28	105.76	103.24	137.22	77.75		620.74	
16																						
17	1.22	2.35	2.11	1.62	7.17	69.72	347.05	117.75	3.38	3.10	27.38	72.31	128.05	10.46	8.27	8.81	8.60	11.43	6.48		51.73	
18																						
19																						
20	3399	52939	515815	23506	46300	190	326	7070	44334	577	46	1838	4316	892	39426	3547	139205	2367	92822		6928456	
21	514	15706	129821	785	13661	831	5218	65137	7246	145	14	320	5684	705	25440	2237	73713	2648	52483		7999662	
22																						
23	15.12	29.06	25.16	3.33	29.51	437.36	1600.61	921.31	16.34	25.17	30.43	17.41	131.69	79.03	64.52	63.06	52.95	111.87	56.54		115.46	
24																						
25	1.37	2.64	2.29	0.30	2.68	39.76	145.51	83.76	1.49	2.29	2.77	1.58	11.97	7.18	5.87	5.73	4.81	10.17	5.14		10.50	
26																						

STATISTICAL REPORT OF THE UNITED LUTHERAN CHURCH IN AMERICA—1931
1931 and 1930 Gains Compared
Also 11 and 12 Years Comparisons, Percentages and Averages—Concluded

FINANCIAL

Index Number	Valuation: Endowment	Valuation: Other Property	Valuation: Total Valuation	Valuation: Indebtedness	Cong. Expenses: Current	Cong. Expenses: Unusual	Cong. Expenses: Total	Apportioned: Paid	Apportioned: Excess	Apportioned: Deficit	Cong. Benevolence: Education	Unapportioned: Foreign Missions	Unapportioned: Home Missions	Unapportioned: Inner Missions	Other Benevolence	Total Un-apportioned Benevolence	Summary: Total Benevolence	Summary: Total Expenditures
1	146988	172272	1703856	64047	470011	1262535	1732547	198200	415	449132	3916	68945	14353	360341	34516	482071	680271	2412818
2	321447	197351	2431026	701297	127911	1397532	1269620	96416	7282	116851	18186	9675	11615	335263	69748	388765	485181	1754801
3	174459		727170	637250	597922	134697	462927	101784	6867	332281	22102	78620	2738	25078	35232	93306	195090	658017
4																		
5																		
6																		
7	1032292	369623	42383332	4527913	4984795	1916749	6901544	1344202			76		5459	70	902981	908586	2252788	9154332
8	2422702		116419345	19605741	6340685	3192918	9533604	854994			200400		118784	838517	571008	906534	1761528	11295132
9																		
10																		
11																		
12	234.69		274.68	432.99	127.20	166.57	138.13	63.60			263157.89		2175.92	1197881.42	63.23	99.77	0.70	123.38
13	21.34		24.97	39.36	11.57	15.14	12.56	5.78			23923.44		197.81	108896.95	5.75	9.07	0.06	11.22
14	2569690		118123201	19669788	5870674	1930383	7801057	656794			196484		104431	478176	605524	424463	1081257	8882314
15																		
16																		
17																		
18	248.93		278.70	434.41	117.77	100.71	113.03	48.86			258531.57		1913.00	683108.57	67.05	46.71	47.99	90.00
19	20.74		23.22	36.20	9.81	8.39	9.42	4.07			21544.29		159.42	56925.71	5.59	3.89	4.00	7.50
20	2065974		70142813	5581845	5630943	2968750	8599693	1206115			612129		36017	233909	983743	1865798	3071913	11671606
21	1536008		90363720	18615856	5224526	878382	6102908	794881			415569		73873	244337	686286	532749	262132	6365040
22																		
23																		
24																		
25	74.34		128.82	333.50	92.78	30.00	70.96	65.90			67.88		205.10	104.45	69.76	28.55	8.53	54.53
26	6.76		11.71	30.32	8.43	2.73	6.45	5.99			6.17		18.65	9.50	6.34	2.60	0.78	4.96

PAROCHIAL REPORT OF THE UNITED LUTHERAN CHURCH IN AMERICA—PERCENTAGES AND AVERAGES—1922-1931—Inclusive

Index Number		PASTORS	PARISHES	PAROCHIAL									
				MEMBERSHIP				CHILDREN		ACCESSIONS — ADULT			
				Congregations	Baptized	Confirmed	Communing	Baptism	Otherwise	Baptism	Confirmation	Certificate	Otherwise
1	1 Year's Percentage Gain	3.56	0.43	0.58	1.85	1.44	1.38	0.41	10.08	5.92	0.96	7.09	2.30
2	1 Year's Percentage Decrease												
3	2 Years' Percentage Gain	3.89	0.51	1.02	3.66	3.12	1.59	1.81	3.05	4.48	3.74	13.00	6.19
4	2 Years' Percentage Decrease												
5	2 Years' Average Percentage Gain	1.94	0.26	0.51	1.83	1.56	0.80	0.90	1.53	2.24	1.87	6.50	3.10
6	2 Years' Average Percentage Decrease												
7	3 Years' Percentage Gain	3.94	0.93	1.51	5.88	5.51	2.18	5.63	7.84	2.12	2.19	10.63	4.14
8	3 Years' Percentage Decrease												
9	3 Years' Average Percentage Gain	1.31	0.31	0.50	1.96	1.84	0.73	1.88	2.61	0.71	0.73	3.54	1.38
10	3 Years' Average Percentage Decrease												
11	4 Years' Percentage Gain	6.81	2.78	2.16	9.75	7.26	2.23	11.11	3.88	7.35	2.67	20.09	16.14
12	4 Years' Percentage Decrease												
13	4 Years' Average Percentage Gain	1.70	0.69	0.54	2.44	1.82	0.56	2.78	0.97	1.84	0.67	5.02	4.04
14	4 Years' Average Percentage Decrease												
15	5 Years' Percentage Gain	8.76	2.14	2.29	10.27	9.23	2.11	5.69	7.97	3.43	29.52	11.38	15.16
16	5 Years' Percentage Decrease												
17	5 Years' Average Percentage Gain	1.75	0.43	0.45	2.05	1.84	0.42	1.13	1.59	0.68	5.90	2.27	3.13
18	5 Years' Average Percentage Decrease												
19	6 Years' Percentage Gain	12.95	4.34	2.32	10.54	12.93	3.27	7.68	13.90	9.68	6.09	13.93	9.31
20	6 Years' Percentage Decrease												
21	6 Years' Average Percentage Gain	2.16	0.72	0.37	1.75	2.15	0.54	1.28	2.31	1.61	1.01	2.32	1.55
22	6 Years' Average Percentage Decrease												
23	7 Years' Percentage Gain	14.01	4.57	3.55	17.17	16.97	7.09	7.24	35.24	12.98	6.27	13.67	7.23
24	7 Years' Percentage Decrease												
25	7 Years' Average Percentage Gain	2.00	0.65	0.50	2.45	2.42	1.01	1.03	5.03	1.85	0.89	1.95	1.03
26	7 Years' Average Percentage Decrease												
27	8 Years' Percentage Gain	16.31	7.71	4.01	20.75	19.33	9.23	3.67	52.84	11.80	16.94	4.19	4.06
28	8 Years' Percentage Decrease												
29	8 Years' Average Percentage Gain	2.04	0.96	0.50	2.59	2.41	1.15	0.46	6.60	1.47	2.11	0.52	0.50
30	8 Years' Average Percentage Decrease												
31	9 Years' Percentage Gain	17.27	10.51	6.24	24.57	22.25	11.35	9.50	49.35	10.69	6.49	8.55	2.06
32	9 Years' Percentage Decrease												
33	9 Years' Average Percentage Gain	1.92	1.16	0.69	2.73	2.47	1.26	1.05	5.48	1.18	0.72	0.95	0.23
34	9 Years' Average Percentage Decrease												
35	10 Years' Percentage Gain	17.79	10.91	4.25	26.48	24.99	15.70	12.85	61.16	5.69	8.19	9.17	1.70
36	10 Years' Percentage Decrease												
37	10 Years' Average Percentage Gain	1.77	1.09	0.42	2.65	2.49	1.57	1.28	6.11	0.56	0.81	0.91	0.17
38	10 Years' Average Percentage Decrease												

PAROCHIAL REPORT OF THE UNITED LUTHERAN CHURCH IN AMERICA— PERCENTAGES AND AVERAGES—1922-1931, Inclusive—Continued

PAROCHIAL

Index Number	Children Death	Children Otherwise	Adult Death	Adult Certificate	Adult Otherwise	No. Sub. to Official Papers	No. S.S. Papers Distributed	No. Sub. to Other Ch. P'rs	Sunday Number	Sunday Officers and Teachers	Sunday Scholars	Home Dep't	Cradle Roll	Weekday Number	Weekday Teachers	Weekday Scholars	Catechumens	Ministry	Deaconess	In Lutheran Institutions	In Non-Luth. Institutions
1	3.17	5.03	2.11	5.98	8.77	9.55	5.04	4.84	5.44	1.95	0.71	3.78	0.11	9.40	6.28	0.30	5.33	7.44	6.25	11.19	0 48
2																					
3	10.71	4.38	5.86	12.31	4.52	11.81	6.32	0.52	7.16	2.76	1.49	7.50	5.15	3.31	13.83	6.05	3.14	9.22	81.81	18.10	10.69
4																					
5	5.36	2.19	2.93	6.15	2.26	5.91	3.16	0.26	3.58	1.38	0.75	3.75	2.58	1.66	6.92	3.03	1.57	4.61	40.90	9.05	5.35
6																					
7	15.02	7.19	3.17	8.89	10.28	14.93	4.65	2.95	6.59	4.85	3.31	12.76	8.85	1.16	22.84	10.87	0.72	1.83	36.40	19.41	11.52
8																					
9	5.01	2.40	1.06	2.96	3.43	4.98	1.55	0.98	2.20	1.62	1.10	4.25	2.95	0.39	7.61	3.62	0.24	0.61	12.13	6.47	3.84
10																					
11	15.57	19.23	0.70	15.48	17.09	19.02	4.19	18.03	7.17	6.90	0.51	12.02	8.51	10.02	32.53	23.44	5.64	176.62	15.38	17.82	19.93
12																					
13	3.89	4.81	0.17	3.87	4.27	4.75	1.05	4.51	1.79	1.72	0.12	3.00	2.13	2.50	8.13	5.86	1.41	44.15	3.84	4.45	4.98
14																					
15	13.86	37.57	8.57	10.69	25.47	29.83	7.15	52.46	11.03	9.64	6.14	16.80	9.07	57.80	75.60	59.16	6.85	15.15	24.05	18.00	32.36
16																					
17	2.77	7.51	1.71	2.13	5.09	5.96	1.43	10.49	2.20	1.92	1.23	3.36	1.81	11.56	15.12	11.83	1.37	3.03	4.81	3.60	6.47
18																					
19	14.77	42.63	11.45	15.44	19.68	29.90	10.81	62.90	10.81	14.52	9.39	19.39	8.74	56.83	105.02	70.41	4.80	12.59	33.33	15.40	48.08
20																					
21	2.46	7.10	1.90	2.57	3.28	4.98	1.80	10.48	1.80	2.42	1.56	3.23	1.45	9.47	17.50	11.73	0.80	2.09	5.55	2.56	8.01
22																					
23	3.82	77.39	13.47	13.84	22.65	29.19	4.06	48.99	11.32	15.94	12.92	18.93	6.08	83.30	170.30	85.98	4.60	12.80	11.76	14.70	71.20
24																					
25	1.97	11.05	1.92	1.97	3.23	4.17	0.58	6.99	1.61	2.27	1.84	2.70	0.87	11.90	24.33	12.28	0.65	1.83	1.68	2.10	10.17
26																					
27	23.88	79.75	10.83	7.03	12.62	25.31	1.77	69.50	13.75	20.71	16.77	2.51	3.28	95.23	238.46	153.91	14.01	3.21	10.44	9.36	85.11
28																					
29	2.98	9.97	1.35	0.88	1.57	3.16	0.22	8.68	1.72	2.59	2.09	0.31	0.41	11.90	29.80	19.24	1.75	0.40	1.30	1.17	10.64
30																					
31	26.82	87.76	8.76	6.33	11.68	27.81	7.47	73.32	12.92	24.06	16.22	20.12	1.17	108.36	281.55	187.11	46.07	0.69	1.69	7.09	121.23
32																					
33	2.98	9.75	0.97	0.70	1.29	3.09	0.83	8.14	1.43	2.67	1.80	2.23	0.13	12.04	31.28	20.79	5.12	0.07	0.18	0.78	13.47
34																					
35	28.59	97.33	15.51	10.75	12.40	3.80	31.57	174.12	6.27	26.49	23.52	13.08	14.98	172.26	481.13	311.81	51.55	24.05	29.41	26.05	132.99
36																					
37	2.85	9.73	1.55	1.07	1.24	0.38	3.15	17.41	0.62	2.64	2.35	1.30	1.49	17.22	48.11	31.18	5.15	2.40	2.94	2.60	13.29
38																					

PAROCHIAL REPORT OF THE UNITED LUTHERAN CHURCH IN AMERICA
PERCENTAGES AND AVERAGES—1922-1931, Inclusive,—Concluded

Index Number	PAROCHIAL — Men's Number	Men's Members	Women's Number	Women's Members	Young P. Number	Young P. Members	FINANCIAL — Church Edifices	Parsonages	School and Parish Houses	Endowment	Other Property	Total Valuation	Indebtedness	Current	Unusual	Total	Paid	Excess	Deficit	Education	Foreign Missions	Home Missions	Inner Missions	Other Benevolence	Total Unapportioned Benevolence	SUMMARY Total Benevolence	Total Expenditures
1	2.43	1.84	2.79	0.17	5.42	2.37	1.45		0.58	4.25	1.97	1.07	0.28	4.15	24.70	10.54	9.01	2.13	63.49	1.95	21.55	11.55	42.97	10.39	26.55	16.94	11.71
2	8.56	1.67	5.39	1.23	6.70	5.58	2.77	0.72	6.00	14.94	0.28	2.64	3.26	3.05	40.87	16.95	12.83	28.02	95.84	7.82	19.10	19.11	59.25	25.95	39.51	25.90	18.76
3	4.28	0.84	2.70	0.62	3.35	2.79	1.39	1.60	3.00	7.47	0.14	1.32	1.63	1.52	20.44	8.48	6.42	14.01	47.92	3.91	9.55	9.56	29.63	12.98	19.76	12.95	9.38
4	11.21	1.91	8.68	1.69	14.36	9.16	8.27	0.80	26.95	22.84	12.72	7.93	24.62	0.87	47.02	18.55	5.12	13.08	45.54	27.41	1.38	17.15	71.42	38.33	52.78	32.40	21.52
5	3.74	0.64	2.89	0.56	4.79	3.05	2.76	1.11	8.98	7.61	4.24	2.64	8.21	0.29	15.67	6.18	1.71	11.03	15.18	9.14	0.46	5.72	23.81	12.78	17.59	10.80	7.17
6	15.47	2.72	11.63	2.36	25.81	8.69	13.74	0.37	39.14	30.60	13.65	14.15	35.30	5.49	52.11	20.61	7.20	40.32	85.48	54.80	21.75	15.05	0.47	42.33	29.14	17.42	20.04
7	3.87	0.68	2.91	0.59	6.45	2.17	3.43	2.25	9.78	7.65	3.41	3.54	8.82	1.37	13.03	5.15	1.80	10.08	21.37	13.70	5.44	3.76	0.12	10.58	7.28	4.35	5.01
8	23.41	9.58	19.75	6.53	30.76	11.30	24.05	0.56	82.83	41.41	14.90	24.45	58.15	14.95	55.52	18.74	7.97	36.78	151.22	34.65	6.68	9.82	51.97	30.35	6.52	1.66	15.61
9	4.68	1.91	3.95	1.30	6.15	2.26	4.81	7.53	16.56	8.28	2.98	4.89	11.63	2.99	11.10	3.75	1.59	7.35	30.24	6.93	1.33	1.96	10.39	6.07	1.30	0.33	3.12
10	31.87	14.01	28.10	15.41	41.38	18.73	43.61	1.50	142.52	51.12	26.98	43.40	111.18	25.10	45.15	6.63	9.41	53.97	153.41	68.58	14.62	0.79	18.48	43.52	29.21	10.17	7.04
11	5.31	2.33	4.68	2.57	6.89	3.12	7.27	19.11	23.75	8.52	4.49	7.26	18.53	4.18	7.52	1.15	1.57	8.99	25.57	11.43	2.43	0.13	3.08	7.25	4.87	1.69	1.17
12	31.65	14.59	34.27	17.34	47.50	20.80	57.80	3.18	203.02	57.89	47.26	58.33	161.17	34.99	43.57	3.75	14.45	57.27	196.44	38.66	2.21	31.57	34.96	55.73	24.42	5.07	1.82
13	4.52	2.08	4.89	2.47	6.78	2.97	8.25	4.80	29.00	8.27	6.75	8.33	23.02	4.99	6.22	1.05	2.06	8.18	28.06	5.52	0.31	4.51	4.77	7.96	3.49	0.72	0.26
14	40.45	20.77	39.33	41.99	56.71	25.55	74.60	43.32	285.74	79.46	71.93	76.78	225.01	46.94	17.01	22.28	24.65	60.35	205.55	38.19	10.17	26.65	83.20	50.16	10.44	7.76	9.31
15	5.05	2.59	4.91	2.75	7.09	3.09	9.32	5.41	35.71	9.93	9.99	9.59	28.12	5.86	2.12	2.78	3.18	7.54	25.69	4.77	1.27	3.33	10.40	6.27	1.30	0.97	2.41
16	44.91	23.49	44.13	22.88	60.12	26.09	88.90	61.60	499.98	94.58	131.00	95.80	243.36	59.25	51.96	35.81	32.24	57.97	213.62	32.84	61.24	5.78	104.97	61.71	12.92	9.52	30.04
17	4.99	2.61	4.90	2.54	6.68	2.89	9.87	6.84	55.55	10.51	14.55	10.64	27.04	6.58	5.77	3.98	3.59	6.44	23.73	3.65	6.80	65.57	11.66	6.85	1.43	1.05	3.33
18	65.14	37.86	59.86	38.89	35.76	35.99	96.09	83.42	982.03	89.99	256.16	109.79	302.52	63.94	0.31	40.00	38.00	69.50	237.84	65.48	78.96	6.55	98.50	66.36	29.90	0.23	30.71
19	6.51	3.78	5.98	3.88	3.57	3.59	9.60	8.34	98.20	8.99	25.61	10.97	30.25	6.39	0.03	4.06	3.80	6.95	23.78	6.54	7.89	6.55	9.85	6.63	2.99	0.02	3.07
20																											
21																											
22																											
23																											
24																											
25																											
26																											
27																											
28																											
29																											
30																											
31																											
32																											
33																											
34																											
35																											
36																											
37																											
38																											

YEARLY GAINS AND DECREASES WITH PERCENTAGES—1919-1931.

Index Number	Year & Type	Pastors	Parishes	Congregations	Baptized (Membership)	Confirmed (Membership)	Communing (Membership)	Children Baptism	Children Otherwise	Adult Baptism	Adult Confirmation	Adult Certificate	Adult Otherwise
1	1919-1920 Total Gain	31		302	23785	14818	105465	1653		434	1735	1330	5336
2	1919-1920 Total Decrease												
3	1919-1920 Percentage Gain	1.09		8.69	2.17	1.90	22.22	4.75		9.86	6.27	9.55	57.78
4	1919-1920 Percentage Decrease												
5	1920-1921 Total Gain	75	45	28	29069	9850	17750	965		468	1087	1242	1929
6	1920-1921 Total Decrease												
7	1920-1921 Percentage Gain	2.66	1.80	0.74	2.60	1.24	3.06	2.64		9.68	3.69	8.16	13.23
8	1920-1921 Percentage Decrease												
9	1921-1922 Total Gain	9		25	5459	9457	18938	1181	255	240	184	14	587
10	1921-1922 Total Decrease												
11	1921-1922 Percentage Gain	0.31		0.65	0.47	1.18	3.16	3.15	2.16	4.52	0.60	0.08	3.55
12	1921-1922 Percentage Decrease												
13	1922-1923 Total Gain	24	65	80	36851	20216	12061	2629	285	1127	2766	745	320
14	1922-1923 Total Decrease												
15	1922-1923 Percentage Gain	0.82	2.59	2.14	3.16	2.46	1.94	7.29	2.24	20.12	8.93	4.55	1.94
16	1922-1923 Percentage Decrease												
17	1923-1924 Total Gain	59	77	17	36608	16901	12652	1751	1610	1274	2832	1714	1965
18	1923-1924 Total Decrease												
19	1923-1924 Percentage Gain	2.01	3.00	0.44	3.04	2.01	1.99	5.24	12.96	28.48	10.04	10.98	12.18
20	1923-1924 Percentage Decrease												
21	1924-1925 Total Gain	28	6	46	38167	30660	23859	169	2629	210	51	52	414
22	1924-1925 Total Decrease												
23	1924-1925 Percentage Gain	0.83	0.22	1.20	0.82	3.58	3.69	0.48	18.73	3.65	0.16	0.30	2.28
24	1924-1925 Percentage Decrease												
25	1925-1926 Total Gain	116	57	1	39444	30018	7592	745	915	358	5620	500	1277
26	1925-1926 Total Decrease												
27	1925-1926 Percentage Gain	3.85	2.15	0.02	3.09	3.38	1.13	2.11	5.49	6.46	18.08	2.87	6.35
28	1925-1926 Percentage Decrease												
29	1926-1927 Total Gain	57	17	5	6160	16792	791	2106	691	219	8420	1838	231
30	1926-1927 Total Decrease												
31	1926-1927 Percentage Gain	1.82	0.62	0.12	0.46	1.83	0.11	6.09	3.99	4.22	33.08	10.89	1.16
32	1926-1927 Percentage Decrease												
33	1927-1928 Total Gain	88	101	25	48403	15538	343	2138	670	501	1615	1979	2506
34	1927-1928 Total Decrease												
35	1927-1928 Percentage Gain	2.76	3.75	0.64	3.66	1.66	0.05	5.83	3.66	9.28	4.76	10.58	12.52
36	1927-1928 Percentage Decrease												
37	1928-1929 Total Gain	2	40	19	29225	21999	3997	1335	818	339	1991	456	383
38	1928-1929 Total Decrease												
39	1928-1929 Percentage Gain	0.06	1.43	0.48	2.13	2.31	0.59	3.86	4.64	6.92	6.17	2.72	2.18
40	1928-1929 Percentage Decrease												

YEARLY GAINS AND DECREASES WITH PERCENTAGES—1919-1931—Continued

Index Number	PAROCHIAL																				
	Losses					Church Papers			Church Schools									Students			
	Children		Adult						Sunday					Weekday			Catechetical				
	Death	Otherwise	Death	Certificate	Otherwise	No. Sub. to Official Papers	No. S. S. Papers Distributed	No. Sub. to Oth'r Ch. P'rs	Number	Officers and Teachers	Scholars	Home Dep't	Cradle Roll	Number	Teachers	Scholars	Catechumens.	Ministry	Deaconess	In Lutheran Institutions	In Non-Luth. Institutions
1				946	3083						891	4487	13072	113	348	4165	7645	51	32	1600	3705
2			2519						13	585											
3				8.87	13.14						0.17	23.48	40.56	83.08	238.35	76.60	20.83	7.69	228.57	686.59	606.38
4			17.89						0.38	1.09											
5									283	1329	6876	2636	5848	185	628	10464		5			
6			499	135	1065												10300		1	121	24
7									8.32	2.51	1.33	11.21	12.63	97.36	192.63	148.00		0.87			
8			0.43	1.62	4.01												23.23		2.08	6.60	0.55
9		491	670		506	10656	23377	10197		843	28016	1902	6940	99	421	6810	567	148	15	272	221
10	82			457					237												
11		5.50	6.06		1.98	28.82	19.78	47.52		1.62	5.35	7.27	13.30	26.40	44.12	38.83	1.66	25.42	33.33	15.88	5.14
12	3.42			3.98					6.43												
13		418		82			8100	841		1533			2731	33	185	3289	9927	29	8	366	882
14	90		223		214	1649			25		2638	1282									
15		4.47		0.74			5.79	2.48		2.77			4.60	6.73	12.73	13.07	28.11	4.04	13.55	18.16	19.51
16	3.85		1.89		0.83	3.34			0.72		0.47	4.50									
17		130		871		2606	9306	4762	75	2342	18865	864	1858	34	413	10386	4072	182		149	439
18	262		268		2080																
19		1.32		7.96		5.47	6.09	13.72	2.18	4.11	3.41	3.18	2.99	6.50	25.21	36.52	9.00	24.39		6.25	8.12
20	11.67		2.32		8.17																
21	22	2417	204	224	579	511	12370		16	735	18432	159	1853	94	653	3548			22	21	912
22								3370									94	2			
23	1.10	24.36	1.81	1.88	2.47	1.01	7.63		0.45	1.24	3.22	0.56	2.90	16.87	31.83	9.14			32.35	0.83	15.61
24								8.53									0.19	0.24			
25		454	304					2472		2669	18092		232		453	2994		25		81	802
26	21			644	1104	51	6989		7			878		4			944		11		
27		3.68	2.65					6.84		4.45	3.06		0.35		16.75	7.06		3.02		3.17	11.87
28	1.04			5.31	4.61	0.10	4.00		0.19			3.11		0.61			1.98		12.22		
29	40	1983	919	650	1633			11252	127	1603	5602			281	1026	13125	551				783
30						6767	5172					1483	394					90	67	6	
31	2.01	15.50	7.81	5.66	7.15			29.17	3.60	2.56	0.92			43.43	32.49	28.93	1.14				10.36
32						13.35	3.08					5.43	0.59					10.57	34.17	0.22	
33		1641	507		1512		781	7298	20	1253	11045	220	243	105	330	6632	2389			52	629
34	13			876		2108												52	8		
35		11.10	3.99		6.18		0.48	14.64	0.54	1.95	1.79	0.85	0.37	11.31	7.88	11.33	4.89			1.98	7.54
36	0.64			7.22		4.79												19.92	15.38		
37		442	377	437	1430		2913	1382	544	1335	11213			23	357	2959					67
38	97					1480						1482	2569				1603	48	11	43	
39		2.69	2.85	3.88	5.50		1.78	2.41	14.81	2.03	1.79			2.22	7.91	4.53					0.74
40	4.82					3.53						5.68	3.90				2.34	6.77	25.0	1.60	

YEARLY GAINS AND DECREASES WITH PERCENTAGES—1919-1931—Continued

Index Number	PAROCHIAL — CHURCH SOCIETIES						FINANCIAL — VALUATION OF CHURCH PROPERTY						
	Men's Number	Men's Members	Women's Number	Women's Members	Young People's Number	Young People's Members	Church Edifices	Parsonages	School and Parish Houses	Endowment	Other Property	Total Valuation	Indebtedness
1	184	6876	736	34445	253	11076	28153935	4857263		1033682		27759481	953932
2	25.99	21.12	26.18	32.88	11.96	13.54	193.66	234.46		100.13		65.49	21.06
3	75	7626	71	14884	327	14020	13165411	2209977	540100	170176	1412694	6364302	429627
4	8.89	19.34	2.00	10.69	13.81	15.10	24.42	31.89	61.48	8.23	58.84	9.07	7.69
5	122	4925	368	18077	366	7438	2313462	943961	879820	55259	1271688	5154958	885170
6	12.61	10.46	10.17	11.73	13.58	6.96	3.66	11.59	55.53	2.09	34.35	6.73	14.72
7	35	1181	138	1265	68	492	5372527	1178030	672650	155893	833163	8857958	394106
8	3.17	2.24	3.43	0.73	2.17	0.42	8.19	12.75	27.29	8.42	15.74	10.80	5.59
9	95	2899	156	6912	200	4551	7554195	1203536	783469	274221	927385	10537765	823837
10	8.47	5.39	3.75	3.96	6.25	3.93	10.64	11.55	24.97	13.66	15.97	11.60	11.07
11	2	287	208	3026	147	2013	7762777	913040	1279446	102221	707965	10487892	2192906
12	0.16	0.50	4.83	1.66	4.32	1.67	9.88	7.85	32.64	4.48	10.51	10.34	23.45
13	83	2298	315	15380	278	8172	13606033	1349558	1631981	164394	81815	17107396	3842120
14	6.85	4.03	6.97	8.33	7.83	6.67	15.76	10.76	31.39	6.89	1.09	15.20	33.53
15	89	3956	351	8148	161	3130	9062160	716573	655864	210803	62286	11645606	2583821
16	6.87	6.68	7.26	4.07	1.61	4.20	9.07	5.16	9.60	8.27	0.82	9.03	16.88
17	53	500	141	1315	399	577	5490201	166248	1479929	174309	939956	8091991	1532980
18	3.83	0.79	2.72	0.63	10.01	0.42	5.03	1.13	19.76	6.32	12.38	5.75	8.57
19	35	153	166	1010	313	4519	6127370	406420		201372		7668790	4015447
20	2.43	0.24	3.11	0.48	7.13	3.39	5.17	2.75		6.86		5.15	20.68

YEARLY GAINS AND DECREASES WITH PERCENTAGES—1919-1931—Continued

FINANCIAL

	Congregational Expenses			Apportioned			Congregational Benevolence	Unapportioned				Summary		
Index Number	Current	Unusual	Total	Paid	Excess	Deficit	Education	Foreign Missions	Home Missions	Inner Missions	Other Benevolence	Total Un-apportioned Benevolence	Total Benevolence	Total Expenditures
1	646148	1052001	1698149	138087								957212	819125	2517274
2	12.96	54.88	24.60	10.27								105.35	36.36	27.49
3	990325	866385	1856710	295840			42608		30352	7072	139722	36682	269879	2126589
4	17.58	29.18	21.50	25.85			9.60		84.27	3.02	16.74	1.96	8.78	18.22
5	137919	148108	286027	61184	11627	22673	293119	9314	5856	26671	148788	412696	351512	65485
6	2.08	3.86	2.73	4.24	18.57	6.62	51.46	6.64	8.82	11.07	21.42	21.70	10.51	0.47
7	571194	626575	1197769	92213	2732	9799	23374	72119	14475	27726	180114	42420	49793	1247562
8	8.37	7.82	11.06	6.09	6.02	2.65	7.98	46.34	20.02	11.88	23.18	2.77	1.63	8.99
9	653746	2182700	2836446	143057	3465	11626	4392	28869	73835	93286	75134	275516	418573	3255019
10	8.84	47.07	23.59	8.91	7.20	3.07	1.38	12.67	85.10	35.73	12.58	18.80	13.52	21.46
11	635421	196242	831663	80414	3200	68223	302668	37706	49831	49302	145300	119133	199547	1031210
12	7.91	2.87	5.59	4.59	7.17	17.48	94.45	14.69	31.03	13.93	21.62	6.75	5.68	5.61
13	766418	1636350	2402768	24464	11257	1999	322196	49994	10703	88941	85116	457062	432598	1970170
14	8.83	23.32	15.31	1.33	27.19	0.43	51.70	22.84	9.66	22.03	16.15	24.27	11.65	10.15
15	973956	1120265	146309	303166	1787	163149	134097	51772	29296	165834	74211	455210	758376	1185411
16	11.05	9.44	2.36	16.35	5.92	35.44	44.57	19.25	29.27	52.69	18.79	31.92	23.12	5.54
17	274251	772355	469723	47368	3455	171079	164141	73192	32.81	1193179	33437	941971	894603	424880
18	2.56	9.61	2.53	2.19	10.82	27.43	37.74	22.82	2.53	248.30	6.48	50.07	22.15	1.88
19	436317	754670	346735	186589	1722	204068	88486	62711	3218	499860	80659	619357	432768	779503
20	4.05	10.39	1.92	8.84	6.04	25.68	32.67	25.34	2.42	29.86	16.72	21.93	8.77	3.39

YEARLY GAINS AND DECREASES WITH PERCENTAGES—1919-1931—Continued

PAROCHIAL

Index Number		Pastors	Parishes	MEMBERSHIP				ACCESSIONS						
								CHILDREN		ADULT				
				Congregations	Baptized	Confirmed	Communing	Baptism	Otherwise	Baptism	Con-firmation	Certificate	Otherwise
41	1929-1930 Total Gain	10	2	17	24978	16044	1331	465	1176	513	1597	1094	712
42	1929-1930 Total Decrease												
43	1929-1930 Percentage Gain	0.30	0.07	0.43	1.78	1.64	0.19	1.40	6.38	9.79	4.66	6.36	3.98
44	1929-1930 Percentage Decrease												
45	1930-1931 Total Gain	117	12	23	26368	14289	9460	136	1738	278	315	1141	396
46	1930-1931 Total Decrease												
47	1930-1931 Percentage Gain	3.56	0.43	0.58	1.85	1.44	1.38	0.41	10.08	5.92	0.96	7.09	2.30
48	1930-1931 Percentage Decrease												

YEARLY GAINS AND DECREASES WITH PERCENTAGES—1919-1931—Continued

PAROCHIAL

Index Number	LOSSES					CHURCH PAPERS			CHURCH SCHOOLS										STUDENTS			
	CHILDREN		ADULT			No. Sub. to Official Papers	No. S. S. Papers Distributed	No. Sub. to Other Ch. Pr's	SUNDAY					WEEKDAY			Cate-chu-mens		Ministry	Deaconess	In Lutheran Institutions	In Non-Luth. Institutions
	Death	Otherwise	Death	Certificate	Otherwise				Number	Officers and Teachers	Scholars	Home Dep't	Cradle Roll	Number	Teachers	Scholars						
41	149	105	520	785	1070	898	2230	3303	504	529	4932	949	3189	71	346	4345	4476		11	31	205	918
42																						
43	7.78	0.62	3.83	6.72	3.90	2.22	1.34	5.64	11.95	0.79	0.77	3.86	5.04	6.72	7.10	6.38	8.95		1.66	93.93	7.77	10.16
44																						
45	56	844	275	652	2311	3868	8264	2997	202	1316	4583	894	68	106	328	220	2905		50	4	272	48
46																						
47	3.17	5.03	2.11	5.98	8.77	9.55	5.04	4.84	5.44	1.95	0.71	3.78	0.11	9.40	6.28	0.30	5.33		7.44	6.25	11.19	0.48
48																						

YEARLY GAINS AND DECREASES WITH PERCENTAGES—1919-1931—Continued

PAROCHIAL (CHURCH SOCIETIES) / **FINANCIAL** (VALUATION OF CHURCH PROPERTY)

Index Number	Men's Number	Men's Members	Women's Number	Women's Members	Young People's Number	Young People's Members	Church Edifices	Parsonages	School and Parish Houses	Endowment	Other Property	Total Valuation	Indebtedness
41	88	108	139	2230	59	4309	1565020	134412	482620	321447	197351	2431026	701297
42	5.99	0.16	2.53	1.06	1.25	3.13	1.29	0.88	5.39	10.25	2.31	1.55	2.99
43													
44													
45	38	1175	157	360	258	3372	1781906	108459	55693	146988	172272	1703356	64047
46	2.43	1.84	2.79	0.17	5.42	2.37	1.45	0.72	0.58	4.25	1.97	1.07	0.26
47													
48													

YEARLY GAINS AND DECREASES WITH PERCENTAGES—1919-1931—Concluded

FINANCIAL (CONGREGATIONAL BENEVOLENCE) / **SUMMARY**

Index Number	Congregational Expenses: Current	Unusual	Total	Apportioned: Paid	Excess	Deficit	Education	Unapportioned: Foreign Missions	Home Missions	Inner Missions	Other Benevolence	Total Unapportioned Benevolence	Total Benevolence	Total Expenditures
41	127911	1397532	1269620	96416	7282	116851	18186	9675	11615	335263	69748	388765	485181	1754801
42	1.14	21.47	7.17	4.20	27.22	19.78	9.97	3.11	8.41	28.56	17.36	17.63	10.78	7.00
43														
44														
45	470011	1262535	1732547	198200	415	449132	3916	68945	14353	360341	34516	482071	680271	2412818
46	4.15	24.70	10.54	9.01	2.13	63.49	1.95	21.55	11.55	42.97	10.39	26.55	16.94	11.71
47														
48														

UNITED LUTHERAN CHURCH IN THE UNITED STATES AND CANADA

COMPARISON OF TOTALS OF ACCESSIONS AND LOSSES, NET VALUATION AND PER CAPITA

COMPARISON OF TOTALS OF ACCESSIONS AND LOSSES

1931 Total Accessions	121,260	1931 Total Losses	70,956
1930 Total Accessions	120,602	1930 Total Losses	68,784
1931 Increase in Accessions	658	1931 Increase in Losses	2,172
1930 Decrease in Accessions	5,557	1930 Decrease in Losses	2,629
1931 Net Increase in Accessions	6,215	1931 Net Increase in Losses	4,801

1931 Accessions Gain Over Losses........................,...... 50,304
1930 Accessions Gain Over Losses............................ 51,818

1931 Loss in Accessions Gain Over Losses...................... 1,514
1930 Loss in Accessions Gain Over Losses...................... 2,928

1931 Net Gain.. 1,414

NET VALUATION

1931 Total Valuation	$160,506,533	1927 Net Valuation	$122,725,940
1931 Total Indebtedness	24,197,701	1926 Net Valuation	113,664,155
		1925 Net Valuation	100,398,878
1931 Net Valuation	136,308,832	1924 Net Valuation	92,103,946
1930 Net Valuation	134,669,023	1923 Net Valuation	83,389,965
		1922 Net Valuation	74,926,113
1931 Gain Net Valuation	1,639,809	1921 Net Valuation	70,495,643
		1920 Net Valuation	64,560,968
1929 Net Valuation	132,938,294	1919 Net Valuation	37,855,419
1928 Net Valuation	129,284,951		

PER CAPITAS

	Current Expenses	Unusual Expenses	Total Congregational	Apportionment Benevolence Paid	Total Benevolence	Total Expenditures
1931 Per Capita..........(1,001,520 cf.m.)	$10.83	$3.84	$14.68	$2.00	$3.32	$18.01
1930 Per Capita............(987,231 cf.m.)	11.06	5.17	16.64	2.22	4.06	20.71
1931 Gain Per Capita....................						
1931 Loss Per Capita....................	.23	1.33	1.96	.22	.74	2.70
1929 Per Capita............(971,187 cf.m.)	11.42	6.70	18.23	2.36	4.63	22.86
1930 Gain Per Capita....................						
1930 Loss Per Capita....................	.36	1.53	1.59	.14	.57	2.15
1928 Per Capita............(949,188 cf.m.)	11.33	7.65	19.01	2.22	5.11	24.21
1927 Per Capita............(933,650 cf.m.)	11.23	8.59	19.84	2.31	4.32	24.16
1926 Per Capita............(916,858 cf.m.)	10.30	9.44	19.73	2.02	3.58	23.31
1925 Per Capita............(886,840 cf.m.)	9.78	7.91	17.69	2.06	4.19	21.31
1924 Per Capita............(856,180 cf.m.)	9.39	7.96	17.36	2.04	4.10	21.46
1923 Per Capita............(839,279 cf.m.)	8.80	5.52	14.33	1.91	3.52	18.00
1922 Per Capita............(819,063 cf.m.)	8.32	4.89	13.21	1.84	3.71	16.93
1921 Per Capita............(801,250 cf.m.)	8.26	4.79	13.05	1.79	4.17	17.22
1920 Per Capita............(791,400 cf.m.)	7.15	3.75	10.90	1.52	3.88	14.78
1919 Per Capita............(776,582 cf.m.)	6.42	2.46	8.88	1.73	2.90	11.78

STATISTICAL REPORT OF OTHER COUNTRIES OUTSIDE U. S. A. AND CANADA
(United Lutheran Church in America)

PAROCHIAL

Index Number	Country	Province	When Organized	Pastors	Membership — Baptized	Confirmed	Communing	Congregations	Accessions Children — Baptism	Children — Otherwise	Accessions Adult — Baptism	Adult — Confirmation	Adult — Certificate	Adult — Otherwise	Losses Children — Death	Children — Otherwise	Losses Adult — Death	Adult — Certificate	Adult — Otherwise	Church Papers
1	India	Madras	1842	Ord. Miss. 26, Nat. 72, Workers 2779, Unord. men & wom. 56	154721	67981	67981	1591			9932	4796		3641			2985		10306	
2	Africa	Liberia	1860	Ord. Miss. 6, Workers 27, Unord. men and women 19	350	260	260	7				23								
3	Japan	Kyushu-Hondo.	1892	Ord. Miss. 14, Workers 20, Unord. men and women 23	3359	1261	1261	28	66			406					140			17
4	China	Shantung.	1898	Ord. Miss. 6, Nat. 1, Workers 132, Unord. men and women 13	1595	1288	1288	34				259	7		37		30			
5	Virgin Islands		1666	U. L. C. 5.	2168	1047	931	6				68				8	36	24		
6	British Guiana	Berbice.	1889	Ord. Miss. 1, Workers 13.	588	34		8				34		8						
7	Puerto Rico.		1898	U. L. C. 9.	1834	1089	706	21	87	21	11	164	12		26	16	19	26		28
8	Argentina	Buenos Aires.	1908	Ord. Miss. 2, Nat. 6, Workers 44, Unord. women 2.	1389	894	894	13				228								
9	Ttls. Outside U.S.A. & Can.			Pastors 148, Workers 3015, Unord. 123.	166004	73820	73321	1708	153	21	9943	5978	19	3649	63	24	3210	50	10306	45

STATISTICAL REPORT OF OTHER COUNTRIES OUTSIDE U. S. A. AND CANADA—Concluded
(United Lutheran Church in America)

PAROCHIAL / FINANCIAL

Index Number	Church Schools Sunday — Number	Sunday — Officers and Teachers	Sunday — Scholars	Weekday — Number	Weekday — Teachers	Weekday — Scholars	Catechumens (Catechetical)	Students — Ministry	Students — Deaconess	Students — In Lutheran Institutions	Students — In Non-Luth. Institutions	Church Societies Men's — Number	Men's — Members	Women's — Number	Women's — Members	Young P. — Number	Young P. — Members	Valuation — Church Edifices	Parsonages	School and Parish Houses	Other Property	Total Valuation	Congregational Expenses	Total Benevolence	Total Expenditures
1	1088		49806	1058		36656	15617	46				515	11368	397	8047						1200000	1200000	130000	24000	154000
2	3		201	13		310	148														80000	80000	3900	558	4458
3	28		3365	10		1250	379							17	252	20	498				650000	650000	12000	890	12890
4	30	92	1340	35	12	1487		12			8			3	57	2	72	115000	15000		30000	160000	2758	2260	5018
5	6		1124	4		155	74	4													185000	185000	3200	1040	4240
6	9		567	2		102	109	1		1				6	64	2	212				61200	61200	2912	1851	4763
7	20	118	2516	6	17	232	76	1		2	10			1	33	7	48	110000	40000	11750	28000	189750	3145	950	4095
8	7		482	8		814	52														220000	220000	28000	3750	31750
9	1191	210	59401	1136	29	41006	16455	64		3	18	515	11368	424	8453	31	830	225000	55000	11750	2454200	2745950	185915	35299	221214

NOTE—For completed totals see tables on pp 38 and 39.

U.L.C. in A.
MEMBERSHIPS
U.S. and CANADA
1919–1931

Increase 12 yrs. %

Baptized — 32.59

Confirmed — 28.96

Sunday Schools — 28.53

Communing — 45.74

1,500,000
1,400,000
1,300,000
1,200,000
1,100,000
1,000,000
900,000
800,000
700,000
600,000
500,000
0

1919 1920 1921 1922 1923 1924 1925 1926 1927 1928 1929 1930 1931

U.L.C. in A.
NUMBER of PASTORS, PARISHES, CONGREGA-TIONS, SCHOOLS, STUDENTS, and ORGANIZATIONS
U.S. and CANADA
1919–1931

Increase 12 yrs. %

Thousand

Women's Societies — 105.76

Young People's Societies — 137.22

Congregations — 14.17

Sunday Schools — 14.68

Pastors — 19.66

Parishes — 10.91

Men's Societies — 125.56

Students - Ministry — 836.69

Weekday Schools — 37.26

Deaconess Students — 328.57

6
5
4
3
2
1
0

1919 1920 1921 1922 1923 1924 1925 1926 1927 1928 1929 1930 1931

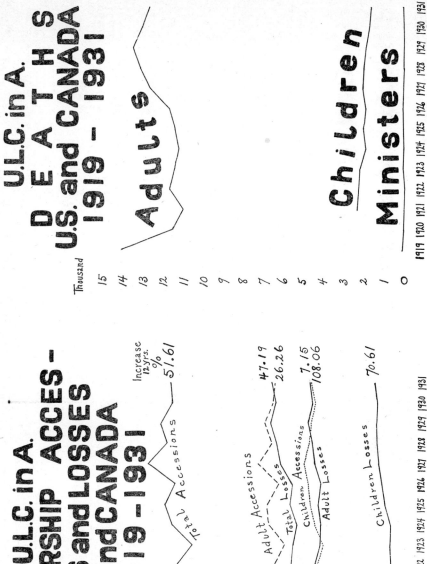

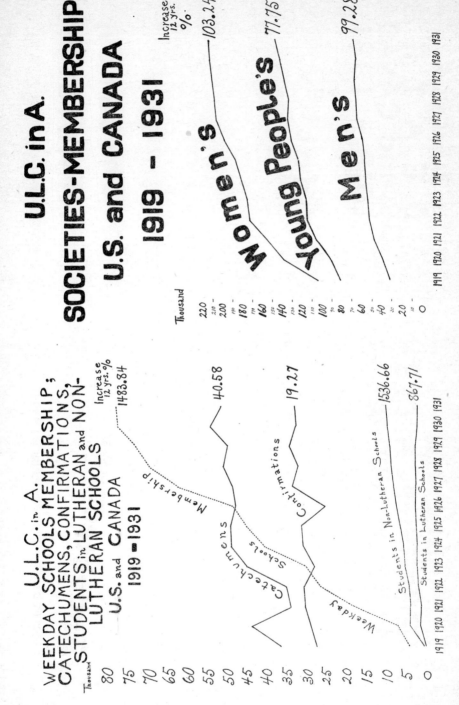

U.L.C. in A.
SOCIETIES-MEMBERSHIP
U.S. and CANADA
1919 - 1931

Increase 12 yrs. %

Women's — 103.24

Young People's — 77.75

Men's — 99.28

Thousand

U.L.C. in A.
WEEKDAY SCHOOLS MEMBERSHIP;
CATECHUMENS, CONFIRMATIONS,
STUDENTS in LUTHERAN and NON-
LUTHERAN SCHOOLS
U.S. and CANADA
1919 - 1931

Increase 12 yrs. %

Membership — 1483.84
Catechumens — 40.58
Confirmations — 19.27
Students in Non-Lutheran Schools — 1536.66
Students in Lutheran Schools — 867.71
Weekday Schools

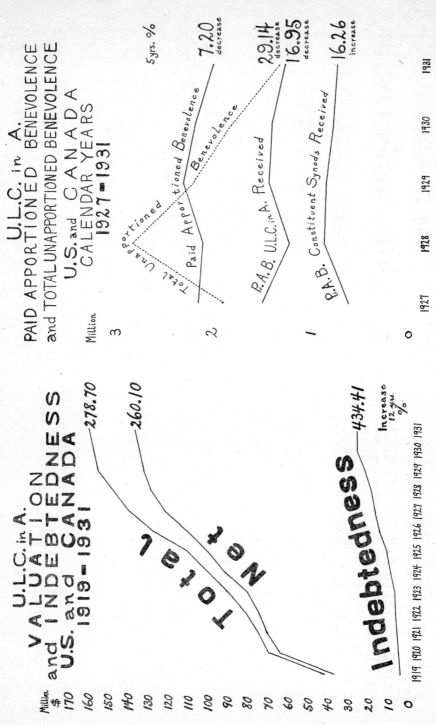

U.L.C. in A.
PAID APPORTIONED BENEVOLENCE
and TOTAL UNAPPORTIONED BENEVOLENCE
U.S. and CANADA
CALENDAR YEARS
1927 - 1931

Million

3

2

1

0

5 yrs. %

7.20 decrease

29.14 decrease

16.95 decrease

16.26 increase

Total Unapportioned Benevolence

Paid Apportioned Benevolence

P.A.B. U.L.C. in A. Received

P.A.B. Constituent Synods Received

1927   1928   1929   1930   1931

U.L.C. in A.
VALUATION
and INDEBTEDNESS
U.S. and CANADA
1919 - 1931

Millin. $
170
160
150
140
130
120
110
100
90
80
70
60
50
40
30
20
10
0

278.70

260.10

434.41

Total

Net

Indebtedness

Increase 12 yrs. %

1919 1920 1921 1922 1923 1924 1925 1926 1927 1928 1929 1930 1931

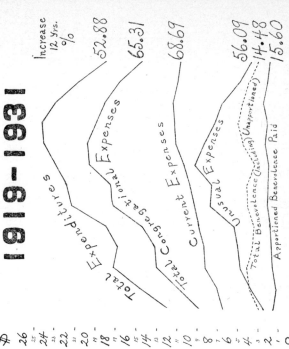

U.L.C. in A.

PER CAPITAS

U.S. and CANADA

1919-1931

Increase 12 yrs. %

Total Expenditures   52.88

Total Congregational Expenses   65.31

Current Expenses   68.69

Unusual Expenses   56.09

Total Benevolence (including Unapportioned)   14.48

Apportioned Benevolence Paid   15.60

1919 1920 1921 1922 1923 1924 1925 1926 1927 1928 1929 1930 1931

$ 26 25 24 23 22 21 20 19 18 17 16 15 14 13 12 11 10 9 8 7 6 5 4 3 2 1 0

U.L.C. in A.

EXPENDITURES

U.S. and CANADA

1919 – 1931

Million $ 24 22 20 18 16 14 12 10 8 6 4 2 0

Increase 12 yrs. %

Total Expenditures   90.00

Total Congregational Expenses   113.03

Current Expenses   117.77

Unusual Expenses   100.71

Total Benevolence   47.99

Apportioned Benevolence Paid   48.86

1919 1920 1921 1922 1923 1924 1925 1926 1927 1928 1929 1930 1931

Dr. Schnur presented the Rev. G. L. Kieffer, Statistical Secretary of the Church, who addressed the Convention.

Recommendations 1, 2, 3, 4, 5, 6, 7, 8, 9, 10 and 11 were adopted.

The Rev. I. F. Frankenfield presented the following resolutions which were adopted:

1. That this Convention record hereby its deep appreciation of the efficient work done by the Rev. G. H. Schnur in editing the Year Book of the United Lutheran Church in past years.

2. That this Convention also pay tribute to the significance of the work of the Rev. G. L. Kieffer as Statistical Secretary of The United Lutheran Church in America and to his untiring efforts and unflagging zeal in that office.

The report of the Committee on German Interests, received by the Convention through the Bulletin, is as follows:

REPORT OF THE COMMITTEE ON GERMAN INTERESTS

The Committee on German Interests held the following meetings during the past biennium: January 7, 1931, Zion Church, Baltimore, Md., the Rev. F. O. Evers, pastor; May 15, 1931, Zion Church, Brooklyn, N. Y., the Rev. E. C. J. Kraeling, D.D., pastor; November 23, 1931, Zion Church, Philadelphia, Pa., the Rev. K. Molzahn, pastor; April 4, 1932, St. Johannis Church, Reading, Pa., the Rev. Robert H. Ischinger, pastor.

All matters referred to this committee by the various agencies of the Church were promptly discussed and acted on.

The College and Seminary at Saskatoon, Saskatchewan, Canada, and the Martin Luther Seminary at Lincoln, Nebraska, being in special need, the committee with the permission of the Executive Board and the Board of Education raised a special offering among the German congregations of The United Lutheran Church in America during and after the season of Whitsunday, 1931. As a result, $1,156.33 was collected for the institution at Saskatoon and $997.09 for Martin Luther Seminary. A total of $2,153.42. This was disbursed through the treasurer of The United Lutheran Church in America with the exception of $50 which was handed directly to the representative of Saskatoon.

With the sanction of the Executive Board the committee called and prepared the program of the "Seventh General German Conference of The United Lutheran Church in America" to meet in the historic and always hospitable Zion Church, Philadelphia, the Rev. K. Molzahn, pastor. This conference was notable in many ways. All sections of the German constituency of The United Lutheran Church in America were represented, including Texas, Nebraska, the Manitoba and Canada Synods, the Wartburg Synod alone remaining unrepresented. One hundred and ten clergymen and twenty-seven laymen answered the roll call, this being the largest attendance in years. In addition to the honored president of The United Lutheran Church in America it was most encouraging to note the presence of the presidents of the Pennsylvania Ministerium, the United Synod of New York and the Pittsburgh Synod. At the opening service the Rev. R. Mosig, of New Hamburg, Ontario, Canada, preached an inspiring sermon on Eph. 3:20-21. This was followed by the administration of Holy Communion. Dr. E. A. Tappert, divisional secretary of the Board of American Missions on linguistic interests, read a paper on German Home Mission Work which elicited a prolonged discussion of the special needs on our own fields, particularly on the territory of the Manitoba Synod. A second paper on "German Literature for the Use of the Congregation" was submitted by Dr. C. R. Tappert. In the discussion following the need of a new German "Agende" and "Fibel" were stressed. Dr. H. Brueckner read a third paper on "The Relations and Exchange of Delegates between The United Lutheran Church in America and the Allgemeine Lutherische Konferenz in Germany." It was clearly evident from the discussion which followed the presentation of this paper, that there is a desire on the part of the German constituency of The United Lutheran Church in America for a closer bond between The United Lutheran Church in America and the Allgemeine Lutherische Konferenz in Germany.

The widespread interest in this meeting of the General German Conference of The United Lutheran Church in America, the unusual number of delegates attending, are proof that this medium for the expression of sentiments on the part of the German congregations in The United Lutheran Church in America is greatly needed and will continue to grow in importance in direct ratio as the German congregations make use of it.

The committee co-operated with the Board of Ministerial Pensions and Relief in connection with claims for pensions and special grants to deserving brethren formerly engaged in specific German work. Matters pertaining to German Home Mission Work in Canada likewise occupied the attention of the committee. Various problems and difficulties found a ready solution through co-operation with the Board of American Missions.

At present a sub-committee is at work to edit a new German "Agende," the need of which was voiced at the meeting of the General German Conference. Another sub-committee has been appointed to consider ways and means of publishing a "Fibel," another great need in the various German congregations of The United Lutheran Church in America.

Respectfully submitted,

E. C. J. KRAELING, *Chairman.*

ROBERT H. ISCHINGER, *Secretary.*

The report of the Committee on Publicity was presented by the Rev. H. R. Gold, Chairman of the Committee.

REPORT OF THE COMMITTEE ON PUBLICITY

The Committee on Publicity in co-operation with the News Bureau of the National Lutheran Council conducted the publicity work in connection with the Convention of the Church held in Milwaukee in 1930. Several members of the Committee and members of the staff of the News Bureau gave service preceding the Convention and during the period of the Convention. Results obtained were on the whole satisfactory and compared favorably with the publicity obtained in connection with other conventions.

A conference of the members of the Committee, representatives of Synodical Publicity Committees and representatives of the National Lutheran Council, together with others interested particularly in Church publicity and advertising was held at the time of the Milwaukee Convention. Several recommendations were made by the Committee to the Convention. (See minutes 1930, page 209.) These grew out of resolutions passed by the New York and other synods.

It has not been possible, for lack of funds, to carry out plans which the Committee has made from time to time. However, it is still hoped that at least the "Publicity Manual" recommended to the Church may be published somehow. Members of the Committee would gladly take the time to provide the copy for such a book if the means for publishing it could be found. It is believed that the Church would willingly authorize the publishing of it.

To many Church publicity means news in the public press. That is but a part of Church publicity and advertising. By far the larger field for Church publicity is in local churches and communities, within the congregation itself, and through the various agencies of the Church at large. An inexpensive manual setting forth the principles and some tried methods of publicity and advertising would undoubtedly be of great value to the Church and its extensive activities.

HOWARD R. GOLD, *Chairman.*

The following resolution, presented by Dr. Gold on behalf of the Committee on Publicity, was adopted:

That the Convention authorize the development of a nation-wide organization for the purpose of stimulating favorable Church publicity of a national, sectional or local character throughout the synods and the congregations of the United Lutheran Church, and that the Convention request the Executive Board to appropriate the modest sum required to accomplish this.

The report of the Counselling Commission of Churches with the Y. M. C. A. was presented by the Rev. Paul E. Scherer, Chairman of the Committee.

REPORT OF THE COUNSELLING COMMISSION OF CHURCHES WITH THE Y. M. C. A.

Since the organization of the General Counselling Commission of the Churches, on the initiation of the Young Men's Christian Association in 1924, there have been seven annual meetings, with representatives of the International Committee and its successor, the National Council of the Y. M. C. A., the last meeting held in January, 1931. These meetings have been of interest and advantage in the better understanding which has resulted to the respective purposes and programs of the Churches and the Association.

It did not seem practicable to get the Counselling Commission together either in the fall or in the spring of 1931-32. The next meeting is planned for the fall of 1932.

There seems to be increasing emphasis on the Christian Message and purpose among those higher up in the Councils of the organization. The difficulty lies in the almost complete autonomy often allowed to individual associations and secretaries.

The meeting of the World's Alliance of the Y. M. C. A. took place in Toronto, July 28-August 2, 1931. The Twentieth World's Conference was held at Cleveland, August 4-9, with the Forty-third International Convention of the North American Y. M. C. A.'s. The resulting pamphlet on religious emphasis and social issues should be of significance for the future program of the Association.

The annual reports from Associations on May 1st a year ago showed, for the first year of the depression, percentage increases in activities over the previous year as follows:

1. Total organized groups increased by 35 per cent. There are now over 25,000 organized groups in Associations.
2. Young Men's groups increased 78 per cent. 83,000 young men are enrolled in organized groups.
3. Employed boys' group increased by 95 per cent.
4. Hi-Y groups increased 16 per cent. There are now 156,000 high school boys in the groups.
5. Ninety-eight thousand positions were secured by Y. M. C. A. employment service. A slight increase over the previous year.
6. Bible study and discussion groups increased by 16 per cent.
7. There was a gain of 56 per cent in the number of vocational interviews reported.
8. Lectures and talks were increased by 40 per cent.

9. Participation in physical education activities went up to 23 per cent.
10. The total number of directors and committeemen increased 5 per cent.

Your Commission recommends the continuance of the contact afforded by membership in the General Counselling Commission.

Respectfully submitted,

PAUL SCHERER, Chairman.

The recommendation was adopted.

The report of the Transportation Committee was presented by the Rev. A. R. Wentz, Secretary of the Committee, and the thanks of the Convention were voted to Dr. Bramkamp and Mr. Miller.

REPORT OF TRANSPORTATION COMMITTEE

Special mention should be made of the services of the Rev. J. M. Bramkamp, D.D., Western Secretary of the Committee. He has secured a number of passes, both annual and trip, which have resulted in great saving to the Church.

The Committee succeeded in securing from all of the railway passenger associations special rates to this convention. It also secured combinations of special rates to the convention of the Women's Missionary Society in Baltimore, the convention of the Brotherhood in Harrisburg, and this convention of The United Lutheran Church in America. The Chairman of the Committee, Mr. Harvey C. Miller, has rendered valuable service in connection with the transportation of delegates to this convention, and in facilitating the validation of their tickets. The thanks of the convention are due to Dr. Bramkamp and Mr. Miller.

ABDEL ROSS WENTZ, Secretary.

The report of the Archivist was presented by the Rev. L. D. Reed.

REPORT OF THE ARCHIVIST

The following items were received during the biennium 1930-32 and placed in the Archives:

Ordination certificate of E. G. Ernst.
Official correspondence between the Presidents of the General Council, the General Synod and the United Synod in the South before the formation of the United Lutheran Church.
Papers of the Commission on Theological Education.

In addition to the above items clippings from Church papers of obituary notices of pastors and prominent laymen have been mounted and filed.
Official protocol of the Erie Convention, 1928.
Correspondence of President Knubel, 1927-1928.

Respectfully submitted,

LUTHER D. REED, *Archivist.*

The Rev. Samuel Trexler, Chairman of the Committee on Place of the Next Convention, reported that the Committee recommended Savannah, Ga., as the place of the 1934 convention. The recommendation was unanimously adopted.

The Rev. A. R. Wentz presented the Minutes of the Lutheran Historical Society, which were received as follows:

MINUTES OF THE LUTHERAN HISTORICAL SOCIETY

BENJAMIN FRANKLIN HOTEL,
Philadelphia, Pennsylvania.
October 17, 1932.

The Society was called to order by President Manhart.

The report of the Curator, Professor A. R. Wentz, was read and adopted as follows:

During the past summer a complete change was made in the facilities for housing the valuable collection of the Society. The entire library of the Seminary at Gettysburg was thoroughly renovated and made completely fireproof. This has doubled the capacity of the library and made all the equipment conform to the most modern requirements of libraries. The basement floor of the library, which for some years has been the home of the Historical Society's collection, was equipped with fire-doors, steel shelving and a large vault with a capacity of 2,500 volumes. These improvements reduce to a minimum all hazards from fire and theft and at the same time provide space for enlargement and for more convenient classification.

The work of card-indexing was continued during the past biennium. Our collection has come to be widely known. The Curator received many inquiries for information and research students from various quarters visited the library of the society in quest of information on Lutheran history.

The report of the treasurer, Mr. J. Elmer Musselman, together with the report of the auditors, was presented and adopted, showing a balance of $133.59.

The following officers were elected:

President—Rev. F. P. Manhart, D.D., LL.D.; Vice-Presidents—Mr. H. M. M. Richards, Litt.D.; Rev. W. J. Finck, D.D.; Rev. S. W. Herman, D.D.; Curator—Rev. A. R. Wentz, Ph.D., D.D.; Secretary—Rev. Prof. H. C. Alleman, D.D.; Treasurer—Mr. J. Elmer Musselman; extra members of the Executive Committee—Rev. Pres. G. Morris Smith, D.D.; Rev. Henry Anstadt, D.D.

The minutes were read and approved.

The Society adjourned.

W. A. WADE, *Secretary pro tem.*

The report of the Lutheran Church Book and Literature Society was presented by Mr. H. Torrey Walker, Treasurer of the Society.

REPORT OF THE LUTHERAN CHURCH BOOK AND LITERATURE SOCIETY

During the biennium the Society has, in a quiet way, created new interests among individuals, and especially among our Luther Leagues.

With the limited funds on hand, consisting of income from an endowment fund of $1,000 and annual contributions of a dollar from about 500 members, the Society has distributed 750 Common Service Books, 250 Parish School Hymnals, 200 Hymns and Prayers and also a number of tracts. These were sent to mission congregations in Texas, Colorado, Virginia, South Carolina, New York, Montana, Washington, Missouri and Illinois.

Among the beneficiaries were a Home for the Aged and a hospital.

The Society hopes to stimulate distribution of Lutheran literature in libraries and other public institutions, and solicits the support of the members in congregations of the church.

The officers are: Honorary President, Rev. F. H. Knubel, D.D.; President, the Rev. P. Z. Strodach, D. D.; Secretary, Rev. G. H. Bechtold; Treasurer, Mr. H. Torrey Walker. Headquarters are in the Muhlenberg Building, 1228 Spruce Street, Philadelphia, Pa.

Respectfully submitted,

G. H. BECHTOLD, *Secretary.*

The Rev. O. F. Blackwelder, a member of the Committee on Associations of Young People, presented the Rev. P. M. Kinports, Executive Secretary of the Luther League, who addressed the Convention and called attention to his report as follows:

REPORT OF THE EXECUTIVE SECRETARY OF THE LUTHER LEAGUE OF AMERICA

The Luther League of America deals particularly with the youth of our Church. Upon the youth of our Church depends the future of our Church organization. How important that our youth be thoroughly acquainted with and educated in all those things which shall go to help them live consecrated Christian lives and to make them thorough and efficient Lutherans.

There is a definite reason for the existence of the Luther League in its three departments, Junior, Intermediate and Senior. If we hope to have good

Senior Leaguers, young people who will take part in the meetings and become leaders in the Senior Department, we must begin with the boys and the girls. A connecting link between the Junior and Senior Departments is the Intermediate League. To carry out a complete program there should be the three departments for the youth of the congregation.

Through the Luther League, young folks are receiving a fine training which prepares those who take the training seriously for leadership in local congregations, teachers in Sunday schools, members of Church councils, members of boards in synods and the United Lutheran Church. There are hundreds of leaders in the Church today who point with pride to the excellent training and preparation they received in the League to assume leadership in, and render service to, the Church.

PERSONNEL

Officers and Executive Committee for 1931-33 are as follows: Honorary Members: Rev. L. M. Kuhns, D.D., Litt.D.; Hon. E. F. Eilert, C. S. D.; Mr. Harry Hodges; Rev. A. J. Traver, D.D.; Officers: President, Mr. Herbert W. Fischer; Vice-President, Mr. John George Kurzenknabe; Second Vice-President, Mr. Alvin H. Schaediger; Recording Secretary, Miss Eva Peeler; Treasurer, Mr. Charles W. Fuhr; Executive Secretary, Rev. Paul M. Kinports; Educational Secretary, Rev. Paul M. Kinports; Missionary Secretary, Miss Winnie Butt; Life Service Secretary, Rev. Chester S. Simonton; Intermediate Secretary, Rev. R. J. Wolf; Junior Secretary, Miss Brenda L. Mehlhouse. Members at large: Mr. C. C. Dittmer, Mrs. S. T. Peterson, Rev. C. P. Harry, D.D., Rev. C. M. Teufel, D.D., Rev. Rudolph G. Schulz, Jr., Mr. Ray F. Anderson, Mr. Austin W. Howard, Rev. A. W. Mehlenbacher, Mr. Harold Sundberg, Miss Irene Schaeffer, and Chairman of the Committee on Associations of Young People, Rev. H. C. Roehner, D.F.

ORGANIZATION

It is difficult to detail the work of such an organization as the Luther League in such a way as to enable those who are not definitely interested to visualize its possibilities. To attempt to describe the work done takes away the element of spiritual dynamic which is the real reason for the League's existence. The strength of the Luther League does not lie in its working units, important as they may be in themselves, but it lies in the fact that it is built on the truth of the Word of God. The League constantly challenges its membership, with the saving message that Jesus Christ is the only Saviour of the world, and that those who want to live lives that really count must live the Christ life. The controlling power and driving force back of all our League work is this life in Christ.

A PROGRAM "FOR THE CHURCH"

This is the mission of the League. The program outlined by the Luther League of America is Education, Missions and Life Service. In every local, district and synodical league, there should be a secretary for each department.

Through the Educational Department the League trains our youth in Bible study, reading religious literature, discussion of vital religious problems and the study of topics of vital interest to the development of spiritual life.

Through the Missionary Department the League informs the youth of the missionary work of the Church at home and abroad, stressing monthly missionary Devotional, Mission Study classes and a Biennial Missionary Objective. The results are that our young people become missionary-minded and take a deep interest in the missionary work of the Church. The last biennial objective was the Training School at Monte Flores, Puerto Rico. The goal of $25,000 was raised and paid over in full amount to the Board of American Missions. The present objective is the appropriation of $15,000 for the Administration Building of the Lutheran Theological Seminary, Tokyo, Japan. During the last biennium, the Leagues gave $32,677 for benevolent purposes to the Church.

Through the Life Service Department our youth are directed to the worth of a God-planned life. Vocational and avocational guidance is given in co-operation with the Board of Religious Education. This department suggests programs and encourages responsibilities in the work of the local congregation.

AGE DEPARTMENTS

The Luther League is divided into three departments: Junior, 8-12 years with supplementary program for Little Leaguers under 8 years; Intermediate, 13-16; and Senior 17 plus. The Executive Secretary is in charge of the Senior Department, Rev. R. J. Wolf, the Intermediate, and Miss Brenda L. Mehlhouse, the Junior Department.

The Intermediate Department is seeking to satisfy some of the many interests and activities peculiar to the teen age.

This is done by a direct approach through a church-centered program to more than 15,000 boys and girls enrolled in 550 Intermediate Luther Leagues, and to countless others not affiliated with the Luther League of America by various program suggestions; and by an indirect approach to still larger numbers in non-sectarian organizations, such as the Boy Scouts of America, Girl Scouts, etc.

The Intermediate program offers weekly devotional study; participation in practical work in the local congregation; co-operation in mutual Luther League activities; promotion of individual and group hobbies, etc. The gist of Intermediate Luther League programing is to service the teen age youth for self, the Church and Christ.

The Intermediate Department denotes action. The teen age youth's line of action follows the line of conception of its leaders. The leaders of the Intermediate Department, among whom many ministers are included, are finding the teen age youth responsible and responsive to understanding guidance. Our prayer is for more of such leaders.

The Junior Department: The Junior Luther Leagues care for over 17,000 children in 665 Junior Leagues (8-12 years) and 100 "Little Leaguers" groups (under 8). During the biennium 147 new organizations were added.

It has two major aims, (1) the education of the children in the things of the Church, and (2) their enlistment in service in the Church.

Over $8,000 was contributed in the last biennium for the local and benevolent work of the Church; $1,014 was contributed to the Puerto Rico Objective of the Luther League, and $1,134 to its Sustaining Membership, in addition to gifts of money and service for all kinds of Inner, Home and Foreign Mission enterprises.

This year's special objective is $300 for the furnishing of the kindergarten in Puerto Rico.

Seventy-five State and District Secretaries direct the local superintendents, for whom two national, four state and numerous district Junior Institutes were held.

A weekly program with Junior Topics, Junior Topics Booklets, and leaflet literature, teaches the children the Bible, the Church, Missions, the story of Luther and the work of the Luther League. The missionary topics once a month are the Light Brigade program supplied by the Women's Missionary Society.

The Junior League is the training school for the Senior Department, and the work of the Church.

REGIONAL SECRETARIES

Three synods at the present time provide full time secretaries: Ohio, New York and Virginia. Part time secretaries are maintained by North and South Carolinas, Illinois and Pennsylvania. These secretaries are engaged in the promotion of the work among young people with splendid results to the Church.

PUERTO RICO, SOUTH AMERICA, INDIA

The development of young people's work in Puerto Rico, South America and India has followed the general program for the Luther League. Active Leagues have been established with large memberships in these respective mission fields. In India, Rev. R. D. Philip Augustus, the full time Secretary for the A. E. L. C. in connection with Sunday school work, has organized many new Leagues, and reports 142 Senior and 224 Junior Leagues with a membership of 10,206. An appropriation toward his salary is made by the Luther League of America.

FINANCES

With the rapid growth of the Luther League, demands for literature, constructive program and greater opportunities for service, the income of the League is meager. The budget of the League is $21,000.00. In comparison to other young people's organizations in other communions, this is by far the smallest budget.

The United Lutheran Church appropriates $8,000 per year to the Leauge. Dues paid by the State and synodical organizations are $7,000. The remainder of the budget is supported by Sustaining Memberships.

PUBLICATIONS

The monthly *Review* in view of reports of the decrease in subscriptions to other Church publications, has but a slight decrease in subscribers. The *Topics Quarterly,* edited by Rev. C. P. Harry, D.D., is distributed in quantities of 11,550 per quarter. These publications are practically self-supporting, due to the fact that there is no expense for editorial service.

The *Intermediate Quarterly Helps* and the *Junior Topics Booklets,* new publications, have a distribution of 11,500. Thousands of separate pieces of literature as aids to program building and organization work were distributed by the six departments in the last biennium. This literature is sold at a minimum cost or provided for in the budget for free distribution.

1931 NATIONAL CONVENTION

The Nineteenth Biennial Convention was held July 2-6, 1931, at Reading, Pennsylvania. From twenty-seven states and seven countries delegates in numbers exceeding by far any prvious convention, came to participate in an exceptionally prepared and finely executed program. The registrations were 1173.

The convention demonstrated that a distinctively spiritual appeal is one that can hold youth even today. It was a Lutheran youth confession to the Church and the world that youth is willing to face God's challenge in all its truth and seriousness; that youth believes in the Bible and its Christ; and that youth loves its Church.

Our Church leaders recognizing the opportunity afforded by closer contact with the rising generation of Church workers have been generous indeed in giving their services in connection with convention programs. We recognize this fact and appreciate the spirit back of it. Our leaders have no better friends than the young people who attend these conventions.

The Twentieth Biennial Convention will be held in Detroit, Michigan, July 7-12, 1933. Plans for the convention are under way, and widespread interest is being manifested in the next general meeting of the League.

INSTITUTES

The Secretaries of the League are at present working on a definite plan of sponsoring League institutes in all sections of the Church. In some sections of our Church the League program is not understood. Where institutes have been held there is every indication that they are bringing about better work in the Leagues and a far more intelligent understanding of League problems than heretofore. At such meetings, secretaries have a chance to discuss with Leaguers the whole cause of Christian young people's work as it affects the individual, the league and the Church. We believe these institutes will assist in training active, intelligent young people to be leaders in the League and Church.

ACKNOWLEDGEMENT

The Luther League expresses its deep appreciation and hearty thanks to the United Lutheran Church for the support given during the past biennium to carry on an enlarged program in an ever extending field of service.

Pastors and Church workers, the Luther League has proven its practical value in the local congregation and Church at large. What the League shall be and do in the future depends in no small measure upon us. The League needs your help, guidance, co-operation and prayers.

Respectfully submitted,

PAUL M. KINPORTS, *Executive Secretary.*

The Rev. P. M. Kinports introduced Miss B. Mehlhouse, Secretary of the Junior Department of the Luther League, and the Rev. R. J. Wolf, Secretary of the Intermediate Department of the Luther League, who addressed the Convention.

Items of unfinished business were next taken up.

The report of the Committee on the Office of the Ministry was presented by the Rev. M. L. Stirewalt, Secretary of the Committee.

REPORT OF THE COMMITTEE ON THE OFFICE OF THE MINISTRY

(For action on the recommendations in this report see p. 541)

REASONS FOR THE APPOINTMENT OF THE COMMITTEE

The Erie Convention of the United Lutheran Church received from the Ministerium of Pennsylvania the following memorial and approved the following reply:

"Resolved, That the Ministerium of Pennsylvania petition the United Lutheran Church to amend the Formula for Ordination so as to read, 'I commit unto thee the office of the Word and Sacraments, according to the faith of the Evangelical Lutheran Church.'"

"Reply: The committee recommends that this petition be referred to the Common Service Book Committee." Minutes, 1928, pp. 136, 137.

The Milwaukee Convention received the following in the report of the Common Service Book Committee on the Order for Ordination and adopted the resolution as quoted with reference to that part of the report:

"The Erie Convention referred to the Common Service Book Committee a request from the Ministerium of Pennsylvania to amend the Formula for Ordination. As it now stands the Order provides that the officiating minister when laying hands upon the candidate shall say:

" 'I now commit unto thee the Holy Office of the Word and Sacraments; I ordain and consecrate thee a minister of the Church; In the Name of the Father, and of the Son, and of the Holy Ghost.'

"The Ministerium asked that this be changed to read:

" 'I commit unto thee the office of the Word and Sacraments according to the faith of the Evangelical Lutheran Church,' etc.

"After careful consideration the Common Service Book Committee recommends that the change asked for by the Ministerium of Pennsylvania be not made. In connection with the subject of Ordination the Common Service Book Committee further recommends:

" 'That the United Lutheran Church recommend to its constituent synods that the practice of the Church be:

" 'When a minister of another communion applies for reception into a synod of the Church, he, having first been received as a member of one of its congregations, shall be ordained.'

"The Rev. C. M. Jacobs submitted the following resolution concerning the section of the report in regard to the Order for Ordination:

"Resolved, That these recommendations be referred to a special committee with instructions that they be studied in the light of the Lutheran doctrine of the ministry and that report be made to a subsequent convention of the Church." Minutes, 1930, pp. 434, 435.

It seemed to the committee that the basic problem herein referred is: Shall ministers from other communions who apply for admission to the Lutheran Church and her ministry be ordained in every case by the Synod of the Lutheran Church to which they apply? The other question with reference to the change in formula depends upon the solution of the basic problem. These two questions are to be studied "in the light of the Lutheran doctrine of the ministry." The committee held four meetings. The general field of our investigation was sub-divided into four areas and assigned to the members of the committee for study and report. Each report was studied by all members of the committee and the summarized conclusions are presented with this report.

THE TEACHING OF THE SCRIPTURE CONCERNING THE MINISTRY AND ORDINATION

1.

For the teaching of the Scripture concerning the ministry and ordination, we may confine ourselves to the New Testament. The Prophetic Ministry of the Old Testament prefigures the Ministry of the New Testament, but in itself, and apart from the Ministry of the New Testament, it is peculiar to the Old Testament Dispensation.

2.

The New Testament does not teach an explicit doctrine of the Ministry and Ordination. But the New Testament lays down the fundamental principles upon which an explicit doctrine of the Ministry and Ordination can be based. Any doctrine or conception of the Ministry and Ordination which is not in harmony with these principles must be regarded as unscriptural and unevangelical.

3.

The fundamental principles by which the doctrine of the Ministry and Ordination is determined are derived from the teaching of the New Testament:

(a) Concerning Christ and His work;
(b) Concerning the Gospel and its meaning;
(c) Concerning the Church and her relation to Christ and the Gospel.

A correct interpretation of the teaching of the New Testament concerning these three fundamental articles of faith will lead to a correct doctrine of the Ministry and Ordination.

4.

There would be no Ministry if there were no Church. There would be no Church, if there were no Gospel. There would be no Gospel, if there were no Christ who was delivered for our offenses and raised again for our justification (Romans 4:25; I Cor. 15:3f). The work of Christ's Redemption and Reconciliation is the objective foundation and the living source of the Gospel, of the Church and of the Ministry in its relation to both the Church and the Gospel.

5.

The first fruit of Christ's work of redemption and reconciliation is the Gospel, the message of salvation, the proclamation of God's forgiveness and grace to all who believe in the Lord Jesus Christ. But the preaching of the Gospel requires a ministry (diakonia) of the Gospel, through which the preaching of the Gospel is realized. The ministry is therefore essentially a service rendered to Christ in the sphere of the Gospel, and its aim is to make the work of Christ's redemption and reconciliation effective in the hearts and lives of men. For this reason it is called by the Apostle Paul the ministry of a new testament or the ministry of reconciliation, and for the same reason the apostle writes: We are ambassadors of Christ (II Cor. 3:6; 5:20). The Ministry of the New Testament, in itself, is nothing apart from the Gospel: whatever it is, whatever power and authority it has, comes from the Gospel, is derived from it, is inherent in it.

6.

As the Gospel and the Gospel Ministry are the fruit of Christ's work of redemption and reconciliation, so the Church is His creation and the fruit of His work of redemption and reconciliation. For the Gospel is "the power of God unto salvation to everyone that believeth" (Rom. 1:16; I Cor. 1:18) and the Church is the communion of believers, the congregation of all who call upon the name of our Lord Jesus Christ in every place (I Cor. 1:2). This communion of believers is present wherever the Gospel is preached, and wherever two or three are gathered together in the name of the Lord Jesus Christ. It is Christ's own creation, it is His body and the temple of His Spirit; but it is distinct from any external organization; it is neither identical with any local organization nor with any larger church body which represents a number of local congregations, although it may be present in both. To this communion of believers has been given the Gospel, the Christ of the Gospel, the preservation and propagation of the Gospel through the Gospel Ministry, and the Power of the Keys.

7.

It is Christ Himself who is ever present in His Church as her living Head, and who builds, preserves and defends His Church so that the gates of Hell shall not prevail against her. It is Christ Himself who in and through His Church appoints and sets apart for the Gospel Ministry those whom He Himself has chosen (Eph. 4:11f). As the work of the ministry is Christ's work, so is also the call to the ministry His call. Therefore, when the Church, as an external organization, appoints and sets apart for the Gospel ministry certain persons whom she has found to be well qualified for the task, and puts her seal of approval upon them by the rite of ordination, with prayer, the reading of the Scripture, and the laying on of hands, according to the example of the Apostolic Church, she acts in the name of the Lord Jesus Christ Himself in so far as she, as an external organization, also represents the communion of believers.

THE TEACHING OF THE LUTHERAN CONFESSIONS

The Teaching of the Lutheran Confession is found in the references to the Church, the Ministry, and Ordination.

The doctrine of the Church is stated chiefly in the Augsburg Confession, Articles VII and VIII; the Apology, Chapter IV, Articles VII and VIII; the Smalcald Articles, Part III, Article XII; and the Small and Large Catechisms, The Creed, Article III.

Augsburg Confession, Article VII. "Also they teach, that one holy Church is to continue forever. But the Church is the congregation of saints, in which the Gospel is rightly taught, and the Sacraments rightly administered.

"And unto the true unity of the Church, it is sufficient to agree concerning the doctrines of the Gospel and the administration of the Sacraments. Nor is it necessary that human traditions, rites, or ceremonies instituted by men, should be alike everywhere; as St. Paul saith: 'There is one faith, one baptism, one God and Father of all.'"

In this life, true believers and hypocrites and evil persons are mingled together in the Church. "Both the Sacraments and the Word are effectual by reason of the institution and commandment of Christ, notwithstanding they are administered by evil men." A. C., Art. VIII. The existence of the Church and the efficacy of the means of grace are not annulled by the presence of wicked persons in the Church.

The Church is the communion of true believers scattered throughout the whole world without regard to land, nation, outward government, or the presence of hypocrites and wicked persons with them. In this sense the term is used only in the singular; however, we may designate local groups within the Church by the use of the plural form.

The doctrine of the Ministry is stated chiefly in the Augsburg Confession, Articles V and XIV; the Apology, Chapter VII, Article XIV; and in the Smalcald Articles, Appendix, "The Power and Primacy of the Pope."

"That we may obtain this faith, the Office of Teaching the Gospel and administering the Sacraments was instituted." A. C., Art. V.

"Of Ecclesiastical Order, they teach, that no one should publicly teach in the Church or administer the Sacraments, unless he be regularly called." A. C., Art. XIV.

Canonical orders may be valid and useful but are not essential. To be rightly called to the Office of the Ministry does not require canonical ordination. When bishops refuse to ordain because they do not allow our doctrine, or make unjust demands of candidates for the ministry, "it is necessary for the Church to retain the authority to call, elect, and ordain ministers." "Thus the cruelty of the bishops is the reason why that canonical government, which we greatly desired to maintain, is in some places dissolved." The Apology, Art. XIV.

"Furthermore, the ministry of the New Testament is not bound to persons and places, as the Levitical ministry, but it is dispersed throughout the whole world and is there where God gives His gifts, prophets, pastors, teachers; neither does this ministry avail on account of the authority of any person, but on account of the Word given by Christ." The Smalcald Articles, Appendix.

Those rightly called to the office of the ministry have authority to teach the Gospel, to administer the Sacraments, and to exercise discipline in the service of Christ and in accordance with the requirements of the word. The ministry is not a priesthood mediating sacrificially for sinners nor having authority to bind consciences aside from the Word. The work of the ministry is efficacious through the Word even though evil may be present in the minister and the Church.

The subject of ordination is treated chiefly in the Apology, Chapter VII, Article XIII; the Smalcald Articles, Part III, Article X and Appendix, "The Power and Primacy of the Pope."

In the Apology, Article XIII, we read: "But if ordination be understood as applying to the ministry of the Word, we are not unwilling to call ordination a sacrament. For the ministry of the Word has God's command and glorious promises (Rom. 1:16): 'The Gospel is the power of God unto salvation to everyone that believeth.' Likewise (Isa. 55:11): 'So shall my word be that goeth forth out of my mouth: it shall not return unto me void, but it shall accomplish that which I please.' If ordination be understood in this way, neither will we refuse to call the imposition of hands a sacrament. For the Church has the command to appoint ministers, which should be most pleasing to us, because we know that God approves this ministry, and is present in the ministry. And it is of advantage, so far as can be done, to adorn the ministry of the Word with every kind of praise against fanatical men, who dream that the Holy Ghost is given not through the Word, but because of certain preparation of their own, if they sit unoccupied and silent in obscure places, waiting for illumination; as the enthusiasts formerly taught, and the Anabaptists now teach."

In the Smalcald Articles, Appendix, Part II, 341, we read: "Where there is, therefore, a true Church, the right to elect and ordain ministers necessarily exists." This follows from the gift to the Church of the Power of the Keys, Matt. 18:19f; His gifts to the Church in general, Eph. 4:8f; and from the Priesthood of all believers, I Peter 2:9.

Also, Idem, Part III, Article X, we read: " . . . . as the ancient examples of the Church and the Fathers teach us, we ourselves will and ought to ordain suitable persons to this office; and (even according to their own laws) they have not the right to forbid or prevent us. For their laws say that those ordained even by heretics should be regarded and remain as ordained, ..."

In the absence of a specific definition of ordination in the Confessions it may be interesting to note that Gerhard, the Lutheran dogmatician, says: "Ordination is a public and solemn declaration or testification, through which the ministry of the Church is committed to a suitable person, called thereto by the Church, to which he is consecrated by prayer and the laying on of hands, rendered more certain of his lawful call, and publicly, in the sight of the entire Church, solemnly and seriously admonished concerning his duties."

THE PRACTICE OF THE LUTHERAN CHURCH IN RECEIVING MINISTERS FROM OTHER COMMUNIONS

A questionnaire was sent to the presidents of thirty-three constituent synods of The United Lutheran Church in America. Twenty-nine presidents responded. The responses from six of the synods state that they require ordination of ministers applying from other communions while the responses from twenty-two synods state that they receive applicants from evangelical communions without ordination. One president states that the synod receives such applicants on recommendation, but that ordination is open and optional. All presidents report that the synods have strict re-

quirements for the examination of such applicants by the examining committees.

A questionnaire was also sent to the presidents of seven of the other
general Lutheran bodies. Three of these consider ordination to be to the
Lutheran Ministry only, while three consider ordination to be to the Christian Ministry in general, and one has no settled rule or practice on the
question. Further, two of these bodies re-ordain applicants from other communions, while five receive such applicants by some form of transfer without ordination.

There is little agreement in positions and uniformity in practice in The
Lutheran Church in America in receiving ministers from other communions who apply for admission into the Lutheran Ministry. All synods
require examination of such candidates. In a majority of the cases ordination is not required. In some cases it is.

The Practice of the Other Protestant Churches in America in Receiving Ministers from Other Communions

Your committee consulted leaders in the major Protestant Churches concerning the practice of their Communions in receiving ministers from other
denominations (with the exception of the Protestant Episcopal Church,
whose position on the question is well known). As a rule, ordination by
another Communion is recognized, but each case is decided on its own
merits by the presbytery, classis, conference, or regional association, the
judicatory in each instance having powers corresponding to our synod.

The following statement, written in reply to our inquiry, by Bishop E. G.
Richardson, of the Methodist Episcopal Church, may be taken as fairly
representative of the general position of all these bodies:

"The rule of our Church is, that duly ordained ministers in good standing
in other evangelical churches can be received into our ministry by recognition of their credentials. We do not re-ordain such ministers. There
never has been a list made of the Churches whose ordination we recognize.
The question is left to the judgment of the conference by whose vote the
recognition is made. Rulings have been adopted to the effect that we do
not recognize orders from the Roman Catholic Church, from the Christian
Science Organization, from the Quakers, and from the Salvation Army. It
has also ruled that in general we should recognize as Churches only
those organizations which by their history, their work, the number of
their members, and their requirements for admission to the ministry have
clear church standing. Another ruling of our Church is, that the term,
'Evangelical Churches' is applicable to Churches that adhere to the fundamental doctrines of Evangelical Christianity. Where men come to us from
other Churches they are required to accept our doctrines and form of government by answering the questions which we ask of those seeking Ordination. You will find a general statement of our law in the Discipline of Our
Church (1928), paragraphs 168, 169, 170. There are also Rulings which
have been adopted at various times by our General Conferences. These
rulings are meant to elucidate our laws. To find them would involve a
good deal of research in the General Conference Journals covering a con-

siderable number of years. I trust that this answer will give you the information you are seeking.

"Perhaps one other statement should be made. We have two Orders— Deacon, and Elder. When a man comes to us from a Church that has only one Order, the Annual Conference that recognizes the Credential has the privilege of recognizing it as either that of a Deacon, or of an Elder, as they think best."

RECOMMENDATIONS

After reviewing the questions referred to us in the light of the Lutheran doctrine of the Ministry, we submit the following resolutions to the convention of the United Lutheran Church for consideration and recommendation to the constituent synods:

1. That a minister of another communion applying for admission to the ministry of the Lutheran Church be required to unite with a congregation of the synod to which the application has been made.

2. That the examining committees of the synods be instructed to continue the practice of examining such applicant as to his acceptance of the faith and Confessions of the Evangelical Lutheran Church and his fitness for the work of the ministry.

3. That the favorable recommendation of the Examining Committee concerning the faith, fitness, and previous ordination of such applicant and its acceptance by the synod be deemed an adequate testification of the applicant's call to the Christian Ministry, and that the Common Service Book Committee be instructed to prepare an appropriate form for the use of the synods in the public reception of such applicants. [Supplemented by the Convention, see p. 542.]

4. That, if a synod should find that the communion by which an applicant was ordained does not represent the Christian Church and does not require, in connection with ordination, subscription to the essentials of the Gospel, or if the applicant should request it, the synod of the Lutheran Church to which the application has been made shall ordain such applicant.

5. That the present formula in the Order for Ordination be retained unchanged as follows: "I now commit unto thee the Holy Office of the Word and Sacraments; I ordain and consecrate thee a minister of the Church; In the Name of the Father, and of the Son, and of the Holy Ghost."

HENRY ANSTADT, *Chairman.*
M. L. STIREWALT, *Secretary.*

Recommendations 1 and 2 were adopted.

Recommendation 3 was divided. It was moved and seconded to adopt the first part:

"That the favorable recommendation of the Examining Committee concerning the faith, fitness, and previous ordination of such applicant and its acceptance by the synod be deemed an adequate testification of the applicant's call to the Christian Ministry."

It was moved and seconded to amend by striking the words "and previous ordination" and by inserting the word "may" between "synod" and "be." The amendment was lost. The first part of recommendation 3 as presented by the Committee was on motion adopted.

It was moved and seconded to adopt the second part of recommendation 3

"that the Common Service Book Committee be instructed to prepare an appropriate form for the use of the synods in the public reception of such applicants."

It was moved and carried that the second part be amended by adding the words

"and that this form be reported for approval to a convention of the United Lutheran Church before publication."

The second part as amended was adopted. The entire recommendation 3 as amended was declared adopted.

Recommendations 4 and 5 were adopted.

The preamble was adopted.

The recommendations with the preamble were adopted as a whole.

President Knubel announced the presence of the Rev. G. E. Lenski, of Washington, D. C., official representative of the American Lutheran Church. Dr. Lenski presented the greetings of his body and the following telegram of greetings from President C. C. Hein of the American Lutheran Church:

"Your greetings sent to our body in convention assembled in Fond du Lac, Wis., were received with marked attention and cordiality. We recognize a bond of fellowship in Christ Jesus and thank God for it. We note with special satisfaction your emphasis upon our mutual subscription to the same Confessions and we trust that these Confessions become actualities in the life of the Church and the factor which in the providence of God and with the guidance of His Holy Spirit will unite our whole Lutheran Church in America and make it the power in our land to which by reason of its doctrine, its history and its numbers it is entitled. We look hopefully into the future. May God abundantly bless your work."

C. C. HEIN,
President of the American Lutheran Church.

The President called on the Rev. C. M. Jacobs to respond to the greetings of the American Lutheran Church.

The report of the Common Service Book Committee was presented by the Rev. L. D. Reed, Chairman of the Committee.

REPORT OF THE COMMON SERVICE BOOK COMMITTEE

A Distinguished Life and Service

The committee, with a deep sense of personal loss in the death of its senior member, records its appreciation of the distinguished services in the liturgical field of Dr. Henry Eyster Jacobs. Appointed a member of the Church Book Committee of the General Council in 1882, he took part in the preparation of the Common Service which appeared in 1889. Numerous articles in the Church periodicals and his book, "The Lutheran Movement in England," were the direct result of his early historical and liturgical studies. His scholarly researches, fine taste and exact knowledge of the Church were constantly at the service of the Joint Committee during the eight or more years of intensive work in the preparation of the Common Service Book. His greatest contributions probably were made in comprehensive studies in the field of hymnology and in the study of sources and the preparation of complete reports as a basis for committee work on the Occasional Services. Upon the completion of the latter, the Joint Committee formally expressed its sincere appreciation of "the unparalleled contribution of labor and learning made by Dr. Jacobs in his investigations and preparation of material." His interest in the worship of the Church was unabated to the end, and the record of his fifty years of continuous and conspicuous service as a member of the liturgical committees of the Church is without parallel. The value of his life and work will be increasingly recognized and his memory will be affectionately cherished by all who knew and labored with him.

Two meetings of the committee were held during the biennium—the first January 27, 28, 29, and the second, April 27, 28, 29, 1932. At the first meeting Dr. Luther D. Reed was elected chairman and Dr. H. D. Hoover secretary.

A Book of Collects and Prayers

The principal work of the committee centered upon the preparation of a book of collects and prayers. This has grown under its hands and promises to be an important and useful collection.

Desire has frequently been expressed for a comprehensive collection of prayers to supplement the material in the Common Service Book for use in the regular services of the Church. Additional General Prayers for the Seasons and Festivals of the Church Year would be serviceable. Special needs and occasions not within the scope of our present liturgical material, should be provided for. Because of the lack of adequate sources, to which they may turn for suggestion in the preparation of prayers of special character, ministers often introduce questionable material or resort to free prayer with results that are unsatisfactory and which destroy the integrity of the liturgical service.

A sub-committee consisting of Drs. Reed, Strodach and E. E. Fischer, held twenty or more meetings preparing material for the committee itself to consider. The entire field of published prayers, ancient and modern, was investigated, many prayers translated and many original prayers composed. The committee itself critically examined and edited this material and determined the text of approximately three hundred collects and prayers. As an indication of the scope of the collection the following condensed summary of subjects is given.

The Church.—World-wide mission; the Church and the community; the Church and the social order; the Church and education; church unity; the ministry; for those who administer the affairs of the Church; the Choir; Conferences of Christian People, etc.

The Parish. — For a parish without a pastor; for men's organizations; women's organizations; young people's organizations, etc.

Divine Worship. — For the spirit of worship; fruitful hearing of the Word; those worshiping with us; for reverence; before and after communion, etc.

The Church Building.—For the builders of a church; for anniversaries, etc.

Missions.—For evangelistic work; inner missions, city missions, etc., for home missions, foreign missions, etc.; for workers, medical missions, the native church, etc.

Education.—For parish schools; schools and colleges; student pastors; students in college and seminary; benefactors, etc.

Home, Friends and Country.—For the families of the land; the marriage estate; neighbors, children, friends, etc.

Gifts and Graces.—For a right use of Scripture; communion with God; love, repentance, forgiveness, courage, purity, truth and honor; for temperate living; the right use of leisure, Christian service, etc.

Our Daily Life. — For the study of God's Word; our daily work; all workers, husbandmen, seamen, fishermen, miners, artisans, industrial workers, etc. For employers; industrial peace, etc.

Special Necessities.—For the sick and suffering; in time of distress, peril, failure, etc. For those in sorrow; in commemoration of the departed.

All Sorts and Conditions of Men.—For the aged, poor, neglected, deaf, blind, tempted, lonely, etc.

For Hospitals, Medical Men and Nurses.

For Holiday and Travel by Land, Sea and Air.

For National and Local Government.—For Congress; for our city; in time of elections; for the Army, Navy, for world peace, international accord, memorial days, etc.

Morning and Evening.

Prayers for the above rubrics and others have been adopted. The committee hopes to complete its work upon the additional General Prayers during the coming year. The collection will constitute a volume of possibly

150 pages. Even though some of the material may have to be adapted to conditions in actual use, it should prove suggestive and helpful.

AN ORDER FOR GOOD FRIDAY

Recognizing the general observance of the Three-hour Devotion on Good Friday, and conscious of the fact that published services from many sources are urged upon our pastors, the committee has outlined a service which includes an appropriate Introduction and an Order based upon the "Seven Words from the Cross." Each part contains a hymn, a psalm, a lesson (from the Sixth Part of the Passion History), a Meditation, the Litany, Hymn of the Passion (Hymn 84), and appropriate Prayers. In accordance with Good Friday tradition, the prayers are arranged for possible use as Bidding Prayers. After Silent Prayer the Order concludes with the *Dignus est Agnus* and the Benediction.

The committee has adopted the general plan of this service and most of the material.

OFFICES FOR LAY ORGANIZATIONS

In response to requests, particularly from general officers of the Women's Missionary Society, the committee prepared two offices for conventions of Lay-Organizations of the Church. These are intended particularly for general, synodical or conference conventions. The first office provides for the opening and the second for the closing of a convention. The forms include versicles and responses, petitions and intercessions appropriate for men's organizations, women's organizations, young people's organizations and Church school organizations respectively.

These offices have been published by the Publication House and used by various organizations during the past year.

MISCELLANEOUS

By appointment of President Knubel, the chairman accepted membership on the Committee of Worship of the Federal Council of Churches. The first meeting of this committee was held in New York, April 26, 1932. Representatives were present from practically all of the Protestant Communions and great earnestness was shown in the effort to inaugurate historical and comparative studies which might prove helpful in encouraging a different conception of worship, particularly in the non-liturgical groups. A strong desire was expressed to overcome the "disorderly informality" found in many sections; to increase the sense of reverence and devotion and "an awareness of the presence of God"; and to emphasize the importance of worship itself apart from other values in Christian assembly such as edification, social programs, etc. It is hoped that the work of the committee as it progresses may make a substantial contribution to essential Christian unity in a new recognition of the fundamental importance of worship in the life and thought of all Protestant Communions.

The committee reviewed an "Office for Induction of Officers and Teachers in a Church School," submitted by the Parish and Church School Board. Inasmuch as this provides for a form to be used in connection with the regular services of the congregation, the committee was glad to co-operate with the Board and offered constructive suggestions.

RESOLUTION

Resolved, that the proposed Book of Collects and Prayers and the Order for the Three-Hour Devotion on Good Friday be approved, and the committee authorized to publish the same when completed.

Respectfully submitted,
LUTHER D. REED, *Chairman.*
HARVEY D. HOOVER, *Secretary.*

The resolution was adopted.

The report of the Committee on Leave of Absence was presented by the Rev. E. E. Fischer, Chairman of the Committee.

REPORT OF COMMITTEE ON LEAVE OF ABSENCE

The Committee on Leave of Absence makes the following report:

The following synods have a perfect record of attendance (a complete delegation present and a perfect record of attendance of all delegates at all sessions):

Georgia-Alabama	Manitoba
California	Pacific
Rocky Mountain	Nova Scotia

Florida

The following synods have reported as follows concerning the absence of delegates from the convention:

New York—two excused
Ohio—two excused
Canada—one excused
Kansas—two excused
Nebraska—one excused
Wartburg—two excused
German Nebraska—four excused
Northwest—two excused

The following synods have reported as follows concerning excuses granted for absence of delegates from sessions of the Convention (each excuse represents the absence of one man from one session):

Miniterium of Pennsylvania—ninety-nine excused; two unexcused
New York—twenty excused
North Carolina—sixteen excused
Maryland—nine excused
South Carolina—seven excused
West Pennsylvania—nine excused
Virginia—two excused
Ohio—thirty-one excused
East Pennsylvania—two excused
Alleghany—thirteen excused
Pittsburgh—thirty-eight excused
Indiana—one excused
Illinois—sixteen excused
Texas—three excused
Susquehanna—seven excused
Mississippi—one excused
Iowa—four unexcused
Michigan—twenty excused
Canada—four excused; four unexcused
Kansas—five excused
Nebraska—one excused
Wartburg—three excused; five unexcused
Northwest—five excused
West Virginia—one excused; one unexcused
Slovak Zion—three excused

The committee recommends that the secretary of the United Lutheran Church prepare a recapitulation sheet for use in tabulating the results.

The committee also desires to express its appreciation of the splendid co-operation which it received from the chairmen of the various delegations.

E. E. FISCHER, *Chairman.*

The report was received and the recommendation adopted.

The report of the Committee of Reference and Counsel was presented by the Rev. A. R. Wentz.

Report of the Committee of Reference and Counsel

With a view to discharging more faithfully our profound debt of gratitude to two eminent servants of the Church, and to render it possible for the constituency of The United United Lutheran Church in America to become better acquainted with their eminent services for the Kingdom of God, be it

Resolved, That we request the publication in *The Lutheran* of the two splendid addresses delivered in St. Matthew's Church, on Monday evening, October 17th:

A Tribute to the Rev. Dr. M. G. G. Scherer by the Rev. Dr. A. G. Voigt and

A Tribute to the Rev. Dr. H. E. Jacobs by the Rev. Dr. N. R. Melhorn.

The recommendation was adopted.

On motion the printing of the Minutes was referred to the Executive Board.

The Convention was closed at 12.15 P. M. with the Order for the Closing of Synods.

ABDEL ROSS WENTZ, *Secretary.*

LIST OF BOARDS AND ELECTIVE COMMITTEES

1. Executive Board.
2. Commission of Adjudication.
3. Board of Foreign Missions.
4. Board of American Missions.
5. Board of Northwestern Missions.
6. Immigrants Mission Board.
7. West Indies Mission Board.
8. Board of Education.
9. Inner Mission Board.
10. Board of Publication.
11. Board of Ministerial Pensions and Relief.
12. Parish and Church School Board.
13. Board of Deaconess Work.
14. National Lutheran Home for the Aged.
15. Committee on Church Papers.
16. Executive Committee of the Laymen's Movement.

LIST OF STANDING COMMITTEES, COMMISSIONS, ETC.

1. Statistical and Church Year Book Committee.
2. Committee on Common Service Book.
3. Committee on Church Music.
4. Committee on German Interests.
5. Committee on Lutheran Brotherhoods.
6. Committee on Women's Work.
7. Committee on Associations of Young People.
8. Committee on Army and Navy Work.
9. Committee on Moral and Social Welfare.
10. Committee on Evangelism.
11. Committee on Church Architecture.
12. Committee on Publicity.
13. Committee on Transportation.
14. Necrologist.
15. Archivist.
16. Such other Standing Committees as may be provided for from time to time.

SPECIAL COMMITTEES

1. Committee to Conduct the Opening and Closing Services of Each Session.
2. Committee on Leave of Absence.
3. Committee on Proceedings of District Synods.
4. Committee of Reference and Counsel.
5. Committee to Nominate Executive Committee of Laymen's Movement.
6. Committee to Nominate Members of Boards.
7. Committee to Nominate Members of Executive Board and all Elective Commissions or Committees.
8. Committee of Tellers.

BOARDS AND ELECTIVE COMMITTEES
EXECUTIVE BOARD

President—Rev. F. H. Knubel, D.D., LL.D., S.T.D., 39 East Thirty-fifth Street, New York City.

Secretary—Rev. W. H. Greever, D.D., LL.D., 39 East Thirty-fifth Street, New York City.

Treasurer—E. Clarence Miller, LL.D., 1508 Walnut Street, Philadelphia, Pa.

Term Expires 1936

Rev. E. B. Burgess, D.D., LL.D.; Rev. E. P. Pfatteicher, D.D., Ph.D., LL.D.; Rev. A. Steimle, D.D.; Hon. Wm. E. Hirt; Robbin B. Wolf, Esq.; Hon. John L. Zimmerman, LL.D.

Term Expires 1934

Rev. Marion J. Kline, D.D.; Rev. J. L. Morgan, D.D.; Rev. Rees Edgar Tulloss, D.D., Ph.D., LL.D.; Mr. John Greiner, Jr.; Mr. B. B. Miller; Mr. Wm. H. Stackel.

COMMISSION OF ADJUDICATION

President—Rev. A. G. Voigt, D.D., LL.D., Columbia, S. C.

Vice-President—Rev. Luther Kuhlman, D.D., 106 Carlisle St., Gettysburg, Pa.

Secretary—Rev. H. C. Roehner, D.D., 30 S. Mulberry St., Mansfield, Ohio.
Clerk—Hon. E. K. Strong, Columbia City, Ind.

Term Expires 1938
Rev. Luther Kuhlman, D.D.; Rev. W. F. Rangeler, D.D.; Hon. C. M. Efird, LL.D.

Term Expires 1936
Rev. E. B. Burgess, D.D., LL.D.; Rev. H. C. Roehner, D.D.; Robbin B. Wolf, Esq.

Term Expires 1934
Rev. George Gebert, D.D.; Rev. A. G. Voigt, D.D., LL.D.; Hon. E. K. Strong.

BOARD OF FOREIGN MISSIONS
President—Rev. S. W. Herman, D.D., 121 State St., Harrisburg, Pa.
Vice-President—Rev. G. A. Greiss, D.D., 38 S. 8th St., Allentown, Pa.
Executive Secretary—Rev. Paul W. Koller, D.D., 18 E. Mt. Vernon Place, Baltimore, Md.
Recording Secretary—Rev. George Drach, D.D., 18 E. Mt. Vernon Place, Baltimore, Md.
Treasurer—Mr. Geo. R. Weitzel, 18 E. Mt. Vernon Place, Baltimore, Md.
General Secretaries in Charge of Departments of Work—Rev. George Drach, D.D., Literature, India and Japan; Rev. L. B. Wolf, D.D., Home Base, China and South America; Rev. M. Edwin Thomas, D.D., Special Gifts and Africa.

Term Expires 1938
Rev. Robert D. Clare, D.D.; Rev. Charles A. Dennig; Rev. S. W. Herman, D.D.; Rev. S. T. Nicholas, D.D.; Mr. John J. Bruns; Mr. Chas. H. Dahmer; Mr. Claude L. Peterman.

Term Expires 1936

Rev. Oscar A. Benson; Rev. E. E. Fischer, D.D.; Rev. P. E. Monroe, D.D.; Rev. Clarence M. Snyder; Rev. H. W. Snyder, D.D.; Mr. Frank Howard; Mr. H. Torrey Walker.

Term Expires 1934

Rev. H. C. Brillhart, D.D.; Rev. G. A. Greiss, D.D.; Rev. E. R. Jaxheimer; Rev. L. C. Manges, D.D.; Paul Van Reed Miller, Esq.; Mr. M. P. Moller, Jr.; Mr. W. A. Rast.

BOARD OF AMERICAN MISSIONS

President—Rev. J. B. Markward, D.D., 914 N. Fountain Ave., Springfield, Ohio.

Vice-President—Rev. H. W. A. Hanson, D.D., LL.D., Gettysburg, Pa.

Secretary—Mr. H. F. Heuer, 52 E. Sedgwick St., Philadelphia, Pa.

Executive Secretary—Rev. F. F. Fry, D.D., 39 East Thirty-fifth St., New York City.

Treasurer—Rev. Zenan M. Corbe, D.D., 39 East Thirty-fifth St., New York City.

Divisional Secretary of English Missions—Rev. J. F. Seibert, D.D., 860 N. Wabash Ave., Chicago, Ill.

Divisional Secretary, Linguistic Interests—Rev. E. A. Tappert, D.D., 39 E. 35th St., New York City.

Departmental Secretary of Church Extension and Finance—Rev. Zenan M. Corbe, D.D., 39 E. 35th St., New York City.

Term Expires 1938

Rev. F. O. Evers; Rev. L. H. Larimer, D.D., LL.D.; Rev. H. J. Pflum, D.D.; Rev. L. W. Steckel, D.D.; Mr. Horace W. Bikle; Mr. Henry F. Heuer; John A. Hoober, Esq.

Term Expires 1936

Rev. G. A. Benze, D.D.; Rev. H. W. A. Hanson, D.D., LL.D.; Rev. J. B. Markward, D.D.; Rev. Jacob Maurer, D.D.; Mr. A. Raymond Bard; Grant Hultberg, D.C.L.; Mr. H. L. Snyder.

Term Expires 1934

Rev. A. E. Bell, D.D.; Rev. C. A. Freed, D.D.; Rev. G. K. Rubrecht, D.D.; Rev. J. C. Seegers, D.D.; Mr. A. H. Durboraw; Mr. Wm. Eck; Mr. S. F. Telleen.

BOARD OF NORTHWESTERN MISSIONS

Term Expires 1938

Rev. F. O. Evers; Rev. L. H. Larimer, D.D., LL.D.; Rev. H .J. Pflum, D.D.; Rev. L. W. Steckel, D.D.; Mr. Horace W. Bikle; Mr. Henry F. Heuer; John A. Hoober, Esq.

Term Expires 1936

Rev. G. A. Benze, D.D.; Rev. H. W. A. Hanson, D.D., LL.D.; Rev. J. B. Markward, D.D.; Rev. Jacob Maurer, D.D.; Mr. A. Raymond Bard; Grant Hultberg, D.C.L.; Mr. H. L. Snyder.

Term Expires 1934

Rev. A. E. Bell, D.D.; Rev. C. A. Freed, D.D.; Rev. G. K. Rubrecht, D.D.; Rev. J. C. Seegers, D.D.; Mr. A. H. Durboraw; Mr. Wm. Eck; Mr. S. F. Telleen.

IMMIGRANTS MISSION BOARD

Term Expires 1938

Rev. F. O. Evers; Rev. L. H. Larimer, D.D., LL.D.; Mr. Horace W. Bikle; Mr. Henry F. Heuer.

Term Expires 1936

Rev. H. W. A. Hanson, D.D., LL.D.; Rev. J. B. Markward, D.D.; Mr. A. Raymond Bard; Grant Hultberg, D.C.L.

Term Expires 1934

Rev. A. E. Bell, D.D.; Rev. C. A. Freed, D.D.; Mr. Wm. Eck; Mr. S. F. Telleen.

WEST INDIES MISSION BOARD

President—Rev. H. W. A. Hanson, D.D., LL.D.
Secretary—Mr. Henry F. Heuer.

Term Expires 1938

Rev. F. O. Evers; Rev. L. H. Larimer, D.D., LL.D.; Rev. H. J. Pflum, D.D.; Rev. L. W. Steckel, D.D.; Mr. Horace W. Bikle; Mr. Henry F. Heuer; John A. Hoober, Esq.

Term Expires 1936

Rev. G. A. Benze, D.D.; Rev. H. W. A. Hanson, D.D., LL.D.; Rev. J. B. Markward, D.D.; Rev. Jacob Maurer, D.D.; Mr. A. Raymond Bard; Grant Hultberg, D.C.L.; Mr. H. L. Snyder.

Term Expires 1934

Rev. A. E. Bell, D.D.; Rev. C. A. Freed, D.D.; Rev. G. K. Rubrecht, D.D.; Rev. J. C. Seegers, D.D.; Mr. A. H. Durboraw; Mr. Wm. Eck; Mr. S. F. Telleen.

BOARD OF EDUCATION

President—Rev. H. R. Gold, D.D., 15 Vaughn Ave., New Rochelle, New York.

Recording Secretary—Rev. Gould Wickey, Ph.D., 744 Jackson Place, N. W., Washington, D. C.

Treasurer—Mr. Thomas P. Hickman, 744 Jackson Place, N. W., Washington, D. C.

Executive Secretary—Rev. Gould Wickey, Ph.D., 744 Jackson Place, N. W., Washington, D. C.

Secretaries—Rev. C. P. Harry, D.D.; Miss Mary E. Markley, Litt.D.; Miss Mildred E. Winston, 744 Jackson Place, N. W., Washington, D. C.

Term Expires 1938

Rev. G. M. Diffenderfer, D.D.; Rev. P. H. Krauss, D.D.; Rev. W. H. Traub, D.D.; Rev. A. R. Wentz, Ph.D., D.D.; Mr. C. J. Driever; Mr. L. C. Hassinger; Prof. Ralph D. Owen, Ph.D.

Term Expires 1936

Rev. H. J. Black, D.D.; Rev. Franklin K. Fretz, D.D., Ph.D.; Rev. H. R. Gold, D.D.; Rev. W. H. Greever, D.D., LL.D.; Henry W. Bikle, LL.D.; Mr. Frederick Henrich; Prof. R. S. Saby, Ph.D.

Term Expires 1934

Rev. Henry H. Bagger; Rev. E. C. Herman, D.D.; Rev. M. L. Stirewalt, D.D.; Rev. A. A, Zinck, D.D., S.T.D.; Mrs. Adelaide Burge; W. J. Showalter, Sc.D.; Hon. Charles Steele.

INNER MISSION BOARD

President—Carl M. Distler, Esq., 401 American Life Bldg., Baltimore, Md.

Vice-President—Rev. F. B. Clausen, D.D., Waterloo College, Waterloo, Ont., Canada.

Executive Secretary and Treasurer—Rev. Wm. Freas, D.D., 39 East Thirty-fifth St., New York City.

Secretary for Immigrant Work—Rev. E. A. Sievert, 218 Seventh Ave., New York City.

Term Expires 1938

Rev. S. E. Greenawalt, D.D.; Rev. Harold S. Miller; Rev. J. L. Sieber, D.D.; Mr. Robert F. Bowe; H. C. Hoffman, M.D.

Term Expires 1936

Rev. G. H. Bechtold; Rev. Herman Brezing, D.D.; Rev. P. D. Brown, D.D.; Carl M. Distler, Esq.; Mr. T. C. Rohrbaugh.

Term Expires 1934

Rev. F. B. Clausen, D.D.; Rev. J. F. Fedders, D.D.; Rev. R. E. Kern; Mr. A. H. Durboraw; Mr. Thos. P. Hickman.

BOARD OF PUBLICATION

President—Mr. D. F. Yost, 1616 DeKalb St., Norristown, Pa.

Vice-President—Mr. E. G. Hoover, 25 North Third St., Harrisburg, Pa.

Secretary—Rev. S. W. Herman, D.D., 121 State St., Harrisburg, Pa.

Business Manager—Grant Hultberg, D.C.L., 1228 Spruce St., Philadelphia, Pa.

Term Expires 1938

Rev. Henry Anstadt, D.D.; Rev. John W. Horine, D.D.; Rev. Paul E. Scherer, D.D.; Rev. Russell D. Snyder; Charles Baum, M.D.; Mr. M. P. Moller, Jr.; Hon. Claude T. Reno.

Term Expires 1936

Rev. Oscar F. Blackwelder, D.D.; Rev. Stewart W. Herman, D.D.; Rev. J. J. Scherer, Jr., D.D.; L. Russell Alden, Esq.; F. Wm. Cappelmann, Esq.; Mr. E. G. Hoover; Mr. Einar Schatvet.

Term Expires 1934

Rev. H. C. Alleman, D.D.; Rev. A. H. Holthusen, Ph.D.; Rev. G. W. Nicely, D.D.; Mr. J. C. Lynch; Mr. Otto W. Osterlund; Mr. W. G. Semisch; Mr. D. F. Yost.

BOARD OF MINISTERIAL PENSIONS AND RELIEF

President—Mr. Paul F. Myers, Munsey Bldg., Washington, D. C.

Vice-President—Hon. Henry W. Harter, 1543 Market St., Canton, Ohio.

Executive Secretary—Mr. Harry Hodges, 1228 Spruce St., Philadelphia, Pa.

Treasurer—Mr. Peter P. Hagan, Kensington Ave. and Butler St., Philadelphia, Pa.

Term Expires 1938

Mr. Paul F. Myers; Mr. Francis Seiberling; Mr. Albert F. Sittloh; Mr. Belding B. Slifer; Mr. D. F. Yost.

Term Expires 1936

Rev. J. H. Reble; Rev. Ross H. Stover, D.D.; Wm. A. Granville, Ph.D., LL.D.; Mr. H. J. Herbst; W. T. Stauffer, Esq.

Term Expires 1934

Rev. Otto Kleine; Mr. A. Raymond Bard; Mr. J. L. Fisher; Hon. Henry W. Harter; Mr. M. P. Moller, Sr.

PARISH AND CHURCH SCHOOL BOARD

President—Rev. F. M. Urich, D.D., 2336 S. 18th St., Philadelphia, Pa.

Vice-President—Rev. F. R. Knubel, 330 Barrington St., Rochester, N. Y.

Secretary—Rev. D. Burt Smith, D.D., 1228 Spruce St., Philadelphia, Pa.

Treasurer—George M. Jones, Esq., 52 N. Fourth St., Reading, Pa.

Executive Secretary—Rev. S. White Rhyne, 1228 Spruce St., Philadelphia, Pa.

Term Expires 1938

Rev. J. D. M. Brown, Litt.D.; Rev. M. Hadwin Fischer, Ph.D., Th.D.; Rev. F. R. Knubel; George M. Jones, Esq.

Term Expires 1936

Rev. Paul H. Heisey, Ph.D., D.D.; Rev. George H. Rhodes, D.D.; Rev. Wm. C. Schaeffer, Jr., D.D.; Mr. Clarence C. Dittmer.

Term Expires 1934

Rev. P. D. Brown, D.D.; Rev. A. J. Turkle, D.D.; Rev. F. M. Urich, D.D.; Grant Hultberg, D.C.L.

BOARD OF DEACONESS WORK

President—Rev. William A. Wade, D.D., 505 Harwood Ave., Baltimore, Md.

Vice-President—Rev. U. S. G. Rupp, D.D., 1501 Bolton St., Baltimore, Md.

Secretary—Rev. Foster U. Gift, D.D., 2500 W. North Ave., Baltimore, Md.

Treasurer—Frederick J. Singley, Esq., 215 N. Charles St., Baltimore, Md.

Term Expires 1938

Rev. George N. Lauffer, D.D.; Rev. Wm. A. Wade, D.D.; Mr. Harry R. Hagerty; Mr. I. Searles Runyon; Edgar W. Young, Esq.

Term Expires 1936

Rev. Allen L. Benner, D.D.; Rev. J. J. Schindel, D.D.; Rev. L. A. Thomas, D.D.; Mr. E. S. Gerberich; Frederick J. Singley, Esq.

Term Expires 1934

Rev. Earl J. Bowman, S.T.M.; Rev. U. S. G. Rupp, D.D.; Rev. W. C. Schaeffer, Jr., D.D.; Prof. J. C. Kinard, LL.D.; Mr. Frederick H. Wefer.

NATIONAL LUTHERAN HOME FOR THE AGED

President—Rev. John Weidley, D.D., 233 Second St., S. E., Washington, D. C.

Vice-President—Rev. J. E. Harms, D.D., Hagerstown, Md.

Recording Secretary—Rev. Richard Schmidt, D.D., 3540 N. 11th St., Philadelphia, Pa.

Corresponding Secretary—W. H. Finckel, Esq., 918 F St., N. W., Washington, D. C.

Treasurer—H. T. Domer, Litt.D., 1745 Q St., N. W., Washington, D. C.

Term Expires 1934

Rev. Henry Anstadt, D.D.; Rev. Oscar F. Blackwelder; Rev. J. L. Frantz; Rev. J. E. Harms, D.D.; Rev. John T. Huddle, D.D.; Rev. Richard Schmidt, D.D.; Rev. H. E. Snyder; Rev. F. R. Wagner, D.D.; Rev. John Weidley, D.D.; L. Russell Alden, Esq.; W. K. Butler, M.D.; Mr. F. E. Cunningham; D. P. Deatrick, D.D.S.; H. T. Domer, Litt.D.; Mr. W. H. Finckel; F. W. Kakel; Mr. Harry L. Snyder.

COMMITTEE ON CHURCH PAPERS

Chairman—Rev. H. Offermann, D.D., 7206 Boyer St., Mt. Airy, Philadelphia, Pa.

Secretary—Rev. E. P. Pfatteicher, D.D., Ph.D., LL.D., 1228 Spruce St., Philadelphia, Pa.

Term Expires 1938

Rev. M. R. Hamsher; Rev. E. P. Pfatteicher, D.D., Ph.D., LL.D.; Mr. Henry Streibert.

Term Expires 1936

Rev. John Aberly, D.D.; Rev. A. J. Holl, D.D.; Wm. J. Showalter, Sc.D.

Term Expires 1934

Rev. C. E. Gardner, D.D.; Rev. W. H. Greever, D.D., LL.D.; Rev. H. Offermann, D.D.

EXECUTIVE COMMITTEE OF THE LAYMEN'S MOVEMENT

Chairman—Mr. J. L. Clark, Ashland, Ohio.

Vice-Chairman—Mr. E. J. Young, Wadsworth, Ohio.

Executive Secretary—Mr. Arthur P. Black, 1000 Our Home Life Bldg., Washington, D. C.

Treasurer—Mr. P. H. Glatfelter, Spring Grove, Pa.

Chairman of the Administrative Committee—Mr. Wm. H. Hager, Lancaster, Pa.

Term Expires 1934

Mr. H. J. Albrecht; Mr. J. L. Clark; Mr. Peter P. Hagan; Hon. Henry W. Harter; Mr. E. G. Hoover; E. Clarence Miller, LL.D.; Mr. Harvey C. Miller; George E. Neff, Esq.; Mr. Charles Steele; Hon. John L. Zimmerman, LL.D.

STANDING COMMITTEES

STATISTICAL AND YEAR BOOK COMMITTEE

Rev. G. H. Schnur, D.D., (Convener), 709 East 11th St., Erie, Pa.; Rev. Ira F. Frankenfield; Rev. G. L. Kieffer, D.D., Litt.D.; Rev. J. D. Krout, D.D.; Rev. C. W. Leitzell, D.D.; Rev. C. J. Rockey, D.D.; Mr. Harry E. Pugh; also Secretary of The United Lutheran Church in America (ex-officio).

COMMITTEE ON COMMON SERVICE BOOK

Rev. L. D. Reed, D.D., (Convener), 7204 Boyer St., Mt. Airy, Philadelphia, Pa.; Rev. R. D. Clare, D.D.; Rev. E. E. Fischer, D.D.; Rev. Carl R. Simon; Rev. H. D. Hoover, Ph.D., D.D., S.T.D.; Rev. J. C. Mattes, D.D.; Rev. J. F. Ohl, D.D., Mus. D.; Rev. George R. Seltzer; Rev. A. Steimle, D.D.; Rev. M. L.

Stirewalt, D.D.; Rev. P. Z. Strodach, D.D.; Rev. C. P. Swank, S.T.D.; Rev. H. J. Pflum, Jr., D.D.; Rev. J. F. Krueger, Ph.D., D.D., LL.D.; Rev. E. F Keever, D.D.

COMMITTEE ON CHURCH MUSIC

Rev. G. C. Rees, D.D., (Convener), 211 South Main St., North Wales, Pa.; Rev. C. T. Benze, D.D.; Rev. J. D. M. Brown, Litt.D.; Rev. E. F. Krauss, D.D.; Rev. H. K. Lantz; Rev. George R. Seltzer; Rev. E. A. Trabert; Rev. H. Grady Davis; Prof. Frederick Lewis Bach, MusD.; Mr. William Benbow; Mr. Ralph P. Lewars; Harold K. Marks, Mus.D.; Mr. Rob Roy Peery; Prof. Carl P. Pfatteicher, Th.D.; Mr. Henry F. Seibert; Harry A. Sykes, Mus.D.

COMMITTEE ON GERMAN INTERESTS

Rev. E. C. J. Kraeling, D.D., (Convener), 132 Henry St., Brooklyn, N. Y.; Rev. G. A. Benze, D.D.; Rev. F. H. Bosch, D.D.; Rev. S. G. R. von Bosse; Rev. F. O. Evers; Rev. R. H. Ischinger; Rev. O. Kleine; Rev. J. L. Neve, D.D., D.Th.; Rev. F. E. Oberlander, D.D.; Rev. T. O. Posselt, D.D.; Rev. J. Reble; Rev. C. R. Tappert, D.D.; Rev. J. A. Weyl, D.D.; Rev. L. A. Fritsch; Rev. E. H. von Hahmann, Ph.D., D.D.

Corresponding Members—The Presidents of the German Nebraska, Manitoba, Texas and Wartburg Synods.

COMMITTEE ON LUTHERAN BROTHERHOODS

Rev. David A. Davy, D.D., (Convener), 860 N. Wabash Ave., Chicago, Ill.; Rev. J. S. Blank; Rev. Mark O. Heller; Rev. W. C. Schaeffer, Jr., D.D.; Rev. J. Earl Spaid; Mr. William B. Ahlgren; Mr. P. R. Boubel; Mr. J. Milton Deck; Mr. Paul T. Fretz; Mr. E. B. Graeber; Mr. George H. Hollenberg; Dr. T. J. Seiler; Mr. W. B. Shealy; Mr. Joseph Tate; Mr. Karl Weichers; Hon. John L. Zimmerman, LL.D.; Mr. A. M. Cooper.

COMMITTEE ON WOMEN'S WORK

Rev. Frank M. Urich, D.D., (Convener), 2336 S. 18th St., Philadelphia,Pa.; Rev. W. G. Boomhower, D.D.; Rev. S. J.

McDowell, D.D.; Rev. J. E. Rudisill; Rev. D. Bruce Young, D.D.; Rev. W. C. Ney, D.D.

COMMITTEE ON ASSOCIATIONS OF YOUNG PEOPLE

Rev. H. C. Roehner, D.D., (Convener), 30 S. Mulberry St., Mansfield, Ohio; Rev. Oscar F. Blackwelder, D.D.; Rev. G. Franklin Gehr, D.D.; Rev. L. M. Kuhns, D.D., Litt.D.; Rev. L. H. Lesher; Rev. H. L. Saul; Rev. John Schmieder; Rev. Chester Simonton; Rev. Ross H. Stover, D.D.; Mr. Austin Howard; Mr. Alvin Schaediger.

COMMITTEE ON ARMY AND NAVY WORK

Rev. Charles D. Trexler, D.D., (Convener), 28 E. 73rd St., New York City; Rev. J. F. Fedders, D.D.; Rev. Wm. Freas, D.D.; Rev. R. H. Gearhart; Rev. Henry Manken, Jr.; Rev. H. S. Miller; Rev. Emil W. Weber; Mr. C. H. Dahmer; Mr. W. A. G. Lape.

COMMITTEE ON MORAL AND SOCIAL WELFARE

Rev. C. B. Foelsch, Ph.D., (Convener), 43 Wentworth St., Charleston, S. C.; Rev. O. E. Brandorff; Rev. E. C. Dinwiddie, D.D.; Prof. E. E. Flack, S.T.D.; Rev. J. H. Harms, D.D.; Rev. P. H. Heisey, Ph.D., D.D.; Rev. W. A. Sadtler, Ph.D., D.D.; Rev. N. Willison, Litt.D.; Rev. F. A. Dressel, D.D.; Rev. W. C. Zimmann; Mr. W. H. Hager.

COMMITTEE ON EVANGELISM

Rev. A. Pohlmann, D.D., M.D., (Convener), 5143 Race St., Philadelphia, Pa.; Rev. Russell F. Auman; Rev. W. C. Davis, D.D.; Rev. Franklin C. Fry; Rev. G. Arthur Fry, D.D.; Rev. C. F. Stickles; Rev. F. Wolford, D.D.; Rev. F. W. Otterbein; Rev. R. Homer Anderson; Mr. F. Stussy, Jr.

COMMITTEE ON CHURCH ARCHITECTURE

Rev. L. D. Reed, D.D., (Convener), 7204 Boyer St., Mt. Airy, Philadelphia, Pa.; Rev. Wm. H. Cooper; Rev. J. L. Deaton, Jr.; Rev. H. S. Kidd; Rev. E. F. Krauss, D.D.; Rev. G. H. Schnur,

D.D.; Rev. E. A. Trabert; Mr. Charles Z. Klauder; Prof. Warren P. Laird, Sc.D.; Mr. Luther M. Leisenring; Mr. Charles F. Obenhack; Mr. Charles A. Scheuringer; Mr. Frank P. Albright.

COMMITTEE ON PUBLICITY

Secretary of The United Lutheran Church in America, ex-officio, (Convener); Rev. Howard R. Gold; Rev. M. Luther Canup, D.D.; Rev. C. K. Fegley; Rev. G. F. Genszler; Rev. Arthur Herbert; Rev. A. F. Klepfer; Rev. Geo. C. Koehler; Rev. A. R. Naus; Rev. L. W. Rupp; Mr. Edward E. Croll; Mr. Jesse R. Hildebrand; Mr. Oscar H. Lindow; Wm. J. Showalter, Sc.D.

COMMITTEE ON TRANSPORTATION

Mr. Harvey C. Miller, (Convener), Broad Street Station Bldg., Philadelphia, Pa.; Rev. J. M. Bramkamp, D.D., 4114 N. Tripp Ave., Chicago, Ill., and the Secretary of The United Lutheran Church in America (ex-officio).

NECROLOGIST

Rev. James F. Lambert, D.D., 415 Howertown Ave., Catasauqua, Pa.

ARCHIVIST

Rev. L. D. Reed, D.D., 7204 Boyer St., Mt. Airy, Philadelphia, Pa.

COMMISSIONERS TO THE NATIONAL LUTHERAN COUNCIL

Rev. P. W. Koller, D.D., (Convener), 18 E. Mt. Vernon Place, Baltimore, Md.; Rev. E. B. Burgess, D.D., LL.D.; Rev. C. A. Freed, D.D.; Rev. J. A. W. Haas, D.D., LL.D.; Rev. E. P. Pfatteicher, Ph.D., D.D., LL.D.; Rev. L. W. Steckel, D.D.; Rev. C. E. Krumbholz, D.D.; Rev. M. R. Hamsher; Hon. E. F. Eilert, C.S.D.; G. F. Greiner, Esq.

REPRESENTATIVE ON THE ADVISORY COMMITTEE OF THE AMERICAN BIBLE SOCIETY

Rev. H. C. Alleman, D.D., Gettysburg, Pa.

CONSULTATIVE REPRESENTATIVES TO COMMISSIONS OF THE FEDERAL COUNCIL OF CHURCHES

Administrative Committee—Rev. G. U. Wenner, D.D., LL.D., L.H.D., 355 E. 19th St., New York City; Rev. A. Steimle, D.D.

Washington Committee—Rev. Wm. Freas, D.D., 39 E. 35th St., New York City; Rev. Henry Manken, Jr.; Rev. Emil W. Weber.

Commission on International Justice and Good Will—Rev. E. H. Delk, D.D., 35 W. Phil-Ellena St., Philadelphia, Pa.; Rev. L. B. Wolf, D.D.

Committee on Mercy and Relief—Rev. F. H. Knubel, D.D., LL.D., S.T.D., 39 E. 35th St., New York City; Rev. Amos J. Traver, D.D.

COMMITTEE ON CONFERENCE WITH Y. M. C. A.

Rev. Paul E. Scherer, D.D., (Chairman), 3 W. 65th St., New York City; Rev. R. E. Tulloss, Ph.D., LL.D., D.D.; Mr. W. H. Hager; Robbin B. Wolf, Esq.

COMMITTEE TO PREPARE A STATEMENT CONCERNING RELATIONS OF CHURCH AND STATE

Rev. C. M. Jacobs, D.D., LL.D., L.H.D., 7335 Germantown Ave., Mt. Airy, Philadelphia, Pa.; Rev. J. A. W. Haas, D.D., LL.D.; Rev. F. K. Fretz, Ph.D., D.D.; Rev. A. R. Wentz, Ph.D., D.D.

COMMISSION ON WORLD CONFERENCE ON FAITH AND ORDER

(To be elected by the Executive Board).

COMMISSION ON LUTHERAN CHURCH UNITY

Rev. Paul E. Scherer, D.D., 3 W. 65th St., New York City; Rev. C. M. Jacobs, D.D., LL.D., L.H.D.; Rev. R. E. Tulloss, Ph.D., D.D., LL.D.; Hon. E. F. Eilert, C.S.D.; W. A. Granville, Ph.D., LL.D.; Mr. J. K. Jensen.

COMMISSION ON INVESTMENTS

Chairman—E. Clarence Miller, LL.D., 1508 Walnut Street, Philadelphia, Pa.

Secretary—Grant Hultberg, D.C.L., 1228 Spruce Street, Philadelphia, Pa.

Members elected by the Executive Board:

Robbin B. Wolf, Esq., Term Expires 1937

Mr. Wm. H. Stackel, Term Expires 1936

Mr. W. G. Semisch, Term Expires 1935

Mr. S. F. Telleen, Term Expires 1934

Members Ex-Officio:

President of The United Lutheran Church in America—Rev. F. H. Knubel, D.D., LL.D., S.T.D.

Treasurer of The United Lutheran Church in America— E. Clarence Miller, LL.D.

Members elected by their respective Board or Agency:

Miss Flora Prince, the Women's Missionary Society

Rev. S. W. Herman, D.D., the Board of Foreign Missions

Grant Hultberg, D.C.L., the Board of American Missions

Hon. Charles Steele, the Board of Education

Mr. Paul F. Meyers, the Board of Ministerial Pensions and Relief

COMMITTEE ON WOMEN AS CONGREGATIONAL REPRESENTATIVES

(To be appointed later).

COMMITTEE ON PLAN OF APPORTIONMENT

Rev. E. B. Burgess, D.D., LL.D., (Convener), 73 Haldane St., Crafton, Pittsburgh, Pa.; Rev. Herbert A. Bosch; Rev. C. B. Foelsch, Ph.D.; Rev. Robert H. Ischinger; Mr. Arthur P. Black; Mr. Robert F. Bowe; Mr. J. Milton Deck; Mr. J. K. Jensen; Mr. E. Clarence Miller, LL.D.; Hon. Charles Steele.

APPENDIX

CORPORATE TITLES

The United Lutheran Church in America, 39 East 35th Street, New York City.

The Board of Foreign Missions of the United Lutheran Church in America, 18 East Mt. Vernon Place, Baltimore, Md.

The Board of American Missions of the United Lutheran Church in America, 39 East 35th St., New York City.

The Board of Education of the United Lutheran Church in America, 744 Jackson Pl., N. W., Washington, D. C.

The Inner Mission Board of the United Lutheran Church in America, 39 East 35th Street, New York City.

The Board of Publication of the United Lutheran Church in America, 1228 Spruce Street, Philadelphia, Pa.

Board of Ministerial Pensions and Relief of the United Lutheran Church in America, 1228 Spruce St., Philadelphia, Pa.

The Parish and Church School Board of the United Lutheran Church in America, 1228 Spruce Street, Philadelphia, Pa.

The Board of Deaconess Work of the United Lutheran Church in America, 2500 W. North Avenue, Baltimore, Md.

The Women's Missionary Society of the United Lutheran Church in America, 1228 Spruce Street, Philadelphia, Pa.

———————•———•———————

Evangelical Lutheran Seminary of Canada, Waterloo, Ontario, Canada.

The Theological Seminary of the Evangelical Lutheran Church at Chicago, Ill., 11th Avenue & Harrison Street, Maywood, Ill.

The Theological Seminary of the General Synod of the Evangelical Lutheran Church in the United States and of the United Lutheran Church in America, Gettysburg, Pa.

The Hartwick Seminary, 259 Washington Avenue, Brooklyn, N. Y.

Martin Luther Seminary of the German Evangelical Lutheran Synod of Nebraska, Lincoln, Nebr.

Northwestern Lutheran Theological Seminary, 1018 Nineteenth Avenue, N. E. Minneapolis, Minn.

Pacific Theological Seminary of the Evangelical Lutheran Church, 4300 E. 45th Street, Seattle, Wash.

The Lutheran Theological Seminary at Philadelphia, 7301 Germantown Avenue, Mt. Airy, Philadelphia, Pa.

The Lutheran College and Seminary, Saskatoon, Sask., Canada.

Trustees of the Lutheran Theological Southern Seminary, at Columbia, S. C.

The Western Theological Seminary of the United Lutheran Church in America, Fremont, Nebr.

Carthage College, Carthage, Ill.

North Carolina College (called Collegiate Institute), Mt. Pleasant, N. C.

Gettysburg College, Gettysburg, Pa.

Irving Female College, Mechanicsburg, Pa.

Lenoir-Rhyne College, Hickory, N. C.

Marion Female College (known as Marion Junior College), Marion, Va.

Midland College of the United Lutheran Church in America, Fremont, Nebr.

Muhlenberg College, Located at Allentown, Lehigh County, Pennsylvania.

Newberry College, Newberry, S. C.

The Trustees of Roanoke College, at Salem, Va.

Susquehanna University, Selinsgrove, Pa.

Trustees of Thiel College of the Evangelical Lutheran Church, Greenville, Pa.

Wagner Memorial Lutheran College, Staten Island, N. Y.

The Board of Directors of Wittenberg College, Springfield, Ohio.

Hartwick College, Oneonta, N. Y.

Hartwick Academy, Hartwick Seminary, N. Y.

Lutheran Orphans' Home in Berks County, Pennsylvania.

Tressler Orphans' Home of the Evangelical Lutheran Church of the General Synod in the United States of America, Loysville, Pa.

The Zelienople Orphans' Home Board of Directors of the Pittsburgh Synod of the Evangelical Lutheran Church, Zelienople, Pa.

The Oesterlen Orphans' Home of the United Lutheran Church of North America located at Springfield, Ohio.

The Lutheran Orphan Home of the South, located at Salem, Va.

The Nachusa Lutheran Orphanage, Nachusa, Ill.

Wartburg Orphans' Farm School of the Evangelical Lutheran Church, in the State of New York, Mount Vernon, N. Y.

Evangelical Lutheran St. John's Orphan Home at Buffalo and Sulphur Springs, N. Y., "Station D," Buffalo, N. Y.

Old People's Home of the Pittsburgh Synod of the Evangelical Lutheran Church, at Zelienople, Pa.

Evangelical Lutheran Charities Society of Charleston, S. C., (for The Jacob Washington Franke Lutheran Hospital and Home), Charleston, S. C.

The Association of the Lutheran Church Home for the Aged and Infirm of Buffalo, N. Y.

The Lutheran Church Home for the Aged and Infirm of Central New York, Inc., Clinton, N. Y. (Office at Utica, N. Y.)

The National Lutheran Home for the Aged, Washington, D. C.

The Feghtly Lutheran Home, Tippecanoe City, Ohio.

Lowman Home for Aged and Helpless, White Rock, S. C.

Lutheran Home for the Aged, of Erie, Pennsylvania.

Lutheran Inner Mission Society of the State of Connecticut, Inc. Owner of "Lutheran Home for the Aged, Southbury, Conn."

Tabitha Home, Lincoln, Nebr.

Emaus Orphan House, Middletown, Pa.

Orphans' Home and Asylum for the Aged and Infirm of the Evangelical Lutheran Church, Philadelphia, 6950 Germantown Avenue, Philadelphia, Pa.

The Good Shepherd Home, Allentown, Pa.

The Auxiliary Board of the Passavant Memorial Homes for the Care of Epileptics, Rochester, Pa.

Bethesda Home of the Pittsburgh Synod of the Evangelical Lutheran Church, Crawford Co., Pa.

INDEX